HARRIET TUBMAN

Wisconsin Studies in Autobiography Series

HARRIET TUBMAN

The Life and the Life Stories

JEAN M. HUMEZ

THE UNIVERSITY OF WISCONSIN PRESS

The University of Wisconsin Press
1930 Monroe Street
Madison, Wisconsin 53711

www.wisc.edu/wisconsinpress/

3 Henrietta Street
London WC2E 8LU, England

1   3   5   4   2

Printed in the United States of America

Library of Congress Cataloging-in-Publication Data
Humez, Jean McMahon, 1944–
Harriet Tubman: the life and the life stories / Jean M. Humez.
p. cm. — (Wisconsin studies in autobiography)
Includes bibliographical references and index.
ISBN 0-299-19120-6 (cloth : alk. paper)—
ISBN 0-299-19124-9 (pbk.: alk. paper)
1. Tubman, Harriet, 1820?–1913. 2. Slaves—United States—Biography.
3. African American women—Biography. 4. Underground railroad.
5. Slaves—United States—Biography—History and criticism.
6. African American women—Biography—History and criticism.
7. Autobiography—African American authors. 8. Autobiography—
Women authors. I. Title. II. Series.

E444.T82 H86 2003
973.7'115—dc21

2003005676

IN MEMORY OF MY BROTHER

Thomas McMahon

(1943–1999)

CONTENTS

ILLUSTRATIONS

ACKNOWLEDGMENTS

My decision to work on Tubman's life stories was inspired by discussions with students in a course on spiritual autobiographies I taught during a year spent at the Harvard Divinity School (1990–1991). I thank my students in that seminar and Connie Buchanan, then director of the Women's Studies in Religion program, for a wonderful year in which the seed of this book was sown.

I contacted William L. Andrews about the original idea in 1993. His enthusiastic response then and over subsequent years has sustained me as I struggled to shape the final volume. I have been very fortunate to have the benefit of his experience, wisdom, and patience throughout the entire life-span of this project. Other colleagues, often writing books on related subjects, have offered valuable information and insights, including Harriet Alonso, Randall Burkett, Jean Fagan Yellin, Dick Newman, Ann Braude, Mary Helen Washington, Jim Livingston, Sherry Penney, and Milton Sernett.

I have accumulated many other debts—quite a few of them to people I have yet to meet in person (thanks to the ease of Internet communications). I am grateful to Charles Blockson not only for information about his Underground Railroad research collection at Temple University but also for the suggestion that I call James McGowan. An independent scholar and author who had been working on Harriet Tubman for years himself, Jim immediately offered to collaborate with me on this book. He has shared documents from his research and carefully reviewed my drafts and answered queries, all the while encouraging me to remember why this work was important. I am tremendously in his debt. It was also my great good fortune to meet doctoral candidate Kate Larson, whose research skills are truly impressive—and matched only by her canny analysis and her generous attitude as a fellow researcher. As was also true with Jim McGowan, where I might have found a competitor, I found a true collegial relationship. Kate's zealous pursuit of primary documentation and willingness to share her information before publication enabled me to find and correct many a fallacious assumption embedded in earlier versions of the book—whatever errors remain, needless to say, are my own.

I gratefully acknowledge the work of the anonymous readers of the massive first draft I sent to the University of Wisconsin Press—thanks to their empathetic but tough-minded comments, I steeled myself to trim 250 pages from the original manuscript and make other changes that I think have improved the book. Mary Gilmore of the Seymour Library in Auburn went far beyond the call of duty, helping me find materials before, during, and after my research visits. Arden Phair of the St. Catharines Museum helped me with my specific information and put me in touch with Dennis Gannon, a skilled independent researcher with a special interest in the Canadian Underground Railroad refugees, who has become another major contributor to my primary source list. Reference and Interlibrary Loan staff of my own Healey Library at the University of Massachusetts have been very helpful, as always, on this project. I also want to thank Melissa Gilmartin, my former graduate student assistant, who did many Internet research tasks for me, as well as Rebecca Green, undergraduate research assistant at Swarthmore College, who transcribed passages from the Emily Howland diaries. Dozens of skilled and attentive research librarians of other collections have also provided invaluable aid.

I am grateful to Ann Froines, Lois Rudnick, Judith Smith, and other UMB colleagues who have supported my scholarly work in too many ways to list. Chrissie Atkinson provided me with a quiet place to plug in my computer one summer in Maine. And final heartfelt thanks go to my friends and family, who have patiently endured my expense of time on this project when I might have been doing other things in life—you know who you are.

The Life and the Life Stories

INTRODUCTION

One of the teachers lately commissioned by the New-England Freedmen's Aid Society is probably the most remarkable woman of this age. That is to say, she has performed more wonderful deeds by the native power of her own spirit against adverse circumstances than any other. She is well known to many by the various names which her eventful life has given her; Harriet Garrison, General Tubman, etc.; but among the slaves she is universally known by her well-earned title of Moses,—Moses the deliverer. She is a rare instance, in the midst of high civilization and intellectual culture, of a being of great native powers, working powerfully, and to beneficent ends, entirely unaided by schools or books.

—EDNAH CHENEY, "Moses"

Her name (we say it advisedly and without exaggeration) deserves to be handed down to posterity side by side with the names of Joan of Arc, Grace Darling, and Florence Nightingale; for not one of these women has shown more courage and power of endurance in facing danger and death to relieve human suffering, than has this woman in her heroic and successful endeavors to reach and save all whom she might of her oppressed and suffering race, and to pilot them from the land of Bondage to the promised land of Liberty.

—SARAH HOPKINS BRADFORD, *Scenes in the Life of Harriet Tubman*

In the twenty-first century we continue to be inspired by the larger-than-life figure of Harriet Tubman (1820–1913), still the most famous African American female hero. In her own day she was called "the most remarkable woman of this age" for her courage and success in guiding fugitive slaves out of slave territory in the 1850s and for her Union army service behind Confederate lines. The frontispiece illustration of the first full-length Tubman biography captured her in a pose as war scout holding a rifle at rest and looking directly and unsmilingly out at the viewer[1]— an image that would convey to later generations both African American militant resistance to racial oppression and African American female dignity, strength, and empowerment.

Harriet Tubman in Civil War scout attire. This is the woodcut frontispiece (by J. C. Darby of Auburn) from Sarah Bradford's *Scenes in the Life of Harriet Tubman* (1869).

Her life history has been told and retold many times, by both black and white biographers, as part of the political effort to construct and pass on a history of effective African American resistance to white supremacist attitudes, policies, and institutions.[2] Her celebrity today, as in her own time, also reflects her violation of dominant gender norms. She was one of very few women whose escape from slavery was widely publicized in her own time among antislavery activists, and she was virtually the only woman celebrated as a guide for fleeing fugitives. Though other women certainly were involved in the rescue of bondspeople, she was unique in repeating so many times, over many years, the secret rescue work that put her own life in danger.[3]

Her celebrity in her own day was based both on her unusual career itself and on her ability to form and keep close relationships with a group of well-connected white antislavery activists in the North, upon whom she relied for both funding and the opportunities to transmit her story in public. Her three earliest biographers, Franklin B. Sanborn, Ednah Cheney, and Sarah Hopkins Bradford, were among her many white Northern political allies, and as it turned out, all remained loyal supporters during her long lifetime.[4] They all inserted editorial commentary on her personality and character into their biographies—much of which reflects white racial attitudes of the times that are highly repellent today—and to different degrees they distorted her spoken narratives, summarizing longer accounts by leaving out detail and using nonstandard English spellings to reproduce what they heard as uneducated Southern dialect. Yet all three were in genuine awe of her abilities and accomplishments, and all considered her life story to be one for the ages.

Tubman herself wrote none of the biographical texts on which our culture's collective memories of her life are based. As a child in the 1820s, she was a slave in Dorchester County, Maryland. She had no access to formal education, and she remained a bondswoman until she was nearly thirty years of age. After her escape from slavery in 1849, she readily found political allies in the North who would read correspondence aloud to her and pen her replies from dictation.[5] She may have been inspired by participating in this process of committing her words to paper to think about learning to read and write. One of her early biographers tells us that she indeed made an effort to learn to read and write in the late 1850s, when visiting among abolitionist friends in Concord, Massachusetts (Sanborn, 1913).[6] And during the Civil War, she told another early biographer that she planned to acquire the power of telling her own story in writing

(Cheney, 1865). Yet she never did find the necessary time to devote to such an arduous self-improvement project in her middle age, and it may well be that she came to feel that she could exercise sufficient control over the pen by carefully choosing the writer with whom she would work and asking that writer to read the final product aloud.

If she did not use the pen herself, is it really possible to claim that she produced a self-authored life story? I believe, as I argue in part 2, "The Life Stories," that in the most important senses she did "write" her auto-biography, using all the resources available to her as a skilled oral story-teller and a well-connected African American celebrity. Her self-expressive legacy has been fragmented and obscured by the mediated forms in which it was recorded, and this is undoubtedly the major reason why she has not been included as yet in the lively contemporary scholarly discussion of nineteenth-century African American women's narratives. Still, she was clearly an active participant in the creation of the public Harriet Tubman story, and I believe that she had a larger part in the shaping of her legacy than has yet been understood. Even in the more formal storytelling sessions with Sarah Bradford that became the basis for the most detailed biography of Tubman written during her lifetime, Tubman clearly exerted significant control over the shape of the text through choosing which stories to tell and how to tell them.[7]

Harriet Tubman told stories, sang songs, and performed dramatic re-enactments of many of the life experiences she considered most significant (and most entertaining as well) on public platforms, in private gatherings, in formal interviews, and in conversations with close associates, family members, and visiting strangers over a span of more than sixty years in the North. Her early storytelling performances were memorable events for her listeners, as many of them testified afterward. These sessions helped create a market for the collaborative biography she produced with Sarah Hopkins Bradford three years after the war, a narrative of nearly a hundred pages called *Scenes in the Life of Harriet Tubman* (1869). This was actually a patchwork collection of interview-based stories and documentary materials, prepared in haste. Later Bradford revised and expanded it twice, in 1886 and 1901, and renamed it *Harriet, the Moses of Her People*. Taken together, the three versions of the Bradford biography contain almost all the important stories of her Underground Railroad career and war service that have survived.[8] All later biographers, even if they also interviewed Tubman, relied at least in part on information (and misinformation) from Bradford.

The present volume offers a hypothetical version of Tubman's "auto-biography" in part 3, "Stories and Sayings." Here I have assembled every individual life history story I was able to locate, most of them excavated from the three early biographies created with Tubman's help during her lifetime. The vast majority of her own stories cover the period of her initial celebrity. Through attending to the stories she chose to tell (many of them repeatedly) and the way she told them, readers can create for themselves the closest possible approximation of her own storytelling voice.[9] I have also included a selection of "Documents" (part 4)—primary source material from Tubman's lifetime that helps us understand the impact of her personality and actions on others, including her early biographers.[10] Some of these documents provide telling glimpses of her long postwar life in Auburn, New York, when she faced economic and social challenges with characteristic energy, resourcefulness, and generosity.

I have selected and edited the story texts and other documents with the overriding goal of illuminating Harriet Tubman's own perspectives on her experience as a nineteenth-century American woman and as an anti-slavery activist. Together, her story texts and the documents enable us to witness key moments in the creation and early evolution of her celebrity. They allow us to appreciate some of the problems fame brought a female "race hero" in the nineteenth-century context, and to understand the strategies she adopted for dealing with these problems, at a time when asserting social, economic, legal, and political rights for African Americans was still very much a radical, unpopular, and even dangerous activity.

By making these stories and documents widely accessible, I hope to contribute to a fresh and more multifaceted understanding of the private woman whose life has virtually disappeared behind the heroic public icon. There have been many popular biographies of Tubman for adults and children produced since her death, but only one work based on careful research into the original sources has as yet appeared: *General Harriet Tubman* (1943a) by the politically progressive white writer Earl Conrad, still the standard biography of Tubman. Conrad's book is both carefully documented and passionately written, yet his Harriet Tubman is still very much a larger-than-life figure. Conrad, a journalist who became interested in black history through experience as a labor organizer in the 1930s, minimized her spirituality and maximized her role as a militant, an African American woman warrior.[11]

In providing my own biographical overview in this book (part 1, "The Life"), I invite readers to contemplate some of the complexities of the life of the historical woman within the setting of nineteenth-century social and political conflict over the institution of slavery. I build on the work of her former biographers, but with the great advantage of a much larger number of primary sources to work from than were available to any of them.[12] I am very much aware that my retelling of her life story cannot be definitive. Where the "facts" are still not fully known, I hope students of African American history and literature and American culture will be inspired to continue the research. My own experience during the more than ten years in which I did research for this book suggests that many other fascinating lost documents will turn up in libraries and archives in the future, to reward the persistent, imaginative, and lucky explorer.

A full list of primary sources is included in the bibliography as a resource for those who want to explore more thoroughly the manuscript and printed sources most relevant to Tubman's life story.[13]

PART I

The Life

THE SLAVERY YEARS

Harriet Tubman was born into American slavery, a complex legal, social, economic, cultural, and psychological world that had evolved in the colonies of the eastern seaboard over nearly two hundred years.[1] After the Revolutionary War and the federal abolition of the slave trade in 1808, the legal institution was well on its way to gradual extinction in the North, primarily for economic reasons, but also because of growing religion-based antislavery organizing by Quakers and others. In contrast, the development of a cotton-based economy expanded and reinforced the grip of the slavery system upon all aspects of the culture of the Southern states. When Tubman was a child in Maryland in the 1820s and 1830s, the slave-owning elite of the South were closing ranks to defend the institution, in response both to the threat of slave insurrection and to a newly militant antislavery movement in the United States, represented in the pages of William Lloyd Garrison's newspaper the *Liberator*, which thundered out an uncompromising fire-and-brimstone message about the evils of slave ownership and called for immediate emancipation. The proslavery ideology of the Southern states deepened as she grew into womanhood, and there was less and less room for dissenting voices among Southern whites—even though only a small minority of the residents of Southern states were themselves slave owners, with a strong economic interest in keeping slavery intact.

Tubman experienced the particular slave system of the border state of Maryland, where the geographical proximity to the free states of Pennsylvania and New Jersey allowed more opportunities to flee successfully than in the states of the Deep South, and the Underground Railroad developed many stations. Yet she did not escape the profound psychologically and

spiritually shaping effects of a plantation slave culture during her childhood and young womanhood, as is evident from some of the stories she
later told about her youth.[2]

She testified in later years that she had been born in Cambridge,
Maryland, in Dorchester County (Tubman, 1894b). She did not know the
exact date of her birth. The best current evidence suggests that Tubman
was born in 1820, but it might have been a year or two later.[3] The documentary record is contradictory about her lineage: her earliest biographer
says that she was a "grand-daughter of a slave imported from Africa, and
has not a drop of white blood in her veins" (Sanborn, 1863).[4] Another,
much later sketch asserts: "She knows that her mother's mother was
brought in a slave-ship from Africa, that her mother was the daughter of
a white man, an American, and her father a full-blooded Negro" (Miller,
1912).[5] We do know that her maternal grandmother's name was Modesty
and that her parents' names were Benjamin Ross and Harriet (Rittia,
Ritta, Rit, or Ritty) Green (Sanborn, 1863). Her own name in the South
is said by various sources to have been Araminta Ross, and she is listed
in one important early document as Minty (Thompson, 1853). In affidavits later in life she testified both that her "maiden name was Aramitta
Ross" and that she was known as Harriet Ross before her marriage to
John Tubman.[6]

She lived for most of her young life with her family on a plantation
owned by the Brodess family near the town of Bucktown, not far from
Cambridge, in Dorchester County, Maryland.[7] Her mother worked as a
cook for the Brodess family. Her father was owned by Anthony Thompson until 1840, when he was legally freed.[8] Fifteen years later, in 1855,
Benjamin Ross was able to purchase his wife from Eliza Ann Brodess,
presumably through savings accumulated over the years of toil.

The two white slaveholding families that controlled the lives of
Tubman's parents and siblings intermarried, and the resulting "blended
family" relationships have bedeviled her biographers and are still confus-
ing to explain. Her mother had become the property of Mary Pattison at
the death of Mary's grandfather Athow Pattison. Mary Pattison married
Joseph Brodess, March 19, 1800, but Joseph Brodess died in 1803, leaving Mary with a two-year-old son, Edward (b. June 1801). Mary Pattison
Brodess then married a neighboring widower, Anthony Thompson (October 11, 1803), who also had a son, then ten-year-old Anthony C. Thompson.
Very likely it was at this time, when the Brodess and Thompson households were united by marriage, that Benjamin Ross and Harriet Green

Ross began to establish a family together.[9] Their eldest daughter, Linah, was born around 1808. When Mary Pattison died in 1809 or 1810, her slave property, including Harriet Ross and her children, passed to Edward, and the elder Anthony Thompson became the legal guardian of his underage stepson.[10] Edward Brodess reached his legal maturity in 1822, perhaps two years after Tubman's birth.

Anthony C. Thompson, the stepbrother of Edward Brodess, figured prominently in Harriet Ross's family's life in the 1840s and 1850s. He hired several of the Ross family members to work for him, paying first Edward Brodess for their labor and then his widow Eliza Ann Brodess. Tubman lived with Dr. Thompson during her last two years in Maryland, and though he was not her legal owner, he appears frequently as a comic figure in her stories about tricking the "master."

Tubman believed, and told all three of her early biographers, that her mother had been kept in slavery illegally. In about 1845, a year after her own marriage to John Tubman, she "paid a lawyer $5 to look up the will of my mother's first master" (Bradford, 1869). The lawyer did indeed find the will, dated January 18, 1791, in which "Rittia" and her "increase" were given to the master's granddaughter, Mary Pattison, to serve her and her offspring only until the servants reached the age of forty-five. Harriet Ross should have been legally emancipated in 1834 or so, when she turned forty-five.[11] The anecdote indicates Tubman's own interest, as a relatively young woman, in securing her family's liberation, and it is also a valuable example of the willingness of some enslaved people living in Maryland in the immediate prewar era to seek justice under the law.

Harriet Ross's work as cook in the plantation "big house" kept her out of her own family's home until "late nights." Like most girl children in slave families, Harriet Tubman at an early age cared for a younger brother and a baby.[12] We know nothing about her father's role in her preadolescent childhood. Even her mother appears only briefly in her later stories of childhood, leaving us to infer the quality of the relationship between mother and daughter based on very little evidence. In several stories, Ritta Ross emerges as fiercely protective of her children. We also know from her actions in her later life that Tubman was among the most dutiful of daughters.[13]

One of the most universally feared experiences of slavery happened in the Ross family during Tubman's young years in Maryland. Two older sisters were sold south, as she testified in 1855 in Canada: "I had two sisters carried away in a chain-gang—one of them left two children. We were always uneasy" (Tubman, 1856).[14] The dread of further repetitions of this particularly destructive exercise of arbitrary power by the slaveholding family figured prominently in Tubman's accounts of her decision to risk the dangers of an attempted escape. This terrible experience of helplessly enduring the loss of her elder sisters helps explain her extraordinary drive to protect her remaining family members at all costs.

The religious life of her family during their years in Maryland can only be glimpsed fitfully in the stories she told and the contemporary documents. They certainly received religious instruction of some kind, most probably in a Methodist church setting.[15] In the 1860s she told one interviewer about her parents' religious fasting on Fridays and Sundays, saying they were "taught to do so down South." "Good Friday, and five Fridays hand [?] going from Good Friday, my father never eats or drinks, all day— fasting for the five bleeding wounds of Jesus. All the other Fridays of the year he never eats till the sun goes down; then he takes a little tea and a piece of bread. . . . He says if he denies himself for the sufferings of his Lord and Master, Jesus will sustain him."[16]

Like many other enslaved people who later testified critically about the hypocrisy of Southern antebellum churches and white churchgoers, Tubman and her brothers were highly indignant about the misappropriation of Christianity by slaveholder culture to justify unchristian practices against other human beings. The Christian religious beliefs and spiritual practices of her family, however acquired, were nonetheless vital resources upon which they could draw for psychological survival.

Tubman was hired out during her youth to work for several white employers outside the Brodess family. As a young child, she was apprenticed briefly to a weaver, and the weaver's husband, James Cook, employed her "watching his musk-rat traps, which compelled her to wade through the water," even when sick with measles, according to Sanborn. (This was one occasion when her mother came to her defense.) Later she was hired out as a house maid or nurse maid to a series of neighboring families— possibly on a trial basis for possible purchase. She suffered whippings that left scars on her back and neck, when her work did not satisfy those who had hired her time.

She was partially disabled by a head injury, probably in her early teens, when an overseer threw a heavy weight at another slave.[17] The disability was described by her biographers as "somnolence," or the tendency to fall briefly into a deep sleep in the midst of daily activities.[18] Later in her teenage years she was hired out to work for a builder named John Stewart, who had hired Benjamin Ross's services as well. Sanborn reported that she often "worked for her father, who was a timber inspector, and super-intended the cutting and hauling of great quantities of timber for the Bal-timore ship-yards," and he emphasized her ability to use the hiring-out system to put aside enough money to invest in her own livestock. In a situation where she had first to earn enough to repay Dr. Thompson for the value of her labor, she was able to "buy a pair of steers' worth forty dollars." (Her early biographers viewed her performance of heavy field-work—"man's work" to them—from a variety of conflicting perspectives, as I discuss in part 2, "The Life Stories.")

She married a free man named John Tubman in 1844, when she would have been about twenty-four years old (Sanborn, 1863). Nothing is known about how they came to marry or what their feelings may have been on the occasion. Very possibly her physical disability and her laborious work assignments both played a role in delaying the age at which she married. Many enslaved girls were informally married at a much younger age. Historian Deborah Gray White points out that because it was in the slave owner's interests, young enslaved women were encouraged to reproduce early and often, sometimes by the assignment of lighter tasks to pregnant women. Prolific slave women were sometimes given material rewards, and those who resisted reproduction could be threatened with punishments. The mothers of slave daughters, on the other hand, often attempted to slow "the pace of courtship" of their daughters, and it is possible that the protective Harriet Ross played a role in delaying the age at which her daughter married John Tubman.

No information has as yet surfaced about any possible pregnancies or miscarriages that may have ensued, and according to her own later testi-mony, Tubman remained childless during the four or five years of her first marriage (and, indeed, throughout her whole life). We do not know what this may have meant to her personally, but we do know that childless-ness greatly increased her chances for successful escape and made her later Underground Railroad and war work more easily possible.[19] Her relation-ship with John Tubman must have been complicated by the fact that she was the legal property of a white man, while her husband was his own master. Very little has come down in her own words to flesh out the story of their feelings for one another, but what we have suggests that her attachment to him was stronger than his to her.[20]

On March 9, 1849, Edward Brodess died, leaving a will specifying that his widow, Eliza Ann Brodess, should have "the use and hire of [Harriet

Ross and her children] . . . during her life, for the purpose of raising his children."[21] Tubman was working at that time for Dr. Thompson (Sanborn said she had been living with Thompson for two years). The death of any slave owner raised the specter of the sale of enslaved "property" to pay estate-related expenses, and Tubman's decision to try to escape is linked in all the early biographies to her fear that she and other family members would be sold into Southern slavery around this time.[22]

The escape in 1849 began as a joint venture with two or three of her brothers, but the brothers eventually decided not to continue.[23] According to Bradford's 1869 account, it was Harriet Tubman who had "persuaded" the brothers to join her, "but they had not gone far when the brothers, appalled by the dangers before and behind them, determined to go back, and in spite of her remonstrances dragged her with them. In fear and terror, she remained over Sunday," setting out by herself a few days later.[24] Whatever the number of brothers and whatever the reason for the brothers' change of mind, the early sources all agree that Tubman finally took the important step of pursuing freedom on her own.

In the earliest published version of the escape story, it is recorded that "she found a friend in a white lady, who knew her story and helped her on her way" (Sanborn, 1863). This is undoubtedly a less "heroic" version of the escape than the one fixed in our cultural memory by later biographers (following Bradford) that she simply "followed the North Star," impelled by visionary dreams. On reflection, however, we can see that it does seem highly likely that she would have had help in her initial steps toward freedom. (A similar role was played by a white woman neighbor in the Harriet Jacobs narrative *Incidents in the Life of a Slave Girl.*)

Acknowledgment of the likelihood of a white woman's help does not diminish Tubman's own achievement, in my view. On the contrary—it makes it easier to understand Tubman's ability to form apparently affectionate relationships with politically allied white women afterward, despite her experience of physical and psychological mistreatment by white slaveholding women such as those whose whippings scarred her neck and back. This "white lady, who knew her story" may have been someone in the immediate neighborhood, perhaps even a friend of the Brodess family. Helen Woodruff Tatlock, the daughter of white friends of Tubman's in Auburn, told Earl Conrad in 1939 that Tubman gave this woman who helped her a prized bed quilt, "which she did not dare to give to any of the slaves, for if this was found in their possession, they would be questioned and punished for having known about her plans. . . . The white woman

Thomas Garrett, Quaker abolitionist and Underground Railroad agent based in Wilmington, Delaware. Garrett was among the first to document Tubman's secret work on behalf of escaping fugitives. Courtesy Chester County Historical Society, West Chester, Pennsylvania.

gave her a paper with two names upon it, and directions how she might get to the first house where she would receive aid"(Tatlock, 1939a).

Tubman's escape route in 1849 may have taken her through several towns in the slave state of Delaware on her way to Wilmington.[25] There Thomas Garrett, a dedicated white Quaker Underground Railroad operative, maintained close correspondence with the Philadelphia Vigilance Committee, an interracial fugitive aid group.[26] All sources agree that once in Philadelphia, she found work and contacts with the organized antislavery movement and within a year or two had begun to formulate a plan to return south to guide other family members to freedom.

UNDERGROUND
RAILROAD YEARS

EARLY RESCUES

During the early 1850s, as Harriet Tubman began her work with the Underground Railroad, the slavery question came to dominate national political debate. Antislavery sentiment, once confined to a tiny minority of radicals in the North, spread dramatically, and soon national dissolution came to seem inevitable. Several important legal developments help us understand this dramatic shift in popular opinion in the years leading up to the Civil War.

The decade began with the enactment of the Fugitive Slave Law (1850), which put the Northern states in the position of aiding and abetting the slaveholding class of the South. Suddenly many white Northerners who had previously not been personally involved in the slavery question began to resent the power of the Southern states to dictate federal policy on fugitives, and white participation in Underground Railroad networks to aid fugitive slaves in the North dramatically increased. Then, in 1854, Congress passed the Kansas-Nebraska Act, which included an explicit repeal of earlier legislation restricting the expansion of slavery in new territories seeking statehood. This opened Kansas to a prolonged period of struggle between proslavery and antislavery forces. When President Pierce recognized a proslavery territorial government there in 1856, the struggle turned increasingly violent. The antislavery town of Lawrence, Kansas, was attacked, burned, and looted by "border ruffians." In retribution, the antislavery guerilla John Brown and a small band of supporters committed the "Pottawatomie massacre" in the late spring of that year.[1]

The violence spread east into the halls of Congress. During debate

on the Kansas questions, antislavery senator Charles Sumner of Massachusetts gave a speech bitterly denouncing South Carolina senator A. P.
Butler. A congressman related to Butler beat Sumner almost to death
two days later in the Senate chamber. The following year, when a new
Democratic president took office, the Supreme Court added further fuel
to the fires of discord by rendering its infamous Dred Scott decision, effectively denying U.S. citizenship to blacks as well as overturning the Missouri Compromise's ban on slavery in new Northern states.[2] By 1858,
John Brown was recruiting and fund-raising for an armed insurrection of
Southern slaves. A severe split within the Democratic Party, as well as
growing "mainstream" antislavery sentiment in the North, was preparing
the way for the election of the antislavery Republican president Abraham
Lincoln in 1860.[3]

When Harriet Tubman successfully escaped from Maryland slavery in
1849, she must have been heartened to discover the strength of the radical
or "immediate abolition" wing of the U.S. antislavery movement, founded
by William Lloyd Garrison, which had been organizing resistance to the
slave power for a full generation. National and regional antislavery societies were numerous and well organized—including the female antislavery
societies that had begun to play an important part in encouraging social
activism and political thinking among U.S. women on behalf of women
as a disenfranchised group.[4] Thanks to the sustained activism of these networks, slavery was publicly denounced as a great moral evil throughout
the North, from pulpits, in lecture halls, and in the pages of antislavery
newspapers such as Garrison's *Liberator* or Frederick Douglass's several
independent newspapers.

Tubman's initial contact with the antislavery movement after arriving
in Philadelphia in 1849 was probably through William Still, an African
American antislavery activist who worked as a clerk in the American
Anti-Slavery Society's Office in Philadelphia and received and interviewed
fugitives sent on by Thomas Garrett on behalf of the Philadelphia Vigilance Committee.[5] Tubman frequently stayed at Still's house when passing through Philadelphia on her missions in the 1850s. James and Lucretia
Mott, white Quaker antislavery and women's rights activists, were also
members of the Philadelphia Vigilance Committee, and along with Garrett
they were likely to have been among Tubman's earliest white Northern
antislavery associates. Tubman described Lucretia Mott in later years as
someone who "stood by them when there was no one else" (M. C. Wright,
1868j). Still or one of the Motts, perhaps impressed with her ability to

William Still, antislavery activist and Underground Railroad operative in Philadelphia. Still helped bring fugitives through Philadelphia and later published accounts of some of Harriet Tubman's rescues in *The Underground Rail Road* (1872). Courtesy Chester County Historical Society, West Chester, Pennsylvania.

engineer her own successful escape, may even have recruited Tubman for Underground Railroad work.

In Philadelphia, and in the nearby summer resort of Cape May, New Jersey, she found wage work (probably primarily as a hotel cook and laundress) that enabled her to support herself and put aside some money. She made an initial return to Maryland to rescue her niece Keziah and two children from Baltimore in December 1850—a rescue planned in collaboration with the husband of her niece, a free black man named John Bowley.[6] Clearly Tubman had established a reliable mode of communication with her family members in Maryland as early as the year after her own escape.[7] There may have been a second rescue from Baltimore of "a brother and two other men" in the spring of 1851—this was reported by Sanborn, but it is otherwise undocumented.

Tubman made her first journey to her "old home" in the fall of 1851, on what Sanborn called her "third expedition into Maryland" (Sanborn, 1863). Her purpose was to fetch her husband, John Tubman, and bring him

Executive Committee of the Pennsylvania Anti-Slavery Society, circa 1851. Tubman's contacts included J. Miller McKim (standing, second from right), Oliver Johnson (seated, far left), and James and Lucretia Coffin Mott (seated, far right). She also may have known Robert Purvis (seated, third from right). Courtesy Friends Historical Library of Swarthmore College, Swarthmore, Pennsylvania.

north, but she learned when she arrived that he had taken a new wife.[8] As she told the story afterward, only after a mighty struggle with her own feelings of anger and jealousy was she able to change course and abandon her former strong attachment to John Tubman. This was an important personal turning point for Harriet Tubman, it seems, one that allowed her to focus all her energy on a newly articulated mission for the next decade—the rescue of her entire family from slavery.[9]

Three brothers who still remained in Maryland exerted themselves strenuously on behalf of their own emancipation during the early 1850s with the help of their father, Benjamin Ross, and perhaps a white friend, according to the testimony one of them later gave in Canada in 1863. The brother, "Henry Stewart," told how he and his brothers made one attempt to get away, "but got surrounded and went back" (H. Stewart, 1863). They hid for a while and then tried to negotiate for their freedom through "a white gentleman," but they were rebuffed by "our mistress," Eliza Ann Brodess. Benjamin Ross also got involved, trying unsuccessfully to find someone who could transport them to freedom. Ultimately, Henry Stewart said, "we had to turn round & go back to our owners, after we had been gone six months." They remained at home another year, "and then we were to be sold," which brought Tubman to get them, Stewart testified, "but we wouldn't go."[10] Finally, the daring rescue of Christmas 1854 took place, and at least two (and probably three) of Tubman's brothers were successfully brought to Philadelphia as part of a larger party.[11] In the story of this rescue collected by Sarah Bradford, Ritta Ross was said to be kept in the dark about Tubman's plans so to that she would not "raise an uproar" in her efforts to keep her sons at home.[12] Benjamin Ross secretly brought food to Tubman and her brothers, who were hidden in an outbuilding. Cunningly, he tied a handkerchief over his eyes so that he could credibly testify to authorities later that "he hasn't seen one of his children this Christmas." Six months after Tubman had spirited away the three Ross brothers, Benjamin Ross purchased Ritta Ross from Eliza Ann Brodess on June 11, 1855, for the sum of $20.[13] Though Tubman's parents were now both legally free, they continued to live in their old neighborhood, where Benjamin Ross continued to support the efforts of other would-be fugitives.

By this time Tubman was well on the way to celebrity in transatlantic Quaker antislavery networks. She began to appear very regularly in Thomas Garrett's letters to Eliza Wigham, the secretary of the Edinburgh Ladies Emancipation Society, which was helping to raise funds to support Underground Railroad work in America. In this initial sketch of Tubman's career

as of the end of 1855, Garrett speaks of "4 successful trips to the neighborhood she left" and the rescues of "17 of her brothers, sisters, & friends"
(Garrett, 1855).[14] Garrett's sketch makes it clear that Tubman knew the risk
she ran of being returned to slavery "for life" if captured, and indicates
her unwavering focus on rescuing her one remaining "sister" or niece, as
well as a sister-in-law and the children of both women. Interestingly, he
quotes her as anticipating an early retirement: "She says if she gets them
away safely, she will be content." Her strong attachment to her family,
rather than an abstract idea of liberating "her people," drove Tubman to
run such great risks.[15]

A CANADIAN HOME BASE

The Canada West settlement of St. Catharines, just across the Suspension
Bridge from Buffalo, New York, became an initial home base for Tubman,
her brothers, and her niece's families, perhaps from as early as 1851 (as
Sanborn reported).[16] The growing black community drew the attention of
the ex-fugitive slave writer and speaker William Wells Brown, who enthusiastically described those fortunate ones who had been in Canada long
enough to acquire property and money: "Each family has a good garden,
well filled with vegetables, ducks, chickens, and a pig-pen, with at least
one fat grunter getting ready for Christmas. . . . The houses in the settlement are all owned by their occupants, and from inquiry I learned that the
people generally were free from debt."[17]

When Tubman and her brothers (who were now using the surname
Stewart[18]) established a home in St. Catharines, their experience was quite
different from this rosy picture: "The first winter was terribly severe for
these poor runaways. They earned their bread by chopping wood in the
snows of a Canadian forest; they were frostbitten, hungry, and naked.
Harriet was their good angel. She kept house for her brother, and the poor
creatures boarded with her. She worked for them, begged for them, prayed
for them, . . . and carried them by the help of God through the hard
winter" (Sanborn, 1863). But they survived, and later two of the brothers
tried to establish themselves as farmers. According to Henry Stewart (1863):
"At first I made pretty good headway, and then my brother and I rented
a farm, for which we paid $200 a year, and we got into some trouble and
left that, and my brother went to Berlin, and I undertook to buy six acres
of land out in the country; and am now living on it."[19]

The family of Tubman's niece was also settled in St. Catharines in the early 1850s. Harkless Bowley, the grandnephew who gave Earl Conrad so much information about the family many years later, was born in St. Catharines. James Bowley, an older grandnephew, had become Tubman's special protégée while she was still working in Philadelphia and Cape May. She sent this grandnephew to school with money she raised by "working out two years at a dollar a week." After the war, James Bowley returned south to work as a schoolteacher for freed people and later held elective office in the legislature of Reconstruction South Carolina.

Tubman was interviewed in St. Catharines by the Bostonian antislavery journalist Benjamin Drew when he visited in the summer of 1855. Remarkably, given the danger she faced in her Underground Railroad work, the brief testimonial she dictated about her experience in slavery was published over her own name.[20] She did not reveal her clandestine role as a liberator of her family and friends, of course—as a matter of fact, she even claimed, somewhat disingenuously (given that she had already made several trips back to Dorchester Country to rescue family), that she had "no opportunity to see my friends in my native land." This testimony, though brief, is a strong expression of her antislavery views: "Now I've been free, I know what a dreadful condition slavery is. I have seen hundreds of escaped slaves, but I never saw one who was willing to go back and be a slave. . . . I think slavery is the next thing to hell. If a person would send another into bondage, he would, it appears to me, be bad enough to send him into hell, if he could" (Tubman, 1856).

When she brought fugitives to St. Catharines in 1857, they were received by the Reverend Hiram Wilson, of the Canada Mission (of the American Missionary Society). Wilson reported: "In another instance 4 of the sable pilgrims of liberty came having a remarkable colored heroine for their conductress from the land of oppression to the 'land of Promise,' and to the bright noontide of British Freedom. . . . We could not but admire the courage and fortitude of their benevolent guide nor refrain from cautioning her against too much adventure & peril, as this was but one of many instances of her deeds of daring" (H. Wilson, 1857). [21]

She retained her connection to the fugitive relief efforts in St. Catharines even after she had resettled in Auburn, New York, in 1858–1859. A notice in the *Liberator* from December 20, 1861, indicates that a new association, the Fugitive Aid Society of St. Catharines, would accept donations of clothing and money to "relieve such fugitive slaves as may be suffering from sickness or destitution."[22] Tubman and her brother William H. Stewart were listed as committee members. This new organization, controlled at least in part by the fugitive community itself, may have been a practical response of the Boston antislavery friends to a complaint she lodged about Hiram Wilson's management of the donations a year or two earlier.[23]

During Tubman's early years in St. Catharines (between 1851 and 1855), a substantial church building was erected by the independent black British Methodist Episcopal (B.M.E.) Church to serve the African Canadian community.[24] The church was located near the site of a boardinghouse Tubman is known to have rented in 1858,[25] and it seems very likely that she and her family members attended this church when in St. Catharines (O. Thomas, 1999, 39).

RESETTLEMENT IN AUBURN

Harriet Tubman's northern Underground Railroad escape route—from Philadelphia to New York, then to Albany, Syracuse, Rochester, and across the Niagara Falls suspension bridge to St. Catharines, Canada West—brought her into contact with antislavery activist networks in western New York State.[26] A key site where she found many political allies was the town of Auburn, which had an active Underground Railroad community. Her Philadelphia antislavery associate Lucretia Mott probably provided an introduction to her sister in Auburn, Martha Coffin Wright.[27] Wright and her lawyer husband, David, became staunch allies and lifelong friends of Tubman's, as did two of their daughters (one of whom married a son of William Lloyd Garrison). Through the Wrights Tubman would have met New York politician and statesman William H. Seward, who also played a significant role in her life history. Seward's wife, Frances Miller Seward, and her widowed sister, Lazette Miller Worden, were close friends of Martha Coffin Wright. The Seward family, like the Wrights, helped raise relief funds and find work for some of the fugitives Tubman brought to Auburn.[28]

William H. Seward, a former New York governor, was elected U.S. senator in the year of Tubman's self-liberation, 1849. After an unsuccessful bid for the Republican presidential candidacy in 1860, he was appointed Secretary of State by the newly elected Republican president, Abraham Lincoln. Seward had an impressive record of political antislavery leadership among Northern white liberals at the time Tubman first met him in the mid-1850s, although he would later compromise on his antislavery politics in order to position himself better for the run for the Republican nomination for president. He had opposed the Fugitive Slave Law in his first speech in the Senate in March 1850, appealing to a "higher law" than the Constitution. The American Anti-Slavery Society distributed ten thousand copies of this speech, which helped to establish Seward as a major national mouthpiece for antislavery sentiment in the 1850s. He had led the opposition in the Senate to the repeal of the Missouri Compromise provided in the Kansas-Nebraska Act of 1854. In his second term as senator from New York he had introduced a bill that would have admitted Kansas to the union with an antislavery constitution. He harshly criticized the president and the Southerners on the Supreme Court for collusion in the Dred Scott decision. Finally, in a well-publicized speech made on October 1858 in Rochester, Seward warned of an impending "irrepressible conflict" between the slave labor and free labor systems of the South and North. Because of this speech, the *New York Herald* labeled him an "arch agitator." His apparent antislavery radicalism made him attractive as a future Republican presidential candidate to some abolitionists who were later disappointed in his compromises (J. M. Taylor, 1991, 76–118).

Even given the support of such influential antislavery friends, the decision to settle down in a Northern state while she was still a fugitive with a price on her head was a risky one, and Tubman based it entirely on family considerations. In June 1857, she was virtually compelled to bring her elderly parents out of the South on short notice, because Benjamin Ross's antislavery activism had brought him into immediate danger of arrest. He had sheltered eight fugitive slaves who had broken out of jail in Dover, Delaware, in March, but he was betrayed to the authorities. Thomas Garrett reported at the time that "The old man Ross had to flee. . . . They were preparing to have Benjamin arrested when his master secretly advised him to leave"(Garrett, 1857d).

Who was the white man referred to by Garrett as the "master" who "secretly advised" Benjamin Ross that he was about to be arrested, and what was this man's motivation? Might Dr. Anthony Thompson, though an ungenerous taskmaster, have been capable of acting upon a complex "family feeling" when it did not affect his own pocketbook? Could the warning have come from the shipbuilder John Stewart, who had been a kind of surrogate "master" to Benjamin Ross and Harriet Tubman in the past?[29] As with so many other crucial details of Tubman's life history, this mystery remains to tantalize her biographers.

Tubman had learned of Benjamin Ross's vulnerability in Philadelphia, and by the end of March 1857 was planning the trip south. It was challenging to transport her elderly parents, who could not be expected to travel on foot. For this rescue, she manufactured a primitive horse-drawn carriage, "fitted out in a primitive style with a straw collar, a pair of old chaise wheels, with a board on the axle to sit on, another board swung with ropes, fastened to the axle, to rest their feet on" (Garrett, 1868). She successfully brought Ritta and Benjamin Ross to Canada, with Garrett's assistance, but they did not spend much time there. Ritta Ross, in particular, made no secret of her misery in Canada West over the winter of 1857–58 (Sanborn, 1863). The following year Tubman began to look for a location for a family home, and by the spring of 1859 she had located one in Auburn. William H. Seward agreed to sell Tubman a house and seven acres of land on South Street for $1,200.[30] Her friends referred to Seward's sale price and mortgage terms as "generous." Nevertheless, Tubman was hard-pressed to keep up her quarterly payments on the debt she owed Seward.[31]

In November 1859, after a five-month absence in New England, Tubman received a letter from her brother John Stewart in Auburn, reminding her of the many needs of her dependent family there and informing her that "Seward has received nothing as payment since the 4th of July that I know of." The elders may have only recently moved into the South Street house at this time—Benjamin Ross still wanted to fetch goods left behind in Canada, and they did not yet have a stove. The letter implies that Tubman was the acknowledged head of the household. Her advice was eagerly sought by both her father and her brothers—a double-edged sword for her, perhaps, given the other concerns she had in this year of the failed Harpers Ferry uprising. "Please write as soon as possible and not delay. We three are alone. I have had a good deal of trouble with them as they are getting old and feeble. . . . Catharine Stewart has not come yet but wants to very bad send what things you want father to bring if you think best for him to go. . . . Write me particularly what you want me to do as I want to hear from you very much" (John Stewart, 1859).[32]

By the time she had settled her parents in Auburn, Tubman was widely known and respected in Northern antislavery networks. There were many organizations and politically allied individuals nearby to whom she could turn for financial aid, both for the support of her Northern household and to underwrite the expenses of her rescue trips south. One important backer was Gerrit Smith (a cousin of Elizabeth Cady Stanton's), who lived in Peterboro, New York, and whom Tubman had visited on several occasions by the later 1850s. A wealthy reformer with a particular interest in antislavery politics, Smith had set aside a tract of 120,000 acres of land in the Adirondacks for homesteading by black families who wished to become self-sufficient farmers. Smith was a steady source of funds for antislavery work during the 1840s and 1850s.

Tubman also knew and worked with prominent African American antislavery activists in New York State, and she may have received some financial support from these networks, as well as shelter in their homes when needed. She had undoubtedly come into contact with the famous antislavery lecturer Frederick Douglass in the early 1850s, as she brought fugitives through his home city of Rochester on their way to Canada West.

Frederick Douglass, former fugitive, abolitionist orator, writer, and publisher, and Underground Railroad operative in Rochester. Tubman probably brought fugitives to his house in the 1850s, and Douglass later testified to her daring.

By the time she had escaped from Maryland in 1849, Douglass had established himself as the editor of his own antislavery newspaper in Rochester
and was well known as the author of a well-received fugitive slave autobiography.[33] Douglass almost certainly referred to Tubman in 1858, though
without using her name: "one coloured woman, who escaped from Slavery
eight years ago, has made several returns at great risk, and has brought out,
since obtaining her freedom, fifty others from the house of bondage. She
has been spending a short time with us since the holidays. She possesses
great courage and shrewdness, and may yet render even more important
service to the Cause" (Douglass, 1858).

Tubman's likely visit to Douglass in 1858 took place during the period
when John Brown was intensively consulting with prominent African
American abolitionists, including Douglass and the Reverend Jermain Wesley Loguen of the Fugitive Aid Society of Syracuse, New York.[34] Douglass's
reference to the "even more important service for the Cause" in Tubman's
future is surely based on his knowledge of John Brown's hope to use her
in the Virginia campaign—what was soon to be known as the Harpers
Ferry Raid.

THE JOHN BROWN ASSOCIATION AND
BOSTON ANTISLAVERY CIRCLES

Frederick Douglass had been acquainted with John Brown since 1848, and
both were present at the founding conference of the Radical Abolitionist
Party, in Syracuse, New York, in June 1855—an enterprise heavily backed
by Gerrit Smith.[35] In the guerilla war between antislavery and proslavery
forces over "bleeding Kansas" in 1855–1856, John Brown and his sons had
made a fearsome name for themselves as defenders of the antislavery settlers, willing to risk their own lives and to shed the blood of proslavery
forces in a cause sanctioned by their egalitarian and militant understanding of Christianity. Now Brown had come east both to cultivate alliances
and to raise funds and procure rifles to continue his Kansas activities on
behalf of the free-state settlers.

Gerrit Smith sent Brown to Boston to meet prominent Boston-area
abolitionists in January 1857. There Brown contacted twenty-five-year-
old antislavery idealist and Concord schoolteacher Franklin B. Sanborn,
then in Boston acting as the secretary of the Massachusetts State Kansas
Committee.[36] Sanborn was immediately enthralled with Brown and his

Jermain Loguen, former fugitive and Underground Railroad operative in Syracuse. Loguen may have introduced John Brown to Tubman in Canada. Courtesy Onondaga Historical Association.

uncompromising antislavery actions and introduced him to many prominent antislavery speakers and writers in Boston and nearby Concord—
including Theodore Parker, William Lloyd Garrison, Wendell Phillips,
Ralph Waldo Emerson, and Henry David Thoreau (Sanborn, 1878). John
Brown and William Lloyd Garrison argued heatedly over a central tenet
of Garrisonian abolitionism—its "nonresistance" or nonviolence policy,
which Brown repudiated. The other Bostonian antislavery luminaries were
highly impressed with Brown's moral integrity and courage and saw in
him a man of action whom they could support with both rifles and
pledges of funds.

Brown returned to Kansas but was back in the East the following
winter, spending three weeks in Frederick Douglass's home in Rochester
(from January 27 to February 17, 1858). During this second visit, he was
ripening his new, larger plan—for an armed slave rebellion to begin in
Virginia.[37] He went on to Gerrit Smith's Peterboro home for a meeting
in February in which Sanborn first heard Brown reveal in outline form the
plans for his Virginia campaign. Gerrit Smith and Sanborn both pledged
their support, and Sanborn went on to organize a secret group of six co-
conspirators who agreed to fund Brown's planned slave uprising.[38] Meanwhile, Loguen brought John Brown to Tubman in St. Catharines in April
1858 to enlist her help in recruiting guerilla fighters from among the former fugitives there.[39] Loguen was quoted by an antislavery associate as
having said admiringly of Tubman, "Among slaves she is better known
than the Bible, for she circulates more freely."[40]

The contemporary documents amply record the mutual admiration
of Harriet Tubman and John Brown. In a letter to his son, Brown wrote
enthusiastically: "Harriet Tubman hooked on his whole team at once. He
is the most of a man, naturally, that I ever met with." (John Brown, 1858b).
Brown's enigmatic use of the masculine pronoun apparently represents his
respect, though Tubman might not have appreciated the implied denigra-
tion of womanhood—"Harriet Tubman said in Worcester I should make
a good woman, which she meant as a compliment," wrote Sanborn to his
friend Benjamin Smith Lyman (1859d). On her side, Tubman would have
had good reason to be impressed with John Brown's reputation before
meeting him. She would have known not only of his bloody guerrilla warfare against proslavery forces in Kansas, but also of his spectacular rescue of
a slave party of eleven people from Missouri, at gunpoint, in the winter of
1858. When they met in April, in fact, Brown had just completed his successful journey with this party to Canada, "an eighty-two day wintertime

John Brown, antislavery crusader and leader of the attack on the Harpers Ferry federal arsenal in 1859. Tubman met Brown in Canada in April 1858 and helped him contact potential African Canadian recruits.

trek of over 1000 miles while harassed for a time by troops," according to Quarles (1974, 54).

At least two separate face-to-face meetings between Tubman and Brown are documented in St. Catharines in April 1858.[41] Tubman introduced Brown at this time to members of the St. Catharines fugitive slave community who were potential recruits for his Virginia campaign. According to one source, their first meeting included a strange ritualistic greeting by John Brown, in tribute to Tubman's history of leadership of bands of escaping fugitives: "When John Brown entered he shook hands with her three times, saying, 'The first I see is General Tubman, the second is General Tubman, and the third is General Tubman.' . . . When John Brown bade Harriet good by, he again called her 'General' three times, and informed her that she would hear from him through Douglass"(Wyman, 1896).

Tubman did not attend the secret convention of Brown supporters held in Chatham, Canada West, in early May 1858, however—nor did Douglass or Loguen, who had both been invited.[42] At the Chatham convention, twelve members of John Brown's company met with thirty-four African American men thought to be potential supporters of the Virginia uprising, including Martin R. Delany. Brown revealed his plan to begin a war to end slavery by provoking an armed uprising of the slaves in Virginia, Tennessee, and Alabama, beginning within a very few weeks or months. Together, the group discussed and approved the "provisional constitution" (drafted by Brown during his three-week sojourn with Frederick Douglass in February) by which the liberated territory would be governed.[43] As it turned out, the Chatham compact never bore its intended fruit. A year's postponement of the Virginia campaign became necessary because of a breach in security.[44] By the time John Brown was back in the East the next year looking for assistance from the Afrrican Canadian recruits, those who attended the Chatham convention had scattered or lost enthusiasm for the project—or they were simply were not kept informed of the new plans. Only one African Canadian recruit traveled to Harpers Ferry to join John Brown's daring but unsuccessful raid.[45]

Tubman and John Brown met once again, in Boston, in late May of 1859, probably for the last time. On May 30, Franklin Sanborn wrote to Thomas Wentworth Higginson, an antislavery Unitarian minister based in Worcester, Massachusetts, who was also a pledged member of the Secret Six John Brown co-conspirators. Sanborn informed Higginson of the presence in Boston of the two notable guests.[46] "I wonder if you have rec'd two letters from me about Capt. Brown who has been here for three weeks—

and is soon to leave—having got his $2,000 secured. He is at the U.S. hotel; and you ought to see him before he goes—for now he is to begin. Also you ought to see Harriet Tubman, the woman who brought away 50 slaves on 8 journies made to Maryland; but perhaps you have seen her—She is the heroine of the day. She came here Friday night and is at 168 Cambridge St. . . . Even you would be amazed at some of her stories" (Sanborn, 1859a).

John Brown brought Tubman to the home of the Bostonian antislavery orator Wendell Phillips around this time. Phillips later quoted John Brown as saying: "Mr. Phillips, I bring you one of the best and bravest persons on this continent—General Tubman, we call her" (Phillips, 1868). Brown may have brought Tubman up-to-date on his new version of the Virginia uprising plan, although given his penchant for secrecy, this is far from certain.[47] Sanborn wrote to Higginson on June 4 that John Brown "is desirous of getting someone to go to Canada and collect recruits for him among the fugitives, with H. Tubman, or alone, as the case may be, & urged me to go,—but my school will not let me. Last year he engaged some persons & heard of others, but he does not want to lose time by going there himself now. . . . Now is the time to help in the movement, if ever, for within the next two months the experiment will be made" (Sanborn, 1859b). Brown left Boston with funds secured from the Secret Six, but it sounds as though there was no clear commitment for Tubman to go to Canada for him.

Her own reason for coming to Boston in late May 1859 was to raise money for the mortgage debt owed to Seward and for her next Underground Railroad rescue. Like John Brown the year before, she had arrived in Boston with a letter of introduction from Gerrit Smith to Sanborn. As Sanborn later remembered it, "She brought a few letters from her friends in New York, but she could herself neither read nor write, and she was obliged to trust to her wits that they were delivered to the right persons. One of them, as it happened, was to the present writer, who received it by another hand, and called to see her at her boarding house. It was curious to see the caution with which she received her visitor until she felt assured that there was no mistake. One of her means of security was to carry with her the daguerreotypes of her friends, and show them to each new person. If they recognized the likeness, then all was well" (Sanborn, 1863).

Franklin Sanborn's patronage unquestionably opened many doors for Tubman and contributed to her sudden celebrity in Massachusetts antislavery circles in 1859. When she visited Thomas Wentworth Higginson

GEORGE L. STEARNS

GERRIT SMITH

FRANK B. SANBORN

T. W. HIGGINSON

THEODORE PARKER

SAMUEL G. HOWE

JOHN BROWN'S NORTHERN SUPPORTERS

John Brown's Secret Six financial backers: George L. Stearns, Gerrit Smith, Franklin B. Sanborn, Thomas W. Higginson, Theodore Parker, and Samuel G. Howe. Sanborn, who arranged Tubman's visits in Boston and Concord in 1859 and 1860, was also Tubman's first biographer. Courtesy Boston Public Library.

in Worcester, he wrote enthusiastically to his mother, describing her as "the greatest heroine of the age" (Higginson, 1859). Sanborn brought her to meet many of Concord's antislavery literary intellectuals, including Thoreau, Emerson, William Ellery Channing, and Bronson Alcott's family.[48] Through Sanborn she came to know Ednah Littlehale Dow Cheney, her second biographer and a lifelong benefactor.[49]

Cheney arranged a reception at which Tubman made a vivid impression on Boston antislavery women, as a letter from a friend of antislavery writer Lydia Maria Child indicates: "Yesterday afternoon I missed through my weather caution of a unique entertainment, to which I had been kindly invited by Mrs. Bartoll, who at the request of Mrs. Cheney opened her doors for a gathering of friends, to ascertain who might be disposed to aid a real heroine. Where Mrs. Cheney found her, I do not know, but her name is Harriet. She is coal black, and was a slave only three years ago, but within that time she has taken leg bail herself, & assisted no fewer than fifty others to do the same. Two or three times she has returned to the very plantation where she had served, & brought away with her companies of her relations and friends. Her old father & mother she had helped out of bondage, & the object of this gathering was to assist her to buy a little place for them in Auburn" (Osgood, 1859).

During her time in Boston Tubman also met Maria Weston Chapman, who was one of the original founders of the Boston Female Anti-Slavery Society in 1832, a leader in the Massachusetts Anti-Slavery Society, and a strong supporter of William Lloyd Garrison's philosophy and work.[50] Chapman gave Tubman a letter of introduction to an antislavery friend in the seaport city of New Bedford, Massachusetts ("where many of her proteges are hiding"), suggesting that she might be "the suitable person to undertake to bring off the children of Charles, about whom I had so fruitless a correspondence with the Philadelphia Vigilance Committee & others" (Chapman, 1859).[51]

As she had done in Philadelphia and New York, Tubman made contact with black antislavery activists in Boston and New Bedford. On more than one occasion when in Boston, she stayed with Dr. John S. Rock, who in 1865 became the first black lawyer admitted to the bar of the Supreme Court.[52] She also knew Lewis Hayden, an ex-fugitive who sheltered other fugitives in his home in Boston. As she began to appear on antislavery platforms in Worcester, Framingham, and Boston, she frequently shared the stage with other already recognized African American abolitionist speakers. One of these was William Wells Brown, former Underground

Railroad conductor, antislavery lecturer, and author of a well-known slave narrative. Brown later published a brief tribute to Harriet Tubman in his book *The Rising Son* (1874)—one of the few early biographical sketches of Tubman authored by an African American writer.[53]

During her Boston visit, Tubman progressed from telling her life story in private and semipublic gatherings such as the reception given by Mrs. Bartoll to performing it on the public antislavery platform.[54] She quickly worked out a narrative that she knew would both entertain and educate her audience, as a prelude to her necessary appeal for funds. When she mounted the platform to address the Massachusetts Anti-Slavery Society at its Fourth of July meeting in Framingham in 1859, at the invitation of Higginson, "She spoke briefly, telling the story of her suffering as a slave, her escape, and her achievements on the Underground Railroad, in a style of quaint simplicity, which excited the most profound interest in her hearers. . . . A collection was taken in her behalf, amounting to thirty-seven dollars, for which, at the conclusion of the meeting, in a few earnest and touching words, she spoke her thanks" (Yerrington, 1859).

Giving a more overtly political talk against the African colonization movement at the New England Colored Citizens' Convention held in Boston in early August 1859, Tubman was still clearly conscious of the value of being entertaining in her delivery.[55] The reporter in her audience was able to capture a wonderful political "parable" she told: "Miss Harriet Garrison was introduced as one of the most successful conductors on the Underground Railroad.[56] She denounced the colonization movement and told a story of a man who sowed onions and garlic on his land to increase his dairy production; but he soon found the butter was strong, and would not sell and so he concluded to sow clover instead. But he soon found the wind had blown the onions and garlic all over his field. Just so, she said, the white people had got the 'niggers' here to do their drudgery, and now they were trying to root 'em out and send 'em to Africa. 'But,' said she, 'they can't do it; we're rooted here, and they can't pull us up.' She was much applauded" ("New England Colored Citizens' Convention," 1859).

Her whereabouts for several months after this convention are as yet undocumented. It is a crucial period of absence, for John Brown's supporters were diligently, even desperately, trying to locate her from late summer of 1859 into September, and she was not to be found. A letter from Sanborn in late August suggested that he thought she may have been ill and out of action temporarily, perhaps in New Bedford during the crucial last weeks of preparation. Sanborn continued in vain to expect her to turn up in Boston throughout September.[57] The possibility has been raised by historian Benjamin Quarles that by October 1859 Brown's supporters may have actually succeeded in contacting her. If so, and if she was aiming at the new date most recently set for the raid—"around October 25," as Sanborn later remembered it—she could actually have been recruiting in West Canada at the time the raid took place, prematurely, on October 16.[58] However, her friend Martha Wright later reported, "She told me that John Brown . . . wanted her to go with him on his expedition, but when he sent a message for her, she was not at home" (M. C. Wright, 1869a). Moreover, Sanborn later said that on the day of the Harpers Ferry Raid (October 16) she was in New York and was able to predict to her "hostess" that something had happened to John Brown (Sanborn, 1863). For better or for worse, Tubman did not play a significant role personally or even through gathering recruits for John Brown's paramilitary action at Harpers Ferry.

The story of the raid itself is quickly told. Eighteen of John Brown's band of twenty-one followers, five of them black, temporarily took possession of the federal arsenal at Harpers Ferry, Virginia, in a surprise attack on October 16. The three others waited at the base camp, called the Kennedy Farm, while the raid took place. The invaders were defeated just over twenty-four hours later when federal troops under Robert E. Lee arrived, and no slave uprising occurred. Ten of the party were killed, including two of John Brown's sons, Oliver and Watson, in the retaking of the arsenal by the troops. Seven were captured, including John Brown. Five escaped, including Owen Brown, one of John Brown's sons, and Osborne Anderson, the one black Canadian recruit. John Brown and four surviving captured associates, two of them black, were quickly tried, condemned, and executed—amid a vast outpouring of publicity, north and south. Several of the Secret Six co-conspirators and other associates of Brown fled to Canada to avoid possible arrest and treason trials in Virginia.[59]

A Senate committee led by James Mason of Virginia investigated Brown's activities by interviewing white witnesses and combing through captured documents. The committee expected to find evidence of widespread complicity in a plot to foment slave insurrection, but failed to do so.[60] Martyr Day ceremonies were held across the North and in Canada on December 2, the day John Brown was executed. Brown's dignity and religious conviction, as conveyed in the many newspaper accounts of his trial, imprisonment, and execution, helped transform him from a "fanatic" to a martyr in the eyes of the antislavery community of the North.[61] His body was returned to his widow, who accompanied it to the family home-stead in North Elba, Ohio. Wendell Phillips gave the eulogy at the funeral held there on December 8.

Tubman's reaction to the execution of John Brown and his captured asso-ciates was remembered a few years afterward by Ednah Cheney. Tubman came to Cheney's room on the day of the execution of Brown's compan-ions (December 16, 1859), needing to talk: "'I've been studying and study-ing upon it,' she said, 'and it's clear to me, it wasn't John Brown that died on that gallows. When I think how he gave up his life for our people, and how he never flinched, but was so brave to the end, it's clear to me that it wasn't mortal man, it was God in him. When I think of all the groans and tears and prayers I've heard on the plantations, and remember that God is a prayer-hearing God, I feel that his time is drawing near'" (Cheney, 1865).

Tubman told Sanborn that she had anticipated meeting John Brown in a repeated visionary dream, which she did not fully understand until his death: "She thought she was in a 'wilderness sort of place, all full of rocks and bushes,' when she saw a serpent raise its head among the rocks, and as it did so, it became the head of an old man with a long white beard, gazing at her 'wishful like, just as if he were going to speak to me,' and then two other heads rose up beside him, younger than he,—and as she stood looking at them, and wondering what they could want with her, a great crowd of men rushed in and struck down the younger heads, and then the head of the old man, still looking at her so 'wishful'" (Sanborn, 1863). When she talked with Martha Wright about him in the late 1860s, she emphasized his military discipline and his "moderation." "His orders was not to destroy property, nor to hurt men, women or children, but to fetch away the slaves when they could, and if they couldn't get them to get their masters, and keep them in the Mts till their frnds wd give slaves in exchange." But she also pointed to the galvanic effect of his martyrdom on the antislavery movement: "he done more in dying than 100 men would have, in living" (M. C. Wright, 1869a).

Although her brief but intense relationship with John Brown did not ultimately lead to her participation in the Harpers Ferry Raid, there is no doubt that she would have been a courageous and physically able com-panion in this kind of paramilitary action. Just six months later, in Troy, New York, she demonstrated her ability and willingness to lead a spon-taneous uprising in orchestrating the mob rescue of a fugitive named Nalle.[62] An angry mob had gathered outside the commissioner's office where Nalle was held captive prior to being turned over to slave catchers.

As the newspaper account described the "mob," "many of them were black, and a good share were of the female sex" ("Fugitive Slave Rescue," 1860). As the prisoner was being moved to another location,

> Harriet Tubman, who had been standing with the excited crowd, rushed amongst the foremost to Nalle, and running one of her arms around his manacled arm, held on to him without ever loosening her hold through the more than half-hour's struggle to Judge Gould's office, and from Judge Gould's office to the dock, where Nalle's liberation was accomplished. In the melee, she was repeatedly beaten over the head with policemen's clubs, but she never for a moment released her hold, but cheered Nalle and his friends with her voice, and struggled with the officers until they were literally worn out with their exertions, and Nalle was separated from them. . . . Harriet crossed the river with the crowd, in the ferry-boat, and when the men who led the assault upon the door of Judge Stewart's office, were stricken down, Harriet and a number of other colored women rushed over their bodies, brought Nalle out, and putting him in the first wagon passing, started him for the West. (Townsend, 1868)

Shortly after this dramatic episode, Tubman began her first public association with the fledgling women's rights movement (which was still largely contained within the Garrisonian antislavery networks).[63] She attended the New England Anti-Slavery Society Conference in Boston in May 1860, and her speech at an associated Drawing Room Convention of feminist antislavery activists was mentioned briefly in the *Liberator*: "A colored woman of the name of Moses, who, herself a fugitive, has eight times returned to the slave States for the purpose of rescuing others from bondage, and who has met with extraordinary success in her efforts, was then introduced. She told the story of her adventures in a modest but quaint and amusing style, which won much applause" ("Woman's Rights Meetings," 1860). The recent move to Auburn had brought her into regular contact with passionate women's rights organizer Martha Coffin Wright, sister of her Underground Railroad ally Lucretia Mott. Wright may have suggested to her the importance of the women's rights networks as a place to meet potential new allies.

One feminist admirer who heard Harriet Tubman tell her Underground Railroad rescue stories in the spring of 1860 in Boston was a young fledgling writer named Louisa May Alcott—later to become nationally known as the author of *Little Women*. The Alcott family's home in Concord was an Underground Railroad station, and Louisa's father, Bronson Alcott, had been involved in planning Concord's "martyr" service for John Brown on the date of his execution, December 2, 1859 (Shepard, 1966). Very likely Louisa originally heard about Tubman from Sanborn, and she may have been in the audience when Tubman spoke in "the vestry" of a church in Concord in early June 1859. Louisa May Alcott was an ardent writer of antislavery stories[64] and may have used Tubman as the model for a character in the novel *Work*, published in 1873.[65]

THE LAST TRIP TO MARYLAND

By the summer of 1860, Tubman had completed eight or nine successful clandestine trips to Maryland.[66] Her most recent trips had been motivated by her desire to rescue a last "sister" and her children, but as Garrett had reported in 1856, "She went for them at the time proposed, & had one or more interviews with her sister, but after waiting some ten days, found she could not get her and all three of the children, as two were placed at some distance from the mother—The mother was in hopes they would be permitted to visit her during the holidays, which generally last from Christmas to New Year's day, and Harriet agreed to be in the neighborhood at that time, ready to bring all away together, as her sister would not leave without having all her children with her" (Garrett, 1856f).

Another attempt the next summer had also failed "to get them all away together"—"two of the children are separated some twelve miles from their mother, which has caused the difficulty," wrote Garrett in August 1857. A third attempt was in the planning stages in August 1860 when Tubman asked Wendell Phillips (probably among others) for the financial help she needed to rescue this family (Tubman, 1860). In December she brought a party of seven fugitives north from Maryland, but this group did not include the "sister," who had died before Tubman could collect the whole family together.[67] According to Cheney, the group did not include the "sister's" children either. "She had to leave her sister's two orphan children in slavery the last time, for the want of thirty dollars. . . . She would never allow more to join her than she could properly care for" (Cheney, 1865).

The last Maryland mission nevertheless succeeded in another way, as we hear in a letter from Martha Coffin Wright: "We have been expending our sympathies, as well as congratulations, on seven newly arrived slaves that Harriet Tubman has just pioneered safely from the southern part of

Maryland—One woman carried a baby all the way, & brot two other children that Harriet & the men helped along, they brot a piece of old comfort[er] & blanket in a basket with a little kindling, a little bread for the baby, with some laudanum, to keep it from crying during the day—They walked all night, carrying the little ones, and spread the old comfort[er] on the frozen ground, in some dense thicket, where they all hid, while Harriet went out foraging & sometimes cd not get back till dark, fearing she wd be followed—Then if they had crept further in, & she couldn't find them, she wd whistle, or sing certain hymns, & they wd answer" (M. C. Wright, 1860).

The dramatic details of the story of the final trip to Maryland fascinated Tubman's audiences, including her early biographers, and the final rescue became one of the most emblematic of her stories, as her celebrity grew in the postwar years. The drugged baby (or babies), the walking by night and hiding by day, and the song codes for secret communication—all these were much-loved and much-repeated elements in the later iconography of the Underground Railroad heroine.

THE WAR YEARS

OUTBREAK OF WAR

As Tubman prepared for her last Maryland rescue trip, the nation plunged toward civil war. The election of Abraham Lincoln a president on the Republican Party ticket in November 1860 (backed by all but one of the free states, but with only 40 percent of the popular vote) touched off what historians have called the "secession crisis." Reacting to the prospect of what they saw as an antislavery administration, seven Southern states, led by South Carolina on December 20, left the Union within six weeks. In a desperate effort to forestall further secession, Senator William H. Seward, Tubman's influential neighbor, introduced a "compromise" bill in Congress on December 24 that was highly conciliatory toward the Southern states. This measure provided for the return of fugitive slaves, the prosecution of those who conducted slaves to freedom, and a congressional guarantee of slavery in existing slave states; predictably, abolitionists were outraged.[1]

Tubman's reaction to Seward's compromise efforts has not come to light, but we do know what many of her antislavery associates thought.[2] During the secession crisis, fearing that Seward might sacrifice her for political reasons, Tubman's radical friends warned her to flee to Canada. Martha Coffin Wright wrote to her sister Lucretia Mott, probably in February 1861, describing the anxious activity of Tubman's upstate New York friends on her behalf: "I called at Mrs. Seward's on my way home, D. [David Wright, her husband] . . . lent me a letter to shew them, enquiring after Harriet Tubman written by Chas. Mills of Syracuse, saying that she left Canistota en route to Auburn, & that a slaveholder was there the day before enquiring as to the possibility of retaking slaves here—Mr. Mills sd. they cd. learn nothing about Harriet & wished to know if she was here— He also sent a word of caution to fugitives here. D. sent the letter to Mr. Hosmer, & he read it Harriets folks—She has not been heard from, but I told one of her slaves that I tho't most likely Mr. Smith had sent her to Canada" (M. C. Wright, n.d.). Tubman soon sent back word that she was safe; she asked the Wright family in Auburn to send a barrel of flour to her family, "and she wd pay us on her return."

Given that her family lived in Auburn at this time, a mile from the Seward household, and that they were in frequent contact with members of the Seward family and their friends, Tubman would certainly have known about his role in national politics—including his hope to secure the young Republican Party's presidential nomination the year before. It is hard to imagine her being uninformed about what historian Richard Sewell has characterized as Seward's "waffling on the slavery question" in the months leading up to the Republican convention (1988, 74–75). Whatever she thought privately about Seward's swerve to the political center, however, she does not appear to have felt personally threatened. According to Sanborn, who told the story in the first published biography (1863), when she was "hurried . . . off to Canada," it was "sorely against her will."[3] Nor did she express distrust of Seward by relocating her parents and other dependents from the newly established Auburn base on the property formerly owned by Seward.[4]

The federal union continued to unravel. In early February 1861, around the time Tubman was on her way to Canada, delegates from six lower Southern states met in Montgomery, Alabama, to create the provisional constitution of the Confederacy. Two weeks later, president-elect Lincoln, having been warned of a possible assassination attempt in Baltimore, journeyed incognito on the train to Baltimore and Washington as he went to take office. Though Maryland had not seceded, it was a slave state hostile to a Republican presidency, and mob violence was very much a real possibility. When Lincoln's inauguration took place on March 4, 1861, Seward assumed the post of Secretary of State. Only a month later, the Confederacy fired the first shots of the Civil War, shelling Fort Sumter in the harbor at Charleston, South Carolina. The Confederate capture of the federal fortress led to Union retaliation and to four more states joining the Confederacy.

The outbreak of war was exhilarating to those in antislavery networks who saw the war as inevitably leading to the destruction of the institution of slavery. The day after the Fort Sumter hostilities began, Lincoln called up 75,000 state militia in the free states to deal with the insurrectionary forces, and not long after this Tubman's New England antislavery friends began to think about how she might be of service to the Union. George L. Stearns of Boston, one of the Secret Six John Brown co-conspirators, wrote to Sanborn on April 26, 1861, that he was asking John Brown Jr. and Harriet Tubman to come to Boston, all expenses paid. "Glorious times, these are," Stearns exulted to Sanborn. "They will show that our Republic is worth saving." Even committed "nonresistants" (pacifists) such as William Lloyd Garrison had experienced elation at the outset of the war, believing that if slavery could be destroyed in no other way, war could be seen as "righteous violence" (Sewell, 1988, 85).

What were Tubman's activities during the first six months or so of the war? Biographers have contradicted each other, and the facts have not yet been clearly established. Earl Conrad asserted that she "followed General Butler's army as it marched through Maryland on the way to the defense of Washington during the months of April and May 1861, when Maryland debated whether to secede and when the Federal troops met with violence at Baltimore" (Conrad, 1942a, 153).[5] However, if she did in fact follow this hastily assembled all-white federal army in some sort of clandestine role, neither of Tubman's earliest biographers, her close associates Ednah Cheney and Franklin Sanborn, ever heard about it—and they would almost certainly have recorded it, had she told them about it. Sanborn reported that she came to New England, perhaps with another Southern rescue mission in mind, sometime following the outbreak of war.[6]

One intriguing possibility is that during the early months of the war Tubman took the opportunity to slip into Maryland to visit the family of a "brother," bringing one of the brother's daughters north with her when she returned by ship. Her great-grandniece, Alice Brickler, told Earl Conrad a fascinating story in 1939 about Tubman "kidnapping" Margaret Stewart (Brickler's mother) "from her home on the Eastern Shore of Maryland, when she was a little girl eight or nine years old":

[Aunt Harriet] fell in love with the little girl who was my mother. . . . When her visit was ended, she, secretly and without so much as a by-your-leave, took the little girl with her to her northern home. . . . They made the trip by water as that was what impressed Mother so greatly that she forgot to weep over the separation from her twin brother, her mother & the shiny carriage she liked so much. Aunt Harriet must have regretted her act for she knew she had taken the child from a sheltered good home to a place where there was nobody to care for her. . . . She gave the little girl, my mother, to Mrs. William H. Seward, the Governor's wife. This kindly lady brought up Mother—not as a servant but as a guest within her home. . . . Whenever Aunt Harriet came back, Mother was dressed and sent in the Seward carriage to visit her. (Brickler, 1939c)[7]

Although her whereabouts in the spring, summer, and early fall of 1861 are as yet undocumented, by late October 1861 Tubman was again in Concord with Sanborn, bringing useful information about how the war's early days were affecting those still in slavery: "she represents the number escaping from Maryland and Virginia as unusually great. Emancipation would check this exodus," Sanborn wrote in November (1861b).[8] Perhaps one reason for her Boston visit in the fall was a desire to attend an upcoming meeting of African American leaders opposed to Haitian emigration.[9] In early November, a Boston meeting on this issue produced resolutions rebuking "misguided colored men and white men" who were trying "to induce free colored persons, resident in the United States and in the Canadas, to emigrate to Hayti under the mistaken policy of bettering their condition" (McPherson, 1965, 85).

Tubman may also have attended the thirtieth anniversary convention of the Massachusetts Anti-Slavery Society, held in Boston on January 23, 1862. She had talked recently with Lydia Maria Child, at any rate, because Child quoted her in a letter to poet John Greenleaf Whittier dated January 21, 1862. Child had heard her criticize President Lincoln's failure to emancipate the slaves as a wrong-headed and immoral policy that would make a Union victory impossible: "They may send the flower of their young men down South, to die of the fever in the summer, and the ague in the winter. . . . They may send them one year, two years, three years, till they are tired of sending, or till they use up all the young men. All no use! God's ahead of Master Lincoln. God will not let Master Lincoln beat the South till he do the right thing" (1862a).[10]

The Lincoln administration had placed its highest priority first on preserving, and then on restoring, the rupturing union of Northern and Southern states—rather than on ending the immoral institution of slavery. As Fort Sumter was being taken by Confederate troops, Lincoln was writing a letter to representatives of the Virginia secession convention, reminding them that "I have no purpose, directly or indirectly, to interfere with the institution of slavery in the States where it exists. I believe I have no lawful right to do so, and I have no inclination to do so" (Sewell, 1988, 161). Lincoln was still unprepared to issue an Emancipation Proclamation, and though he was personally convinced that slavery was a great evil, like many other whites brought up to hold racist views, he did not envision a postwar world in which blacks and whites could live together amicably as equals. Even after he had decided to use emancipation as a political tool to aid in winning the war, Lincoln articulated a separatist philosophy to a group of African American men from the District of Columbia who had asked to speak with him on August 14, 1862. During this meeting he suggested a scheme for colonizing U.S. black families in a coal-mining area of Central America. The story of this interview, published in the Northern antislavery press, evoked angry reactions from the antislavery community, including Frederick Douglass, who wrote in response: "In this address Mr. Lincoln assumes the language and arguments of an itinerant Colonization lecturer, showing all his inconsistencies, his pride of race and blood, his contempt for Negroes and his canting hypocrisy."[11]

Tubman's chief reason for visiting Boston in late fall of 1861 was a summons for a private discussion of possible war service from the abolitionist governor of Massachusetts, John A. Andrew. (Sanborn later remembered that she had been brought to meet Andrew by her Boston antislavery friends George and Mary Stearns and Ednah Cheney.) Governor Andrew may have been thinking of her as a possible Union army spy and scout even before the federal occupation of the Sea Islands of South Carolina, Georgia, and Florida in November, but it was the occupation of the islands by Union forces that brought immediate and pressing opportunities for several kinds of war service for antislavery activists.[12] Her experience with dangerous secretive missions, as well as her absolute antislavery loyalty, obviously made her an exceptionally useful resource for the Union army in the coastal South.[13]

The capture of the Sea Islands was an important milestone in the evolutionary erosion of slavery in the South that gradually persuaded Lincoln to issue the Emancipation Proclamation. The occupation also led directly to the use of black soldiers in Union army service. Tubman's two and half years of war service took place largely in the Sea Islands and neighboring coastal areas as far south as Fernandina, Florida. Here she had a history-making opportunity to play an essential part in the conduct of significant military campaigns.[14]

SERVICE IN PORT ROYAL

The South Carolina Sea Islands were a fertile and productive plantation area that stretched along the coast from Charleston to Savannah, Georgia. The town of Beaufort on Port Royal Island was taken by Union forces on December 8 of 1861. Troops of the Union army's Department of the South were headquartered on nearby Hilton Head Island, at the head of Port Royal Sound. The relatively small white planter population fled the islands as the federal occupation began. Ten thousand formerly enslaved people remained, with the ambiguous status of "contraband of war"—free by virtue of military action rather than by civil law.[15]

These Sea Islanders, although rid of their former masters, faced dire poverty, as they lacked employment, property, and formal educational institutions of their own. The call went out for Northern educators and abolitionist reformers to come south and help the former slaves make the transition to an entirely new way of life. Antislavery communities in Boston, New York, and Philadelphia were particularly eager to participate in what would eventually be called the "Port Royal Experiment"—an improvisational social and economic reform project that abolitionists hoped would demonstrate to the doubting white Northern majority the feasibility of emancipation.[16]

In response to the federal call for volunteers to serve in Port Royal, seventeen Bostonians, including Governor Andrew and Ednah Cheney, formed an organization dedicated to "the industrial, social, intellectual, moral and religious elevation of persons released from Slavery in the course of the War for the Union" (Rose, 1976, 35). Originally called the Boston Educational Commission and renamed the New England Freedmen's Aid Society, it was a fundraising and oversight agency for the Port Royal Experiment. Ednah Cheney played a leadership role in the society, recruiting, training, and sending minimal wages to the Northern teachers of the freed people, as well as dispensing clothing and other items collected for the temporary economic relief of the former slaves. An initial group of missionary teachers (including twelve women) was sent from Boston on March 3, and two months later Tubman was dispatched to Beaufort as well.

It seems very likely that the humanitarian mission was a convenient "cover story" to conceal her secret assignment as a spy. According to the friend in Auburn to whom she later dictated a story of her war service, "Harriet Tubman was sent to Hilton Head—she says—in May 1862, at the suggestion of Governor Andrew, with the idea that she would be a valuable person to operate within the enemies' lines—in procuring information & scouts" (Wood, 1868). She also later told her neighbor Emma Paddock Telford that she agreed to Governor Andrew's request to "act as spy, scout or nurse as circumstances required . . . but before she got started (I tell this story in her own words), 'they change[d] their program and wanted me to go down and [dis]tribute clothes to the contrabands who were coming in to the Union lines night and day'" (Telford, n.d.). Her closest associates seem to have understood that her actual mission from the beginning was spying for the military. Martha Coffin Wright, in a letter to her son Frank written May 28, 1862, reported on Tubman's recent departure: "Harriet is at Port Royal, on some secret service."

Before leaving Boston in January, Tubman consulted with her friends there about how to support her parents and other dependents in Auburn in her absence.[17] Ednah Cheney helped Tubman prepare financially for her extended absence. When Tubman accepted the assignment, Cheney said, "The only condition she made was, that her old parents should be kept from want. It was wonderful to see with what shrewd economy she had planned all their household arrangements. She concluded that thirty dollars would keep them comfortable through the winter" (Cheney, 1865).[18] Among her preparations for the extended absence was her placement of her ten-year old niece, Margaret Stewart, in the care of Frances Miller Seward's widowed sister, Lazette Miller Worden.[19]

While Tubman was preparing to leave for service in the South, the Lincoln administration retreated from the use of limited emancipation as a tool of war. General David Hunter, commander of the Department of the South, issued an order in early May that freed the slaves in the territories under martial law—in effect all of the islanders in occupied territories of South Carolina, Georgia, and Florida. But Lincoln revoked Hunter's order on May 19, fearing this would alienate the border states and perhaps cause further secession. More thoroughgoing Northern abolitionists such as Frederick Douglass were outraged by Lincoln's act. Douglass challenged Lincoln's motives in a bitter Fourth of July speech, which was delivered shortly after Tubman had arrived in the Sea Islands:

> He [President Lincoln] has steadily refused to proclaim, as he had the constitutional and moral right to proclaim, complete emancipation to all the slaves of rebels who should make their way into the lines of our army. He has repeatedly interfered with and arrested the anti-slavery policy of some

of his most earnest and reliable generals. . . . It is from such action as this,
that we must infer the policy of the Administration. To my mind that policy is simply and solely to reconstruct the union on the old and corrupt-
ing basis of compromise, by which slavery shall retain all the power that it
ever had, with the full assurance of gaining more, according to its future
necessities.[20]

Governor Andrew of Massachusetts provided for Tubman's transportation to Beaufort and her assignment to Major General David Hunter
at the army camp at Hilton Head. Hunter wrote on her military pass:
"Harriet was sent to me from Boston, by Gov. Andrew, of Mass., and is
a valuable woman" (D. Hunter, 1863). Tubman later told Emma Paddock
Telford that she was supposed to pose as the servant of a "gentleman from
New York" on her journey south, but she decided she didn't like his
looks and "went on alone to Baltimore and General Hunt[er] sent for me
to go to Beaufort, and the vessel that was going there didn't sail for two
days, awaiting for me till the General's orders were fulfilled. I first took
charge of the Christian Commission House at Beaufort" (Telford, n.d.).
Her caution in refusing to accompany a "gentleman" she didn't trust into
the South made very good sense, since she was still a fugitive (from the
Confederate point of view) with a price on her head.[21] Throughout her
war service, she continued to trust her own judgment rather than follow
bureaucratic procedures—an advantage of her informal, irregular connection to the military. (Later the informality of the connection made for
problems, when she needed to assert a claim on the federal government
for a veteran's pension.)

STATIONED AT BEAUFORT

When she arrived in the village of Beaufort, she found that a "thoroughgoing abolitionist of the radical sort," General Rufus Saxton, was in charge
of the federal enterprises at Port Royal (Rose, 1976, 152–153). But despite
the presence of firmly antislavery leadership, that summer of 1862 was a
hard one for the Port Royal residents. Several of the missionaries died
because of unexpected heat and disease, including a nephew of Wendell
Phillips. The early efforts made by General Hunter to organize a regiment of freed men were high-handed and resented both by the men and
their families, according to Laura Towne, a Northern schoolteacher who

recorded these events. The men had been promised freedom from coercion, and the families were depending on the help of the men with raising crops (146–148, 187–188). By June, Towne relented in the severity of
her criticism after viewing the regiment: "They looked splendidly, and the
great mass of blackness, animated with a soul and armed so keenly, was
very impressive. . . . The men seemed to welcome General Hunter and to
be fond of him. The camp was in beautiful order" (Towne, in Holland,
1969, 70–71).

Hunter tried unsuccessfully throughout June and July to win official
recognition and pay for the First South Carolina Volunteers. With no support forthcoming from Washington, he disbanded the regiment in early
August, ironically just after Congress finally empowered the president to
employ "persons of African descent" to suppress the rebellion, in a provision of the Confiscation Act passed on July 17, 1862. Largely because of
heavy Union battle losses throughout 1861 and 1862, which had greatly
reduced early patriotic enthusiasm in the North and diminished the numbers of white recruits available to the Union armed forces, public opinion
had at last begun to shift in favor of arming black men. Lincoln himself
was still opposed to arming black men in August, both on political grounds
and because he, like the majority of whites, did not believe former slaves
could become effective soldiers (McPherson, 1965, 164–165). At last, however, on August 24, Rufus Saxton was authorized by the War Department
to put together five regiments of black troops from the Sea Island contraband residents and refugees. These troops would enable the army to mount
expeditions from the islands into the coastal mainland of the South to
encourage the further desertion of the slaves behind Confederate lines
(Rose, 1976, 190). This historic shift of policy occurred under Tubman's
direct observation, and she was well acquainted with the major characters
of the drama on the Sea Islands. Unquestionably she applauded the arming of black men and deplored the shabby treatment the colored troops
received during their first months of military service.[22] Before long she
had the opportunity to express in public her pride in the service of the
black soldiers on the Combahee River expedition.

Excitement ran high among Tubman's abolitionist friends in the North-
east when the call came to train black troops. Antislavery activists had
been arguing that war service would quickly allow black men to prove
their mettle. Many had been chafing impatiently for this policy since
the beginning of the war and had expressed puzzlement and frustration
over the delay. Writing in the *Liberator* of January 30, 1863, William Lloyd

Garrison pointed out that "another reason why the war has lingered has been the unwillingness to employ the free colored and slave population in the military service of the government" (cited in Cain, 1995).

Thomas W. Higginson, the Secret Six John Brown co-conspirator who had been so thrilled to hear Tubman tell her story in Boston in 1859, was now invited by General Saxton to lead a regiment made up of newly freed black soldiers on the Sea Islands. Two weeks after his arrival in Beaufort to begin service as a colonel with the First South Carolina Volunteers (Rose, 1976, 193) he wrote to his wife, "Who should drive out to see me today but Harriet Tubman who is living in Beaufort as a sort of nurse & general care taker; she sent her regards to you" (Higginson, 1862b). The abolitionist Higginson was eager to prove the "superiority" of black soldiers. He reported glowingly on his regiment's first action, in January 1863, on St. Mary's River (McPherson, 1965, 167). Colonel James Montgomery, another John Brown supporter and a veteran of the Kansas antislavery guerrilla wars, arrived soon after Higginson to form a second regiment of colored troops. Montgomery impressed schoolteacher Laura Towne as "a fiery westerner, full of fight and with sufficient confidence in himself" (Towne in Holland, 1969, 103). Montgomery led the famous Combahee River Raid the following June, with Tubman's very substantial help.[23]

Lincoln's Preliminary Emancipation Proclamation was finally issued on September 22, 1862, just a few months into Tubman's Southern war service. The new war policy of emancipating those slaves whose owners were in open rebellion against the government as of January 1, 1863, had been approved by Lincoln's cabinet in July. However, the public announcement was withheld so that the policy would not appear to be forced upon the Union by impending defeat. It was the pragmatic William Seward who had suggested this delay (Sewell, 1988, 165–173). The scope of the Emancipation Proclamation was limited, of course. It exempted all slave states that had remained loyal to the union, for example. Nevertheless, when it became law there was heartfelt rejoicing among former slaves and antislavery workers throughout the north, and also among the now clearly emancipated residents in the Sea Islands.

Tubman was very likely present at the celebration at Camp Saxton. The events were described breathlessly and enthusiastically by Northern missionary schoolteacher Charlotte Forten in her diary (1863):

> As I sat on the stand and looked around on the various groups, I thought I had never seen a sight so beautiful. There were the black soldiers, in their

blue coats and scarlet pants, the officers of this and other regiments in their handsome uniforms, and crowds of lookers-on, men, women and children, grouped in various attitudes, under the trees. . . . Immediately at the conclusion, some of the colored people—of their own accord sang "My Country Tis of Thee." It was a touching and beautiful incident, and Col. Higginson, in accepting the flags made it the occasion of some happy remarks. . . . He seemed inspired. Nothing c'ld have been better, more perfect. . . . Ah what a grand, glorious day this has been. The dawn of freedom which it heralds may not break upon us at once; but it will surely come, and sooner, I believe, than we have ever dared hope before. My soul is glad with an exceeding great gladness.[24]

Tubman's humanitarian duties for the New England Freedmen's Aid Society included helping newly freed women in the refugee camps adapt to a new life working for wages. She told Charles P. Wood in 1868 that she had invested $200 (the entire amount of pay drawn for her government service to date) in "the erection of a wash-house, in which she spent a portion of her time in teaching the freed women to do washing—to aid in supporting themselves instead of depending wholly on Gov't aid."[25] But her relationship with the freed people was jeopardized by her apparent privileged position as a government employee during the early days of her service. As Charles P. Wood relates, "When she first went to Beaufort, she was allowed to draw rations as an officer or soldier, but the freed people becoming jealous of this privilege accorded her—she voluntarily relinquished this right and thereafter supplied her personal wants by selling pies and root beer—which she made during the evening and nights—when not engaged in important service for the Gov't" (Wood, 1868).

The "jealousy" of the freed people probably stemmed from their observation of the highly anomalous position of Harriet Tubman at Beaufort. She was certainly not an officially appointed "officer" in the Union army—no woman was or could be. Even the men of her race who were finally in the military service still worked for the most part in "nonmilitary and semi military roles" as "laborers, teamsters, cooks, carpenters, nurses, or scouts" (McPherson, 1965, 143–159). Moreover, pay was a serious problem in the newly organized Sea Islands economy. The freed people who were doing agricultural labor on the Sea Islands plantations (now for the Union Treasury Department under the supervision of the Port Royal missionaries) were often paid months after the work had been done (Rose, 1976, 177). There might have been less bad feeling about her pay if the freed people

had known Tubman's reputation as the Underground Railroad heroine
"Moses." Their "jealousy" suggests that she successfully kept this identity
secret, probably so as not to undermine her ability to pass undetected into
country occupied by Confederate troops.

After she stopped accepting pay from the Union army, she worked hard
at a variety of women's traditional economic enterprises to support her own
activities, as well as to save money to send north. According to Bradford,
she baked and brewed refreshments nightly for sale to the troops, including "a great quantity of gingerbread, and two casks of root beer. These
she would hire some contraband to sell for her through the camps, and
thus she would provide her support for another day" (Bradford, 1869).

Charlotte Forten, who had met Harriet Tubman for the first time just
a few weeks after Emancipation, understood that Tubman was "keeping
an eating house" in Beaufort.[26] Forten, as an educated Northerner in an
anomalous position herself among the white Port Royal missionary teaching force, was clearly less interested in Tubman's work for her daily bread
than in her glorious past as an antislavery heroine: "In Beaufort we spent
nearly all our time at Harriet Tubman's, otherwise 'Moses.' She is a wonderful woman—a real heroine. Has helped off a large number of slaves, after
taking her own freedom. . . . How exciting it was to hear her tell the story"
(Forten, 1863). Interestingly, Forten also noted: "she wants to go North,
and will probably do so ere long." But both Tubman and Forten were
mistaken about how soon Tubman would be allowed to return to the work
of supporting her family.

THE COMBAHEE RIVER RAID

The Combahee River Raid on June 2, 1863, resulted in the capture of
about eight hundred slaves with no injuries to the Union forces. Given the
raid's later prominence in the stories of Tubman's exploits, it is surprising to find that a soldier just arrived in Beaufort from Massachusetts (a
member of the Massachusetts 54th Colored Regiment) described the raid
in a letter published in a New Bedford newspaper, without mentioning
her role at all:

> The 2nd South Carolina volunteers have made a successful expedition. Col.
> Montgomery left with his regiment May 1st [actually June 1st], in three
> small steamers . . . the next morning he anchored in the Combahee River,

thirty miles from Beaufort and twenty from Charleston. . . . Thirty-four large mansions, belonging to notorious rebels, were burned to the ground. After scattering the rebel artillery, the Harriet A. Weed [a U.S. Army steamboat] tied up opposite a large plantation. . . . The white inhabitants, terrified at seeing armed Negroes in their midst, fled in all directions, while the blacks ran for the boats, welcoming the soldiers as their deliverers. After destroying all they could not bring away, the expedition returned to Beaufort Wednesday evening, with over $15,000 worth of property and 840 slaves. Over 400 of the captured slaves have been enlisted in the 3rd S.C. regiment; the rest of the number being women and children and old men. (Gooding, 1865)[27]

Her invisibility in this report is especially puzzling because we would expect the soldier, as a black man in uniform, to take special pride in the unusual part played in a military raid by a woman of his race. Perhaps full details had not yet reached him—or he may simply have doubted the accuracy of the report he heard, so unprecedented was the idea of a woman in a military leadership position.

The Combahee River Raid of the Second South Carolina Volunteers, in which Harriet Tubman played an extraordinary role as "commander" of a group of scouts. The action was depicted by an artist in *Harper's Weekly*, July 4, 1863.

Bradford said that General Hunter asked Tubman to participate in the raid, and "she said she would go if Col. Montgomery was appointed to the command" (Bradford, 1869). It is also possible that she actually suggested the location and sketched the plan for the raid, as a routine part of her work as "spy and scout," as a newspaper account of the raid implied.[28] By January 1863 Tubman was issued $100 in "secret service money" by the Department of the South (Guterman, 2000, 165). Presumably she used this money to pay the group of "eight or nine" reliable scouts she had recruited to inform her of the Confederate troop movements and fortifications on the shoreline just beyond the Union pickets.[29] Clearly by this time she had begun her clandestine work with the "fiery westerner" Colonel James Montgomery.[30] For the Combahee River raid, Tubman directed the advance spying activities of the scouts, and together they determined where the Confederate forces had placed torpedoes. She and "several men under her" were on the lead gunboat with Colonel Montgomery, helping to pilot the Union boats safely. She also played a central role in persuading the frightened contrabands to come aboard the alien boats.

Tubman's name quickly was associated in the North with this story of a triumphant Union army action featuring black soldiers. Tubman's Concord friend Franklin Sanborn, now the editor of the Boston antislavery newspaper *Commonwealth*, was particularly excited by the news of Tubman's role in the raid when it reached him, because of their former association. He immediately reprinted the eyewitness story of the Beaufort celebration of the raid that appeared first in a Wisconsin antislavery newspaper. Headlined "Colonel Montgomery's raid—The Rescued Black Chattels—A Black She 'Moses'—Her Wonderful Daring and Sagacity," this piece breathlessly made Tubman's role the central one:

> I doubt whether this church was ever before filled with such a crowd of devout worshippers—whether it was ever before appropriated to so good a purpose—whether so true a gospel had ever before been preached within its walls. I certainly never felt such swelling emotions of gratitude to the Great Ruler as at this moment. Col. Montgomery and his gallant band of 300 black soldiers, under the guidance of a black woman, dashed into the enemies' country, struck a bold and effective blow, destroying millions of dollars worth of commissary stores, cotton and lordly dwellings, and striking terror to the heart of rebellion, brought off near 800 slaves and thousands of dollars worth of property, without losing a man or receiving a scratch. . . . The Colonel was followed by a speech from the black woman who led the raid,

Col. James Montgomery, with whom Tubman worked on the Combahee River Raid and other forays into Confederate territory while stationed at Beaufort, South Carolina. Courtesy Kansas State Historical Society, Topeka.

and under whose inspiration it was originated and conducted. For sound sense and real native eloquence, her address would do honor to any man, and it created quite a sensation. ("From Florida," 1863)[31]

Sanborn worked up his own biographical sketch of Tubman based on his memories (and perhaps journal notes, correspondence, or newspaper clippings as well) by the following week. He also published parts of a dictated letter he had received from Tubman, dated June 30, 1863, in the same issue of the *Commonwealth* in which his sketch appeared.

Her letter to Sanborn is exceptionally interesting, both in its contents and in its bookish style (probably provided by one of the New England missionaries acting as her scribe):

Last fall, when the people here became very much alarmed for fear of an invasion from the rebels, all my clothes were packed and sent with others to Hilton Head, and lost; and I have never been able to get any trace of them since. I was sick at the time, and unable to look after them myself. I want, among the rest, a bloomer dress, made of some coarse, strong material, to wear on expeditions. In our late expedition up the Combahee River, in coming on board the boat, I was carrying two pigs for a poor sick woman, who had a child to carry, and the order "double quick" was given, and I started to run, stepped on my dress, it being rather long, and fell and tore it almost off, so that when I got on board the boat, there was hardly anything left of it but shreds. I made up my mind then I would never wear a long dress on another expedition of the kind, but would have a bloomer as soon as I could get it. . . . You have, without doubt, seen a full account of the expedition I refer to. Don't you think we colored people are entitled to some credit for that exploit, under the lead of the brave Colonel Montgomery? We weakened the rebels somewhat on the Combahee River, by taking and bringing away seven hundred and fifty-six of their most valuable live stock, known up in your region as "contrabands," and this, too, without the loss of a single life on our part. . . . Nearly or quite all the able-bodied men have joined the colored regiments here. (Tubman, 1863b)

Tubman's own modestly stated claim to reflected glory—"Don't you think we colored people are entitled to some credit?"—suggests her delight in the historic occasion. Though she described herself here as "under the lead of the brave Colonel Montgomery," she knew the value of her own role. Later, in her 1898 affidavit in her pension claim case, she specifically referred to herself as "commander of several men (eight or nine) as scouts during the late War of the Rebellion" (Tubman, 1898). Another notable feature of this letter is her casual request for a "bloomer dress"—the costume worn by a few brave dress reform feminists who criticized the showy, expensive, and unhealthy fashions of middle-class ladies of the day. The request suggests how thoroughly comfortable she was with the claims made on behalf of women's rights in the elite Garrisonian antislavery circles in which she had become a "heroine" in the 1850s and 1860s. Finally, it is interesting to find her characterizing the relief work she was doing among recently freed people as a necessary precursor to both financial independence and racial pride: "Among other duties which I have, is that of looking after the hospital here for contrabands. Most of those coming from the mainland are very destitute, almost naked. I am trying to find places for those able to work, and provide for them as best I can, so as to lighten the burden on the Government as much as possible, while at the same time they learn to respect themselves by earning their own living." Here she sounds fully committed to the social worker's role in which she was cast by the New England Freedmen's Aid enterprise—the emphasis on saving government money indicates canny knowledge of her thrifty Northern audience.

Sanborn did not publish the portion of the letter in which she reminded him of his personal promise of funds: "You will recollect having said to me some time ago that you would help me with a small sum of money every year to help me carry on my work" (Cameron, 1982, 24). She told him she had also "written a dunning letter to our friend Wendell Phillips" for the same reason. She added: "I have now been absent two years almost, and have just got letters from my friends in Auburn, urging me to come home. My father and mother are old and in feeble health, and need my care and attention. I hope the good people there will not allow them to suffer, and I do not believe they will" (Tubman, 1863b).

UNION ARMY NURSING SERVICE IN SOUTH CAROLINA AND FLORIDA

Shortly after the Combahee River Raid, Tubman contributed to the war effort in the less glorious but vital role of nurse for those wounded in the assault on Fort Wagner in Charleston Harbor by the 54th Massachusetts Volunteers. Colonel Robert Gould Shaw, for whom Tubman may have cooked during his short time in Camp Saxton, was killed leading the charge at this battle, which took place on July 18, 1863.[32] The Confederate troops expressed their contempt for a white officer of a black regiment by throwing his body into a mass grave with the bodies of many of his troops. Although the loss of life at Fort Wagner was terrible, the assault was symbolically important in proving the bravery and competence of the newly recruited African American soldiers fighting for the North.

Very probably Tubman heard the gunfire and saw the sky alight from where she was stationed, at the army encampment at Camp Saxton, only one mile away from Battery Wagner. She was sent to help bury the dead and nurse the survivors of that assault almost immediately afterward. One survivor, later an Auburn resident, dated the beginning of his fifty-year acquaintance with her to that time.[33] Tubman vividly described the unsanitary wartime hospital conditions to Bradford: "Well, Missus, I'd go to the hospital, I would, early every morning. I'd get a big chunk of ice, I would, and put it in a basin, and fill it with water; then I'd take a sponge and begin. First man I'd come to, I'd thrash away the flies, and they'd rise, they would, like bees round a hive. Then I'd begin to bathe the wounds, and by the time I'd bathed off three or four, the fire and heat would have melted the ice and made the water warm, and it would be as red as clear blood. Then I'd go and get more ice, I would, and by the time I got to the next ones, the flies would be round the first ones black and thick as ever" (Bradford, 1869).

Separate hospital facilities were maintained for white and black soldiers.[34] The Sea Islands missionary school teacher Laura Towne wrote: "[July 28] Brought home from school to-day a heavy load of watermelons . . . that we can send to the hospitals for the wounded soldiers; we sent the fruit to the colored hospitals, . . . because the other hospitals have more friends to care for them" (Towne, in Holland [1969], 115–116). Tubman may very well have met Clara Barton, founder of the American Red Cross, at this time. Barton and Susie King Taylor also nursed the wounded African American soldiers who had stormed Fort Wagner.[35]

Interestingly, in that rural Southern world where a tremendous amount of traditional knowledge of local plant characteristics must already have existed in the local population, Tubman became known as a maker of particularly effective herbal remedies. She later told both Bradford and Telford of her success in curing dysentery in Fernandina, Florida, just over the border with South Carolina, where she was sent sometime in 1863–1864 specifically for medical work.

When dysentery in its worst form attacked the camp at Fernandina, the surgeon in charge was down with the disease and ordinary remedies proved absolutely worthless. Harriet, who had acquired quite a reputation for her skill in curing this disease by a decoction which she prepared from roots which grew near the water which gave the disease, was sent for. "I went down there," she quaintly says, "and found them that bad with chronic dysentery, that they was dying off like sheep. I dug some roots and herbs and made a tea for the doctor and the disease stopped on him. And then he said, 'Give it to the soldiers.' So I boiled up a great boiler of roots and herbs, and the General [de]tailed a man to take two cans and go round and give it to all in the camp that needed it, and it cured them."[36] (Telford, n.d.)

GOING ON LEAVE

For almost a full year after the Combahee River Raid, Tubman continued to serve in her multiple capacities in the Sea Islands and to support herself by extra work in the informal economy of the military camp.[37] A son of William Lloyd Garrison who was a lieutenant with the Massachusetts 55th Regiment (a second African American regiment recruited at the same time as the 54th) met her in the winter of 1863–1864. He recorded both her desire to go north (a strong theme in the documentation of her war years) and the reluctance of the army to lose her intelligence-gathering services.

She no sooner saw me than she recognized me at once, and instantly threw her arms around me, and gave me quite an affectionate embrace, much to the amusement of those with me. We had a very interesting conversation with her. She is just now cooking and washing clothes at Gen. Terry's quarters, who is now in command of Morris and Folly islands. She wants to go North, but says Gen. Gilmore will not let her go, only on condition that she will return back to this department. He thinks her services are too valuable to lose. She has made it a business to see all contrabands escaping from the rebels, and is able to get more intelligence than anybody else. She is just now working hard to lay up a little money for her parents, and to pay off some debt that she owes. She has a chance of making a good deal of money here, and can easily get fifty times more work than she can do. She had the misfortune to have fifty dollars stolen from her the other day.

What money she had left, Mr. Severance took from her to send North. (G. Garrison, 1864)

In the summer of 1864 she finally went north. Wendell Garrison, another of William Lloyd Garrison's sons, reported her arrival in Brooklyn, New York, in a letter dated June 20: "Moses Garrison, alias Harriet alias General Tubman has just arrived up from Port Royal. What times. She has seen George, he was in good health." She was in Boston in August (staying at the home of John Rock). A brief story in the *Commonwealth* reported at that time that she "left Florida to come north in the latter part of June." As usual she was in need of money: "Her services to her people and to the army seem to have been very inadequately recompensed by the military authorities, and such money as she has received, she has expended for others as her custom is. Any contributions of money or clothing sent to her at this office will be received by her, and the givers may be assured that she will use them with fidelity and discretion for the good of the colored race" ("Harriet Tubman," 1864a).

Tubman fell ill during the leave of absence and did not return south until the following year, shortly before the end of the war. She was in the North during Lincoln's reelection campaign and at the time of the passage of the Thirteenth Amendment (abolishing slavery throughout the United States) on January 31, 1865. This was a culminating moment in the long antislavery struggle that touched off rejoicing in the House of Representatives: "The packed galleries, which included many black people formerly excluded by congressional rules, burst into delirious cheering and weeping that had previously occurred at mass meetings but never before in the House itself, where members embraced and literally danced with joy in a raucous display of emotion" (Mayer, 1998, 575–576). She may have been present when William Lloyd Garrison spoke in a Jubilee meeting in Boston that week of the "liberation" of both four million blacks and thirty-four million whites, but as with so much else about her activities during the last months of the war this has not yet been documented.

AT THE WAR'S END

Tubman intended to return to the Port Royal area to continue work with the freed people on the Sea Islands. According to a report of the New England Freedmen's Aid Society's Committee on Teachers, published in the *Freedmen's Record* for April 1865, "Harriet Tubman, whose earnest labors for her race are well known, is employed at a small salary to go among her own people and aid in their practical education" (Cheney, 1865, 54–55).[38] And indeed she was listed as a "practical teacher" at Hilton Head in the *Freedmen's Record* through November.[39] Yet instead of returning to the Sea Islands she spontaneously decided on the trip south to work as a nurse in military hospitals in Virginia from March through July.[40] According to her postwar account recorded by Charles P. Wood, "she was intercepted in Philadelphia[41] by some members of the Sanitary Commission who persuaded her to go instead to the James River Hospitals—where there was pressing need of such service as she could give in the Gov't Hospitals. And relinquishing her plan of returning to the Dept. of the South—without a thought as to the unfortunate pecuniary result of this irregular proceeding she went to the Hospitals of the James River, and at Fortress Monroe or Hampton—where she remained until July 1865. In that month she went to Washington again to advise the Gov't of some dreadful abuses existing in one or more of the Hospitals there" (Wood, 1868).[42]

While in Washington in March 1865, Tubman was asked to assist Martin Delany in a remarkable government-approved plan to raise a black army by recruiting slaves behind the lines in South Carolina—an effort cut short by the end of the war.[43] In the first week of April she visited Camp William Penn in Philadelphia, where she told her inspirational stories to newly recruited black soldiers stationed there ("For the Christian Recorder," April 15, 1865). But the rebellion was nearly over as she spoke. Richmond, the capital of the Confederacy, fell to Union forces, and Robert E. Lee surrendered. Many of Tubman's antislavery associates, including William Lloyd Garrison, Martin Delany, and a group of missionaries and freed people from Beaufort, were present at Fort Sumter for the victory celebration and Union flag-raising ceremony that took place on April 14.[44] The joyous feelings expressed by the antislavery celebrants at Fort Sumter were short-lived, however. As they soon learned, an assassin had fatally shot Abraham Lincoln on the evening of the very day of celebration. Lincoln's Secretary of State, William Seward, had also been targeted for assassination on April 14, but the attempt failed; Seward, though badly injured, had survived.

In mid-July Tubman went to Washington to report on the abuses in the hospitals. She also took the opportunity to visit Seward, who was then still recovering from both an earlier carriage accident and from the knife wounds he suffered in the assassination attempt. Moreover, his

Ednah Cheney, the Bostonian secretary of the New England Freedmen's Aid Society during the last years of the Civil War. Cheney wrote the second important biographical sketch of Tubman for the Society's journal (1865). Courtesy Concord Free Public Library, Concord, Massachusetts.

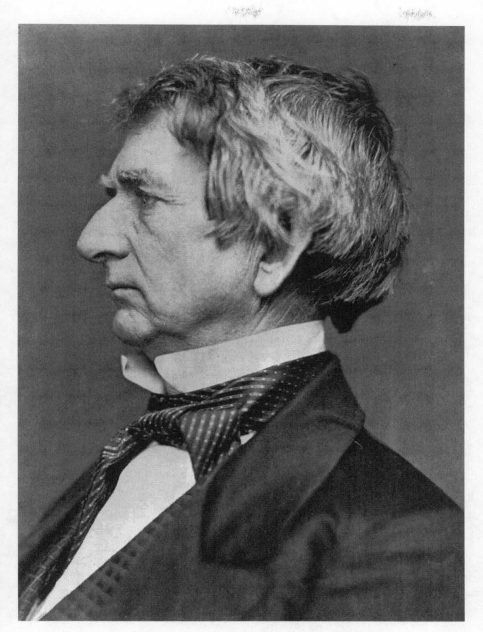

William H. Seward, former governor of New York and Lincoln's secretary of state. Seward sold Tubman a small farm in Auburn near his own residence, and his family provided various kinds of support for Tubman's activities during her long residence in Auburn.

wife, Frances Miller Seward, had died on June 21, just three weeks before Tubman's visit. Whatever feelings Tubman may have had on seeing Seward suffering from these severe recent blows, she accomplished her practical goal of obtaining his support for her claim to back pay for her military service.[45] Seward wrote at this time to General Hunter on her behalf, in a much quoted character assessment: "Harriet Tubman, a colored woman, has been nursing our soldiers during nearly all the war. She believes she has claims for faithful services to the command in South Carolina, with which you are connected, and she thinks that you would be disposed to see her claim justly settled. I have known her long as a noble, high spirit, as true as seldom dwells in the human form. I commend her therefore to your kind attention."

However eloquent Seward's letter, no back pay was forthcoming as Tubman left government service sometime in the fall of 1865.[46] Charles P. Wood, the Auburn banker who assisted Tubman in 1868 in assembling the documentary support she needed to put in a formal pension claim, thought that the root of the problem was bureaucratic: "that she held no commission, and had not in the regular way and at the proper times and places, made proof and application of and for, her just compensation. On such certificates as she holds she should have it without further delay" (Wood, 1868). Tubman's own war service was never to be acknowledged by the award of a veteran's pension—and it took twenty-eight more years before her sporadically renewed campaign for just treatment by the national government would produce a small war widow's annuity. Despite her unprecedented history and celebrity in antislavery networks, Tubman entered a postwar life in which it was impossible to translate her achievements into economic security.

POSTWAR YEARS
IN AUBURN

RECONSTRUCTION BEGINS

As Harriet Tubman was returning to Auburn in the fall of 1865, travel-ing on a government pass on a train from Philadelphia to New York, a conductor tried to remove her from a car and in strenu-ously resisting she suffered both insult and injury. Bradford's account of the event was highly indignant on her behalf: "When the conductor looked at her ticket, he said, 'Come, hustle out of here! We don't carry niggers for half fare.' Harriet explained to him that she was in the employ of the gov-ernment, and was entitled to transportation as the soldiers were. But the conductor took her forcibly by the arm, and said, 'I'll make you tired of try-ing to stay here.' She resisted, and being very strong, she could probably have got the better of the conductor, had he not called three men to his assistance. The car was filled with emigrants, and no one seemed to take her part. The only words she heard, accompanied with fearful oaths, were 'Pitch the nigger out!' They nearly wrenched her arm off, and at length threw her, with all their strength, into a baggage car. She supposed her arm was bro-ken, and in intense suffering she came on to New York" (Bradford, 1869).

Martha Coffin Wright captured an intriguingly different version of the racial insult Tubman resented. "How dreadful it was for that wicked conductor to drag her out into the smoking car & hurt her so seriously, disabling her left arm, perhaps for the Winter—She still has the misery in her Shoulder & side & carries her hand in a sling—It took three of them to drag her out after first trying to wrench her finger and then her arm— She told the man he was a copperhead scoundrel,[1] for which he choked her.... She told him she didn't thank any body to call her cullud pusson—

An informal portrait of Harriet Tubman (possibly from the 1860s), reproduced in Sanborn's *Recollections of Seventy Years* (1909).

She wd he called [her] black or Negro[2] —She was as proud of being a black woman as he was of being white" (M. C. Wright, 1865).

Tubman mobilized several of her antislavery friends to pursue the possibility of suing the New Jersey–based railroad company. In April 1866 Wright wrote to her husband in Philadelphia, asking him to "stop in New York long enough to see Smalley & Parker Pillsbury at the Anti Slavery Office, & find out whether anything can be done about the Camden & Amboy [railroad company]—If not there should at least be an account of the outrage published in the Independent—William sd she told him they wd have suffered for food, the past winter, as she was disabled, if it had not been for the work of a woman in the house—They had to burn their fences for fire-wood—I wish something could be done, for her faithful services during the war, certainly deserve some recompense."

Nothing seems to have come of this effort to right the wrong, but activists in antislavery circles seized upon the opportunity to draw attention to the issue of racial discrimination in public transportation in the North. Frances Ellen Watkins Harper, abolitionist feminist writer and speaker, used the experience to exemplify a pattern of insulting and discriminatory treatment of black women in a speech at the Eleventh Women's Rights convention sponsored by the National Woman Suffrage Association in May 1866. Harper spoke of the need to make visible "the wrongs of black women," in ironic juxtaposition to "the rights of white women."

> You white women speak here of rights. I speak of wrongs. I, as a colored woman, have had in this country an education which has made me feel as if I were in the situation of Ishmael, my hand against every man, and every man's hand against me. Let me go to-tomorrow morning and take my seat in one of your street cars—I do not know that they will do it in New York, but they will in Philadelphia—and the conductor will put up his hand and stop the car rather than let me ride.
>
> A Lady—They will not do that here.
>
> Mrs. Harper—They do in Philadelphia. Going from Washington to Baltimore this spring, they put me in the smoking car. (Loud Voices—"Shame.") Aye, in the capital of the nation, where the black man consecrated himself to the nation's defense, faithful when the white man was faithless, they put me in the smoking car!

The treatment of the antislavery heroine was Harper's culminating example: "We have a woman in our country who has received the name of

Frances E. W. Harper.

Frances E. Watkins Harper, African American feminist lecturer and novelist. She spoke about the injuries Harriet Tubman sustained when ejected from a railroad car immediately after the war, in a speech at the Eleventh Women's Rights Convention sponsored by the National Woman Suffrage Association in May 1866. Courtesy Boston Public Library.

'Moses,' not by lying about it, but by acting it out (applause)—a woman who has gone down into the Egypt of slavery and brought out hundreds of our people into liberty. The last time I saw that woman, her hands were swollen. That woman who had led one of Montgomery's most successful expeditions, who was brave enough and secretive enough to act as a scout for the American army, had her hands all swollen from a conflict with a brutal conductor, who undertook to eject her from her place."[3]

Antislavery lecturer Sallie Holley also referred to the incident in a letter published in the *National Anti-Slavery Standard*—though she placed the main emphasis on the generosity of the antislavery luminaries who had provided financial aid:

> The other day at Gerrit Smith's, I saw this heroic woman, whom the pen of genius will yet make famous as one of the noblest Christian hearts ever inspired to lift the burdens of the wronged and the oppressed, and what do you think she had to tell me? She had been tending and caring for our Union black soldiers in hospital during the war, and, at the end of her labors, was on her way home, coming in a car through New Jersey. A white man, the conductor, thrust her out of the car with such violence that she has not been able to work scarcely any since; and as she told me of the pain she had and still suffered, she said she did not know what she should have done for herself and old father and mother she takes care of if Mr. Wendell Phillips hadn't sent her $80 that kept them warm through the Winter. . . . Gerrit Smith, in his tireless, unceasing benevolence, has just given her money. (Holley, 1867b)

The railway car incident clearly signaled the beginning of a new set of challenges for the celebrated heroine and war veteran—social and economic challenges that were in some respects more difficult for her to meet than the dangers and obstacles she had encountered in her Underground Railroad and war service. In the postwar period, the stark moral and religious touchstone issue of human enslavement had vanished along with emancipation.[4] There was no national consensus on how the newly emancipated population would be integrated into the economic, political, and social life of the United States after the war was over. Indeed, there was no national consensus on what shape the new United States itself would take, now that the states formerly in rebellion had been defeated by military force but not persuaded of the rightness of the Union's cause.

What is called the "Reconstruction" period actually began during the war, when the executive and legislative branches of the federal government began to formulate policies by which the defeated Confederate states would be readmitted to the Union.[5] The assassination of Lincoln dramatically shifted the relationship of the antislavery radicals to the government. When Andrew Johnson, a ticket-balancing War Democrat vice president from Tennessee, assumed the presidency in 1865, antislavery stalwarts were dismayed.[6] Johnson increasingly alienated the antislavery Radical Republicans by proposing lenient measures for the restoration of the Southern states to the Union. The congressional Radical Republicans countered with proposed bills that would protect the civil rights of the newly emancipated Southern blacks, delaying the readmission of the former Confederate states until such protections were in place.

Frederick Douglass, who had begun to campaign actively for universal suffrage at the National Convention of Colored Men that met in Syracuse in September 1864 during Lincoln's reelection campaign, continued to see the ballot as an absolutely necessary weapon that newly enfranchised Southern blacks would need to use once Southern whites had reclaimed political power. When he and a committee of prominent black men met with President Andrew Johnson in early February 1866, Johnson clearly expressed opposition to mandating black suffrage in the South. The committee publicized the contents of the interview through a letter to a Washington newspaper, and this publicity contributed to a hardening of positions on both sides. Johnson vetoed the first version of the Freedmen's Bureau Bill, but Congress passed another in July 1866 and overrode his veto of a Civil Rights Bill in April. Johnson also vetoed a bill that enfranchised the black population of the District of Columbia, but this veto was immediately overridden by Congress. In the fall of 1868, Johnson and the Democrats suffered defeat at the polls, and the Republican candidate, Ulysses S. Grant, was elected president (Quarles, 1976, 228–235).

The political enfranchisement of former slaves was a burning and divisive national issue that created conflict within the Republican Party ranks as well as between Democrats and Republicans. At the Republican national convention in September 1866 there was a strongly prosuffrage wing, and the black suffrage plank was ultimately adopted, but Northern Republicans were initially less than enthusiastic. Even among the Radical Republicans there was disagreement over the best political strategy by which black suffrage could be won. One of the most important divisions within the ranks of former antislavery allies occurred when feminists disagreed among themselves about whether to support the Fourteenth and Fifteenth Amendments to the Constitution.[7]

The Fourteenth Amendment established broad civil rights protections and a new rule that based a state's representation in Congress on the number of "adult male citizens" with access to the ballot—but it did not specifically make black men eligible to vote. Nevertheless, it failed ratification the first time, in 1866, when the legislatures of ten Southern states rejected it. When the Republicans won veto-proof two-thirds majorities in both houses in the 1866 elections, Congress was able to pass the Reconstruction Acts of 1867. These authorized federal troops in the South to enroll black voters under military law—in order to create "new state governments that would ratify the Fourteenth Amendment" (Mayer, 1998, 611). By July 1868 the Fourteenth Amendment was in place, and the struggle over the Fifteenth Amendment had begun.

The feminist wing of the abolitionist movement had initially attempted to link black suffrage with women's suffrage. At the Woman's Rights Convention in May 1866 where Frances Watkins Harper spoke about "the wrongs of black women," Susan B. Anthony offered a resolution changing the name of the organization to the American Equal Rights Association. She gave a stirring statement linking the female suffrage struggle with the broader "human rights" movement: "The duty of Congress at this moment is to declare what shall be the basis of representation in a republican form of government. There is, there can be, but one true basis; and that is that taxation must give representation; hence our demand must now go beyond woman—it must extend to the farthest bound of the principle of the 'consent of the governed,' the only authorized or just government. We, therefore, wish to broaden our Woman's Rights platform, and make it in name—what it ever has been in spirit—a Human Rights platform" (*Proceedings of Eleventh Woman's Rights Convention*, 1866, 48). Lucretia Mott, Elizabeth Cady Stanton, and Martha Coffin Wright all made clear statements of support for the broader goals of the new organization.

This alliance between the two suffrage causes did not last long, however. The Fourteenth Amendment's use of the word "male" introduced sex discrimination into the women's rights struggle. The feminists' Republican antislavery allies in Congress, Charles Sumner and Wendell Phillips, made the political judgment that the ballot for women would have to wait, and told Stanton that it was "the Negro's hour." Stanton and Anthony were determined to keep women's suffrage politically visible and to take whatever advantage might be made of the postwar shifts in political power. Although Stanton and Anthony did not actively oppose the Fourteenth Amendment in 1867, they did campaign in Kansas for a state women's suffrage bill with the help of George F. Train, a Democrat who worked to defeat a Republican black suffrage bill in the same campaign and used racist arguments to do so.[8]

Meanwhile African American feminists began to speak out forcefully on the danger of losing black suffrage entirely in the South, if supporters were to cling to a universal suffrage strategy. Frederick Douglass, one of the three vice presidents of the new American Equal Rights Association, was a long-time proponent of the women's rights movement, having participated at the Seneca Falls convention of 1848, and he reminded the organization at a meeting in Albany in 1866 of the extreme dangers facing impoverished and politically powerless blacks in the postwar South. At the founding meeting of the New England Woman Suffrage Association in Boston in November of 1868, both Douglass and Harper argued the priority of black men's claim to the ballot. But in May 1869, the Equal Rights Association failed to support a resolution for the Fifteenth Amendment, which mandated black male suffrage.

At the initiative of Stanton and Anthony, the organization's name was changed again, this time to the National Woman Suffrage Association (NWSA). Dissenting feminist abolitionists (including Harper) broke away and went on to create a rival organization under the leadership of Lucy Stone and Abby Foster Kelley, the American Woman Suffrage Association (AWSA). The AWSA supported the Fifteenth Amendment and received considerable support over the next few years from Garrison, Higginson, and Douglass. The NWSA under Stanton and Anthony opposed the Fifteenth Amendment "unless accompanied immediately by a Sixteenth Amendment that would enfranchise women" (Mayer, 1998, 612). When the Fifteenth Amendment was ratified (April 1870), members of the American Anti-Slavery Association declared their work complete and dissolved the organization, but the two separate national women's rights organizations worked on separately (and relatively unsuccessfully) for another twenty years, before finally merging in 1890 in a successor organization, the National American Woman's Rights Association (NAWSA). NAWSA ultimately devised a winning political strategy for women's suffrage—one that again focused exclusively on gender discrimination but turned a blind eye to racist politics.[9]

On the grassroots level, meanwhile, the struggle for such resources as work, land, education, and social services for the newly emancipated population went on. In the Southern states, despite (and sometimes because of) the presence of federal troops, there were many incidents of race-related violence. In South Carolina, for example, there were "three major race riots" between July 1865 and November 1866 (two involving white Union soldiers), as well as vigilante white groups organized as "home police" (Williamson, 1986, 258). John Tubman, Harriet Tubman's faithless first husband, was one of the victims of the violence of this period. As the story was reported in a Reconstruction-era Baltimore newspaper, "A colored man, named John Tubman, was shot and instantly killed yesterday evening, by Robert Vincent, a white man. The shooting took place on the county road, about 6 miles from Cambridge. A difficulty had occurred in the morning relative to the removal of some ashes from a tenant-house on Vincent's farm, and the parties again met about sundown on the public road, when the shooting took place"("Fatal Shooting Affray," 1867).

The trial and acquittal of John Tubman's murderer by an all-white jury was also the subject of indignant Radical Republican newspaper coverage, which used the incident to urge the necessity of black male suffrage. "That Vincent murdered the deceased we presume no one doubts; but as no one but a colored boy saw him commit the deed, it was universally conceded that he would be acquitted, the moment it was ascertained that the jury was composed exclusively of Democrats. The Republicans have taught the Democrats much since 1860. They thrashed them into at least a seeming respect for the Union. They educated them up to a tolerance of public schools. They forced them to recognize Negro testimony in their courts. But they haven't got them to the point of convicting a fellow Democrat for killing a Negro. But even that will follow when the Negro is armed with the ballot" ("Acquittal of a Murderer," 1867).

Tubman would have been made aware of the murder and the trial through her connections in Maryland, but the subject was never mentioned by Bradford or later biographers who interviewed her—which strongly suggests that she herself chose to be silent on this question.[10]

SETTLING DOWN IN AUBURN

In the autumn of 1865 Harriet Tubman returned to the house she had arranged to purchase on mortgage from the Seward family on South Street in the thriving city of Auburn.[11] In the very first of the postwar years, still disabled from her recent injuries, she was hard-pressed to provide for the most basic needs of her elderly parents and other dependents, in addition to her own.[12] Her household included a variety of kinfolk living with her for longer or shorter periods, as well as boarders and refugees who could contribute little toward their own support. A sister-in-law from Canada, called "Catherine" by Sarah Bradford, lived with Tubman and helped out with the elders for a while.[13] The "kidnapped" niece from Maryland, Margaret Stewart, whom Tubman had placed in the Seward family during the war, may have lived with Tubman for a few years before marrying Henry Lucas and establishing her own household nearby.[14] Other relatives returning from Canada, including her niece Keziah Bowley's family, lived temporarily in the South Street household and then moved further south. Tubman sheltered and provided subsistence farming work for an extended family throughout her long life in the North. Occasionally she charged a small boarding fee for children placed in her care, but according to all testimony, those in need, including some whom she had brought north during the Underground Railroad years, were never turned away (Tatlock, 1939a, 1939b).[15]

The Wright, Osborne, and Seward families and others in the antislavery networks helped out in a variety of ways in the hard early years. A donation by a Mrs. Birney added $50 yearly to Tubman's income, and other cash gifts were forthcoming at times from Wendell Phillips, Gerrit Smith, and William Lloyd Garrison.[16] Tubman and her household members grew and sold (or bartered) vegetables, planted fruit trees, and raised chickens. She herself also made baskets, cooked, cared for children, and even hired out to do spring cleaning in her white friends' homes.[17]

Martha Coffin Wright's diaries and letters suggest this web of economic exchange between Tubman and her politically allied neighbors in the late 1860s and early 1870s:

> [August 31, 1868] Harriet came to see Ellen [Wright Garrison] and the babies, & brot them some fresh eggs—I engaged her late peas.
> [May 2, 1870] Harriet Tubman came to clean—Had her to help wash, & then she & Mary cleaned front parlor—Frank Round's man helped Lawrence shake carpet & Mary & Harriet got it down again in time for Mary & Lizzie to go to a wedding after tea was ready.
> [May 3, 1870] Had Harriet Tubman to clean round front door & entry steps & take nails out of front chamber carpet.
> [January 14, 1871] Saturday . . . Too muddy to go out—Harriet Tubman came & bro't hoop basket. pd. her 62½c.
> [October 1872] Harriet Tubman came yesterday & got a large basket full of pears & Apples.—

A Wright family portrait, probably from the early 1870s, including Lucretia Coffin Mott of Philadelphia; her sister, Martha Coffin Wright of Auburn; Wright's daughter, Eliza Wright Osborne, a key friend in Tubman's later years in Auburn; and one of the Osborne daughters. Courtesy Friends Historical Society, Swarthmore College, Swarthmore, Pennsylvania.

Tubman's own household's economic stability was not her only concern, of course. In the early postwar days she had an active charitable interest in two schools for freed people in South Carolina, probably through her schoolteacher grandnephew, James Bowley. In September 1868, Martha Coffin Wright reported that Bowley was preparing to take clothing and other donations south with him when he left Auburn: "He lived in Canada till the War, & now teaches the freedmen in S. Carolina—He was one of the first that Harriet rescued from Slavery." A year later Wright noted that this grandnephew was now "a member of the S. Carolina legislature!" (M. C. Wright, 1869h). Bowley was one of the pioneer black men elected to serve in state legislatures in the South in the late 1860s when the Southern states qualified for reentrance into the union.[18] Several blacks were sent to Congress in 1870 during the period that came to be known as Radical Reconstruction.[19] Educated Northern black men with an ambition for political leadership were drawn to South Carolina in particular after the war, because of its majority black population (Williamson, 1965). Some of them started as schoolteachers and went on to run for office, as did Tubman's grandnephew. (Freed women, although not formally enfranchised in the Southern states during Reconstruction, found informal ways of engaging in political activity, as recent scholarship has shown.[20])

Tubman's Auburn friends were well aware that she was engaged in various kinds of social service work related to her antislavery convictions. In the early postwar days they frequently pitched in to support her efforts. For example, in the fall of 1868, she and a group of close friends in Auburn worked on organizing what Martha Coffin Wright called "Harriet Tubman's fair," a major fund-raising bazaar based on the familiar model of the antislavery fair.[21] Wright worked long hours for several months on handicraft contributions, and she provided a lively description of the event, strategically scheduled for just before Christmas: "Fanny has been active at the Fair—-they took a little more than last yr. a little over $500, after two days of very hard work for a few—Eliza Townsend & Debby Ann were indefatigable & Anne & Anna & the Carries busy at the tables—they made a good many fancy things wh. sold well, & they have orders for a good many more—I sent my 38 aprons 9 bags—lap bags for children, & rag bags & knitting needle elastics—3 tomatoes (pincushions) & one needle book— Eliza sent holders—rag babies (large) & towels—the babys were soon sold at 3 dollars each—" (M. C. Wright, 1866–1870, diary entry for December 16, 1868).

Full-length standing studio portrait of Harriet Tubman, probably from the late 1860s. (Photographer: H. R. Luidley, Auburn, New York.) Courtesy the Cayuga Museum and Chase Research Laboratory, Auburn, New York.

Studio portrait of Harriet Tubman, circa late 1860s, (head and shoulders, voluminous white neck cloth).

THE TUBMAN/BRADFORD
BIOGRAPHY PROJECT OF 1868

The first extended biography of Harriet Tubman originated as a fund-raising project. Tubman and her friends knew that a book-length narrative could be profitably sold at fairs, conventions, and other gatherings of the antislavery network. The proceeds would be devoted to Tubman's household's financial support and, in particular, to the regular payment of the mortgage interest on the property purchased from Seward.[22] For this project, Sarah Hopkins Bradford of Geneva, New York, was recruited sometime in the spring of 1868.[23] Bradford was the sister of Samuel Hopkins, a professor of church history at the Auburn Theological Seminary. She had met Tubman's parents in the Sunday school class she taught in Auburn while visiting her brother's household during the war. Though Bradford had not known Tubman long at the time of the collaboration, her experience as a writer of published moral children's stories (including one about a fugitive slave) probably made her seem qualified to help Tubman produce the narrative.

As they began work on the project, Tubman presented Bradford with a collection of documents attesting to her war service and letters of reference from notable antislavery associates. They also solicited additional testimonial letters from Gerrit Smith, Wendell Phillips, Franklin Sanborn, Thomas Garrett, the Reverend Henry Fowler (pastor of the antislavery Central Presbyterian Church of Auburn), Lucretia Mott, and Frederick Douglass.[24] (Mott's letter was not included in the final volume, and there may have been others that came too late as well.[25]) Bradford explicitly asked people to comment on Tubman's truthfulness—apparently anticipating that readers might react skeptically to uncorroborated accounts of derring-do of the kind that would be contained in the sketch. Douglass's eloquent letter comparing her courage favorably to his own has been frequently quoted:

> The difference between us is very marked. Most that I have done and suffered in the service of our cause has been in public, and I have received much encouragement at every step of the way. You, on the other hand, have labored in a private way. I have wrought in the day—you in the night. I have had the applause of the crowd and the satisfaction that comes of being approved by the multitude, while the most that you have done has been witnessed by a few trembling, scarred, and foot-sore bondmen and women,

Sarah Bradford, of Geneva and later Rochester, New York; Tubman's third biographer. Bradford, a writer of children's books, met Tubman and her family through visits to her brother, Samuel Miles Hopkins, of the Auburn Theological Seminary. In her late years, Tubman relied on Bradford to help republish her biography.

whom you have led out of the house of bondage, and whose heartfelt "God
bless you" has been your only reward. The midnight sky and the silent stars
have been the witnesses of your devotion to freedom and of your heroism.
Excepting John Brown—of sacred memory—I know of no one who has willingly encountered more perils and hardships to serve our enslaved people
than you have. (Douglass, 1868)

Bradford invited Tubman to her home in Geneva for interviews (Brad-
ford, 1869), and they may also have talked at the home of Martha Coffin
Wright or Eliza Wright Osborne. The narrative was hastily put together in
the late summer, while Bradford was preparing for an extended trip to
Europe with her children. Wright reported in a letter to her sisters, "A
Mrs. Bradford of Geneva is writing a memoir of her [Tubman]—as well
as she can, with Harriets disjointed materials" (M. C. Wright, 1868f).
Bradford seems to have judged that a fundraising project aimed at a predominantly white audience should present the intended beneficiary as an
object of charity rather than make a social justice argument.[26] Accordingly, *Scenes in the Life of Harriet Tubman* begins and ends with sentimental depictions of Tubman as a kind of suffering saint: "Worn down
by her sufferings and fatigue, her health permanently affected by the cruelties to which she has been subjected, she is still laboring to the utmost
limit of her strength for the support of her aged parents, and still also for
her afflicted people ... never obtruding herself, never asking for charity,
except for 'her people.' ... This woman of whom we have been reading is
poor, and partially disabled from her injuries, yet she supports cheerfully
and uncomplainingly herself and her own parents, and always has several
poor children in her house, who are dependent entirely upon her exertions" (Bradford, 1869, 2, 103–104).

Although its official publication date is 1869, *Scenes in the Life of Harriet
Tubman* was available in time to be sold at the Harriet Tubman Fair in
December 1868. Martha Coffin Wright noted that "the price was too
high—$1 a copy for a small book," yet "60 or 70 sold & more perhaps
will." The Wright family helped with further distribution of the book.
Ellen Wright Garrison, in Boston, received her copies around Christmas.
She had some criticisms to make of Bradford's "effort" but promised her
mother to help call attention to it. When Martha Coffin Wright was visiting her sister Lucretia in Philadelphia the next month, she wrote home
for six more copies to be sold at the upcoming American Anti-Slavery
Society meeting and also reported that she had "sold the copy I bro't, to

Mr. Purvis."[27] Other friends of Tubman's also exerted themselves to get the book sold. Sanborn reviewed it favorably in the *Springfield Republican.* Bradford later reported that sales of the 1869 book had brought in $1,200, enabling Tubman to pay off the mortgage debt she owed Seward.[28]

MARRYING A SECOND HUSBAND

Three months after the Bradford book was published, on March 18, 1869, Harriet Tubman married her second husband, Nelson Davis, a Civil War veteran about twenty-five years old who had boarded in her household for three years.[29] She herself was then in her late forties. The ceremony took place in the predominantly white Central Presbyterian Church in Auburn, with many of her antislavery friends and neighbors in attendance. As with Tubman's first husband, very little information about Davis survives.[30] We know that he was born near Elizabeth City, North Carolina, and that he was another successful fugitive from slavery. He was known both as Nelson Charles (his slave name and the name he used in the army) and Nelson Davis; he married as Charles Nelson Davis ("he said Davis was his correct name," Tubman testified in 1890). He enrolled in the army (Tubman thought he was drafted) in Oneida County, New York, on September 25, 1863, when she was in the Sea Islands, and he received his discharge in Brownsville, Texas, November 10, 1865. He was 5′11″ tall and dark skinned. One photographic image of him survives, a household group photograph including Tubman and several others (see page 87).

Nelson Davis was also a brickmaker. Harkless Bowley, who lived with Tubman and Davis for several years, remembered working in his brickyard: "He and Harriet was carrying on the business together." Davis lived to be only forty-four, dying in October 1888 of tuberculosis. Tubman testified, "I never had any children nor child by the soldier nor by John Tubman" (Tubman, 1894b).

THE END OF RECONSTRUCTION

When the Fifteenth Amendment was ratified in 1870, the American Anti-Slavery Society disbanded, after celebrating the apparent accomplishment of the organization's major postwar goal. But the national commitment to Reconstruction faltered and faded quickly, and by the early 1870s "the force of a great movement for social reform seemed to be spent, and its leadership was being lost" (Stampp, 1971, 43–44). Antislavery Republicans in Congress had died or retired, allowing the passage in May 1872 of an Amnesty Act that empowered the majority of ex-Confederates to hold elective office again. Anti-black propaganda was used by Democrats in political campaigns north and south. Physical violence was threatened and used by white terrorist organizations, including the Ku Klux Klan, to undermine the Radical Republican governments in the South.[31] Northern business interests were less concerned with black civil rights than with a Southern political stability that would be favorable to investment. Following a business panic in 1873 came an economic depression that further distracted Northerners from Reconstruction. Disillusionment with President Grant allowed Democrats to win a majority in the House of Representatives in 1874. Finally, in 1877, when the election of Republican president Rutherford Hayes was so close as to be contested by Southern Democrats,

Outdoor photograph of Harriet Tubman and her household, circa 1887. Handwritten identifications, from left: Harriet Tubman, Gertie Davis, Mr. [Nelson] Davis, Lee Chaney, Alexander, Walter Green, Sara Parker, and Dora Stewart. (Photographer: William H. Cheney, South Orange, New Jersey.) Courtesy Friends Historical Library of Swarthmore College, Swarthmore Pennsylvania.

Republicans in Congress agreed to remove federal troops from the South. This assured the end of Radical Republican government there (Stampp, 1971, 42–57).[32]

During the Reconstruction era, Tubman would have been well aware of both the temporary political advances of black men in the Reconstruction South and the diminishing Northern support for civil rights. No evidence has yet come to light that suggests that she attempted to influence the course of national politics during these years, however. Her attention was sufficiently absorbed by her responsibilities for her elderly parents and older dependents. Benjamin Ross died in 1871, perhaps increasing her mother's need for care from the one remaining daughter. Her Auburn friends made another unsuccessful effort through two members of Congress to secure her a government pension in 1874.[33]

THE GOLD SWINDLE INCIDENT OF 1873

Tubman was in an anomalous position in Auburn, just as she had been at Port Royal. On the one hand, she was an aging, uneducated subsistence farmer with a large and impoverished extended family, and she was a black woman. On the other hand she was the still celebrated heroine of Underground Railroad and war adventures, befriended by many politically prominent and wealthy white families. In theory, this was a position of relative privilege—but in practice there were sharp limits to the uses that she could make of her good connections, and her celebrity could actually make her vulnerable at times. This is evident in the events surrounding the "gold swindle" of 1873, when she emerged from relative obscurity into the local Auburn limelight—but this time in an uncharacteristically disempowered public role. The incident received extensive coverage in the local paper and was widely discussed among her white antislavery friends. It definitely reveals the vulnerability of her position in the town.

The events are quickly retold. In 1873, her brother John Stewart was approached by a pair of clever African American con men, who promised to exchange Confederate gold worth $5,000 for $2,000 in ready cash. They evidently knew he would turn to his famous sister, who, because of her reputation for complete integrity with several wealthy and respected white families, might be able to persuade wealthy friends to advance money for the scam. The primary con man passed himself off as an acquaintance of a South Carolina nephew of Tubman's (the name was rendered in the newspaper account of the story as Alfred Boly).[34] Significantly, her influential friends the Wrights and Osbornes declined to advance any money and warned her that the scheme might be fraudulent. The newspaper account said that it was her brother who found a wealthy Auburn man who was prepared to make a profit in this slightly shady deal.

Anthony Shimer, whom Alice Brickler recalled as "a junk dealer . . . known as Old Man Shimer" (also noting, "I believe he was a Jew,")[35] provided Tubman and John Stewart with the $2,000 in cash. The con men specified that only Tubman should bring the money to a secret meeting place in the woods. Several different versions of what happened next have survived, but all agree that after a period of solitude in the woods she became fearful.[36] She was then set upon by the thieves, who rendered her unconscious (probably using chloroform, guessed Martha Coffin Wright). They robbed her of the money, tied and gagged her, and successfully escaped. Still bound and gagged, she struggled back to where her party was waiting for her and gave an account of what happened that—because it involved ghosts—"was generally accepted as a romance," according to the newspaper account. Martha Coffin Wright put it more delicately: "They took her to the tavern, but she became insensible & a mystery."

From the close questioning of the principal parties reported in the newspaper accounts, one gathers that Tubman and her brother may have been briefly suspected of making a deal with the thieves to help steal Shimer's money. Both of them assured the authorities that "no other arrangement was made, than that of giving Shimer the benefit of the difference between greenbacks and gold."[37] Shimer claimed that he had lent them the money "secured by Harriet's house," Martha Coffin Wright wrote in a letter to Ellen Wright Garrison. Evidently this was one time when Tubman's reputation among her white friends for strict integrity (combined with poor judgment in money matters), served her in good stead.[38] She and her brother weathered the potentially dangerous situation they were in and were cleared of suspicion, but it was at the cost of Tubman's appearing in the public eye in Auburn as a "superstitious" elderly woman.

What do we make of this strange incident, with its jarring erosion of her previously heroic public image? Although we can only speculate as to her motives in telling the "ghost stories," I believe it would be naive in the extreme to accept them at face value. She may have had a very particular self-protective strategy in mind. The clever trickster of the Underground Railroad days could undoubtedly resurface in an emergency, when her own economic security, reputation, and even physical safety—and that of her brother—might depend on presenting a highly nonthreatening appearance to a suspicious white community. In other words, I believe she may have been playing the fool, in order to divert suspicion and avoid danger.

This interpretation is suggested by the glimpse we get of her storytelling in Emily Howland's diary. Tubman spent some time immediately after the events recuperating at the nearby home of Slocum Howland, a wealthy Quaker neighbor with an Underground Railroad history. Slocum Howland's daughter Emily Howland, who later became one of Tubman's benefactors, wrote down a joke Tubman told on this visit:

> Harriet Tubman came, pleasant and bright, and entertaining with her accounts of adventure in camp and forest in leading her fellow bondmen to freedom and in nearly equally perilous military service. Her shrewdness appeared in her tact to ward off danger when imminent. Ready wit led her when peril impended to turn suspicion from herself and her company by starting a chat with the dangerous person on a subject of absorbing general interest, matrimony. Once she and a band of eleven when crossing a bridge came upon a company of Irish laborers: what to do? She stepped bravely up and began about Christmas. Being asked what was her business, she said her present speculation was getting a husband. She had had one colored husband and she meant to marry a white gentleman next time. This made a great laugh so they went on thro' the town all together laughing and talking. (Howland, 1873)

She told this story just a few days after telling the "ghost stories" that averted the suspicions of the white community as to her own or her brother's possible culpability in the gold swindle robbery. Clearly the story she told Howland displayed her own "shrewdness . . . to ward off danger when imminent" and her "ready wit . . . to turn suspicion from herself and her company." Nothing is said directly about the events of the gold swindle robbery, but the parallels between the Underground Railroad strategy in the story she told Howland and her own telling of ghost stories are too strong to ignore. In all likelihood, then, her quick thinking and habits of concealment produced the ghost stories that would allow whites in her adopted Northern home to dismiss her as lovably pathetic, rather than see her or her brother as a potentially criminal menace.[39] The gold swindle story, if I am right, gives a rare view of Tubman adapting her Underground Railroad concealment skills to survival in the increasingly tense racial environment of the postwar era.

THE LATER YEARS

BLACK INSTITUTION BUILDING IN THE
POST-RECONSTRUCTION ERA

Industrial, technological, and economic expansion followed the Civil
War in the North, but the sharecropping system that developed in the
still largely agricultural South locked the majority of the landless rural
black population there into deep economic dependency and poverty. The
continuing economic exploitation was backed up by new strategies of
political disenfranchisement. After the end of Federal Reconstruction in
1877, Southern states moved to create legal restrictions that would curtail
the voting rights of Southern black males, as well as a system of racial
intimidation based on terrorism. By the 1890s, the Jim Crow system of
racial segregation had been developed throughout the South, and the U.S.
Supreme Court had ruled that such a system was constitutional (*Plessy v.
Ferguson*, 1896). Racial segregation was rationalized by a "scientific" theory
of race heavily influenced by Social Darwinism, which elevated "Anglo-
Saxons" (whites of English ancestry) and other northern European popula-
tions over such racial groups deemed less civilized and therefore genetically
inferior. This included Eastern and Southern Europeans, the Irish, Jews,
Asians, and members of the African Diaspora. White mob intimidation
and lynching of Southern blacks who threatened the racial order could
now be understood as simple justice, enacted by knights of threatened
white civilization upon those who were dangerously "brutal."

Northern African American communities enlarged as Southern migrants
sought less restrictive and dangerous lives in Northern cities, but race-based
discrimination in public service, housing, education and employment

was widely practiced in the North as well. Although white women were streaming into previously male-only clerical and sales occupations in these decades, most African American women wage earners in the North were restricted to live-in domestic service or laundry work. (Black workers were barred from factory employment until World War I.)

Yet during these same years African American and white educational leaders built schools and colleges for the under-served black population in the South; substantial advances were made by black professionals (many of whom were the early products of these schools and colleges); and many other black social and cultural institutions and businesses sprang up to serve the black communities, North and South.[1] The independent black churches played key roles as multipurpose community institutions during a time when white religious and social institutions, with a few notable exceptions, abdicated responsibility for helping to serve the needy within the emancipated black population.[2]

Harriet Tubman also came to rely on an African American church organization for spiritual and sociopolitical needs as the racial social divide widened in Auburn, as it was doing in the rest of the industrial North. In the early days of her family's residence in Auburn, Tubman and her parents (though raised as Methodists) had attended the (antislavery) Central Presbyterian Church along with many of her white political allies.[3] She was married there in 1869. Sometime in the 1870s she also began to attend the African Methodist Episcopal Zion Church.[4] Her new husband, Nelson Davis, was elected a trustee of the church on August 6, 1870, and she may have decided to attend church with him. Tubman was an active member of the A.M.E. Zion congregation at the end of the decade, according to Rev. James E. Mason of Livingstone College, South Carolina. He remembered being impressed with her religious fervor when he first met her at a service in "the long one-aisled frame Zion A.M.E. Church on Washington Street," in around 1878 or 1879.[5] "At the close of a thrilling selection she arose and commenced to speak in a hesitating voice. . . . In a shrill voice, she commenced to give testimony to God's goodness and long suffering. Soon she was shouting, and so were others also. She possessed such endurance, vitality, and magnetism that I inquired and was informed it was Harriet Tubman—the 'Underground Railroad Moses.' . . . Service ended, I greeted her. She said, 'Are you saved?' I gave an affirmative reply. She remarked: 'Glory to God,' and shouted again"("Pays Tribute to Harriet Tubman," June 6, 1914).

Another rare glimpse of Tubman's ecstatic spirituality in the postwar period occurs in an Auburn newspaper story in 1884. She was reported as overpowered by religious feeling when praying for Moses Stewart, a kinsman who had been arrested.[6] "A considerable amount of excitement was caused upon Court Street at 1:45 yesterday afternoon, by shouting and crying about the jail. It was found that Harriet Tubman, whose reputation is national, had been making a Sunday call upon 'Moses' Stewart at the jail and had there prayed and sung with him. When she came out she was seized with what is familiarly known as the 'power,' and began shouting and singing. Deputy Sheriff Stiles took her down to the office where Dr. F. M. Hamlin succeeded in quieting her, after a time" ("A Considerable Amount of Excitement" October 13, 1884).

Her involvement with the church community may have helped inspire the idea to build a permanent social service institution aimed providing shelter and nursing care for the impoverished elderly of the African American community—a home she originally planned to name the John Brown Hall.[7] Tubman certainly knew the need for such a home from her own experience caring for the sick, disabled, and aging in her own house on South Street. Many families broken up during slavery times and war had never reconnected with lost kinfolk, and many people faced aging and death without family members to care for them. Historian Dorothy Salem has pointed out that "care of the race's aged was the first type of organized reform initiated by small groups of local black women." There were very few institutions that accepted the impoverished black elderly, and those that existed, founded by whites, "displayed the difficulties inherent in one race dominating the services to another race." Black-founded institutions, especially those founded by women without very powerful support networks, often did not survive long, for lack of sufficient resources (Salem, 1990, 67–68).[8]

INITIATING THE
JOHN BROWN HALL PROJECT

Even before the death of her second husband Nelson Davis in October 1888 Tubman was managing an informal self-help community out of her own home, employing the able-bodied members of her household in a wide variety of tasks to contribute to the economic stability of the entire group. To the brickyard operation and vegetable and fruit gardens she had added a pig farm, apparently contracting with the city of Auburn to collect its garbage for her hogs. A newspaper story from the early 1880s reported her loss of forty hogs, apparently to rat poison carelessly discarded by the householders whose garbage she had used to feed her animals ("Harriet Tubman's Hogs," 1884). When she was interviewed for a magazine story in 1886, the visitor described Tubman's South Street residence as "a very plain little home which is an asylum for the poor people of her own color. Sometimes she has three or four invalids at a time for whom she is caring" (Holt, 1886). Ten years later, another interviewer drew a similar picture of Tubman's informal caregiving establishment: "She is very poor; but she devotes herself to the succor of colored men and women more aged and wretched than herself, and she cares for helpless children who are allied to her race. Her house is a hospital for the infirm and sick" (Wyman, 1896).

It was in the late 1880s that she took an important step toward transforming her informal asylum into a more formal caregiving institution that might outlive her and carry on this work. In June 1886, completely on her own initiative, she bid in auction on an adjacent twenty-five-acre farm property, with several buildings. She did not worry about the financing in advance.[9] Her story of the auction, as told to Bradford for the 1901 edition of the biography, offers a rare insight into her sense of being "a stranger in a strange land" by virtue of her race, in the white-controlled community in the North where she had lived for over thirty years. Her story emphasizes her recklessness in bidding on the land, the insulting attitudes expressed by the white bidders at the auction, and her triumphant success: "They was white folks but me there, Missus, and there I was like a blackberry in a pail of milk, but I was hid down in a corner, and no one knowed who was bidding. The man began pretty low, and I kept going up by fifties; he got up to twelve hundred, thirteen hundred, fourteen hundred, and still that voice in the corner kept going up by fifties. At last it got up to fourteen hundred and fifty,[10] and then others stopped bidding, and the man said, 'All done! who is the buyer?' 'Harriet Tubman,' I shouted. 'What! That old nigger?' they said. 'Old woman, how [are] you ever going to pay for that lot of land?' 'I'm going home to tell the Lord Jesus all about it,' I said" (Bradford, 1901, 149–150).

She turned to her church connections, asking the bishop of the A.M.E. Zion church conference then at Syracuse to help locate funds for a down payment ($350) as well as a bank mortgage loan for $1,000. This new financial obligation caused her great anxiety and privation over the next ten years—but it also spurred her on to a remarkable series of public appearances in which she again told her life story.

We don't know just when she approached Sarah Bradford with the idea of collaborating on a new edition of the biography—it may have been earlier in the year, as she was looking for a way to expand her physical facilities for the John Brown Hall project.[11] Bradford did very little new research, but she rewrote much of the material in the original book, introducing more literary touches and a few errors.[12] When *Harriet, the Moses of Her People* came out in October 1886, Tubman visited Boston to publicize the event. Sanborn acted as her host and arranged to have her photographed at this time, possibly at her request, since photographs could be sold to supplement her income from the book.[13] Sanborn and other friends also helped with the distribution of the new book.

THE WOMEN'S SUFFRAGE
CONNECTION RENEWED

To raise funds for the John Brown Hall, Harriet Tubman began to speak at gatherings promoting women's suffrage in Auburn and the surrounding area, and Auburn's white feminists seemed happy to have Tubman as a living embodiment of female ability and equal achievement.[14] The new version of the Bradford book had obviously helped stimulate interest in Tubman's career among younger women in particular, as did a biographical sketch by Rosa Belle Holt called "A Heroine in Ebony," which appeared in the *Chatauquan* the same year. When she told her story at the Non-Partisan Society of Political Education for Women in Auburn in March 1888, she received admiring coverage in the local paper: "In view of Mrs. Tubman's services in the late war, in freeing and helping to emancipate her down trodden and oppressed race, the ladies of the society requested that she say a few words before the society. . . . Her recital of the brave and fearless deeds of women who sacrificed all for their country and moved in battle when bullets mowed down men, file after file, and rank after rank, was graphic. Loving women were on the scene to administer to the injured, to bind up their wounds and tend them through weary months of suffering in the army hospitals. If those deeds do not place woman as man's equal, what do? The speaker said that her prayers carried her through and they would eventually place woman at the ballot box with man, as his equal. Her speech, though brief, was very interesting, and was listened to with rapt attention by all" ("Suffragists," 1888).

She also spoke at regional meetings of the NWSA, the Stanton/Anthony

Studio portrait of Harriet Tubman with checked head cloth, circa 1895, Courtesy the Cayuga Museum and Case Research Laboratory, Auburn, New York.

national suffrage organization.[15] Martha Coffin Wright, Wright's daughter Eliza Wright Osborne, and Emily Howland were all close allies of Susan B. Anthony and Elizabeth Cady Stanton, the preeminent leaders of the NWSA throughout this period.[16] Tubman's invitations to speak may have come through them. Unlike Sojourner Truth or Frances Watkins Harper, two highly visible African-American feminists she had met at various times, Tubman was not a major prosuffrage activist associated with a national suffrage organization.[17] She focused her social change energies on her local community during her postwar life, although she did accept invitations to travel to meetings in Washington or Boston on behalf of black women's organizations.

It was a tremendous financial struggle to pay taxes on both properties as well as the mortgage interest on the new land for the John Brown Hall. Tubman remortgaged her own house and land in 1892.[18] But she continued to push for the home for the elderly, sometimes delicately reminding her wealthy friends of the need. For example, in a letter written for her by Jane Kellogg (a friend of Eliza Wright Osborne's) to Ednah Cheney, dated April 9, 1894, we hear that "Harriet Tubman has asked me to write you for her to send her love to you and to say that she shall always remember you most 'lovingly to the day of her death.' Harriet is very well for a woman of her advanced years and is as busy as ever going about doing good to every body her home is filled with 'odds and ends' of society and to every one outcast she gives food and shelter. She is still trying to establish a home for old colored women but as yet has succeeded very slightly in collecting funds for that purpose—yet she is not discouraged but is working always with that object still in view. . . . She remembers you with great affection and thanks you always for your kindness to her'" (Tubman, 1894a). Cheney responded as intended with a check, calling it a birthday gift to herself and expressing the wish, as many of Tubman's white benefactors did over the postwar years, "that she should use the money for her own comfort."[19]

At other times Tubman spoke directly both about her own charity work in Auburn and about the plans she had for generating more money for the John Brown Hall project. In May 1896, she dictated a letter to a Mrs. Mary Wright (a friend of Ednah Cheney's), recording her relief at turning over the financial burden of the mortgage on the John Brown Hall property to a board of directors[20] and thanking Wright for recent donations: "I received the trunk and package which you sent me and I am very thankful to you for them. I have been appointed by the pastors of the first

M.E. and the A.M.E. Churches of Auburn, to collect clothes for the destitute colored children[21] and the things which you have sent are very acceptable. The four dollars which you sent me was also very acceptable for it was in a very needy time." She went on to relay her newest plan for fund-raising and to ask Wright's assistance: "I would like for you to see Miss Edna Cheny for me. I would like to get out another edition of books. The editor says he can let [me] publish a five hundred of books for $100 before he destroyed the plates. I would like to have another set of books published to take to the Methodists Centennial at New York this fall. I can raise fifty dollars and if Miss Cheny can see Mr. Sanburn and some of those Anti-Slavery friends and have them raise fifty dollars more that will enable me to get the books out before the editor destroys the plate. If they will help me raise the money they can hold the books until I can sell enough to pay them back . . . Miss Cheny has done very well by me and I do not wish to ask for money [but] if through her influence I can get the friends to help me I shall be ever thankful."[22]

"MOTHER TUBMAN"
AMONG AFRICAN AMERICAN CLUB WOMEN

Harriet Tubman made a well-publicized appearance at the founding convention of the National Association of Colored Women (NACW) in Washington, D.C., a conference at which a merger of two predecessor organizations took place.[23] The creation of the new national umbrella organization for local women's clubs was an important milestone on the road to development of what historian Rosalyn Terborg-Penn has called "nationalist feminist" sentiment among elite black women of this era. A new generation of leaders had emerged in the 1890s, one that had bene-fited from the establishment of collegiate institutions for black women as well as from church-related associational work. They built upon tradi-tions of grassroots activism to develop strategies to publicize pressing civil rights issues during a period when race relations slid to what has been called the "nadir" or lowest point since Emancipation.[24] Taking some les-sons from the national organizational successes of the Women's Christian Temperance Union and the white women's club movement with which they had had some experience, leaders of the black women's club move-ment created a structure that facilitated networking, political strategizing, and publicizing social issues. The NACW provided support for local and regional "race uplift" social service and charitable work. At the same time a national organization made it possible to exert greater moral and political pressure on the elite white community to reconsider its exclusionary policies, through organizational and individual participation in other organizations by representatives of the NACW. [25]

Race and gender pride were very much part of the "nationalist feminist" culture being developed in the NACW, which duly lionized "race heroines." Tubman was certainly one of the beneficiaries of this impulse. Journalist and clubwoman Victoria Earle (Mathews) used Tubman's celebrity status among the younger generation of educated African American women to promote advance interest in the 1896 meetings in Washington and to express intergenerational solidarity. Writing in the Boston club's newspaper, the *Woman's Era*, in June 1896, she summarized Tubman's Underground Railroad and Civil War achievements and predicted: "It will be an inspiration for the rising generation to see and clasp hands with this noble mother in Israel! . . . We expect to reproduce her photograph on our souvenir programme. This alone will make them valuable. . . . All over our country, thousands of women are awakening to the fact that a new day is dawning for our people, and that a tidal wave of deep heartfelt anxiety for better and purer homes, healthier and better trained children, broader and more helpful educational and missionary work is sweeping over the great body of Afro-American Women. So at the very beginning of this new day let us all meet in the benign presence of this great leader, in days and actions, that caused strong men to quail" (Earle [Mathews], 1896).

Tubman was welcomed warmly into the company of the clubwomen as a symbolic figure of past heroism. Her own participation at the conference included storytelling, singing, and, inevitably, making a speech appealing for funds for the John Brown Hall project. "When Mrs. [Victoria Earle] Mathews retired to take the chair of the presiding officer, and Mrs. Tubman stood alone on the front of the rostrum, the audience, which not only filled every seat, but also much of the standing room in the aisles, rose as one person and greeted her with the waving of handkerchiefs and the clapping of hands. This was kept up for at least a minute, and Mrs. Tubman was much affected by the hearty reception given her. When the applause had somewhat subsided, Mrs. Tubman acknowledged the compliment paid her in appropriate words, and at the request of some of the leading officers of the Convention related a little of her war experience. Despite the weight of advancing years, Mrs. Tubman is the possessor of a strong and musical voice, which last evening penetrated every portion of the large auditorium in which the Convention was held, and a war melody which she sang was fully as attractively rendered as were any of the other vocal selections of the evening" (National Association of Colored Women's Clubs, 1902).

In the role of the venerated "Mother Tubman" she was asked to introduce to the crowd the newborn baby of Ida B. Wells Barnett, the anti-lynching journalist and pioneer clubwoman. Rosetta Douglass-Sprague (daughter of Frederick Douglass) used Tubman's example in a speech designed to spur the clubwomen on to build new social institutions: "From the log cabins of the South have come forth some of our most heroic women, whose words, acts and deeds are a stimulus to us at this hour. . . . Women who have endured untold misery for the betterment of the condition of their brothers and sisters. While the white race have chronicled deeds of heroism and acts of mercy of the women of pioneer and other days, so we are pleased to note in the personality of such women as Phyllis Wheatley, Margaret Garner, Sojourner Truth and our venerable friend, Harriet Tubman, sterling qualities of head, heart and hand, that hold no insignificant place in the annals of heroic womanhood. . . . This is indeed the women's era, and we are coming" (National Association of Colored Women's Clubs, 1902).[26]

"The women's era" celebrated at this conference is part of the broader social movements of the Progressive Era, and Tubman's ambitious work on behalf of the John Brown Hall should be understood as a contribution in this context. Legal and institutional reforms were evidently needed to mitigate the impact of untrammeled capitalism on industrial growth and urban life in particular. In the decades bridging the beginning of the twentieth century, newly educated and organized women played a major part in "social housekeeping" based on their presumed special interests and talents as "social mothers." White and black women's clubs advocated for "playgrounds, kindergartens, compulsory education laws, child labor laws, protective laws, pure food laws, juvenile courts, and other items on the progressive reform agenda" (Woloch, 1996, 194). Jane Addams (founder of Chicago's famous Hull House) and Nannie Helen Burroughs (founder of the National Training School for Women and Girls) were among the women who left important institutional legacies as part of this collective history of Progressive Era social motherhood.[27]

Tubman appeared at the New York State Women's Suffrage Association meetings in Rochester in November. This was the occasion on which she was introduced by Susan B. Anthony and made a memorable joke

(solemnly inscribed on a memorial tablet after her death): "Yes, ladies . . .
I was the conductor of the Underground Railroad for eight years, and I
can say what most conductors can't say—I never run my train off the track
and I never lost a passenger" (Bradford, 1901). The following spring Ednah
Cheney helped organize a reception in Boston for Tubman by the Massachusetts Women's Suffrage Association to publicize the release of the 1897
reprint of the 1886 Bradford book. To attend the reception, "she had sold
a calf to get here from where she lives in New York State," according to
the journal entry of Helen Tufts Bailie, who attended the reception.

Frances E. Watkins Harper, who had made the fiery speech about the
wrongs of colored women and used the railroad conductor's treatment of
"Moses" as a stirring example of intolerable prejudice thirty years earlier,
also attended this reception.[28] Harper had sided with the Lucy Stone AWSA
faction in 1869 when the antislavery feminist coalition split over the priority of black male suffrage (Collier-Thomas, 1997, 41–65). Harper's most
recent organizational work had been as superintendent of the colored
division of the Women's Christian Temperance Union, from 1883 until
1890—work that had led to the formation of many black WCTU branch
organizations. Tubman and Harper had many occasions to meet over the
years, most recently at the NACW founding conference.[29] Linked by
their histories as prominent black female antislavery activists of an earlier
era, they would almost certainly have spoken with each other on this
occasion, but it may be that barriers of education and social class would
have limited their ability to form an ongoing personal relationship. At
any rate, no evidence has as yet emerged to suggest that they ever had
friendly ties.

RACIAL POLITICS AND
THE HARRIET TUBMAN HOME

During the decade or so when Tubman managed the new property herself, she lived next door, continuing her subsistence farming operations
with the help of those who lived with her.[30] By the mid 1890s she had realized that she would not be able to raise enough money through her own
fund-raising efforts to refurbish the buildings on the farm or to hire staff
needed to make the John Brown Hall a reality. Her income, even when
supplemented by donations brought in by her influential Auburn friends
and help from her brother William Henry Stewart, was never sufficient for

the free institution she had in mind.[31] She decided at last to try to donate
the land and the proposed institution to the A.M.E. Zion church.[32]

According to the memory of one participant at the A.M.E. Zion western New York convention in Syracuse at which Tubman spoke in 1896:
"During the singing of a hymn, Harriet shouted up and down the aisles
of the church. Later she was introduced to the Conference and related that
she had purchased a farm at the outskirts of the city of Auburn, New York,
for $1250 which she wished to dedicate as a home for aged people, espe-
cially ministers. . . . She now requested the Conference to give her financial assistance and invited the members to go to Auburn to inspect the
property. . . . The Bishop and Conference gave the matter their endorse-
ment, but instructed Harriet to retain the title for awhile" (Brooks, n.d.).

With hindsight we can see that she was of two minds when she made
her appeal to the church conference. On the one hand she fervently hoped
to divest herself of the burden of financial management. At the same time
she wanted to retain control over the development of the institution, so
that her vision would be realized. In the next several years, however, it
became apparent that her goals for the target population and the overall
shape of the institution differed from those of the church organization. The
wish to have the home serve "ministers" seems only to have been stated in
the context of this appeal to a body of ministers. Otherwise, Tubman's service focus was always on the destitute elderly, women in particular. Even
more problematic was the question of funding. She always maintained
idealistically that the home should provide fully subsidized shelter and care,
rather than charging a fee.[33] At one point she even considered turning the
enterprise and property over to the secular women's club movement, but
because the property was not "unencumbered," members at the NACW
meeting in Chicago in 1899 declined to accept responsibility for it.[34]

Tubman now actually had two groups attempting to help her transform
the informal "home" she was running into a financially stable institution.
Unfortunately there was considerable friction between the two, and this
played out as racial politics to some extent. One largely white group consisted of longstanding antislavery friends and their offspring, including
the Osbornes, Sewards, and Emily Howland. The other group consisted
primarily of A.M.E. Zion clergy—some of them distinguished outsiders
from black educational institutions in the South, including James Mason
and Robert Taylor. A.M.E. Zion laypeople from Auburn were also part of
the latter group, which was now increasingly involved in the planning and
management of the Home.

Tubman reached an understanding with the church by 1896 that they would take over the mortgage on the land for the John Brown Home project, but the official transfer of property did not happen until 1903. Meanwhile, fund-raising efforts by both groups of supporters continued. The delays were related to the complexities of her debt, as well as to conflict between the two groups over the exact terms of the transfer deed, according to a detailed narrative submitted to the church conference in 1904 by Rev. Wheeler, the first A.M.E. Zion supervisor of the property: "As some of Aunt Harriet's white friends were bitterly opposed to her deeding the property to us, we had to make generous provisions for her in drawing the deed.[35] I stipulated in the deed that . . . she is to have a life interest in all money accruing from rents, on conditions that she pay the taxes and keep up the insurance, but that these rents should cease when we needed the property" (Wheeler, 1904).

The report also touched on a strong difference of opinion among Tubman's black and white friends, as to the best uses to which the John Brown Hall might be put. "The public are in great sympathy with the work, and if the General Conference can arrange to let the superintendent give his whole time to the work, this home will soon be developed into a great institution for the aged and infirm colored people, who are constantly seeking shelter under its roof. . . . The deed conveying the property to the church stipulates that when the trustees see their way clear to do so, they shall establish on the ground beside the home, a school of domestic science where girls may be taught the various branches of industrial education. This feature of the work is particularly popular with the white people in this western part of the state of New York" (Wheeler, 1904).

By this time a tense debate had arisen between advocates of "industrial education" (vocational training institutions) and those who supported collegiate education for black people. The John Brown Hall project was almost derailed because of the broader issues it raised for Tubman's black and white supporters. Booker T. Washington, the former slave who founded the Tuskegee Institute in Alabama, was a nationally known advocate of industrial education. He had risen to preeminent political influence in Washington by the 1890s through what many of his critics saw as an overly accommodationist stance toward wealthy white donors. The white power elite supported industrial education such as that at Tuskegee more eagerly than schools with a classical curriculum as part of a strategy to "keep the race down," it was argued.[36] More radical voices led by Harvard-educated sociologist W. E. B. Du Bois articulated an alternative vision of racial justice, including academic education for African Americans and a more outspoken and directly critical stance toward white supremacy. The Niagara Movement, precursor of the National Association for the Advancement of Colored People (NAACP), also attracted anti-lynching crusader and Chicago clubwoman Ida B. Wells.[37]

But the industrial education question was not a simple one, and African American women's organizations, as well as other "race" organizations, took a variety of perspectives on it.[38] Industrial education had been high on the wish list for social services articulated at the founding convention of the NACW in 1896 in the speech by Rosetta Douglass-Sprague. She referred to the need for schools "where labor of all kinds is taught, enabling our boys and girls to become skilled in the trades." Nannie Helen Burroughs's National Training School for Women and Girls supplied "professional" training for domestic work as part of a pragmatic strategy for "racial uplift." Given that masses of working African American women were already employed in domestic service work, Burroughs saw a clear need to win respect for the workers and increase the status of domestic work as a "profession."[39] Burroughs persuaded the Baptist Women's Convention to help fund this working-class black woman's educational institution.

In the case of the Harriet Tubman Home (as it was now being called in the newspaper stories) the problem was that the initiative for a "domestic science school" seemed to reflect a "keep them in their place" perspective: "It is well known that the field of operation for the colored girl is to be in the family and here is an almost unlimited opportunity. The demand today for competent domestic help is widespread. The object of the domestic science school is to so train and fit colored girls as to be able to do everything belonging to household service. They are to be fitted in every way to make them reliable and know their duty and responsibilities. . . . The plot of ground given by Mrs. Harriet Tubman and the buildings thereon are to be used for this purpose, the houses are to be repaired for the work and used until a more suitable building is erected" ("Plans for Tubman Home," 1907).[40] Yet there was also a push from national black industrial education leaders to use Tubman's name in fund-raising for "an industrial school of the type of Tuskegee and Hampton," according to a newspaper story the year after the home had actually opened.[41]

What did Tubman think about using the home for this purpose? We have no direct evidence of this, but it is perhaps possible that at one time she approved of the idea of adding this component to the services provided by her John Brown Hall.[42] After all, despite her personal dislike of indoor domestic work as a child, she had supported herself, in part, by such work from the time she had come north. She may well have felt that no stigma should be attached to any kind of honest work. Certainly she would have wanted young black women to have access to the kind of education that would enable them to escape the indignities and drudgery of domestic service in white homes in an increasingly Jim Crow world. Yet, like Nannie Helen Burroughs, she might have seen a domestic science school as a step toward professionalizing service work and thus protecting workers.

Just a few months later, another newspaper article reframed yet again the objective of the institution, called the Harriet Tubman Home and Training School[43]: "The Harriet Tubman Home will soon be a reality. . . . The home is for worthy indigent, aged colored people of the state of New York, and elsewhere. It will also be a place of temporary retreat for younger people." The article also reported that a "committee of lady managers" was now beginning a fund-raising effort directed at the black community: "The colored people throughout the state of New York are asked to give one dollar each for the benefit of the home" ("Harriet Tubman Home Meeting," June 14, 1907).

The churchwomen's role in the last push of fund-raising was crucial, as Evelyn Higginbotham (1993) has found was generally true in church-based charity work of this time period. According to the summary history of the project published when the Harriet Tubman Home opened in 1908, "Less than two years ago Rev. Mr. Carter came and found no funds in the treasury. The friends of Aunt Harriet had lost all hope of ever seeing the home open, but Rev. Mr. Carter is not the man to surrender to obstacles without a strong effort. After a hard struggle the work of fitting up the building was commenced nearly a year ago, but owing to the stringency of money matters the work was delayed until a few weeks ago, when the board of lady managers took hold of the work with the result that the home was so auspiciously opened yesterday. Much credit is due the board of lady managers under the direction of Mrs. C. A. Smith" ("Dedication of Harriet Tubman Home," 1908).

The dedication ceremony was vividly described in several local newspaper accounts. Evidently it was an occasion of pride and joy for much of the African American community in the western New York region.

Marshal Frank H. Prime led the procession on a prancing bay horse which gave him a chance to show off his good horsemanship. Next came Comrade Perry Williams in white coat and blue trousers, and proudly bearing the national flag. He was followed by another Grand Army man, the Rev. C. A. Smith. Next came the pride of the outfit, the Ithaca colored band, John O. Wye, leader, with 20 men. The band hit off some lively quicksteps which were kept time to by a long column of young colored people, all dressed in their Sunday best, who marched in the parade. Following was a long string of carriages containing prominent colored people of the city who are connected with the organization and care of the home. In the first carriage rode 'Aunt Harriet' Tubman and her brother William Stewart, Mrs. R. Jerome Jeffreys of Rochester,[44] and Major H. Ross of Norwich. ("Tubman Home Dedicated," 1908)

The next day both Auburn newspapers covered the remainder of the festivities, taking the occasion to remind readers of Tubman's heroic past:

With the stars and stripes wound about her shoulders, a band playing national airs and a concourse of members of her race gathered about her to pay tribute to her lifetime struggle in behalf of the colored people, aged Harriet Tubman Davis, the Moses of her people, yesterday experienced one of the happiest moments of her life. . . . When called upon by the chairman for a few words of welcome the aged woman stated that she had but started the work for the rising generation to take up. "I did not take up this work for my own benefit," said she, "but for those of my race who need help. The work is now well started and I know God will raise up others to take care of the future. All I ask is united effort, for "united we stand, divided we fall." ("Tubman Home Open," 1908)

The funding plan devised for the Tubman Home was now more realistic than in the past, when Tubman had relied entirely on contributions from the local African American community and her white friends. "At the present time the sum of $150 gives the applicant life privileges," the newspaper account report. The phrasing does not make it clear, however, whether any subsidized or free beds were also available. The A.M.E. Zion regional conference had "voted to take an annual collection for the maintenance fund of the Home, and it is estimated that this sum will not be less than $200 per year." It was a relatively modest facility: only five bedrooms had been furnished for occupancy when the dedication ceremony took place. Tubman was the only female member of the board of trustees, now dominated by ministers, but there was a board of lady managers, and three of the four were apparently wives of ministers on the board.[45]

At the age of eighty-eight, Tubman experienced one of the most significant public tributes to her life's work to date, and one of the few to
take place in a predominantly black gathering.[46] No longer merely a figure
brought on stage to evoke a glorious past, she was now representing the
energetic agency of the black Northern communities as they moved to
identify and find solutions for their own problems. It was a well-deserved
moment of community self-celebration, one that lifted Tubman briefly up
out of her everyday life into the realm of cultural politics.

COPING WITH POVERTY

When Congress finally passed a bill making widows of Civil War soldiers eligible for pensions, in June 1890, Harriet Tubman immediately applied, and after several years and much paper work, she received a tiny award of $8 a month.[1] This amount was inadequate for her needs. Moreover, a widow's pension was an unsatisfactory substitute for the veteran's pension to which her own war service entitled her. In 1898, she submitted an affidavit to the Committee on Invalid Pensions, testifying to the accuracy of the account of her war services that had been written in 1868 by Charles P. Wood and stating simply, "My claim against the U.S. is for three years' service as nurse and cook in hospitals, and as commander of several men (eight or nine) as scouts during the late War of the Rebellion, under direction and orders of Edwin M. Stanton, Secretary of War, and of several Generals. I claim for my services above named the sum of eighteen hundred dollars" (Tubman, 1898). Auburn's congressman recommended the approval of her claim, and there was actually a brief committee debate on a bill that would have granted her a pension for her work as a nurse. Taking the bureaucratically easier path, however, the committee decided simply to increase her monthly widow's pension allocation from $8 to $20 (Conrad, 1943a, 218–220).[2] The final failure of the U.S. government to acknowledge her war services in her own right after so many years of petitions was a bitter pill. A comment captured by a friendly interviewer ten years later expressed her disgust: "It was not plaintively, but rather with a flash of scorn in her dulling eyes, that she remarked to the writer last week: 'You wouldn't think that after I served the flag so faithfully I should come to want under its folds'" (F. C. Drake, 1907).

Various friends expressed concerns about her health and welfare as she aged in poverty.[3] Robert Taylor's *Heroine in Ebony* (1901) spoke of her inability to care for the "two friendless old women and two homeless orphans" in her household "because the hand of affliction has rested heavily upon her for more than a year. There was a time when she traveled a great deal, and whatever requests she made of her white friends were granted. Many of her old friends have 'crossed the bar,' while others, I am sure, know not of her present condition. Just now her lot is a hard one—dependent entirely on what may be handed her by occasional callers and the scant earnings of her brother, several years her senior" (Taylor, 1901, 15–16). Around the first years of the new century, Tubman, now just turned eighty, requested head surgery from a doctor in a Boston hospital in an effort to relieve the symptoms associated with the old head injury of childhood. She later described undergoing the operation as lying down "like a lamb for the slaughter, and he sawed open my skull, and raised it up, and now it feels more comfortable" (Bradford, 1901, 151–152).[4]

Bradford became increasingly concerned about Tubman's health and vulnerability to what she saw as exploitation by her dependents. In an undated letter probably written during this time, Bradford reported to Franklin Sanborn on a disturbing recent visit to Tubman, with whom she was apparently collaborating in plans for distributing the biography: "I have been to see Harriet & found her in a deplorable condition, a pure wreck, [mind?] & body—& surrounded by a set of beggars who I fear fleece her of every thing sent her—She drew all the money I had sent for her, & I fear had little good of it—I am keeping the money I get for her now—& will pay her bills—& I send her a little at a time as she needs it— If I could only get her into a home where she would be well cared for I should be so glad, but she will not leave her beloved darkies."[5] In 1901 Bradford brought out the last version of the biography, enhanced with a few additional stories about Tubman in old age. Emily Howland, now well launched in her career as a philanthropist—she was known particularly for her support of black educational institutions, including Tuskegee[6]— pitched in to help distribute copies as gifts to friends at Christmas time in 1901. She also visited Tubman in January and recorded her own concern at Tubman's situation in her diary: "Jan. 18, 1902 . . . Miss Bradley & I went to Auburn. I took H. Tubman a piece of pork, found her looking pale & feeble. 2 little children and a sick woman up stairs were her family."

There was some truth to Bradford's idea that the aging Tubman was an easy mark for unscrupulous guests in her household, in part because of her

Emily Howland, one of the network of women's suffrage supporters friendly with
Susan B. Anthony and Eliza Wright Osborne, also helped Tubman with fund-raising
in later years.

connections with wealthy white patrons. For example, in October 1905 Howland was taken in by a con man, who falsely claimed Tubman had sent him to her and told a story of having been shot in the back by lynchers in North Carolina. He was able to enlist Howland's sympathy sufficiently to cheat her out of nearly $600. Howland learned soon afterward from Tubman that "the man was a 'highway robber.' Two months ago a col'd man brought this man to her to shelter. She kept him all [night] he had a revolver. She rather feared him or did not want her brother to know he was in the house. She sat up all night. He wanted money. She got a friend to give her $5 for him. He scorned so small a sum. The last time she saw him he was intoxicated. She never mentioned my name to him. That with all the rest was a lie." Howland lost a large sum of money, but it was Tubman who had to sit up all night in anxiety over the revolver-wielding stranger in her own house.[7]

Two years later Tubman was robbed of $34 in cash received as a Christmas gift, perhaps by someone then living in her household. According to the story in the local newspaper, "Harriet said she carried the money home Christmas day, safely hidden in her clothing. The next morning while her brother was eating his breakfast, Harriet showed him her present. Hearing the approach of someone at the outside door, she gathered the money and purse which contained it, up in her apron and went up stairs. At the head of the stairs, she said, she was overcome by a sort of dizziness and sat down to recover herself. When she came to, her money was gone. Harriet thinks she dropped her purse from her apron as she went up stairs and some one passing through the hall picked it up. She has her suspicions as to who the guilty one is and came to town today to see if steps could not be taken to have her money returned" ("Harriet Tubman's Money Gone," 1907).[8]

CELEBRITY IN THE LAST YEARS

By the early twentieth century, many people were taking a new interest in Tubman's past. Her antislavery associates had already included a few comments about her in their memoirs in the 1870s and 1880s, but she was now interviewed by younger historians of the reform and antislavery movements.[9] She was also sought out by younger-generation liberals, black and white, for magazine and feature newspaper articles.[10] Pauline Hopkins included an article titled "Harriet Tubman ('Moses')" in her series on "Famous Women of the Negro Race" for the *Colored American Magazine* (1902).

She ended with the usual reference to Tubman's financial need—but in a rather more political vein than some: "The government has never assisted Mrs. Tubman in any way. Are Republics ungrateful?"

Tubman was asked to lend her name to a new African American social service facility in Boston by a group associated with the Women's Christian Temperance Union, and she attended their fund-raising reception in her honor on May 26, 1905. "Mrs. Tubman has come to be regarded as one of the great benefactors of her race. . . . During the evening this rare old woman told extremely interesting reminiscences of the exciting events in which she participated. For a woman of so great age she is remarkably erect, her voice is clear, her manner bright and her wit keen. . . . She arrived in town yesterday morning from Auburn, N.Y., and told her friends she guessed it would be the last time she would be up this way. . . . An interesting concert was given, and the funds received went to the aid of the Harriet Tubman Women's Temperance Union of this city. Before the concert Mrs. Tubman received the congratulations of some of the very people who she had helped to escape years ago" ("Harriet Tubman at the Hub," 1905).[11]

She was less able to contribute to her own support and that of her dependents by physical labor as she aged, and her poverty had undermined her farming operation as well. In 1908, a fund-raising appeal by the Tubman Home in a Boston suffrage journal cannily blamed the forgetfulness of her "former friends" as well: "Aunt Harriet, as she is known by her people, has at her home an old man who depends on her for his daily bread, and an old lady totally blind who has no other home.[12] . . . Mrs. Tubman's only brother (that she knows anything about) is dependent on her. The blind woman and the old man referred to all eat at her table. She can no longer go out and bring in money, and the small pension she receives from the government is about all she has to depend on for support. Her little place of seven acres was once the resource by which she fed so many. Then she raised pigs, chickens and ducks. She sold vegetables, fruit and milk from her cows. Through old age and other causes, she is deprived of these helps. Many of her former friends have forgotten her; hence her condition" (G. C. Carter, 1908).

Illness finally forced Harriet Tubman to move into the Tubman Home on May 19, 1911. Private nursing assistance cost $10 per week, while her newly enlarged widow's pension amounted to only $20 monthly. Appeals for donations were now made to private individuals such as Booker T. Washington.[13] Letters were also sent to newspapers and newsletters of

Oval studio portrait of an aging Tubman, published in "The Moses of Her People," *New York Sun* (May 2, 1909). Courtesy the Cayuga Museum and Case Research Laboratory, Auburn, New York.

organizations likely to contribute funds to her support.[14] Major newspaper articles on Tubman's history and current poverty and disability appeared in the *New York World,* the *Evening Sun,* and T. Thomas Fortune's "race" paper, the *New York Age* in June 1911. Organized African American women began to mobilize to raise funds for Tubman's care. The West 136th Street branch of the YWCA (an African American women's service organization) announced a "dramatic and musical entertainment . . . for the benefit of Harriet Tubman and the YWCA" in the *New York Age* in September ("News of Greater New York," 1911). The Empire State Federation of Women's Clubs (combining clubs from Buffalo and New York City) recognized the need for sustained contributions.[15] Mary Burnett Talbert[16] of Buffalo, elected president of the Federation in 1912, took a particular interest in Tubman.[17]

Tubman lived for two more years and continued to tell the story of her life to those who visited her in the Tubman Home. Rev. E. A. U. Brooks

Group photograph outside the Harriet Tubman Home, circa 1912, published with "Death of Aunt Harriet" (March 11, 1913). Harriet Tubman is seated, with white shawl, seventh from left.

Close-up of Tubman seated, with white shawl, taken on the same occasion as the group photo outside the Harriet Tubman Home. Courtesy Conrad Collection, Cayuga Community College.

conducted a service there shortly after she had arrived—a service at which she was still able to deliver "an interesting talk on her experiences during the Civil War," according to newspaper coverage ("Zionists Are Active," 1911). A magazine article published by a West Indian student visitor shortly after her admission to the home depicts her as sprightly and feisty, physically weak but possessing an "astonishingly fresh and active mind.[18] It offers a poignant glimpse of her efforts to maintain independence in her life as an inmate of the home: "On the day of my visit she had without assistance gone down stairs to breakfast, and I saw her eat a dinner that would tax the strength of a gourmand. A friend had sent her a spring chicken and had the pleasure of seeing it placed before her with rice and pie and cheese and other good things. 'Never mind me,' Aunt Harriet replied to the friend's remark that the conversation was interfering with the dinner, 'I'll eat all you give me, but I want you to have some of this chicken first.' . . . She resented the suggestion that someone should feed her. She only wanted the nurse to cut the chicken and place the tray on her lap" (Clarke, 1911).

Friends continued to help out with gifts of money. Just a few weeks before Tubman's death, Josephine F. Osborne acknowledged the receipt of a check from Emily Howland for Tubman's support. Her thank-you letter suggests how tightly the funds had to be stretched and provides an example of Tubman's notorious penchant for spending her money on others before herself. "I telephoned awhile ago to ask how Harriet had been, the matron said she was about the same as before I went away, she has been in bed all winter is very thin and weak so emaciated that her nurse can lift her about very easily. . . . Thank you again for the checque. The pension Harriet gets goes toward paying her nurse but it isn't quite enough I think. The annuity she receives in the fall she will not let me use for that purpose.[19] She wants to keep that on hand for her own personal use. She gave the last that she had to pay for a cow for the Harriet Tubman Home, a nice fine cow she is too, gives a lot of milk they told me" (J. F. Osborne, 1913).

Harriet Tubman died on March 10, 1913. She had been "ill with pneumonia for nearly a year and her death was not unexpected," one local newspaper reported the day after her death ("Death of Aunt Harriet," 1913). Just prior to her death,

Harriet asked for her friends, Rev. Charles A. Smith and Rev. E. U. A. Brooks, clergymen of the Zion A.M.E. Church. They, with Eliza E. Peterson, national superintendent for temperance work among colored people of the WCTU, who came here from Texarkana, Tex., to see Harriet, and others, joined in a final service which Harriet directed.[20] She joined in the singing when her cough did not prevent, and after receiving the sacrament she sank back in bed ready to die. To the clergymen she said, 'Give my love to all the churches' and after a severe coughing spell she blurted out in thick voice this farewell passage which she had learned from Matthew: "I go away to prepare a place for you, and where I am ye may be also". ("Harriet Tubman Is Dead," 1913)

Aware of the responsibility of her celebrity even on her deathbed, it seems, she enacted a gallant final public profession of her faith and ties to the local church communities.

Her grandniece, Alice Brickler, provided Earl Conrad with a more private and intimate memory of the day of her death: "For sometime before her death, Aunt Harriet had lost the use of her legs. She spent her time in a wheel chair and then finally was confined to her bed. It is said that on the day of her death, her strength returned to her. She arose from her bed with little assistance, ate heartily, walked about the rooms of the Old Ladies' Home which she liked so much and then went back to bed and her final rest. Whether this is true or not, it is typical of her. She believed in mind [over] matter. Regardless of how impossible a task might seem, if it were her task she tackled it with a determination to win. I've always enjoyed believing this story as a fitting finish chapter to her life. It was right that her sun should go down on a bright day out of a clear sky" (Brickler, 1939b).

It had been both an extraordinary and an ordinary life. In the Underground Railroad years, Harriet Tubman had seized the opportunity to do dangerous work to emancipate her family and establish them in the North. Having experienced the satisfactions of success and believing "God's time" was near, she had gone on to put her ingenuity, fearlessness, and caution to work in the service of a war to bring about the end of slavery. In extraordinary times, she had made extraordinary commitments and had won fame among her astonished Northern friends as a woman capable of adventurous leadership outside the home on behalf of family, race, and the ideal of emancipation. In the postwar years she showed both desire and talent for "ordinary" domestic life.[21] She settled in a small city in upstate New York, put down roots, owned a piece of land and a home (however precariously), found a new partner, made a living for herself

Tubman's niece Margaret Stewart Lucas and her daughter Alice Lucas (later Brickler). Lucas and her husband helped Tubman apply for a government pension as a Civil War veteran in her old age. Alice Brickler was one of Earl Conrad's informants for his 1943 biography of Tubman. Courtesy Schomburg Collection, New York Public Library.

and her dependents, and made herself available to help a large extended family whenever they needed her. She also raised funds to help support the displaced and impoverished and brought to fruition the ambitious John Brown Hall project—charitable work that clearly had roots in family feeling.

The celebrity she earned in the extraordinary times was sometimes a tool and just as often a mixed blessing as she lived out the more ordinary life of an African American subsistence farmer in an increasingly race-conscious North. Whatever her private feelings, Tubman continued to act as though she believed many whites were committed to the work for more humane social institutions for those who were formerly enslaved, and their offspring. Through the sheer force of her willpower and personality she attracted others in her local community to her vision of a more caring society, and in so doing she demonstrated the heroism of the ordinary life.

TUBMAN AS A SYMBOL IN TWENTIETH-CENTURY RACE POLITICS

Harriet Tubman was not included in a list of "great race women" generated by an authoritative writer in 1893, as the historian Bettye Collier-Thomas has pointed out: "Of the Negro race in the United States since 1620, there have appeared but four women whose careers stand out so far, so high, and so clearly above all others of their sex, that they can with strict propriety and upon well established grounds be denominated great. These are Phillis Wheatley, Sojourner Truth, Frances Ellen Watkins Harper, and Amanda Smith."[24] Tubman's absence from this list might be surprising to many people today, but as we have seen, the development of the Tubman iconographic race heroine by the organized African American community had only just begun in the 1890s with her appearance at the founding conference of the NACW in 1896. By the time of her death, however, she had become a potent symbol, frequently used in the tense public discourse over the meaning of "race" in American history. Her life story could be and was endowed with different racial and gendered meanings, by political conservatives, liberals, and radicals, by blacks and whites, by women and men. As organized African Americans struggled in various ways to resist the Jim Crow racism that had solidified during the "nadir" period and to hold white America accountable for its failure to live up to its democratic rhetoric during the twentieth century, the iconographic Tubman was an important resource—more potent in some periods of the twentieth century than in others, but always available for reinterpretation and educational use. The story with which we are most familiar crystallized in African American biographical dictionaries in the first half of the twentieth century and was then transplanted into inspirational and edifying children's literature in the second half.[25]

Tubman received recognition in death from both sides of a racially divided local and regional community in upstate New York. The "private services" held at the Tubman home on the morning of March 13 were attended "by several hundred colored residents of Auburn and there were many prominent Negroes from out of town." Then her body lay in state at the Thompson A.M.E. Zion church, and "hundreds of whites and Negroes from all parts of the city came to view the remains during the three hours from noon until three o'clock." A public funeral service was held in the afternoon "attended by a crowd that filled the little church on Parker Street and overflowed into the street." Prominent at these services were A.M.E. Zion clergy and the members of the board and board of lady managers of the Harriet Tubman Home.[22] The pastor of the First Methodist Episcopal Church also spoke, and the newspaper account claimed that Tubman had attended this church "for many years." A letter of tribute was read from John Quincy Adams and Fannie Frances Adams, referring to her as "that Christian and patriotic saint, Mrs. Tubman." The representative of the city of Auburn said, "No one of our fellow citizens of late years has conferred greater distinction upon us than has she," and he spoke about knowing her personally from his childhood.[23]

Mary Talbert was also among the featured speakers. She placed Tubman in a pantheon of race heroines: "Harriet Tubman has fallen asleep—the last star in that wonderful galaxy of noble pioneer Negro womanhood has fallen. Phyllis Wheatley, Sojourner Truth, Frances Ellen Watkins Harper, Fannie Jackson Coppin, Harriet Tubman! A fallen star that has shot across the intricate and twinkling dark, vanished, yet left no sense of loss." Talbert also conveyed some "last words" directed specifically to the organized African American women's community: "One month ago she told me of the sweet spirit in that home and of the happiness she felt was there. As I bent over to listen to her feeble voice she bade me thank the women who were helping to make her last days of earth comfortable. . . . As I arose to go, she grasped my hand firmly and whispered, "I've been fixing a long time for my journey but now I'm almost home, God has shown me the

Golden Chariot, and a voice spoke to me and said, 'Arouse, awake! Sleep no longer, Jesus does all things well.' After a moment's hesitation she said, 'Tell the women to stand together for God will never forsake us,' and finally, as I shook her hand to say good-bye, she smiled that peaceful smile of hers and said, 'I am at peace with God and all mankind'" ("Race of Harriets Would Secure the Future of the Negro," 1913).

The political use of Tubman's name and celebrity intensified in the public discussion of her legacy that was touched off by the unveiling of a bronze memorial tablet in her honor by the city of Auburn in 1914. Booker T. Washington, who spoke at this ceremony, had recognized her value as a symbol for his formula for race progress for almost a decade before her death, including her in his own *The Story of the Negro* (1909). "I think we ought to have a chapter showing what Negroes themselves did to bring about freedom. We could use in this chapter such persons as Douglass, Harriet Tubman, Judge Gibbs and other strong characters that are little known about," he had written to Alphonsus Orenzo Stafford, who assisted in the writing of this work (B. T. Washington, 1907).[26] Washington's address at the June 12, 1914, dedication of the Auburn monument was well publicized. In this speech, after reminding his audience of the western New York region's history of "honoring the great characters of our race" and of its "great heroic souls who believed in liberty for all the people," he went on to frame Tubman as an example of "great power in simplicity" and as a role model, especially for "law-abiding" black people: "In her simplicity, her modesty, her common-sense, her devotion to duty, she has left for us an example which those in the present generation of all races might strive to emulate. In the tens of millions of black people scattered throughout this country there are many great souls, heroic souls, that the white race does not know about. Harriet Tubman brought the two races nearer together and made it possible for the white race to know the black race, to place a different estimate upon it. In too many sections of our country the white man knows the criminal Negro, but he knows little about the law-abiding Negro; he knows much of the worst types of our race, he does not know enough of the best types of our race" (B. T. Washington, 1914).[27]

He again used Tubman's life to support a particular political agenda in the address he gave on the following day at the A.M.E. Zion Church, an address characterized in the Auburn newspaper as "straight from the shoulder" talk to "the colored people of the north."[28] The reporter summarized his speech: "He spoke familiarly to the congregation that filled

the church, uttering words of advice and optimism. He urged all to proclaim the success and progress of the race and to desist from telling their
troubles. . . . He also pointed out to them the good fruits that accrued
from industry and habits of saving and he advised them to turn to the
country more; to own some land and to become producers; he advised
them to go into business in the city and to not be afraid to begin at the
bottom. He told the young men to avoid the saloons and the gambling
places and to put their money in the banks. . . . 'Let us in the future advertise our progress everywhere. And we must stand together and help one
another. Race cooperation is needed. Push one another along. In everything that concerns the mutual progress of the race let us stand together.
You will be measured by the great life of Harriet Tubman and by her great
life all the country is watching you'" ("Booker T. Washington Urges Colored Men to Go on Farms," 1914).

Washington's vocal critic W. E. B. Du Bois had also recognized Tubman's
iconographic value before her death, as well as her actual role in African
American history. He had included a brief section on her life (based on
Bradford) in his biography *John Brown* (1909). In a brief article for the
NAACP's publication the *Crisis* shortly after her death, Tubman's life of
service was compared to that of David Livingstone, the missionary to
Africa: "Both these sincere souls gave their lives for black men. . . . Harriet
Tubman, fought American slavery single handed and was a pioneer in that
organized effort known as the Underground Railroad ([Du Bois], 1913).[29]

The white community of Auburn also weighed in with various interpretations of the significance of Tubman's life among them, in speeches
and newspaper stories and editorials at the time of her funeral. One theme
that her life evoked for the representative of city government was the value
of persistence, which seemed to him to make race a negligible barrier to
achievement: "'Aunt Harriet's' life should be an inspiration to the young
men and to the young women of this congregation, for it points out
that possibilities of human achievement are not limited or distinguished
by race, creed or color. In this workaday world filled with its activities,
what a contrast we find between the average person's life filled with petty
vanities, as compared with the unselfish life of our good sister, filled with
sympathy and devotion to her people. If we take this contrast to heart
the example which she has set will not be entirely lost upon us ("Aunt
Harriet's Funeral," 1913).

The pastor of the First Methodist Episcopal Church in Auburn spoke
about her career in a sermon the next week "under the Freedman's Aid

auspices." In a speech that expressed white Christian "liberalism" of the day, he first pointed to the extreme hostility of many whites toward the black population and then urged white Christians to support missionary efforts to educate and "elevate" the black masses. This project would complete "the work of Harriet Tubman and her mighty contemporaries brought forward by the heroic soldiers of the sixties [that] is yet incomplete":

> The blacks, who were 5,000,000 at the close of the war, have now grown until they are greater than the entire population of the country in 1800. These combined make the problem of the South. What shall we do with them. Some say: "Send them back where they belong." But to what place do they belong more than this. They own their homes, they want to stay and who shall say they shall not? But we cannot spare them. We cannot do the work of the South without them. . . .The church is saying, train into citizens, and connect them into the kingdom of God. They have the ability. No Nation that has come among us has made such a rapid progress as has the colored race for the last 45 years. . . . They have the desire for education and elevation. Who that has read the story of Booker T. Washington can doubt it? . . . No mission field of the world has yielded such splendid results as have our efforts among the colored race of America for the past 45 years. ("Two Timely Topics Discussed by Dr. Rosengrant," 1913)

The unveiling of a bronze memorial tablet for the Auburn Courthouse in Tubman's honor the next year gave the white spokespeople of Auburn a second opportunity for public contemplation of the meaning of Tubman's life. In the days leading up to the ceremonial, the newspapers published several stories about the design of the tablet, the planned program, and the anticipated presence of Booker T. Washington and Mary Talbert.[30] Boy Scouts were notified that to take advantage of the free seats offered by the planning committee, they needed to assemble at 7:30 sharp at the Presbyterian Church. The mayor ordered that flags be displayed on municipal buildings on June 12, and he invited Auburn citizens to fly flags also. A former mayor of the city presented the tablet, stressing in his speech the historic nature of the occasion, given Tubman's gender, race, and class: "'Few memorials have been erected in this land to women,' said Mr. Aiken, 'and few to Negroes. None has been erected to one who was at once a woman, a Negro, and a former slave. Harriet Tubman had the courage of a man. She was wise and unselfish'" ("High Tribute Paid to Harriet Tubman," 1914).

An editorial in a local newspaper on the day of the tablet dedication congratulated white Auburn for its liberalism: "Every thoughtful person in the audience carried away the thought—what a remarkable woman Harriet Tubman must have been to deserve this tribute, an enduring monument from the white race to one of the lowliest and most humble of the blacks! Where has anything like it been recorded?" The writer went on (somewhat incoherently) to offer a character analysis that would justify this breaking of the racial ranking rules: "None who has studied her career will say that the tributes paid her were unmerited. . . . In her illiterate way she plodded through life. She was born in ignorance as a slave and in early life developed only craftiness through the ever increasing hope that some day freedom might be her lot. Becoming the arbiter of her own destiny by a bold stroke, as fugitive slave she rejoiced in her freedom and became a religious zealot. The Scriptures became her guide, and few persons ever interpreted them more faithfully than this humble black woman. . . . Tact, loyalty, intelligent obedience, excellent judgment, resourcefulness and numerous other qualities that only trained and highly educated persons possess came to her in her romantic career. On the matter of self sacrifice it may be said that she was almost a fanatic. . . . How many of the white race exist today who will ever merit equal recognition with Harriet Tubman?" ("Tribute by the White Race to the Black Race," 1914).

Race leaders also spoke again. Mary Talbert pointed to the educational value of the tablet the city had dedicated: "This tablet will stand as a silent but effective monitor teaching the children of Auburn and of the state and of the country to lead such noble, unselfish and helpful lives that they too may leave behind them memories which shall encourage others to live." The Booker T. Washington address was covered fully. The reporter called him "the great educator" and characterized his speech as an oration to which "the large audience listened closely." He was said to have drawn frequent applause and appreciative laughter at "amusing incidents," and he was quoted: "Harriet Tubman he pronounced, in spite of her lack of bookish education, 'One of the best educated persons that ever lived in this country,' an education gained by harsh experiences and hardships" ("High Tribute Paid to Harriet Tubman," 1914). Not to be outdone by the grand display the city of Auburn had made of its public devotion to Tubman's memory, the African American clubwomen of New York raised funds over the next year for a monument to mark her grave in Auburn's Fort Hill cemetery.[31]

Black and white Auburnians could agree that Tubman's life reflected positively on their city. Yet an incident reported in the papers during the week before the dedication of the memorial tablet illustrated again the extent to which Tubman's friends and supporters were polarized along racial lines. Louis K. R. Laird, the white executor of Tubman's estate, sold the seven-acre property on South Street to a white neighbor named Frank Norris, refusing an offer made by William Freeman, a member of the board of directors of the Tubman Home. Freeman and his associates "felt they should have first opportunity to buy" and evidently saw racial discrimination in the executor's refusal. They consulted with visiting dignitary Rev. James E. Mason (for many years associated with the Tubman Home effort), who "took up the matter with a number of colored citizens including the Tubman heirs and said he contemplated hiring a lawyer." Laird claimed that "the people who complain had ample opportunity to buy the property, but declined to pay the price, which the executor had fixed at not less than $1,500." Freeman told the reporter that when Laird was unresponsive to his first offer of $1,400 he offered $1,500. Laird was quoted as saying, "It is not true that any of the heirs offered me anything like what the property sold for." The white neighbor who bought the property refused to reveal what he paid ("Wanted to Buy Tubman Property," 1914), but the property remained with the white neighbor. Most of the money from the sale was used to pay off old debts, according to the executor's report.[32] The incident illustrates how little love was lost between Tubman's two groups of friends in Auburn.

THE HARRIET TUBMAN HOME AS A SHRINE

For a few years, the A.M.E. Zion Church struggled successfully to meet the financial obligations they had accepted along with the deed to the property. In October 1918 the Western New York Conference of the church celebrated on the occasion of the burning of the mortgage on the Harriet Tubman Home, which rendered it "free—free as the heroine for whom it is named" ("Mortgage on the Tubman Home," 1918). There were plans for improving the property with additional buildings at that time, and a later unsuccessful appeal from the Empire State Federation of Colored Women's Clubs to take over the property and establish a "girls home in memory of Mother Tubman," around 1924 (Walls, 1974, 444). The home faltered and failed, and by 1937, when the Empire State Women's Clubs came

Gathering at the dedication of a headstone for Tubman's grave in Fort Hill Cemetery, Auburn, in 1915. Funds for the headstone were raised by the Empire State Federation of Women's Clubs, which included African American women's clubs from Buffalo and New York City, under the leadership of Mary B. Talbert.

to Auburn to erect a new granite monument over Tubman's grave, the Tubman Home had not been used for its original purpose "of late years" ("Monument over Harriet Tubman Grave Unveiled, 1937).

The odds of the Home's success were not very good from the outset. While she was alive, Tubman had fostered a tense coalition between her personally loyal white supporters and the A.M.E. Zion ministers and laypeople to whom the responsibility for the management of the charitable institution had been transferred.[33] After her death this coalition ended, and the black church organization shouldered the financial and managerial burden exclusively. The problems of maintaining a charitable institution through small voluntary donations by church members, year in and year out, overwhelmed the Harriet Tubman Home. Yet as the legacy of a national symbol of racial pride, the Home could not simply be allowed to fail. And so it went through a series of cycles of vacancy, decay, and vandalism, followed by indignant publicity and finger-pointing by city and church representatives, followed by fund-raising and efforts at restoration and renewal, throughout the twentieth century. Ultimately it evolved from a failed rest home into its present identity as historical shrine.[34]

With the renewed national interest in civil rights and black history of the 1960s and 1970s, the Harriet Tubman Home began to function as a pilgrimage site. African American church groups, organized Tubman descendants, and others began to attend annual "homecomings" at the site, featuring memorial ceremonies at the Tubman gravesite as well as musical entertainment and the crowning of a young "Miss Harriet Tubman," homecoming-queen style. A new generation of feminists was drawn to the 1983 tribute. "Several dozen women . . . from the Women's Encampment for a Future of Peace and Justice near the Seneca Army Depot in Romulus," a feminist antimilitary demonstration, came to ceremonies at the Home and went on to Fort Hill Cemetery: "At the gravesite activist Queen Mother Moore spoke for a few moments: 'She is gone, she is no longer with us, her work was revolutionary work,' she said. 'We must work in Harriet Tubman's name. It's not enough to eulogize her; we must work in her spirit.' Again everyone joined hands and as a cool breeze arose, sang, 'We are the flow, we are the ebb, we are the weavers, we are the web'" (Holberg, "Tubman's Life Inspires Women," 1983).

Retellings of Tubman's story, like pilgrimages to her grave, continue. Her life story is used to remind black children and adults of their own heroic potential and to remind white children and adults both of national broken promises and of the powers and agency of the African American community. But it is important to remember that the heroic iconography that inspires us was not merely a creation of her embattled political descendants after her death. During her own lifetime, Harriet Tubman shaped the public story of her heroism for an American audience that was polarized by racial politics. How did she herself understand what her life meant? And how did she choose to present her life story to the world? Her own storytelling practices can help provide answers to these questions. The stories she left behind—stories that are often fragmented and always mediated by the pens of others—are among the most important resources we have for exploring her own perspectives on the political and social world of her time and her place within it.

PART 2

The Life Stories

HARRIET TUBMAN'S
PRACTICES AS A LIFE
STORYTELLER

Harriet Tubman's autobiographical medium was the well-told individual story performed for an audience—not the more private, analytical, and self-reflective commentary characteristic of autobiographers in the habit of reading and writing.[1] She was schooled in her Maryland childhood in the distinctive storytelling practices of an African American subculture within a larger Anglo-American rural culture—both traditions intimately shaped by the power dynamics of the institution of slavery. When she came north she found she was able to put her storytelling skills to good use in her life as a celebrated antislavery heroine. Her experience with living in two cultures in Maryland undoubtedly made it easier for her to operate in the initially alien world of the antislavery networks in Northern cities and towns—the world in which most of her life storytelling took place.

Tubman's motives for public performance of her life stories were a mixture of the practical, the political, and the religious. Her public testimony certainly had economic value, and from the moment she arrived in the North she began to struggle with the problem she would face for the rest of her life—how to feed, clothe, and shelter those who depended on her. Recognition that her telling her life story could help her raise funds did not imply a cynical perspective on the project—as perhaps it might for the celebrity today. She moved in highly idealistic political circles, where former slave testimonial was seen as a powerful tool in the war against the sinful ownership of other human beings. To make sure that at least some of the facts of her experience as a former slave would become part of the public record was a political act, even if it also helped her support herself and her family. Most importantly, her work as a storyteller should be understood within the context of her lifelong personal religiosity. Like other spiritual autobiographers who have been confident of divine guidance in their lives, Tubman believed that telling her life story could be a way of making God's active participation in antislavery work more widely known.

Unlike her acquaintances Frederick Douglass and William Wells Brown, Tubman never acted as a paid lecturer for an antislavery society. Her stories of slavery were not developed into a written "slave narrative" prior to the war, as so often happened with the paid lecturers.[2] Yet like these more "professional" antislavery life story narrators, she provided her politically allied audiences with thrilling and entertaining stories and songs and further stimulus for their political work.[3] As important as the plot and style of the well-told story was the body language—the "wealth of eloquent gesture" Tubman used to enhance the performance (in Telford's phrase). Those who heard her frequently claimed that a mere transcription of her words would be inadequate: "I wish it were possible to give some of her racy stories; but no report would do them justice" (Cheney, 1865, 36). Similarly: "The mere words could do no justice to the speaker; and therefore we do not undertake to give them; but we advise all our readers to take the earliest opportunity to see and hear her" (Yerrington, 1859).

Those who heard her speak in the 1850s were both amazed by the facts of her unusually courageous actions and moved by the impact of her personal presence. Thomas W. Higginson recalled in his memoirs the impact this kind of storytelling had on his generation of antislavery white Northerners:

> I know that my own teachers were the slave women who came shyly before the audience, women perhaps as white as my own sisters,—Ellen Craft was quite as white—women who had been stripped and whipped and handled with insolent hands and sold to the highest bidder as unhesitatingly as the little girl whom I had seen in the St. Louis slave-market; or women who having once escaped, had, like Harriet Tubman, gone back again and again into the land of bondage to bring away their kindred and friends. My teachers were the men whom I first saw walking clumsily across the platform, just arrived from the South, as if they still bore a hundred pounds of plantation soil on each ankle, and whom I saw develop in the course of years into the dignity of freedom. What were the tricks of oratory in the face of men and women like these? We learned to speak because their presence made silence impossible. (Higginson, 1898, 327–328)

Instead of the classical Greek "tricks of oratory" to which the college-educated Higginson refers, Tubman drew upon homelier sources of eloquence, such as scriptures she would have heard preached in the South. She frequently employed a teaching technique made familiar in the New Testament Gospels—the "parable" or narrative metaphor—to make her lessons persuasive and memorable. One example quoted earlier in part 1, "The Life," was a story told as part of an anticolonization movement speech at an African American political convention in Boston in 1859, the story of a farmer who wanted to get rid of the garlic he had sown in his field. Another type of memorable extended metaphor impressed the visiting historian Albert Bushnell Hart: "Her extraordinary power of statement was illustrated in her description of a battle in the Civil War: 'And then we saw the lightning, and that was the guns; and then we heard the thunder, and that was the big guns; and then we heard the rain falling, and that was drops of blood falling; and when we came to get in the crops, it was dead men that we reaped'" (Hart, 1906, 209). Ednah Cheney also admired Tubman's "great dramatic power; the scene rises before you as she saw it, and her voice and language change with her different actors" (Cheney, 1865).

She could easily move her audience to laughter as well. The version of the Joe story recorded by Bradford in 1868 is an example of her unwillingness to spare even the central character of a thrilling fugitive slave story the edge of her wit. Too depressed to appreciate the sight of Niagara Falls as the train passes over the Suspension Bridge, Joe exclaims mournfully, "Only one more journey for me now, and that is to Heaven!" Tubman's punch line: "Well, you old fool you. . . . You might have looked at the Falls first, and then gone to Heaven afterwards." (Bradford censored this element to emphasize the pathos in her 1886 rewriting). Sometimes the joke was at Tubman's own expense. "Mrs. Follen and Miss Putnam shouted at her comic pathos," when she told them about how eagerly she had brought new clothes for her faithless husband, only to be left with the clothes and no husband (Osgood, 1859).

One of Earl Conrad's informants who as a child had known Tubman in her old age reported: "there was never any variation in the stories she told, whether to me or to any other" (Tatlock, 1939a). It is characteristic of the folklore performer trained in an oral culture to tell a story in precisely the right way each time. This is because the story itself is often regarded as a form of knowledge that will educate the young and be passed down through the generations. The storyteller must not weaken the story's integrity with a poor performance. When reporting on Tubman's testimony about her spiritual experience, Ednah Cheney observed something like the same phenomenon (though with obvious impatience): "She loves to describe her visions, which are very real to her; but she must tell them word for word as they lie in her untutored mind, with endless repetitions and details; she cannot shorten or condense them, whatever be your haste" (Cheney, 1865, 36–37).

As Cheney's impatience suggests, Tubman's early biographers as white Northerners were not what today's folklorists would call "culturally competent," despite good intentions, to record or fully understand her oral performances. Her spiritual self-expression was particularly mystifying to her book-educated Northern auditors. Cheney frankly gave up the effort to report the "eloquence" that made such a striking impression upon her the day John Brown's companions were executed. Tubman had told Cheney that Brown's death represented a kind of second crucifixion. She went on:

> "When I think of all the groans and tears and prayers I've heard on the plantations, and remember that God is a prayer-hearing God, I feel that his time is drawing near."
>
> "Then you think," I said, "that God's time is near?"
>
> "God's time is always near," she said; "He gave me my strength, and he set the North Star in the heavens; he meant I should be free."
>
> She went on in a strain of the most sublime eloquence I ever heard; but I cannot repeat it. (Cheney, 1865, 37)

Religious songs embellished Tubman's oral storytelling performances and were frequently central plot elements in her most popular Underground Railroad stories. There was the story of teasing the thick-witted "master" the night before her escape by using a familiar Methodist song, "I'm Bound for the Promised Land," to communicate to her family her intention to run away. Singing was also integral to her much-told story about coded communication with fugitives she had hidden in the woods. "Go Down, Moses" meant "stay hidden," while a "Methodist air," "Hail, oh hail, ye happy spirits," meant "all clear" (Bradford, 1869). Though she was able to capture and reproduce the lyrics for her readers, Bradford was evidently bewildered by Tubman's musical performance in much the same way Cheney was by her spiritual testimony: "The air sung to these words was so wild, so full of plaintive minor strains, and unexpected quavers, that I would defy any white person to learn it, and often as I heard it, it was to me a constant surprise" (Bradford, 1886, 35–36).

The much-told story of "Joe" culminated in her imitating his performance of a joyful hymn when he touched Canadian soil:

Glory to God and Jesus too,
One more soul is safe!
Oh, go and carry the news
One more soul is safe. (Bradford, 1869)

Charlotte Forten recorded the emotional impact of the final song when
Tubman told the Joe story to an audience at Port Royal: "How exciting it
was to hear her tell the story. And to hear the very scraps of jubilant hymns
that he sang. She said the ladies crowded around them, and some laughed
and some cried. My own eyes were full as I listened to her" (Forten, 1863).
     The Combahee River Raid story also culminated in a song, one Tubman
had improvised on the spur of the moment to reassure the plantation's
slave population that the Yankees would provide support. A visitor in 1911
who watched Tubman perform this story (at age ninety-one!) reported on
the athleticism of her rendition: "At the refrain 'come along,' Aunt Harriet
waved her withered arm with an imperious gesture. After nearly fifty years
it had not lost its appeal. To illustrate the effect of her song upon the slaves
who first heard it, the African Joan [Joan of Arc] clapped her hands and
thumped her feet upon the floor" (Clarke, 1911).
     Her singing voice even in old age was impressive. Florence Carter,
widow of the pastor of the A.M.E. Zion Church Tubman attended in her
later years, remembered, "She had a fine voice, that was very feminine,
and when she sang, as she often did, her lungs opened up widely and she
would shout, and she could shout as loudly as anyone I heard." Samuel
Hopkins Adams, the grandson of Samuel Hopkins and nephew of Sarah
Bradford, remembered the voice from his boyhood as low in pitch but
powerful: "The old Negress would clap her stringy hands upon her bony
knees, rock her powerful frame, snap her eyes, and raise a voice that re-
sounded up to the cupola. It was baritone rather than contralto, that voice,
and produced a strangely moving effect of mingled challenge and appeal.
'Farewell, old master, don't think hard of me, I'm on my way to Canaday,
where all the slaves is free'" (S. H. Adams, 1989).
     When retelling her war stories to close friends and family, Tubman
would often spontaneously add further dramatic gestures, such as the one
remembered by her grandniece Alice Brickler: "She and Mother were talking as they sat in the yard. Tiring of their conversation, I wandered off in

the tall grasses to pick the wild flowers. Suddenly I became aware of something moving toward me through the grass. So smoothly did it glide and with so little noise, I was frightened! Then reason conquered fear and I knew it was Aunt Harriet, flat on her stomach and with only the use of her arms and serpentine movements of her body, gliding smoothly along. Mother helped her back to her chair and they laughed. Aunt Harriet then told me that that was the way she had gone by many a sentinel during the war" (Brickler, 1939b).

Dramatic performances of the most popular stories and songs enabled her to repay friends, family members, and associates in her later years in Auburn for small kindnesses. Tubman knew by experience which stories would most interest these private audiences. Always aware of her own value as an entertainer, she could occasionally joke about the insatiable demand for her stories. "'And so you wants to hear the story of Harriet's life all over again?' she said when calling recently at the little brick cottage after a long absence from the city. 'Pears like you has heard it so many times you could tell that story yourself.' . . . In her own home Harriet delights to welcome any who may come, opening her treasury of story and song for their benefit" (Telford, n.d., 3–5).

Perhaps there were moments of feeling herself on exhibition as a curiosity, rather than eagerly anticipated as a respected freedom fighter. A Bradford story is suggestive of this. Bradford intended this story to illustrate her own view that Tubman's "expressions are often very peculiar." It also seems to reveal a sly critique of the postwar debasement of her former glorious role as antislavery storyteller: "Some ladies of a certain church who had become interested in her wished to see her, and she was invited to come to their city, and attended the sewing circle, where twenty or thirty of them were gathered together. They asked her many questions, and she told stories, sang songs, danced, and imitated the talk of the Southern Negroes; and went away loaded with many tokens of the kind interest of these ladies. On the way home she said: 'What nice, kind-looking ladies they was, Missus. I looked in all their faces, and I didn't see nothing venomous in one of them'" (Bradford, 1901).

FROM STORYTELLING TO TEXT CREATION

She says, when the war is over she will learn to read and write, and then will write her own life. The trouble in her head prevents her from applying closely to a book. It is the strong desire of all her friends that she should tell her own story in her own way at some future time. We think it affords a very cogent answer to the query, "Can the Negro take care of himself?'" (Cheney, 1865, 38)

We do not know exactly why Tubman did not pursue the project of learning to read and write after the war.[4] The most likely reason is that providing for her dependents took all of her time and energy in those days. Her age and physical condition, including the liability to seizure or sudden bouts of sleep ("the trouble in her head" mentioned by Cheney), may also have been factors. Whatever the reasons, the result was that she depended on the assistance of others when she converted her oral life history narrative into textual forms.[5]

The storytelling texts she produced in collaboration with Bradford, as well as others produced by her associates, can be usefully placed within the context of former slave narrative literature in its broadest definition, which includes narratives gathered in oral historical interviews and other highly collaborative or "mediated" life stories. Historians of American culture have long since identified the "slave narrative" (which is more accurately called the former- or ex-slave narrative) as a foundational genre in the history of African American self-expression and self-representation.[6] Such narratives illuminate the complex processes of self-discovery, self-invention, and public assertion of individual and group identity of African Americans emerging from the world of chattel slavery during the eighteenth and nineteenth centuries. Literary historian John Sekora has argued, "The (ex-slave) narrative is the only moral history of American slavery we have. Outside its pages, slavery for black Americans was a wordless, nameless, timeless time. . . . The written narrative encouraged a recollection that could be tested, corrected, replenished. Such recollection could then be united with other life stories to inscribe a history, a time beyond personal memory, a time beyond slaveholders' power. The narrative is both instrument and inscription of a powerful collective memory" (Sekora, 1988, 111). But we must "engage in radical strategies to hear the imposed silences of the narratives, . . . attend to the gaps, the elisions, the contradictions, and especially the violations" in order to understand this history from the perspective of those who lived it.

Because most enslaved people were denied access to literacy as a matter of policy and law, scribal and editorial mediation, most often by well-intentioned whites, affects the vast majority of texts in which former slaves offer accounts of their own experience.[7] In many cases where mediation by a white scribe and editor was involved, the editor clearly contributed a number of literary elements that would not have been present had the former slave been in control of the pen.[8] Sarah Bradford's influential 1886 biography in particular needs to be seen as a highly mediated text of this kind. Its literary framework was created entirely by Bradford. Valuable oral historical material gathered from Tubman in interviews has been embedded within this framework—though often in significantly altered forms. We can borrow some valuable strategies for reading the Bradford texts from the work of historians of slavery using highly mediated twentieth-century interviews of aging former slaves.

Between 1936 and 1938, the federal Works Projects Administration employed interviewers to conduct 2,194 interviews with former slaves, two-thirds of whom were at least eighty years old at the time of the interview. The WPA texts are invaluable sources of information about the daily material lives and culture and even, to a lesser extent, the emotional lives of survivors of slavery—especially those who were children in the immediate prewar period. This kind of information can be acquired in no other way, now that this generation of living survivors of slavery is gone. But such texts cannot be read at face value. A critical awareness of how the texts were created allows us to understand just what kind of truths these texts can tell.

The interview situation in the segregated Great Depression South involved dramatic imbalances in social power between interviewer and interviewee. According to historian John Blassingame, "Often the white interviewer-author's actions and demeanor led to distortions and limitations of what the black informant-author told him. Many of the blacks played it safe; they claimed that they remembered very little about slavery, and gave one- or two-page interviews. Even the informants who gave the longest, most candid interviews refused to talk about certain things" (Blassingame, 1975, 84–86). Another substantial body of interview material collected by black interviewers based in the historically black Southern colleges of Hampton Institute, Fisk University, and Southern University provides an important comparative perspective.[9] Blassingame found that "The former slaves who talked to black interviewers presented an entirely different portrait of their treatment. . . . The informants talked much more freely to black than white interviewers about miscegenation, hatred of whites, courtship, marriage and family customs, cruel punishments, separation of families, child labor, black resistance to whites, and their admiration of Nat Turner"(Blassingame, 1975, 91).[10]

When the interviewer was white, as in the WPA projects, former slaves might resort to subterfuges learned in relationships with whites developed during slavery. As Paul Escott points out, "storytelling was a skill used effectively by some former slaves to divert the conversation and avoid giving offense; it reached a high level of development as a survival tactic" (Escott, 1985, 43). The reader of mediated texts like these needs to look for textual clues to the power dynamic that may have existed between the former slave and the interviewer (such features as the form of address used by the narrator or the degree of responsiveness of the narrator to questions). Escott also urges us to look for ways to separate factual content from "declarations of feeling that were designed to satisfy the racial etiquette of the day." He has found it useful to rely on "described events as indicators of feeling rather than on patterned and otherwise unsupported statements. . . . In general, recollections that were convincing were specific and fleshed out with individual circumstances and detail" (43–44).

The mediated storytelling texts in this book were created under circumstances that were far more favorable for Tubman. Often the initiative was hers or that of close political allies and friends concerned with her survival, and the scribes were always supportive of her mission. Yet we still need to be aware of possible distortions in the transmission of her experience resulting from conscious or unconscious racial (and often social class) power dynamics between the speaker and the writer. The modern reader of the Bradford/Tubman texts, in particular, is like the critical reader of the WPA interview material, conscious of hearing the voices of "two authors" simultaneously (Blassingame, 1975). Escott's emphasis on "described events as indicators of feeling," as the textual site least likely to be "contaminated" by deference to the interviewer's agenda, is similar to my own emphasis on the individual story texts as the place to seek the most authentic embodiments of her own values and political and religious perspectives.

Then there is the question of what was lost or changed as the spoken language was recorded in written form. In the case of the WPA former slave narrative texts, what purports to be first-person quotation generally is summary (not literal transcription) based on handwritten notes taken at the interview—a far cry from the accurate transcriptions of tape-recorded conversations that we routinely expect as the basis of oral history texts today.[11] Similarly, the "quotations" attributed to Tubman in all the mediated sources must be understood as highly approximate. The written rendition of her speech style—her grammar, diction, and Southern accent in particular—varies tremendously from one mediated text to another, and this variation serves as an immediate warning to the reader that we are always hearing her through another person's ears.[12]

Tubman's voice is represented in several different genres or types of collaborative text—each with distinctly different levels of "authority" or likely reliability. Among the most authoritative (because they are the least mediated) are texts that she dictated. On a half dozen occasions Tubman made factual statements about her life in situations where there was no need to entertain or amuse and there was no personal relationship with the scribe. These include the 1855 interview in Canada with Benjamin Drew, the 1863 testimony in the court-martial case of a Union Army official at Port Royal, and several legal affidavits supporting her various claims to the government for a pension. Even these dictated texts are, of course, "mediated" in the sense that she did not compose them herself, but we can presume that the content of these texts was completely under her own control, even if the scribe did not capture the exact language used. The affidavits were very much her own project, but they also probably involved a clerk making a digest of the facts after a discussion with her. While not particularly revealing of her personal feelings, they are exceptionally valuable sources for reconstructing her wartime service and the facts of her second marriage. The Port Royal testimony may be the closest thing we have to a literal transcription of what was actually said on a specific occasion, but it is very brief: she answers a few questions related to the sales of government stores of sugar. The Drew testimonial provides one of the most explicit condemnations of the institution of slavery ever attributed to her, yet it is still mediated in two ways. Drew very likely shaped the discussion by asking specific questions, and he certainly produced a spare summary of what she may actually have said at great length on the occasion. We have what is probably the gist of her answers including a quoted phrase every now and then.

Her letters are the next most authoritative texts representing her voice. She must have produced dozens, and perhaps hundreds, of dictated letters during her lifetime, though only a small percentage were saved, to be turned up by research in the archived papers of her associates.[13] Tubman also dictated affectionate messages to individuals to be written in copies of gift books.[14] The history of her dictated correspondence suggests that she derived pleasure and perhaps a sense of mastery through the increasing access to the pen she gained over the years, even if the pen was in the hand of someone else. We know that at first in her Underground Railroad work she relied on trusted antislavery associates such as Thomas Garrett, William Still, Oliver Johnson, or Franklin Sanborn to pass on crucial information to others in the networks. For example, Garrett informed Tubman that he had heard of someone wishing to donate money from Eliza Wigham; Garrett later informed Wigham of Tubman's request for "five pound sterling to aid her in her trustworthy calling" (Garrett, 1856b). Tubman also sent both oral and encoded written messages through Underground Railroad associates to Maryland friends and relations, as we hear in accounts of the Christmas rescue of 1854 and the rescue of her parents in 1857. At some point fairly early in the 1850s, however, she began to dictate her own correspondence as well. "She got a friend in New York to write to me," Thomas Garrett reported in a letter to Mary Edmundson in March 1857 (1857c). When she was traveling in the fall of 1859, she and her brother John Stewart exchanged dictated letters, and during the war she was able to correspond in the same way with her antislavery associates in Boston and her family and friends in Auburn. The fact that the four letters known to have survived are, among other things, "dunning letters," as she herself called a letter to Wendell Phillips asking for money to support her activities, suggests that their contents must be read with some awareness of her current relationship to the person addressed.[15]

Although we can probably rely on the accuracy of the information in the letters, we must be cautious not to make assumptions with respect to language. One interesting example is the well-known letter to Sanborn following the Combahee River Raid publicity, written in a highly educated diction that contrasts strongly with the Southern dialect in which her speech is usually rendered by Northern biographers. The language suggests that one of her white Sea Islands associates from the North bent over backward to avoid the indignity of dialect. The scribe has written: "You have without doubt seen a full account of the expedition I refer to. Don't you think we colored people are entitled to some credit for that exploit, under the lead of the brave Colonel Montgomery?" Yet we know from Martha Coffin Wright's version of the railway assault incident in 1865 that the term "colored person" was a euphemism Tubman actually found insulting.

In later life she developed an interesting way of asserting her authorship over the dictated letters, perhaps even "controlling the pen" herself: "Her letters are all written by an amanuensis, and she seems to have an idea that by laying her hand on this person, her feelings may be transmitted to the one to whom she is writing. These feelings are sometimes very poetically expressed. I have by me some of these letters, in one of them she says, 'I lay my hand on the shoulder of the writer of this letter, and I wish for you, and all your offsprings, a through ticket in the gospel train to glory.' In another letter she has dictated this sentence: 'I ask of my Heavenly Father, that when the last trump sounds, and my name is called, I may stand close by your side, to answer to the call'" (Bradford 1901, 148–149). Flowery benedictions of this kind were customarily included in letters to friends, it seems. Certainly we see examples in the small number of texts that have survived, including one addressed to Mary Wright in 1896: "Remember me in your prayers as your father did before you. If I never see you again I hope to see you in the kingdom."

Less authoritative than dictated letters but much more full of potentially illuminating details are the contemporary renditions of her stories and style of speech by first-hand observers in private literature such as letters and journals, or even in more public literature such as newspaper summaries of her speeches and early biographical sketches in antislavery journals. The embedded stories and sayings in these sources must be assumed to reflect the writer's ideas of what was valuable in what she said, even when the writer was highly trustworthy and had known her for an extended period. (Later sketches of this sort tended to rely heavily on earlier published accounts without specifying what information was based on fresh interviews, so it is difficult to determine how authoritative a story found in one of these later biographical sketches may be.) Finally, perhaps least authoritative but still very interesting and potentially useful are stories found in accounts by those who knew her as an old woman when they themselves were young. I am thinking especially of Adams, Bowley, Brickler, and Tatlock. These twentieth-century gleanings could very well have been influenced by the hearing or reading of versions of stories already in wide circulation, and, of course, they could also have been remolded by tricks of memory during the many years of the informant's own adulthood.[16]

Mediated texts, then, inevitably reflect a tension between two alternative perspectives on the significance of the events retold, and all the stories and sayings of Tubman come to us in the form of mediated texts. The more we know, both about the type of mediated source and about the social and political ideas of the writer, the better guess we can make about what she likely said on a given occasion, and even how she might have said it.

IDENTIFYING THE PERSPECTIVES OF HARRIET TUBMAN'S EARLIEST COLLABORATORS

Fortunately we know quite a bit about Tubman's three earliest biographical collaborators. Franklin B. Sanborn (1831–1917), her first biographer, was a New Hampshire–born Harvard graduate and schoolteacher in nearby Concord. He become passionately involved in antislavery politics as a secretary of the Massachusetts Free Soil Association, an organization that supported the entry of Kansas into the Union as a free state. He met Tubman through his John Brown support work, and he acted as her host on several of her visits to the Boston area before and after the Harpers Ferry Raid. Editor of the Boston antislavery newspaper *Commonwealth*, Sanborn wrote his first biographical sketch of Tubman in order to correct mistaken facts in a published report on the Combahee River Raid in the *Wisconsin State Journal* ("From Florida: Colonel Montgomery's Raid," 1863, June 20). Sanborn's feature article "Harriet Tubman" appeared on July 17, 1863, and allowed him, as her initial New England "discoverer," to share in the reflected glory of Tubman's celebrity. Sanborn's sketch was based on at least five years' acquaintance with Tubman, but we should remember that she had been in South Carolina for over a year when he wrote it on one week's notice. Thus he must have relied on old notes and letters, and perhaps a journal, as he put together the earliest published biographical narrative on Tubman. He had no opportunity to refresh his memory by speaking with her before it was published. After the war he continued to write weekly for the *Springfield Republican*, and he also wrote many books and magazine articles about John Brown and about literary friends and associates from Concord (Alcott, Emerson, Thoreau, and Hawthorne). He remained a staunch defender of the radical wing of abolitionism of the 1850s, of which he had been a part, long after it was generally fashionable. He wrote about Tubman several more times, often in order to contribute to her material support,[17] and his treatment of her career in his writings was consistently admiring—though his character assessment after her death acknowledged her "flaws."

Her second biographer, Ednah Dow Littlehale Cheney (1824–1904), also had an elite education for a woman of her day. Just a few years younger than Tubman, Cheney moved in the same circles as Sanborn, whose deceased wife had been her girlhood friend. Cheney came from a relatively prosperous Universalist family and was very much influenced by the ideas and culture of the "transcendentalist" philosophers and writers of Concord and Boston—including Margaret Fuller, as well as Bronson Alcott, Ralph Waldo Emerson, and Theodore Parker. She was a member of an unchurched liberal group called the Free Religious Association.

Ednah Cheney's "Moses" was written for the March 1865 issue of the *Freedmen's Record* (the journal of the New England Freedmen's Aid Society, of which she was secretary).[18] The article, probably written shortly before Tubman returned to war service in the South after nearly a year's leave of absence, drew upon conversations Cheney had had with Tubman over the six or seven years of their acquaintance, including some very recent ones.[19] Cheney had read Sanborn's sketch and relied extensively upon information from it.

Cheney was also a reliable political ally for Tubman throughout the postwar years. In her career as reformer and philanthropist in the post-Reconstruction years, she supported African American education and civil rights, giving "money and moral support to Atlanta University and Hampton and Tuskegee Institutes" and opposing segregation.[20] She was active in the New England women's club movement and women's suffrage campaigns in Massachusetts and was a supporter of the New England Hospital for Women and Children. Like Sanborn, Cheney came to Tubman's assistance in various ways in later years, and in her old age Cheney again wrote about Tubman for her *Reminiscences* (1902), for the most part relying heavily on her own earlier biography.

The sketches by Sanborn and Cheney were each a few columns of newsprint written hastily during the war years for audiences of passionately committed antislavery readers. The first biography of real scope was Bradford's *Scenes in the Life of Harriet Tubman*, which appeared over three years after the war and twenty years after Tubman's original escape from Maryland. Sarah Hopkins Bradford (1818–1912), the daughter of a New York State lawyer, legislator, and judge, grew up in Geneva and Albany, New York, and in 1839 married another lawyer, John Bradford, with whom she had six children. Her husband left the family to move to Chicago in 1857, and Bradford ran a school for girls and young women in her own home in Geneva from 1861 until early 1869 (Johnston, 1944). A writer of historical and moral tales, Bradford had already published several collections of stories for children in the 1850s, including "Poor Nina, the Fugitive" (1855), which revealed her antislavery sympathies and her opposition to the Fugitive Slave Act.[21] Bradford told how she met Tubman in the first version of the biography,

The writer of this story has till very lately known less personally of the subject of it, than many others to whom she has for years been an object of interest and care. But through relations and friends in Auburn, and also through
Mrs. Commodore Swift of Geneva, and her sisters, who have for many years
known and esteemed this wonderful woman, she has heard tales of her deeds
of heroism which seemed almost too strange for belief, and were invested
with the charm of romance. During a sojourn of some months in the city
of Auburn, while the war was in progress, the writer used to see occasionally in her Sunday-school class the aged mother of Harriet, and also some
of those girls who had been brought from the South by this remarkable
woman. She also wrote letters for the old people to commanding officers at
the South, making inquiries about Harriet, and received answers telling of
her untiring devotion to our wounded and sick soldiers, and of her efficient
aid in various ways to the cause of the Union. (Bradford, 1869, 46–47)

Bradford's *Scenes in the Life of Harriet Tubman* was based on Bradford's
interviews with Tubman in 1868, at least some of which took place in
Bradford's home in Geneva. The 1868 interviews generated most of the
surviving Underground Railroad and Civil War stories.[22] Later biographers
of Tubman are all to a greater or lesser degree dependent on the Bradford
book (especially the 1886 revision). Therefore it is of critical importance
to look carefully at the 1868 interview situation in order to evaluate the
strengths and weaknesses of the story texts that emerged from this collaborative context.

Harriet Tubman enjoyed some clear advantages over the former slaves
interviewed in the 1930s for the WPA oral history project. Her memory of
the events was far fresher, because much less time had intervened. Unlike
most of the twentieth-century informants, she had known and could
speak from both a child's and an adult's perspective on slavery.[23] Moreover,
it seems likely that she took the initiative in the storytelling with Bradford
once they were together and to a large degree set the agenda herself. I infer
this from several facts we know about their relationship. First, Tubman
herself was already a highly experienced oral autobiographer at the time
the project began (having begun to use her life history material to inform
and entertain in the late 1850s). Bradford, in contrast, was an inexperienced interviewer/scribe and was distracted by other concerns, such as her
approaching trip to Europe. She is unlikely to have made preparations to
control the interviews tightly with a list of carefully thought-out questions.

Most significantly, however, is Tubman's own state of mind and her accustomed storytelling practices, previously discussed. She was highly motivated to work on the project, and as Cheney had said, she had plenty of practice telling stories in her own way, "no matter what your haste." I think she decided which stories were appropriate to put in the public record through Bradford, and this was her clear agenda in the interviews.

To give Bradford due credit, she tells us that she did her best to avoid relying strictly on the interviews for the facts. Luckily for historians, she wrote candidly about her improvisational research methods in the hastily assembled volume. Like the cautious oral historian of today, she attempted to corroborate Tubman's memories. "Much has been left out which would have been highly interesting, because of the impossibility of substantiating by the testimony of others the truth of Harriet's statements. But whenever it has been possible to find those who were cognizant with the facts stated, they have been corroborated in every particular" (Bradford, 1869, 3–4).[24] She solicited testimonial letters from a list supplied by Tubman: "Many of the stories told me by Harriet, in answer to questions, have been corroborated by letters, some of which will appear in this book. Of others, I have not been able to procure confirmation, owing to ignorance of the address of those conversant with the facts" (Bradford, 1869, 36–37). Bradford also pointed out that Tubman had plenty of corroborating documentation, some of which was copied directly into the book manuscript: "Of the many letters, testimonials and passes, placed in the hands of the writer by Harriet, the following are selected for insertion in this book, and are quite sufficient to verify her statements" (Bradford, 1869, 64).

Lacking sufficient time to do the necessary research and to organize her materials into a coherent chronological narrative, Bradford both apologized for the disorderly narrative and farmed some of the work out to Charles P. Wood, a local Auburn banker in the antislavery orbit.[25] She turned over to him Tubman's war-related documents for this purpose, and Wood did indeed complete a narrative mentioned by Bradford in the 1869 text as having been "of very material assistance" to her—but the narrative itself, somewhat puzzlingly, was not included in the book (Conrad, 1950). Most of Sanborn's 1863 sketch made it into the book (without attribution to him by name). Apparently Bradford did not notice or did not have the time to deal with the contradictions between several parts of Sanborn's account and her own.[26]

When she rewrote the narrative thoroughly for the 1886 edition, *Harriet, the Moses of Her People*, Bradford gathered only a modest amount of new material. She did visit New York City to interview and solicit a testimonial letter from Oliver Johnson, who "remembered her coming into his office with Joe, as I have stated it" (Bradford, 1886, 90).[27] Bradford's brother, the professor at Auburn Seminary, also wrote a testimonial letter for the revision. More significant than the new material in 1886 were the changes Bradford made in the material already published. She made many minor changes in "facts"—notably inflating the figures on the rewards offered for Joe and Tubman and on the numbers of fugitives helped by Thomas Garrett (see appendix B, "A Note on the Numbers"). She changed significant details in the story of Tubman's escape.[28] Bradford systematically took out all references to Tubman's racial politics.[29] She also changed many of the original stories to make them more "literary," reorganizing the narrative substantially and in the process increasing her own authorial control and editorial interference in Tubman's storytelling. Bringing into play her habits as a writer of moralistic children's literature, Bradford added dramatized scenes and rhetorical asides to the reader.[30] She renarrated in the third person the stories that she had originally captured as told in the first person. And by so doing, she censored aspects of Tubman's witty and salty persona, as well as her politics.[31]

In all fairness to Bradford, it might be argued that her rewriting of the earlier narrative was intended to eliminate anything that might mar the image of a saintly self-sacrificing African American heroine—an image she wanted to offer her white readers in an era of increasingly virulent white racism.[32] From today's perspective, we can see that the strategy she followed—of trying to "elevate" her heroine by emphasizing how different she was from other former slaves—merely fed into the racist climate Bradford may have believed she was fighting on Tubman's behalf.[33] Certainly this strategy is not one that Tubman would have adopted or approved—as we have seen in part 1, "The Life," she took every opportunity offered to express racial pride.

For the final edition of the book, published in 1901, Bradford reprinted the 1886 narrative (already reprinted in 1897, at Tubman's request) and added a new appendix, with a few stories gathered between 1886 and 1901 and "some interesting and amusing incidents which I have related to my friends" (Bradford, 1901).[34] Again she indicated that she had not done the research she might have: "Probably many of her friends and correspondents might contribute facts and incidents in Harriet's life quite as interesting as any I have mentioned, but I have no way of getting at them" (Bradford, 1901, 33–34, 149).[35]

What do we know about Sarah Bradford's motivation for working on the book and for her continuing relationship with Tubman as they both aged? Unlike Sanborn and Cheney, Bradford was not part of an unconventional alternative intellectual culture centered in Massachusetts. She was brought up within the social reform milieu of evangelical Protestantism in the "burned over district" of western New York, an area where the influential revivalist preaching of Presbyterian Charles G. Finney had stirred up Christian anxiety and social reform energy in the late 1820s and early 1830s. Garrisonian abolitionism found many converts eager to do battle with the great sin of owning human property in this part of New York State.[36] As the sister of a professor at Auburn Theological Seminary, Bradford would have been well aware, at least in a general way, of Underground Railroad support activities going on in Auburn and the surrounding towns and cities in the 1850s, and her commitment to antislavery support work would have had clear religious motivation.

Yet Bradford was also a captive of the middle-class Anglo-American norms of female respectability of her era. As a proper single mother of three girls, author of children's literature, and head of a private school for young ladies, she was concerned about her own reputation when she acted as Tubman's public biographer. Even as early as 1869 her voice sounds defensive about the project of publicizing a black heroine's life to a largely white audience: "There are those who will sneer, there are those who have already done so, at this quixotic attempt to make a heroine of a black woman, and a slave; but it may possibly be that there are some natures, though concealed under fairer skins, who have not the capacity to comprehend such general and self-sacrificing devotion to the cause of others as that here delineated, and therefore they resort to scorn and ridicule, in order to throw discredit upon the whole story" (Bradford, 1869, 3).[37] The "lady bountiful" role Bradford played in Tubman's life in later years was part of the cultural complex of Victorian female respectability, only temporarily undermined by the religiously motivated desire to end national complicity with the sin of slaveholding.

Bradford has rightly been taken to task for many failings as a writer and biographer. Knowing something of Bradford's own history as Tubman's accidental biographer and later self-appointed protector, we are in a good position to make critical use of the valuable oral historical material captured in her 1868 interviews. The Bradford/Tubman texts remain among the most important repositories of Tubman's storytelling performance. Especially valuable are those produced in 1868–69, when Tubman's memories of her slavery years and antislavery heroism were freshest—and when Bradford's editorial interference was minimal.

LATER BIOGRAPHICAL INTERVIEWS

After 1886, writers of biographical magazine and newspaper articles tended to use Bradford heavily, even when they also interviewed the elderly Tubman.[38] Several of these later writers were younger-generation relatives of her longstanding antislavery friends: Frank Drake was the journalist husband of Emily Hopkins Drake, Bradford's niece; Anne Fitzhugh Miller was the granddaughter of Gerrit Smith and the daughter of suffragist Elizabeth Smith Miller;[39] and Samuel Hopkins Adams was a grandson of Bradford's brother Samuel Hopkins. Emma Paddock Telford was an Auburn neighbor who wrote more than one biographical sketch and who was also an author of cookbooks. References in several unsigned stories in the Auburn newspapers also imply a writer who was very familiar with Tubman's history—perhaps through personal acquaintance as well as through reading their own files of clippings.

A very few writers who did not already have a strong history of acquaintance with Tubman collected a bit of new material or new detail about old stories in her later years. For example, Rosa Belle Holt, who published "A Heroine in Ebony" in the *Chatuaquan* of July 1886, came to Auburn as the guest of someone who knew Tubman well—probably Eliza Wright Osborne—and described the encounter admiringly: "It has been my pleasure to have three long talks with Harriet Tubman. The last one was during the past month, when my hostess invited her to spend the day with us. Modest and quiet in demeanor, a stranger would never guess what depths there are in her nature" (Holt, 1886, 461).[40] During Holt's visit, Tubman retold some of her childhood stories, including the one about the head injury. Holt also gathered two versions of the story of Tubman's call from God.[41] "She said: 'Long ago when the Lord told me to go free my people I said, "No, Lord! I can't go—don't ask me." But he came another time. I saw him just as plain. Then I said again, "Lord, go away—get some better educated person—get a person with more culture than I have; go away, Lord." But he came back a third time, and speaks to me just as he did to Moses, and he says, "Harriet, I wants you." And I knew then I must do what he bid me. Now do you suppose he wanted me to do this just for a day, or a week? No! The Lord who told me to take care of my people

meant me to do it just so long as I live, and so I do what he told me to'"
(Holt, 1886).

The narrative produced by Holt gives a glimpse of Tubman's long-ago
spiritual experience, closely patterned on the Old Testament story of the
Lord's call to Moses to take up the mantle of leadership. But even more
intriguing is the context in which this story of the call was gathered. Holt
introduces the story by saying that Tubman frequently had to deal with
someone who "remonstrates with her for giving to others what has been
sent to supply her own needs" (probably Eliza Wright Osborne or Sarah
Bradford). On "a recent occasion in reply to such a remark," Tubman
retold the story of her call. Holt captured a valuable glimpse of Tubman
using one of her classic autobiographical mini-narratives to deflect well-
meaning but intrusive advice on how to live her life.

Another later interviewer was Lillie Buffum Chace Wyman, whose
sketch appeared in the *New England Magazine* in March 1896. Wyman
was the daughter of notable Quaker abolitionists and had asked Eliza
Wright Osborne to interview Tubman for her several years before, when
she was writing a book on women's participation in the antislavery movement.[42] She wrote that she had "once heard Harriet describe" the departure of John Brown from Tubman's house in St. Catharines, indicating
at least one other meeting in the past.[43] Though the sketch is heavily indebted to Bradford as well as several other published sources, Wyman did
capture a nice detail from the Underground Railroad years that either had
eluded Bradford or perhaps was censored out of "delicacy": "A toothache
tormented her during one of her journeys. She took a stone or bit or iron
and knocked the offending tooth out of her mouth (Wyman, 1896, 113).

One of Tubman's later interviewers wrote from an African American
organizational perspective.[44] Robert Taylor, Tuskegee Institute's financial
agent, was also involved in Tubman's John Brown Hall project and candidly described his fund-raising goal in the preface to *Harriet Tubman:
The Heroine in Ebony*: "Some weeks ago I sent out an appeal through
several colored newspapers, with the hope that this amount would be
raised; but at this writing only seventy-seven dollars have been sent in.
The net proceeds from the sale of this sketch will be applied on this mortgage; and it is earnestly hoped that each one in whose hands this falls
will not only read it, but will make himself or herself a missionary for the
cause of Harriet Tubman" (R. W. Taylor, 1901, 4).[45] Taylor mentioned two
specific details that are not in Bradford, probably from stories Tubman
told to him.[46] Otherwise, his sketch relied on Bradford's information. It

emphasizes the cruelty of her treatment in slavery, the brilliance of her planning and execution of rescues, and the importance of her activism on behalf of her people.

The only other sketch clearly based on interviews that was not mediated by a white writer was that of the British West Indian James B. Clarke. A Cornell student who was very much involved in organizing against American racism, Clarke visited Tubman in the Harriet Tubman Home in the company of Anne Fitzhugh Miller.[47] Although Clarke's article does not contain any new stories from her career as Underground Railroad heroine and Civil War scout, it is a fascinating and valuable depiction of her sociability and political consciousness in the waning years of her life, particularly valuable because it is not mediated by the perspective of a white American writer.

NEW SOURCES OF STORIES IN THE TWENTIETH CENTURY

After Harriet Tubman's death, very little new material based on her storytelling was published until Conrad's major biography in 1943. Earl Conrad (Earl Cohen) was a journalist and author who had grown up in Auburn and then moved to New York City in 1934, where he was drawn into labor activism. Like many other politically progressive writers of this time, he was involved in the Federal Writers Project for a while. When he decided upon doing a biography of Tubman in the late 1930s, as he told Harkless Bowley, Tubman's grandnephew, it was because he was looking for just the right black history subject[48]: "For a long while I organized truckdrivers on the waterfront; and it was here that I established my first contacts with Negroes: I found that most of the people who interested me were the Negro porters and truckdrivers, and I found myself calling upon them in Harlem. . . . In my spare time I studied Negro history, and I took a class or two in Harlem from a Negro teacher, and then, at one time, when my health was weakening from too much running about I decided to resume writing—but this time on a Negro subject. I looked over the various Negro figures and I came to the conclusion that Harriet was the greatest and the one about whom, for her stature, the least was known. I believed that through presenting Harriet I could show also the contribution of the Negro people—and I am of course in the middle of that now" (Conrad, 1940c).

Conrad was a scrupulous nonacademic historian. His journalism training led him to check his facts thoroughly and to create a dramatic storyline
that would impress his version of Tubman indelibly on the imaginations
of his readers. A thoroughgoing social democrat who wanted history to
belong to "the people," he donated his substantial collection of documents
and copies of his research correspondence to the Schomburg black history
collection at the Harlem branch of the New York Public Library. It took
many months to find a publisher for *General Harriet Tubman* because of
its overtly radical politics. The publisher that finally took it was the black-
owned Associated Publishers of Washington, D.C.[49]

Conrad's research process in 1939–1941 is very well documented in his
correspondence in the Conrad/Tubman collection at the Schomburg. He
was not able to travel much, beyond two research visits to Auburn, where
he read through old newspapers and did several interviews. But he wrote
many letters to libraries and to individuals he believed would have information about Tubman. Realizing the importance of supplementing the
fragmentary documentary record with oral historical interviews and correspondence with elderly kin and associates of Tubman, he also put advertisements in the African American press, seeking informants. Once he
had found one Tubman descendant willing to talk with him, he was introduced to several others. Ultimately he located and either interviewed or
received written testimony from several dozen relatives and acquaintances.

Conrad's own politics clearly influenced the questions he asked his informants. He openly discussed his political views when asked about himself by his correspondents, including Harkless Bowley, Alice Brickler, and
Carrie Chapman Catt, the former national leader of NAWSA. Looking
for ways of combating racism among whites and for increasing racial pride
among blacks in the context of the Great Depression, Conrad wanted to
paint the portrait of a militant black heroine, in the worker-hero 1930s
style of socialist realist painting. He was highly struck by Tubman's military service and made this a central concern in his research and writing—
and he was highly skeptical about her spirituality, perhaps viewing religion
from a broadly socialist perspective as a force responsible for the contain-
ment of popular rebellion against political oppression.[50]

Three informants who contributed new stories or distinct variations of
classic stories spoke from African American perspectives: Alice Brickler,
Harkless Bowley, and Florence Carter.[51] Though their testimony should
be used cautiously on matters of fact, where memory is notoriously un-
reliable, all three made significant contributions to our understanding of

Tubman's life, particularly within the contexts of family and church in Auburn. Helen Woodruff Tatlock, daughter of a white Auburn family friendly to Tubman, provided some new details for other classic stories (including the escape story), as well as interesting memories of the elderly Tubman from the perspective of a white child and later a young woman.[52]

Brickler and Bowley were key informants for Conrad. They provided several fascinating stories—both their own stories about interacting with Tubman and remembered stories she had told them or their parents. Obviously their own memories of experiences with her are of tremendous value for the biographer. We need to be more cautious, however, about their memories of her life stories, some of which were conveyed to them secondhand through older relatives. A good example is Alice Brickler's false memory of a "happy ending" to the gold swindle story probably conveyed to her by her mother (see part 3, "Stories and Sayings").

Alice Lucas Brickler, Tubman's grandniece, was living with her husband and two children in the university town of Wilberforce, Ohio, when a friend sent her Conrad's published request for information on Tubman. She began by sending Conrad suggestions for people to interview along with newspaper clippings that might interest him. Soon she began to reminisce about Tubman and wrote a series of thoughtful, occasionally expansive and even somewhat personal letters, including news of her husband and children. (One has the impression that she may have been very interested in writing herself and seized upon the opportunity Conrad offered to correspond with an author from New York.) Brickler was aware of the Bradford book—though she reported that their family's copies had long ago been destroyed in a fire. She was also clearly diffident about the accuracy of her memory: "As you must know," she wrote, "many of Aunt Harriet's interesting stories were never written down but were told. . . . I can close my eyes now and feel again the thrills of adventure & terror as my mother used to tell me the stories of Aunt Harriet. I can get the sensation, parts of the stories, but most of the plots have left me with my girlhood" (Brickler, 1939a).

Yet Brickler argued her own interpretation of the meaning of Tubman's spiritual life to Conrad, in answer to one of his questions: "I may be wrong but I believe that every age, every country and every race, especially during the darkest history, has had its unusual Souls who were in touch with some mysterious central originating Force, a comprehensive stupendous Unity for which we have no adequate name. Aunt Harriet was one of those unusual Souls. Her religion, her dreams or visions were so bound together that nobody, and I certainly should not attempt it, could separate them. Aunt Harriet was a member of an oppressed race. She had the ruggedness and common sense of one whose very existence depended upon wits. In her, one found a stubborn tenacity of purpose. Her real strength was in the inspiration of the mystic as well as sagacity" (Brickler, 1940b).[53]

Through Brickler Conrad was able to contact Harkless Bowley, then eighty-one years old and living with a son in Baltimore. Bowley responded enthusiastically to Conrad's inquiries with a series of letters, retelling some of Tubman's stories spontaneously and offering other information in answer to Conrad's later specific questions. He had photos and newspaper clippings and mentioned a family Bible that had been lost or misplaced, but he did not seem to know about the Bradford book until he wrote to Katie Stewart Northrup, another Tubman sibling descendant, in Philadelphia to tell her about Conrad's project. He then reported, "Katie said there was a book already out in Auburn" (H. Bowley, 1940b). Bowley acknowledged difficulty remembering details: "There is so many things she told me which might be helpful to you if I could think of them it has been so long now and I am forgetful now" (H. Bowley, 1939b).

IDENTIFYING TUBMAN'S OWN POLITICAL AND SOCIAL AGENDA

In order to be confident of the differences between the collaborator's contributions to the storytelling texts and Tubman's own words, we also need to look carefully for evidence of her own political and social agenda. Though relatively few of her explicit political comments are preserved in the least mediated kinds of sources, we can make careful use of these to construct a probable portrait of Tubman as a political and social thinker and activist.

As we noted in reviewing her life history in part 1, she condemned slavery in her earliest surviving dictated testimonial (Tubman, 1856), and throughout her life she spoke of slavery as an evil. Along with Frederick Douglass and many others, she opposed emigration schemes and supported full civil rights for former slaves after emancipation. Her brief association with John Brown suggests that she recognized that an armed uprising might be necessary to end the institution of slavery. Unlike many Garrisonian abolitionists with whom she worked, she did not interpret the Christian message as requiring "nonresistance" or pacifism. Her enthusiastic participation in the Union Army's guerilla warfare in the South (in partnership with the firebrand Colonel Montgomery) makes it unlikely that she questioned the justice of the destruction of Confederate property in such campaigns—unlike her friend Thomas W. Higginson, who criticized Montgomery for this policy. She had working associations with both Frederick Douglass and Martin Delany, two antebellum race leaders who were ultimately divided on many issues of race politics.[54]

It is important to bear in mind the fact that most of the Tubman storytelling texts reflect a post-1860 perspective on her earlier experience with slavery. Literary critics who have studied the slave narrative genre have noted significant differences between the "classic" antebellum narratives produced prior to the Civil War with the aid of antislavery editors and the various narratives produced after the war—many of which were more thoroughly self-authored by the former slave. Although the horrors of slavery are presented as the "norm" in the politicized antebellum genre, a more complex portrait of life in a slave culture emerges after emancipation. William L. Andrews has pointed out that postwar ex-slave autobiographers frequently "take pride in having endured slavery without having lost their sense of worth or purpose and without having given in to the despair that the antebellum narrator pictures as the lot of so many who languished in slavery."[55] To the extent that the Tubman storytelling texts can be assimilated into the slave narrative genre, then, they are especially relevant to the ongoing recovery of the postwar perspectives of former slaves.

After the war, Bradford quoted Tubman as saying that the cruelty of slave owners was simply the result of their conditioning in Southern culture—perhaps she "forgave" a sin whose evil was not fully understood by those who committed it.[56] In the same period, she fought back against racial discrimination in public transportation in the North, both physically resisting expulsion from the railroad car in New Jersey and pursuing the matter into the courts, and repeatedly claimed her own rights as a veteran of army service. She identified herself as allied with women's rights initiatives as early as 1860. After the Combahee River expedition, she announced her plan to wear bloomers on future scouting expeditions. She told her life story in women's organizational venues,[57] both predominantly white and predominantly black, over the remainder of her life, perhaps in part because she was aware of the need of nineteenth-century women for what twentieth-century feminism has called "role models."

IDENTIFYING "CORE STORIES"
WITHIN MEDIATED TEXTS

One key method for deciphering Tubman's own perspective within the interview-based biographical texts is to attend especially closely to the embedded mini-narratives I call her "core stories," in which she not only plays a role as a character but also controls the narrative point of view. Although the larger chronological superstructure and editorial commentary is clearly supplied by the bookish biographers (Cheney, Sanborn, Bradford, and others), the individual mini-narrative delivered orally is Tubman's own creation. Like a joke or folktale, a spoken core story is artfully structured to be entertaining, with an economical setup and sequence of events that build inexorably to a satisfying conclusion. The collaborating writer can choose different words but cannot easily tamper with the basic structure lest the story lose its point and entertainment value entirely—just as a joke told without its punch line is disappointing and meaningless. Moreover, an artfully structured spoken mini-narrative can contain details that may not be fully understood by the recording collaborator and therefore can evade censorship by that person. The self-contained brief mini-narratives stand out like gleaming nuggets of wit and wisdom in the biographies. Somewhat like the hymns she sang during her rescues, the core stories potentially can convey coded meanings to those "in the know." At any rate they are an excellent place to look for possibly "subversive" and relatively authentic expressions of Tubman's own ideas, values, worldview, and self-concept (if not her exact language).

She had a favorite group of stories of resistance to persecution and of valiant adventure, told repeatedly over the years. The core story texts that I have gathered together in part 3, "Stories and Sayings," include many favorites or classics from the public repertoire, but there are also some that were recorded only in more private interview settings. Even these more private core story texts should be read with an awareness of their limitations as a medium for representing the subjectivity or inner life of the historical woman, however. The former slave who became a successful Underground Railroad operative and Civil War spy and scout was deeply cautious, well aware throughout her life of the potential dangers of revealing too much about her private feelings to the wrong person. Just as we are aware of at least two kinds of potential censorship by the writer—intentional "protective" changes or omissions and unintentional distortions resulting from cultural "incompetence"—we must be prepared to acknowledge the possibility of both intentional and unconscious kinds of self-censorship on the side of the storyteller.

THE QUESTION OF SILENCES IN THE TEXTS

Recent biographers of Sojourner Truth have questioned what may lie behind certain silences in the mediated autobiographical *Narrative of Sojourner Truth* (1850). Olive Gilbert, the white woman with whom Truth collaborated on the narrative, explicitly said that it was Truth's own decision to censor certain material: "There are some hard things that crossed Isabella's (Sojourner Truth's) life while in slavery, that she has no desire to publish, for various reasons. First, because the parties from whose hands she suffered them have rendered up their account to a higher tribunal, and their innocent friends alone are living, to have their feelings injured by the recital; secondly, because they are not all for the public ear, from their very nature" (Titus and Gilbert, 1991, 82). Historian Nell Irvin Painter has challenged historians of slavery to investigate the complexity of patriarchal familial relationships within "families" that included both owners and the enslaved.[58] As Painter argues, "Historians already realize that including enslaved workers as part of the American working classes recasts the labor history of the United States; similarly, envisioning slaves as people who developed psychologically sheds new light on the culture of violence in which they matured" (Painter, 1991, 131).[59] It is a "radical strategy to hear the imposed silences" of the texts as called for by John Sekora. I return to Painter's challenge later, when interpreting some of Tubman's stories of childhood.

Darlene Clark Hine has argued, influentially, "Rape and the threat of rape influenced the development of a culture of dissemblance among Black women. By dissemblance I mean the behavior and attitudes of Black women that created the appearance of openness and disclosure but actually shielded the truth of their inner lives and selves from their oppressors. . . . A secret, undisclosed persona allowed the individual Black woman to function, to work effectively as a domestic in white households, to bear and rear children, to endure the frustration-born violence of frequently under- or unemployed mates, to support churches, to found institutions, and to engage in social service activities, all while living within a clearly hostile white, patriarchal, middle-class America" (Hine, 1989, 912, 916).

When we attempt to look for Tubman's own point of view in the mediated texts, Hine's insight about a "culture of dissemblance" arising specifically from African American women's vulnerable social, economic, and
physical situations in the nineteenth century should be on our minds.
The conventions of nineteenth-century autobiographical narrative for
public figures in general, and women in particular, guaranteed silences on
topics related to sexuality anyway, of course. But if we contrast the classic
autobiographical stories told repeatedly by Tubman with the fuller life
history we glimpse in the contemporary documents, we do become aware
of many important silences related not only to sexuality, but also to her
closest family relationships. Beyond the story of her husband's betrayal
and her own struggle with jealousy, she tells us almost nothing about her
private emotional life. She did not speak of her private reactions to the
murder of John Tubman. She did not comment on her childlessness, discuss the kidnapping of her niece, give any indication of her reasons for
marrying Nelson Davis, or give a retrospective account of what happened
in the gold swindle scheme.

"WEARING THE MASK"

Concealment of the inner self—"wearing the mask"—was a behavioral
skill developed by both men and women in slavery. It was also a rhetorical
feature developed by the former-slave narrator in slave narrative literature.
Literary critic Keith Byerman (1982) has highlighted "the use of deceit
and the trickster motif as thematic, stylistic, and structural elements" in
such texts. The slave's use of deceit and trickery is shown to be justified by
the "moral dishonesty" of the slave owner. Writing for a Northern white
audience, the former-slave narrator must seem to accommodate the values
of that audience: "religious piety, moral conventions (such as honesty,
frankness, and chastity), political democracy, rationality, some racial bias,
and economic individualism." But as Byerman argues, "the accommodation is a form of masking" because "the narrators' values are much closer
to those of Afro-American culture" as created in the Southern world of
slavery. This folkloristic approach to the "wearing of the mask" in life and
in literary texts by the former slave in the North is particularly helpful for
explaining the prominence of the trickster elements in many of Tubman's
core story texts. Steeped in narrative models of Southern African American
oral culture, she would have known not just the styles and structures of

biblical stories, as well as Methodist conversion testimonials and hymns, but also many entertaining folkloric forms, such as trickster tales.[60] In this narrative tradition, the withholding of information would have been understood by the listener as part of a clever strategy to outwit the antagonist.

Like some of the fugitive narrators discussed by Byerman, Tubman probably experienced her freedom in the North at least initially as a kind of life in exile from home. Certainly in the early prewar years in the North, while still legally a fugitive, she would have been highly alert to the possibility of betrayal in every interaction. The wariness would have extended even to black associates she did not know well, since the reward-punishment system of slavery corrupted some slaves into betraying those who expressed resistance. Tubman had had experience with this kind of betrayal as an Underground Railroad conductor. Then she chose to live in Auburn, in an environment utterly different from that in which she was raised. Her close associates were primarily antislavery activists or at least sympathizers before the war, yet these middle-class Northern whites were still culturally foreign, and in all probability even her closest Northern friends were never entirely trusted, never fully allowed to see behind "the mask."

In the light of Nell Painter's discussion of the psychodynamics of childhood in patriarchal slave-owning families, it makes sense to look more closely at some of Tubman's personal relationships with whites in the North. Perhaps some of the surrogate family relationships she developed with her political allies (including her three major biographers) resonated psychologically against her Southern extended-family upbringing. In many letters, diary entries, and other documents included in this book, we glimpse these relationships from the viewpoint of members of the Wright, Osborne, Garrison, Seward, and Hopkins/Bradford families. In this context we observe outward behavior suggestive of the role of the sometimes willful surrogate child who is indulgently patronized by affectionate (but condescending) surrogate parents. This role-playing comes across particularly strongly in the 1901 additions Bradford made to the biography. Tubman is even quoted as referring to the Hopkins clan as "my family" in a story about how she responded when introduced to the new husband of one of Bradford's daughters. "He told her how glad he was to see her, as he had heard so much about her. She made one of her humble courtesies, and said: 'I'm pleased to see you, sir; it's the first time I've had the pleasure making your acquaintance since you was adopted into my family'" (Bradford, 1901, 146). Did Tubman unconsciously cast herself in such a role—or was she merely playing along with a script devised by the white family?

We also see behavior that seems to suggest strong emotional attachment to many members of these families. For example, Bradford gives us in 1886 an account meant to be touching of Tubman's attendance at William Seward's funeral. "The great man lay in his coffin. Friends, children, and admirers were gathered there. . . . Just before the coffin was to be closed, a woman black as night stole quietly in, and laying a wreath of field flowers *on his feet*, as quietly glided out again. This was the simple tribute of our sable friend, and her last token of love and gratitude to her kind benefactor. I think he would have said, 'This woman hath done more than ye all'" (Bradford, 1886, 89–90). We also have accounts of her weeping at the funerals of Theodore Pomeroy (Telford, n.d.) and Mrs. Samuel Hopkins (S. H. Adams, 1989, 278), and of her humoring and chiding the Hopkins grandchildren (S. H. Adams, 1989). Similarly, in the Wright/Garrison/Osborne family references to Tubman, there are many instances in which she is portrayed in surrogate family behavior: disappointed to miss the visit of one of the adult children to Auburn, hugely delighted to be remembered with a visit, warmly embracing the younger generation when she meets them, and so on. How should we "read" such surrogate family behavior? Should we understand her as a matter of course to be "wearing the mask" in such behavior in such relationships, to be part of the "culture of dissemblance" identified by Hines? Or should we understand her to be (perhaps without full consciousness of the fact) in the grip of the psychodynamics of her childhood, still anxiously needing close relationships to white familial authority figures—as Nell Painter might see it? Of course, both interpretations may have some degree of validity—perhaps there was both "real" deep-seated emotional attachment as well as many less-than-candid displays of the excessive personal loyalty that was required of the black surrogate child by the racial etiquette of even the progressive Northern household in the postwar years.

The behavior and expressed attitudes of some of her closest white antislavery associates also suggest conflicting feelings—though the source of their difficulties was not a complex mixed-race childhood upbringing. For the Northerners, there was a sharp dissonance between the religiously based emphasis on the equality of all souls before God and the white person's actual experience of "difference"—by color, regional and ethnic culture, and social class—when socializing with the former slave. Such a dissonance evidently made many white antislavery Northerners personally uncomfortable even in the prewar period, but certainly so after the war as the perception of Reconstruction's "failures" permeated the political discourse in the North and the new scientific racism gained cultural currency. Several of Tubman's long-term white associates, including Bradford, felt themselves to be playing a "surrogate parent" role toward Tubman (and through her constant charitable activities, they also played that role toward other impoverished survivors of slavery). For these white Northerners, Tubman's lifelong poverty may very well have felt like a reproach to themselves—a reproach to which some reacted by blaming her for her "improvidence." Some of the stories her associates told about Tubman suggest tension around money issues in particular. They shed a strong light on the context within which her performances of her own core stories took place.

RACE AND RELATIONSHIPS IN THE NORTH

A consciousness of Tubman's cultural and racial "otherness" is present in her white collaborators' perspectives on her life, though this consciousness varied somewhat according to the religious ideology and political perspective of the individual and the era. In part her "otherness" was a matter of the cultural distance between the Northerners and the Maryland native, between the formally educated intellectual and the informally educated former field hand. Her spiritualistic religiosity was also a major element in the equation. Even those who admired and tried to understand her apparent ability to make direct contact with God found this practice "foreign." Samuel Hopkins, church historian and professor at Auburn Theological Seminary, spoke of her story as offering an "example . . . to show what a lofty and martyr spirit may accomplish, struggling against overwhelming obstacles" (S. M. Hopkins, 1886). In using the term "martyr spirit" and in likening her to the French Catholic mystic peasant Joan of Arc, Hopkins reveals how utterly mysterious her spirituality was to him. In a similar vein, an editorial writer for an Auburn newspaper, evidently someone who knew Tubman personally, wrote, "on the matter of self-sacrifice it may be said that she was almost a fanatic" ("To a Most Heroic Negress," 1914). However honorifically intended, this emphasis on her "saintly" simplicity was an expression of wonder at her difference from ordinary human beings.

But it was her African ancestry (as signified by her skin color) that rendered her most "foreign" to her white antislavery associates. Those who recorded private reactions in the 1850s always mentioned her dark skin color—perhaps because they were surprised to meet a fugitive slave speaker who was not "mulatto," or of evidently mixed racial ancestry. "She is coal black," wrote Lucy Osgood to Lydia Maria Child (1859); "She is jet black and cannot read or write, only talk, besides acting," Thomas W. Higginson told his mother (1859); "She is thoroughly Negro, and very plain," said Ednah Cheney (1865). Remembering her introduction to antislavery Bostonians in the 1850s, William Lloyd Garrison II later described her as "the little woman of black complexion and African stamp" and admiringly spoke of the (momentary) equality of "the flower of Massachusetts culture" (Wendell Phillips) and "the product of the slave whip and the plantation" (W. L. Garrison, 1897b, April 13). Interestingly, Helen Woodruff Tatlock, who grew up as a white child when Jim Crow attitudes were becoming normalized in Auburn, described Tubman's physical appearance in very positive terms (though still racially "other") as "a magnificent looking woman, true African, with a broad nose, very black, and of medium height" (Tatlock, 1939a).

The emphasis her associates placed on her African "blood" could enhance antislavery arguments, of course. If someone so evidently gifted with courage and other noble qualities had "not a drop of white blood in her veins" (as Sanborn asserted in 1863), this was evidence that the brutalizing institution of slavery had not been able to degrade (entirely) a "naturally" noble people. In this spirit, Samuel Miles Hopkins gave a "noble savage" reading of the meaning of her African ancestry: "She has all the characteristics of the pure African race strongly marked upon her, though from which one of the various tribes that once fed the Barracoons, on the Guinea coast, she derived her indomitable courage and her passionate love of freedom I know not; perhaps from the Fellatas, in whom these traits were predominant" (Bradford, 1886).

Still, white Northerners were all influenced to one degree or another by a complex system of taboos governing social interaction between the races (and between social "superiors" and "inferiors" of other kinds as well). As early as 1865, Ednah Cheney commented upon how Tubman reacted to the inconsistent and unpredictable rules of racial separation encountered in the North: " She is not sensitive to indignities to her color in her own person; but knows and claims her rights. She will eat at your table if she sees you really desire it; but she goes willingly to the kitchen" (Cheney, 1865).[61] Sarah Bradford, who regarded herself as one of Tubman's reliable friends and defenders, was also clearly influenced by the post-Reconstruction national dialogue on race, which from today's vantage point obviously "blames the victim." The following passage from the revised biography of

1886 represents Bradford's confused effort to elevate her "sable heroine" in the esteem of Northern readers who were clearly presumed to have white supremacist views:

> I have often heard it said by Southern people that "niggers had no feeling; they did not care when their children were taken from them." I have seen enough of them to know that their love for their offspring is quite equal to that of the "superior race," and it is enough to hear the tale of Harriet's endurance and self-sacrifice to rescue her brothers and sisters, to convince one that a heart, truer and more loving than that of many a white woman, dwelt in her bosom. I am quite willing to acknowledge that she was almost an anomaly among her people, but I have known many of her family, and so far as I can judge they all seem to be peculiarly intelligent, upright and religious people, and to have a strong feeling of family affection. There may be many among the colored race like them; certainly all should not be judged by the idle, miserable darkies who have swarmed about Washington and other cities since the War. (Bradford, 1886, 68–69)[62]

Bradford also gives us a glimpse of the kind of inconsistent enforcement of racial separation taboos that Tubman would have encountered increasingly as the idealism of Reconstruction faded. In the 1901 edition of the biography, Bradford tells about Tubman's visit to the Hopkins/Bradford family at the Hopkins summerhouse on Owasco Lake: "It was after lunch, and my brother ordered a table to be set for her on the broad shaded piazza and waited on her himself, bringing her cups of tea and other good things, as if it were a pleasure and an honor to serve her. There is a quiet dignity about Harriet that makes her superior or indifferent to all surrounding circumstances; whether seated at the hospitable board of Gerrit Smith or any other white gentleman, as she often was, or sent to the kitchen, where the white domestics refused to eat with a 'nigger,' it was all the same to Harriet; she was never elated, or humiliated; she took everything as it came, making no comments or complaints. And so she sat quietly eating her lunch, and talking with us" (Bradford, 1901). Although Bradford says overtly that Tubman's "indifference" to being waited on by Samuel Hopkins, a "white gentleman," is an example of her "quiet dignity," her own language in describing the scene suggests that Bradford was unsettled by her brother's radical Christian disregard for racial and class hierarchy, his "bringing her cups of tea and other good things, *as if it were a pleasure and an honor to serve her*" (italics mine).

Even Franklin Sanborn, otherwise one of Tubman's most reliable associates for fifty years, thought about her in racial terms. He commented
casually in a letter to a friend when he first met her that she was a "thorough 'nigger'—but a striking person, and I esteem it an honor to know
her" (Sanborn, 1859c). He used more euphemistic language in his obituary
sketch but expressed his racial ideology just as clearly. There he described
her as being "as pure a Negress as could then be found in Maryland" and
judged her to be "the type of her race, loyal to the death, secretive as the
grave; but never with hatred in her heart for the worst oppressors. Mercy
and patience, those two qualities which the blacks display in excess,
accompanied with deceit and indifference in moral matters, were Harriet's
outstanding qualities, together with a courage and self-sacrifice that martyrs
and angels might envy" (Sanborn, 1913a). While he praises her for "mercy,"
"patience," "courage," and "self-sacrifice," he also speaks of "deceit and
indifference in moral matters" as race-related traits and judges Tubman to
be "the type of her race."

Of course, Sanborn and other white antislavery associates were well
aware that Tubman practiced "deceit" as a survival strategy, as an enslaved
worker, as a fugitive, and as a conductor of other fugitives. Some of them
expressed admiration for her playacting skills. For example, Thomas
Wentworth Higginson, describing the storytelling of one of the older
men in the regiment he commanded in the Sea Islands, revealed his sense
of Tubman as a skilled actress: "It was a narrative, dramatized to the last
degree, of his adventures in escaping from his master to the Union vessels;
and even I, who have heard the stories of Harriet Tubman, and such wonderful slave-comedians, never witnessed such a piece of acting."[63] The
storyteller displayed "a succession of tricks beyond Moliere, of acts of
caution, foresight, patient cunning, which were listened to with infinite
gusto and perfect comprehension by every listener. . . . Yet tomorrow
strangers will remark on the hopeless, impenetrable stupidity in the daylight faces of many of these very men, the solid mask under which Nature
has concealed all this wealth of mother-wit" (Higginson, 1862a).[64]

Because Sanborn had originally met Tubman in the context of the
secret John Brown conspiracy, he was highly aware that she "wore the
mask" of "simplicity" when necessary. When they met, "It was curious to
see the caution with which she received her visitor until she felt assured
that there was no mistake. One of her means of security was to carry with
her the daguerreotypes of her friends, and show them to each new person.
If they recognized the likeness, then it was all right" (Sanborn, 1863). Even

Ednah Cheney observed and commented upon Tubman's gifts as an actor: "She has needed disguise so often, that she seems to have command over her face, and can banish all expression from her features, and look so stupid that nobody would suspect her of knowing enough to be dangerous; but her eye flashes with intelligence and power when she is roused" (Cheney, 1865).

Despite their firsthand knowledge of her "trickster" abilities and history, Sanborn, Cheney, and others joined in a chorus of public testimony in the 1860s to Tubman's complete honesty and integrity—often linking this alleged "truthfulness" with her religious worldview. For example, Ednah Cheney quoted a "clergyman" who said "that [Tubman's] stories convinced you of their truth by their simplicity, as do the gospel narratives" (Cheney, 1865). Similarly, for the first Bradford biography Sanborn supplied a rather cautiously worded testimonial to Tubman's veracity, saying, "I never had reason to doubt the truth of what Harriet said in regard to her own career, for I found her singularly truthful,"[65] and adding that all the Concord literary luminaries to whom he had introduced her "admired and respected her, and nobody doubted the reality of her adventures. She was too *real* a person to be suspected." Gerrit Smith, who wrote three letters of reference for Tubman in the 1860s, put it this way—perhaps more wholeheartedly: "I am confident that she is not only truthful, but that she has a rare discernment, and a deep and sublime philanthropy" (1868). William Seward lavished praise on her in a similar vein: "I have known her long, and a nobler, higher spirit, or a truer, seldom dwells in the human form" (1868).

Tubman's associates worked hard to create this public image of her as a model truth teller, in part because they anticipated (and wished to defend her against) the racist assumption that as a former slave and now an impoverished black person, she could not be trusted. Some of her friends may also have convinced themselves that although she might readily deceive others in situations where she perceived danger, she was unlikely to feel the need for concealment with her trusted political allies. Cheney, for example, described Tubman as one who "has a very affectionate nature, and forms the strongest personal attachments. She has great simplicity of character" (Cheney, 1865). Sanborn's assessment in his obituary sketch of Tubman also emphasized what he took to be her lack of cunning in dealing with "her friends": "She was ignorant, partial—could never see any fault in her friends; if money was given her, she would give it away, often to the undeserving; her soul was generous, her judgment defective, but never perverse"(Sanborn, 1913a). Samuel Hopkins referred obliquely to the gold swindle events of 1873, events that were never mentioned by the protective Bradford: "Harriet's simplicity and ignorance have, in some cases been imposed upon, very signally in one instance in Auburn, a few years ago; but nobody who knows her has the slightest doubt of her perfect integrity" (S. M. Hopkins, 1886).

In the post-Reconstruction era, the memory of Tubman's resourceful playacting faded, and some of her white Northern associates clearly came to interpret the "simplicity" of her behavior not so much as a "mask" shaped by the institution of slavery but rather as her "nature." But this understanding of Tubman as a transparent truth teller whose naive "simplicity" was a guarantee of complete honesty was certainly not the whole truth.

THE STRUGGLE OVER
MONEY MANAGEMENT

Bradford gives us several stories that portray Tubman's behavior as a fundraiser for "her people" in a curiously ambivalent fashion. Such stories seem to express Bradford's fear that her protégée might be taking advantage of her surrogate family relationships with white associates to use donations and money earned from the Bradford book in ways disapproved of by Bradford. Why couldn't Tubman be as saving and thrifty in money matters, as "practical" as Bradford and other white Northerners were? Was it because she had a mind of her own about how resources should be distributed in an equitable way? Or was it that Tubman was an easy mark, a victim of the unworthy poor, the "idle, miserable darkies who have swarmed about Washington and other cities since the war"?

Friction and tension over Tubman's control of donations of money were evident within antislavery networks even in the Underground Railroad days, to judge from a story Bradford obtained about her from Oliver Johnson of the New York Anti-Slavery Society. The necessity of rescuing her parents in 1857 on very short notice had forced Tubman to put considerable pressure on her antislavery allies for funds, in a way that apparently produced discomfort on both sides. She resorted to a very forceful fundraising technique—very like a modern political movement's hunger strike or sit-in. Bradford's retelling of the story suggests that such techniques could have strained Tubman's relationship with her white antislavery supporters, at least temporarily: "When she received one of her intimations that the old people were in trouble, and it was time for her to go to them, she asked the Lord where she should go for the money. She was in some way, as she supposed, directed to the office of a certain gentleman in New York. When she left the house of her friends to go there, she said, 'I'm going to Mr. ——'s office, and I ain't going to leave there, and I ain't going to eat or drink till I get enough money to take me down after the old people.'" Bradford represents Tubman as stubborn and willful in her pursuit of the needed money—her lack of deference to Oliver Johnson, in whose office she had camped out, even brings her perilously close to "crossing the line" of racial/class etiquette:

> "What do you want, Harriet?" was the first greeting.
> "I want some money, sir."
> "You do? How much do you want?"
> "I want twenty dollars, sir."
> "*Twenty dollars!* Who told you to come here for twenty dollars?"
> "The Lord told me, sir."
> "Well, I guess the Lord's mistaken this time."
> "I guess he isn't, sir. Anyhow, I'm going to sit here till I get it."

The tension generated in Bradford and her presumed white reader is resolved when the narrator assures us that what could otherwise be understood as threatening stubbornness ("I'm going to sit here until I get it") must be read within the context of a "simple" Christian certainty of religious guidance ("The Lord told me so"). Bradford's narrator makes this religious certainty seem naive and Tubman herself unthreatening, and the story ends happily: "She does not know all that happened, for deep sleep fell upon her; but probably her story was whispered about, and she roused at last to find herself the happy possessor of sixty dollars, which had been raised among those who came into the office. She went on her way rejoicing, to bring her old parents from the land of bondage" (Bradford, 1869, 110–111). This naivete is reassuring to those who ultimately give her money within the story and presumably to those reading the Bradford book, who are also being asked to give her money. No, she could not be a clever deceiver merely pretending to sleep, as part of a conscious strategy to hold out until money is forthcoming. Rather, because she genuinely believes herself to be on a divinely guided mission to save her parents, she is an appropriate recipient of Christian charity.

A key feature of the story for the presumed audience of this text (and others by her associates on the same theme) is that Tubman was not "begging for herself." The idea recurs in the 1886 letter by Samuel Hopkins, where she is said to have "too much pride and too much faith to beg." The "deserving" poor are by definition either those who do not beg at all, or those who only beg in extreme necessity, as when the welfare of the immediate family is endangered. Several other stories told by Bradford represent Tubman as hating to call upon friends for money even when desperate to support her dependent household—including her aged parents. In one story of her postwar poverty, for example, Bradford emphasized Tubman's reluctance to ask for a loan of a quarter "at the house of one of her firm and fast friends," when her own household had been snowed in. The story causes Tubman to ask for the money four times, with tears in her eyes by the time she can finally bring herself to utter the words. Bradford calls it "one more little incident" showing "Harriet's extreme delicacy in asking anything for herself" (Bradford, 1869, 111–112).

Tubman's white friends, including Bradford, sent contradictory messages about the conditions under which they would make donations. On some occasions, even as early as in the immediate postwar years when Tubman was working to send money south as part of the freedmen's relief campaign, her antislavery friends expressed irritation with her relentless fund-raising for the former slaves and urged her (inconsistently) to "beg for herself" instead. Bradford gives us another story in which William Seward utters a sentiment of which Bradford clearly approved: "But though so timid for herself, she is bold enough when the wants of her race are concerned. Even now, while friends are trying to raise the means to publish this little book for her, she is going around with the greatest zeal and interest to raise a subscription for her Freedmen's Fair. She called on Hon. Wm. H. Seward, the other day, for a subscription to this object. He said 'Harriet, you have worked for others long enough. It is time you should think of yourself. If you ask for a donation for *yourself*, I will give it to you; but I will not help you to rob yourself for others" (Bradford, 1869, 112). Though Bradford's narrating voice does not say so directly, the implication is that Tubman's excessive "zeal" in soliciting funds for the fair was diverting charitable contributions that might otherwise be available to support the biography project. Ironically, Seward might have been persuaded to donate if the money were devoted to the project of paying off the mortgage loan owed to himself.

Bradford sometimes presents herself as generously going along with what she clearly regards as Tubman's extremely naive religious fantasy that "God would provide." For example, in the appendix to the 1901 edition, Bradford told two stories in which she played the role of "lady bountiful" to the improvident but pious Tubman. In each story, the punch line is Tubman's comment that she understood the gift Bradford sent as coming from God. In the longer story, Bradford represents herself as passing through Auburn by train and deciding on the spur of the moment to "drive out to see what were the needs of my colored friend, and to take her some supplies. On leaving, I said to her: 'If you will come out to the carriage, Harriet, there are some provisions for you.' She turned to one of her poor dependents and said: 'What did you say to me this morning? You said, "We hadn't got nothing to eat in the house," and what did I say to you? I said, "I've got a rich Father!"'" (Bradford, 1901, 139). On the surface this story points to the "admirable," if slightly comic, piety of Tubman. But it also shows Tubman displacing onto God a gratitude to which Bradford may have felt entitled as "lady bountiful." As a Christian herself, Bradford could hardly object, but she could retaliate by adopting a view of Tubman's religiosity as childishly unsophisticated, in comparison with her own.

The "poverty stories" Bradford told about Tubman can be read to suggest that each woman was unsatisfied with the way the other played her racialized class role in this "nadir" period of American racial politics. Bradford expected a personal gratitude she did not get from Tubman, but given her own self-concept as a Christian lady she was unable to express her own irritation with Tubman directly. Instead she drew an ambivalent and incoherent portrait of Tubman in these texts, as a Joan of Arc who was also a harmless religious "primitive," a slightly comic victim of her own improvidence, a person who could survive only because of the charity of her friends. Tubman, on her side, appears to have successfully avoided adopting a deferential attitude toward Bradford—whatever her undoubtedly complex feelings for her and other white women who played a similar "lady bountiful" role. This refusal of gratitude may express indirectly Tubman's critique of a clearly unjust distribution of economic, political, and social power in the post-Reconstruction North.[66] Certainly her own vision of a just society as embodied in her communal extended-family household in the North was radically different from that of her middle-class neighbors and friends, however dutiful in their church attendance and charitable activities. By giving credit for the "charity" of her better-off white associates to a cosmic force beyond their control, she was offering them a lesson about the limits of their own powers. The strong ideology of economic individualism in which they were raised, as well as the new scientific racism that developed in the postwar era to help justify economic exploitation of "darker races" and imperial expansion globally, made it unlikely that Tubman's Northern associates could fully understand or profit from this lesson.

READING THE CORE
STORIES FOR HARRIET
TUBMAN'S OWN PERSPECTIVE

STORIES OF CHILDHOOD

Many of the childhood stories collected and published by Cheney, Sanborn, and Bradford emphasize, in the manner of the classic abolitionist slave narrative, the heartless cruelty of the various white employers to whom Harriet Tubman was hired out and do not reveal much about her own family life or her private emotional world. However, a few stories captured later in her life by her white Auburn neighbor Emma Paddock Telford offer a less politicized, more intimate glimpse of her life as a playful, even mischievous, child.[1]

Tubman's earliest memory was of lying in a cradle, suddenly caught up "in the air" by "the young ladies in the big house where my mother worked." She pictured herself to Telford as enjoying caring for a baby brother a few years later, while her mother was working: "I used to be in a hurry for her to go, so as I could play the baby was a pig in a bag, and hold him up by the bottom of his dress. I had a nice frolic with that baby, swinging him all round, his feet in the dress and his little head and arms touching the floor, because I was too small to hold him higher. It was late nights before my mother got home, and when he'd get worrying I'd cut a fat chunk of pork and toast it on the coals and put it in his mouth. One night he went to sleep with that hanging out, and when my mother come home she thought I'd done kill[ed] him (Telford, n.d.). The story is a kind of joke, emphasizing her pride in herself for creating a pacifier and her success in getting the baby to sleep. The mother's shock when she got home and found the sleeping baby apparently "dead" is recorded, though not the consequences for the babysitter. Did Ritta Ross whip her for this, or was she so relieved that she overlooked the offense? The storyteller goes on, "I nursed that there baby till he was so big I couldn't tote him any more, and I got so mischievous about the house that they put me out to learn to be a weaver."

Even from the perspective of her old age, however, Tubman remembered the experience of being sent away from home to learn the trade of weaving as being traumatic. She conveyed vividly to Telford the embarrassment ("shame") she felt at being in domestic proximity to strange whites for the first time: "The man came after me riding horseback. I hadn't any clothes, but I was anxious to go, and the mistress made me a petticoat and the man took me up in front of him on the horse and off we went. When we got there, they was at the table eating supper. I'd never eat in the house where the white people was, and I was shamed to stand up and eat before them. The mistress asked me if I done want some milk to drink? But I was that shamed to drink before her, that I said, No, I never liked sweet milk no how. When the truth was I was as fond of milk as any young shoat. But all the time I was there I stuck to it, that I didn't drink sweet milk" (Telford, n.d.).

The story leaves us with more questions than it answers about Tubman's adult perspective on her childhood self, however. Did she see this "shame" as foolish in retrospect? Or might she have taken pride in looking back at her instinctive effort to resist psychological identification with the white family? Certainly the stubbornness with which her child self stuck to the lie reminds us of later instances of self-denial, in which she triumphed over her bodily appetites by sheer willpower. Her homesickness in the story is also revealing: "I used to sleep on the floor in front of the fireplace and there I'd lie and cry and cry. I used to think all the time, 'If I could only get home and get in my mother's bed!' And the funny part of that was, she never had a bed in her life. Nothing but a board box nailed up against the wall and straw laid on it. I stayed there two years" (Telford, n.d.). Her mother's body is remembered vividly as a symbol of home and safety.

A suggestive theme in several of the childhood stories is Tubman's strong dislike of indoor work under the supervision of the white woman of the house. According to Sanborn's version of the story of the weaver family, Ritta Ross's intervention when the child fell ill helped bring her back after two years from a place where she was desperately unhappy. However, it was actually the child who engineered her final escape from the weaver family, using the classic passive resistance technique of the otherwise disempowered: "Another attempt was made to teach her weaving, but she would not learn, for she hated her mistress, and did not want to live at home, as she would have done with a weaver, for it was the custom then to weave the cloth for the family, or a part of it, in the house" (Sanborn, 1863).

She resisted housework as well, and for the same reason, it would appear. The arbitrary cruelty of the white mistress is captured in Bradford's story of Miss Susan, who failed to instruct her young helper in how to do her work properly and then whipped her when the work failed to satisfy. Bradford also captured her story of attempting to flee punishment for stealing a lump of sugar by hiding for a week in a pigpen. The story confirms the ultimate power of the white family to punish and control childish resistance, but the storyteller's voice emerges after the ending with a slyly ironic comment, undermining the post-Reconstruction Southern view of slavery as a beneficent institution: "Now mind you, Missus, that wasn't the way on all of the plantations; there was good masters and misuses, as I've heard tell; but I didn't happen to come across them" (Bradford, 1901).

Ednah Cheney preserved a childhood story that emphasized Tubman's clever ability to protect herself, both from physical abuse and from the slaveholder's distortion of Christian religion. This is a good example of an autobiographical "trickster tale"—a story about Tubman's life that is modeled on an African American folktale genre: "When quite young she lived with a very pious mistress, but the slaveholder's religion did not prevent her from whipping the young girl for every slight or fancied fault. Araminta found that this was usually a morning exercise; so she prepared for it by putting on all the thick clothes she could procure to protect her skin. She made sufficient outcry, however, to convince her mistress that her blows had full effect; and in the afternoon she would take off her wrappings, and dress as well as she could. When invited into family prayers, she preferred to stay on the landing, and pray for herself; 'and I prayed to God,' she says, 'to make me strong and able to fight, and that's what I've always prayed for ever since'" (Cheney, 1865). [2]

Perhaps the most frequently retold story of Tubman's childhood is about how she received her head injury. She told the story to many people and routinely reassured them about the symptoms of her resulting disability. Underground Railroad historian Wilbur Siebert described to Earl Conrad how impressed he had been over fifty years earlier, hearing Tubman's account of this injury and its effects: "When she first began to talk, she said that as a girl of perhaps twelve years of age she had been sent to the store on an errand. In a quarrel between the storekeeper and another man, one of them had thrown a weight lying on the counter and it had hit her on the head and left a permanent dent. She had me feel it. This caused her at frequent intervals (say of half an hour or so) to lose consciousness for three or four minutes. She explained that her head would drop and she would become silent, but I was not to become alarmed, she would arouse and continue her talk without losing the thread of her conversation" (Siebert, 1940). Florence Carter told Conrad, "I often witnessed those sleeping fits she was seized with, and she had the strange power of knowing, in a good measure, what was going on even though you could hear her snoring as she slept. She could get up from one of those sleeps and tell you about what was going on" (F. L. Carter, 1939).

Contradictory variants and interpretations of the story of the accident appear in every major biographical sketch. Some say it was the master who threw the weight, and others say the overseer; some cast her as an innocent bystander, and others as a heroic participant in a conflict between a male slave and an enraged master. Her grandnephew Harkless Bowley understood that it was the accident and resulting disability that led to her later employment at heavy agricultural labor, but Sanford understood that she had already been hired out to do fieldwork when the accident occurred. Her twentieth-century biographers attempted to connect the head injury and the resulting disability to her later religious visions (F. C. Drake, 1907) or present it as a turning point in her consciousness of the cruelty of slavery, leading to her determination to escape (S. H. Adams, 1989)—despite the fact that she was probably about thirteen at the time of the injury and did not try to escape until she was nearly thirty. Drake implied that she took advantage of the injury to conceal her own sharp-witted competence thereafter from the whites: "The white people on the plantation thought she was half-witted—a theory she did not seek to disturb" (F. C. Drake, 1907). Although her listeners transmitted the details of the story in a variety of ways, they generally agreed that she was permanently changed by the event—damaged in her monetary value to her owners because of the disability she suffered after the head wound healed. Her memory of the way her owners talked about her after her injury was captured late in her life: "She don't worth the salt that seasons her grub" (R. W. Taylor, 1901, 7–8).

In the version of the head injury story she told to Telford, she casts herself neither as the pathetic victim (à la Bradford) nor as the heroic resistance fighter (à la Drake). Instead she offers some unusually gritty detail about her daily life experience when hired out as a temporary worker to "the worst man in the neighborhood" and about her physical suffering as a result of the head blow: "My hair had never been combed and it stood out like a bushel basket, and when I'd get through eating I'd wipe the grease off my fingers on my hair. And I expect that there hair saved my life. One night I went out with the cook to the store to get some things for the house. I had a shoulder shawl of the mistress's over my head, and when I got to the store I was shamed to go in, and [I saw] the overseer raising up his arm to throw an iron weight at one of the slaves and that was the last I knew. That weight struck me in the head and broke my skull and cut a piece of that shawl clean off and drove it into my head. They carried me to the house all bleeding and fainting. I had no bed, no place to lie down on at all, and they lay me on the seat of the loom, and I stayed there all that day and next, and the next day I went to work again and there I worked with the blood and sweat rolling down my face till I couldn't see" (Telford, n.d.).

This story, like the other one about "shame" recorded by Telford, suggests her strong desire to preserve her dignity and integrity in situations where her power to do so was limited. In this case, the adolescent Tubman's embarrassment at her unkempt appearance, with hair that "had never been combed," keeps her in the doorway of the store, just as the overseer is throwing an iron weight at one of the male slaves. The adult Tubman who is reminiscing about this incident seems to be commenting ironically on the fact that the deprivation she experienced had a providential effect—the thickly matted ungroomed hair under the hand-me-down shawl cushioned the blow sufficiently to save her life. Despite the matter-of-fact tone of the retelling, the anger of the storyteller emerges in the details as she contemplates the unfeeling treatment of her child self: the fact that she was deposited on "the seat of the loom" for two days, before being sent back to work, and the fact that she was made to work while still bleeding.

This is a good moment to return to the question raised by Nell Painter about what kinds of abuse by the powerful might be concealed by "silences" in the accounts of childhood later told by the relatively powerless.[3] We should be alert to the possibility of sexual abuse by a member of the slaveholding family in particular, given the nearly absolute power conveyed by the system of chattel slavery in Southern states. Is this kind of abuse likely to have been a "family secret" in Tubman's early life? Of course, no definitive answer is possible, and there are certainly large gaps in her history as a young woman. In my own view, however, sexual abuse by the

white master, or even by an overseer or surrogate master when she was
hired out, is unlikely. She had two loving parents on the scene, each with
a certain degree of power over their children's lives. She lived with one or
both parents, generally in close proximity to her fiercely protective mother,
until she was about twenty-four years old, at which time she married a
free man of color. Her disability, her assignment as an adolescent to work
as a field hand, including assisting her father in lumbering work—all these
may have provided measures of protection against sexual predation.[4] Those
whose work as house servants put them in a domestic setting in daily close
proximity to the white slaveholding family members were much more
likely to be vulnerable to such exploitation.

Yet Tubman was certainly emotionally affected by the physical abuse she
endured at the hands of those to whom she was hired out in childhood, as
this story of the head injury told to Telford makes clear. Bradford tells us
that she had compassion for those raised in a culture of violence (see the
"Twelve Gates to the Celestial City" conversation in part 3, "Stories and
Sayings"). At the same time she clearly knew she had been scarred by her
childhood in slavery. Beyond the physical lash marks on her neck and
back that she often displayed as evidence of slavery's evil, there was the
damage to her sense of trust. As she testified in Canada just a few years
after her escape, "I grew up like a neglected weed,—ignorant of liberty,
having no experience of it. Then I was not happy or contented, every time
I saw a white man I was afraid of being carried away."[5] The Brodess family may not have used the whip directly on Tubman, but they had hired
her out to those who did, and in many other ways (selling her sisters and
threatening to sell other siblings) they raised and betrayed expectations of
adult protection in the Ross children.

As we read Tubman's stories of adolescence and young womanhood,
when she worked as a field hand, we may wonder how she felt about this
work. Several of her later biographers editorially deplore the "tyranny" of
putting a woman to "out door drudgery" (Bradford, 1886; Miller 1912;
H. Bowley, 1939a). Her mother, it will be remembered, was a house servant and may well have conveyed to her children the greater prestige of
such work within the plantation labor system.[6] But how did Tubman
experience her assignment to heavy fieldwork? Was it work to be ashamed
of, a violation of the womanhood norms of the slave community or of
her family? The stories she told about this time do not provide an answer
to this question, but they do shed light on the way she felt about the work
many years later, in her antislavery activist years.

Sanborn gives a detailed account of hired work "in the rudest labors," emphasizing what for him was a violation of gender norms. He tells us that she "drove oxen, carted, plowed, and did all the work of a man,—sometimes earning money enough in a year, beyond what she paid her master, 'to buy a pair of steers' worth forty dollars. The amount exacted of a woman for her time was fifty or sixty dollars,—of a man, one hundred to one hundred and fifty dollars. Frequently Harriet worked for her father, who was a timber inspector, and superintended the cutting and hauling of great quantities of timber for the Baltimore ship-yards. Stewart, his temporary master, was a builder, and for the work of Ross used to receive as much as five dollars [a] day sometimes, he being a superior workman. While engaged with her father, she would cut wood, haul logs, etc. Her usual "stint" was half a cord of wood in a day" (Sanborn, 1863).

Sanborn's early account presumably captures fairly accurately the "women's rights" perspective Tubman would have had on her own labor history by the time she told him her life story in 1859–1860. At that time she had lived in the North for almost a decade among Garrisonian abolitionists, many of whom were feminists, and it was she who supplied Sanborn with the telling information about the differential between male and female "wages" in Maryland's hiring-out system. She may have wanted to highlight the ironic contradictions in a labor system where a year's work by the kind of woman who could do "all the work of a man" was valued at less than half a man's wage. The retrospective account certainly conveys the pride of the middle-aged woman looking back at the younger woman's ability to earn money for herself through her own unusual physical strength, thus disproving the Brodess family's assumption that after her accident she wasn't "worth her salt."

What she told Sanborn suggests that she wished to have the facts about her own competence and endurance at this demanding work—as well as her father's "superiority" as a skilled woodsman and supervisor—placed in the historical record. Bradford captured Tubman's view that the physical strength built up by this heavy manual labor was providential: "She had worked only as a field-hand for many years, following the oxen, loading and unloading wood, and carrying heavy burdens, by which her naturally remarkable power of muscle was so developed that her feats of strength often called forth the wonder of strong laboring men. Thus was she preparing for the life of hardship and endurance which lay before her, for the deeds of daring she was to do" (Bradford, 1869, 9–10).[7]

Very few surviving stories illuminate Tubman's feelings in relation to

her family in later childhood and early womanhood. This makes one brief
glimpse of her in early adolescence (about age thirteen) all the more precious. Unlike other surviving childhood stories it can be dated precisely.
"In 1833, 'when the stars fell,' referring to a great meteoric shower of the
time, 'Aunt Harriet' was a grown woman and doing a man's work in the
fields, plowing, haying, and wood cutting. She often recalled the time,
telling of going to a neighboring plantation to visit her mother at night,
which was against orders. Her brother remained outside the cabin to see
that the guards did not surprise her. He called her to come out and see the
stars. 'They were all shooting whichway.' All thought the end of the world
had come" (Thomas Freeman, quoted in "Aunt Harriet Was Very Old,"
1913). Clearly she was still highly attached to Ritta Ross and able to visit
her secretly with the connivance of one of her brothers.

What Tubman made of the spectacular sight of the shooting stars or
the possibility of the end of the world was not recorded, but perhaps she
read it as a message of oncoming judgment on the unjust.[8] Her visionary
imagination was often at work in this period of hard physical labor out-
doors, according to Cheney: "She once said, 'We'd been carting manure all
day, and the other girl and I were going home on the sides of the cart, and
another boy was driving, when suddenly I heard such music as filled all the
air;' and she saw a vision which she described in language which sounded
like the old prophets in its grand flow; interrupted now and then by what
the other girl said, by Master's coming and calling her, to wake up, and
her protests that she wasn't asleep" (Cheney, 1865). Here her visionary experience takes place within a trancelike state that appeared to others to be
"sleep." The "somnolence" resulting from her head injury may or may not
have facilitated such mystical moments, but she spoke matter-of-factly in
dozens of conversations with Northern associates after her escape from slavery of her special gifts of foresight (knowledge of the future) and of her spiritual practice of directly consulting God for guidance on daily decisions.[9]

Of course, Tubman was not alone in her ability to use religious vision
as a spiritual, psychological, and even political resource. African Methodist Episcopal women in the Northern states regularly cultivated spiritual
awakening and visionary guidance through praying bands meeting in each
other's homes in the wake of revival, as well as in the more formal settings of Methodist class meetings and churches. Those nineteenth-century
women who experienced the call to preach often did so on the basis of religious vision, which enabled them to bypass man-made (and male) authority by directly claiming the guidance of the divine.[10] While there is less

plentiful documentation of the autonomous religious and spiritual activities of those living under slavery at the same time, there is plenty of informal evidence that a vital, distinctly African American form of evangelical Christianity flourished in the part of the slave's cultural world that was beyond the direct control of the slaveholders' churches.[11]

Sarah Bradford was highly impressed with Tubman's spirituality and documented what we in a more secular age might call "out of body experiences" during Tubman's sleeping seizures:

> When these turns of somnolence come upon Harriet, she imagines that her 'spirit' leaves her body, and visits other scenes and places, not only in this world, but also in the world of spirits. And her ideas of these scenes show, to say the least of it, a vividness of imagination seldom equaled in the soarings of the most cultivated minds. Not long since, the writer, on going into Harriet's room in the morning, sat down by her and began to read that wonderful and glorious description of the heavenly Jerusalem in the two last chapters of Revelations. When the reading was finished, Harriet burst into a rhapsody which perfectly amazed her hearer—telling of what she had seen in one of these visions, sights which no one could doubt had been real to her, and which no human imagination could have conceived, it would seem, unless in dream or vision. (Bradford, 1869, 55–56)

Bradford was also able to capture two spiritual awakening stories in her interviews with Tubman in 1868—stories suggesting that if she had found a collaborator adequate to the task, Tubman's self-liberation narrative might have been a spiritual autobiography.[12]

READING THE ESCAPE AND SPIRITUAL TRANSFORMATION STORIES

The first spiritual awakening story captured by Bradford was an account of Tubman's own "dark night of the soul"—the classic stage in Christian conversion experience in which the seeker feels a deep "conviction of sin," a sense of profound worthlessness, creating a barrier between her soul and the desired union with God. According to Bradford's 1869 text, when Tubman learned that the master was attempting to sell her, a sharp spiritual crisis ensued, in which she prayed for the "change of heart" in the master that would stop him from committing this wickedness, and simultaneously for her own purification: "'Appears like I prayed all the time,' said Harriet, 'about my work, everywhere, I prayed and groaned to the Lord. When I went to the horse-trough to wash my face, I took up the water in my hand and I said, 'Oh Lord, wipe away all my sin!' When I took the broom and began to sweep, I groaned, 'Oh Lord, whatsoever sin there be in my heart, sweep it out, Lord, clear and clean!' . . . Then we heard that some of us was going to be sold to go with the chain-gang down to the cotton and rice fields, and they said I was going, and my brothers and sisters. Then I changed my prayer. First of March I began to pray, 'Oh, Lord, if you aren't never going to change that man's heart, kill him, Lord, and take him out of the way.'"

As if in answer to prayer, Edward Brodess died shortly thereafter. The self-purification not only brought her closer to God (as in the classic Protestant conversion pattern), but it also enabled her to participate directly in the miraculous dispensation of divine justice. The story ends on a note that at first seems puzzling. She told Bradford, "Next thing I heard old master was dead, and he died just as he lived. Oh, then, it appeared like I'd give all the world full of gold, if I had it, to bring that poor soul back. But I couldn't pray for him no longer." Having prayed for his death, is it likely that she would now wish she could "bring that poor soul back"? The key is her belief that a sinner who died without experiencing the saving grace that would make him resolve to change his sinful ways ("he died just as he lived") would go straight to hell. While justice required that God "take him out of the way," she probably regretted her own personal responsibility for sending a soul into eternal torment.[13]

The second spiritual awakening story represents Tubman's moment of transformation into a "liberator" after her own escape, the moment when she realizes God has given her a specific mission. It begins with descriptions of the dream landscapes she saw in the weeks and months between the master's death and her own escape. "But still Harriet in fancy saw the horsemen coming, and heard the screams of terrified women and children. 'And all that time, in my dreams and visions,' she said, 'I seemed to see a line, and on the other side of that line were green fields, and lovely flowers, and beautiful white ladies,[14] who stretched out their arms to me over the line, but I couldn't reach them no how. I always fell before I got to the line.'" The moment she stepped into free territory and consecrated herself to the mission of rescuing her family and friends, a great change took place, she told Bradford:

"When I found I had crossed that line," she said, "I looked at my hands to see if I was the same person. There was such a glory over every thing; the sun came like gold through the trees, and over the fields, and I felt like I was in Heaven . . . I had crossed the line. I was free; but there was no one to welcome me to the land of freedom. I was a stranger in a strange land; and my home, after all, was down in Maryland; because my father, my mother, my brothers, and sisters, and friends were there. But I was free, and they should be free. I would make a home in the North and bring them there, God helping me. Oh, how I prayed then," she said; "I said to the Lord, "I'm going to hold steady on to you, and I know you'll see me through." (Bradford, 1869, 13–20)

In portraying her inner transformation as external, as visible brightness, "a glory over everything," this story echoes other conversion accounts in Protestant evangelical religious autobiography.[15] It seems only fitting that her moment of transfiguration through self-emancipation should be strongly linked with her "call," the discovery of the mission to emancipate others. However, is this really how she herself experienced these two spiritual events? Or should we suspect the pious intervention of Sarah Bradford?

We get a much more secular account of how Tubman assumed the mantle of a liberator from the less conventionally Christian biographer Ednah Cheney. According to Cheney, Tubman's mission became clear to herself two years after her own self-liberation, when she returned to Maryland intending to rescue her husband.

She remained two years in Philadelphia, working hard and carefully hoarding her money. Then she hired a room, furnished it as well as she could, bought a nice suit of men's clothes, and went back to Maryland for her husband. But the faithless man had taken to himself another wife. Harriet did not dare venture into her presence, but sent word to her husband where she was. He declined joining her. At first her grief and anger were excessive. She said, "she did not care what master did to her, she thought she would go right in and make all the trouble she could, she was determined to see her old man once more," but finally she thought "how foolish it was just for temper to make mischief" and that "if he could do without her, she could without him," and so "he dropped out of her heart" and she determined to give her life to brave deeds. Thus all personal aims died out of her heart; and with her simple brave motto, "I can't die but once," she

began the work which has made her Moses—the deliverer of her people.
(Cheney, 1865, 35)

Cheney's account reminds us of the comic and self-deprecating story of
the discovery of her husband's infidelity, told in Boston in 1859: "The
object of her first return journey was to liberate her husband. All her travelling by the way has been performed in the cars by night, but when she
went for her husband, she had carefully provided herself with clothing to
make him, she said, fit to be seen among folks.—Lo! however the recreant
had taken to himself another helpmeet, & strongly advised her to give
up the nonsense of freedom, & 'I had his clothes,' said she, 'but no husband!'" (Osgood, 1859).

How, then, do we reconcile the highly contrasting stories of Tubman's
moment of transformation into the liberator, as collected by Cheney and
Bradford? Might the contradictions simply indicate Tubman's artful ability
to adapt her autobiographical storytelling to the occasion and the expectations of the particular audience? Did she tell a comic story about her
jealousy to her freethinking Boston associates and a more elevated story
about spiritual transformation to the more sentimental and pious Bradford? Or is this an instance of censorship? Did Bradford take it upon herself to omit the frank revelation of John Tubman's betrayal and Tubman's
own emotional reactions and transfer the moment of dedication to an
earlier time?[16]

There is a third possibility as well. The self-transformation process
may have been difficult and nonlinear, beginning with what felt like a new
birth at the moment of crossing the line into the North, followed by a
falling back into "selfishness" and then a later "rededication"—this is also
a pattern that is found in many Protestant spiritual awakening narratives
(Brereton, 1991). When she had to face her own continuing passion for a
faithless husband, her "selfish" weakness, her anger at his rejection of her,
she probably had a second, more painful, experience of self-transformation,
this time through her own resolution. It was clearly necessary to find a
new purpose in life, and this she did through the renunciation of personal
desire.[17]

As we read the 1869 Bradford text of the escape story, we find negative
characterizations of both John Tubman and, to a lesser extent, Ritta Ross,
and again the question arises, whose perspective is likely to be reflected
here—Bradford's or Tubman's? In the case of John Tubman, we hear that
when Tubman received visionary forewarning of the threat of the chain

gang that was to take her and her siblings away, John Tubman, who believed the danger to be over, derided her as foolish. "She would start up at night with the cry, 'Oh, they're coming, they're coming, I must go.' Her husband called her a fool, and said she was like old Cudjo, who when a joke went round, never laughed till half an hour after everybody else got through, and so just as all danger was past she began to be frightened." In Ritta Ross's case, she is seen as too emotional to be let in on the plans. Bradford tells us that Tubman did not let her mother know about the upcoming separation, "because she knew that she would raise an uproar and prevent her going, or insist upon going with her, and the time for this was not yet." In contrast, the narrative shows that Tubman did feel that she could trust a "sister" who worked in the "big house" with her mother. Tubman stages a "frolic" with this sister in order to get her alone and confide in her the news of her impending journey.

Tubman almost surely provided the critical perspective on John Tubman. The story she told Bradford about how he treated her fears suggests that she may still have been angry at his later betrayal. Sufficient time had passed to allow her to get over her passion for him, and as a matter of fact, by the time she talked with Bradford in the summer of 1868, she may have already formed an attachment to Nelson Davis, whom she married only nine months later. But the negative characterization of Ritta Ross does not seem to have come from her daughter. Although the information that Ritta Ross was kept in the dark about the escape plan came from Tubman, it seems very likely that the negative construction placed upon this fact was Bradford's.[18] Bradford saw Ritta Ross as a "bad mother" when she was living as a dependent in Tubman's household in the postwar years. Many years afterward she frankly described Tubman's mother as "nearly a hundred years old and enfeebled in mind, . . . querulous and exacting, and most unreasonable in her temper, often reproaching this faithful daughter as the Israelites did Moses of old, for 'bringing them up into the wilderness to die there of hunger.' There came a day when everything eatable was exhausted, and the prospect was dark, indeed. The old mother had no tobacco and no tea—and these were more essential to her comfort than food or clothing; then reproaches thick and fast fell upon Harriet" (Bradford, 1901, 143–144).

Bradford's attitude toward Ritta Ross was part and parcel of her self-appointed role as protector of the overly generous, self-sacrificing Tubman. But Tubman and her brother, Henry Stewart, saw their mother's character quite differently.[19] Ritta Ross's fierce protectiveness and daring in facing down the white man who came to buy her children are presented as highly admirable in the story told by her son: "And then, late at night, he came to the door, and asked the mother to let him come in, but she was suspicious and she says, 'What do you want?' Says he, 'Mr. Scott wants to come in to light a cigar.' She ripped out an oath, and said, 'You are after my son; but the first man that comes into my house, I will split his head open.' That frightened them, and they would not come in. So she kept the boy hid until the Georgia man went away, and then she let him out" (H. Stewart, 1863). In circumstances like these, the absence of self-restraint in a protective mother was clearly a highly valuable quality. Tubman probably easily forgave her mother's liability to "raise an uproar" when faced with the prospect of losing more of her children—even if they were fleeing to the North.

The most frequently quoted part of the escape story was Tubman's high-spirited "trickster" joke on the "Doctor"—the singing of a farewell song with a double message. Cheney's version captured the daring insolence that was the essence of the joke:

> The evening before she left, she wished very much to bid her companions farewell, but was afraid of being betrayed, if any one knew of her intentions; so she passed through the street singing,—
>
>   Good bye, I'm going to leave you,
>   Good bye, I'll meet you in the kingdom,
>
> And similar snatches of Methodist songs. As she passed on singing, she saw her master, Dr. Thompson, standing at his gate, and her native humor breaking out, she sung yet louder, bowing down to him,—
>
>   Good bye, I'm going for to leave you.
>
> He stopped and looked after her as she passed on; and he afterwards said that, as her voice came floating back in the evening air it seemed as if—
>
>   A wave of trouble never rolled
>   Across her peaceful breast.
>   (Cheney, 1865, 35)

In the deep comic bow Tubman would have performed when she told this story to an appreciative audience, she encapsulated the duplicity that the slave system had taught the enslaved—a mischievous duplicity in which the storyteller clearly takes pride. This emphasis on the daring arts

of deception is brought to full flower in her repertoire of favorite stories
from the Underground Railroad years.

READING THE UNDERGROUND
RAILROAD STORIES

The largest number of the core story texts are about Harriet Tubman's
adventures as a conductor of fugitive slaves. This work was what most
amazed her antislavery supporters in the North and brought her both
celebrity as a heroine and needed financial support. These were the stories
her audiences most wanted to hear in private and public gatherings in the
1850s and 1860s and again from the late 1880s until her death. In these
stories, as in the escape and transformation stories, her intense spirituality
is juxtaposed in a sometimes uneasy fashion with her down-to-earth wit.

A few of the stories that later became classics appear first in summary
form in the private writings of her antislavery associates in the late 1850s.
For example, Thomas Garrett recorded in summary form a story Tubman
told many times afterward of appearing unrecognized under her former
master's nose. Garrett's is the only version I have found that captures her
ironic comment that the lighter skin color that resulted from her freedom
from outdoor field work actually functioned as a disguise on this occasion:
"She, in one instance, was in the immediate neighborhood of her Master
for three months, before she could get off safely with her friends, . . . She
twice in that time met her master in open day, in the fields, but he did
not know her, having always worked in the open air fields, her color had
changed so much [since leaving the South], that her own brother & sister
did not know her" (Garrett, 1855).

Her close personal relationship with a protective and just God was a
primary theme in several of the rescue stories.[20] For example, divine intervention in response to prayer played a central role in the story of the rescue of "Tillie," the light-skinned ladies' maid who was fleeing an enforced
marriage in the South. Confronted with an unexpected problem in getting a travel pass for the boat trip across the Chesapeake Bay to Baltimore,
Tubman prayed fiercely for divine aid and received it, in the form of the
desired tickets (Bradford, 1886, 57–61). In a version of the story remembered after Tubman's death, an even more dramatic vision of the Savior is
included: "On one occasion when she was standing on a steamer sailing
north, she did not have the passports for her runaway girls. On the shore

she saw men that were looking for her, she had asked the captain for passports and he had refused them. She went to the stern of the vessel and
leaned over and said, 'Lord, I am serving thee and I want them passports,'
and suddenly she saw in the water the face of the thorn-crowned Jesus and
heard him say, 'My child, your passports are all right.' She went to the
captain and asked again, and he handed them out and she walked off in
triumph" ("Two Timely Topics Discussed by Dr. Rosengrant," 1913).

She believed in the power of prayer to bring aid in emergencies, but she
also took many precautions to keep emergencies from occurring—thus
bearing out Sanborn's view of her as "the most shrewd and practical person in the world."[21] One precaution she regularly took may have been
the carrying of a gun, but we must approach this question critically. The
evidence is not conclusive, either in the core story texts or in the documentary record.

Tubman holds a Civil War musket in the picture reproduced for the
first Bradford book, but it is a revolver that appears in one of the Underground Railroad adventure stories, and the revolver may or may not have
been in her own hands. Bradford's 1869 version includes the revolver and
her line, "Dead niggers tell no tales. . . . Go on or die, " but in the earlier
published version by Cheney, it is not Tubman who holds and points the
revolver. Instead, she orders others in the party to shoot theirs:

> This expedition was governed by the strictest rules. If any man gave out, he
> must be shot. "Would you really do that?" she was asked. "Yes," she replied,
> "if he was weak enough to give out, he'd be weak enough to betray us all,
> and all who had helped us; and do you think I'd let so many die just for one
> coward man?" "Did you ever have to shoot any one?" she was asked. "One
> time," she said, "a man gave out the second night; his feet were sore and
> swollen, he couldn't go any further; he'd rather go back and die, if he must."
> They tried all arguments in vain, bathed his feet, tried to strengthen him,
> but it was of no use, he would go back. Then she said, "I told the boys to
> get their guns ready, and shoot him. They'd have done it in a minute; but
> when he heard that, he jumped right up and went on as well as anybody."
> (Cheney, 1865, 36).

Cheney's version also transmitted an interesting detail about Tubman's
traveling gear on rescue missions: "By day they lay in the woods; then she
pulled out her patchwork, and sewed together little bits, perhaps not more
than an inch square, which were afterwards made into comforters for the

fugitives in Canada." Significantly, it was the revolver she may not have carried herself, rather than the patchwork that she definitely did carry, that has become an essential part of the heroic iconography of Tubman, especially in the twentieth century, when the gun came to signify a militant attitude toward the civil rights struggle.

Her Underground Railroad rescue stories often convey the pleasure she took in making fools of her former "masters": "Sometimes, when she and her party were concealed in the woods, they saw their pursuers pass, on their horses, down the high road, tacking up the advertisements for them on the fences and trees. 'And then how we laughed,' said she. 'We was the fools, and they was the wise men, but we wasn't fools enough to go down the high road in the broad daylight'" (Bradford, 1869, 25). Her most popular stories were the trickster tales—as when she pinched the chickens she was carrying under her arm in order to create a distracting disturbance when passing her master; or when she pretended to read to foil pursuers who knew she was illiterate; or when, faced with posters offering a reward for her, she deliberately took a train heading south to avoid suspicion; or when she used her songs to distract the gentlemen in her stagecoach from their questions.

One of the most dramatic core stories of the Underground Railroad years, the Troy rescue, features Tubman using her trickster repertoire as well as her unusual physical courage and strength. As captured by Bradford, this story suggests that she actually worked in collaboration with a group of black women and men (the newspaper account lays emphasis on the women). Yet despite its obvious dramatic entertainment value, this story virtually dropped out of her repertoire after the publication of the Bradford book, perhaps because the spectacle of black "mob" action to thwart a legal transfer of a prisoner may have been too much for post-Reconstruction audiences. Whatever the reasons, either Tubman herself told the story more selectively in later years, or those who heard it were more selective about reproducing it in printed accounts of her life.[22]

One Underground Railroad story apparently survived only in oral transmission until many years after her death: a story of an attempted betrayal by a black accomplice, as recalled by an A.M.E. Zion minister: "On one occasion as she was journeying north with a group in a wagon, they stopped at the home of a supposed colored friend. He was not at home upon their arrival, but his wife fed them and put them to bed in the attic of the house. Harriet was awake when the husband arrived home and his wife informed him of the presence of the group in the attic, for

she heard him remark, 'There is a reward offered for the capture of Harriet
and I am going to get it.' Thereupon he ate his supper and then went in
search of the police. As soon as his steps died away, however, Harriet
aroused her comrades and they quickly vacated the premises and proceeded
safely on their way without apprehension" (Brooks, n.d.). Good reasons
for censoring such a story come quickly to mind, whether the censorship
took place during the antebellum antislavery years, during Reconstruction,
or during the post-Reconstruction "nadir" in race relations. But its survival
in purely oral form (assuming we can rely on Reverend Brooks to have
remembered and told its essence accurately) also raises a provocative question. Could an "underground" repertoire of taboo core stories have been
preserved as a kind of "family secret" within black community networks
in the twentieth century? This story, and perhaps others similarly threatening to black political solidarity, might have been inappropriate to tell to
potentially hostile "outsiders" but important to preserve and retell within
community circles as valuable insider wisdom. Certainly when the story
was published in the 1950s it was intended for a black church readership,
and presumably it was retold as a monitory tale about the importance of
race solidarity ("Never betray a sister or brother as this man was prepared
to do to our race heroine, Harriet Tubman").

WAR STORIES AND THE POSTWAR YEARS

Like many other war veterans, Tubman took pleasure in telling war stories
to enthralled audiences. As a female veteran, she could count on the extra
excitement generated by her violation of gender norms in her roles as
scout and spy. Very few of her war stories survive in text form, however,
and those that do have a more "modern" reportial quality than the
stories from the Underground Railroad era. No reference to her experiencing divine guidance during the war years survives, for example, nor do
we have accounts in which she is the wily deceiver pitted against a Confederate antagonist. In stories from the Sea Islands she even appears in
the role of a Northerner and honorary anthropologist or folklorist—an
outsider who records the peculiar speech patterns and unusual "primitive"
customs of the folk.[23]

We see her in this role in the account of the Combahee River Raid
produced by both Bradford and Emma Paddock Telford.[24] In the Telford
version of the story, Colonel Montgomery assumes that Tubman will be

better able to communicate with the Sea Islands rice farmers than he would be, despite her present identity as a "Yankee soldier," domiciled most recently in Canada and upstate New York: "At last the Captain looked at them and he called me. They called me 'Moses Garrison' down there. Said he, 'Moses, come here and speak a word of consolation to your people!' 'Well, they wasn't my people any more than they was his— only we was all Negroes—[be]cause I didn't know any more about them than he did. So I went when he called me on the gunboat, and they on the shore. They didn't know any thing about me and I didn't know what to say.'" Of course her quick wits come to her rescue in this situation, as usual, and she plays the "trick" that will help the Yankees rescue the contrabands. The trick involves taking advantage of their cultural "primitivism"—by singing a song that will excite a physical expression of their emotional response, distract them, and cause them to release their fearful grip on the rowboats:

> I look at them about two minutes, and then I sung to them:
>
>> Come from the East
>> Come from the West
>> 'Mong all the glorious nations
>> This glorious one's the best.
>> Come along; come along; don't be alarmed
>> For Uncle Sam is rich enough
>> To give you all a farm.
>
> Then they threw up their hands and began to rejoice and shout Glory! and the rowboats would push off.
> I kept on singing until all were brought on board. (Telford, n.d.)

The joke may cut more than one way here, of course. As a storyteller Tubman may seem to be collaborating with the perspective of her white friends (Colonel Montgomery and Emma Paddock Telford), viewing the Sea Islanders as amusingly gullible in their enthusiastic response to her song. (We are reminded of her similar joke about the excessive emotionalism of Joe, the fugitive who refused to look at Niagara Falls when he had the chance.) But we should also notice the ironic spearing of Montgomery's assumption that all "Negroes" are alike: "I didn't know any more about them than he did," she told Telford.

The other type of "war story" she told was about the less glamorous "women's work" of nursing the wounded and diseased. Bradford conveyed a memorable description of her bathing the fly-infested wounds of the soldiers, many of whom were wounded in the disastrous Fort Wagner assault, but the only real core story of nursing to have made it into text form is one Telford gives about Tubman "curing the doctor." This is not a particularly entertaining story, but it does show off her skill as an herbalist: "'I went down there,' she quaintly says, 'and found them that bad with chronic dysentery, that they was dying off like sheep. I dug some roots and herbs and made a tea for the doctor and the disease stopped on him. And then he said, "Give it to the soldiers." So I boiled up a great boiler of roots and herbs, and the General [de]tailed a man to take two cans and go round and give it to all in the camp that needed it, and it cured them'" (Telford, n.d.).

Most of the stories recorded about Tubman's postwar life either do not express her own point of view or are too undeveloped to qualify as core stories. Two possible exceptions are the account of her fierce resistance to racial insult on the railroad car and the self-deprecating story of her bidding on the property that would later become the site of the Tubman Home (both discussed in part 1, "The Life"). Both stories convey valuable information about her pride in her color and her recognition that racism was a pervasive and possibly unexpected element of the new life she would forge after emancipation. Neither one became part of her public repertoire for an obvious reason: both show the Underground Railroad heroine and Civil War spy and scout as the target of white racism in the North, and thus they strike a chord that her post-Reconstruction Northern audience definitely did not want to hear.

TUBMAN'S LEGACY:
THE LIFE AND THE LIFE STORIES

Among very few other nineteenth-century texts that originate in the perspective of a female fugitive from slavery, Tubman's story texts help disrupt or at least complicate the classic linkage in antebellum fugitive slave narratives of masculinity and the quest for freedom.[25] Both in Tubman's actions as a "character" in her life history stories and in her narrator's voice, genteel Victorian gender norms are implicitly (and even sometimes explicitly) questioned. The Tubman life story texts offer a window onto the self-understanding and the self-transformation of this extraordinary yet ordinary nineteenth-century African American woman. Transformed by her own actions from her former identity as a disabled worker "not worth her salt" and the wife of a man who thought her a fool into a much-praised female hero, Tubman reinvented herself in the foreign world of the North. Her life stories had both monetary and historic value in this new world.

The power dynamics of the institution of slavery significantly shaped Tubman's storytelling as well as her personality. Hard experience in the complex and dangerous bicultural world of the Maryland plantation taught her to "wear the mask" to protect herself from the arbitrary use of violence and the betrayal of trust in white surrogate family relationships. Not surprisingly, many of her life stories express pride in her own clever jokes at the expense of powerful but thick-witted authorities. Her habits of self-protection can also be seen in the dynamics of her collaborative biographical projects. She had the ability to tell a tightly structured, entertaining story of adventure and quick-witted problem solving that charmed and disarmed the listener, thus resisting editorial interference. This skill enabled her to pass on to posterity a remarkable collection of tales of wit and wisdom, of "fooling the master" and successfully praying for divine intervention in human affairs.

These stories have come down to us largely because Tubman was "in the right place at the right time" to become a black female hero. Her historic actions were real, but they might never have been celebrated if her escape had not occurred in the formative years of organized feminism within Garrisonian abolitionist networks. She was "news" at first because her Underground Railroad work so strikingly challenged the genteel gender norms by which her Northern political allies lived, at a time when feminist protest against such norms of femininity had just barely begun. Tubman's "unladylike" daring in a cause so clearly right could be assimilated by her allies into a pre-existing Euro-American "woman warrior" tradition, one that combined militance with sainthood—that of Joan of Arc. Because they saw her in this light, her biographical collaborators believed fervently in the historic value in her stories and sayings, even when they may not have fully understood her meaning (as is especially true of Sarah Bradford), and they performed the important historical service of turning her speech into texts.

In the post-Reconstruction period, the militance waned and the sainthood gained ascendancy. This change was initiated by Bradford's revision of the earlier biography, but a fuller reshaping of the meaning of her heroism took place, as we have seen, in the "Woman's Era" of the 1890s, in the context of the women's club campaigns for temperance and suffrage and new social services and against lynching and other forms of race terrorism and discrimination. The fact that Tubman had focused her energy on the creation of a local social service institution for the elderly poor of her race added to her value as a role model, a symbol that could be used to combat both complacency and hopelessness. Club leader Mary Church Terrell used Tubman in her list of race heroines in a speech given in 1916—one of the "great women who'd done their work in the yesteryears."[26]

Throughout Tubman's life as a celebrity, her autobiographical storytelling enabled her to function as a public political figure, to instruct and persuade others, to earn money, to repay social debts, to forge social alliances and friendships, and to connect with new generations as she aged. Through telling about her experiences she was able to speak about the evils of bondage, the resourcefulness of the oppressed, and the justice of a benevolent God. At the end of her life, in interviews with trusted neighbors, church associates, and second-generation members of her "surrogate families" in Auburn, Tubman may have derived some of the more private, personal psychological benefits of reflecting freshly on past experience from the vantage point of a later stage in life.[27]

Her autobiographical storytelling to biographers initiated the collaborative creation of a larger-than-life symbol of female heroism in resistance to the oppression of slavery and racism. The life story narrative of Harriet Tubman has been a complex, evolving cultural resource, much used in political debate and organizing from the 1860s to the present day. The history of how her public icon functioned in the long march of twentieth-century racial and gender politics remains to be fully told. In the "Stories and Sayings" texts collected in part 3 of this volume, we hear her own voice as captured by her earliest and closest listeners, and so we come to understand more fully the contribution of this complex historic woman to the collective creation of the Tubman legend.

PART 3

Stories and Sayings

A NOTE ON THE SELECTION AND
EDITING OF STORY TEXTS

When selecting from several recorded versions of a core story text, I have preferred those of writers who knew Harriet Tubman well or at least had documented interviews with her. In most cases I have chosen earlier recorded versions of stories over later ones—not only because they probably reflect a fresher memory of the events retold, but also because there is less probable "contamination" by other printed versions of the story.[1] I have occasionally violated this rule when a later-told or later-written story seemed to add something distinctly new and valuable (as in the case of the material on Tubman's childhood memories gathered by Emma Paddock Telford, discussed in the previous section).

In editing excerpts from manuscripts and nineteenth-century publications I have generally preserved spellings and punctuations of the original texts, occasionally adding paragraph breaks for the relief of the modern reader, along with ellipses (. . .) to indicate editorial omissions within quotations. Exceptions to this practice, made for the convenience of the reader, are noted on individual excerpts.

I have had to wrestle long and hard with the question of whether to preserve the "dialect" spellings used by many writers to render the sounds of Tubman's Southern English. Dialect writing from dictation or memory by scribes arguably reveals more about the ideas and ear of the scribe than it does about the actual sound of the historical spoken word. It is immediately evident when we compare the many inconsistent versions of Tubman's dialect used in these texts, as well as inconsistencies of dialect writing within the same texts, that there is no way of determining which, if any, of the written texts accurately captured the sounds of her speech—even assuming that her "dialect" did not vary according to location, occasion, and time. At any rate, given that my goal is to minimize the "mediation" of the biographers, in texts aimed not at language historians but at the general public, I have not attempted to preserve all these inconsistent, distracting, and (because of the racist history of dialect writing) potentially disturbing examples of dialect writing. I was guided in part by the advice of Sterling A. Brown, who made suggestions to the state WPA oral history narrative editors in 1936. Brown wrote that "simplicity in recording the dialect is to be desired in order to hold the interest and attention of the readers. . . . Truth to idiom is more important . . . than truth to pronunciation. . . . In a single publication, not devoted to a study of local speech, the reader may conceivably be puzzled by different spellings of the same word. . . . Most important are the turns of phrase that have flavor and vividness" (S. A. Brown, 1985, 37–39). When a text rendered Tubman's speech in dialect, I removed nonstandard spellings meant to indicate Southern pronunciation, but I retained distinctive grammatical usage that seemed to preserve "turns of phrase that have flavor and vividness."

STORYTELLING PERFORMANCES DESCRIBED

S1. Lucy Osgood (1859)

Yesterday afternoon I missed through my weather caution of an unique entertainment, to which I had been kindly invited by Mrs. Bartoll, who at the request of Mrs. Cheney opened her doors for a gathering of friends, to ascertain who might be disposed to aid a real heroine. Where Mrs. Cheney found her, I do not know, but her name is Harriet. She is coal black, and was a slave only three years ago, but within that time she has taken leg bail herself, & assisted no fewer than fifty others to do the same. Two or three times she has returned to the very plantation where she had served, & brought away with her companies of her relations & friends. Her old father & mother she has helped out of bondage, & the object of this gathering was to assist her to buy a little place for them in Auburn. Her course had not always been smooth. The object of her first return journey was to liberate her husband. All her travelling by the way has been performed in the cars by night, but when she went for her husband, she had carefully provided herself with clothing to make him, she said, fit to be seen among folks—Lo! however the miscreant had taken to himself another helpmeet [wife], & strongly advised her to give up the nonsense of freedom, & "I had his clothes," said she, "but no husband!"—Mrs. Follen and Miss Putnam shouted at her comic pathos—They dubbed her Moses the deliverer instead of Harriet. Mrs. Holman my neighbour gave me this account (Osgood, 1859).

S2. *Thomas W. Higginson (1859)*

We have had the greatest heroine of the age here, Harriet Tubman, a black woman, and a fugitive slave, who has been back eight times secretly and brought out in all sixty slaves with her, including all her own family, besides aiding many more in other ways to escape. Her tales of adventure are beyond anything in fiction and her ingenuity and generalship are extraordinary. I have known her for some time and mentioned her in speeches once or twice—the slaves call her Moses. She has had a reward of twelve thousand dollars offered for her in Maryland and will probably be burned alive whenever she is caught, which she probably will be, first or last, as she is going again. She has been in the habit of working in hotels all summer and laying up money for this crusade in the winter. She is jet black and cannot read or write, only talk, besides acting (Higginson, 1859).

S3. *Fourth of July Speech (1859)*

The President [Thomas W. Higginson] then said that he wished to introduce to the audience a conductor on the Underground Railroad, who, having first transformed herself from a chattel into a human being, had since transformed sixty other chattels into other human beings, by her own personal efforts. It was rather hard to introduce her. She came here from a place in the slave States; she came by land, and had been here a reasonable time. (Laughter) At the South, she was called "Moses"—after an ancient leader, who took men and women into the promised land. (Applause.)

"Moses," the deliverer, then stood up before the audience, who greeted her with enthusiastic cheers. She spoke briefly, telling the story of her sufferings as a slave, her escape, and her achievements on the Underground Railroad, in a style of quaint simplicity, which excited the most profound interest in her hearers. The mere words could do no justice to the speaker, and therefore we do not undertake to give them; but we advise all our readers to take the earliest opportunity to see and hear her.

Mr. Higginson stated that this brave woman had never asked for a cent from the Abolitionists, but that all her operations had been conducted at her own cost, with money earned by herself. Now, however, having brought her father and mother out of slavery, she found that the labor required for their support rendered her incapable of doing any thing in the way of business, and she therefore desired to raise a few hundred dollars to enable her to buy a little place where her father and mother could support themselves, and enable her to resume the practice of her profession! (Laughter and applause.)

A collection was taken in her behalf, amounting to thirty-seven dollars, for which, at the conclusion of the meeting, in a few earnest and touching words, she spoke her thanks (Yerrington, 1859).

54. Charlotte Forten (1863)

January 31, 1863. In B[eaufort] we spent nearly all our time at Harriet Tubman's otherwise "Moses." She is a wonderful woman—a real heroine. Has helped off a large number of slaves, after taking her own freedom. She told us that she used to hide them in the woods during the day and go around and get provisions for them. Once she had with her a man named Joe, for whom a reward of $1500 was offered. Frequently, in different places she found handbills exactly describing him, but at last they reached in safety the Suspension Bridge over the Falls and found themselves in Canada. Until then, she said, Joe had been very silent. In vain had she called his attention to the glory of the falls. He sat perfectly still—moody it seemed, and w'ld not even glance at them. But when she said, "Now we are in Can.[ada]" he sprang to his feet—with a great shout and sang and clapped his hands in a perfect delirium of joy. So when they got out, and he first touched free soil, he shouted and hurrahed "as if he were crazy"—she said.

How exciting it was to hear her tell the story. And to hear the very scraps of jubilant hymns that he sang. She said the ladies crowded around them, and some laughed and some cried. My own eyes were full as I listened to her—the heroic woman! A reward of $10,000 was offered for her by the Southerners,[2] and her friends deemed it best that she sh'ld, for a time find refuge in Can.[ada]. And she did so, but only for a short time. She came back and was soon at the good brave work again. She is living in B.[eaufort] now; keeping an eating house. But she wants to go North, and will probably do so ere long. I am glad I saw her—very glad. At her house we met one of the Superintendents from P[ort] R[oyal] I[sland], a Boston man—Mr. S.—who is intelligent and very agreeable (Forten, 1863).

S5. Ednah Cheney (1865)

She loves to describe her visions, which are very real to her; but she must
tell them word for word as they lie in her untutored mind, with endless
repetitions and details; she cannot shorten or condense them, whatever be
your haste. She has great dramatic power; the scene rises before you as she
saw it, and her voice and language change with her different actors. . . .

I wish it were possible to give some of her racy stories; but no report
would do them justice (Cheney, 1865, 36, 37).

S6. Emily Howland (1873)

October 4, 1873. Harriet Tubman came, pleasant and bright, and entertaining with her accounts of adventure in camp and forest in leading her
fellow bondmen to freedom and in nearly equally perilous military service. Her shrewdness appeared in her tact to ward off danger when imminent. Ready wit led her when peril impended to turn suspicion from
herself and her company by starting a chat with the dangerous person on
a subject of absorbing general interest, matrimony. Once she and a band
of eleven when crossing a bridge came upon a company of Irish laborers:
what to do? She stepped bravely up and began about Christmas. Being
asked what was her business, she said her present speculation was getting
a husband. She had had one colored husband and she meant to marry
a white gentleman next time.[3] This made a great laugh so they went on
thro' the town all together laughing and talking. Harriet's husband came
about noon for her, looking utterly dejected, and anxious to get home.
(E. Howland, 1873).

S7. Sarah H. Bradford (1901)

Her expressions are often very peculiar; some ladies of a certain church
who had become interested in her wished to see her, and she was invited
to come to their city, and attended the sewing circle, where twenty or
thirty of them were gathered together. They asked her many questions,
and she told stories, sang songs, danced, and imitated the talk of the
Southern Negroes; and went away loaded with many tokens of the kind
interest of these ladies. On the way home she said:

"What nice, kind-looking ladies they was, Missus. I looked in all their
faces, and I didn't see nothing venomous in one of them!"

As has been said, Harriet can neither read nor write; her letters are all
written by an amanuensis, and she seems to have an idea that by laying

her hand on this person, her feelings may be transmitted to the one to whom she is writing. These feelings are sometimes very poetically expressed. I have by me some of those letters; in one of them she says: "I lay my hand on the shoulder of the writer of this letter, and I wish for you, and all your offsprings, a through ticket in the Gospel train to Glory."

In another letter she has dictated this sentence: "I ask of my Heavenly Father, that when the last trump sounds, and my name is called, I may stand close by your side, to answer to the call" (Bradford, 1901, 148–149).

S8. Emma Paddock Telford (circa 1905)

As a raconteur, Harriet herself has few equals and the story of her life taken from her own lips as I have so often heard it, enriched by the picturesque Southern dialect and embellished by a wealth of eloquent gesture peculiarly her own, gives a unique picture of the ante-bellum days and the stirring events which followed. . . .

In her own home Harriet delights to welcome any who may come, opening her treasury of story and song for their benefit. Among the quaint old Negro folk songs which I have heard her sing many a time are the following. The first one she explains is the one with which Frederick Douglass used to electrify his audiences in the old ante-bellum days:

> Come saints and sinners, hear me tell
> How pious priests with Jack and Nell
> Women buy and children sell
> And preach all sinners down to hell
> But save this glorious union.
>
> They'll whip you if you nip a dram
> They'll damn you if you steal a lamb
> They'll rob old Tony, Doll and Sam
> Of human rights and bread and ham
> But save this glorious union.
>
> They'll roar and bleat, they'll baa like goats,
> Gorge down black sheep and strain at motes
> And rare [array?] their backs in fine black coats
> And seize the Negroes by their throats
> And choke for heavenly union.

Another winning preacher spoke
Whose heart was once for sinners broke
He made a prayer both loud and long
He taught the right but did the wrong
And prayed for heavenly union. (Telford, n.d. 3, 23–24)

S9. Agnes Garrison (1899)

Yesterday morning Aunt L. [Lidy][4] got Harriet Tubman up here and she told me stories of her youth which a stenographer took down as best she could. . . . Impossible to unravel the chronology. . . . She refused refreshments because it was Friday "and she always fasts until 12 on that day— until the Lord comes down from de cross.". . .

. . . We had another bout with Harriet yesterday . . . she got warmed up to her narrative yesterday and acted out parts of it, crawling on the floor, gesticulating and singing one of the old songs in a curious, nasal, mournful voice (A. Garrison, 1899a, 1899b).

S10. Alice Brickler (1939)

After Aunt Harriet was confined to her chair, Mother and I used to go visit her very often and to take her sweets which she liked so well. On one of these visits, Aunt Harriet was feeling especially well. She and Mother were talking as they sat in the yard. Tiring of their conversation, I wandered off in the tall grasses to pick the wild flowers. Suddenly I became aware of something moving toward me through the grass. So smoothly did it glide and with so little noise, I was frightened! Then reason conquered fear and I knew it was Aunt Harriet, flat on her stomach and with only the use of her arms and serpentine movements of her body, gliding smoothly along. Mother helped her back to her chair and they laughed. Aunt Harriet then told me that that was the way she had gone by many a sentinel during the war. Seeing the swaying grass, she was mistaken for an animal or in the dim flicker of the camp fire, she appeared only as a small shadow (Brickler, 1939b).

S11. Samuel Hopkins Adams (1947)

The adventure about which Harriet would talk most expansively was a publicly conducted rescue in Troy, New York. Passing through that town on her way to a prewar Abolitionist rally at which she was to speak, she learned that an escaped Negro, Charles Nalle, was in local custody and was to be restored to his master. She gathered a crowd and harangued them with the fervid eloquence always at her command. The town fire bell was rung by her sympathizers, and the street outside the United States Commissioner's office filled up with blacks and whites. When the marshall, backed by his deputy and the local police, ill-advisedly undertook to transfer the prisoner to another court, Harriet rushed him. A policeman clubbed her.

"I knock him squawking," she told us gleefully.

The deputy grappled with her.

"I choke him till his tongue stick out like that." Harriet's imitation of a strangling man was extremely graphic.

Nalle was knocked senseless in the struggle.

"I throw him across my shoulder like a bag of meal and tote him away out of there."

Here enters an element of mystery and an ellipsis. In Harriet's veracious, if incomplete, account, rescuer and rescued presently turned up in Schenectady, fourteen miles away, in a buggy drawn by a blooded horse.

"Where did you get the horse and buggy, Aunt Harriet?"

"I find him."

"Where?"

"A gentleman in Troy had him."

"Did he give it to you?"

"I got him."

"Who was the gentleman?"

"I didn't stop to ask, but he was a good judge of horseflesh," Aunt Harriet would say complacently (S. H. Adams, 1989, 275–276).[5]

THE SLAVERY YEARS AND THE ESCAPE

S12. Paid a Lawyer to Uncover Mother's History (1869)

On asking Harriet particularly as to the age of her mother, she answered, "Well, I'll tell you, Missus. Twenty-three years ago, in Maryland, I paid a lawyer $5 to look up the will of my mother's first master. He looked back sixty-five years, and said it was time to give up. I told him to go back further.["] He went back sixty-five years, and there he found the will— giving the girl Ritty to his grand-daughter (Mary Patterson) to serve her and her offspring till she was forty-five years of age. This grand-daughter died soon after, unmarried[6]; and as there was no provision for Ritty, in case of her death, she was actually emancipated at that time. But no one informed her of the fact, and she and her dear children remained in bondage till emancipated by the courage and determination of this heroic daughter and sister (Bradford, 1869, 107–108).

S13. In the Cradle and Playing with Younger Siblings (circa 1905)

The first thing I [re]member, was lying in the cradle. You has seen these trees that are hollow? Take a big tree, cut it down, put a bode [board?] in each end, make a cradle of it and call it a "gum". I [re]member lying in that there, when the young ladies in the big house where my mother worked come down, catch me up in the air before I could walk.

The next thing I [re]member was when I was four or five years old, my mother cooked up to the big house and left me to take care of the baby and my little brother. I used to be in a hurry for her to go, so as I could play the baby was a pig in a bag, and hold him up by the bottom of his dress. I had a nice frolic with that baby, swinging him all round, his feet in the dress and his little head and arms touching the floor, because I was too small to hold him higher.

It was late nights before my mother got home, and when he'd get worrying I'd cut a fat chunk of pork and toast it on the coals and put it in his mouth. One night he went to sleep with that hanging out, and when my mother come home she thought I'd done kill[ed] him.

I nursed that there baby till he was so big I couldn't tote him any more, and I got so mischievous about the house that they put me out to learn to be a weaver (Telford, n.d. 3–4).

S14. Resistance While Apprenticed to a Weaver (1863)

When Harriet was six years old, she was taken from her mother and carried ten miles to live with James Cook, whose wife was a weaver, to learn the trade of weaving. While still a mere child, Cook set her to watching his musk-rat traps, which compelled her to wade through the water. It happened that she was once sent when she was ill with the measles, and, taking cold from wading in the water in this condition, she grew very sick, and her mother persuaded her master to take her away from Cook's until she could get well.

Another attempt was made to teach her weaving, but she would not learn, for she hated her mistress, and did not want to live at home, as she would have done as a weaver, for it was the custom then to weave the cloth for the family, or a part of it, in the house (Sanborn, 1863).

S15. Ashamed and Homesick at Weaver's Home (circa 1905)

The man came after me riding horseback. I hadn't any clothes, but I was anxious to go, and the mistress made me a petticoat and the man took me up front of him on the horse and off we went.

When we got there, they was at the table eating supper. I'd never eat in the house where the white people was, and I was shamed to stand up and eat before them. The mistress asked me if I done want some milk to drink? But I was that shamed to drink before her, that I said No, I never liked sweet milk no how. When the truth was I was as fond of milk as any young shoat. But all the time I was there I stuck to it, that I didn't drink sweet milk.

I stayed there awhile and then I got homesick. I was like the boy on the Sewanee River, "no place like my old cabin home." Whenever you [see] a child worse homesick than I was, you see a bad one.

I used to sleep on the floor in front of the fireplace and there I'd lie and cry and cry. I used to think all the time, ["]If I could only get home and get in my mother's bed!["] And the funny part of that was, she never had a bed in her life. Nothing but a board box nailed up against the wall and straw laid on it.

I stayed there two years (Telford, n.d. 4–5).

S16. Hired Out to "Miss Susan" (1869)

The first person by whom she was hired was a woman who, though married and the mother of a family, was still "Miss Susan" to her slaves, as is customary at the South. This woman was possessed of the good things of this life, and provided liberally for her slaves—so far as food and clothing went. But she had been brought up to believe, and to act upon the belief, that a slave could be taught to do nothing, and *would* do nothing but under the sting of the whip. Harriet, then a young girl, was taken from her life in the field, and having never seen the inside of a house better than a cabin in the Negro quarters, was put to house-work without being told how to do anything.

The first thing was to put a parlor in order. "Move these chairs and tables into the middle of the room, sweep the carpet clean, then dust everything, and put them back in their places!" These were the directions given, and Harriet was left alone to do her work. The whip was in sight on the mantel-piece, as a reminder of what was to be expected if the work was not done well. Harriet fixed the furniture as she was told to do, and swept with all her strength, raising a tremendous dust. The moment she had finished sweeping, she took her dusting cloth, and wiped everything "so you could see your face in them, they shone so," in haste to go and set the table for breakfast, and do her other work. The dust which she had set flying only settled down again on chairs, tables, and the piano. "Miss Susan" came in and looked around. Then came the call for "Minty"—Harriet's name was Araminta at the South.

She drew her up to the table, saying, "What do you mean by doing my work this way, you —!" and passing her finger on the table and piano, she showed her the mark it made through the dust. "Miss Susan, I done sweep and dust just as you told me." But the whip was already taken down, and the strokes were falling on head and face and neck.

Four times this scene was repeated before breakfast, when, during the fifth whipping, the door opened, and "Miss Emily" came in. She was a married sister of "Miss Susan," and was making her a visit, and though brought up with the same associations as her sister, seems to have been a person of more gentle and reasonable nature. Not being able to endure the screams of the child any longer, she came in, took her sister by the arm, and said, "If you do not stop whipping that child, I will leave your home, and never come back!" Miss Susan declared that "she *would* not mind, and she slighted her work on purpose."

Miss Emily said, "Leave her to me a few moments;" and Miss Susan left the room, indignant. As soon as they were alone, Miss Emily said: "Now, Minty, show me how you do your work." For the sixth time Harriet removed all the furniture into the middle of the room; then she swept; and the moment she had done sweeping, she took the dusting cloth to wipe off the furniture. "Now stop there," said Miss Emily; "go away now, and do some of your other work, and when it is time to dust, I will call you." When the time came she called her, and explained to her how the dust had now settled, and that if she wiped it off now, the furniture would remain bright and clean. These few words an hour or two before, would have saved Harriet her whippings for that day, as they probably did for many a day after.

While with this woman, after working from early morning till late at night, she was obliged to sit up all night to rock a cross, sick child. Her mistress laid upon her bed with a whip under her pillow, and slept; but if the tired nurse forgot herself for a moment, if her weary head dropped, and her hand ceased to rock the cradle, the child would cry out, and then down would come the whip upon the neck and face of the poor weary creature. The scars are still plainly visible where the whip cut into the flesh. Perhaps her mistress was preparing her, though she did not know it then, by this enforced habit of wakefulness, for the many long nights of travel, when she was the leader and guide of the weary and hunted ones who were escaping from bondage.

"Miss Susan" got tired of Harriet, as Harriet was determined she should do, and so abandoned her intention of buying her, and sent her back to her master (Bradford, 1869, 10–13).

S17. Hiding from a Whipping among the Pigs (1901)

"I often think, Missus, of things I wish I had told you before you wrote the book. Now, as I come up on the boat I thought of one thing that happened to me when I was very little.

"I was only seven years old when I was sent away to take care of a baby. I was so little that I had to sit down on the floor and have the baby put in my lap. And that baby was always in my lap except when it was asleep, or its mother was feeding it.

"One morning after breakfast she had the baby, and I stood by the table waiting till I was to take it; just by me was a bowl of lumps of white sugar. My Missus got into a great quarrel with her husband; she had an awful temper, and she would scold and storm, and call him all sorts of names. Now you know, Missus, I never had nothing good; no sweet, no sugar, and that sugar, right by me, did look so nice, and my Missus's back was turned to me while she was fighting with her husband, so I just put my fingers in the sugar bowl to take one lump, and maybe she heard me, and she turned and saw me. The next minute she had the raw hide down; I gave one jump out of the door, and I saw they came after me, but I just flew, and they didn't catch me.

I run, and I run, and I run, I passed many a house, but I didn't dare to stop, for they all knew my Missus and they would send me back. By and by, when I was clear tuckered out, I come to a great pig-pen. There was an old sow there, and perhaps eight or ten little pigs. I was too little to climb into it, but I tumbled over the high board, and fell in on the ground; I was so beat out I couldn't stir.

"And there, Missus, I stayed from Friday till the next Tuesday, fighting with those little pigs for the potato peelings and other scraps that came down in the trough. The old sow would push me away when I tried to get her children's food, and I was awful afraid of her. By Tuesday I was so starved I knowed I'd got to go back to my Missus, I hadn't got no where else to go, but I knowed what was coming. So I went back."

"And she gave you an awful flogging, I suppose, Harriet?"

"No, Missus, but *he* did."

This was all that was said, but probably that flogging left some of those scars which cover her neck and back to his day.

Think of a poor little helpless thing seven years old enduring all this terror and suffering, and yet few people are as charitable to the slave-holders as Harriet. "They don't know no better, Missus; it's the way they was brought up. 'Make the little nigs mind you, or flog them,' was what was said to the children, and they was brought up with the whip in the hand. Now, mind you, Missus, that wasn't the way on all the plantations; there was good masters and missuses, as I've heard tell, but I didn't happen to come across them" (Bradford, 1901, 135–137).

S18. Resisting a Cruel Mistress (1939)

She showed me a knot in her side by being struck by one cruel man with a rope with a knot in one end. She was working about the house and for some trivial offense the woman attempted to whip her, to which she would not submit. When the man came home his wife told him he would not attack her at that time, but sent her upstairs to roll some carpets. When she was thus engaged he crept up behind her and dealt an awful blow. The knot end of the rope struck her in the side, a wound that pained her all of her life (H. Bowley, 1939a).[7]

S19. Clever Resistance and Childhood Prayer for Strength to Fight (1865)

When quite young she lived with a very pious mistress; but the slave-holder's religion did not prevent her from whipping the young girl for every slight or fancied fault. Araminta found that this was usually a morning exercise; so she prepared for it by putting on all the thick clothes she could procure to protect her skin. She made sufficient outcry, however, to convince her mistress that her blows had full effect; and in the afternoon she would take off her wrappings, and dress as well as she could. When invited into family prayers, she preferred to stay on the landing, and pray for herself; "and I prayed to God," she says, "to make me strong and able to fight, and that's what I've always prayed for ever since." It is in vain to try to persuade her that her prayer was a wrong one. She always maintains it to be sincere and right, and it has certainly been fully answered (Cheney, 1865, 34).

S20. *Clever Resistance to Housework (1939)*

She was employed on the plantation in various ways. She would do house-work. When she was sent to the bedrooms to make up the beds, she would beat up the feather beds, make believe she was working hard, and when she had blown them up she would throw herself in the middle of them (Tatlock, 1939a).

S21. *Intellectual Aptitude and Physical Resistance to Tyranny (1950?)*

While still a young girl, she was chosen to work in "the big house" as the master's home was called. One of her duties was to escort the master's chil-dren to and from school, and during nice weather she sat on the doorstep of the schoolhouse to wait for the children. One day the teacher called for a volunteer to spell the word "baker:" None of the scholars responded, so Harriet stood up in the doorway and called out in a loud voice, "B-A-K-E-R, B-A-K-E-R". She was very alert and possessed a splendid memory in spite of the fact that she had had no formal schooling.

On one occasion her master punished her for breach of one of his rules and she in turn bit his knee. From that time forward, he did not punish her again declaring that she had too much temper (Brooks, n.d.).

S22. *Disabled in Early Teens—Sanborn's Version (1863)*

Soon after she entered her teens she was hired out as a field hand, and it was while thus employed that she received a wound which nearly proved fatal, from the effects of which she still suffers. In the fall of the year, the slaves there work in the evening, cleaning up wheat, husking corn, etc. On this occasion, one of the slaves of a farmer named Barrett, left his work, and went to the village store in the evening. The overseer fol-lowed him, and so did Harriet. When the slave was found, the overseer swore he should be whipped, and called on Harriet, among others, to help tie him. She refused, and as the man ran away, she placed herself in the door to stop pursuit. The overseer caught up a two-pound weight from the counter and threw it at the fugitive, but it fell short and struck Harriet a stunning blow on the head. It was long before she recovered from this, and it has left her subject to a sort of stupor or lethargy at times; coming upon her in the midst of conversation, or whatever she may be doing, and throwing her into a deep slumber, from which she will presently rouse herself, and go on with her conversation or work (San-born, 1863).

S23. Disabled in Early Teens—Telford (circa 1905)

After I left that man I was put out again for victuals and clothes to the worst man in the neighborhood, and he set me to breaking flax. My hair had never been combed and it stood out like a bushel basket, and when I'd get through eating I'd wipe the grease off my fingers on my hair, and I [e]xpect that there hair saved my life.

One night I went out with the cook to the store to get some things for the house. I had a shoulder shawl of the mistress's over my head and when I got to the store I was shamed to go in and [saw] the overseer raising up his arm to throw an iron weight at one of the slaves and that was the last I knew. That weight struck me in the head and broke my skull and cut a piece of that shawl clean off and drove it into my head. They carried me to the house all bleeding and fainting. I had no bed, no place to lie down on at all, and they lay me on the seat of the loom, and I stayed there all that day and next, and the next day I went to work again and there I worked with the blood and sweat rolling down my face till I couldn't see" (Telford, n.d., 5).

S24. Employed with Her Father (1863)

After this she lived for five or six years with John Stewart, where at first she worked in the house, but afterwards "hired her time," and Dr. Thompson, son of her master's guardian, "stood for her," that is, was her surety for the payment of what she owed. She employed the time thus hired in the rudest labors,—drove oxen, carted, plowed, and did all the work of a man,—sometimes earning money enough in a year, beyond what she paid her master, "to buy a pair of steers," worth forty dollars. The amount exacted of a woman for her time was fifty or sixty dollars,—of a man, one hundred to one hundred and fifty dollars. Frequently Harriet worked for her father, who was a timber inspector, and superintended the cutting and hauling of great quantities of timber for the Baltimore shipyards. Stewart, his temporary master, was a builder, and for the work of Ross used to receive as much as five dollars a day sometimes, he being a superior workman. While engaged with her father, she would cut wood, haul logs, etc. Her usual "stint" was half a cord of wood in a day (Sanborn, 1863).

S25. Employed in "Man's Work" (1869)

She had worked only as a field-hand for many years, following the oxen, loading and unloading wood, and carrying heavy burdens, by which her naturally remarkable power of muscle was so developed that her feats of strength often called forth the wonder of strong laboring men. Thus was she preparing for the life of hardship and endurance which lay before her, for the deeds of daring she was to do, and of which her ignorant and darkened mind at that time never dreamed (Bradford, 1869, 9–10).

S26. Feats of Strength (1907)

As Harriet grew older she became a marvelous specimen of physical womanhood, and before she was nineteen years old was a match for the strongest man on the plantation of the new master to whom she now belonged. He would often exhibit her feats of strength to his friends as one of the sights of his place. She could lift huge barrels of produce and draw a loaded stone boat like an ox (F. C. Drake, 1907).

S27. The 1833 Shower of Meteors (1913)

In 1833, "when the stars fell," referring to a great meteoric shower of the time, "Aunt Harriet" was a grown woman and doing a man's work in the fields, plowing, haying and wood cutting. She often recalled the time, telling of going to a neighboring plantation to visit her mother at night, which was against orders. Her brother remained outside the cabin to see that the guards did not surprise her. He called her to come out and see the stars. "They were all shooting whichway." All thought the end of the world had come ("Aunt Harriet Was Very Old," 1913).

S28. Visions before Escape—Sanborn's Version (1863)

She declares that before her escape from slavery, she used to dream of flying over fields and towns, and rivers and mountains, looking down upon them "like a bird," and reaching at last a great fence, or sometimes a river, over which she would try to fly, "but it appeared like I wouldn't have the strength, and just as I was sinking down, there would be ladies all dressed in white over there, and they would put out their arms and pull me across." There is nothing strange in this, perhaps, but she declares that when she came North she remembered those very places as those she had seen in her dreams, and many of the ladies who befriended her were those she had been helped by in her visions (Sanborn, 1863).

S29. Visions before Escape—Cheney's Version (1865)

Often these visions came to her in the midst of her work. She once said, "We'd been carting manure all day, and the other girl and I were going home on the sides of the cart, and another boy was driving, when suddenly I heard such music as filled all the air;" and she saw a vision which she described in language which sounded like the old prophets in its grand flow; interrupted now and then by what the other girl said, by Master's coming and calling her, to wake up, and her protests that she wasn't asleep (Cheney, 1865, 36).

S30. Resolution Not to Be Sold (1863)

In 1849 the young man died, and the slaves were to be sold, though previously set free by an old will. Harriet resolved not to be sold, and so, with no knowledge of the North—having only heard of Pennsylvania and New Jersey—she walked away one night alone (Sanborn, 1863).

S31. She Prays for the Master's Change of Heart—or His Death (1869)

Disabled and sick, her flesh all wasted away, she was returned to her *owner*. He tried to sell her, but no one would buy her. "They said they wouldn't give a sixpence for me," she said.

"And so," she said, "from Christmas till March I worked as I could, and I *prayed* through all the long nights—I groaned and prayed for old master: 'Oh Lord, convert master!' 'Oh Lord, change that man's heart!'

"Appears like I prayed all the time," said Harriet; "about my work, everywhere, I prayed and I groaned to the Lord. When I went to the horse-trough to wash my face, I took up the water in my hand and I said, 'Oh Lord, wash me, make me clean!' Then I take up something to wipe my face, and I say, 'Oh Lord, wipe away all my sin!' When I took the broom and began to sweep, I groaned, 'Oh Lord, whatsoever sin there be in my heart, sweep it out, Lord, clear and clean!'"

No words can describe the pathos of her tones, as she broke out into these words of prayer, after the manner of her people. "And so," said she, "I prayed all night long for master, till the first of March; and all the time he was bringing people to look at me, and trying to sell me. Then we heard that some of us was going to be sold to go with the chain-gang down to the cotton and rice fields, and they said I was going, and my brothers, and sisters. Then I changed my prayer. First of March I began to pray, 'Oh Lord, if you [aren't] never going to change that man's heart, kill him, Lord, and take him out of the way.'

"Next thing I heard old master was dead, and he died just as he lived. Oh, then, it appeared like I'd give all the world full of gold, if I had it, to bring that poor soul back. But I couldn't pray for him no longer."

The slaves were told that their master's will provided that none of them should be sold out of the state. This satisfied most of them, and they were very happy. But Harriet was not satisfied; she never closed her eyes that she did not imagine she saw the horsemen coming, and heard the screams of women and children, as they were being dragged away to a far worse slavery than that they were enduring there.

Harriet was married at this time to a free Negro, who not only did not trouble himself about her fears, but did his best to betray her, and bring her back after she escaped.[8]

She would start up at night with the cry, "Oh, they're coming, they're coming, I must go!" Her husband called her a fool, and said she was like old Cudjo, who when a joke went round, never laughed till half an hour after everybody else got through, and so just as all danger was past she began to be frightened.

But still Harriet in fancy saw the horsemen coming, and heard the screams of terrified women and children. "And all that time, in my dreams and visions," she said, "I seemed to see a line, and on the other side of that line were green fields, and lovely flowers, and beautiful white ladies,[9] who stretched out their arms to me over the line, but I couldn't reach them nohow. I always fell before I got to the line."

One Saturday it was whispered in the quarters that two of Harriet's sisters had been sent off with the chain-gang. That morning she started, having persuaded three of her brothers to accompany her, but they had not gone far when the brothers, appalled by the dangers before and behind them, determined to go back, and in spite of her remonstrances dragged her with them. In fear and terror, she remained over Sunday, and on Monday night a Negro from another part of the plantation came privately to tell Harriet that herself and brothers were to be carried off that night. The poor old mother, who belonged to the same mistress, was just going to milk. Harriet wanted to get away without letting her know, because she knew that she would raise an uproar[10] and prevent her going, or insist upon going with her, and the time for this was not yet.

But she must give some intimation to those she was going to leave of her intention, and send such a farewell as she might to the friends and relations on the plantation. These communications were generally made by singing. They sang as they walked along the country roads, and the chorus was taken up by others, and the uninitiated knew not the hidden meaning of the words—

When that old chariot comes,
   I'm going to leave you;
I'm bound for the promised land,
   I'm going to leave you.

These words meant something more than a journey to the Heavenly Canaan.

Harriet said, "Here, mother, go along; I'll do the milking tonight and bring it in." The old woman went to her cabin. Harriet took down her sun-bonnet and went on to the "big house," where some of her relatives lived as house servants. She thought she could trust Mary, but there were others in the kitchen, and she could say nothing.

Mary began to frolic with her. She threw her across the kitchen, and ran out, knowing that Mary would follow her. But just as they turned the corner of the house, the master to whom Harriet was now hired, came riding up on his horse. Mary darted back, and Harriet thought there was no way now but to sing.

But "the Doctor," as the master was called, was regarded with special awe by his slaves; if they were singing or talking together in the field, or on the road, and "the Doctor" appeared, all was hushed till he passed. But Harriet had no time for ceremony; her friends must have a warning; and whether the Doctor thought her *impertinent* or not, she must sing him farewell. So on she went to meet him, singing:

I'm sorry I'm going to leave you,
   Farewell, oh farewell;
But I'll meet you in the morning,
   Farewell, oh farewell.

The Doctor passed on, and she bowed as she went on, still singing:

I'll meet you in the morning,
   I'm bound for the promised land,
On the other side of Jordan,
   Bound for the promised land.

She reached the gate and looked round; the Doctor had stopped his horse, and had turned around in the saddle, and was looking at her as if there might be more in this than "met the ear." Harriet closed the gate, went on a little way, came back, the Doctor still gazing at her. She lifted up the gate as if she had not latched it properly, waved her hand to him, and burst out again:

> I'll meet you in the morning,
>   Safe in the promised land,
> On the other side of Jordan,
>   Bound for the promised land (Bradford, 1869, 13–19)

S32. A "White Lady" Assists Her Escape—Sanborn's Version (1863)

She found a friend in a white lady, who knew her story and helped her on her way. After many adventures, she reached Philadelphia, where she found work and earned a small stock of money (Sanborn, 1863).

S33. A "White Lady" Assists Her Escape—Tatlock's Version (1939)

Harriet and her brothers—I think it was two—started out. Harriet knew the North Star. That is one thing she insisted that she was always sure of. But the brothers disagreed with her about directions, and she returned. Harriet did not want to go on alone apparently.

But afterward Harriet decided she would go. The only person she told was a white woman who lived nearby. This white woman must have been a Quaker, as it was the Quakers who then gave escaping Negroes the most aid. Harriet had a bed quilt which she highly prized, a quilt she had pieced together.[11] She did not dare to give this to any of the slaves, for if this was found in their possession, they would be questioned and punished for having known about her plans. She gave this bed quilt to the white woman. I recall that Harriet even told me this woman's name but what it was I do not remember. The white woman gave her a paper with two names upon it, and directions how she might get to the first house where she would receive aid.

Harriet reached this first house. When she arrived and showed the woman of the house the paper, Harriet was told to take a broom and sweep the yard. This surprised Harriet, but she asked no questions. Perhaps she suspected camouflage. Anyone passing the house would not suspect the Negro girl working in the yard of being a runaway slave. The husband, who was a farmer, came home in the early evening. In the dark he loaded his wagon, put her in it, well covered, and drove to the outskirts of another town. Here he told her to get out, and directed her to a second station. Such stations existed in Maryland. She was handed on from one to another until she got north.

In the north she began to think about her family. The desire to aid them out of their bondage became strong, and she started her career as an operator of the Underground Railroad (Tatlock, 1939a, 6–9).

S34. Self-Liberation, Spiritual Transformation, and Mission (1869)

And she started on her journey, "not knowing whither she went," except that she was going to follow the north star, till it led her to liberty. Cautiously and by night she traveled, cunningly feeling her way, and finding out who were friends; till after a long and painful journey she found, in answer to careful inquiries, that she had at last crossed that magic "line" which then separated the land of bondage from the land of freedom; for this was before we were commanded by law to take part in the iniquity of slavery, and aid in taking and sending back those poor hunted fugitives who had manhood and intelligence enough to enable them to make their way thus far towards freedom.

"When I found I had crossed that *line*," she said, "I looked at my hands to see if I was the same person.[12] There was such a glory over every thing; the sun came like gold through the trees, and over the fields, and I felt like I was in Heaven."

But then came the bitter drop in the cup of joy. She said she felt like a man who was put in state prison for twenty-five years.[13] All those twenty-five years he was thinking of his home, and longing for the time when he would see it again. At last the day comes—he leaves the prison gates—he makes his way to his old home, but his old home is not there. The house has been pulled down, and a new one has been put up in its place; his family and friends are gone nobody knows where; there is no one to take him by the hand, no one to welcome him.

"So it was with me," she said. "I had crossed the line. I was *free*; but there was no one to welcome me to the land of freedom. I was a stranger in a strange land; and my home, after all, was down in Maryland; because my father, my mother, my brothers, and sisters, and friends were there. But I was free, and *they* should be free. I would make a home in the North and bring them there, God helping me. Oh, how I prayed then," she said; "I said to the Lord, 'I'm going to hold steady on to *you*, and I *know* you'll see me through'" (Bradford, 1869, 19–20).

S35. *Guided by the North Star (1939)*

She also told me of her escape. After being so ill treated she decided to run away. Hearing the people talk about the north and how some was guided by the North Star, she determined to strike out, so one dark night she left home guided by the north star when she could see the stars, hiding in the woods in the day.

She crossed the line into Delaware finding some friends who helped her through to New Jersey into Pennsylvania, a free woman. She thought of her father and mother, sister and three brothers. Having found some friends, telling them of her escape and determination, they were much impressed with her courage and daring, [and] enlisted her services with the Underground Railroad[14] (H. Bowley, 1939a).

INDIVIDUAL RESCUES FROM MARYLAND

S36. *A "Sister" Rescued from Auction at Cambridge (1939)*

She told me of the plan to get my mother[15] away from Cambridge and [she] was sold twice in one day. When she [was] sold the first time, my uncle bidding her off, and while the auctioneer went to dinner she was hid in a lady's house only a five minute's walk from the court house. When the auctioneers returned, mother was gone. Then they sold her sight unseen.

My father John Bowley took mother and two children in a small boat to Baltimore. My uncle met them there. Aunt Harriet had a hiding place there for her, in a few days took her and the children and several others aboard the Underground Railroad into Canada (H. Bowley, 1939a).

S37. *Story of Return to Rescue Her Husband (1863)*

After many adventures, she reached Philadelphia, where she found work and earned a small stock of money. With this money in her purse, she traveled back to Maryland for her husband, but she found him married to another woman, and no longer caring to live with her. This, however, was not until two years after her escape, for she does not seem to have reached her old home in her first two expeditions.

In December 1850, she had visited Baltimore and brought away her sister and two children, who had come up from Cambridge in a boat, under charge of her sister's husband, a free black.

A few months after she had brought away her brother and two other men, but it was not till the fall of 1851 that she found her husband and learned of his infidelity. She did not give way to rage or grief, but collected a party of fugitives and brought them safely to Philadelphia (Sanborn, 1863).

S38. Story of Husband's Infidelity Linked to Transformation of Mission (1865)

She remained two years in Philadelphia working hard and carefully hoarding her money. Then she hired a room, furnished it as well as she could, bought a nice suit of men's clothes, and went back to Maryland for her husband. But the faithless man had taken to himself another wife. Harriet did not dare venture into her presence, but sent word to her husband where she was. He declined joining her. At first her grief and anger were excessive. She said, "she did not care what master did to her, she thought she would go right in and make all the trouble she could, she was determined to see her old man once more;" but finally she thought "how foolish it was just for temper to make mischief;" and that "if he could do without her, she could without him," and so "he dropped out of her heart,"[16] and she determined to give her life to brave deeds. Thus all personal aims died out of her heart; and with her simple brave motto, "I can't die but once," she began the work which has made her Moses,—the deliverer of her people (Cheney 1865, 35).

S39. Christmas Rescue of Brothers (1869)

At one time, Harriet was much troubled in spirit about her three brothers,[17] feeling sure that some great evil was impending over their heads. She wrote a letter, by the hand of a friend, to a man named Jacob Jackson, who lived near there. Jacob was a free Negro, who could both read and write, and who was under suspicion at that time, as it was thought he had something to do with the disappearance of so many slaves. It was necessary, therefore, to be very cautious in writing to him. Jacob had an adopted son, William Henry Jackson, also free, who had come South; and so Harriet determined to sign her letter with his name, knowing that Jacob would be clever enough to understand, by her peculiar phraseology, what meaning she intended to convey to him. She, therefore, after speaking of indifferent matters, said, "Read my letter to the old folks, and give my love to them, and tell my brothers to be always *watching unto prayer*, and when *the good old ship of Zion comes along, to be ready to step aboard.*"

The letter was signed "William Henry Jackson." Jacob was not allowed to have his letters till the self-elected inspectors had had the reading of them, and studied into their secret meaning. They, therefore, got together, wiped their glasses, and got them on, and proceeded to a careful perusal of this mysterious document. What it meant, they could not imagine; William Henry Jackson had no parents or brothers, and the letter was incomprehensible. White genius having exhausted itself, black genius was called in, and Jacob's letter was at last handed to him. Jacob saw at once what it meant, but tossed it down, saying "That letter can't be meant for me, no how. I can't make head nor tail of it," and walked off and took immediate measures to let Harriet's brothers know secretly that she was coming, and they must be ready to start at a moment's notice for the North.

When Harriet arrived there, it was the day before Christmas, and she found her three brothers, who had attempted to escape, were advertised to be sold on Christmas day to the highest bidder, to go down to the cotton and rice fields with the chain gang. Christmas came on Sunday, and therefore they were not to be sold till Monday. Harriet arrived on Saturday, and gave them secret notice to be ready to start Saturday night, immediately after dark, the first stopping-place to be their father's cabin, forty miles away. When they assembled, their brother John was missing; but when Harriet was ready, the word was, "Forward!" and she "never waited for no one."

Poor John was almost ready to start, when his wife was taken ill, and in an hour or two, another little inheritor of the blessings of slavery had come into the world. John must go off for a "Granny," and then he would not leave his wife in her present circumstances. But after the birth of the child, he began to think he must start; the North and Liberty, or the South and life-long Slavery—these were the alternatives, and this was his last chance.

He tried again and again to steal out of the door, but a watchful eye was on him, and he was always arrested by the question, "Where are you going, John?" At length he told her was going to try to see if he couldn't get hired out on Christmas to another man. His wife did not think that he was to be sold. He went out of the door, and stood by the corner of the house, near her bed, listening. At length, he heard her sobbing and crying, and not being able to endure it, he went back. "Oh! John," said his wife, "You're going to leave me; but, wherever you go, remember me and the children."[18]

John went out and started at full speed for his father's cabin, forty miles away. At daybreak, he overtook the others in the fodder house near the cabin of their parents.

Harriet had not seen her mother there for six years, but they did not dare to let the old woman know of their being in her neighborhood, or of their intentions, for she would have raised such an uproar in her efforts to detain them with her, that the whole plantation would have been alarmed. The poor old woman had been expecting the boys all day, to spend Christmas with her as usual. She had been hard at work, had killed a pig, and put it to all the various uses to which [swine's][19] flesh is doomed, and had made all the preparations her circumstances admitted of, to give them a sumptuous entertainment, and there she sat watching.

In the night, when Harriet and two of her brothers and two other men, who had escaped with them, arrived at the fodder house, they were exhausted and famished. They sent the two strange men up to the house to try and speak to "Old Ben," their father, but not to let their mother know of their being in the neighborhood. The men succeeded in rousing old Ben, who came out, and as soon+ as he heard their story, he gathered together a quantity of provisions, and came down to the fodder house, and slipped them inside the door, taking care not to *see* his children. Up among the ears of corn they lay, and one of them he had not seen for six years.

It rained very hard all that Sunday, and there they lay all day, for they could not start till night. At about daybreak, John joined them. There were wide chinks in the boards of the fodder house, and through them they could see their father's cabin; and all day long, every few minutes, they would see the old woman come out, and, shading her eyes with her hand, take a long look down the road to see if her children were coming, and then they could almost hear her sigh as she turned into the house, disappointed.

Two or three times the old man came down, and pushed food inside the door, and after nightfall he came to accompany them part of the way upon their journey. When he reached the fodder house, he tied his handkerchief tight over his eyes, and two of his sons taking him by each arm, he accompanied them some miles upon their journey. They then bade him farewell, and left him standing blind-fold[ed] in the middle of the road. When he could no longer hear their footsteps, he took off the handkerchief, and turned back.

But before leaving, they had gone up to the cabin, to take a silent farewell of the poor old mother. Through the little window of the cabin, they saw the old woman sitting by her fire with a pipe in her mouth, her head on her hand, rocking back and forth as she did when she was in trouble, and wondering what new evil had come to her children. With streaming eyes, they watched her for ten or fifteen minutes; but time was precious, and they must reach their next station before daybreak, and so they turned sadly away.

When the holidays were over, and the men came for the three brothers to sell them, they could not be found. The first place to search was of course the plantation where all their relatives and friends lived. They went to the "big house," and asked the "Doctor" if he had seen anything of them. The Doctor said, "No, they mostly came up there to see the other niggers when they came for Christmas, but they hadn't been round at all. "Have you been down to Old Ben's?" the Doctor asked. "Yes." "What does Old Rit say?" "Old Rit says not one of them came this Christmas. She was looking for them most all day, and most broke her heart about it." "What does Old Ben say?" "Old Ben says that he hasn't seen one of his children this Christmas." "Well, if Old Ben says that, they haven't been round." And so the man-hunters went off disappointed.

One of the brothers, William Henry, had long been attached to a girl named Catherine, who lived with another master; but her master would not let her marry him. When William Henry made up his mind to start with Harriet, he determined to bring Catherine with him. And so he went to a tailor's, and bought a new suit of men's clothes, and threw them over the garden fence of Catherine's master. The garden ran down to a run, and Catherine had been notified where to find the clothes. When the time had come to get ready, Catherine went to the foot of the garden and dressed herself in the suit of men's clothes. She was soon missed, and all the girls in the house were set to looking for Catherine. Presently they saw coming up through the garden, as if from the river, a well-dressed little darkey, and they all stopped looking for Catherine to stare at him. He walked directly by them round the house, and went out of the gate, without the slightest suspicion being excited as to who he was. In a fortnight from that time, the whole party were safe in Canada.[20]

William Henry died in Canada, but Catherine has been seen and talked with by the writer, at the house of the old people (Bradford, 1869, 57–64).

S40. First Winter in Canada (1863)

But the first winter was terribly severe for these poor runaways. They earned their bread by chopping wood in the snows of a Canadian forest; they were frost-bitten, hungry, and naked. Harriet was their good angel. She kept house for her brother, and the poor creatures boarded with her.

She worked for them, begged for them, prayed for them, with the strange familiarity of communion with God which seems natural to these people, and carried them by the help of God through the hard winter (Sanborn, 1863).

S41. Story of Rescue of "Tilly" (1886)

At one time, as she was on her way South for a party of slaves, she was stopped not far from the southern shore of the Chesapeake Bay, by a young woman, who had been for some days in hiding, and was anxiously watching for "Moses," who was soon expected to pass that way.[21]

This girl was a young and pretty Mulatto, named Tilly; she had been lady's maid and dressmaker, for her Mistress. She was engaged to a young man from another plantation, but he had joined one of Harriet's parties, and gone North. Tilly was to have gone also at that time, but had found it impossible to get away. Now she had learned that it was her Master's intention to give her to a Negro of his own for his wife; and in fear and desperation, she made a strike for freedom. Friends had concealed her, and all had been on the watch for Moses.

The distress and excitement of the poor creature was so great, and she begged and implored in such agonized tones that Harriet would just see her safe to Baltimore, where she knew of friends who would harbor her, and help her on the way, that Harriet determined to turn about, and endeavor to take the poor girl thus far on her Northward journey.

They reached the shore of Chesapeake Bay too late to leave that night, and were obliged to hide for a night and day in the loft of an old out-house, where every sound caused poor Tilly to tremble as if she had an ague fit. When the time for the boat to leave arrived, a sad disappointment awaited them. The boat on which they had expected to leave was disabled, and another boat was to take its place. At that time, according to the law of Slavery, no Negro could leave his Master's land, or travel anywhere, without a pass, properly signed by his owner. Of course this poor fugitive had no pass; and Harriet's passes were her own wits; but among her many friends, there was one who seemed to have influence with the clerk of the boat, on which she expected to take passage; and she was the bearer of a note requesting, or commanding him to take these two women to the end of his route, asking no questions.

Now here was an unforeseen difficulty; the boat was not going; the clerk was not there; all on the other boat were strangers. But forward they must go, trusting in Providence. As they walked down to the boat, a gang of lazy white men standing together, began to make comments on their appearance.

"Too many likely looking Niggers traveling North, about these days." "Wonder if these wenches have got a pass." "Where are you going, you two?" Tilly trembled and cowered, and clung to her protector, but Harriet put on a bold front, and holding the note given her by her friend in her hand, and supporting her terrified charge, she walked by the men, taking no notice of their insults.

They joined the stream of people going up to get their tickets, but when Harriet asked for hers, the clerk eyed her suspiciously, and said: "You just stand aside, you two; I'll attend to your case bye and bye."

Harriet led the young girl to the bow of the boat, where they were alone, and here, having no other help, she, as was her custom, addressed herself to the Lord. Kneeling on the seat, and supporting her head on her hands, and fixing her eyes on the waters of the bay, she groaned:

"Oh, Lord! You've been with me in six troubles, *don't* desert me in the seventh!"

"Moses! Moses!" cried Tilly, pulling her by the sleeve. "Do go and see if you can't get tickets now."

"Oh Lord! You've been with me in six troubles, *don't* desert me in the seventh."

And so Harriet's story goes on in her peculiarly graphic manner, till at length in terror Tilly exclaimed:

"Oh, Moses! The man is coming. What shall we do?"

"Oh Lord, you've been with me in six troubles!"

Here the clerk touched her on the shoulder, and Tilly thought their time had come, but all he said was:

"You can come now and get your tickets," and their troubles were over. (Bradford, 1886, 57–60).[22]

S42. Story of the Rescue of "Joe" (1869)

Of the very many interesting stories told me by Harriet, I cannot refrain from telling to my readers that of *Joe*,[23] who accompanied her upon her seventh or eighth[24] journey from Maryland to Canada.

Joe was a noble specimen of a Negro, and was hired out by his master to a man for whom he worked faithfully for six years, saving him the expense of an overseer, and taking all trouble off his hands. At length this man found him so absolutely necessary to him, that he determined to buy him at any cost. His master held him proportionably high. However, by paying a thousand dollars down for him, and promising to pay another thousand in a certain time, Joe passed into the hands of his new master.

As may be imagined, Joe was somewhat surprised when the first order issued from his master's lips, was, "Now, Joe, strip and take a whipping!" Joe's experience of *whippings*, as he had seen them inflicted upon others, was not such as to cause him particularly to desire to go through the same operation on his own account; and he, naturally enough, demurred, and at first thought of resisting. But he called to mind a scene which he had witnessed a few days before, in the field, the particulars of which are too horrible and too harassing to the feelings to be given to my readers, and he thought it best to submit; but first he tried remonstrance.

"Master," said he, "haven't I always been faithful to you? Haven't I worked through sun and rain, early in the morning and late at night; haven't I saved you an overseer by doing his work; have you anything to complain of against me?"

"No, Joe; I've no complaint to make of you; you're a good nigger, and you've always worked well; but the first lesson my niggers have to learn is that I am *master*, and that they are not to resist or refuse to obey anything I tell them to do. So the first thing they've got to do, is to be whipped; if they resist, they get it all the harder; and so I'll go on, till I kill them, but they've got to give up at last, and learn that I'm master."

Joe thought it best to submit. He stripped off his upper clothing, and took his whipping without a word; but as he drew his clothes up over his torn and bleeding back, he said, "This is the last!"[25] That night he took a boat and went a long distance to the cabin of Harriet's father, and said, "Next time Moses comes, let me know." It was only a week or two after that, that the mysterious woman whom no one could lay their finger on appeared, and men, women, and children began to disappear from the plantations. One fine morning Joe was missing, and his brother William, from another plantation; Peter and Eliza, too, were gone; and these made part of Harriet's next party, who began their pilgrimage from Maryland to Canada, or as they expressed it, from "Egypt to the land of Canaan."

Their adventures were enough to fill a volume; they were pursued; hey were hidden in "potato holes," while their pursuers passed within a few feet of them; they were passed along by friends in various disguises; they scattered and separated, to be led by guides by a roundabout way, to a meeting-place again. They were taken in by Sam Green, the man who was afterwards sent to State Prison for ten years for having a copy of "Uncle Tom's Cabin" in his house; and so, hunted and hiding and wandering, they came at last to the long bridge at the entrance of the city of Wilmington, Delaware. The rewards posted up everywhere had been at first five hundred dollars for Joe, if taken within the limits of the United States; then a thousand, and then fifteen hundred dollars, "and all expenses clear and clean, for his body in Easton Jail." Eight hundred for William, and four hundred for Peter, and twelve thousand for the woman who enticed them away.[26] The long Wilmington Bridge was guarded by police officers, and the advertisements were everywhere. The party were scattered, and taken to the houses of different colored friends, and word was sent secretly to Thomas Garrett, of Wilmington, of their condition, and the necessity of their being taken across the bridge.

Thomas Garrett is a Quaker and a man of wonderfully large and generous heart, through whose hands, Harriet tells me, two thousand self-emancipated slaves passed on their way to freedom. He was always ready, heart and hand and means, in aiding these poor fugitives, and rendered most efficient help to Harriet on many of her journeys back and forth. A letter received a few days since by the writer, from this noble-hearted philanthropist, will be given presently.

As soon as Thomas Garrett heard of the condition of these poor people, his plan was formed. He engaged two wagons, filled them with brick-layers, whom of course he paid well for their share in the enterprise, and sent them across the bridge. They went as if on a frolic, singing and shouting. The guards saw them pass, and of course expected them to re-cross the bridge. After nightfall (and fortunately it was a dark night) the same wagons went back, but with an addition to their party. The fugitives were on the bottom of the wagons, the bricklayers on the seats, still singing and shouting; and so they passed by the guards, who were entirely unsuspicious of the nature of the load the wagons contained, or of the amount of property thus escaping their hands. And so they made their way to New York.

When they entered the anti-slavery office there, Joe was recognized at once by the description in the advertisement. "Well," said Mr. Oliver Johnson, "I am glad to see the man whose head is worth fifteen hundred dollars." At this Joe's heart sank. If the advertisement had got to New York, that place which it had taken them so many days and nights to reach, he thought he was in danger still. "And how far is it now to Canada?" he asked. When told how many miles, for they were to come through New York State, and cross the Suspension Bridge, he was ready to give up.

"From that time Joe was silent," said Harriet; "he sang no more, he talked no more; he sat with his head on his hand, and nobody could amuse him or make him take any interest in anything." They passed along in safety, and at length found themselves in the cars, approaching the Suspension Bridge. The rest were very joyous and happy, but Joe sat silent and sad. Their fellow-passengers all seemed interested in and for them, and listened with tears, as Harriet and all their party lifted up their voices and sang:

I'm on my way to Canada,[27]
    That cold and dreary land;
The sad effects of slavery
    I can't no longer stand.
I've served my master all my days,
    Without a dime's reward;
And now I'm forced to run away,
    To flee the lash abroad.
Farewell, old master, don't think hard of me,
I'll travel on to Canada, where all the slaves are free.

The hounds are baying on my track,
    Old master comes behind,
Resolved that he will bring me back,
    Before I cross the line;
I'm now embarked for yonder shore,
    There a man's a man by law;
The iron horse will bear me o'er
    To shake the lion's paw.
Oh, righteous Father, wilt thou not pity me
And aid me on to Canada where all the slaves are free.

Oh, I heard Queen Victoria say,
    That if we would forsake
Our native land of slavery
    And come across the lake;
That she was standing on the shore
    With arms extended wide,
To give us all a peaceful home
    Beyond the rolling tide,
Farewell, old master, etc.

The cars began to cross the bridge. Harriet was very anxious to have her companions see the Falls. William, Peter, and Eliza came eagerly to look at the wonderful sight; but Joe sat still, with his head upon his hand.

"Joe, come look at the Falls. Joe, you fool you, come see the Falls! It's your last chance." But Joe sat still and never raised his head. At length Harriet knew by the rise in the center of the bridge, and the descent on the other side, that they had crossed "the line." She sprang across to Joe's seat, shook him with all her might, and shouted, "Joe, you've shook the lion's paw!" Joe did not know what she meant. "Joe, you're *free!*" shouted Harriet. Then Joe's head went up, he raised his hands on high, and his face, streaming with tears, to heaven, and broke out in loud and thrilling tones:

"Glory to God and Jesus too,
    One more soul is safe!
Oh, go and carry the news
    One more soul got safe."

"Joe, come and look at the Falls!" called Harriet

"Glory to God and Jesus too,
    One more soul got safe"

was all the answer. The cars stopped on the other side. Joe's feet were the first to touch British soil, after those of the conductor.

Loud roared the waters of Niagara, but louder still ascended the anthem of praise from the overflowing heart of the freeman. And can we doubt that the strain was taken up by angel voices, and that through the arches of Heaven echoed and re-echoed the strain:

"Glory to God in the Highest,
Glory to God and Jesus too,
    One more soul is safe."

"The ladies and gentlemen gathered round him," said Harriet, "till I couldn't see Joe for the crowd, only I heard 'Glory to God and Jesus too!' louder than ever." William went after him, and pulled him, saying, "Joe, stop your noise! You act like a fool!" Then Peter ran in and jerked him most off his feet,—"Joe, stop your hollering! Folks'll think you're crazy!"

But Joe gave no heed. The ladies were crying, and the tears like rain ran down Joe's sable cheeks. A lady reached over her fine cambric handkerchief to him. Joe wiped his face, and then he spoke.

"Oh, if I'd felt like this down South, it would have taken *nine* men to take me;[28] only one more journey for me now, and that is to Heaven!" "Well, you old fool you," said Harriet, with whom there seems but one step from the sublime to the ridiculous, "you might have looked at the Falls first, and then gone to Heaven afterwards." She has seen Joe several times since, a happy and industrious freeman in Canada (Bradford, 1869, 27–35).

S43. Rescue of Tubman's Parents—Bradford's Version (1869)

It was a wise plan of our sagacious heroine to leave her old parents till the last to be brought away. They were pensioned off as too old to work, had a cabin, and a horse and cow, and were quite comfortable. If Harriet had taken them away before the young people, these last would have been sold into Southern slavery, to keep them out of her way. But at length Harriet heard that the old man had been betrayed by a slave whom he had assisted, but who had turned back, and when questioned by his wife, told her the story of his intended escape,+ and of the aid he had received from "Old Ben." This woman, hoping to curry favor with her master, revealed the whole to him, and "Old Ben" was arrested. He was to be tried the next week, when Harriet appeared upon the scene, and, as she says, "saved them the expense of the trial, and removed her father to a higher court, by taking him off to Canada." . . .

It has been mentioned that Harriet never asks anything for herself, but whenever her people were in trouble, or she felt impelled to go South to guide to freedom friend or brother, or father and mother, if she had not time to work for the money, she was persistent till she got it from somebody. When she received one of her *intimations* that the old people were in trouble, and it was time for her to go to them, she asked the Lord where she should go for the money. She was in some way, as she supposed, directed to the office of a certain gentleman in New York. When she left the house of her friends to go there, she said, "I'm going to Mr. ——'s[29] office, and I ain't going to leave there, and I ain't going to eat or drink till I get enough money to take me down after the old people."

She went into this gentleman's office.

"What do you want, Harriet?" was the first greeting.

"I want some money, sir."

"You do? How much do you want?"

"I want twenty dollars, sir."

"*Twenty dollars*! Who told you to come here for twenty dollars?"

"The Lord told me, sir."

"Well, I guess the Lord's mistaken this time."

"I guess he isn't, sir. Anyhow, I'm going to sit here till I get it."

So she sat down and went to sleep. All the morning and all the afternoon she sat there still, sleeping and rousing up—sometimes finding the office full of gentlemen—sometimes finding herself alone. Many fugitives were passing through New York at that time, and those who came in supposed that she was one of them, tired out and resting. Sometimes she would be roused up with the words, "Come, Harriet, you had better go. There's no money for you here." "No, sir. I'm not going till I get my twenty dollars."

She does not know all that happened, for deep sleep fell upon her; but probably her story was whispered about, and she roused at last to find herself the happy possessor of *sixty dollars*, which had been raised among those who came into the office. She went on her way rejoicing, to bring her old parents from the land of bondage.

She found that her father was to be tried the next Monday, for helping off slaves; so, as she says, she "removed his trial to a higher court," and hurried him off to Canada (Bradford 1869, 47–48, 109–111).

S44. Thomas Garrett's Memory of the Rescue of the Parents (1868)

She brought away her aged parents in a singular manner. They started with an old horse, fitted out in primitive style with a *straw collar*, a pair of old chaise wheels, with a board on the axle to sit on, another board swung with ropes, fastened to the axle, to rest their feet on. She got her parents, who were both slaves belonging to different masters,[30] on this rude vehicle to the railroad, put them in the cars, turned Jehu herself,[31] and drove to town in a style that no human being ever did before or since; but she was happy at having arrived safe. Next day, I furnished her with money to take them all to Canada. I afterwards sold their horse, and sent them the balance of the proceeds (Garrett, 1868).[32]

S45. Failure of Final Mission to Maryland in December 1860—Cheney (1865)

She never went to the South to bring away fugitives without being provided with money; money for the most part earned by drudgery in the kitchen, until within the last few years, when friends have aided her. She had to leave her sister's two orphan children in slavery the last time, for the want of thirty dollars. Thirty pieces of silver; an embroidered hand-kerchief or a silk dress to one, or the price of freedom to two orphan chil-dren to another! She would never allow more to join her than she could properly care for, though she often gave others directions by which they succeeded in escaping (Cheney, 1865, 35–36).

S46. Last Rescue—Sanborn (1863)

Her last visit to Maryland was made after this, in December 1860; and in spite of the agitated condition of the country, and the greater watchful-ness of the slaveholders, she brought away seven fugitives, one of them an infant, which must be drugged with opium to keep it from crying on the way, and so revealing the hiding place of the party.

She brought these safely to New York, but there a new difficulty met her. It was the mad winter of compromises, when State after State, and politician after politician, went down on their knees to beg the South not to secede. The hunting of fugitive slaves began again. Mr. Seward went over to the side of compromise. He knew the history of this poor woman; he had given his enemies a hold on him, by dealing with her; it was thought he would not scruple to betray her. The suspicion was an unworthy one, for though the Secretary could betray a cause, he could not surely have put her enemies on the track of a woman who was thus in his power, after such a career as hers had been. But so little confidence was then felt in Mr. Seward, by men who had voted for him and with him, that they hurried Harriet off to Canada, sorely against her will (Sanborn, 1863).

S47. Help from Quaker on Last Trip to Maryland (1886)

On one of her journeys to the North, as she was piloting a company of refugees, Harriet came, just as morning broke, to a town, where a colored man had lived whose house had been one of her stations of the under-ground, or unseen railroad.[33] They reached the house, and leaving her party huddled together in the middle of the street, in a pouring rain, Harriet went to the door, and gave the peculiar rap which was her customary signal to her friends. There was not the usual ready response, and she was obliged to repeat the signal several times. At length a window was raised, and the head of a *white man* appeared, with the gruff question, "Who are you?" and "What do you want?" Harriet asked after her friend, and was told that he had been obliged to leave for "harboring niggers."

Here was an unfortunate trouble; day was breaking, and daylight was the enemy of the hunted and flying fugitives. Their faithful leader stood one moment in the street, and in that moment she had flashed a message quicker than that of the telegraph to her unseen Protector, and the answer came as quickly; in a suggestion to her of an almost forgotten place of refuge. Outside of the town there was a little island in a swamp, where the grass grew tall and rank, and where no human being could be suspected of seeking a hiding place. To this spot she conducted her party; she waded the swamp, carrying in a basket two well-drugged babies (these were a pair of little twins, whom I have since seen well grown young women), and the rest of the company following. She ordered them to lie down in the tall, wet grass, and here she prayed again, and waited for deliverance. The poor creatures were all cold, and wet, and hungry, and Harriet did not dare to leave them to get supplies; for no doubt the man at whose house she had knocked, had given the alarm in town; and officers might be on the watch for them. They were truly in a wretched condition, but Harriet's faith never wavered, her silent prayer still ascended, and she confidently expected help from some quarter or other.

It was after dusk when a man came slowly walking along the solid pathway on the edge of the swamp. He was clad in the garb of a Quaker; and proved to be a "friend" in need and indeed; he seemed to be talking to himself, but ears quickened by sharp practice caught the words he was saying:

"My wagon stands in the barn-yard of the next farm across the way. The horse is in the stable; the harness hangs on a nail." And the man was gone. Night fell, and Harriet stole forth to the place designated. Not only a wagon, but a wagon well provisioned stood in the yard; and before many minutes the party were rescued from their wretched position, and were on their way rejoicing, to the next town. Here dwelt a Quaker whom Harriet knew, and he readily took charge of the horse and wagon, and no doubt returned them to their owner. How the good man who thus came to their rescue had received any information of their being in the neighborhood Harriet never knew. But these sudden deliverances never seemed to strike her as at all strange or mysterious; her prayer was the prayer of faith, and she *expected* an answer. (Bradford, 1886, 53–57)

STORIES OF CLEVER EXPLOITS AND TRICKS

S48. Her Caution to Avoid Capture (1865)

She always came in the winter when the nights are long and dark, and people who have homes stay in them. She was never seen on the plantation herself; but appointed a rendezvous for her company eight or ten miles distant, so that if they were discovered at the first start she was not compromised. She started on Saturday night; the slaves at that time being allowed to go away from home to visit their friends,—so that they would not be missed until Monday morning. Even then they were supposed to have loitered on the way, and it would often be late on Monday afternoon before the flight would be certainly known. If by any further delay the advertisement was not sent out before Tuesday morning, she felt secure of keeping ahead of it; but if it were, it required all her ingenuity to escape.

She resorted to various devices, she had confidential friends all along the road. She would hire a man to follow the one who put up the notices, and take them down as soon as his back was turned. She crossed creeks on railroad bridges by night, she hid her company in the woods while she herself not being advertised went into the towns in search of information. If met on the road, her face was always to the south, and she was always a very respectable looking darkey, not at all a poor fugitive. She would get into the cars near her pursuers, and manage to hear their plans.

By day they lay in the woods; then she pulled out her patchwork,[34] and sewed together little bits, perhaps not more than an inch square, which were afterwards made into comforters for the fugitives in Canada (Cheney, 1865, 36).

S49. Divine Guidance Leads Her into a River in March (1868)

She mostly had her regular stopping places on her route; but in one instance, when she had two stout men with her, some 30 miles below here, she said that God told her to stop, which she did; and then asked him what she must do. He told her to leave the road, and turn to the left; she obeyed, and soon came to a small stream of tide water; there was no boat, no bridge; she again inquired of her Guide what she was to do. She was told to go through. It was cold, in the month of March; but having confidence in her Guide, she went in; the water came up to her arm-pits; the men refused to follow till they saw her safe on the opposite shore. They then followed, and if I mistake not, she had soon to wade a second stream; soon after which she came to a cabin of colored people, who took them all in, put them to bed, and dried their clothes, ready to proceed next night on their journey. Harriet had run out of money, and gave them some of her underclothing to pay for their kindness.[35] When she called on me two days after, she was so hoarse she could hardly speak, and was also suffering with violent toothache. The strange part of the story we found to be, that the master of these two men had put up the previous day, at the railroad station near where she left, an advertisement for them, offering a large reward for their apprehension; but they made a safe exit (Garrett, 1868).

S50. Contacting a Party of Hidden Fugitives with Songs (1869)

At one time she left her party in the woods, and went by a long and round-about way to one of the "stations of the Underground Railway," as she called them. Here she procured food for her famished party, often paying out of her hardly-gained earnings, five dollars a day for food for them. But she dared not go back to them till night, for fear of being watched, and thus revealing their hiding-place. After nightfall, the sound of a hymn sung at a distance comes upon the ears of the concealed and famished fugitives in the woods, and they know that their deliverer is at hand. They listen eagerly for the words she sings, for by them they are to be warned of danger, or informed of safety. Nearer and nearer comes the unseen singer, and the words are wafted to their ears:

Hail, oh hail ye happy spirits,
    Death no more shall make you fear,
No grief nor sorrow, pain nor anger (anguish)[36]
    Shall no more distress you there.

Around him are ten thousand angels,
    Always ready to obey command.
They are always hovering round you,
    Till you reach the heavenly land.

Jesus, Jesus will go with you,
    He will lead you to his throne;
He who died has gone before you,
    Trod the wine-press all alone.

He whose thunders shake creation;
    He who bids the planets roll;

He who rides upon the temple (tempest)
  And his scepter sways the whole.

Dark and thorny is the desert,
  Through the pilgrim makes his ways [*sic*]
Yet beyond this vale of sorrow,
  Lies the fields of endless days.

I give these words exactly as Harriet sang them to me to a sweet and simple Methodist air.[37] "The first time I go by singing this hymn, they don't come out to me," she said, "till I listen if the coast is clear; then when I go back and sing it again, they come out. But if I sing:

Moses go down in Egypt
  Tell old Pharaoh let me go;
Hadn't been for Adam's fall,
  Shouldn't have to died at all.

Then they don't come out, for there's danger in the way" (Bradford, 1869, 25–27).

S51. Carrying and Quieting Babies (1943)

I have heard her tell how she carried a ticking bag around her waist. If there were babies to be brought north, as often there were, she gave them paregoric to stop their crying, and put them in this bag, when near farms or homes so they might not cry and so attract notice (Tatlock, 1943a).

S52. Knocking Out a Bothersome Tooth (1896)

She tolerated no weakness in herself or in her followers. A toothache tormented her during one of her journeys. She took a stone or bit of iron and knocked the offending tooth out of her mouth (Wyman, 1896, 113).[38]

S53. Hiding in Potato Holes (1913)

On one occasion [she] hid herself and six fugitive slaves in "potato holes" dug in the fields, the runaways covering themselves completely with dirt ("Harriet Tubman Is Dead," 1913).

S54. She Tells the Others to Shoot the Weak Fugitive (1865)

The expedition was governed by the strictest rules. If any man gave out, he must be shot. "Would you really do that?" she was asked. "Yes," she replied, "if he was weak enough to give out, he'd be weak enough to betray us all, and all who had helped us; and do you think I'd let so many die just for one coward man?" "Did you ever have to shoot any one?" [she] was asked. "One time," she said, "a man gave out the second night; his feet were sore and swollen, he couldn't go any further; he'd rather go back and die, if he must." They tried all arguments in vain, bathed his feet, tried to strengthen him, but it was of no use, he would go back. Then she said, "I told the boys to get their guns ready, and shoot him. They'd have done it in a minute; but when he heard that, he jumped right up and went on as well as anybody" (Cheney, 1865, 36).[39]

S55. Variant: "Dead Niggers Tell No Tales" (1869)

Sometimes members of her party would become exhausted, foot-sore, and bleeding, and declare they could not go on, they must stay where they dropped down, and die; others would think a voluntary return to slavery better than being overtaken and carried back, and would insist upon returning; then there was no remedy but force; the revolver carried by this bold and daring pioneer would be pointed at their heads. "Dead niggers tell no tales," said Harriet; "Go on or die;" and so she compelled them to drag their weary limbs on their northward journey (Bradford, 1869, 24–25).

S56. Avoiding Capture with Fluttering Chickens (1886)

With a daring almost heedless, she went even to the very village where she would be most likely to meet one of the masters to whom she had been hired; and having stopped at the Market and bought a pair of live fowls, she went along the street with her sun-bonnet well over her face, and with the bent and decrepit air of an aged woman. Suddenly on turning a corner, she spied her old master coming towards her. She pulled the string which tied the legs of the chickens; they began to flutter and scream, and as her master passed, she was stooping and busily engaged in attending to the fluttering fowls. And he went on his way, little thinking that he was brushing the very garments of the woman who had dared to steal herself, and others of his belongings (Bradford, 1886, 34–35).

S57. Laughing at Enemies (1889)

Sometimes, when she and her party were concealed in the woods, they saw their pursuers pass, on their horses, down the high road, tacking up the advertisements for them on the fences and trees. "And then how we laughed," said she. "*We* was the fools, and *they* was the wise men; but we wasn't fools enough to go down the high road in the broad daylight" (Bradford, 1869, 25).

S58. Taking Railroad South to Avoid Capture (1896)

Once she sent her company of fugitives onward by some secret route, and started North herself on a railroad train. There were posters in the car offering $40,000 for her head.[40] The passengers read these papers aloud, so that she learned their purport. At the next station, the dauntless woman left the car and took a train going South, feeling convinced that no one would suspect that a woman upon whose life a price was set would dare turn her face in that direction. The reward was promised by the slave-holders of the region she was accustomed to visit (Wyman, 1896, 113).

S59. Avoiding Capture by Pretending to Read (1939)

At another time when she heard men talking about her, she pretended to read a book which she carried. One man remarked, "This can't be the woman. The one we want can't read or write." Harriet devoutly hoped this book was right side up (Tatlock, 1939a).

S60. Singing to Distract Potential Enemies (1913)

At another time she was being questioned too closely on a stage coach, by men who were looking for her and she said: "Gentlemen, let me sing for you"—she had a great voice for song—then sang on for mile after mile till they came to the next station, then bade them good-bye and left the stage ("Two Timely Topics Discussed by Doctor Rosengrant," 1913).

S61. Treachery of Supposed Friends (1950?)

On one occasion as she was journeying north with a group in a wagon, they stopped at the home of a supposed colored friend. He was not at home upon their arrival, but his wife fed them and put them to bed in the attic of the house. Harriet was awake when the husband arrived home and his wife informed of the presence of the group in the attic, for she heard him remark, "There is a reward offered for the capture of Harriet and I am going to get it!" Thereupon he ate his supper and then went in search of the police. As soon as his steps died away, however, Harriet aroused her comrades and they quickly vacated the premises and proceeded safely on their way without apprehension (Brooks, n.d.).

SAYINGS REMEMBERED FROM UNDERGROUND RAILROAD YEARS

S62. Rejecting Uncle Tom's Cabin Performance in Philadelphia (1869)

While Harriet was working as cook in one of the large hotels in Philadelphia, the play of "Uncle Tom's Cabin" was being performed for many weeks every night. Some of her fellow-servants wanted her to go and see it. "No," said Harriet, "I haven't got no heart to go and see the suffering of my people played on the stage. I've heard 'Uncle Tom's Cabin' read, and I tell you Mrs. Stowe's pen hasn't begun to paint what slavery is as I have seen it at the far South. I've seen the real thing, and I don't want to see it on no stage or in no theater" (Bradford, 1869, 21–22).

S63. Choice of Canada as Escape Destination (1869)

But after the passage of the Fugitive Slave law, she said, "I wouldn't trust Uncle Sam with my people no longer; I brought them all clear off to Canada" (Bradford, 1869, 27).

S64. Kindness of Gerrit Smith's Son (1911)

"I remember," she said, "once after I had brought some colored people from the South. I went up to Peterboro to the Big House. Gerrit Smith's son, Greene, was going hunting with his tutor and some other boys. I had no shoes. It was a Saturday afternoon and—would you believe it?—those boys went right off to the village and got me a pair of shoes so I could go with them" (J. B. Clarke, 1911).

S65. Right to Death or Liberty (1869)

Fearlessly she went on, trusting in the Lord. She said, "I started with this idea in my head, There's *two* things I've got a *right* to, and these are, Death or Liberty—one or the other I mean to have. No one will take me back alive; I shall fight for my liberty, and when the time has come for me to go, the Lord will let them kill me" (Bradford, 1869, 21).

THE TROY RESCUE (1860)

S66. Cheney's Account (1865)

She gives a most vivid description of the rescue of a slave in Troy. She fought and struggled so that her clothes were torn off her; but she was successful at last. Throughout all she shouted out her favorite motto, "Give me liberty or give me death," to which the popular heart never fails to respond. When she was triumphantly bearing the man off, a little boy called out, "Go it, old aunty! You're the best old aunty the fellow ever had" (Cheney, 1865, 37).

S67. Bradford's Version (1869)

In the Spring of 1860, Harriet Tubman was requested by Mr. Gerrit Smith to go to Boston to attend a large Anti-Slavery meeting. On her way, she stopped at Troy to visit a cousin, and while there, the colored people were one day startled with the intelligence that a fugitive slave, by the name of Charles Nalle, had been followed by his master (who was his younger brother, and not one grain whiter than he), and that he was already in the hands of the officers, and was to be taken back to the South. The instant Harriet heard the news, she started for the office of the U.S. Commissioner, scattering the tidings as she went.

An excited crowd were gathered about the office, through which Harriet forced her way, and rushed up stairs to the door of the room where the fugitive was detained. A wagon was already waiting before the door to carry off the man, but the crowd was even then so great, and in such a state of excitement, that the officers did not dare to bring the man down. On the opposite side of the street stood the colored people, watching the window where they could see Harriet's sun-bonnet, and feeling assured that so long as she stood there, the fugitive was still in the office. Time passed on, and he did not appear.

"They've taken him out another way, depend upon that," said some of the colored people. "No," replied others, "there stands 'Moses' yet, and as long as she is there, he is safe." Harriet, now seeing the necessity for a tremendous effort for his rescue, sent out some little boys to cry *fire*. The bells rang, the crowd increased, till the whole street was a dense mass of people. Again and again the officers came out to try and clear the stairs, and make a way to take their captive down; others were driven down, but Harriet stood her ground, her head bent down, and her arms folded.

"Come, old woman, you must get out of this," said one of the officers; "I must have the way cleared; if you can't get down alone, some one will help you." Harriet, still putting on a greater appearance of decrepitude, twitched away from him, and kept her place.

Offers were made to buy Charles from his master, who at first agreed to take twelve hundred dollars for him; but when that was subscribed, he immediately raised the price to fifteen hundred. The crowd grew more excited. A gentleman raised a window and called out, "Two hundred dollars for his rescue, but not one cent to his master!" This was responded to by a roar of satisfaction from the crowd below.

At length the officers appeared, and announced to the crowd that if they would open a lane to the wagon, they would promise to bring the man down the front way.

The lane was opened, and the man was brought out—a tall, handsome, intelligent *white* man,[41] with his wrists manacled together, walking between the U.S. Marshal and another officer, and behind him his brother and his master, so like him that one could hardly be told from the other.

The moment they appeared, Harriet roused from her stooping posture, threw up a window, and cried to her friends: "Here he comes—take him!" and then darted down the stairs like a wild-cat. She seized one officer and pulled him down, then another, and tore him away from the man; and keeping her arms about the slave, she cried to her friends: "Drag us out! Drag him to the river! Drown him! but don't let them have him!"

They were knocked down together, and while down she tore off her sun-bonnet and tied it on the head of the fugitive. When he rose, only his head could be seen, and amid the surging mass of people the slave was no longer recognized, while the master appeared like the slave. Again and again they were knocked down, the poor slave utterly helpless, with his manacled wrists streaming with blood.

Harriet's outer clothes were torn from her, and even her stout shoes were all pulled from her feet, yet she never relinquished her hold of the man, till she had dragged him to the river, where he was tumbled into a boat, Harriet following in a ferry boat to the other side. But the telegraph was ahead of them, and as soon as they landed he was seized and hurried from her sight.

After a time, some school children came hurrying along, and to her anxious inquiries they answered, "He is up in that house, in the third story." Harriet rushed up to the place. Some men were attempting to make their way up the stairs. The officers were firing down, and two men were lying on the stairs, who had been shot. Over their bodies our heroine rushed, and with the help of others burst open the door of the room, dragged out the fugitive, whom Harriet carried down stairs in her arms.

A gentleman who was riding by with a fine horse, stopped to ask what the disturbance meant; and on hearing the story, his sympathies seemed to be thoroughly aroused; he sprang from his wagon, calling out, "That is a blood-horse; drive him till he drops."

The poor man was hurried in; some of his friends jumped in after him, and drove at the most rapid rate to Schenectady (Bradford, 1869, 88–91).

THE JOHN BROWN ASSOCIATION

S68. Harriet Tubman First Approached by Brown in Canada in Spring 1858 (1896)

John Brown and a colored man named Loguen went to St. Catherine's in Canada to see Harriet, when Brown was making preparations for his Virginia campaign.[42] Gerrit Smith paid the expenses of this trip. Loguen found Harriet's house in this town, and informed her privately that Brown was in the place, and asked her whether she would go to the hotel and see him or whether it would do for him to come to see her. Harriet declares that she was forewarned by dreams that John Brown was to come to her, and she answered Loguen that the old man might visit her home, for nobody would hurt them there. She also sent for some of the colored people in the neighborhood to come and see him.

When John Brown entered he shook hands with her three times, saying: "The first I see is General Tubman, the second is General Tubman, and the third is General Tubman."[43]

He sat down and explained his purposes to her and to the Negroes who came in. As is well known, his first intention was to establish a camp in the Virginia mountains, and gather together and run off fugitive slaves; and he urged Harriet's friends to aid him. He promised to send them word when and where to join him. He said that in any raid they were to be called upon to make, they were not to destroy property, injure children or insult women. He also said that if in the conflicts which he evidently anticipated, white men were taken prisoners, they would be released on condition that they would send to his party colored men in numbers equal to their own families.[44]

John Brown remained in St. Catherine's several days, and saw Harriet more than once. It is stated, moreover, that he framed his Constitution in her house.[45] He told her, as he told many other persons, that God had called him to do something for the black man, and he declared that he was not born to be killed by a Sharpe's rifle or a bowie knife.

Many of the Negroes in that town promised to go to Brown when he sent orders; but as the world knows, he changed his plans afterwards, attacked Harper's Ferry, and never sent for his Canadian recruits. At this time, however, he seems to have had no doubt as to what he should do . . .

When John Brown bade Harriet good by, he again called her "General" three times, and informed her that she would hear from him through Douglass. This was probably the parting which the writer once heard Harriet describe,[46] when she stood on her doorstep and gazed after him as long as she could see him, and then watched the omnibus which he had entered till it was out of sight. They were two souls who dealt in action, but were alike moved by impulses from mystical and hidden sources (Wyman, 1896, 116–117).

S69. Tubman's Visionary Dream of John Brown's Death (1863)

Before she left [Boston], however, she had several interviews with Captain Brown, then [1859] in Boston. He is supposed to have communicated his plans to her,[47] and to have been aided by her in obtaining recruits and money among her people. At any rate, he always spoke of her with the greatest respect, and declared that "General Tubman," as he styled her, was a better officer than most whom he had seen, and could command an army as successfully as she had led her small parties of fugitives.

Her own veneration for Captain Brown has always been profound, and since his murder, has taken the form of a religion. She had often risked her own life for her people, and she thought nothing of that; but that a white man, and a man so noble and strong, should so take upon himself the burden of a despised race, she could not understand, and she took refuge from her perplexity in the mysteries of her fervid religion.[48]

Again, she laid great stress on a dream which she had just before she met Captain Brown in Canada. She thought she was in a "wilderness sort of place, all full of rocks and bushes," when she saw a serpent raise its head among the rocks, and as it did so, it became the head of an old man with a long white beard, gazing at her "wishful like, just as if he were going to speak to me," and then two other heads rose up beside him, younger than he,—and as she stood looking at them, and wondering what they could want with her, a great crowd of men rushed in and struck down the younger heads, and then the head of the old man, still looking at her so "wishful." This dream she had again and again, and could not interpret it; but when she met Captain Brown, shortly after, behold, he was the very image of the head she had seen. But still she could not make out what her dream signified, till the news came to her of the tragedy of Harper's Ferry, and then she knew the two other heads were his two sons.

She was in New York at that time,[49] and on the day of the affair at Harper's Ferry, she felt her usual warning that something was wrong—she could not tell what. Finally she told her hostess that it must be Captain Brown who was in trouble, and that they should soon hear bad news from him. The next day's newspaper brought tidings of what had happened (Sanborn, 1863).

S70. Comments about John Brown on the
Day of His Companions' Execution (1865)

She was deeply interested in John Brown; and it is said, that she was fully acquainted with his plans, and approved them.[50] On the day when his companions were executed, she came to my room. Finding me occupied, she said, "I am not going to sit down, I only want you to give me an address;" but her heart was too full, she must talk.

"I've been studying and studying upon it," she said, "and it's clear to me, it wasn't John Brown that died on that gallows. When I think how he gave up his life for our people, and how he never flinched, but was so brave to the end; it's clear to me it wasn't mortal man, it was God in him. When I think of all the groans and tears and prayers I've heard on the plantations, and remember that God is a prayer-hearing God, I feel that his time is drawing near."

"Then you think," I said, "that God's time is near?"

"God's time is always near," she said; "He gave me my strength, and he set the North star in the heavens; he meant I should be free."

She went on in a strain of the most sublime eloquence I ever heard; but I cannot repeat it (Cheney, 1865, 37).[51]

S71. Harkless Bowley Remembers
Tubman's Comment on John Brown's Intent (1939)

She said it was not John Brown's idea to murder the white people but stir the slaves so as to attract the attention [of the] country and to strike for freedom (H. Bowley, 1939b).

WARTIME ADVENTURES

S72. How Her War Service Began—Telford (circa 1905)

In 1862, Governor Andrew of Massachusetts knowing Harriet's intrepidity
and wisdom sent for her and asked if she could go South at once to act as
spy, scout or nurse as circumstances required. To this Harriet agreed; but
before she got started (I tell the story in her own words) "they change[d]
their program and wanted me to go down and [dis]tribute clothes to the
contrabands who were coming in to the Union lines night and day.

"They wouldn't let no colored people go down South then, unless they
went with some of the officers as a servant, so they got a gentleman from
New York to take me as a servant. He was stopping at a big hotel on
Broadway and I went to the parlor and they sent for him and he came
down, but I didn't like that man no how. He look[ed] at me and said,
'Well, I guess you're young enough. You go to the quartermaster and tell
him I sent you.' But I made up my mind that I wasn't going with that
man. He looked brave and noble enough to be a gentleman if looks made
one, strutting about, but I went out and I ain't seen the quartermaster
yet, nor him neither. So I just went on alone to Baltimore, and General
Hunt[er] sent for me to go to Beaufort, and the vessel that was going there
didn't sail for two days, awaiting for me till the General's orders were fulfilled. I first took charge of the Christian Commission House at Beaufort."
(Telford, n.d., 15).

S73. The Combahee River Raid—Bradford's Version (1869)

When our armies and gun-boats first appeared in any part of the South,
many of the poor Negroes were as much afraid of "the Yankee Buckra" as
of their own masters. It was almost impossible to win their confidence, or
to get information from them. But to Harriet they would tell anything;
and so it became quite important that she should accompany expeditions
going up the rivers, or into unexplored parts of the country, to control and
get information from those whom they took with them as guides.

Gen. Hunter asked her at one time if she would go with several gun-
boats up the Combahee River, the object of the expedition being to take
up the torpedoes placed by the rebels in the river, to destroy railroads and
bridges, and to cut off supplies from the rebel troops. She said she would
go if Col. Montgomery was to be appointed commander of the expedition.
Col. Montgomery was one of John Brown's men, and was well known to
Harriet. Accordingly, Col. Montgomery was appointed to the command,

and Harriet, with several men under her, the principal of whom was
J. Plowden, whose pass I have, accompanied the expedition.

   Harriet describes in the most graphic manner the appearance of the
plantations as they passed up the river; the frightened Negroes leaving
their work and taking to the woods, at sight of the gun-boats; then coming to peer out like startled deer, and scudding away like the wind at
the sound of the steam-whistle. "Well," said one old Negro, "Master said
the Yankees had horns and tails, but I never believed it till now." But the
word was passed along by the mysterious communication existing among
these simple people, that these were "Lincoln's gun-boats come to set
them free." In vain, then, the drivers used their whips, in their efforts to
hurry the poor creatures back to their quarters; they all turned and ran
for the gun-boats. They came down every road, across every field, just as
they had left their work and their cabin; women with children clinging
around their necks, hanging to their dresses, running behind, all making
at full speed for "Lincoln's gun-boats." Eight hundred poor wretches at
one time crowded the banks, with their hands extended towards their
deliverers, and they were all taken off upon the gun-boats, and carried
down to Beaufort (Bradford, 1869, 38–40).

S74. The Combahee River Raid—
Telford's First-Person Version (circa 1905)

"They gave us Colonel Montgomery, one of John Brown's men, to command the expedition," says Harriet, *"and three gunboats and all colored
soldiers and we found where the torpedoes was and saw that we could find
another channel.*[52] *When we went up the river in the morning, it was just
about light, the fog was rising over the rice fields and the people was just done
their breakfast and was going out to the field.*

   *"I was in the forward boat where the Colonel and Captain and the colored
man that was to tell us where the torpedoes was. The boats was a quarter of
a mile apart, one after the other, and just about light, the Colonel blowed
the whistle and stopped the boat and the Captain and a company of soldiers
went ashore. About a quarter of an hour after, he done blowed the whistle, and
when the sun got clear, so that the people could see the boats, you could look
over the rice fields, and see them coming to the boat from every direction.
I never see such a sight."*

   And here Harriet invariably becomes convulsed with laughter at the
recollection—"Some was getting their breakfasts, just taking their pots
of rice right off the fire, *and they'd put a cloth on top their head and set that*

on, rice a smoking, young one hanging on behind one hand round the mother's forehead to hold on, the other hand digging into the rice pot, eating it with all its might. Some [had] white blankets on their heads with their things done up in them and them that hadn't a pot of rice would have a child in their arms, sometimes one or two holding on to their mother's dress; some carrying two children, one astride of the mother's neck, holding on her forehead and another in her arms; [it ap]pears like I never see so many twins in my life. Some had bags on their backs with pigs in them; some had chickens tied by the legs, and so child squalling, chickens squawking, and pigs squealing they all come running to the gun boats through the rice fields just like a procession. *Thinks I, 'These here puts me in mind of the children of Israel, coming out of Egypt.'* When they got to the shore, they'd get in the rowboat, and they'd start for the gun boat; but the others would run and hold on so they couldn't leave the shore. They wasn't coming and they wouldn't let any [no] body else come. The soldiers beat them on the hands but they wouldn't let go. They was afraid the gun boats [would] go off and leave them. At last the Captain looked at them and he called me. *They called me 'Moses Garrison' down there.* Said he, 'Moses, *come here and speak a word of consolation to your people!*

"*Well, they wasn't my people any more than they was his—only we was all Negroes—[be]cause I didn't know any more about them than he did. So I went when he called me on the gun boat, and they on the shore. They didn't know any thing about me and I didn't know what to say. I look at them about two minutes,* and then I sung to them:

Come from the East
   Come from the West
'Mong all the glorious nations
   This glorious one's the best.
Come along; come along; don't be alarmed
   For Uncle Sam is rich enough
To give you all a farm.

"Then they threw up their hands and began to rejoice and shout Glory! and the rowboats would push off.

"I kept on singing until all were brought on board. We got 800 people that day, and we tore up the railroad and fired the bridge, *and we went up to a big house and catched two pigs* and named the white pig Beauregard and the black pig Jeff Davis.

"*When we got back to Hilton Head in the morning and landed there 900 contrabands I took 100 of the men to the recruiting office and they enlisted in the army. Colonel Whittle said I ought to be paid for every soldier as much as a recruiting officer; but laws! I never done got nothing*" (Telford, n.d., 17–19).

S75. Bowley's Version: "Landed from a Gunboat in the Darkness of the Night" (1939)

She was cautious, cunning and brave. She penetrated the Rebel lines, told of their movements, brought back other information of great value. Landed from a gunboat in the darkness of the night on the shore of a river in a section of the country unknown to her, she made her way to the cabins of the slaves, talked with them, and found the men who had helped place torpedoes in Combahee River to keep the Union boats from ascending, brought them to the spot where she was landed and many women and children. The men with the officers went up the river and took the torpedoes up thus opening up the river for the Union boats to ascend and cut off the supplies of the Rebel armies (H. Bowley, 1939a).

S76. Hospital Work during War (1869)

At this time, her manner of life, as related by herself, was this:

"Well, Missus, I'd go to the hospital, I would, early every morning. I'd get a big chunk of ice, I would, and put it in a basin, and fill it with water; then I'd take a sponge and begin. First man I'd come to, I'd thrash away the flies, and they'd rise, they would, like bees round a hive. Then I'd begin to bathe the wounds, and by the time I'd bathed off three or four, the fire and heat would have melted the ice and made the water warm, and it would be as red as clear blood. Then I'd go and get more ice, I would, and by the time I got to the next ones, the flies would be round the first ones black and thick as ever."

In this way she worked, day after day, till late at night; then she went home to her little cabin, and made about fifty pies, a great quantity of ginger-bread, and two casks of root beer. These she would hire some contraband to sell for her through the camps, and thus she would provide her support for another day; for this woman never received pay or pension, and never drew for herself but twenty days' rations during the four years of her labors.[53]

At one time she was called away from Hilton Head, by one of our officers, to come to Fernandina, where the men were "dying off like sheep,"
from dysentery. Harriet had acquired quite a reputation for her skill in
curing this disease, by a medicine which she prepared from roots which
grew near the waters which gave the disease. Here she found thousands
of sick soldiers and contrabands, and immediately gave up her time and
attention to them. At another time, we find her nursing those who were
down by hundreds with small-pox and malignant fevers. She had never
had these diseases, but she seems to have no more fear of death in one
form than another. "The Lord would take care of her till her time came,
and then she was ready to go" (Bradford, 1869, 37–38).

S77. Curing the Doctor in Union Army Camp, Fernandina, Florida (circa 1905)

When dysentery in its worst form attacked the camp at Fernandina, the surgeon in charge was down with the disease and ordinary remedies proved
absolutely worthless. Harriet, who had acquired quite a reputation for her
skill in curing this disease by a decoction which she prepared from roots
which grew near the water which gave the disease, was sent for. "I went
down there," she quaintly says, "and found them that bad with chronic
dysentery, that they was dying off like sheep. I dug some roots and herbs
and made a tea for the doctor and the disease stopped on him. And then
he said, 'Give it to the soldiers.' So I boiled up a great boiler of roots and
herbs, and the General [de]tailed a man to take two cans and go round
and give it to all in the camp that needed it, and it cured them" (Telford,
n.d., 16).[54]

S78. A Story of Army Nursing Remembered by Grandson of Samuel Hopkins (1947)

Some of the reminiscences of her work as a volunteer nurse were delight-
fully gory. There was one account of an amputation that began, "Tie down
his arms. Stick a bullet in his mouth."

"What for?" one of us would ask.

"To bite on. Saw his leg off."

"Didn't he yell?"

"Yell and kick and flounce. Bit the bullet clean through. I had to hold
him down."

"You must have been awful strong."

"I could tote a flour barrel on one shoulder" (Adams, 1989, 277).

SAYINGS FROM WAR YEARS

S79. Her Joke about the National Obsession with Slavery (1865)

She said once, just before the war, when slavery was the one theme agitating the country,—"They say the Negro has no rights a white man is bound to respect; but it seems to me they send men to Congress, and pay them eight dollars a day, for nothing else but to talk about the Negro" (Cheney, 1865, 37).

S80. War Will Bring Black "Call for Justice" Home to Whites (1865)

She says, "The blood of her race has called for justice in vain, and now our sons and brothers must be taken from our hearts and homes to bring the call for justice home to our hearts" (Cheney, 1865, 37).

S81. Sent by God to Help "Deliver My People" (1869)

When the war broke out she felt, as she said, that "the good Lord has come down to deliver my people, and I must go and help him" (May, 1869, 406).

S82. Conversation with Sojourner Truth about President Lincoln (1886)

When asked if she had ever met Lincoln she replied, "No, I'm sorry now, but I didn't like Lincoln in them days. I used to go see Missus Lincoln,[55] but I never wanted to see him. You see we colored people didn't understand then [that] he was our friend. All we knew was that the first colored troops sent south from Massachusetts only got seven dollars a month, while the white regiment got fifteen.[56] We didn't like that. But now I know all about it, and I is sorry I didn't go to see Master Lincoln.

"It was Sojourner Truth told me Master Lincoln was our friend. Then she went to see him, and she thanked him for all he had done for our peoples.[57] Master Lincoln was kind to her, and she had a nice visit with him, but he told her he had done nothing himself; he was only a servant of the country. Yes, I is sorry now I didn't see Master Lincoln and thank him" (Holt, 1886, 462).

S83. Tubman's Comment on Her Later View of Lincoln (1939)

I remember very clearly Harriet saying, and repeating very often, that she did not know Lincoln. It was a deep sorrow and regret of her later years. She never recovered from that in a way. During the war she had been opposed to some of the things Lincoln did; she had been prejudiced against him at first (Tatlock, 1939a).

POSTWAR YEARS

S84. Assaulted and Insulted by a
Conductor on the Amboy Railroad (1869)

The last time Harriet was returning from the war, with her pass as hospital nurse, she bought a half-fare ticket, as she was told she must do; and missing the other train, she got into an emigrant train on the Amboy Railroad. When the conductor looked at her ticket, he said, "Come, hustle out of here! We don't carry niggers for half fare." Harriet explained to him that she was in the employ of the government, and was entitled to transportation as the soldiers were. But the conductor took her forcibly by the arm, and said, "I'll make you tired of trying to stay here." She resisted, and being very strong, she could probably have got the better of the conductor, had he not called three men to his assistance. The car was filled with emigrants, and no one seemed to take her part. The only words she heard, accompanied with fearful oaths, were, "Pitch the nigger out!" They nearly wrenched her arm off, and at length threw her, with all their strength, into a baggage-car. She supposed her arm was broken, and in intense suffering she came on to New York.

As she left the car, a delicate-looking young man came up to her, and, handing her a card, said, "You ought to sue that conductor, and if you want a witness, call on me." Harriet remained all winter under the care of a physician in New York; he advised her to sue the railroad company. and said that he would willingly testify as to her injuries. But the card the young man had given her was only a visiting card, and she did not know where to find him, and so she let the matter go (Bradford, 1869, 46–47).

S83. Attempting to Support Her Aging Parents in Postwar Auburn (1901)

Her old father and mother were with her, and the mother, nearly a hundred years old and enfeebled in mind, was querulous and exacting, and most unreasonable in her temper, often reproaching this faithful daughter as the Israelites did Moses of old, for "bringing them up into the wilderness to die there of hunger."

There came a day when everything eatable was exhausted, and the prospect was dark, indeed. The old mother had no tobacco and no tea—and these were more essential to her comfort than food or clothing; then reproaches thick and fast fell upon Harriet. She made no reply, but "went into her closet and shut the door."[58] When she came out she had a large basket on her arm.

"Catherine,"[59] she said, "take off that small pot and put on a large one."

"But, Harriet, there ain't nothing in the house to eat."

"Put on the large pot, Catherine; we're going to have soup today"—and Harriet started for the market.

The day was nearly over, and the market men were anxious to be rid of their wares, and were offering them very cheap. Harriet walked along with the basket on her arm. "Old woman, don't you want a nice piece of meat?" called out one; and another, "Here's a nice piece; only ten cents. Take this soup-bone, you can have it for five cents." But Harriet had not five cents. At length a kind-hearted butcher, judging of the trouble from her face, said, "Look here, old woman, you look like an honest woman; take this soup-bone, and pay me when you get some money"; then another said, "Take this," and others piled on pieces of meat till the basket was full.

Harriet passed on, and when she came to the vegetables she exchanged some of the meat for potatoes, cabbage, and onions, and the big pot was in requisition when she reached home. Harriet had not "gone into her closet and shut the door" for nothing (Bradford, 1901, 143–145).

S84. Borrowing a Quarter from "Miss Annie" (1869)

Last winter ('67 and '68), as we all know, the snow was very deep for months, and Harriet and the old people were completely snowed-in in their little home. The old man was laid up with rheumatism, and Harriet could not leave home for a long time to procure supplies of corn, if she could have made her way into the city. At length, stern necessity compelled her to plunge through the drifts to the city, and she appeared at the house of one of her firm and fast friends, and was directed to the room of one of the young ladies. She began to walk up and down, as she always does when in trouble. At length, she said, "Miss Annie?" "What, Harriet?" A long pause; then again, "Miss Annie?" "Well, what *is* it Harriet?" This was repeated four times, when the young lady, looking up, saw her eyes filled with tears. She then insisted on knowing what she wanted. And with a great effort, she said, "Miss Annie, could you lend me a quarter till Monday? I never asked it before." Kind friends immediately supplied all the wants of the family, but on Monday Harriet appeared with the quarter she had borrowed (Bradford, 1869, 111–112).

S85. Buying Land for John Brown Hall Project (1901)

Harriet had long cherished the idea of having her hospital incorporated, and placed in charge of the Zion African Methodist Church of Auburn, and she was particularly anxious to come into possession of a lot of twenty-five acres of land, near her own home, to present to it as a little farm. This lot was to be sold at auction, and on the day of the sale Harriet appeared with a very little money, and a determination to have the land, cost what it might.

"They was all white folks but me there, Missus, and there I was like a blackberry in a pail of milk, but I hid down in a corner, and no one knowed who was bidding. The man began down pretty low, and I kept going up by fifties; he got up to twelve hundred, thirteen hundred, fourteen hundred, and still that voice in the corner kept going up by fifties. At last it got up to fourteen hundred and fifty, and then others stopped bidding, and the man said, "All done! who is the buyer?" "Harriet Tubman," I shouted. "What! that old nigger?" they said. "Old woman, how you ever going to pay for that lot of land?" "I'm going home to tell the Lord Jesus all about it," I said."

After telling the Lord Jesus all about it, Harriet went down to a bank, obtained the money by mortgaging the land, and then requested to have a deed made out, making the land over to the Zion African Methodist Church. And her mind is easy about her hospital, though with many persons the trouble would be but just beginning, as there is interest on the mortgage to be paid (Bradford, 1901, 149–150).

S86. Appearing at Suffrage Convention in Rochester (1901)

A Woman's Suffrage Meeting was held in Rochester a year or two ago,[60] and Harriet came to attend it. She generally attended every meeting of women, on whatever subject, if possible to do so.

She was led into the church by an adopted daughter, whom she had rescued from death when a baby, and had brought up as her own.[61]

The church was warm and Harriet was tired, and soon after she entered deep sleep fell upon her.

Susan B. Anthony and Mrs. Stanton were on the platform, and after speeches had been made and business accomplished, one of these ladies said:

"Friends, we have in the audience that wonderful woman, Harriet Tubman, from whom we should like to hear, if she will kindly come to the platform."

People looked around at Harriet, but Harriet was fast asleep.

"Mother! mother!" said the young girl; "they are calling for you," but it was some time before Harriet could be made to understand where she was, or what was wanted of her. At length, she was led out into the aisle and was assisted by one of these kind ladies on to the platform.

Harriet looked around, wondering why so many white ladies were gathered there. I think it was Miss Anthony who led her forward, saying:

"Ladies, I am glad to present to you Harriet Tubman, 'the conductor of the Underground Railroad'."

"Yes, ladies," said Harriet, "I was the conductor of the Underground Railroad for eight years, and I can say what most conductors can't say—I never run my train off the track and I never lost a passenger." The audience laughed and applauded, and Harriet was emboldened to go on and relate portions of her interesting history, which were most kindly received by the assembled ladies" (Bradford, 1901, 141–143).

S87. Skull Surgery in Boston (1901)

Harriet's friends will be glad to learn that she has lately been for some time in Boston, where a surgical operation was performed upon her head, the skull (which was crushed by a weight thrown by her master more than seventy years before) being successfully raised. Harriet's account of this operation is rather amusing.

"Harriet," said Professor Hopkins, "What is the matter with your head? Your hair is all gone!"

"Why, that's where they shaved it off before they cut my head open."

"Cut your head open, Harriet? What do you mean?"

"Well, sir, when I was in Boston I walked out one day, and I saw a great big building, and I asked a man what it was, and he said it was a hospital. So I went right in, and I saw a young man there, and I said, "Sir, are you a doctor?" And he said he was; then I said, "Sir, do you think you could cut my head open?"

"What do you want your head cut open for?" he said.

"Then I told him the whole story, and how my head was giving me a powerful sight of trouble lately, with aching and buzzing, so I couldn't get no sleep at night."

"And he said, "Lay right down on this here table," and I lay down."

"Didn't he give you anything to deaden the pain, Harriet?"

"No, sir; I just lay down like a lamb for the slaughter, and he sawed open my skull, and raised it up, and now it feels more comfortable."

"Did you suffer very much?"

"Yes, sir, it hurt, of course; but I got up and put on my bonnet and started to walk home, but my legs kind of [gave?[62]] out under me, and they sent for an ambulance and sent me home" (Bradford, 1901, 151–153).

CONVERSATIONS IN HER OLD AGE RECALLED

S88. "Someday I'll Plant Apple Trees" (1907)

It was not plaintively, but rather with a flash of scorn in her dulling eye, that she remarked to the writer last week:—"You wouldn't think that after I served the flag so faithfully I should come to want under its folds."[63] Then, looking musingly toward a nearby orchard, she asked suddenly, "Do you like apples?"

On being assured that I did, she said, "Did you ever plant any apple trees?" With shame I confessed I had not. "No," said she, "but somebody else planted them. I liked apples when I was young, and I said, Some day I'll plant apples myself for other young folks to eat, and I guess I done it."

Then she laughed as though a sudden comical recollection had come to her and throwing back her furrowed face, burst into a wild melody, beating the time with her hands upon her knees and gleefully swaying to and fro:

There's cider and brandy in the cellar,
And the darkies they'll have some;
Must be now the kingdom's coming
And the year of Jubilum!

. . . Harriet is very proud of the fact that she is a member of the Grand Army of the Republic, Woman's Auxiliary, and as I came away she said, with a laugh, "You can put me in the paper feet and head down, but don't forget to put in it, too, for I sure belong to the G.A.R." (F. C. Drake, 1907).

S89. Comments over a Meal in the Tubman Home (1911)

Her failing strength has obliged her to share with four or five old women the modest home that she had established on the adjoining land. But, in spite of her advanced age, she is not ready to be oslerized.[64] On the day of my visit she had without assistance gone down stairs to breakfast, and I saw her eat a dinner that would tax the stomach of a gourmand. A friend had sent her a spring chicken and had the pleasure of seeing it placed before her with rice and pie and cheese and other good things. "Never mind me," Aunt Harriet replied to the friend's remark that the conversation was interfering with the dinner, "I'll eat all you give me, but I want you to have some of this chicken first." And when the lady protested that she was not hungry, but would taste the rice, Aunt Harriet extended her hospitable invitation to another visitor to share her favorite viand. She resented the suggestion that someone should feed her. She only wanted the nurse to cut the chicken and place the tray on her lap.

. . . Although her face is furrowed and her hand has lost its one-time vigor, Harriet Tubman's mind is astonishingly fresh and active. She not only remembers things that happened when most people's grandmothers were little girls; she has the newspapers read to her and she follows with great interest the important events of the day. Hearing of the coronation of King George V, she requested Miss F. Miller, the granddaughter of Gerrit Smith, to send her congratulations to the king, whose grandmother, the late Queen Victoria, sent a medal and a letter to the old Negro woman who had brought so many of her people to the free soil of Canada.

No such medal or letter is mentioned in the biography of Harriet Tubman, so Miss Miller visited her to obtain further information about this mark of appreciation from the "Great White Mother," as Queen Victoria was affectionately called by her black subjects in Africa. Aunt Harriet said: "It was when the queen had been on the throne sixty years, she sent me the medal. It was a silver medal, about the size of a dollar. It showed the queen and her family. The letter said, 'I read your book to Her Majesty, and she was pleased with it. She sends you this medal.' She also invited me to come over for her birthday party, but I didn't know enough to go. The letter was worn to a shadow, so many people read it. It got lost, somehow or other. Then I gave the medal to my brother's daughter to keep."

I afterwards found, on inquiring at the home of her niece, that Aunt Harriet had made no mistake in describing the medal. It is of silver and bears the likenesses of Queen Victoria, her son, grandson and great grandson, the present Prince of Wales. Such medals were circulated throughout the British Empire in commemoration of the Diamond Jubilee of Queen Victoria in 1897, but there can be no doubt that the Queen personally directed one to be sent to Harriet Tubman, whose "book" had been read to her. This explains why this token from the greatest white woman of the nineteenth century is not mentioned in the biography of the greatest black woman, for the book of Harriet Tubman by Mrs. Sarah H. Bradford closed with the Civil War.

Satisfied that her honored friend had reasonable ground to congratulate the grandson of Queen Victoria on his coronation, Miss Miller assured Aunt Harriet that she would send a letter to the King of England, but that she would ask me to write it for her, as a British subject from the West Indies, I might be more familiar with the proper form of address. And Aunt Harriet immediately replied, "I knew where he came from as soon as I heard him speak."

Aunt Harriet's ready wit is one of her most pleasant qualities. Wishing to make her an honorary member of the Geneva Political Equality Club, Miss Miller said, "I remember seeing you years ago at a suffrage convention in Rochester."

"Yes," the old woman affirmed, "I belonged to Miss Susan B. Anthony's Association."

"I should like to enroll you as a life member of our Geneva Club. Our motto is Lincoln's declaration: 'I go for all sharing the privileges of government who assist in bearing its burdens, by no means excluding women.' You certainly have assisted in bearing the burdens. Do you really believe that women should vote?"

Aunt Harriet paused a moment as if surprised at this question, then quietly replied, "I suffered enough to believe it."

When Miss Miller asked her full name she answered in solemnly measured tones, "Harriet Tubman Davis."

"Shall I write it with or without Mrs?"

"Any way you like, just so you get the Tubman," the woman responded.

Aunt Harriet proved by this answer that she is a good suffragette and an independent, self-assertive woman (Clarke, 1911).

S90. A Warning to Hopkins Grandchildren (1947)

When my cousins Julia and Winthrop visited Auburn and went to call on Harriet, they found her vigorously tidying up the yard. She was then well over ninety, but the broom strokes were powerful and rhythmical. The place was run-down, but well kept. Poverty was evident, but no real want, since Harriet was receiving a belated pension. . . .

Leaning on her broom handle, she addressed the visitors with calm dignity. "Good morning. Who is you?"

"We're Dr. Hopkins' grandchildren," answered Julia.

Harriet fixed her with a beady eye.

"Don't go and think you can ride to Heaven hanging to your grand-daddy's coattails," she warned. It was her way of putting the younger generation in its place (Adams, 1989, 278–279).

S91. Her "Last Words" to Mary B. Talbert

As I arose to go, she grasped my hand firmly and whispered: "I've been fixing a long time for my journey but now I'm almost home. God has shown me the Golden Chariot, and a voice spoke to me and said, 'Arouse, Awake! Sleep no longer, Jesus does all things well.'" After a moment's hesitation she said, "Tell the women to stand together for God will never forsake us," and finally, as I shook her hand to say good-bye, she smiled that peaceful smile of hers and said, "I am at peace with God and all mankind" ("Race of Harriets Would Secure the Future of the Negro," 1913).

RECALLING HARRIET TUBMAN: STORIES FROM FRIENDS, ASSOCIATES, AND KINFOLK

SPIRITUAL LIFE

S92. Her Father's Religious Fasting (1869)

On asking Harriet where they [her parents] got anything to eat on Sunday, she said, in her quiet way, "Oh! The old folks never eats anything on *Sunday*, Missus! We never has no food to get for them on Sunday. They always fasts; and they never eats anything on Fridays. Good Friday, and five Fridays hand [?] going from Good Friday, my father never eats or drinks, all day—fasting for the five bleeding wounds of Jesus.[65] All the other Fridays of the year he never eats till the sun goes down; then he takes a little tea and a piece of bread." "But is he a Roman Catholic, Harriet?" "Oh no, Missus; he does it for *conscience*; we was taught to do so down South. He says if he denies him self for the sufferings of his Lord and Master, Jesus will sustain him"(Bradford, 1869, 108–109).

S93. Foreknowledge of Danger (1863)

Then she says she always knows then there is danger near her,—she does not know how, exactly, but "It [ap]pears like my heart go flutter, flutter, and then they may say, 'Peace, Peace,' as much as they like, I know it's going to be war!' She is very firm on this point, and ascribes to this her great impunity, in spite of the lethargy before mentioned, which would

seem likely to throw her into the hands of her enemies. She says she inherited this power, that her father could always predict the weather, and
that he foretold the Mexican war (Sanborn, 1863).

S94. Foreknowledge of Emancipation (1886)

This war our brave heroine had expected, and its result, the emancipation of the slaves. Three years before, while staying with the Rev. Henry
Highland Garnet in New York, a vision came to her in the night of the
emancipation of her people. Whether a dream, or one of those glimpses
into the future, which sometimes seem to have been granted to her, no
one can say, but the effect upon her was very remarkable.

She rose singing, *"My people are free!" "My people are free!"* She came
down to breakfast singing the words in a sort of ecstasy. She could not
eat. The dream or vision filled her whole soul, and physical needs were
forgotten.

Mr. Garnet said to her:

"Oh, Harriet! Harriet! You've come to torment us before the time; do
cease this noise! My grandchildren may see the day of the emancipation of
our people, but you and I will never see it."

"I tell you, sir, you'll see it, and you'll see it soon. My people are free!
My people are free!"

When, three years later, President Lincoln's proclamation of emancipation was given forth, and there was a great jubilee among the friends
of the slaves, Harriet was continually asked, "Why do you not join with
the rest in their rejoicing!" "Oh," she answered, "I had *my* jubilee three
years ago. I rejoiced all I could then; I can't rejoice no more" (Bradford,
1886, 92–93).

S95. Other Instances of Foreknowledge (1901)

Sitting in her house one day, deep sleep fell upon her, and in a dream or
vision she saw a chariot in the air, going south, and empty, but soon it
returned, and lying in it, cold and stiff, was the body of a young lady
of whom Harriet was very fond [Frances Seward], whose home was in
Auburn, but who had gone to Washington with her father [William H.
Seward], a distinguished officer of the Government there.

The shock roused Harriet from her sleep, and she ran into Auburn, to
the house of her minister, crying out: "Oh, Miss Fanny is dead!" and the
news had just been received.[66]

She woke from a sleep one day in great agitation, and ran to the houses of her colored neighbors, exclaiming that a "dreadful thing was happening somewhere, the ground was opening, and the houses were falling in, and the people being killed faster than they was in the war—faster than they was in the war."

At that very time, or near it, an earthquake was occurring in the northern part of South America, for the telegram came that day, though why a vision of it should be sent to Harriet no one can divine (Bradford, 1901, 147–148).

S96. Canadian Refugees Believe "Moses Has Got the Charm" (1874)

While in Canada, in 1860, we met several whom this woman had brought from the land of bondage, and they all believed that she had supernatural power. Of one man we inquired, "Were you not afraid of being caught?"

"O, no," said he, "Moses has got the charm."

"What do you mean?" we asked.

He replied, "The whites can't catch Moses, [be]cause she's born with the charm. The Lord has given Moses the power."

Yes, and the woman herself felt that she had the charm, and this feeling, no doubt, nerved her up, gave her courage, and made all who followed her feel safe in her hands (W. W. Brown, 1874, 538).

S97. Conversation with a Boston Lady about Divine Protection (1886)

He [Oliver Johnson] said, "You know Harriet never spoke of anything she had done, as if it was at all remarkable, or as if it deserved any commendation, but I remember one day, when she came into the office there was a Boston lady there, a warm-hearted, impulsive woman, who was engaged heart and hand in the Anti-Slavery cause.

Harriet was telling, in her simple way, the story of her last journey. A party of fugitives were to meet her in a wood, that she might conduct them North. For some unexplained reason they did not come. Night came on and with it a blinding snow storm and a raging wind. She protected herself behind a tree as well as she could, and remained all night alone exposed to the fury of the storm.

"Why, Harriet!" said this lady, "didn't you almost feel when you were lying alone, as if there was *no God?*" "Oh, no! Missus," said Harriet, looking up in her child-like, simple way, "I just asked Jesus to take care of me, and He never let me get *frost-bitten* one bit" (Bradford, 1886, 90–91).

S98. God Visited Her Three Times to Confirm Her Call (1886)

Occasionally some one remonstrates with her for giving to others what has been sent to supply her own needs. On a recent occasion, in reply to such a remark,[67] she said: "Long ago when the Lord told me to go free my people, I said, 'No, Lord! I can't go—don't ask me.' But he come another time. I saw him just as plain. Then I said again, 'Lord, go away—get some better educated person,—get a person with more culture than I have; go away, Lord.' But he came back the third time, and speaks to me just as he did to Moses, and he says, 'Harriet,[68] I want you.' I knew then I must do what he bid me. Now do you suppose he wanted me to do this just for a day, or a week? No! the Lord who told me take care of my people meant me to do it just so long as I live, and so I do what he told me to" (Holt, 1886, 461–462).

S99. Her Many Reports of Talking with God (1868)

I never met with any person, of any color, who had more confidence in the voice of God, as spoken direct to her soul. She has frequently told me that she talked with God, and he talked with her every day of her life, and she has declared to me that she felt no more fear of being arrested by her former master, or any other person, when in his immediate neighborhood, than she did in the State of New York, or Canada, for she said she never ventured only where God sent her, and her faith in a Supreme Power truly was great (Garrett, 1868).

S100. A Prediction Come True (1865)

Once an old silk dress was given her among a bundle of clothes, and she was in great delight. "Glory," she exclaimed; "Didn't I say when I sold my silk gown to get money to go after my mother, that I'd have another some day?" (Cheney, 1865, 37).

S101. Visionary Spirituality Admired by Bradford (1869)

Of the "dreams and visions" mentioned in this letter [Garrett's], the writer might have given many wonderful instances; but it was thought best not to insert anything which, with any, might bring discredit upon the story. When these turns of somnolency come upon Harriet, she imagines that her "spirit" leaves her body, and visits other scenes and places, not only in this world, but in the world of spirits. And her ideas of these scenes show, to say the least of it, a vividness of imagination seldom equaled in the soarings of the most cultivated minds.

Not long since, the writer, on going into Harriet's room in the morning, sat down by her and began to read that wonderful and glorious description of the heavenly Jerusalem in the two last chapters of Revelations.
When the reading was finished, Harriet burst into a rhapsody which per-
fectly amazed her hearer—telling of what she had seen in one of these
visions, sights which no one could doubt had been real to her, and which
no human imagination could have conceived, it would seem, unless in
dream or vision. There was a wild poetry in these descriptions which
seemed to border almost on inspiration, but by many they might be characterized as the ravings of insanity. All that can be said is, however, if this
woman is insane, there has been a wonderful "method in her madness"
(Bradford, 1869, 55–56).

S102. *Twelve Gates to the Celestial City (1869)*

When asked, as she often is, how it was possible that she was not afraid
to go back, with that tremendous price upon her head, Harriet always
answers, "Why, don't I tell you, Missus, it wasn't me, it was the Lord!" I
always told him, 'I trust to you. I don't know where to go or what to do,
but I expect you to lead me,' and he always did."

At one time she was going down, watched for everywhere, after there
had been a meeting of slaveholders in the court-house of one of the large
cities of Maryland, and an added reward had been put upon her head,
with various threats of the different cruel devices by which she should be
tortured and put to death; friends gathered round her, imploring her not
to go on directly in the face of danger and death, and this was Harriet's
answer to them:

"Now look here! John saw the City, didn't he?"[69] "Yes, John saw the
City." "Well, what did he see? He saw twelve gates—Three of those gates
was on the north; three of them was on the east; and three of them was
on the west; but there was three of them on the south, too; and I reckon,
if they kill me down there, I'll get into one of them gates, don't you?"
(Bradford, 1869, 35–36).

S103. *"God's Time Is Always Near" (1902)*

I shall never forget the eloquence of her expression on the day when John
Brown's men were executed. "It's clear to me," she said, "that it wasn't John
Brown that was hung on that gallows—it was God in him." And again,
"When I think of the prayers and groans I've heard on them plantations,
and remember that God's a prayer-hearing god, I feel that His time is

near." "Then you feel that 'God's time'[70] is near?" said I. "God's time is always near," she replied. "He set the North Star in the heavens; He gave me the strength in my limbs; He meant I should be free." Her first prayer was "God make me strong and able to fight," and it was answered (Cheney, 1902, 81–82).[71]

S104. Friends' Gifts Attributed to God's Providence (1901)

One day, in passing through Auburn, I was impelled to stop over a train, and drive out to see what were the needs of my colored friend, and to take her some supplies.

Her little house was always neat and comfortable, and the small parlor was nicely and rather prettily furnished. The lame, the halt, and the blind, the bruised and crippled little children, and one crazy woman, were all brought in to see me, and "the blind woman" (she seemed to have no other name), a very old woman who had been Harriet's care for eighteen years, was led into the room—an interesting and pathetic group.

On leaving, I said to her: "If you will come out to the carriage, Harriet, there are some provisions there for you."

She turned to one of her poor dependents and said: "What did you say to me this morning? You said we hadn't got nothing to eat in the house, and what did I say to you? I said, 'I've got a rich Father!'"

Nothing that comes to this remarkable woman ever surprises her. She says very little in the way of thanks, except to the Giver of all good. How the knowledge comes to her no one can tell, but she seems always to know when help is coming, and she is generally on hand to receive it, though it is never for herself she wants it, but only for those under her care. . . .

I hope I may be excused for sometimes telling my story in the first person, as I cannot conveniently do it in any other way. In getting ready a Thanksgiving box to send to Harriet, a few years ago, I had ordered a turkey to be sent for it, but as the weather grew quite warm, I was advised to send a ham instead. That box was lost for three weeks, and when I saw Harriet again and told her that I had intended to send a turkey in it, she said, "Well, there was a clear Providence in that, wasn't there, Missus?"

A friend, hearing that I was preparing a Christmas box in New York for this needy household, sent me a quantity of clothing and ten dollars for them. As my box was not quite full, I expended three dollars of that money in groceries, and sent seven dollars to a lady in Auburn who acted as a treasurer for Harriet, giving her money as it was needed; for Harriet's heart is so large, and her feelings are so easily wrought upon, that it was never wise to give her more than enough for present needs.

Not long after, I received a letter from a well-known physician—a woman—in Auburn, in which she said:

"I want to tell you something about Harriet. She came to me last Friday, and said, 'Doctor, I have got my taxes and insurance to pay tomorrow, and I haven't a cent. Would you lend me seven dollars till next Tuesday?' More to try her than anything else, I said, 'Why, Harriet, I'm a poor, hard-working woman myself; how do you know you'll pay me seven dollars next Tuesday?' 'Well, Doctor, I can't just tell you how, but I'll pay you next Tuesday.' On Tuesday my letter with seven dollars enclosed arrived in Auburn, and Harriet took the money to the friend who had lent it to her. Others thought this strange, but there was nothing strange about it to her" (Bradford, 1901, 138–139, 145–146).

S105. Conversation about the Dead Remembered (1939)

She was always religious, but she had no superstitions.[72] As an example of this, I lived on Ross Place and the usual street route from my place to where Harriet lived was a long trip, but a direct cross-lot trip was across Fort Hill Cemetery. One moonlit night Harriet had come down and talked with a group of us, sitting with us on the piazza. After she told us some stories, she started walking home, but in a direction that would take her toward the cemetery.

"Why are you going that way?" we asked.

"I'm going across the cemetery."

"Why?" we remonstrated with her. What we were worried about was that she might fall asleep on route; as she often did from her illness, or she might stumble and fall, and so hurt herself.

"They're all quiet there," she said. "All peaceful" (Tatlock, 1939a).

IMPRESSIONS OF HER CHARACTER AND APPEARANCE

S106. Ednah Cheney's Character Assessment (1865)

She has a very affectionate nature, and forms the strongest personal attachments. She has great simplicity of character; she states her wants very freely, and believes you are ready to help her; but if you have nothing to give, or have given to another, she is content. She is not sensitive to indignities to her color in her own person; but knows and claims her rights. She will eat at your table if she sees you really desire it; but she goes as willingly to the kitchen. She is very abstemious in her diet, fruit being the only luxury she cares for. Her personal appearance is very peculiar. She is thoroughly Negro, and very plain. She has needed disguise so often, that she seems to have command over her face, and can banish all expression from her features, and look so stupid that nobody would suspect her of knowing enough to be dangerous; but her eye flashes with intelligence and power when she is roused. She has the rich humor and the keen sense of beauty which belong to her race. She would like to dress handsomely. . . .

She is never left in a room with pictures or statuary that she does not examine them and ask with interest about them.[73] . . .

She can tell the time by the stars, and find her way by natural signs as well as any hunter; and yet she scarcely knows of the existence of England or any other foreign country. . . .

She loves action; I think she does not dislike fighting in a good cause; but she loves work too, and scorns none that offers. . . .

She has shown . . . all the characteristics of a great leader: courage, foresight, prudence, self-control, ingenuity, subtle perception, command over others' minds. Her nature is at once profoundly practical and highly imaginative. She is economical as Dr. Franklin, and as firm in the conviction of supernatural help as Mahomet. A clergyman once said, that her stories convinced you of their truth by their simplicity, as do the gospel narratives (Cheney, 1865, 37, 36, 35).

S107. William Lloyd Garrison II Recalls His First Sight of Harriet Tubman (1897)

My own acquaintance with Harriet Tubman dates from about 1858. It was at the house of the venerable Samuel May in Hollis Street, the father of the now venerable Samuel May of Leicester, that I first saw her. There was a small gathering of anti-slavery friends, among whom were John A. Andrew, Wendell Phillips, and my father. I shall never forget the exquisite manner of Mr. Phillips, when, asking the attention of the company, he introduced to them, in a few words of deep feeling and admiration, the little woman of black complexion and African stamp. Had she been a duchess, no courtier could have surpassed that genuinely deferential presentation. Nor can a more striking contrast have been furnished than that between the flower of Massachusetts culture and the product of the slave whip and plantation. That night they stood on equal ground.

Harriet had just returned from one of her periodical incursions in the South, bringing as always her sheaves with her, in the shape of a ransomed company of slaves, personally conducted by her from bondage to freedom. Since 1845 [1854] when that noble friend of the fugitive Negro, Thomas Garrett of Wilmington, Delaware, had first welcomed and assisted Harriet in her early attempts at emancipating her relatives and friends, she had made periodical systematic trips from Canada to the South. John Brown had introduced Harriet to Mr. Phillips, saying, "I bring you one of the best and bravest persons on the continent." If her response was somewhat incoherent, it was enough to know that, with her consummate general-ship, of the probably three hundred persons guided by her to Canada, no one was captured. What made a most pathetic impression upon me was her broken teeth, which had been partially knocked out with a stone in her own hands, because of toothache, while hiding by day on her latest escape (W. L. Garrison, 1897b).[74]

S108. Helen Tatlock Remembers Harriet Tubman's "Matriarchal Phase" (1939)

Harriet when I knew her in her matriarchal phase, was a magnificent look-ing woman, true African, with a broad nose, very black, and of medium height. I used to often sit and listen to her stories when I could get her to tell them. We always gave her something to eat. She preferred butter in her tea to anything else. That was a luxury. She was a compelling charac-ter. She had a soft, typical, colored voice. In her youth she must have sung well. . . . She usually wore black, a full, black skirt, an old black hat. She was not particular about her dress. She was, however, clean. She had a shapeless figure, at least at this time. But she was terribly poor. Her gen-eral appearance bore this out (Tatlock, 1939a).

S109. Florence Carter Remembers Harriet Tubman's Frail Old Age (1939)

She was a very short woman, plain and quite frail. At least in the latter part of her life she was frail. I believe she must have been very slight of build all of her life, although perhaps when she was younger she might have had a stronger build. She had a fine voice, that was very feminine, and when she sang, as she often did, her lungs opened up widely and she would shout, and she could shout as loudly as anyone I heard. She had a sensi-ble, an intelligent look, and she was of few words, except when she had something definite to say. She was a devout Christian, and perhaps that is what partially accounts for her frequent visits to my house when I lived at 18 Parker Street, Auburn, New York (F. L. Carter, 1939).

FUND-RAISING AND MONEY MANAGEMENT

S110. Fund-raising for Education of Former Slaves (1869)

Worn down by her sufferings and fatigue, her health permanently affected by the cruelties to which she has been subjected, she is still laboring to the utmost limit of her strength for the support of her aged parents, and still also for her afflicted people—by her own efforts supporting two schools for Freedmen at the South, and supplying them with clothes and books; never obtruding herself, never asking for charity, except for "her people." . . .

This woman of whom you have been reading is poor, and partially disabled from her injuries; yet she supports cheerfully and uncomplainingly herself and her old parents, and always has several poor children in her house, who are dependent entirely upon her exertions. At present she has three of these children for whom she is providing, while their parents are working to pay back money borrowed to bring them on. . . .

But though so timid for herself, she is bold enough when the wants of her race are concerned. Even now, while friends are trying to raise the means to publish this little book for her, *she* is going around with the greatest zeal and interest to raise a subscription for her Freedmen's Fair. She called on Hon. Wm. H. Seward, the other day, for a subscription to this object. He said, "Harriet, you have worked for others long enough. It is time you should think of yourself. If you ask for a donation for *yourself*, I will give it to you; but I will not help you to rob yourself for others" (Bradford, 1869, 2, 103–104, 112).

S111. Fund-raising Purpose of the Bradford Book Revision (1886)

Secretary Seward, from whom Harriet purchased her little place near Auburn, died. The place had been mortgaged when this noble woman left her home, and threw herself into the work needed for the Union cause; the mortgage was to be foreclosed. The old parents, then nearly approaching their centennial year, were to be turned out to die in a poor-house, when the sudden determination was taken to send out a little sketch of her life to the benevolent public, in the hope of redeeming the little home. This object, through the kindness of friends, was accomplished.[75] The old people died in Harriet's own home, breathing blessings upon her for her devotion to them.

Now another necessity has arisen, and our sable friend, who never has been known to beg for herself, asks once more for help in accomplishing a favorite project for the good of her people. This, as she says, is "her last work, and she only prays the Lord to let her live till it is well started, and then she is ready to go." This work is the building of a hospital for old and disabled colored people; and in this she has already had the sympathy and aid of the good people of Auburn; the mayor and his noble wife having given her great assistance in the meetings she has held in aid of this object.[76] It is partly to aid her in this work, on which she has so set her heart, that this story of her life and labors is being re-written (Bradford, 1886, 78–79).

S112. "Constantly on the Verge of Want" (1947)

Aunt Sarah's idea was that the money [brought in by book sales] should be a sort of current fund for the relief of needy colored people. Harriet's notion was different. Her method of administering a fund was to give away all the money she had upon her at the moment and trust to the good Lord to fill the void. Whatever the amount on hand, it was chronically insufficient. . . .

The postwar ebb of patriotic fervor left her stranded. Nobody wanted to hear her exhortations, which, delivered with the fire and art of the born orator, had been such a popular lecture-platform feature of an earlier generation. Constantly on the verge of want, she did a little nursing, a little cooking—she had not lost her light hand with pastry—and a little assorted choring, and was helped out by the charitable Auburn folk, the Sewards, the Pomeroys, the Osbornes, the Beardsleys, and the Underwoods (S. H. Adams, 1989, 269, 271–272).

SELECTED MEMORIES OF KIN

S113. Alice Brickler's Memory of a "Happy Ending" to the Gold Swindle (1939)

There used to be a junk dealer, I believe he was a Jew, who was known as Old Man Shimer or Sheiner. He and Aunt Harriet had a most harrowing experience with some swindlers. I can't remember the story in the entirety but here is the outline of the plot. It seems the swindlers agreed for a certain amount of money to deliver to Aunt Harriet a box of gold ore. The box was buried out in the woods. She must come to a designated place in woods, alone and at midnight, bringing the money with her.

Of course, she hadn't the money but she went to her friend Mr. Shimer or Sheiner to borrow it. She wasn't supposed to tell anyone about her plan but she had to tell her friend in order to get the money. After hours of argument, Mr. Shimer let her have the money but made his own plans of protection.

The day of the transaction arrived, then the hour of midnight, and to make it most dramatic, it was raining. Aunt Harriet alone, in the rain and with a goodly sum of money, set out for the woods. Farther and farther she went into the silent wood until she became suspicious. She did not turn back because she felt sure some one had been watching her. She said the most weird sounds were to be heard, then she would catch a glimpse of a gray something in the distance. Her first thought was Mr. Shimer's money. What should she do with it? Now here's where the story fades. Skillfully and without attracting unusual attention by her movement, she hid the money. It must have been under her head kerchief which she always wore under her hat. Anyway when she was attacked, her clothes torn off her in a mad search for the money, it was not found by the swindlers. She was beaten, gagged, tied and left in the woods to die.

Hours later, Mr. Shimer came across her, a little muddy bloody ball. He released her and scolded her for being so trusting of strangers. The story ended with the return of the money and Aunt Harriet nursing a bruised head (Brickler, 1939b).

S114. Return of Strength before Death (1939)

For sometime before her death, Aunt Harriet had lost the use of her legs. She spent her time in a wheel chair and then finally was confined to her bed. It is said that on the day of her death, her strength returned to her. She arose from her bed with little assistance, ate heartily, walked about the rooms of the Old Ladies' Home which she liked so much and then went back to bed and her final rest. Whether this is true or not, it is typical of her. She believed in mind [over] matter. Regardless of how impossible a task might seem, if it were her task she tackled it with a determination to win. I've always enjoyed believing this story as a fitting finish chapter to her life. It was right that her sun should go down on a bright day out of a clear sky (Brickler, 1939b).

S115. Alice Brickler Attempts to Help Reconstruct "Family Tree" (1939)

You speak of the "family tree" being re-constructed. What a job you have placed before me. I would not dare to attempt it. You see Aunt Harriet died during the early years of my life and outside of Uncle William Henry, her brother who lived with her, I have never seen the others and know of them only through Mother.

I have heard talk of Grandmother and Grandfather, the parents of Aunt Harriet. On Sunday morning, they and my mother who was a small girl, use to drive from the homestead on the edge of town to the Central Church on William Street for services. Mother said no sooner were they seated comfortably than they both went sound asleep and remain[ed] so until the end of service. Then they would make their way to the pastor's side congratulate him on his splendid sermon & go home. Mother always wondered how they knew the sermon was delivered well.

There were many people whom we knew as "Aunt" & "Uncle." Whether they were of the family or not I do not know but Mother had a cousin near her age, brought up by Aunt Harriet who would know these things if he is alive. He is Mr. Harkless Bowley 705 13th Street N. E. Washington D.C. I have not heard from him since Mother's death. His son, Dr. J. Guy Bowley is a physician in Baltimore Maryland but I do not know his address. Cousin Harkless knew the family well. His branch lived in the north a very short time. They returned to the Eastern Shore, Maryland and Washington D.C. (Brickler, 1939b).

S116. Margaret Stewart's Kidnapping from Baltimore by Harriet Tubman (1939)

My mother's life really began with Aunt Harriet kidnapping her from her home on Eastern Shore Maryland, when she was a little girl eight or nine years old. I say Mother's life began then because her memories of her southern home were very vague. One thing she knew, and that was that neither she, her brothers or her mother had ever been slaves. Her grandfather on her mother's side had bought his wife and children's time which made them free. Her mother's marriage to Harriet's brother, an ex-slave, seems not to have hindered the family's progress for Mother said they had a pair of slick chestnut horses and a shiny carriage in which they rode to church. That was all she remembered of her home.

Her next memory was of Aunt Harriet's visit to the home. She fell in love with the little girl who was my mother. Maybe it was because in Mother she saw the child she herself might have been if slavery had been less cruel. Maybe it was because she knew the joys of motherhood would never be hers and she longed for some little creature who would love her for her own self's sake. Certainly whatever the emotion, it was stronger than her better judgment for when her visit was ended, she, secretly and without so much as a by-your-leave, took the little girl with her to her northern home.

I wonder what her thoughts could have been as she & her little partner stood side by side on the deck of the steamer looking out over the
water. They made the trip by water[77] as that was what impressed Mother
so greatly that she forgot to weep over her separation from her twin
brother, her mother & the shiny carriage she liked so much. Aunt Harriet
must have regretted her act for she knew she had taken the child from a
sheltered good home to a place where there was nobody to care for her.
She must have known that the warmth of this new love was not great
enough to calm her restless soul and turn her into a domestic. She knew
she had violated her brother's home & sorrow & anger were there. I suppose she thought of her white friends in the north and desired to place her
dearest possession in their hands.

She gave the little girl, my mother, to Mrs. William H. Seward, the
Governor's wife. This kindly lady brought up Mother—not as a servant
but as a guest within her home. She taught Mother to speak properly, to
read, write, sew, do housework and act as a lady. Whenever Aunt Harriet
came back, Mother was dressed and sent in the Seward carriage to visit
her. Strange to say, Mother looked very much like Aunt Harriet and there
was hardness about her character in the face of adversity that must have
been hereditary (Brickler, 1939c).

S117. Disparate Kinship Accounts by
Katy Northrup and Alice Brickler (1940)

Mrs. Northrup of Philadelphia has written to say that you are not in
any way related to Harriet. She contends that there are only seven direct
descendants of Harriet and that you are not one of them (Conrad,
1940g)

I have never heard of Mrs. Northrup of Phila. It may be that she knows
more about our family than I. I do not doubt her. Being a member of
the Harriet Tubman family is an empty honor at most but I do have
this to say. Mother was always said by the older heads to be Aunt
Harriet's niece. Gov. Seward's family accepted her on Aunt Harriet's
word as one of the brother's children and when the people of Auburn
planned her memorial services, of all the relatives in and about the
country, Mother's youngest child was selected as the grand niece of
Harriet Tubman to unveil the tablet. At the time of this affair, it was
published far and wide that I was a relative and nobody came forward
to dispute the statement.

Now that you mention it, I do remember a will. You see these events happened at a time when I was not too interested. It must have been back in 1910 or so and I am now 39 years old. The Mary Gaston mentioned in the will died not too long ago. Her mother, Maria Elliott was my mother's elder sister and Mary Gaston always called my mother Aunt Maggie (much to my father's disgust). . . . The Stewart of Boston of whom you spoke, I thought was dead. It may not be the same person. Mr. Bowley would know that also. The Stewart of Boston of which I have heard was married to a white woman and had many children.[78]

. . . I remember when I was in college a very elderly man came to see me and stated that he was a nephew of Aunt Harriet. None of our family knew him so we said, "Is that so?" and let it pass. . . .

Besides being divided into the Stewarts and Rosses, the family is divided as to color. The fair branch is slow in acknowledging the browner branch. Mother used to tell an interesting story along this line. As a little girl, Mother was very proud to the point of being snobbish. In appearance she was short and plump, light brown with long thick Negroid hair. There was a relative living at the home at this time who disliked Mother very much and whenever Aunt Harriet was out of hearing she used to call Mother a "pumpkin-colored hussy." Ha, ha. Many of the family are said to have passed over into the white world. I can't prove this as I know of only one. . . .

P. S. I was neither born in or lived in the home of Harriet Tubman. Mother lived there as a small girl whenever Aunt Harriet was at home but I frequented her home very often. I knew Kate Stewart very well. She should be living in Auburn now. I have not seen her in years (Brickler, 1940d).

S118. Harkless Bowley Reconstructs the Family Tree (1939–1940)

I do not know anything about Aunt Harriets Brothers, only those I told you about in my last letter. One brother James and my family lived in the same House in Chatham. His son and I was born there in the same year, Elijah was born in March and I was born in December. Uncle William lived in St. Catherines. Uncle John lived in Auburn. Uncle John was afflicted with Rheumatism and could not walk. He had a fine team of horses. He hired a man to drive them. This man was sick for a while [and] Uncle John's youngest son worked his team. Both of us were quite young. I helped him load the wagon sometimes. Afterwards Uncle William who still lived in St. Catherine came to live with Aunt Harriet in Auburn and died there. . . .

Now about the sisters, I am a little mixed on this point. I am trying to get at the real *blood* kin. My mother's mother was sold south. Aunt Harriet was my mother's aunt or half sister but mother always called Aunt Harriet "Sister Harriet." . . .

I do not know anything about [the] kidnapping of Mrs. Brickler's mother. Mrs. Brickler's father and mother were very dear friends of mine. I never heard Aunt Harriet mention how she brought Mrs. Brickler's mother to Auburn. . . .

Just a line about kidnapping. Aunt Harriet's brother's son married an Indian girl in Canada. She gave birth to a baby girl. She was about to die in her struggles. She sent for Aunt Harriet. Aunt Harriet went to see her. She asked Aunt Harriet if she would take this child and take care of her. Aunt Harriet promised her she would. She said, "Now I die happy," and passed away. This child is a grown woman living in Philadelphia. I hear from her often. She says she is coming to see me next Sunday. Aunt Harriet kept her promise

Just a word about my father. Uncle John Stewart, Aunt Harriet's brother, left two boys in Talbot county Md when he came north. Uncle John was anxious to have them with him. He asked my father if there was any way he could get those boys. My father visited Talbot county and found those boys. They were bound to a man named Kadaway. Father went across the river at night, brought the oldest boy away, kept him in our own home in Dorchester county, and kept him until he could send him to his father in Auburn. After things quieted down he went back and brought the other boy away and sent him to his father. Wonder if that was [the] kidnapping? (H. Bowley, 1939c)

. . . In regards [to] the Lady Aunt Harriet reared, Katie we call her, came to see me, her daughter also. I gave them the letters I received from you. They said they would write you. Both left here for a visit to Auburn about the first of this month. I do not think they will be gone long. I have been looking for a letter from them. I do not know their address in Auburn. Their Address in Philadelphia [is] 242 N 54th Street. Address Mrs. E. S. Narthrip. I have been quite sick since they left here, and am sick now. Thanks for Alice's address (H. Bowley, 1939d).

. . . Yes, I remember Grandfather and Grandmother Ritty Ross very well. I can see Grandfather now walking the floor praising the Lord. They were living with Aunt Harriet when we came back from Canada. We stayed with Aunt Harriet a year or two before going to Maryland. I do not know anything especial about their talk or ways, for I was quite young then. (H. Bowley, 1940a).

Conrad and Carrie Chapman Catt

S119. No Memory of Harriet Tubman (1939–1940)

I was rather amazed at your letter for, so far as I can recall, I never heard of Harriet Tubman. That does not prove that she was not a great woman.

There were a good many outstanding Negro women who, from time to time, came to the old Women's Rights Convention and sometimes made speeches. There was one who never learned to read or write, but was a very pious woman and spoke often. Her name was Sojourner Truth. . . .

You have aroused my curiosity and I would esteem it a favor if you would let me know in what period of our history she lived. The book Sarah Bradford wrote, "Harriet, the Moses of Her People," I do not know either and I have spent the last two years looking for books on women which are not to be found in ordinary libraries (Catt, 1939a).

I read the manuscript you sent. I take it that this may not, necessarily, be printed, but if it ever is, or anything like it, I will ask you to *leave out my name*, because, to tell the truth, I had never heard of Harriet Tubman when you first wrote me and although I tried to help you a little, I was also interested to find out for myself what could be said of her.

. . . I do not know much about the early anti-slavery days, but I know a great deal about suffragists and how they proceeded during the long campaign. Wherever there were Friends [Quakers], they were always much interested in the Negro and since Harriet Tubman was staying in Auburn, it would be quite natural for Mrs. Osborne and her friends to have invited Harriet Tubman to come to see Miss Anthony and other Friends who may have been gathered there in the interest of woman suffrage. Harriet Tubman undoubtedly agreed with the proposition of the women to gain the vote, but her idea was far away from that as an aim. She did not assist the suffragists or the woman suffrage movement at any time. It was they who were attempting to assist her. That much I know from the nature of things and to make Harriet Tubman a leader in the woman suffrage movement and in all other good movements is quite wrong. There was no leadership on the part of the colored people at that time and there is very little even now. I have not the slightest doubt that she did good things and I hope you can get a good deal of information about her, but do not try to make her what she was not (Catt, 1940b).

S120. Conrad Chastises Catt (1940)

If you were amazed to hear of Harriet Tubman, as you said you were in your first note to me, I was equally amazed to hear what you think of her now that you know something about her contribution. I am even more amazed, even stunned, at your impressions of Negro leadership, or rather, as you say, their lack of it, and I naturally feel that you have dismissed a remarkable woman, together with a whole people, rather too categorically. . . .

What you say, of course, is no more or less than what a small minority within the suffrage movement have said and have apparently believed about the Negro ever since the 1860 convention of the Equal Rights Association, when Susan B. Anthony and Elizabeth Cady Stanton scuttled the organization and split the suffrage movement—wide open—with the Negro remaining as the key question in woman suffrage history from that time onward. It is this stream of conflict that has run through the history of your movement that became reflected in your observations about Harriet and your coolness toward the idea that the Negroes ever had leaders

. . . I think that what you find lacking in the character of Harriet Tubman is this: she could not read or write; she spoke with a dialect; and because of these qualities she retained always an air of simplicity and an untutored manner that, in a woman of your own education and scholarly attainments, she would have seemed what has been called "ignorant." . . . It was Booker T. Washington who best evaluated the contribution of Harriet Tubman when he said, "Harriet Tubman brought the two races nearer together and made it possible for the white race to know the black race, to place a different estimate upon it." That was much for one woman to achieve. Susan B. Anthony achieved no more . . .

Yours for the enfranchisement of all peoples (Conrad, 1940a).

S121. Catt Moderates Her Position (1940)

Your letter indicates that you do not understand me and I presume I have not understood you. . . .

I do not mean at all to underestimate the qualifications of Harriet Tubman. I only meant to say that in your preliminary statement, you had not given the proof and I somewhat doubted your ability to do so. . . .

I do not wish to be understood as opposed to the fame of Harriet Tubman. I only say that I am not yet convinced (Catt, 1940c).

PART 4

Documents

A NOTE ON THE EDITING AND
ARRANGEMENT OF THE DOCUMENTS

L ike the story texts, the document excerpts below generally preserve the original spellings and punctuation, though I have occasionally inserted paragraph breaks for the convenience of the reader. All of Tubman's own letters (and one from her brother John Stewart) are printed in their entirety, but to save space I have included only brief passages from the letters by those who knew her, omitting salutations, closings, and other material not directly relevant to Tubman's life history. The title I have given each excerpt includes the date of the event documented, when known, rather than the date of composition of the excerpt. Thus although William Still's accounts of Tubman's Underground Railroad rescues did not appear in print until 1872, I have included them as documents for the years 1854 and 1857, when the rescues described took place.

TESTIMONY AND LETTERS BY
HARRIET TUBMAN AND HER BROTHERS

D1. *Canadian Testimony of Harriet Tubman (1855)*

I grew up like a neglected weed,—ignorant of liberty, having no experience of it.[1] Then I was not happy or contented; every time I saw a white man I was afraid of being carried away.

I had two sisters carried away in a chain-gang,—one of them left two children. We were always uneasy.

Now I've been free, I know what a dreadful condition slavery is. I have seen hundreds of escaped slaves, but I never saw one who was willing to go back and be a slave.

I have no opportunity to see my friends in my native land. We would rather stay in our native land, if we could be as free there as we are here.

I think slavery is the next thing to hell. If a person would send another into bondage, he would, it appears to me, be bad enough to send him into hell, if he could (Harriet Tubman, testimony, 1856).

D2. Betrayal of Tubman's Family in Maryland by the Master

I was born in Maryland, about a hundred miles below Baltimore. My old boss told us if we served him faithfully, he would give us our freedom after his death. His name was Edward Broadis.

There were some ten of us in the family. I had a sister, who had a young child, about two or three months' old, & the master came after her to sell her to Georgia. Her husband had great confidence in a gentleman, who was a (Methodist) class-leader, & he takes my sister and carries her to him to keep her from her master. He told him,—"Get your wife and bring her to me, and I will take care of her." So he did it. And the same time, the old master had got him to look out and get her, and after her husband carries her there, this man turns round and lets the master understand it, & he comes & gets her & sells her down to Georgia, and leaves that young child; and on his death-bed, sometime after the mother was sold, his greatest cry was, "Take this young child away from me!"

After that, a Georgia man came and bought my brother; and after he had bought him, the master calls to him to come to the house & catch the gentleman's horse, but instead of his coming to catch the horse, my mother, who was out in the field, and knew what the master was doing, comes in. She had a suspicion that they were going to sell the boy, and went to the backside of the house, and heard the master count the money; and after he had counted out the money, the master says, "I ought to have fifty dollars more yet," and then they took and counted the money out and put it all away, and then sent for the boy, as I have told you. When the mother comes, she says, "What do you want of the boy?" He wouldn't tell her, but says to her, "Go and bring a pitcher of water"; and after she brought the pitcher of water, she goes to work again. Then he makes another excuse, & hollers to the boy to come & put the horse into the carriage. But the mother comes again. Then he says, "What did you come for? I hollared for the boy." And she up & swore, and said he wanted the boy for that (ripping out an oath) Georgia man. He called three times, but the boy did not come; and the third time, he came to look for the boy, but the mother had him hid, & kept him hid, I suppose, for a month. The master still kept the money and told the Georgia man, "Before you get ready to make up your flock, I will try to catch the boy someway." The mother had the boy hid, all this time, in the woods, and at friends' houses.

The master had a servant who was working for him, who knew where my brother was, and he got him to betray the boy. He told him to tell the boy to come and bring his dinner to him, in the woods, and he would appear there & catch him. But when the old gentleman said to my mother, "You send my dinner out by the boy," she didn't let on she wouldn't send it, but thought there was something wrong. At noon, he appears in the bush, expecting the boy would be there, with the dinner, but the boy wasn't there. And there, late at night, he came to the door, and asked the mother to let him come in, but she was suspicious and she says, "What do you want?" Says he, "Mr. Scott wants to come in to light a segar." She ripped out an oath, and said; "You are after my son; but the first man that comes into my house, I will split his head open." That frightened them, and they would not come in. So she kept the boy hid until the Georgia man went away, and then she let him come out. Then the master came to the mother, and said he was exceedingly glad she hid the boy, so that he couldn't sell him. He told her, "when we wanted you to send the boy into the woods, we were there to catch him." And then he promised us, that if we would only be faithful, he would leave us all to be free; but at his death, he left us all to be slaves (Henry Stewart, testimony, 1863).

D3. Several Escape Attempts by Tubman's Brothers

We started to come away, but got surrounded, and went back. After we went back, we concealed ourselves, and a white gentleman offered to buy us as we were, but our mistress says, "If I can't keep them, I'd rather see them sold to Georgia." After the gentleman saw she wouldn't sell us to him at any price, he sent us word, "Boys, I can't buy you. If you can get away, get away." We had then been concealed some six or eight months, and advertisements had come out about us, and we didn't know what course to take. Our father abided in Caroline County, and after this friend failed, he took the case up; and after this gentleman told us to get away, we made an effort to start, and our father looked out for a man who said he could carry us away. But when we got to this man, he disappointed us, and we didn't know what to do. We had to turn round & go back to our owners, after we had been gone six months. The old woman was awful glad, & said unto us, "Boys, you have come back again." And after we came back, we had the same resolution to go away we ever had.

We worked there about a year or more, and then we were to be sold.[2] We made ready to go away, but we couldn't get away; and our sister, (the one that is now here) was out in Pennsylvania, and came down after us when she heard we were going to be sold, but we wouldn't go.[3] After she had gone away, our hearts mourned that we didn't go with her. Just after that, we were to be sold again, and she came in good season. She brought us all off together—ten of us[4]—and we rode to Canada, and have been here ever since.

I have been here about eight years. At first, I made pretty good headway, and then my brother and I rented a farm, for which we paid $200 a year, and we got into some trouble there and left that, and my brother went to Berlin, and I undertook to buy six acres of land out in the country; and am now living on it. If slavery remains just as it is, I will stay in Canada. I have no idea of going back unless freedom is established (Henry Stewart, testimony, 1863).

D4. John Stewart's Letter from Auburn (1859)

Sister Harriet Tubman

I am well and hope you are the same Fathers health is very good for him I received your welcome letter yesterday which relieved my uneasiness[5] we thought quite hard of you for not writing before we would like to see you much but if you can do better where you are you had perhaps better stay Father wanted to go to Canada after his things on foot but I would not consent as I thought it would be too much for him and he consents to stay until he gets your advice on the subject as he has no means for going please write as soon as possible and not delay we three are alone, I have a good deal of trouble with them as they are getting old and feeble there was a man by the name of Young that promised father a stove and some things to go to keeping house but has refused to do anything for them Brother John[6] has been with father ever since he left Troy and is doing the best he can Catharine Stewart has not come yet but wants to very bad send what things you want father to bring if you think best for him to go I am going to send a letter to Wm Henry if you wish me to say any thing for You to him let me know when you write Seward has received nothing as Payment since the 4th of July that I know of—write me particularly what you want me to do as I want to hear from you very much I would like to know what luck you have had since you have been gone have heard that you were doing well hope to find it so Direct my letters to me Box 750 Auburn

Truly Yours
John Stewart—

[on reverse side] have you ever written to Canada since you have been gone, let me know (John Stewart to Harriet Tubman, November 1, 1859)

D5. Dictated Fund-raising Letter to Wendell Phillips (1860)

My dear Friend,

I write to let you know that I am about to start on my mission. I shall leave on Tuesday. As you promised if I would let you know in case I did not make up my $100, I will state I lack (after paying my board)[7] 19 or 20 of that amount. I shall not take my money with me but leave it with Mr. Walcott to forward to me at Philadelphia. Whatever you do will be gratefully appreciated by

Harriet Tubman

I am as well as it is usual for me to be and in good spirits (Harriet Tubman to Wendell Phillips, August 4, 1860).

D6. Dictated Letter to Franklin Sanborn
about the Combahee River Raid (1863)

Last fall, when the people here became much alarmed for fear of an invasion from the rebels, all my clothes were packed and sent with others to Hilton Head, and lost; and I have never been able to get any trace of them since. I was sick at the time, and unable to look after them myself. I want, among the rest, a bloomer dress, made of some coarse, strong material, to wear on expeditions. In our late expedition up the Combahee River, in coming on board the boat, I was carrying two pigs for a poor sick woman, who had a child to carry, and the order "double quick" was given, and I started to run, stepped on my dress, it being rather long, and fell and tore it almost off, so that when I got on board the boat there was hardly any thing left of it but shreds. I made up my mind then I would never wear a long dress on another expedition of the kind, but would have a bloomer as soon as I could get it. So please make this known to the ladies if you will, for I expect to have use for it very soon, probably before they can get it to me.

You have without doubt seen a full account of the expedition I refer to. Don't you think we colored people are entitled to some credit for that exploit, under the lead of the brave Colonel Montgomery? We weakened the rebels somewhat on the Combahee river, by taking and bringing away seven hundred and fifty-six head of their most valuable live stock, known up in your region as "contrabands," and this, too, without the loss of a single life on our part, though we had good reason to believe that a number of rebels bit the dust. Of these seven hundred and fifty-six contrabands, nearly or quite all the able-bodied men have joined the colored regiments here.

I have now been absent two years almost, and have just got letters from my friends in Auburn urging me to come home.[8] My father and mother are old and in feeble health, and need my care and attention. I hope the good people there will not allow them to suffer, and I do not believe they will. But I do not see how I am to leave at present the very important work to be done here. Among other duties which I have, is that of looking after the hospital here for contrabands. Most of them coming from the mainland are very destitute, almost naked. I am trying to find places for those able to work, and provide for them as best I can, so as to lighten the burden on the Government as much as possible, while at the same time they learn to respect themselves by earning their own living.

Remember me kindly to Mrs. —— and her daughters; also, if you will, to my Boston friends, Mrs. C., Miss. H., and especially to Mr. and Mrs. George L. Stearns, to whom I am under great obligations for their many kindnesses. I shall be sure to come and see you all if I live to go North. If you write me, please direct your letter to the care of E. G. Dudley, Beaufort, S.C. (Harriet Tubman to Franklin B. Sanborn, June 30, 1863).[9]

D7. Affidavit Testimony in Pension Claim Case (1894)

Sworn by Harriet Tubman, November 10, 1894, State of New York, County of Cayuga.

. . . I was born in Cambridge, Dorchester County, Md.

My residence at the time I became acquainted with the above named soldier [Nelson Davis], was in the Town of Fleming, Cayuga Co., NY (adjoining the city of Auburn, N.Y.). My P.O. address was then and is now Auburn, Cayuga Co., N.Y. There has been no change of my P. O. address nor residence since.

I had known the soldier before my marriage to him a little over three years.

I was married to the soldier in the city of Auburn, N.Y., March 18th 1869 by the Rev. Henry Fowler. See proof of my marriage on file.

I was a slave in the state of Maryland before the war. My owner's name was Edward Broadice. I escaped from slavery before the war and came North. I was not a slave at the time of my marriage to the soldier, I having been freed by the Proclamation of President Lincoln.

My name before I married my first husband John Tubman was Harriet Ross. After my marriage to him my name was Harriet Tubman and so continued and I was known and recognized by that name until my marriage to Nelson Davis. See affidavit of Nov. 28, 1892 and proof of J. Tubman's death dated Nov. 22nd, 1892, all on file with my claim. I have had no husband since the death of the soldier, Nelson Davis.

I have no knowledge as to how he enlisted (or was drafted) but I have heard him say it was at Oneida or Rome, Oneida Co., N.Y. I have his certificate of discharge which shows that he was enrolled Sept. 25, 1863 and discharged at Brownsville, Texas, Nov. 10, 1865 and did not re-enlist.

I never had any children nor child by the soldier nor by John Tubman.

The soldier was born (as he informed me) in or near Elizabeth County, North Carolina. His actual residence when I became acquainted with him was at my house in the town of Fleming, Cayuga Co., N.Y. as a boarder and so continued to live until the date of our marriage and continued to live at the same place as my husband till he died, Oct. 14, 1888, during all of that time his P.O. address was Auburn, Cayuga Co., N.Y. and we were never divorced from each other. I have no knowledge of his change of residence before his enrollment as I did not [know] him till after he was discharged from the service and came to my house to live.

His occupation was that of a brick maker and laborer. His age as given in the certificate of discharge is 21 and in the record of death it is 44. See proof of death on file. His height 5 ft. 11 inches, color of skin black.

The name of his owner (when a slave) was Fred Charles. His father's name was Milford Davis.

The soldier was not a slave at the time of his marriage to me nor at the time of his enrollment he having been freed from slavery by the Proclamation of President Lincoln Sept. 22, 1862 which gave him his freedom on January 1st 1863. He was known as Nelson Charles and

Nelson Davis. He never had any other wife but me. See proof upon this point on file with the claim, and my affidavit of Nov. 28, 1892 . . .

There has been but little change in the character and extent of my property since my former statement [affidavit of February 1, 1892], except my horse has since died and the mortgage of two hundred has been increased to five hundred. See certificate of C. G. Adams of Sept. 4, 1894.

There is no one legally bound for my support.

Harriet (her mark) Davis (Harriet Tubman, affidavit, November 10, 1894)

D8. Dictated Fund-raising Letter to Ednah Cheney (1894)

Harriet Tubman has asked me to write you for her to send her love to you and to say that she shall always remember you most "lovingly to the day of her death." Harriet is very well for a woman of her advanced years and is as busy as ever going about doing good to every body her home is filled with "odds and ends" of society and to every one outcast she gives food and shelter. She is still trying to establish a home for old colored women but as yet has succeeded very slightly in collecting funds for that purpose—yet she is not discouraged but is working always with that object still in view—she certainly deserves success and I trust her many friends will help her as far as possible in accomplishing her object[10]—She remembers you with great affection and thanks you always for your kindness to her (Jane Kellogg[11] [for Harriet Tubman] to Ednah Cheney, April 9, 1894).

D9. Dictated Letter to Mary Wright (1896)

Mrs. Mary Wright,

I received the trunk and package which you sent me and I am very thankful to you for them. I have been appointed by the pastors of the first M.E. and the A.M.E. Churches of Auburn, to collect clothes for the destitute colored children and the things which you have sent are very acceptable. The four dollars which you sent me was also very acceptable for it was in a very needy time.

Please remember me to Lizzie and Marshie Clara to your son & all of the family. The young lawyer sent my papers to me from Washington. Please let me know how many grandchildren you have. I would like for you to see Miss Edna Cheny for me. I would like to get out another edition of books. The editor says he can let [me] publish a five hundred books for $100 before he destroyed the plates. I would like to have another set of books published to take to the Methodists Centennial at New York this fall. I can raise fifty dollars and if Miss Cheny can see Mr. Sanburn and some of those Anti-Slavery friends and have them raise fifty dollars more that will enable me to get the books out before the editor destroys the plate. If they will help me raise the money they can hold the books until I can sell enough to pay them back. I would like to come and see you but my brother is sick and I cannot very well leave home at this time. I am not doing any thing right now as I am not able.

Miss Cheny has done very well by me and I do not wish to ask for money [but] if through her influence I can get the friends to help me I shall be ever thankful. My home is incorporated for an asylum for aged colored people that will hold the mortgage and I won't be trouble[d] now. Remember me in your prayers as your father did before you. If I never see you again I hope to see you in the kingdom.

Goodby. God bless you all, from your friend who loves you all,
Harriet Tubman (Harriet Tubman to Mrs. Mary Wright, May 29, 1896)[12]

D10. Affidavit Testimony in Pension Claim Case (1898)

I am about 75 years of age. I was born and reared in Dorchester County, Md. My maiden name was Araminta Ross. Some time prior to the late War of the Rebellion I married John Tubman who died in the State of Maryland on the 30th day of September 1867. I married Nelson Davis, a soldier of the late war, on the 18th day of March 1869, at Auburn, N.Y.

I furnished the original papers in my claim to one Charles P. Wood, then of Auburn, N. Y., who died several years ago. Said Wood made copies of said original papers which are herewith annexed. I was informed by said Wood that he sent said original papers to one James Barrett, an attorney on 4½ Street, Washington, D.C., and I was told by the wife of said Barrett that she handed the original papers to the Hon. C. D. MacDougall, then a member of the House of Representatives.

My claim against the U.S. is for three years service as nurse and cook in hospitals, and as commander of several men (eight or nine) as scouts during the late War of the Rebellion, under direction and orders of Edwin M. Stanton, Secretary of War, and of several Generals.

I claim for my services above named the sum of eighteen hundred dollars. The annexed copies have recently been read over to me and are true to the best of my knowledge, information and belief (Harriet Tubman, affidavit, January 1, 1898).

DOCUMENTS FROM
UNDERGROUND RAILROAD YEARS

D11. "Moses" Arrives with Six Passengers (1854)

The coming of these passengers[13] was heralded by Thomas Garrett's letter as follows:

Thomas Garrett's letter

Wilmington, 12 mo. 29th, 1854
Esteemed Friend, J. Miller McKim:—We made arrangements last night, and sent away Harriet Tubman, with six men and one woman to Allen Agnew's, to be forwarded across the country to the city. Harriet, and one of the men had worn their shoes off their feet, and I gave them two dollars to help fit them out, and directed a carriage to be hired at my expense, to take them out, but do not yet know the expense . . . Thomas Garrett.

Harriet Tubman had been their "Moses," but not in the sense that Andrew Johnson was the "Moses of the colored people." She had faithfully gone down into Egypt, and had delivered these six bondmen by her own heroism. Harriet was a woman of no pretensions, indeed, a more ordinary specimen of humanity could hardly be found among the most unfortunate-looking farm hands of the South. Yet in point of courage, shrewdness and disinterested exertions to rescue her fellow-men, by making personal visits to Maryland among the slaves, she was without her equal.

Her success was wonderful. Time and again she made successful visits to Maryland on the Underground Rail Road, and would be absent for weeks, at a time, running daily risks while making preparations for herself and passengers. Great fears were entertained for her safety, but she seemed wholly devoid of personal fear. The idea of being captured by slave-hunters or slave-holders, seemed never to enter her mind. She was apparently proof against all adversaries. While she thus manifested such utter personal indifference, she was much more watchful with regard to those she was piloting. Half of her time, she had the appearance of one asleep, and would actually sit down by the road-side and go fast asleep when on her errands of mercy through the South, yet, she would not suffer one of her party to whimper once, about "giving out and going back," however wearied they might be from hard travel day and night. She had a very short and pointed rule or law of her own, which

implied death to any who talked of giving out and going back. Thus, in
an emergency she would give all to understand that "times were very
critical and therefore no foolishness would be indulged in on the road."
That several who were rather weak-kneed and faint-hearted were greatly
invigorated by Harriet's blunt and positive manner and threat of extreme
measures, there could be no doubt.

After having once enlisted, "they had to go through or die." Of course
Harriet was supreme, and her followers generally had full faith in her,
and would back up any word she might utter. So when she said to them
that "a live runaway could do great harm by going back, but that a dead
one could tell no secrets,"[14] she was sure to have obedience. Therefore,
none had to die as traitors on the "middle passage." It is obvious
enough, however, that her success in going into Maryland as she did,
was attributable to her adventurous spirit and utter disregard of
consequences. Her like it is probable was never known before or since.

On examining the six passengers who came by this arrival they were
thus recorded:

December 29th, 1854 . . . Benjamin was twenty-eight years of age,
chestnut color, medium size, and shrewd. He was the so-called property
of Eliza Ann Brodins, who lived near Buckstown, in Maryland. Ben did
not hesitate to say, in unqualified terms, that his mistress was "very
devilish." He considered his charges, proved by the fact that three slaves
(himself one of them) were required to work hard and fare meagerly, to
support his mistress' family in idleness and luxury. The Committee paid
due attention to his *ex parte*[15] statement, and was obliged to conclude
that his argument, clothed in common and homely language, was
forcible, if not eloquent, and that he was well worthy of aid. Benjamin
left his parents besides one sister, Mary Ann Williamson,[16] who wanted
to come away on the Underground Rail Road.

Henry left his wife, Harriet Ann, to be known in future by the name
of "Sophia Brown." He was a fellow-servant of Ben's, and one of the
supports of Eliza A. Brodins.

Henry was only twenty-two, but had quite an insight into matters
and things going on among slaves and slave-holders generally, in country
life. He was the father of two small children, whom he had to leave
behind. . . .

Jane, aged twenty-two, instead of regretting that she had unadvisedly
left a kind mistress and indulgent master, who had afforded her
necessary comforts, affirmed that her master, "Rash Jones, was the worst

man in the country." The Committee were at first disposed to doubt her sweeping statement, but when they heard particularly how she had been treated, they thought Catherine [alias Jane] had good ground for all that she said. Personal abuse and hard usage, were the common lot of poor slave girls.

Robert was thirty-five years of age, of a chestnut color, and well made. His report was similar to that of many others. He had been provided with plenty of hard drudgery—hewing of wood and drawing of water, and had hardly been treated as well as a gentleman would treat a dumb brute. His feelings, therefore, on leaving his old master[17] and home, were those of an individual who had been unjustly in prison for a dozen years and had at last regained his liberty.

The civilization, religion, and customs under which Robert and his companions had been raised, were, he thought, "very wicked." Although these travelers were all of the field-hand order, they were, nevertheless, very promising, and they anticipated better days in Canada. Good advice was proffered them on the subject of temperance, industry, education, etc. Clothing, food and money were also given them to meet their wants, and they were sent on their way rejoicing (Still, 1872, 296–299).

D12. Thomas Garrett's Early Sketch of Harriet Tubman as "Noble Woman" (1855)

I feel as if I could not close this already *too long* letter, without giving some account of the doings of a noble woman, but a *black one*, in whose veins flows not one drop of Caucasian blood. She is strong & muscular, now about 55 years of age; born a Slave, and raised what is termed a *field hand.* She escaped from Slavery some 8 years since; her master lived nearly 100 miles below this. She has made 4 successful trips to the neighborhood she left; & brought away 17 of her brothers, sisters, & friends & has mostly made the journeys down on foot, *alone,* & with her companions mostly *walked back,* traveling the whole distance at *night,* and secreting themselves during the day. She has three times gone to Canada with those she brought, and spent every dollar she could earn, or *get in the cause.* She, in one instance, was in the immediate neighborhood of her Master for three months, before she could get off safely with her friends; & but one family, & they colored, where she stopped, knew her. She twice in that time met her master in open day, in the fields, but he did not know her; having always worked in the

open air fields, her color had changed so much, that her own brother &
sister did not know her.

Last week, after a trip of two weeks, she brought up one man.[18] She
took tea with me, & has left again with a determination (during the
Christmas holidays) to bring away her sister, now the last left in slavery,
& her three children, a sister in law & *her* three children, (the husband
of the latter has been a Year in Canada), & one male friend. She says if
she gets them away safely, she will be content, & give up such hazardous
journeys, but says she will either accomplish it or be arrested, & spend
the remainder of her days in Slavery; for should she be arrested for
assisting a slave, even if she had been *free-born*, she would be sold a *slave
for life*; were a white person, man or woman, to peril life & health, &
spend everything he or she had earned in such a noble & disinterested
cause, the name would be trumpeted over the land; but be sure you *do
not trumpet* her noble deeds in the Newspapers. I can assure you I am
proud of her acquaintance (Thomas Garrett to Eliza Wigham,
December 16, 1855).

D13. *Further Information from Garrett on "The Colored Heroine" (1856)*

Thy kind note of 6th mo. 26th came to hand by the kindness of our
friend, Sarah Pugh,—& I can truly assure thee that it gave me great
pleasure to receive a note from thee. Since the receipt of thine, I had not
known of the colored heroine thou inquired for; till the 8th of this
month, when she very unexpectedly came to my store. She says she
went to Canada some four months since, to pilot two fugitives; & was
taken ill there, & is now just able to travel again. She is to leave this day
for Baltimore, to bring away two slave children; when she returns if
successful, she will set out for her sister & two children, a distance of
eighty miles on the coast of Maryland, near where her *legal master now
lives*. She is quite feeble, her voice much impaired from a cold taken last
winter, which I fear has permanently settled on her lungs.

While sick in Canada, the colored man with whom she had made her
home in Philadelphia, *died*; she had left in his care her clothes & ten
dollars; his widow had broken up house-keeping and returned to
Harrisburg, 120 miles distant. She yet hopes to get all her effects
sometime. She told me if she should be successful in getting the two
from Baltimore & her sister & two children from the eastern shore, she
would be satisfied to remain at home till her health should be restored.
The name this noble woman is now known by is Harriet Tubman, &

she requests me to inform thee that if the friend still feels disposed to send her 5 pound sterling to aid her in her praiseworthy calling, it may be sent to the care of Wm. Still, a clerk in the Anti-Slavery Office Philadelphia, where our friend J. Miller McKim is employed; she will continue to report herself in the office, whenever she is in the city (Thomas Garrett to Eliza Wigham, September 12, 1856).

D14. Thomas Garrett's Account of the Rescue of Joe (1856)

If I recollect rightly, in my last letter I wrote thee that I had handed Harriet Tubman the £5 sterling you sent for her, but I then felt some hesitation about giving you some facts connected with it, which I think might be of interest to your Society, & more particularly, to the donor. In the first place, I may inform you that Harriet has a good deal of the old fashioned Quaker about her, she is a firm believer in spiritual manifestations, but I presume knows nothing about *table rappings*,[19] but she has great confidence God will preserve her from harm in all her perilous journeys, as she says she never goes on her missions of mercy without his consent, or approbation.

At the time I gave her the money thee sent her, she came into our store and asked for me; she was directed to the back counting house, where I was writing. I said to her, "Harriet, I am glad to see thee, thee looks much better than when I saw thee last." Her reply was, "Yes, I thank you, I am now well, & God has sent me to you for money." I said, "Harriet, how is this? I expected thee would want a new pair of shoes as usual when thee hast been on a journey, *those* I can give thee, but thee knows I have a great many calls for money from the coloured people, & thee cannot expect much money from me." Her reply was, "You can give me what I need now, God never fools me."

I said, "Well, Harriet, how much does thee want now," she said it would take 3½ ff [shillings] to get shoes for herself and the friend she had with her, & to pay their expenses to Philadelphia, & she must have 20 ff more to enable her to go for her sister & children making 23½ in all. I said to her, "Harriet, has thee been to Philadelphia lately?" "No, not for several weeks."—"Has anyone told thee I had money for thee?" *"No, nobody but God."* I then gave her 24 ff 31 cents, the proceeds of the £5 thee sent her, and gave her an [account] of where it came from, & how thee came to get it to forward to her, after which she said, "Thank God." I thought seriously of giving thee these facts in my last letter, but do not think I did so, fully.

On mentioning the circumstance last week while at the Fair, to Wm. Lloyd Garrison and Jas. and Lucretia Mott, they encouraged me to write you and give the facts, as near as I can now recollect in her own words which I have endeavored to do;[20] and now for a history of her last mission of love and daring in order to rescue her sister and her children from Slavery.

She went for them at the time proposed, & had one or more interviews with her sister. but after waiting some ten days, found she could not get her and all three of the children, as two were placed at some distance from the mother—The mother was in hopes they would be permitted to visit her during the holidays, which generally last from Christmas to New Year's day, and Harriet agreed to be in the neighborhood at that time, ready to bring all away together, as her sister would not leave without having all her children with her; when she found such was the case, she left with 5 slaves, 4 men and 1 woman, and reached here safely on foot 90 miles thro' the enemy's country having traveled six nights.

Three days before they arrived, the masters of three of them arrived here, and had hand bills printed up and put up about the town (which were torn down by the colored people as fast as they were put up). They also had them distributed at the railway depots & principal towns all the way down to where they left, offering 1500 ff reward for one, 800! for another & 300 for the third—the other man & woman I have never seen any reward offered for.

Four days after leaving here, I rec[eived] a letter from our friend Oliver Johnson, of New York, saying Harriet with her 5 friends had left that morning for Canada, by railroad, since that time I have not heard from her, & I very much fear she is sick, or something has happened [to] her, as she expected when she left to have been here 10 days since on her way to her sister. I feel almost confident she has not passed, as I have not heard of her in Philadelphia at the Anti-Slavery Office since she left for Canada (Thomas Garrett to Eliza Wigham, December 27, 1856).

D15. William Still's Notes on the Testimony of Harriet Tubman's Escaping Parents (1857)

This party stated that Dr. Anthony Thompson had claimed them as his property. They gave the Committee a pretty full report of how they had been treated in slavery, especially under the doctor. A few of the interesting points were noted as follows: The doctor owned about twenty head of slaves when they left; formerly he had owned a much larger number, but circumstances had led him to make frequent sales during the few years previous to their escape, by which the stock had been reduced. As well having been largely interested in slaves, he had at the same time been largely interested in real estate, to the extent of a dozen farms at least. But in consequence of having reached out too far, several of his farms had slipped out of his hands.

Upon the whole, Benjamin pronounced him a rough man towards his slaves, and declared, that he had not given him a dollar since the death of his (the master's) father, which had been at least twenty years prior to Benjamin's escape. But Ben. did not stop here, he went on to speak of the religious character of his master, and also to describe him physically; he was a Methodist preacher, and had been "pretending to preach for twenty years." Then the fact that a portion of their children had been sold to Georgia by this master was referred to with much feeling by Ben and his wife; likewise the fact that he had stinted them for food and clothing, and led them a rough life generally, which left them no room to believe that he was anything else than "a wolf in sheep's clothing." They described him as a "spare-built man, bald head, wearing a wig."

These two travelers had nearly reached their three score years and ten under the yoke. Nevertheless, they seemed delighted at the idea of going to a free country to enjoy freedom, if only for a short time. Moreover some of their children had escaped in days past, and these they hoped to find. Not many of those thus advanced in years ever succeeded in getting to Canada (William Still, 1872, 395–396).

D16. Thomas Garrett's Report on the Escape of Harriet Tubman's Parents (1857)

I lately, say the 4th day of the 6th mo., furnished *Harriet Tubman's* father and mother, Benjamin and Cathrine Ross[21] with 30ff to carry them to Canada, thee maybe seen their names in the arrivals of fugitives in Canada, in last week's Antislavery Standard. Harriet Tubman accompanied them. The old man Ross had to flee, he had been guilty of sheltering in his hut, for one day, those 8 slaves that broke out of Dover jail, early last Spring—a free coloured man who piloted these slaves some 20 miles to his house from Caroline County, was betrayed by one who started with the rest & turned back and informed of the man who piloted them & told where they went to stop over the first day.

The poor fellow was tried, convicted and sentenced to Maryland Penitentiary for ten years. They were preparing to have Benjamin arrested when his master secretly advised him to leave;[22] his wife belonged to another plantation and the old man, wisely concluding it would be more agreeable to have her along, she left without so much as asking leave and with such an experienced guide as Harriet they passed safely on.

Harriet has still one sister and her 3 children yet in slavery. She has tried hard this summer to get them all away together, but two of the children are separated some twelve miles from their mother, which has caused the difficulty, her sister refusing to leave without bringing all her children away with her.

Harriet's health has much improved, & I hope she will be spared many years yet (Thomas Garrett to Mary Edmundson, August 11, 1857).

D17. John Brown Expresses Admiration for Harriet Tubman (1858)

I came on here direct with J. W. Loguen the day after you left Rochester. I am succeeding to all appearance, beyond my expectations. Harriet Tubman hooked on his whole team at once. He is the most of a man, naturally, that I ever met with. There is the most abundant material, and of the right quality, in this quarter, beyond all doubt. Do not forget to write Mr. Case at once about hunting up every person and family of the reliable kind about, at, or near Bedford, Chambersburg, Gettysburg, and Carlisle, in Pennsylvania, and also Hagerstown and vicinity, Maryland, and Harper's Ferry, Va. The names and residences of all, I want to have sent me at Lindenville (John Brown to John Brown Jr., April 8, 1858).

D18. Franklin Sanborn Calls Harriet Tubman the "Heroine of the Day" (1859)

I wonder if you have rec'd two letters from me about Capt. Brown who has been here for three weeks—and is soon to leave—having got his $2000 secured. He is at the U.S. Hotel; and you ought to see him before he goes—for now he is to begin. Also you ought to see Harriet Tubman, the woman who brought away 50 slaves on 8 journies made to Maryland; but perhaps you have seen her—She is the heroine of the day. She came here Friday night and is at 168 Cambridge St. On Wednesday at 4 P.M. she is to meet [Thomas Starr] King at Mrs. [Cyrus A.] Bartol's on Chestnut St—Can you not attend? Even you would be amazed at some of her stories— ... (Franklin B. Sanborn to Thomas W. Higginson, May 30, 1859).

D19. Harriet Tubman's Suggestion of a
Date for the Harpers Ferry Raid (1859)

Mr. Smith has lately written to John Brown at New York to find what
he needed, meaning to supply it. He now sends to him according to
your enclosed address. I suppose you know the place where this matter is
to be adjusted. Harriet Tubman suggested the 4th of July as a good time
to "raise the mill" (Edwin Morton to Franklin B. Sanborn, June 1, 1859).

D20. Harriet Tubman in Boston as
John Brown Leaves for Virginia (1859)

Brown has set out on his expedition, having got some $800 from all
sources except from Mr. Stearns, and from him the balance of $2000;
Mr. Stearns being a man who "having put his hand to the plough
turneth not back." Brown left Boston for Springfield and New York on
Wednesday morning at 8½ and Mr. Stearns has probably gone to N.Y.
today to make final arrangements for him. He means to be on the
ground as soon as he can perhaps so as to begin by the 4th July. . . .

He is desirous of getting some one to go to Canada and collect
recruits for him among the fugitives, with H. Tubman or alone, as the
case may be—and urged me to go, but my school will not let me. Last
year he engaged some persons and heard of others, but he does not want
to lose time by going there himself now. I suggested you to him, for you
have already some acquaintance with the Canada people, and you would
be able to go instantly to the right places and get the right men. Now is
the time to help in the involvement, if ever for within the next two
months the experiment will be made.

Harriet Tubman is here today to spend the Sunday. Next Sunday she
may be in Leicester with Mr. May. Tomorrow young Heywood is to
speak here and to be the guest of Mrs. Brooks, while Harriet goes to
Miss Whiting's; H. T. mentions a matter which some one ought to go
to Canada to look after a society in aid of destitute fugitives at St.
Catharine's which has some reason to complain of Mr. Wilson the
missionary among fugitives in that town—whom you perhaps know—
It is said that the contributions of the friends do not reach the fugitives
at all, and they are desirous to have the matter looked into. How would
you like to take a journey to that region for this double purpose—
. . . H. T. is in Boston at 168 Cambridge St. (Franklin B. Sanborn to
Thomas W. Higginson, June 4, 1859).

D21. Maria Weston Chapman Sends
Harriet Tubman to a Friend in New Bedford (1859)

When I wrote to you yesterday I had not learned what I have just heard—that Harriet Tubman, our black heroine, is about to start for New Bedford where many of her protégés are in hiding.

I venture to furnish her with a letter of introduction to you, in the hope that you may find her the suitable person to undertake to bring off the children of Charles, about whom I had so fruitless a correspondence with the Philadelphia Vigilance Committee & others.

There may be many persons of general humanity in New Bedford who would rejoice to aid this noble woman in her present purpose of securing a home for the parents she has rescued; and if your kind commendation of her to such, should prove the means of success to *her*, it will also be a real obligation to *me*.

Referring to my former letters for her history in brief,[23]
I am, dear Madam
Your obliged & obedient
M. W. Chapman (Maria Weston Chapman to Mrs. Sarah Rotch Arnold, June 4, 1859)

D22. Harriet Tubman's Visit to Concord (1859)

I was to have gone to Leominster last Sunday again but was kept here in part by a heavy rain, and in part by a visit from Harriet Tubman, a fugitive slave who has aided in the escape of fifty slaves—in fact, has brought them under her own care. She is a thorough "nigger"—but a striking person, and I esteem it an honor to know her. Miss Whiting took charge of her while here—and she spoke on Sunday night at a meeting in the vestry—(Franklin B. Sanborn to Benjamin Smith Lyman, June 8, 1859).

D23. Harriet Tubman "Probably in New Bedford, Sick,"
as Harpers Ferry Raid Approaches (1859)

Yours of the 18th has been received and communicated. S. G. H. [Samuel G. Howe] has sent you fifty dollars in a draft on New York, and I am expecting to get more from other sources, perhaps some here, and will make up to you the $300, if I can, as soon as I can, but I can give nothing myself just now, being already in debt. . . . Your son John was in

Boston a week or two since, and I tried to find him, but did not; and, being away from Concord, he did not come to see me. He saw [Samuel G. Howe, George Luther Stearns, Wendell Phillips, Francis Jackson] and everybody liked him. . . .

I conclude that your operations will not be delayed if the money reaches you in the course of the next fortnight, if you are sure of having it there. I cannot certainly promise that you will; but I think so. Harriet Tubman is probably in New Bedford, sick. She has stayed here in N[ew] E[ngland] a long time, and been a kind of missionary.[24] Your friends in C[oncord] are all well; I go back there in a week.

God prosper you in all your works. (Franklin B. Sanborn to John Brown, August 27, 1859)

D24. Letter Found at Harpers Ferry Refers to Harriet Tubman

I received your very kind letter, and would state that I have sent a note to Harriet requesting her to come to Boston, saying to her in the note that she must come right on, which I think she will do, and when she does come I think we will find some way to send her on. I have seen our friend at Concord [Sanborn]; he is a true man. I have not yet said anything to anybody except him. I do not think it is wise for me to do so. I shall, therefore, when Harriet comes, send for our Concord friend, who will attend to the matter. Have you all the hands you wish? Write soon. (L[ewis] H[ayden] to John Brown via Kagi, September 16, 1859).

WARTIME DOCUMENTS

D25. Harriet Tubman's View of Lincoln, before Emancipation Proclamation (1862)

You have doubtless heard of Harriet Tubman, whom they call Moses, on account of the multitude she has brought out of bondage, by her courage and ingenuity. She talks politics sometimes, and her uncouth utterance is wiser than the plans of politicians. She said, the other day[25]: "They may send the flower of their young men down South, to die of the fever in the summer, and the ague in the winter (for tis cold down there, though it is down South). They may send them one year, two years, three years, till they are tired of sending, or till they use up all the young men. All no use! God's ahead of Master Lincoln. God will [not let] Master Lincoln beat the South till he do the right thing. Master Lincoln, he [is a] great man, and I'm a poor nigger, but this nigger can tell Master Lincoln how to save the money and the young men. He [can] do it by setting the niggers free.

"Suppose that was an awful big snake down there on the floor. He bite you, folks all scared cause you die. You send for the doctor to cut the bite; but [the] snake, he rolled up there, and while the doctor [is] doing it, he bite you again. The doctor cut out that bite; but while he [is] doing it, the snake he spring up and bite you again; and so he keep doing, till you kill him. That's what Master Lincoln ought to know"[26] (Lydia Maria Child to John Greenleaf Whittier, January 21, 1862,).

D26. Celebration Service for the Combahee River Raid Victory (1863)

June 6 1863[27]

At Beaufort a few days since, I had the satisfaction of witnessing the return of the gallant Col. Montgomery from a successful raid into the enemy's country, having with him the trophies of war in the shape of 780 black chattels, now recreated and made freemen, and thousands of dollars worth of rice and other property.

As I witnessed the moving mass of recreated black humanity on its way from the boat to the church in Beaufort, where they were quartered for the moment, with the filth and tatters of slavery still hanging to their degraded persons, my heart went up in gratitude to God for the change which had been wrought on South Carolina soil. The emblem of liberty and a nation's glory, as it floated over these poor, defenseless children of oppression, never looked to me so glorious, and never thrilled any heart with a more honest pride. . . .

I doubt whether this church was ever before filled with such a crowd of devout worshippers—whether it was ever before appropriated to so good a purpose—whether so true a gospel had ever before been preached within its walls. I certainly never felt such swelling emotions of gratitude to the Great Ruler as at this moment.

Col. Montgomery and his gallant band of 300 black soldiers, under the guidance of a black woman, dashed into the enemies' country, struck a bold and effective blow, destroying millions of dollars worth of commissary stores, cotton and lordly dwellings, and striking terror to the heart of rebellion, brought off near 800 slaves and thousands of dollars worth of property, without losing a man or receiving a scratch. It was a glorious consummation.

After they were all fairly disposed of in the church, they were addressed in strains of thrilling eloquence by their gallant deliverer; to which they responded in a song—

"There is a white robe for thee."

A song so appropriate and so heartfelt and cordial as to bring unbidden tears.

The Colonel was followed by a speech from the black woman who led the raid, and under whose inspiration it was originated and conducted. For sound sense and real native eloquence, her address would do honor to any man, and it created a great sensation.

And now a word of this woman—this black heroine—this fugitive slave. She is now called "Moses," having inherited the name, for the many daring feats she has accomplished in behalf of the bondmen and the many slaves she has set free. She was formerly a slave in Virginia—she determined upon "freedom or death" and escaped to Canada. She there planned the deliverance of all her kindred, and made nine successful trips to different slave states, effecting the escape of over 180 slaves[28] and their successful establishment in Canada. Since the rebellion she has devoted herself to her great work of delivering the bondmen, with an energy and sagacity that cannot be exceeded. Many and many times she has penetrated the enemy's lines and discovered their situation and condition, and escaped without injury, but not without extreme hazard. True, she is but a woman, and a "nigger" at that, but in patriotism, sagacity, energy, ability and all that elevates human character, she is head and shoulders above all the copperheads in the land, and above many who vaunt their patriotism and boast their philanthropy, swaggering of their superiority because of the cuticle in which their Creator condescended to envelop them ("From Florida: Colonel Montgomery's Raid," *(Madison) Wisconsin State Journal,* June 20, 1863).

D27. George Garrison Meets Harriet Tubman in South Carolina during the War (1864)

I went with Mr. and Mrs. Severance, Miss Iveson, Miss Lee and Col. Hartwell to see Harriet Tubman, who it seems has been on the island some three months, and until Mrs. Severance told me I was not aware she was here. When we entered where she was at work ironing some clothes, Mrs. Severance went to introduce me by saying here is George Garrison. She no sooner saw me than she recognized me at once, and instantly threw her arms around me, and gave me quite an affectionate embrace, much to the amusement of those with me.

We had a very interesting conversation with her. She is just now cooking and washing clothes at Gen. Terry's quarters, who is now in command of Morris and Folly Islands. She wants to go North,[29] but says Gen. Gilmore will not let her go, only on condition that she will return back to this department. He thinks her services are too valuable to loose. She has made it a business to see all contrabands escaping from the rebels, and is able to get more intelligence from them than anybody else.

She is just now working hard to lay up a little money for her parents, and to pay off some debt that she owes. She has a chance of making a good deal of money here, and can easily get fifty times more work than she can do. She had the misfortune to have fifty dollars stolen from her the other day. What money she had left Mr. Severance took from her to send North (George Garrison to William Lloyd Garrison II, February 10, 1864).

POSTWAR DOCUMENTS

D28. Martha Coffin Wright's Account of the Railway Car Incident (1865)

Harriet Tubman was here yesterday—it was quite dark & wet, when she left, but she didn't kear for that[30]—she'd as lief go in de dark as de light—How dreadful it was for that wicked conductor to drag her out into the smoking car & hurt her so seriously, disabling her left arm, perhaps for the Winter—She still has the misery in her Shoulder & side & carries her hand in a sling—It took three of them to drag her out after first trying to wrench her finger and then her arm—She told the man he was a copperhead scoundrel, for which he choked her—she was on the 11 o'cl (p. m.) train between Cambden & South Amboy—She told him she didn't thank any body to call her cullud pusson—She wd he called [her] black or Negro—She was as proud of being a black woman as he was of being white—

It was not tho't best to publish the circumstances till they found whether something cd be got from the Company—D. told her that she could sue the company here, at her home, and he wd write to Mr. Phillips' son-in-law, at the A. S. Office, and enquire whether the witness advertised for, had been found, but if not, her own testimony, & her Drs. wd be sufficient [insert over line: "he has written '————Donalley

Esq.'"]—She shewed me her documents, and told me what Sister L. and Thomas gave her.—She said there was to be a letter sent to me for her, this week, from Mr. Phillips or his son-in-law. So she is coming again— (Martha Coffin Wright to Marianne Pelham Mott, November 7, 1865).

D29. Trial of John Tubman's Killer (1867)

The trial of Robert Vincent for the murder of the colored man John Tubman was brought to a close early on Sunday morning last, by the jury rendering a verdict of "not guilty." That Vincent murdered the deceased we presume no one doubts; but as no one but a colored boy saw him commit the deed, it was universally conceded that he would be acquitted, the moment it was ascertained that the jury was composed exclusively of Democrats. The Republicans have taught the Democrats much since 1860. They thrashed them into at least a seeming respect for the Union. They educated them up to a tolerance of public schools. They forced them to recognize Negro testimony in their courts. But they haven't got them to the point of convicting a fellow Democrat for killing a Negro. But even that will follow when the Negro is armed with the ballot ("Acquittal of a Murderer," *Baltimore American,* December 23, 1867).

D30. Oral History of Harriet Tubman's War Service by Charles P. Wood (1868)

Harriet Tubman was sent to Hilton Head—she says—in May 1862, at the suggestion of Gov. Andrew, with the idea that she would be a valuable person to operate within the enemies lines—in procuring information & scouts. She was forwarded by Col. Frank Howe—the Mass. state agent in New York, by the Gov't transport Atlantic—was sent up to Beaufort, attached to the HQrs of Gen'l Stevens—and rendered much, and very valuable service acting as a spy within the enemies lines—and obtaining the services of the most valued Scouts and Pilots in the Gov't employ in that Department.

Among the original papers in Harriet's possession—is a list of the names of the Scouts and Pilots. . . .

Unconscious of the great value of the official documents she had from the several officers at different times, Harriet has lost some of them—and the first documentary proof we have of her service in the Department of the South is a pass issued by Gen'l Hunter [dated July 1, 1863] . . .

When she came North on leave of absence to see her aged parents residing in this City—she was taken sick and so failed to return to New York City within the time specified in her leave, and for that reason was refused

transportation to Hilton Head. To remedy this difficulty she went to Washington and on representing her case at the War Dep't she was promptly
with the following:

"Pass Mrs. Harriet Tubman (colored) to Hilton Head and Charlestown,
S.C. with free transportation on a Gov't transport, By order of Sec'y of
War . . . Dated Washington, March 20, 1865."

Returning with the intention of embarking at New York—she was intercepted in Philadelphia by some members of the Sanitary Commission
who persuaded her to go instead to the James River Hospitals—where was
pressing need of such service as she could give in the Gov't Hospitals. And
relinquishing her plan of returning to the Dept. of the South—without a
thought as to the unfortunate pecuniary result of this irregular proceeding
she went to the Hospitals of the James River, and at Fortess Monroe or
Hampton—where she remained until July 1865. In that month she went
to Washington again to advise the Gov't of some dreadful abuses existing
in one or more of the Hospitals there. And so great was the confidence of
some officers of the Gov't in her that Surgeon Gen'l Barnes directed that
she be app[ointed] "Nurse or Matron." . . .

It does not appear that she rec'd the appointment above indicated, and
soon after this date she returned to Washington—and thence home— to
devote herself since the countrys need had ceased to her aged Father &
Mother, who still survive at a very advanced age entirely dependent on her.

During the service of more than three years, Harriet states that she
received from the Gov't only two hundred dollars ($200) of pay. This was
paid her at or near Beaufort, and with characteristic indifference to self—
she immediately devoted that sum to the erection of a wash-house, in
which she spent a portion of her time in teaching the freed women to do
washing—to aid in supporting themselves instead of depending wholly
on Gov't aid. During her absence with an important expedition in Florida,
this wash-house was destroyed or appropriated by a Reg't of troops fresh
from the north to make shelter for themselves but without any compensation whatever to Harriet. When she first went to Beaufort she was allowed
to draw rations as an officer or soldier, but the freed people becoming jealous of this privilege accorded her—she voluntarily relinquished this right
and thereafter supplied her personal wants by selling pies and root beer—
which she made during the evenings and nights—when not engaged in
important service for the Gov't. . . .

When in Washington in July 1865 Harriet was in need of money and
applied to Mr. Sec'y Seward to present her claim to the proper Department.

Gen'l Hunter being then in Washington, Mr. Seward referred the matter to him in a note ... But no pay whatever was obtained—and another attempt has been made since—I believe with the same result.

This letter of Mr. Seward shows the estimate of Harriet Tubman by all who know her—she is known throughout this State and New England as an honest, earnest and most self-sacrificing woman. The substance of this statement has been obtained from her lips and in making it up, I have before me the original papers in her possession, which are copied.

That Harriet is entitled to several thousands of dollars pay—there can be no shadow of doubt—the only difficulty seems to lie in the facts that she held no commission, and had not in the regular way and at the proper times and places, made proof and application of and for, her just compensation. On such certificates as she holds she should have it without further delay (Charles P. Wood, manuscript and testimonial materials, 1 June 1868).[31]

D31. Wendell Phillips's Testimonial Letter (1868)

The last time I ever saw John Brown was under my own roof, as he brought Harriet Tubman to me, saying: "Mr. Phillips, I bring you one of the best and bravest persons on this continent—*General* Tubman, as we call her."

He then went on to recount her labors and sacrifices in behalf of her race. After that, Harriet spent some time in Boston, earning the confidence and admiration of all those who were working for freedom. With their aid she went to the South more than once,[32] returning always with a squad of self-emancipated men, women, and children, for whom her marvelous skill had opened the way of escape. After the war broke out, she was sent with endorsements from Governor Andrew and his friends to South Carolina, where in the service of the Nation she rendered most important and efficient aid to our army.

In my opinion there are few captains, perhaps few colonels, who have done more for the loyal cause since the war began, and few men who did before that time more for the colored race, than our fearless and most sagacious friend, Harriet (Wendell Phillips, testimonial letter to Sarah Bradford, June 16, 1868).

D32. Thomas Garrett's Testimonial Letter (1868)

Thy favor of the 12th reached me yesterday, requesting such reminiscences as I could give respecting the remarkable labors of Harriet Tubman, in aiding her colored friends from bondage. I may begin by saying, living as I have in a slave State, and the laws being very severe where any proof could be made of any one aiding slaves on their way to freedom, I have not felt at liberty to keep any written word of Harriet's or my own labors, except in numbering those whom I have aided. For that reason I cannot furnish so interesting an account of Harriet's labors as I otherwise could, and now would be glad to do; for in truth, I never met with any person, of any color, who had more confidence in the voice of God, as spoken direct to her soul. She has frequently told me that she talked with God, and he talked with her every day of her life, and she has declared to me that she felt no more fear of being arrested by her former master, or any other person, when in his immediate neighborhood, than she did in the state of New York, or Canada, for she said she never ventured only where God sent her, and her faith in a Supreme Power truly was great.

I have now been confined to my room with indisposition more than four weeks, and cannot sit to write much; but I feel so much interested in Harriet, that I will try to give some of the most remarkable incidents that now present themselves to my mind. The date of the commencement of her labors, I cannot certainly give; but I think it must have been about [1854];[33] from that time till 1860, I think she must have brought from the neighborhood where she has been held as a slave, from 60 to 80 persons, from Maryland, some 80 miles from here. No slave who placed himself under her care, was ever arrested that I have heard of; she mostly had her regular stopping places on her route. . . .

She at one time brought as many as seven or eight, several of whom were women and children. She was well known here in Chester County and Philadelphia, and respected by all true abolitionists (Thomas Garrett, testimonial letter to Sarah Bradford, June 1868).

D33. *Franklin Sanborn's Testimonial Letter (1868)*

Mr. Phillips has sent me your note, asking for reminiscences of Harriet Tubman, and testimonials to her extraordinary story, which all her New England friends will, I am sure, be glad to furnish.

I never had reason to doubt the truth of what Harriet said in regard to her own career, for I found her singularly truthful. Her imagination is warm and rich, and there is a whole region of the marvelous in her nature, which has manifested itself at times remarkably. Her dreams and visions, misgivings and forewarnings, ought not to be omitted in any life of her, particularly those relating to John Brown.

She was in his confidence in 1858–9, and he had a great regard for her, which he often expressed to me. She aided him in his plans, and expected to do so still further, when his career was closed by that wonderful campaign in Virginia. The first time she came to my house, in Concord, after that tragedy, she was shown into a room in the evening, where Brackett's bust of John Brown was standing. The sight of it, which was new to her, threw her into a sort of ecstasy of sorrow and admiration, and she went on her rhapsodical way to pronounce his apotheosis.

She has often been in Concord, where she resided at the houses of Emerson, Alcott, the Whitneys, the Brooks family, Mrs. Horace Mann, and other well known persons.[34] They all admired and respected her, and nobody doubted the reality of her adventures. She was too *real* a person to be suspected. In 1862, I think it was, she went from Boston to Port Royal, under the advice and encouragement of Mr. Garrison, Governor Andrew, Dr. Howe, and other leading people. Her career in South Carolina is well known to some of our officers, and I think to Colonel Higginson, now of Newport, R.I., and Colonel James Montgomery, of Kansas, to both of whom she was useful as a spy and guide, if I mistake not.[35] I regard her as, on the whole, the most extraordinary person of her race I have ever met. She is a Negro of pure or almost pure blood, can neither read nor write, and has the characteristics of her race and condition. But she has done what can scarcely be credited on the best authority, and she has accomplished her purposes with a coolness, foresight, patience, and wisdom, which in a *white man* would have raised him to the highest pitch of reputation (Franklin B. Sanborn, testimonial letter to Sarah Bradford, n.d. [June 1868]).

D34. *Frederick Douglass's Testimonial Letter (1868)*

Dear Harriet: I am glad to know that the story of your eventful life has been written by a kind lady, and that the same is soon to be published. You ask for what you do not need when you call upon me for a word of commendation. I need such words from you far more than you can need them from me, especially where your superior labors and devotion to the cause of the latterly enslaved of our land are known as I know them. The difference between us is very marked. Most that I have done and suffered in the service of our cause has been in public, and I have received much encouragement at every step of the way. You, on the other hand, have labored in a private way. I have wrought in the day— you in the night. I have had the applause of the crowd and the satisfaction that comes of being approved by the multitude, while the most that you have done has been witnessed by a few trembling, scarred, and foot-sore bondmen and women, whom you have led out of the house of bondage, and whose heartfelt *"God bless you"* has been your only reward. The midnight sky and the silent stars have been the witnesses of your devotion to freedom and of your heroism. Excepting John Brown—of sacred memory—I know of no one who has willingly encountered more perils and hardships to serve our enslaved people than you have. Much that you have done would seem improbable to those who do not know you as I know you. It is to me a great pleasure and a great privilege to bear testimony to your character and your works, and to say to those to whom you may come, that I regard you in every way truthful and trustworthy[36] (Frederick Douglass, testimonial letter to Harriet Tubman, August 29, 1868).

D35. Visit of James Bowley (1868)

Harriet Tubman just came with her mother's great grandson[37]—He lived in Canada till the War, & now teaches the freedmen in S. Carolina— He was one of the first that Harriet rescued from Slavery—She wanted I should ask Mrs. Mott if she would not write a letter, telling what she knew of her, for Mrs. Bradley [*sic*] to put in a book she was writing about her—She had letters from Thos. Garret, Gerritt Smith & others, & Mr. Mott & Mrs. M. came to see her in Phila. & assisted her—so I have done what I promised, & if she dreads it like other skeletons, she needn't bother—I have to look round & find a bundle of blamed things for the Nephew to take to the Freedmen[38]—& get it to Eliza's (Martha Coffin Wright to Anna and Patty Lord, September 11, 1868).

D36. Successes of Harriet Tubman's Freedmen's Fair (1868)

Fanny has been active at the Fair—they took a little more than last yr.[39] a little over $500. after two days of very hard work for a few—Eliza Townsend & Debby Ann were indefatigable & Anne & Anna & the Carries busy at the tables—they made a good many fancy things wh. sold well, & they have orders for a good many more—I sent my 38 aprons 9 bags—lap bags for children, & rag bags—& knitting needle elastics— 3 tomatoes (pincushions) & one needle book—Eliza sent holders—rag babies (large) & towels—the babys were soon sold at 3 dollars each— A large fruit cake that was made by the Annes & Carries brot only $12. hardly what it cost, as it was elaborately ornamented, in imitation of one Carrie had just seen bring $200 at Buffalo—it was bought by 25 ct. contributions for the minister who had the largest number of votes, & Mr. Brainard got it—much to Anne's disgust as he had taken no interest, & Mr. Fowler had given the Ch. & been in, several times. They shd. have decided on him in the first place & not left it to chance—But there is always something in this sublunary sphere, to go wrong—

Anne Wise was very useful, & Mr. Wise very kind in getting Harriet Tubman's Book printed here, & having it bound & ready in time—quite creditably done too,[40] tho' there are some errors, like "sinner's flesh" for "swine's flesh", &c—the price was too high—$1. a copy, for a small book—but 60 or 70 sold & more perhaps will—It is a mistake to mark Fair things too high—We had quite good weather—plenty of snow for sleighing—

Harriet was quite a heroine—An affected sort of piece, enquired at the table for Miss Tub, & when they found who she meant, Harriet was summoned, & her talk to her, was good as a play, Carrie said—among the rest, she thought, if all was true that that book said, she must have a great deal of "sponscientiousness!" Harriet answered her big words at random.—

We didn't have any dinners or teas got, but all ate at the Fair.—I did not go, however, till toward dusk, being nearly laid up, with a bad cold—It was quite refreshing to stay at home, & accomplish a little sewing of my own. (Martha Coffin Wright to Ellen Wright Garrison, December 16, 1868).

D37. What Harriet Tubman Told
Martha Coffin Wright about John Brown (1869)

We all owe you thanks for your efforts to make Harriet Tubman's book known. It was not quite so well arranged as we should have liked—or so interesting as Mrs. Child cd have made it with the same materials, but at the same time, I think Mrs. Bradford deserves credit for having done even so well, almost impossible as it is to understand Harriet's desultory talk—She told me that John Brown staid at her house in Canada, while he was there, & that he wanted her to go with him, in his expedition, but when he sent a message for her, she was not at home. I asked her if she did not feel bad, when she heard of his death—She said "Yes, at first—but he done more in dying, than 100 men would, in living." She said, "His orders was not to destroy property, nor to hurt man woman or children, but to fetch away the slaves when they could & if they couldn't get them to get their masters, & keep them in the Mts [mountains] till their frds [friends] wd give slaves in exchange" (Martha Coffin Wright to William Lloyd Garrison II, January 10, 1869).

D38. An Annuity from Mrs. Birney (1869)

I have just answered a letter from Caroline. She wanted to know how Harriet Tubman's $50. from Mrs. Birney, now ready, should be sent[41]— Perhaps Harriet had a revolution—I meant to say Revelation, for she came, & solved my doubts, saying she was told it was given for her present use, to make her & her parents comfo'ble & she wanted it sent to me—Her garden had failed, by the wet season & the masons[42] turning water on it & they were in need of supplies—(Martha Coffin Wright to Ellen Wright Garrison, October 20, 1869).

D39. Friends Help Manage Donations and
Income from Bradford Book (1869)

I have a letter from Caroline, asking what Harriet Tubman needs most, as Mrs. Tallman has her money from Mrs. Birney, ready for her, so I have to paddle down to Mr. Wise's & see if it is most needed on the Mortgage or in the household. He has been so active in selling her Life, he may know. She was here the other day—greatly disappointed that Mrs. Garrison & the chillen had gone without seeing her. Wm. Generally makes a point of calling on her, but the days flew by & he didn't get there (Martha Coffin Wright, to Anna Brown, October 19, 1869).

D40. News of James Bowley in the
South Carolina Legislature (1869)

Harriet Tubman was here last evening. She shewed us a letter from her nephew[43] whom William met here, once—he is a member of the S. Carolina Legislature!—His letter was well written—How funny it must seem to him[44]—Harriet, after getting him from de Souf[45]— worked out two years at a dollar a week & paid 50 cts a wk for his board, & sent him to school—then she saved up enough to get his Ma away & nursed her thro' a fit of sickness after she came Norf— (Martha Coffin Wright to Ellen Wright Garrison, December 22, 1869).

D41. Wright Family Hires Harriet Tubman for Chores (1870–1871)

May 1870 2nd. Monday—Harriet Tubman came to clean[46]—Had her to help wash, & then she & Mary cleaned front parlor—Frank Round's man helped Lawrence shake carpet & Mary & Harriet got it down again in time for Mary & Lizzie to go to a wedding after tea was ready— . . .

3rd Tuesday— . . . Had Harriet Tubman to clean round front door & entry steps & take nails out of front chamber carpet— . . .

4th Wednesday—air full of dust—Warm—Sun red—Harriet Tub cleaning— . . .

January 1871 Saturday 14th.—Cut carpet rags. Anne McD. called & read letters.—Snow all gone Too muddy to go out—Harriet Tubman came & bro't hoop basket. pd. her 62½ c.—

. . . July 8th Saturday. Very warm—carriage came at 8—Rode with D. & Mr. Garrison, to Eliza's & went with her & Nelly to greenhouse, & without her to Harriet Tubman's— . . . I took charge of $5. from Mr. G. for H. Tubman. paid. Too warm to go out in the p.m.

October 7th Saturday— . . . Wrote to Mrs. Tallman acknowledging rect. of check for $50. for Harriet Tubman—(Martha Coffin Wright, diary entries, 1870–1871).

D42. Contemporary Newspaper Account of Gold Swindle Events (1873)

Harriet Tubman, the celebrated colored philanthropist, whose connection with the "gold" transaction and loss of Shimer's $2,000 in greenbacks which has, for the past week, created so much interest in this city and abroad, returned to her home, near the Fleming toll gate on Saturday afternoon, having so far recovered from the effects of her adventure as to admit of leaving the shelter of Mr. Slocum Howland's roof . . .[47]

From interviews with John Thomas, at Seneca Falls, Harriet and her brother, Mr. John Stewart, who lives on South-St., opposite Gen. Jno. N. Knapp's, and with Mr. Zadoc Bell, an intelligent colored man, who lives on Jefferson street, we are enabled to furnish a more connected and reliable account of the great gold swindle and robbery than has heretofore been attainable. . . .

John Stewart's Story.

John Stewart, who is an honest and industrious man of 55 years, and the brother of Harriet Tubman, is employed as a teamster by D. M. Osborne & Co.[48] He relates that on Friday evening, ten days ago, he was approached in his yard, while caring for his team, by two strange colored men, who introduced themselves as his friends, giving the names of John Thomas and Stevenson, . . . and wanted to have a private talk with him, at the same time making inquiries relative to a colored pastor formerly residing in the city, probably with a view of more effectually "ringing in."[49]

Having finished his work and taken his supper, Mr. Stewart met the strangers in his dooryard, to hear what they had to say. Stevenson, alias Johnson, then asked Stewart if he "did not wish to do something good for himself—to make some money." Stewart replied that he always liked to do good, and to get money honestly.

At this, Stevenson unfolded his business. He said that a contraband had come from near Charleston, South Carolina, and was then but a short distance from them, who had found a large sum of gold in that State, which he had kept since the war—being afraid to use any of it, or to let any white man know of it. The money, he said, was all in five, ten, and twenty dollar gold pieces; that there was five thousand dollars of it, in a trunk; but the man who had it would rather have two thousand dollars in greenbacks, which would be worth more to him in South Carolina than the entire sum of gold. . . . Stewart informed them that he himself could not raise the funds, but that perhaps his sister might be able to effect the transaction with some of her white friends.

Stewart afterward made application to a banker, for aid in the business, but as that gentleman required the gold before paying for it, the application failed.

Stewart met the agents on Saturday morning, near the head of State street, and they afterward proceeded to call on Harriet Tubman, of whom they said they had heard much in the newspapers.[50] Having learned by some means that she had a nephew in South Carolina, Stevenson pretended to be recommended to her by that relative. And here the connection of our story requires the introduction of

Harriet Tubman's Narrative.

The first Harriet saw of John Thomas and Stevenson, alias Johnson, as she relates it to our reporter, was on Saturday morning, following their interviews with Bell and John Stewart. They told her they had seen Bell and had also called on the colored pastor. The latter had been able to promise $400, but that sum was insufficient.

John Thomas told Harriet he belonged in South Carolina, but now lived at Seneca Falls, that Stevenson had just been to South Carolina, and had returned with the contraband who had the trunk full of gold, and represented the amount to be $5,000, which they had been secreting since the war, waiting for a chance to exchange it for greenbacks; that they were afraid to be seen with gold, as all coin belonged to the Government, whose agents would seize it; that after the contraband had received his $2,000 Harriet and her friends could have the rest, as that amount in greenbacks would do him more good in South Carolina than all the gold.

The strangers took lodgings at Harriet's house, Stevenson remaining three nights, and John Thomas two. In the meantime, Harriet called on various bankers and capitalists to aid her colored friends in procuring currency. Among these, she visited ex-Sheriff James Mead, on the Fleming road, who advised her to beware of the strangers, as they were probably robbers, and might eventually take her life. Her belief was too deeply fixed to be shaken, and she saw Dr. E. P. K. Smith, and C. A. Myers, Esq., of the Exchange bank, who drove out to meet the agents in the evening, with $500, thinking to invest that amount, and, if the gold was genuine, to take the balance, which was offered at par. After going to Harriet's house, she told them it was too late to go to the place where the gold was concealed.

John afterward called on Mr. Anthony Shimer, who has known him for many years, and has implicit confidence in his integrity. Mr. Shimer heard the story and agreed to furnish the $2,000 in greenbacks, and to receive in exchange therefor, *dollar for dollar* in gold.

The journey was made on Wednesday afternoon, the cavalcade filing out in vehicles, being first told that the gold was near Fleming Hill, but afterward, that it was a few miles further.

The anxious wait at the tavern, and Harriet's final appearance in speechless and almost unconscious disarray, have been noted previously,[51] and we now give her story from the time of her leaving the house.

Harriet left the tavern with Stevenson, and went toward the railroad, passing a white house on the way, and afterward a house where colored people live. Here Stevenson said he would go in and get his contraband friend. He came back with him in about five minutes, and introduced Harriet to him, saying, "She is the friend Alfred Boly was telling us about," Alfred Boly probably being the nephew in South Carolina.[52]

Harriet then, as she says, talked kindly to the contraband, a very dark man, who appeared scared and troubled, and insisted upon having the money. She refused to give it up until she should get the gold. He complained of being fearful that the family where he was staying would discover that he had the gold; said they had occasion to move the trunk when putting his room in order, and were getting inquisitive concerning it. He was sorry he had not taken Stevenson's advice and gone with him away from this section. Harriet asked him where the gold was, and he said it was over the fields, in the woods. The three then started for the woods, going across plowed ground and over two fences.

On arriving at the woods, the dark man again insisted on having the greenbacks, and commenced to "take on" again, in order to induce Harriet to give up the notes; but he was finally mollified, and then the three began to throw off some rails which were piled over the spot where the trunk was sunk in the ground.

The rails being removed, the trunk was found, covered with leaves, and set into the ground just deep enough to hide its top, which was covered with leaves. The men lifted it out, disclosing an oblong box or trunk, about three feet long by twenty inches high, and covered with canvas.

The dark man then wanted the greenbacks, before he would open the box, but she would not give them until the gold was shown. She exhibited the greenbacks, and after Stevenson had some words with the dark man and Harriet, during which he placed his hands on her shoulders and chest, as she relates, the dark man appeared to be mollified and then said he had forgotten the key, which was at the house. Some discussion ensued between the men, as to who should go to the house for it, when they started off together, telling Harriet to await their return.

She examined the trunk, after they left, and found it to be only a common box. She had seen a trunk full of gold and silver, buried in Beaufort, S.C., during the war, and had that in her mind when this affair came up—the reminiscence aiding her most sanguine imagination in the present instance.

By the dim light of the moon, she continued the examination, and could find no key-hole. This awoke her suspicions for the first time, and she thought that if the affair was, indeed, a plan for robbery, she would stay and see it out. So she waited, but the men did not return. She became nervous, thinking of the stories about ghosts haunting buried treasures, and finally became so "worried" that she took walk in the woods. Here she saw something white, and thought it was a ghost. On approaching the spectre, it proved to be a cow, which became disturbed by her presence and started off in a mad run, which startled up numerous other cows, all joining in a wild prance about the woods.

This added to her fright and tremor—alone in the night, away from all, the money on her person, and, with probable robbers near—and, she became nearly distracted. She looked for a stone with which to break open the box, thinking to assure herself if the gold was there or not, but not finding a stone, she took a piece of a rail, and while striking at the box, all the woods seemed filled with the wild cattle, and spectres, and then it seemed to her that two men were at her side. She sank down grasping for the box, and lost all consciousness.

When she recovered her consciousness she found she was bound and gagged. She says she succeeded in getting over the fences by resting her chin on the top rail, to steady herself while she climbed up, and then dropped to the ground.

The Timid Man Identified . . .

The rest of her story is substantially as published. While at Sherwoods, where she stayed with Slocum Howland's family, her description of the dark man was declared to tally with that of one Harris, who formerly lived in that neighborhood and married a colored girl who had been brought up in Mr. Howland's family. He had disappeared from there and since lived at Seneca Falls. Some of the neighbors reported that he had been about for two weeks previous, with the yellow man, Stevenson, and had bought the box in question, at the store of Sidney Mosher.

The plot looks very "thin" to such as first hear of it through its exposure, and especially so to those who bit at the bait and were "caught."

Harris, if he be the Suspension Bridge swindler, is an old hand at "confidence" games, and if not the man, evinces a knowledge of men's "weak sides" that has gained him a large booty for the investment.

Both John and Harriet insist that no other arrangement was made, than that of giving Shimer the benefit of the difference between greenbacks and gold. John was impressed with the idea after the failure of the plan, that he would have to turn over his team to Mr. Shimer, toward making good the loss of the money. As to passing any agreement or security, he denies all such intention, as do Harriet Tubman and her husband.

They claim that if Mr. Shimer had lent them the money he would not have carried it to Smith's Corners, or Poplar Ridge, in his own possession—as they say he did—and afterward count it out to Harriet at the tavern, from whence she went to meet Harris, the dark, gold man, to effect the exchange.

The journey cost John Stewart the hire of a livery rig, and this expense and loss of time, with the after tribulation and fear of ruin are all that he has realized for his trouble ("The Gold Swindle and the Greenback Robbery," *Auburn [N.Y.] Daily Bulletin*, October 6, 1873).

DOCUMENTS FROM THE LATER YEARS

D43. Speaking to Auburn Suffragists (1888)

The Non-Partisan society for political education for women held their regular meeting in the common council chamber yesterday afternoon. The attendance was not as large as at previous meetings, owing to the fact that several members of the society are ill with severe colds, however, all the seats inside the railing were occupied, over 20 ladies being present. . . .

The president, Mrs. J. M. Pearson, read a selection written by Miss Frances E. Willard, the national president of the W.C.T.U. on the study of school politics for women. Miss Willard advises all women to study politics, especially temperance women. Mrs. Pearson said that words from such a power as Miss Willard, ought certainly to lend encouragement to all women to help along a reform, espoused and supported by the greatest minds of the 19th century.

At this point Harriet Tubman the noted woman, scout and soldier of the late rebellion, called and was introduced by the president to the society. In view of Mrs. Tubman's services in the late war, in freeing and helping to emancipate her down trodden and oppressed race, the ladies of the society requested that she say a few words before the society. With a polite courtesy, the venerable Harriet prefaced her remarks by saying that she had not presented herself before the society to teach them but rather to learn and be taught. The lessons learned in the late war by her, as scout, soldier, nurse, and protector of her people, recited in her graphic and quaint way, added much to the interest of her story; her experience was indeed thrilling. She spoke affectionately of her friends of the late war, most of whom have passed away, among those personally mentioned were the late and honored Secretary William H. Seward, William Lloyd Garrison, John Brown and Wendell Phillips. President Lincoln also championed her cause and secured her an important commission in the war. Her recital of the brave and fearless deeds of women who sacrificed all for their country and moved in battle when bullets mowed down men, file after file, and rank after rank, was graphic. Loving women were on the scene to administer to the injured, to bind up their wounds and tend them through weary months of suffering in the army hospitals. If those deeds do not place woman as man's equal, what do? The speaker said that her prayers carried her through and they would eventually place woman at the ballot box with man, as his equal. Her speech, though brief, was very interesting, and was listened to with wrapped [rapt] attention by all.

Harriet Tubman served 25 years as a slave, 11 years in the work of freeing her race from the bondage of slavery and four years in the late war.

A letter was read by Miss M. B. Fosgate from Miss Emily Howland of Sherwood on the suffrage question and the interest and enthusiasm on this important subject by the women and men in the east ("The Suffragists," *Auburn [N.Y.] Morning Dispatch,* March 15, 1888).

D44. Appearance at Founding Convention of NACW (1896)

July 20, 1896. Morning Session.

The first Annual Convention of the National Federation of Afro-American Women convened in the 19th Street Baptist Church, Washington, D.C., on the above date, Mrs. Booker T. Washington of Tuskegee, Ala., President in the chair, assisted by Mrs. Mary H. Dickerson of Newport, R.I., First Vice-President. . . .

Rev. (Walter H.) Brooks delivered a pleasant address of welcome, declaring that when the best women of the land unite in one mighty company all their force of character, their intelligence and their active services, to lift up and ennoble the womanhood, a brighter and better day was dawning.

Mrs. Rosetta Douglass-Sprague, only daughter of the late Frederick Douglass, responded in behalf of the Afro-American women of the United States.

"From the log cabins of the South have come forth some of our most heroic women, whose words, acts and deeds are a stimulus to us at this hour. We have such women by the score, women in whose hearts philanthropic impulses have burned with ardor; whose love for mankind was second only to their love for God. Women who have suffered death rather than be robbed of their virtue. Women who have endured untold misery for the betterment of the condition of their brothers and sisters.

"While the white race have chronicled deeds of heroism and acts of mercy of the women of pioneer and other days, so we are pleased to note in the personality of such women as Phyllis Wheatley, Margaret Garner, Sojourner Truth and our venerable friend, Harriet Tubman, sterling qualities of head, heart and hand, that hold no insignificant place in the annals of heroic womanhood.

"Our wants are numerous. We want homes in which purity can be taught, not hovels that are police-court feeders; we want industrial schools where labor of all kinds is taught, enabling our boys and girls to become skilled in the trades; we want the dram shops closed; we want the pool rooms and the gambling dens of every variety swept out of existence; we want reform schools for our girls in such cities where the conscience of the white Christian is not elastic enough to take in the Negro child.

"These and many more are the wants we desire gratified. Your words of welcome, your gracious greeting, cheering us on in our endeavor," said Mrs. Sprague, "is an inspiration for us to work with a will and a determination worthy of our cause.

"Our progress depends in the united strength of both men and women—the women alone nor the men alone cannot do the work.

"We have so fully realized that fact by witnessing the work of our men with the women in the rear. This is indeed the women's era, and we are coming." . . .

July 20, Evening Session 8:15 P.M.

The meeting was called to order by the President, who introduced Mrs. Victoria Earle Mathews of New York City as the Chairman of the evening.

Mrs. Mathews gave a vivid account of the work accomplished by the National Federation during the past year, also an account of her visit through the South, which was received with applause by the large audience. . . .

Miss S. Cole and Mr. Jas. T. Walker rendered vocal solos, after which Mother Harriet was introduced to the audience by Mrs. Mathews, who referred briefly to the great services that Mrs. Tubman had rendered to her race.

When Mrs. Mathews retired to take the chair of the presiding officer, and Mrs. Tubman stood alone on the front of the rostrum, the audience, which not only filled every seat, but also much of the standing room in the aisles, rose as one person and greeted her with the waving of handkerchiefs and the clapping of hands. This was kept up for at least a minute, and Mrs. Tubman was much affected by the hearty reception given her.

When the applause had somewhat subsided, Mrs. Tubman acknowledged the compliment paid her in appropriate words, and at the request of some of the leading officers of the Convention related a little of her war experience. Despite the weight of advancing years, Mrs. Tubman is the possessor of a strong and musical voice, which last evening penetrated every portion of the large auditorium in which the Convention was held, and a war melody which she sang was fully as attractively rendered as were any of the other vocal selections of the evening. . . . After the benediction by Rev. Crummell, the meeting adjourned.

July 21, 1896. Afternoon Session. 2 P.M.

. . . Mrs. Mathews stated that both Committees [Committee from the National League and Committee of the National Federation] had agreed upon the name of the new organization [National Association of Colored Women]. Mrs. Fanny Jackson Coppins, Philadelphia, thought the present name of the Federation too long, and that as the race was known in the census as colored people she did not admire the name Afro-American, but colored.

Mrs. Mathews, New York City, replied by permission of the chair, that her preference would always be for Afro-American as the name meant so much to the Negro in America . . . She was not a colored American, but an Afro-American. . . .

Evening Session. 8 P.M.

The evening session was called to order by the President, Mrs. Booker T. Washington. The meeting was opened with Devotional Exercises, after which Mrs. Fanny Jackson Coppins, Philadelphia, spoke of "The Necessity of a Course of Training for the Elevation and Improvement of Domestic Service." . . .

By request, Mother Tubman gave one of her characteristic songs, which thrilled the audience. Mrs. Mathews announced that the Committee on Union had agreed upon a basis of union, and that the two Committees appointed by the two "national bodies" now existed as a Committee of the whole, and that they would elect the officers of the new organization Wednesday. . . .

July 22, 1896. Morning Session.

. . . Reports from six clubs were then read, after which Mrs. Thurman of Michigan made a motion that Baby Barnett be the first Honorary Member of the Federation (Carried).

Suggested by Mrs. B. K. Bruce that as Mother Tubman was the oldest member, that she introduce Baby Barnett to the audience.

Motion, Mrs. Thurman, that Baby Barnett be hereafter known as the Baby of the Federation. (Carried.) . . .

Afternoon Session. 2:30 P.M.

The meeting was called to order by the President . . . Miss Jenny Dean of Manassas Industrial School gave an interesting account of her work. . . .

Mother Tubman spoke of "More Homes for our Aged Ones," and her remarks were listened to attentively, after which Mrs. T. H. Lyles of St. Paul, Minn., pledged $25.00 to the Tubman Home. . . .

Evening Session. 8:15 P.M.

The convention was opened with a chorus of one hundred voices, Prof. J. T. Layton, Director. . . .

"Our Country Women and Children" was the interesting topic of which Miss Georgia Washington of Central Alabama, a graduate of Hampton Institute, Virginia, read a paper. She referred particularly to the situation of the colored women at Mount Meigs, a village near Montgomery, Ala., where a school has been established for Afro-Americans. "Country women," she said, "are suffering for the help and for the influence of her more educated sister of the North and other sections."

A chorus by the pupils of the Girls High School was rendered after which Mrs. Lucy B. Thurman, National Superintendent of the W.C.T.U. work among Afro-Americans, made an earnest appeal for a contribution to assist in defraying the expenses of Mother Harriet Tubman during her visit in Washington.

Mrs. Thurman appointed Mrs. Victoria Earle Mathews, Mrs. B. K. Bruce, Mrs. Rosetta Douglass Sprague, Mrs. T. J. Lyles, Miss L. C. Anthony, Mrs. Ida B. Wells Barnett, Miss Jenny Dean and Miss Georgia Washington to wait upon the audience. The contribution netted $27.42 (National Association of Colored Women's Clubs, *Official Minutes*, 1902, 36–37, 45, 46, 54, 55, 57–58).

D45. Appearance at New York Suffrage Convention (1896)

Certainly the most picturesque, if not the most interesting incident of the afternoon's meeting was the appearance on the rostrum of Susan B. Anthony, the veteran worker of political emancipation for women, leading by the hand an old colored woman. Miss Anthony introduced her as Mrs. Harriet Tubman, a faithful worker for the emancipation of her race, who had reason to revere President Lincoln.[53]

The old woman was once a slave, and as she stood before the assemblage in her cheap black gown and coat and big black straw bonnet without adornment, her hand held in Miss Anthony's, she impressed one with the venerable dignity of her appearance. Her face was black, and old and wrinkled, and strongly marked with her race characteristics, but through it all there shows an honesty and true benevolence of purpose which commanded respect.

She bowed modestly as Miss Anthony presented her and when she commenced to speak, her voice low and tremulous at first, rose gradually as she warmed to her subject, till it was plainly heard throughout the hall.

It is impossible to tell in the woman's own words her pathetic recital of heroism and endurance during the slavery days for her recital was colored with the picturesque Southern dialect. Her phrases ungrammatical though they were, were none the less strong and convincing, and accompanied with gestures which added to the effect.

She told of her escape from slavery in the south, choosing the doubtful experiment of liberty rather than submit to being sold to a new master. A big price was put upon her head, and she came North, where she became one of the strongest workers of the underground railroad, assisted by Frederick Douglass, and William Lloyd Garrison. Advertisements offering a large reward for her return were placed everywhere, and she told how her master was ahead of her posting the bills, and she came along behind and pulled them down.

Sleeping anywhere in the woods, under bushes, along the railroads, in barns or sheds, she pursued the work, and many and many a slave was helped to Canada and freedom through her noble assistance.

She told touchingly of the soldiers of the war and how she ministered to their mangled bodies. In her humility she considered it a great favor that these men should long for her to speak to them a kindly word, or offer them a drink, or wash and dress their wounds. She said, "These men rank over me just the same as the president does over the common people that put him there, yet they called on me, and asked me about their wives or their mothers."[54]

This old woman who can neither read nor write, has still a mission, which is the moral advancement of her race. She makes her home in Auburn, but depends on the kindness of friends to assist her, by a dollar now and then, or a bed, or a meal, as she travels from place to place ("The Fight for the Ballot," *Rochester [N.Y.] Democrat and Chronicle,* November 19, 1896).

D46. Bradford Alerts Sanborn to Tubman's "Deplorable Condition" (1900 or 1901?)

I have been to see Harriet & found her in a deplorable condition, a pure *wreck*, [mind?] & body—& surrounded by a set of beggars who I fear fleece her of every thing sent her—She drew all the money I had sent for her, & I fear had little good of it—I am keeping the money I get for her

now—& will pay her bills—& I send her a little at a time as she needs it—
If I could only get her into *a home* where she would be well cared for I
should be so glad, but she will not leave her beloved darkies—

Two or three persons have written me that I charge too much for the
book. I have always been aware that as *books go* the price is high—but Mrs.
Osborne has always charged $1.00—& it is looked upon I suppose as *a
charity*—I am quite willing to sell it for less—Do you know of any
bookseller who would take a number of the books, & sell them for $.75
Cents taking out a percentage for himself? I would order Mr Little to send
them to him—my way of disposing of them works slowly as I have never
been in this kind of business—& do little towards advertising them—Do
you want one of Harriets photographs?—(Sarah Bradford to Franklin B.
Sanborn, n.d. [May 11, 1900? 1901?]).

D47. Emily Howland Helps with Book Sales (1901–1902)

December 21 1901. . . . I have wrapped H. Tubman books to send to some
of my friends. I sent off 4 copies this a.m. and have 5 more ready to go . . .

Jan. 18 1902. . . . Miss Flanders Miss Bradley & I went to Auburn. I took
H. Tubman a piece of pork, found her looking pale & feeble. 2 little children and a sick woman up stairs were her family. . . .

November 15 1902. A pleasant day in which we rode cheerily on to
Auburn, Miss Bradley, Miss Flanders & I. I dropt my basket at Mrs.
Osborn's & went to town to do my errands returning at 1 p.m. Miss
(Susan B.) Anthony was there. . . .

November 18. My departure this a.m. Harriet Tubman came to see us,
much set upon her home for old col'd folk. Mrs. Kellogg sees me to my
train most kindly, my precious visit ended. Harriet said we should never
all be there again together. (Emily Howland, diary entries, December 1901
to November 18, 1902).

D48. Harriet Tubman's Visit to Boston
to Support Women's Club (1905)

A reception was given last night by the Harriet Tubman's Christian Temperance Union at Parker Memorial Hall to Mrs. Harriet Tubman, colored,
one of the oldest living ex-slaves, who escaped from slavery 28 years before
the civil war, served three years with the Union forces as a government
scout and aided so many fugitives slaves to escape that $40,000 was
offered for her capture by the slaveholders of Maryland. . . .

Mrs. Tubman has come to be regarded as one of the great benefactors of her race. . . . During the evening this rare old woman told extremely interesting reminiscences of the exciting events in which she participated. For a woman of so great age she is remarkably erect, her voice is clear, her manner bright and her wit keen.

She arrived in town yesterday morning from Auburn, N.Y., and told her friends she guessed it would be the last time she would be up this way. Then she beamed from ear to ear, with a peculiar twinkle in her eye, which seemed to say: "But I'll be somewhere else on this good earth for a year or two longer, honey."

An interesting concert was given, and the funds received went to the aid of the Harriet Tubman Women's Temperance Union of this city. Before the concert Mrs. Tubman received the congratulations of some of the very people whom she had helped to escape years ago. None of them seemed to bear the burden of time more lightly than this remarkable old woman ("Harriet Tubman at the Hub," *Auburn [N.Y.] Daily Advertiser,* May 30, 1905).

D49. Confidence Man Uses Tubman's Name to Bilk Emily Howland (1905)

October 14, 1905. While at the supper table a ring at the door and Mrs. Shepard came and said a gentleman wanted to see me, I went, there was little Herman and another dark figure, I led them in and finished my supper little dreaming of the tragedy in wh[ich] I must assist. He was a good looking man from Henderson N. Carolina, in terror & excitement, fleeing from lynchers. His sister had been killed in a car, he shot and had 2 bullets in his back. What he had done I was left to infer.

He had come from Harriet Tubman. She sent him to me for help. He wanted $135. I gave him the money borrowing from Miss Flanders to do so. . . .

October 16 1905 Monday. Another fine day. The dreadful black man appeared again with another story that he went to Auburn that night was nearly caught, fled, and Geo Howland brought him home & let him hide in his barn, now a lawyer had promised to get him clear but he must have $450. I was terribly disturbed but gave him a check for the sum. He said he had been at Harriet Tubman's Sunday night. So I resolved to go to see Harriet.

October 17 1905 Tuesday. Went to Auburn, took Mrs. Shepard, a pleasant drive only I was disturbed. I stopped at Harriet's. She said the man was "a highway robber." Two months ago a col'd man brought this man to her to shelter. She kept him all [night?] he had a revolver. She rather feared him or did not want her brother to know he was in the house. She sat up all night. He wanted money. She got a friend to give her $5 for him. He scorned so small a sum. The last time she saw him he was intoxicated. She never mentioned my name to him. That with all the rest was a lie. I do not feel very comfortable (Emily Howland, diary entries, October 1905).

D50. Ellen Wright Garrison's Visit to Harriet Tubman (1906)

Yester m. we took a fine drive along the Lake— . . .

We stopped on our way home to make a carriage call on Harriet Tubman. We drove into her yard & such a leaking rummage heap as it was! Quantities of old dry goods boxes (for kindling) old cooking utensils sitting on the ground, old wagons & an old buggy in rags & tatters & dozens of other things & I counted five homely cats, four puppies & their dusty Ma, a dirty pig & lots of chickens besides 2 white children eating apples & looking very much at home.

Harriet came out of the kitchen looking quite well & brisk & when she saw Fanny she said "O my Lawd!" & clutched her hand with rapture—We gave her ten minutes or so & then Fanny pressed a bill upon her & we tore ourselves away. She stopped the carriage to shake hands with John [Osborne?] saying "You've always been a good friend to me"—I was glad we took Fanny to see her & now I can wait another year for the next visit (Ellen Wright Garrison to William Lloyd Garrison II, October 22, 1906).

D51. Evolving Plans for Tubman Home (1907)

For a number of years Harriet Tubman and her friends have been waiting for the home and school for colored people to materialize, but no effectual effort has been undertaken, heretofore. It is now proposed to put the institution in operation, and Rev. G. C. Carter has been elected superintendent and financial agent to take up this work. Special effort is now to be given to the opening and maintaining a school for the purpose of training and fitting colored girls for domestic service in this state.

It is well known that the field of operation for the colored girl is to be in the family and here is an almost unlimited opportunity. The demand today for competent domestic help is widespread. The object of the domestic science school is to so train and fit colored girls as to be able to do everything belonging to household service. They are to be fitted in every way to make them reliable and know their duty and responsibilities. It will be a splendid opportunity for the colored girls to place themselves in a position where they can better their condition. The plot of ground given by Mrs. Harriet Tubman and the buildings thereon are to be used for this purpose,[55] the houses are to be repaired for the work and used until a more suitable building is erected ("Plans for Tubman Home," *Auburn [N.Y.] Daily Advertiser,* February 9, 1907).

D52. *Parade Celebrating Dedication of Tubman Home (1908)*

Gala Day for Auburn Afro-Americans—Exercises This Evening

The weather man was good to the colored folks and gave them a beautiful day for "opening day" exercises at the Tubman home on South Street.... Marshal Frank H. Prime led the procession on a prancing bay horse which gave him a chance to show off his good horsemanship. Next came Comrade Perry Williams in a white coat and blue trousers, and proudly bearing the national flag. He was followed by another Grand Army man, the Rev. C. A. Smith. Next came the pride of the outfit, the Ithaca colored band, John O. Wye, leader, with 20 men. The band hit off some lively quicksteps which were kept time to by a long column of young colored people, all dressed in their Sunday best, who marched in the parade. Following was a long string of carriages containing prominent colored people of the city who are connected with the organization and care of the home. In the first carriage rode "Aunt Harriet" Tubman and her brother William Stewart, Mrs. R. Jerome Jeffreys of Rochester, and Major H. Ross of Norwich....

At 9 o'clock this evening there will be a reception at Macabee Hall, addresses on the "Needs and Purposes of the Home" and then the young folks will dance away the rest of the night ("Tubman Home Dedicated," *Auburn [N.Y.] Daily Advertiser,* June 23, 1908).

D53. *History of Tubman Home Planning (1908)*

Local colored society was out in force last evening to attend the dance and reception which brought to an end the dedication day of the Harriet Tubman home....

Among the clergymen present at the afternoon exercises was the Rev. E. U. A. Brooks of Utica, who comes here next Sunday to take up the duties of the local pastorate of Zion.

... It was an occasion of great rejoicing on the part of the colored people gathered at the home. "Aunt Harriet" Tubman the founder of the home was the most conspicuous figure at the ceremonies. She was the subject of many eulogies for her self-sacrifice in her long years of labor for the establishment of the home. Her remarks were listened to with great interest. . . . At the business meeting of the home held after the opening exercises a constitution was adopted and the home is ready for the reception of inmates.

A sketch of the home may be of interest to the readers of the Advertiser. Just 12 years ago this month Harriet Tubman bought the property at a surrogate's sale at the Court house by Judge Turner. The property was bid off to Harriet Tubman for $1,350. The money was to be paid in a few days and Harriet Tubman came to the conference then being held at Syracuse, and desired the bishop to send a committee to Auburn. The committee consisted of Rev. W. A. Ely, Rev. J. E. Mason and Rev. G. C. Carter. After looking around for some one to take a mortgage, the Cayuga County Savings bank finally agreed to take one of $1,000 if the balance of $350 was provided for. The work of raising the $350 fell to the lot of Rev. G. C. Carter and in ten days he had the entire amount raised, and paid into the bank. The property was then deeded to "Aunt Harriet" and for seven years Harriet Tubman looked personally after the property. Mr. Eddy, the real estate dealer, had the buildings fitted up for rent. It sometimes puzzled "Aunt Harriet" to know where the money was to come from to pay the taxes. At one time she had to surrender her cows to get the money to pay taxes. Four years ago Mrs. Tubman deeded the property to the A.M.E. Zion church in America to carry out her cherished wishes, the establishment of a home for aged and infirmed colored people of this state.[56] Several times it was thought the home would be open, but it was not until Rev. G. C. Carter came on the ground that any real step was taken to open the home.

Less than two years ago Rev. Mr. Carter came and found no funds in the treasury. The friends of Aunt Harriet had lost all hope of ever seeing the home open, but Rev. Mr. Carter is not the man to surrender to obstacles without a strong effort. After a hard struggle the work of fitting up the building was commenced nearly a year ago, but owning to the stringency of money matters the work was delayed until a few weeks ago, when the board of lady managers took hold of the work with the result that the home was so auspiciously opened yesterday. Much credit is due the board of lady managers under the direction of Mrs. C. A. Smith. Rev. G. C. Carter is well known in central New York, for the faithful service he has given to Zion church. He has paid debts on churches at Norwich,

Johnstown, Gloversville, Little Falls, Wilkes-Barre, Pa., Binghamton and Watertown ("Dedication of Harriet Tubman Home," *Auburn [N.Y.] Daily Advertiser,* June 24, 1908).

D54. *Tubman's Speech at the Dedication Ceremony for the Tubman Home (1908)*

With the stars and stripes wound about her shoulders, a band playing national airs and a concourse of members of her race gathered about her to pay tribute to her lifetime struggle in behalf of the colored people of America, aged Harriet Tubman Davis, the Moses of her race, yesterday experienced one of the happiest moments of her life, a period to which she has looked forward for a score or more of years, the dedication of a home for aged and friendless colored people. The delays in the consummation of her efforts have been many and tedious, but the Harriet Tubman Home is today an accomplished fact, and her 95 years have at last been crowned with success. . . .

Now the A.M.E. Zion Church of America has taken upon itself the work of establishing the Home on a successful basis and yesterday marked the opening of the home for the reception of those who wish to take advantage of it. At the present time the sum of $150 gives the applicant life privileges.[57] Mr. and Mrs. Asa Lewis have recently been placed in charge of the Home as overseers and managers with their residence upon the property. The property will gradually be improved and the land cultivated as funds will permit. There are an abundance of fruit trees and the entire property is tillable. At the lately adjourned conference of western New York held at Binghamton, it was voted to take an annual collection for the maintenance fund of the Home, and it is estimated that this sum will not be less than $200 per year.

The Home has been tidily fitted up with comfortable furniture, plenty of clean, white linen, enameled beds, etc. The bedrooms, of which there are five, besides those of the overseer and matron, were equipped by the following persons: Mrs. George Belt, Mrs. Thomas Freeman, Mrs. Charles Goodlow, Mrs. Edwards, all of Auburn, and George Brown of Schenectady. The board of Trustees of the home, of which the Reverend E. U. A. Brooks, recently transferred from the Utica church to Auburn, is secretary, is composed of the following members: Bishop A. Walter, Bishop C. R. Harris, Rev. J. E. Mason, secretary of Livingstone College, Salisbury, N. C., Rev. J. C. Walters of Rochester, Rev. M. H. Ross of Norwich, Rev. T. A. Auten of Ithaca, Rev. C. A. Smith, Thomas Freeman, James Dale,

Asa Lewis, and Harriet Tubman Davis of Auburn. All of the trustees were in attendance yesterday, with the exception of Bishop Walters.

Other notable Negro workers present were Mrs. Jerome Jeffrey, president of the Colored Women's Clubs of New York State; Rev. J. W. Brown of Rochester, Rev. J. C. Roberts of Binghamton, and Rev. G. C. Carter.

Upon the arrival of the guests at the Home after the street parade of the Ithaca colored band, dinner was served by the board of lady managers consisting of Mrs. Charles Smith, president, Mrs. M. H. Ross, vice president, Mrs. Henry Johnson, secretary, and Mrs. James Dale, treasurer. One of the most active persons on the grounds was Harriet herself and everywhere she went groups of people gathered about her to listen to her stories of her work.

When called upon by the chairman for a few words of welcome the aged woman stated that she had but started the work for the rising generation to take up. "I did not take up this work for my own benefit," said she, "but for those of my race who need help. The work is now well started and I know God will raise up others to take care of the future. All I ask is united effort, for 'united we stand: divided we fall.'"

Harriet stated that the first payment she made on the present property was a York shilling. As she ceased speaking Perry Williams unfurled the flag behind her and the band played The Star Spangled Banner amid the applause of the throng ("Tubman Home Open," *Auburn [N.Y.] Citizen*, June 24, 1908).

D55. Friends Contribute to Her Care in Last Days (1913)

Your letter with enclosed check is just received, for which in Harriet's name I thank you, I think she will be glad of the money and it was good of you to send it on before selling the books; they do sell for a dollar so Harriet told me.

I found your first letter awaiting me here when I came home last Monday after a months absence, it was put in the letter box here instead of being forwarded with the others, is the reason I didn't answer it; I sent the books to you the day before I went away intending to write you but I didn't for want of time partly and neglect also.

I telephoned awhile ago to ask how Harriet has been, the matron said she was about the same as before I went away, she has been in bed all winter is very thin and weak so emaciated that her nurse can lift her about very easily.

The last time I saw her tho' in bed she was bright and talkative very

clear in her mind, told me what she wanted me to do with her gold
pieces, which were given to her by Mrs. Osborne & her children, in
case she didn't live very long, I thought when she first went to bed she
couldn't live very long she looked so thin & gray and seemed to be so
short in her breathing, but she has gone on like that for three or four
months she may last in that condition for a year or more.

Thank you again for the checque, the pension Harriet gets goes
toward paying her nurse but it isn't quite enough I think, the annuity
she receives in the fall she will not let me use that for that purpose she
wants to keep that on hand for her own personal use, she gave the last
that she had to pay for a cow for the Harriet Tubman home a nice fine
cow she is too, gives a lot of milk they told me. . . .

I shall try and see Harriet Tubman next week (J. F. Osborne to Emily
Howland, February 19, 1913).

AFTER HER DEATH:
DOCUMENTS OF MEMORIAL POLITICS

D56. Local Newspaper Coverage of Her Death (1913)

Harriet Tubman-Davis, Aunt Harriet, died last night of pneumonia at the
home she founded out on South Street road near here. Born lowly, she
lived a life of exalted self-sacrifice and her end closes a career that has taken
its place in American history. Her true services to the black race were never
known but her true worth could never have been rewarded by human
agency.

Harriet's death was indeed the passing of a brave woman. There was
no regret but on the contrary she rejoiced in her final hours. Conscious up
to within a few hours of her passing she joined with those who came to
pray for her and the final scene in the long drama of her life was quite as
thrilling as the many that had gone before.

Yesterday afternoon, when the trained nurse, Mrs. Martha Ridgeway
of Elmira, and Dr. G. B. Mack had decided that her death was but the
question of a few hours, Harriet asked for her friends, Rev. Charles A.
Smith and Rev. E. U. A. Brooks, clergymen of the Zion A.M.E. Church.
They, with Eliza E. Peterson, national superintendent of temperance work
among colored people of the W.C.T.U. who came here from Texarkana,
Tex., to see Harriet, and others, joined in a final service which Harriet
Tubman directed. She joined in the singing when her cough did not

prevent, and after receiving the sacrament she sank back in bed ready to die ("Harriet Tubman Is Dead," *Auburn [N.Y.] Citizen*, March 11, 1913).

D57. The Funeral (1913)

The funeral of Harriet Tubman Davis was held from the A.M.E. Zion church this afternoon at 3 o'clock.[58] The church was crowded and many were turned away long before the hour of the service. Prayer was offered at the home at 11 o'clock this morning. These services were attended by the immediate members of the family and inmates of the Home.

... As the body lay in state hundreds of persons passed before the casket to take a last look at the features which were known so well.

The body was clothed in a black dress and waist on which was pinned a medal which was presented to "Aunt Harriet" by Queen Victoria, in recognition of her great work in freeing the slaves and her remarkable work on the battlefield. She held in her hand a crucifix which was a gift of the late Father Mulheron.

The church was made beautiful by countless floral decorations. The casket was draped with an American flag. The lady managers of the Home acted as a guard of honor while the body was lying in state. The bearers from the Home to the church were Henry T. Johnson, Arthur Smith, Henry Lucas, William Freeman, George Parker and Edward Watkins.

The services in the church were elaborate and fitting. There was scripture reading by Rev. R. F. Fisher of Ithaca and Rev. J. H. Morse of Oneida and prayer was offered by Rev. E. S. Bailey of Syracuse. The Central [Presbyterian] church quartet then sang a selection ["The Sands of Time Are Sinking"].

The city was represented by John F. Jaeckel, president of the Common Council, Mayor O'Neill being away from home.

Mr. Jaeckel Spoke As Follows:

I came here as the representative of our city government and I bring a message of sympathy from Mayor O'Neill and his expressions of keen regret at his inability to be present in person to take part in these services.

It is appropriate that the city give official recognition of the passing of this wonderful woman. No one of our fellow citizens of late years has conferred greater distinction upon us than has she. I may say that I have known "Aunt Harriet" during my whole lifetime. The boys of my time always regarded her as a sort of supernatural being; our youthful imaginations were fired by the tales we had heard of her adventures and we stood in great awe of her. In later years I came to know her more intimately through the relations of business. She was a woman of unusual judgment and great common sense. Her integrity was never questioned. She was slow to make a promise, but once made, she was scrupulous to fulfill it to the letter. She was a woman of deep religious convictions, and she has told me over and over again of her faith in the Master and of the certainty that she would find a place by his side in her eternal home. She seemed to intersperse her ordinary conversations of life with fitting quotations from the Scriptures, and who can say that it was not this faith in divine providence which gave the vital force to the successful termination of her marvelous undertakings in behalf of her people.

Greatness in this life does not come to people through accident or by the caprice of fate or fortune; it is the reward of great zeal accompanied by great faith in the object sought and the persistent fighting against great obstacles and difficulties for its accomplishment. "Aunt Harriet's" life should be an inspiration to the young men and to the young women of this congregation, for it points out that possibilities of human achievement are not limited or distinguished by race, creed or color. In this workaday world filled with its activities, what a contrast we find between the average person's life filled with petty vanities, as compared with the unselfish life of our good sister, filled with sympathy and devotion to her people. If we take this contrast to heart the example which she has set will not be entirely lost upon us.

In conclusion it is pleasant for us to think and to believe that she is now in full and happy reunion with those great spirits who have gone before and who were her contemporaries in a common cause of humanity.

Rev. E. J. Rosengrant, pastor of the First M.E. church briefly eulogized "Aunt Harriet." [who for many years had attended the first M.E. Church.] His talk was followed by another selection by the Central church quartet ["Good Night, I'm Going Home"].

Mrs. Mary B. Talbert, president of the Empire State Federation of Women's Clubs and chairman of the executive committee of the National Federation of Women's clubs told of the last visit she made to the home and of her conversation with "Aunt Harriet." "Aunt Harriet" said to Mrs. Talbert as she was about to leave, "I've been fixing up for the journey for some time."

Rev. J. C. Roberts of Binghamton made a few remarks. A solo by Mrs. George Parker followed ["Safe in the Arms of Jesus"]. Rev. E. U. A. Brooks, pastor of the church told of "Aunt Harriet's" wonderful career and of her life which was one of usefulness. Dr. Brooks then introduced

Bishop G. L. Blackwell, D.D., LL.D., of Philadelphia, Pennsylvania, who delivered the sermon.[59] The Bishop said in part:

"The soldier's happiest day is when he achieves victory. No battle is too hot, no conflict rages too fiercely nor cannonade sound too heavy and long for the soldier who is confident.

"If the colored race in this country could grow a generation of women as resolute as "Aunt Harriet" the future of the race would be secure.

"Her sound mind, native ability, and sterling qualities placed her in the foremost rank of the best women of her race.

"The African Methodist Episcopal Zion church feels honored for having had "Aunt Harriet" as a communicant in its ranks for many years. . . .

A delegation from the Charles H. Stewart Post and the Charles H. Stewart Relief Corps attended the funeral in a body ("Aunt Harriet's Funeral," *Auburn [N.Y.] Daily Advertiser,* March 13, 1913).

D58. Franklin B. Sanborn's Memorial Sketch (1913)

Brutus in Shakespeare's play of "Julius Caesar," hearing in battle of the untimely death of Cassius, says to his loyal Romans: "Friends,—'tis impossible that ever Rome should breed his fellow; I do owe more tears to this dead man than you shall see me pay."

Something like this might I say of Araminta Ross, who became by marriage successively Mrs. Tubman and Mrs. Davis; but whose career was shaped by herself and her Lord, and scarcely influenced at all by her marriages, which were only special instances of her general plan of life,—to exist for the benefit of others, to whom she devoted magnificent powers, ever in readiness to serve the cause of humanity, as she understood it. As I was the first scribe who ever drew from her the story of her life and ancestry [which has been singularly exaggerated by lovers of the marvelous],[60] I will repeat here the facts given by me in a Boston newspaper, 50 years ago, July 17, 1863, when she was in the service of the Union army against the enslavers of her race, who were then fighting to destroy our free Republic, in which she was born a slave near Cambridge, on the Eastern Shore of Maryland, not earlier than 1820, nor later than 1821. . . .

I first met her at a boarding-house in Boston, probably in the summer of 1858,[61] when she had become acquainted with John Brown, and was aiding him in his scheme to raise colored soldiers for his small band of men who were to lessen the value of slaves in Virginia, as she had done in Maryland. For, although I could never count more than 150 slaves brought away from Maryland under her direct lead, yet her example and incitement may have led to the escape of 150 more. I calculate the average market value of the human cattle she led off at $750 a head, as things stood in the 10 years 1849–1859, when her work was done; that means $100,000; and if as many more escaped through her example, another $100,000 may be set down. . . .

She visited me at Concord, in all, four or five times, and always came first to me there. I took her to Emerson's house; but she was never a guest there for more than a day at a time. She was more with Miss Anne Whiting, who vainly tried to teach her to read; she was with the Alcotts, the Brookses, with Mrs. Horace Mann; but her whole stay in Concord, in 30 years, could not have exceeded a fortnight. The Stearnses, Cheneys and others introduced her to Gov. Andrew in 1861, who gave her passes to the South, where my good friend, Elbridge Gerry Dudley, then at the Sea Islands, 1862–3, gave her the means of becoming acquainted with Gens. Hunter and Saxton, Col. Shaw and Col. Montgomery of Kansas. Under his command she did her best service in S. Carolina; but her direct way of interpreting orders, and Montgomery's soldierly way of acting under general orders, offended the more fastidious Col. Higginson, and led to some censures of both Montgomery and Harriet.[62]

Harriet was by no means faultless; she was ignorant, partial,—could never see any fault in her friends; if money was given her, she would give it away, often to the undeserving; her soul was generous, her judgment defective, but never perverse. She was the type of her race, loyal to the death, secretive as the grave, but never with hatred in her heart for her worst oppressors. "With malice toward none, with charity for all," describes her as it hardly describes the most generous white person. Mercy and patience, those two qualities which the blacks display in excess, accompanied with deceit and indifference in moral matters, were Harriet's outstanding qualities; together with a courage and self-sacrifice the martyrs and angels might envy. Many have died and will die who have used greater faculties; none who have consecrated what they had to the cause of the poor with greater zeal or a truer heart (Franklin B. Sanborn, "Concerning Harriet Tubman and Figitive Slaves," *Springfield [Mass.] Republican*, March 19, 1913).

D59. A Canadian Memoir (1913)

Harriet Tubman, the aged colored woman whose work in leading escaped slaves by the "underground railway" from the Southern States to the North and to Canada was one of the romances of the days before the war, died recently. Her death has brought vividly to the recollection of many of the colored people of Canada the great work she did and the inspiration of that work in attracting others to the group of fearless "abolitionists" who operated the underground railway. . . .

The Rev. R. A. Ball of the B.M.E. Church of this city, who was a lad in St. Catharines while the underground railway was in operation, remembers Harriet Tubman's arrival there on her escape from slavery with two of her brothers. On her first rescue venture she led to freedom another brother, William, and his wife and child. On her next she brought her aged father and mother. By that time the desire to help in the destruction of slavery had become the passion of her life. Among the men who acted as "directors" of the underground route to freedom were Rev. G. W. Loguen, Syracuse; the famous Frederick Douglass, Rochester, and Rev. Hiram Wilson, a Presbyterian missionary in charge of the St. Catharines "terminal." Henry Ball of St. Catharines, a brother of Rev. R. A. Ball, was for several years employed by Mr. Loguen of Syracuse as "porter" of the system, and attended to the purchase of tickets and the making of other transportation arrangements. Mr. Ball tells how Harriet Tubman, after getting a party safely over the border—usually at Niagara Falls—would say to them: "Shout, shout, you are free." Some of the refugees in their ecstasy would clap their hands, kneel in prayer, kiss the ground that meant freedom to them, and say, "This is British soil." . . .

Throughout Ontario to-day there are hundreds of colored people whose ancestors were brought out of slavery by the strong arm and keen intellect of Harriet Tubman ("This Is British Soil," *Toronto Globe,* April 2, 1913).

D60. James E. Mason Remembers
First Meeting with Harriet Tubman (1914)

As one of the incorporators of the Tubman home, about 19 years ago, I wish to express my gratitude to your splendid citizenship, for the high estimate of, and of your grand testimonial soon to be given at the unveiling of a tablet in honor of the late Aunt Harriet—widely known as "the Moses of her people." I deeply regret prior engagements prevent me from being present June 12.

Over 35 years have elapsed since I met for the first time this remarkable personality. It was on a beautiful September Sunday morning. The monarch of the day had risen in Oriental splendor. The rich and varied hues of the autumnal woods added their attractions to our environment.

The eloquent Bishop J. J. Clinton was conducting the Genesee Annual Conference in your city.

The early morning exercises were held in the long one-aisled frame Zion A.M.E. Church, on Washington Street. The lovely feast was practically ended but the rapturous songs of Zion were borne outward through the windows, across the avenue and the passerby's listened with rapture and rejoiced.

I entered and was seated near the altar, facing the audience. Singing, soul-stirring and reviving, continued. Seated four pews from the front, on my right, was a woman with shoulders somewhat stooped, and head bent forward. She had a broad forehead, piercing eyes, thin lips and strong, masculine features.

At the close of a thrilling selection she arose and commenced to speak in a hesitating voice. I understood her impediment resulted from a violent blow, which broke her skull, when a child. In a shrill voice, she commenced to give testimony to God's goodness and long suffering. Soon she was shouting, and so were others also. She possessed such endurance, vitality, and magnetism, that I inquired and was informed it was Harriet Tubman—the "Underground Railroad Moses."

Here was a modern Priscilla, a prophetess, telling out of the fullness of her heart God's revelation to her in the secret of His presence.

Service ended, I greeted her. She said, "Are you saved?" I gave an affirmative reply. She remarked: "Glory to God," and shouted again.

We have met on many important occasions during the intervening years. In the cottages of the lowly and the palatial homes of the wealthy; in private and in public place of responsibility. Everywhere she was the same determined, generous, enthusiastic, race-loving, cheerful heroic soul. A many chorded harp was her broadly sympathetic nature, sensitive to every touch of her race's sorest travail.

Her wit, humor and originality were striking compelling characteristics. She was directing a band of fugitives over Mason and Dixon's line, when something unexplainable occurred and they hesitated. She is reported as saying:

"Come along, come along,
Don't be a fool,
Uncle Sam is rich enough
To send us all to school"[63]

("Pays Tribute to Harriet Tubman," *Auburn [N.Y.] Advertiser-Journal,* June 6, 1914)

D61. Unveiling of Auburn's Memorial Tablet (1914)

Glorifying the life of Harriet Tubman, characterizing her courage, constancy and wisdom as models for the races of the world, extolling the Negro race for the great progress it has made along all lines in fifty years of freedom in this country and predicting for it a bright and happy future, Dr. Booker T Washington, president of Tuskegee Institute of Alabama, delivered a splendid oration at the Auditorium last night in connection with the unveiling of the tablet, the gift of the citizens of this city, in memory of the former slave and later the "Moses of her people," Harriet Tubman Davis. . . .

The spacious lower floor of the theater was well filled and all the boxes were occupied when the curtain arose. Upon the stage were the speakers, the members of the Auburn Festival Chorus, an orchestra and other participants and guests. In one box was a group of Civil War veterans; in another a party of prominent Auburn women; in a front seat in one of the lower boxes sat Emily Howland of Sherwood, the philanthropic friend of the Negro race to whom a tribute was paid by Doctor Washington in his address. Delegations representing various Negro societies occupied other boxes. . . .

With a brief speech, former Mayor E. Clarence Aiken formally presented the tablet.

"Few memorials have been erected in this land to women," said Mr. Aiken, "and few to Negroes. None has been erected to one who was at once a woman, a Negro, and a former slave. Harriet Tubman had the courage of a man. She was wise and unselfish." . . .

Then came the actual unveiling. Miss Alice H. Lucas of this city, a grandniece of Harriet Tubman, arose and pulled aside the American flag that had draped the tablet, set for the occasion in a huge shell of papier mache.[64] The theater lights were turned out and the tablet was illuminated by a frame of incandescents. There was a moment of silence before the house lights came on again.

. . . An entertainment and colorful sketch of the life of Harriet Tubman was read by Mrs. Mary B. Talbert of Buffalo, president of the Empire State Federation and chairman of the Executive Board of the National Association of Colored Women.

"This memorial to that great heroine of my race is peculiarly appropriate," Mrs. Talbert began. "It typifies her character and deeds of courage and sacrifice are typified in this bronze tablet." . . .

"This tablet will stand as a silent but effective monitor teaching the children of Auburn and of the state and of the country to lead such noble, unselfish and helpful lives that they too may leave behind them memories which shall encourage others to live."

Mr. Aiken with a few words of tribute to the great educator, introduced Booker T. Washington. The latter's powers as an orator are well known and he spoke with great feeling last night. The large audience listened closely. The oration contained many strong and dramatic statements that called forth applause. And Doctor Washington told of many amusing incidents and related stories that brought bursts of laughter. . . . Harriet Tubman he pronounced, in spite of her lack of bookish education, "One of the best educated persons that ever lived in this country," an education gained by harsh experiences and hardships. . . .

Dance for Visitors

Colored people from other cities who attended the Tubman memorial services were tendered a dance last evening by Elmer and George Cooper at Walsh's Academy. The party was one of the most brilliant and successful of any ever held by the colored people in this city. Guests were present from Syracuse, Rochester, Geneva, Ithaca, Rome and other places in Central New York. . . .

The dancing commenced soon after 11 o'clock and continued until early in the morning. The new steps were danced by the younger people while the older folks enjoyed the old steps. . . . The hall presented a brilliant appearance with the tasty decorations and the beautiful dresses of the ladies ("High Tribute Paid to Harriet Tubman," *Auburn [N.Y.] Advertiser-Journal,* June 13, 1914).

D62. Newspaper Editorial Congratulates Whites of Auburn (1914)

The meeting at the Auditorium last night may be said to rank among the most unique in the history of this State, if not the Nation. Every thoughtful person in the audience carried away the thought—what a remarkable woman Harriet Tubman must have been to deserve this tribute, an enduring monument from the white race to one of the lowliest and most humble of the blacks! Where has anything like it been recorded.

None who has studied her career will say that the tributes paid her were unmerited. . . . In her illiterate way she plodded through life. She was born in ignorance as a slave and in early life developed only craftiness through the ever increasing hope that some day freedom might be her lot. Becoming the arbiter of her own destiny by a bold stroke, as fugitive slave she rejoiced in her freedom and became a religious zealot. The Scriptures became her guide, and few persons ever interpreted them more faithfully than this humble black woman. She translated all of the virtues into realities, and spent her long life thinking first of others, never of herself. Tact, loyalty, intelligent obedience, excellent judgment, resourcefulness and numerous other qualities that only trained and highly educated persons possess came to her in her romantic career. On the matter of self sacrifice it may be said that she was almost a fanatic. . . .

How many of the white race exist today who will ever merit equal recognition with Harriet Tubman? ("A Tribute by the White Race to the Black Race," *Auburn [N.Y.] Advertiser-Journal,* June 13, 1914).

D63. Sale of Tubman's Seven-Acre Property Stirs Up Controversy (1914)

According to Rev. James Edward Mason, who is associated with the Negro school at Salisbury, N.C., various colored people of this city have complained to him that they were unable to purchase a plot of seven acres of land adjourning the Tubman Home. According to Louis K. R. Laird, executor of the Tubman estate, the people who complain had ample opportunity to buy the property, but declined to pay the price, which the executor had fixed at not less than $1,500. The strip was desired by the colored people as an addition to the home property, having originally been a part of it. The seven acres was sold to a Mr. Norris, residing on the South Street Road. Mr. Laird says that Norris paid a better price for it than the colored people who visited him were willing to pay, and that it was necessary to obtain a good price in order to discharge the debts, which far exceeded the sum received, Mr. Laird says.

"Aunt Harriet was a great friend of my father and mother," said Attorney Laird, when asked about it. "In fact, she prepared the supper at their wedding many years ago. I never was intimately acquainted with her, but always when she met me she was accustomed to say I was Doctor Laird's boy. In her last illness my father attended her professionally. Aunt Harriet expressed a desire that I be summoned to take charge of her legal affairs, realizing as she did that she was nearing the great beyond.

"Well, I went up. Aunt Harriet said she wanted me to be her secretary, after her death. I asked her if she meant executor, and she said, 'Well, secretary or executor or whatever you call it, I want you to 'take charge.' I accepted, and found that contrary to the belief of Aunt Harriet's friends there were debts totaling a much larger sum than the property would bring. So I put the price as high as I dared, and kept it there. If I remember right, William Freeman offered me $1,200, which naturally I refused. It is not true that any of the heirs offered me anything like what the property sold for."

William Freeman declared to a reporter that he had bid $1,400 for the seven acres of land adjoining the Tubman home. He said he had been unable to obtain any satisfaction from Executor Laird, and that he enlisted the aid of Samuel C. Swarthout, who according to Mr. Freeman, was authorized to offer and did offer $1,500 for the land. Freeman says he asked Mr. Norris what he paid for it and that Norris told him that the price was a secret.

Rev. James Edward Mason, who was in the city several days ago, took up the matter with a number of colored citizens including the Tubman heirs and said he contemplated hiring a lawyer. So far no move has been made in that direction, it was said today. Aunt Harriet willed the property to Mary Gaston, Katie Stewart and Mrs. Frances P. Smith. Mrs. Smith wrote Surrogate Woodin asking what powers the executor had in the matter and the surrogate advised her that the executor had full power to dispose of the property, at such price and in such manner as might seem most advantageous to the estate.

Professor Mason said colored people here and elsewhere had desired to have the seven acres as part of the Home, and that they felt they should have first opportunity to buy ("Wanted to Buy Tubman Property," *Auburn [N.Y.] Advertiser-Journal,* June 9, 1914).

D64. Booker T. Washington's Talk (1914)

Booker T. Washington in an address at Zion A.M.E. Church yesterday morning talked straight from the shoulder to the colored people of the city; his words were in fact a message to the colored people of the North. It was in one sense the most important speech that the famous educator delivered during his three days in this city.

He spoke familiarly to the congregation that filled the church, uttering words of advice and optimism. He urged all to proclaim the success and progress of the race and to desist from telling their troubles. "Advertise your success not your troubles," he told them. He also pointed out to them the good fruits that accrued from industry and habits of saving and he advised them to turn to the country more; to own some land and to become producers; he advised them to go into business in the city and to not be afraid to begin at the bottom. He told the young men to avoid the saloons and the gambling places and to put their money in the banks. . . .

". . . Let us in the future advertise our progress everywhere. And we must stand together and help one another. Race cooperation is needed. Push one another along. In everything that concerns the mutual progress of the race let us stand together. You will be measured by the great life of Harriet Tubman and by her great life all the country is watching you." . . .

The reception was under the auspices of the Board of Managers of the Harriet Tubman Home, Rizpah Household of Ruth, No. 1,161, St. Peter's Lodge, No. 3,970, G. U. O. O. F [Grand Union of Odd Fellows]. All the speakers spoke highly of the life work of the dead heroine.

H. T. Johnson, one of the officers of Zion Church, said yesterday that the next step along the lines of honoring the memory of Harriet Tubman would probably be toward the erection of a monument over her grave in Fort Hill Cemetery. The matter of procuring the memorial for Harriet Tubman which was unveiled last Friday night was first broached in a conversation Mr. Johnson had with C. G. Adams, secretary of the Business Men's Association, a year ago last April ("Booker T. Washington Urges Colored Men to Go on Farms," *Auburn [N.Y.] Advertiser-Journal,* June 15, 1914).

APPENDIXES
NOTES
BIBLIOGRAPHY
INDEX

APPENDIX A

A NOTE ON HARRIET TUBMAN'S KIN

Assembling accurate basic information about Harriet Tubman's parents and siblings for the period covered by this book—Tubman's own lifetime—has been a challenging task.[1] As I have attempted to do throughout, in what follows I have placed the highest value on the earliest information given by sources that were in the best position to know. Where insufficient documentation was available, or documentary evidence seemed contradictory, I have made an effort to explain the reasoning behind my speculative judgments.

Anne Fitzhugh Miller wrote in her 1912 biographical sketch that Tubman's mother "was the daughter of a white man." Is this true? I have not located any other reference to this possibility, and I am inclined to doubt it. Ritta Ross lived in Tubman's family in Auburn for many years and was well known to Bradford, the Wright and Osborne families, and others who recorded information about Tubman and her parents. If Ritta Ross had a visibly biracial identity, it seems likely this would have been mentioned by Bradford or others. (Bradford does use the term "mulatto" in reference to a sister-in-law of Tubman's). It is barely possible that Tubman might reveal a family secret at the very end of her life to this interviewer, the granddaughter of her trusted longtime abolitionist ally Gerrit Smith. On balance, however, I think it unlikely that Tubman would have wished to keep secret for almost sixty years the kind of fact that could have expanded the catalogue of crimes perpetrated against her family by the oppressive institution of Southern slavery. Unless new documentary evidence becomes available to confirm it, then, I think Miller's statement should be regarded skeptically.

As for the number, names, and migrations of Tubman's brothers and sisters, Kate Larson's research has uncovered important new unpublished documents that will fill in and clarify the fragmentary and contradictory record of the published biographies. Meanwhile, it is clear that at least six siblings were part of her family in Maryland, and four brothers and a niece (and their offspring) were among the kinfolk she successfully brought out of Maryland in the 1850s.[2] Anthony C. Thompson, the "son in law" (stepson) of Mary Pattison Brodess Thompson, testified in a court case in October 1853 (four years after Tubman had escaped) that Rit (Ross) was the mother of only seven children as far as he knew: Linah (then age 45), Soph, Robert (age 37), Minty (Araminta) (32), Ben (30), Harry (28), and Mose (18 or 19). The two sisters, Linah and Soph, he testified, had been sold south by Edward Brodess. Robert, Ben, and Harry were still in the family orbit in Dorchester County, Maryland, while Mose (or Moses) had "run off."[3]

The number of siblings in Thompson's list is smaller than that in other early accounts. For example, Tubman's brother Henry Stewart, when testifying in Canada in 1863, referred to the number in the family as "ten" (but whether he included Tubman and her parents as well in that sum of ten is not clear). Sanborn said in 1863 that "she had ten brothers and sisters, of whom three are now living, all at the North." However, in 1913, when writing an obituary tribute, Sanborn referred to her as "one of a dozen" children of Benjamin Ross and Harriet Green. It is possible, then, that Thompson's list is not definitive.

We also run into problems when we try to reconcile the two sisters Thompson mentions with a variety of "sisters" apparently still part of the family at the time of Tubman's escape or afterward. For example, William Still mentions by name a "sister," Mary Ann Williamson, who was said by Tubman's brother Benjamin to have been left behind when some of the brothers escaped in 1854. Several of Thomas Garrett's letters and documents by other antislavery associates indicate that Tubman made at least two separate trips to Maryland to rescue a "sister" who died before Tubman could reach her in 1860. We also have Sanborn's report in 1863 that Tubman had a "sister" married to a free black man (who helped Tubman rescue his wife from Baltimore in 1851). And Bradford, in retelling Tubman's escape story in 1869, also makes reference to a "sister" Mary with whom she worked in the kitchen.

One or more of the "sisters" in these documents may have been sisters-in-law, wives of one of the brothers.[4] (Thompson's reference to his stepmother Mary Pattison as his "mother-in-law" warns us to be aware of possibly different nineteenth-century usages of kinship terms.) Moreover, Tubman and her family apparently used the term "sister" generously, to include nieces. Tubman's own Canadian testimony, as well as that of her brother Henry Stewart, indicated that one of the older sisters who was sold south left one (or possibly two) children behind.[5] Linah, listed by Thompson as the eldest in Ritta Ross's family, was thirteen years older than Tubman. She could easily have been the mother of one or more daughters only a few years younger than Tubman herself.

At least one of the women called "sisters" was the niece Keziah Bowley, the mother of Harkless Bowley, the "grandnephew" who corresponded with Earl Conrad in the late 1930s.[6] Harkless Bowley told Conrad that he thought his mother was a niece or "half-sister" of Tubman's: "but mother always called aunt Harriet Sister Harriet" (H. Bowley, 1939a). Bowley also said that his mother's mother had been sold south—which suggests strongly that Keziah was the daughter of either Linah or Soph.

It is difficult to count, name, and track the life careers of Tubman's brothers. Thompson's 1853 court testimony gives the birth order and names of four brothers, but because they changed both their surnames and their Christian names as they escaped to the North (sometimes more than once), it is tricky even for members of descendants' families to reconstruct the family tree, as both Harkless Bowley and Alice Brickler testified to Earl Conrad in the 1930s.

Three men with the surname Ross were in the rescue party guided by Tubman to Philadelphia in December 1854, and William Still supplied aliases for two of them: Benjamin Ross (alias James Stewart, age 28) and Henry Ross (alias Levin Stewart, age 22). The third he simply called Robert Ross (age 35). Although Still did not say directly that any of the men was a brother of Tubman, he did say that the first two men named Ross worked for Eliza Ann Brodess. ("Robert Ross," who was probably Tubman's elder brother, may have been working for Dr. Thompson at that time, as he had been the year before, according to Thompson's 1853 testimony). It is significant that the birth order of the brothers as given by Thompson in 1853 is the same as that given by William Still in 1854, though the exact ages are a bit different:

Thompson (1853)
Robert (37), working for Thompson
Ben (30)
Harry (28)

Still (1854)
Robert (35)
Benjamin (28)
Henry (22)

At least two and probably all three of these brothers were in the party of nine or ten that Tubman brought out of Maryland at Christmas in 1854.[7] Eventually at least three and possibly four of the Ross brothers seem to have made it to Canada. Two eventually settled in Auburn. Harkless Bowley (who was born in Chatham, Canada West, in 1856) remembered three brothers of Tubman's in the North: "Uncle James," who lived in Chatham; "Uncle William," who lived first in St. Catharines and quite a bit later in Auburn; and a third brother, "Uncle John," who lived in Auburn near Tubman for most of his life. The easiest of these to trace with confidence is the last: John Stewart (formerly Robert Ross).

A brother using the name John Stewart was living in Auburn as early as fall 1859, helping take care of Tubman's and his parents, Benjamin and Ritta Ross (J. Stewart, 1859). In the immediate postwar period, he lived in Auburn with children of his own, probably including two sons originally left behind in Maryland when he escaped and later brought north by his niece's husband, John Bowley. According to the memory of Harkless Bowley, "Uncle John was afflicted with Rheumatism and could not walk. He had a fine team of horses. . . . Uncle John's youngest son worked his team" (H. Bowley, 1939c). John Stewart had a good job as a teamster and a continuing connection with his sister in Auburn in the 1870s and 1880s, according to various glimpses of his name in the newspaper stories referring to Tubman, in street directories, and in census records.[8] He was the brother who seems to have gotten her into the gold swindle in 1873. John Stewart died in 1889.

James Stewart (formerly Benjamin Ross) may have died in Canada. Harkless Bowley told Conrad that James's family and his own had lived together in the same house in Chatham before the war. Henry Stewart testified in 1863 that he had rented a farm with one brother in Canada for a while, which had not worked out, and that the brother had then "gone to Berlin"—possibly this was James.

The "Henry Stewart" who testified in Canada in 1863 was certainly a brother of Tubman's, but it is not yet certain which brother he was—he may have been "Harry Ross" in Maryland, but it is also possible that he was the youngest brother, Moses Ross.

After the war, one of Tubman's brothers, called William (or William Henry), continued to live in St. Catherines for many years before ultimately moving his family to Auburn.[9] Harkless Bowley testified that "Uncle William lived in St. Catharines. . . . Afterwards Uncle William . . . came to live with Aunt Harriet in Auburn and died there." Alice Lucas

Brickler, born just ten years before Tubman's death, lived in close proximity to her great-aunt for those last years and referred to Uncle William
Henry as "her brother who lived with her." According to an Auburn
descendant, William Henry Stewart had a son by the same name, who also
came to Auburn to live, arriving as early as 1880.[10] Robert Taylor referred
in his 1901 sketch to an "older brother" whose wages helped Tubman out at
this time (although William Henry must have been younger than Tubman).
The name also appears on a "third mortgage" Tubman took out on the
twenty-five-acre property she bought for the John Brown Hall project.
At the time of the legal transfer of the property to the AME Zion Church
in 1903, this mortgage of $350, together with a year's interest, was paid
to "William H. Stewart, a brother of Aunt Harriet," according to Wheeler
(1904). Street directories show a William Stewart living at the same South
Street address as Tubman as early as 1897–1898, and William Henry Stewart is listed in the 1905 census as living with Tubman. An account of her
living situation in 1908 asserts that her "only brother (that she knows anything about) is dependent on her" (G. C. Carter, 1908). William Henry
Stewart was among those who joined Tubman in the first carriage of the
parade celebrating the opening of the Tubman Home ("Tubman Home
Dedicated," 1908). William Henry Sr. died July 1912, just a year before
his sister. (His son William Henry Jr. predeceased both of them, dying in
1906.)[11]

Tubman probably brought at least one sister-in-law north, at first to
Canada West and then to Auburn. There are some indications in the early
documents of a sister-in-law named Catherine. In the letter from John
Stewart to Tubman of November 1, 1859, shortly after the parents had
arrived in Auburn, he says, "Catherine Stewart has not come yet but wants
to very bad." Bradford said in 1869 that "William Henry" had been
"attached to a girl called Catherine," and she told the story of how
William Henry helped in Catherine's escape, providing her with men's
clothes.[12] Bradford also said that "Catherine has been seen and talked with
by the writer, at the house of the old people" in Auburn.

Several nephews and nieces and their offspring played significant parts
in Tubman's life or in preserving her storytelling legacy and life history.
One grandnephew in the Bowley family, James A. Bowley, received a good
basic education through Tubman's efforts.[13] When his family returned to
the South after the war, he became a teacher and then a state representative in Reconstruction South Carolina. Harkless Bowley stayed on with
Tubman in Auburn for "quite awhile" after the rest of his family moved

on to Maryland, and thus he was able to provide Conrad with valuable information about Tubman's household and life in the immediate postwar years.

Although many other nephews and nieces lived in or near Tubman's household for shorter or longer amounts of time in the postwar years, two young kinswomen became "foster children" or surrogate daughters of Tubman. The older of these, Margaret Stewart Lucas, born around 1850 in Baltimore, told her own daughter, Alice Lucas Brickler, that she had been "kidnapped" by Tubman from her family on the eastern shore of Maryland just prior to the Civil War. Margaret Stewart said that her mother (whose parents had been able to purchase their freedom before her mother was born) was married to a "brother" of Tubman's who was "an ex-slave."[14] Alice Brickler referred to her mother, Margaret Stewart Lucas, as Tubman's "favorite niece." "One thing she knew, and that was that neither she, her brothers, or her mother had ever been slaves. . . . Her mother's marriage to Harriet's brother, an ex-slave, seems not to have hindered the family's progress for Mother said they had a pair of slick chestnut horses and a shiny carriage in which they rode to church. That was all she remembered of her home."[15]

Tubman's second foster daughter, actually a grandniece, was Katy Stewart (later Northrup). Her early history as given by Harkless Bowley was almost as dramatic as Margaret Stewart's: "Aunt Harriet's Brother's Son married an Indian girl in Canada. She gave birth to a baby girl. She was about to die. In her struggles she sent for Aunt Harriet. Aunt Harriet went to see her. She asked Aunt Harriet if she would take this child and take care of her. Aunt Harriet promised her she would. She said, 'Now I die happy,' and passed away. This child is a grown woman living in Philadelphia. I hear from her often. She says she is coming to see me next Sunday. Aunt Harriet kept her promise" (H. Bowley, 1939c).[16] Sarah Bradford referred to her in 1901 as Tubman's "adopted daughter" and pictured her as a helper and companion.[17] Katy Stewart appears in the 1905 census for the Town of Fleming as a sixteen-year-old schoolgirl residing with Tubman (suggesting that Tubman adopted her around 1889).

APPENDIX B

A NOTE ON THE NUMBERS

How many journeys into the South did Harriet Tubman make during her Underground Railroad career? How many fugitives did she escort north? And how large was the reward offered for her capture? Most twentieth-century biographies follow Sarah Bradford in speaking of nineteen journeys, at least three hundred fugitives, and a $40,000 reward. Yet the documentary record (at least so far) does not support an estimate even close to those numbers.[1]

Earl Conrad compared accounts in the early biographies and in William Still's book and noted that "actual dated journeys in the Sanborn, Still, Bradford and other accounts total only ten." Yet Conrad went on to say that "there is no reason, in view of Mrs. Bradford's careful check on Harriet's story . . . to question the total of nineteen" (Conrad, 1943a, 232–233). He began with Bradford's report that Tubman said "she made eleven trips from Canada." He then added what he called "the first four trips"—which he believed to have been made before she had established a Canadian base—to this eleven. He also assumed that any trips made after she had settled in Auburn in 1858 should also be added on beyond the eleven, since they also would not have been "from Canada." On the basis of these assumptions he concluded, "there is no reason why a conservative estimate of fifteen excursions should not be acceptable." He estimated the total number of fugitives she rescued at about two hundred to three hundred.

Like James McGowan, I am inclined to be more cautious than Conrad was about Bradford's accuracy—both in asserting a total of nineteen trips and even in reporting Harriet Tubman as saying she had made eleven trips from Canada. I would rather rely *on Tubman's own words as reported at the time and from more than one reliable source, whenever possible.* Tubman herself kept a rough running count of the number of trips she had made, and at various times she conveyed this count to her friends. In 1859–1860, when she was raising funds for her parents' support and for her own journeys south, she would have had no reason to minimize her previous accomplishments. Therefore I think Tubman's reported statements from several different sources in the late 1850s are more likely to be reliable than Bradford's later figures, gathered in haste from her interviews. If we stick closely to the numbers Tubman reported to her closest political associates, such as Thomas Garrett and, when speaking in Boston and Auburn in 1859 and 1860, Franklin B. Sanborn and Thomas W. Higginson, it becomes very difficult to argue that the number of trips overall into slave territories exceeded ten. Similarly, this method suggests that the total number of refugees she personally escorted north could have been as low as fifty-seven.

Once Tubman had become an abolitionist "heroine," in Boston in the spring of 1859, many people listened to her stories and wrote down what they remembered she had said about the number of fugitives rescued. Sanborn's earliest letters are highly enthusiastic about her exploits and therefore not likely to underestimate the magnitude of her accomplishments. He speaks of fifty people rescued on eight journeys, by May or June 1859 (Sanborn, 1859a). Higginson, another John Brown supporter who made Tubman's acquaintance somewhat before the early summer of 1859, wrote to his mother that Tubman had "been back eight times secretly and brought out in all sixty slaves with her, including all her own family" (Higginson, 1859). Higginson agrees with Sanborn on the number of trips Tubman mentioned, though he heard her say "sixty" rather than "fifty" people rescued. Lucy Osgood also heard the number rescued as "fifty" during this early summer 1859 Boston visit. The following year, when Tubman visited Boston again, the account in the *Liberator* also referred to eight journeys into the South (July 6, 1860). The last documented trip was in December 1860. On that occasion she brought out another seven people, according to Sanborn (1863). A highly conservative estimate of the total number of trips, including those to Baltimore and those to Dorchester County, then, would be nine or ten, and a conservative guess as to the total number of people rescued would be fifty-seven. Somewhat higher estimates of both the number of trips and the number of fugitives rescued emerge if we attempt to combine the earliest biographers' statements from the 1860s with the contemporary documents available from the 1850s—

but this is difficult to do with confidence. The accounts are not truly compatible and certainly include some errors, because they are contradictory.

Thomas Garrett understood at the end of 1855 that she had made "four successful trips to the neighborhood she had left and brought away 17 of her brothers, sisters & friends" and "has three times gone to Canada with those she brought" (Thomas Garrett, 1855). The four trips "to the neighborhood she had left" before this date probably include 1) the journey from Philadelphia to rescue her husband in the fall of 1851, which yielded instead a "party of fugitives ... brought ... safely to Philadelphia" (Sanborn, 1863); 2) another trip starting from Cape May in the fall of 1852, from which she brought back nine fugitives (Sanborn, 1863); 3) the Christmas rescue of 1854, with ten or eleven people; and 4) the most recent trip Garrett's letter mentions as "last week" (December 1855), on which she rescued just "one man." The number rescued on these four trips must be somewhat higher than the seventeen Garrett reported (we have twenty or twenty-one in just three trips), but it seems unlikely to exceed thirty.

Sanborn also reported the rescue from the old neighborhood of a "party of eleven" that included "a brother and his wife" and gave the date as December 1851. If we think of this as a separate trip not included in Garrett's four, we would need to increase the trip count by one and the total number of fugitives by eleven. But I think Sanborn, writing in 1863 without Tubman there to ask, may have gotten the date wrong when remembering the Christmas rescue. Certainly the 1854 Christmas rescue involved a large party, and it included more than one brother and probably a brother's wife as well.[2]

Garrett's letter does not mention the two earlier rescues from Baltimore recorded by Sanborn in 1863—that of the "sister" (niece) Keziah Bowley and her two children in December 1850,[3] and that of "a brother and two men" in early 1851. Harkless Bowley said that on the rescue of his mother and two older siblings, Tubman also took "several others aboard the Underground Railroad into Canada" (H. Bowley, 1939b). Assuming that Bowley's memory of the story he had been told was correct, the number rescued on these two earlier trips to Baltimore might be as many as perhaps a dozen. Adding this to the four trips discussed above would bring the total number of trips to six (or seven), and the total number of people rescued on Southern trips by December 1855 would be forty-two to fifty-three.

Four more trips are documented in Garrett's and Still's letters for 1856–1857. William Still reported a rescue of four men "per Harriet Tubman" on May 13, 1856; and Garrett's letters document two more in 1856 ("Tillie" in October, from Baltimore, and a party of ten including "Joe" in late November—substitutes for the "sister" and children she was unable to gather at this time), as well as the rescue of her parents in 1857. This brings us to ten or eleven trips, with fifty-nine to seventy fugitives brought north.[4] Adding the last documented trip (December 1860) with its party of seven would make the grand total, by this conservative method, eleven (or twelve) trips, with sixty-six to seventy-seven rescued.

What about the size of the rewards—the one offered for her own capture and those offered for the capture of her party in the rescue of Joe? In both cases Bradford enlarged the amounts when she revised her book in 1886, and so the later figures should be regarded skeptically. Earlier evidence suggests that the more modest, though still substantial, figures are more accurate.

In describing the "Joe" rescue, Garrett's letter dated November 29, 1856, makes reference to a reward offer published by the *Baltimore Sun* of $2,600 dollars—presumably for the whole party of four men and one woman. In Garrett's letter of December 27, 1856, the reward is broken down into "1500 shillings for one, 800 for another, and 300 for the third— the other man or woman. I have never seen any reward offered for her."[5] In 1869, Bradford wrote: "The rewards posted up everywhere had been at first five hundred dollars for Joe, if taken within the limits of the United States; then a thousand, and then fifteen hundred dollars, 'and all expenses clear and clean, for his body in Easton Jail.' Eight hundred for William, and four hundred for Peter, and twelve thousand for the woman who enticed them away" (Bradford, 1869, 30). Writing in November 1867, Sallie Holley claimed: "Forty-thousand dollars was not too great a reward for the Maryland slaveholders to offer for her" (Holly, 1867b). When writing the first version of her book, Bradford apparently asked Tubman whether Holley's figure was correct and reported: "she did not know whether it was so, but she heard them read from one paper that the reward offered was $12,000" (Bradford, 1869, 22).[6] Assuming Tubman herself to be the source most likely to be accurate—and in the absence of any new primary documentation—I think the figure of $12,000 should be used.

NOTES

INTRODUCTION

1. This woodcut image may have been based on an actual photograph taken during the Civil War. Tubman's grandnephew Harkless Bowley told biographer Earl Conrad, "I did however let a [man?] have one of her photographs, the one she had taken when she was with the Union Army. I have never gotten it back" (Bowley, 1940a).

2. Although Tubman's earliest nineteenth-century biographers were white, many of her African American contemporaries (especially abolitionists and activist writers) left important documentary evidence about her impact, including William Still, Frederick Douglass, William Wells Brown, Charlotte Forten, and Frances Watkins Harper. Dozens of brief biographical articles were produced by black writers in the later years of her life, and since her death hundreds of African American writers, intellectuals, and artists have created influential retellings or visual representations of key stories, in pamphlets, magazine articles, and books aimed both at adults and at children.

3. For example another fugitive slave heroine successfully protected a grandson from being sold south by fleeing with him to Canada and then returned to rescue other children and grandchildren. We get a glimpse of her in a letter dated October 24, 1856, in which Thomas Garrett explained to Eliza Wigham that this heroine was not Harriet Tubman. Garrett mentions a newspaper story in the *Trenton (N.J.) Gazette* as the source of the story (McGowan, 1977, 129–131). Also see Jacqueline Jones (1985), for an instance of a seventy-year-old former slave woman rescuing herself and twenty-two children and grandchildren during the war (47). Deborah Gray White (1985) discusses the reasons "why women were underrepresented in the fugitive population," with particular emphasis on the restrictions entailed by their motherhood roles (70–90).

4. Sanborn and Cheney were closely associated with Tubman in antislavery work in the late 1850s and freedmen's aid work in the 1860s. They continued to respond to her appeals for help with fund-raising projects throughout their long lives. (Sanborn outlived her by just a few years, dying in 1917; Cheney died in 1904; and Bradford died in 1912, one year before Tubman herself.) These biographers' relationships with Tubman are discussed in more detail in part 2, "The Life Stories."

5. I have located four dictated letters from Tubman as well as many references to others. It is very likely that more Tubman letters await discovery in the papers of her antislavery associates at dozens of archives.

6. For an extended discussion of the similar case of Sojourner Truth, another public antislavery ex-slave heroine who did not acquire literacy as a free adult, see Carleton Mabee (1993), 60–66.

7. I have made this argument in more detail in relation to Tubman's impact on the Bradford biography in Humez (1993), 162–182.

8. See part 2, "The Life Stories," for a more extended discussion of how Tubman's storytelling practices affected the mediated autobiographical texts that have come down to us.

9. For a fuller discussion of the language issues raised by oral-historical interview texts, see part 2, "The Life Stories."

10. I have selected those portions of the surviving interview-based biographies that seem likely to have undergone the least transmutation by the collaborator with the pen. For more detail on my editing procedures, see "A Note on the Selection and Editing of Story Texts," in part 3, "Stories and Sayings."

11. Earl Conrad was the pen name chosen by Earl Cohen (1912–1986). Conrad described his political perspectives as a white progressive in a letter to Harkless Bowley (Conrad, 1940c). Also see McHenry (1943).

12. No full-length scholarly biography of Tubman based on new primary research has yet appeared in the nearly sixty years since Earl Conrad's *General Harriet Tubman* (1943a)—though several scholars are currently working on new books. I was initially guided by Conrad's careful research to many important primary texts used in this book.

13. James McGowan, Kate Larson, Milton Sernett and I plan to put a comprehensive collection of unedited primary source material on a website to facilitate future research.

THE SLAVERY YEARS

1. The historical literature on slavery is vast. For an overview, I recommend Eugene Genovesee (1974), Ira Berlin (1998), and Deborah Gray White (1985).

2. See further discussion in part 2, "The Life Stories."

3. Anthony C. Thompson, who hired Tubman and her brothers to work on his farm, estimated the age of "Minty" at thirty-two in 1853, which would suggest a birth date in late 1820 or 1821 (Thompson, 1853). Sanborn, Tubman's earliest biographer, said "she was born, as near as she can remember, in 1820 or in 1821, in Dorchester Country, on the Eastern Shore of Maryland, and not far from the town of Cambridge" (Sanborn, 1863); Sarah Bradford implied she was twenty-five when she escaped "in the last year of James J. Polk's administration" (1869), while Sanborn thought she was twenty-eight or twenty-nine. Near the end of her life, there were other variations in reports of how old she was, many suggesting that she herself was unsure of her date of birth (as was true for many who were born in slavery).

4. In the obituary he wrote about Tubman, Sanborn embellished this ancestry somewhat, saying that her grandfather was "an imported African of a chieftain's

family" (Sanborn, 1913b). Frank C. Drake quoted her as having said she had heard tell that she might be descended from the Ashanti (Drake, 1907). Later biographical sketches may have picked up the hypothetical Ashanti connection from his dramatic newspaper sketch of her life.

5. I discuss my skeptical view of Miller's assertion in appendix A, "A Note on Tubman's Kin."

6. Modesty's name is given in Anthony Thompson's Testimony of 1853, where Tubman is referred to only as "Minty," and Tubman's mother is called "Rit" repeatedly and "Ritty" once. Sanborn (1863) reported that Tubman's mother's name was Harriet Green. No further information about the source of the name Green is available. In an affidavit in 1898 Tubman testified: "I am about 75 years of age. I was born and reared in Dorchester Co Md. My maiden name was Aramitta Ross" (Tubman, 1898, January 1). She also testified in an affidavit in 1894: "My name before I married my first husband John Tubman was Harriet Ross" (Tubman, 1894b, November 10). This might indicate that she rejected the name Araminta (which Sanborn calls "her sounding Christian name") sometime before she came north. Samuel Hopkins Adams, grandson of Harriet Tubman's Auburn friend and benefactor Samuel Miles Hopkins (Sarah Bradford's brother), claimed that "Harriet was her slave name, which she accepted for convenience." In the same passage, Adams tells us: "Her relations with the Deity were personal, even intimate, though respectful on her part. He always addressed her as Araminta, which was her christened name" (S. H. Adams, 1989, 277–278). Conrad and Rose Mary Sadlier (following Conrad) treat the name Araminta as an alias Tubman used when going out to work—on what basis I am not sure.

7. Prior to his manumission, Benjamin Ross was the legal property of the Thompson family, which had several plantations of its own. See Larson (2003) for a carefully documented account of Tubman's family's life in Maryland and relations with the Brodess and Thompson families. Brodess is variously spelled Brodas, Broadis, Broadice, and Brodins in different sources.

8. Sanborn understood correctly that Dr. Anthony C. Thompson's father, Anthony Thompson, owned Benjamin Ross. I am indebted to James McGowan and Kate Larson for establishing and conveying to me the facts of Benjamin Ross's legal status and the date of his manumission.

9. Anthony Thompson, the owner of Benjamin Ross, died in 1837, leaving in his will the instruction "Negro man Ben to serve 5 years and then free." Apparently Ben Ross did not serve the full five years. Although Harriet Green and Benjamin Ross were unable to marry legally, they clearly considered themselves married. I will therefore refer to Tubman's mother henceforth by the married name she is most likely to have used herself while in Maryland, Harriet (or Ritta) Ross.

10. Thanks to Kate Larson for providing biographical information on the two slaveholder families from her Dorchester County research.

11. The Last Will and Testament of Athow Pattison basically confirms the facts as conveyed by Bradford (though she spells the name "Mary Patterson"). The relevant section of the Pattison will reads: "I give and bequeath unto my Grand daughter, Mary Pattison, one negro girl called Rittia and her increase until she and they arrive to forty five years of age" (Pattison, 1791). Despite the pronoun ambiguity, Pattison apparently intended that Rittia and her offspring should all become free, as each one

of them reached the age of forty-five. Thanks to James McGowan for providing me with this document, as well as several others on Tubman's family's history in Maryland. See Larson (forthcoming) for a fuller discussion of manumission in the intertwined histories of the Ross family and their various legal owners.

12. One story from this era suggests both pleasure in this role and the precariousness of the arrangement. See part 2, "The Life Stories," for further discussion.

13. As I discuss in more detail in "The Life Stories," several of Tubman's white antislavery associates and friends expressed an apparently negative attitude toward Ritta Ross, perhaps based on their observations of her later relationship with her daughter in Auburn in the late 1850s and 1860s.

14. Thompson said in 1853 that the sisters (Linah and Soph) were sold south by Edward Brodess. One of Tubman's brothers later told a detailed story about the sale of one of his sisters by treachery, but he did not indicate how long ago the event had taken place (H. Stewart, 1863).

15. Because of its antislavery doctrine and evangelical style, Wesleyan Methodism was very attractive to the enslaved population in the First Great Awakening revivals in the 1740s. "Although after 1785 the church retreated from its original opposition to slavery, the number of black members continued to increase in the lingering aura of Methodist benignity, and as the African Americans experienced the evangelical fervor of the Second Great Awakening at the turn of the century" (Lincoln and Mamiya, 1990, p. 50). African Methodism dates from the 1780s, when black Methodists in Philadelphia objected to segregation in a Methodist Episcopal Church. It is not yet clear how much contact the Ross family and other Dorchester County slave and free black residents would have had with African Methodism in the 1820s and 1830s. For further discussion of Tubman's own religious and spiritual history and practices, see part 2, "The Life Stories."

16. Sarah Bradford, a Presbyterian, wondered if this meant Tubman's family was Roman Catholic (Bradford, 1869, 108–109). Tubman continued to fast on Fridays in observance of this religious custom, as was noted in 1899 by one of the Osborne family members interviewing her about her life history: "She refused refreshments because it was Friday, 'and she always fasts until 12 on that day—until the Lord comes down from the cross'" (A. Garrison, 1899a).

17. Many different versions of this story have been captured (and embroidered upon) by her various early biographers. See part 2, "The Life Stories."

18. It may be impossible at this remove in time to separate out the involuntary aspects of her famous "somnolence" from a possible strategic use of the appearance of unconsciousness. The head injury was certainly real enough—the object left a dent that many people touched and described. In her old age Tubman told of a recent visit to a Boston hospital for surgery to relieve the symptoms (Bradford, 1901).

19. For a discussion of how the maternity of enslaved women affected their motivation to flee or stay, as well as their problems as fugitives, see Deborah Gray White (1985, 70–74). (Also see pages 98–101 for a discussion of slavery's impact on reproductive life and choices.)

20. Sarah Bradford tells us that John Tubman "not only did not trouble himself about her fears" when she anticipated that her family was to be sold, "but did his best to betray her, and bring her back after she escaped" (Bradford, 1869). Bradford is not

an unbiased source, of course. Tubman's own action in returning to Maryland for her husband is difficult to reconcile with her knowledge of such a betrayal. See part 2, "The Life Stories," for a fuller discussion of how Tubman and her early biographers treat John Tubman as a character in her narratives.

21. Because Edward Brodess's will was destroyed in a fire in the Dorchester County Registry office in 1852, we must rely on testimony about its contents offered in 1853 by someone who had attended Brodess in his last illness and acted as the scribe for the will (A. C. Thompson, 1853).

22. Different and contradictory accounts of the rumors that preceded Tubman's escape were given in Bradford's *Scenes in the Life of Harriet Tubman* (1869) and *Harriet, the Moses of Her People* (1886). In general, I take the earlier book to be more likely to be reliable on most matters of fact. In this case, however, the earlier version is in error— it states that it was the impending sale of the two sisters that touched off the escape.

23. In 1869, Bradford said that three of Tubman's brothers started off with her, but when Bradford rewrote the story in 1886, she stated it was two brothers. See appendix A, "A Note on Harriet Tubman's Kin."

24. In the 1886 version they did not "drag her back." Rather, they simply turned back themselves.

25. Priscilla Thompson (1986) points out that there were Quaker meetings in two Maryland towns twenty miles from Bucktown, where Tubman could have found Quaker supporters, and she believes "it is reasonable to think that Tubman crossed into Delaware just north of Sussex County." She notes that Tubman might have stayed with the African American Underground Railroad conductor William Brinkly in Camden (3). Another prominent African American Underground Railroad conductor in Camden was Samuel D. Burris, with whom Tubman may also have stayed (Still, 1872).

26. The Philadelphia Vigilance Committee was founded in 1838 and originally was headed by the distinguished African American abolitionist lecturer Robert Purvis. According to historian Benjamin Quarles, "After 1839 the monthly meetings were no longer attended by whites, so that the committee was all-Negro in its operations and increasingly Negro in its personnel. This committee assisted some three hundred fugitives a year." William Still, who arrived in Philadelphia in 1844, chaired the Acting Committee of its successor organization, the General Vigilance Committee. Quarles characterized the later organization as "more consistently interracial" (Quarles, 1969, 154–155).

UNDERGROUND RAILROAD YEARS

1. John Brown's guerrilla band killed five proslavery settlers in Pottawatomie Creek, Kansas, a widely publicized action that enhanced Brown's reputation as a dangerous fanatic in some quarters and a committed freedom fighter in others.

2. For a fuller discussion of *Dred Scott v. Sandford* and the decision, see Richard H. Sewell (1988), 57–61.

3. Lincoln had spoken forcefully about the immorality of slavery during a campaign for the Senate in 1858, but his later emphasis on preserving the Union over ending slavery disappointed antislavery activists (Sewell, 1988, 68).

4. The first women's rights convention, held at Seneca Falls, New York, in 1848, was organized by antislavery women, notably Lucretia Mott and Elizabeth Cady Stanton, who had suffered exclusion based on gender at the London World Anti-slavery Conference of 1840. For the connections between antislavery and feminist organizing, see especially Blanche Glassman-Hersch (1978), Ann D. Gordon (1997), Shirley J. Yee (1992), Clare Taylor (1995), and Jean Fagan Yellin (1990).

5. William Still also published *The Underground Rail Road* (1872), a major primary documentary source that includes many accounts of Tubman's rescues.

6. Kate Larson has identified this niece as Keziah, "alternately called Mary Ann," the daughter of one of Tubman's older sisters, Linah or Soph. Harkless Bowley, a grandnephew of Tubman's, told Conrad in the 1930s that Tubman had "told me of the plan to get my mother away from Cambridge." His father, John Bowley, arranged to rescue her from auction in Cambridge, Maryland, by hiding her "in a lady's house only a five minute's walk from the court house." The party then went by boat from Cambridge to Baltimore, where they met Tubman. A few days later Tubman guided her niece and niece's two children and "several others" to freedom (H. Bowley, 1939a).

7. By 1854 she was able to send dictated letters to literate confederates in her neighborhood, as we learn from Sarah Bradford's version of the Christmas rescue of 1854. See part 3 in this book, "Stories and Sayings."

8. Earl Conrad learned from the Dorchester, Maryland, County Court that John Tubman's new wife's name was Caroline.

9. See part 2, "The Life Stories," for a fuller discussion of how Tubman articulated this mission to different biographers.

10. This testimony is notable for showing Benjamin Ross's energetic efforts on behalf of his sons, as well as the existence of a "white gentleman" upon whom he was able to call as a resource for negotiating with Eliza Ann Brodess.

11. Contemporary documents suggest that the three Ross brothers that Still greeted in late 1854, Robert, Benjamin, and Henry, were brothers of Tubman. It is fairly certain that Robert Ross became "John Stewart" and Benjamin Ross became "James Stewart" in the North. Kate Larson's new research suggests that either Henry Ross or Moses Ross became William Henry Stewart Sr. (Larson, forthcoming) See appendix A, "A Note on Harriet Tubman's Kin," for a fuller discussion.

12. Bradford's characterization of Ritta Ross's weak emotionality is discussed further in part 2, "The Life Stories."

13. Sojourner Truth sharply criticized her parents' white Northern owners for turning the elderly former slaves out to live on their own resources in their later years. Perhaps Eliza Ann Brodess was also thinking of the expenses she might incur in the years ahead in caring for the aging Ritta Ross. The amount of $20 was considerably more than the $15 per year Brodess had recently earned by hiring out Ritta Ross, according to Anthony C. Thompson (1853).

14. Garrett was probably not counting Tubman's early trips to Baltimore, so his figures are a bit low. See appendix B, "A Note on the Numbers."

15. The following year Tubman was back in Wilmington in September planning to rescue two children from Baltimore (probably a Canadian brother's children) and

"the sister & two children from the eastern shore." This time she told Garrett that once these goals had been achieved, "she would be satisfied to remain home till her health should be restored" (Garrett, 1856b).

16. Garrett reported in 1855 that Tubman said she had already "three times gone to Canada with those she brought."

17. Brown's description of ex-slaves is quoted in Owen Thomas (1999, 57).

18. Those brothers who lived with Tubman in Canada (and later in Auburn, New York) took the surname Stewart in the North, presumably in repudiation of their former slave identities and to conceal themselves from "slave catchers" who might be on their trail. Conrad speculated that they chose the name as a tribute to the shipbuilder for whom Benjamin Ross and Tubman had worked (Conrad, 1943a, 21).

19. Stewart said he had been there about eight years—which would mean since about 1855.

20. Tubman's Canadian testimony consists of a series of summarized answers made to a specific set of questions asked by Drew. This is one of the few early texts that do not use Southern dialect to represent her voice. Kate Larson has identified three other brief interviews by Drew as those of Tubman's brothers John Stewart ("John Seward") and James Stewart ("James Seward") and sister-in-law Catherine Stewart ("Mrs. James Seward").

21. Reverend Wilson received and dispersed funds for emergency relief of the fugitives donated by antislavery contributors. Frederick Douglass refers to Wilson as the agent at St. Catharines to whom he sent fugitives (Douglass, 1881, 330). Wilson also appears as a prominent antislavery activist and advocate for free blacks in various news stories in the *St Catharines Journal* in the 1850s.

22. Contributions were to be sent either to the Boston Anti-Slavery Society or to Rev. William Burns, St. Catharines.

23. Ironically, Tubman came to have her doubts about the effectiveness of Wilson's fugitive relief. Sanborn reported in a letter to Thomas Wentworth Higginson (1859b): "H. T. mentions a matter which some one ought to go to Canada to look after, a society in aid of destitute fugitives at St. Catharines which has some reason to complain of Mr. Wilson the missionary among fugitives in that town—whom you perhaps know—It is said that the contributions of the friends do not reach the fugitives at all, and they are desirous to have the matter looked into."

24. In the earlier decades of the century, the free black and refugee community had established an African Methodist Episcopal (A.M.E.) church (organized in 1816). In 1855 the church added "British" to its name, as an indication of the Canadian (and therefore free) identity of its members (O. Thomas, 1999, 39–40).

25. Tubman's name appears on a town tax assessment list as renting a house owned by Joseph Robinson in St. Catharines in 1858, where she is described as "colored," and her occupation is listed as "labourer" (St. Catharines Assessment Roll, 1858).

26. Frederick Douglass (1881) later named the principal Underground Railroad agents on this route: "Thomas Garrett was the agent in Wilmington; Melloe McKim, William Shill, Robert Purvis, Edward M. Davis, and others did the work in Philadelphia; David Ruggles, Isaac T. Hopper, Napolian, and others in New York City; the Misses Mott and Stephen Myers were forwarders from Albany; Revs. Samuel J. May

and J. W. Loguen were the agents in Syracuse; and J. P. Morris and myself received and dispatched passengers from Rochester to Canada, where they were received by Rev. Hiram Wilson" (pp. 329–330).

27. The sisters Lucretia Coffin Mott and Martha Coffin Wright were among Elizabeth Cady Stanton's and Susan B. Anthony's closest associates in the early years of organizing for women's rights.

28. Martha's husband David Wright was an attorney and antislavery activist. The Wrights' adult children later also became "patrons" of Tubman's—especially the daughters, Ellen Wright Garrison (who married William Lloyd Garrison II in 1864 and moved to the Boston area) and Eliza Wright Osborne (who married David Munson Osborne in 1851, stayed in Auburn, and helped to found one of the elite families there). The Osbornes became wealthy in the postwar period when the automated farm harvester developed by David Munson Osborne's company began to be distributed widely. He was elected alderman (1871–1874) and then mayor of Auburn (1879–1880); his son Thomas Mott Osborne was a prison reformer and then warden of Sing-Sing prison (located in Auburn) for a period. Eliza Osborne (and her brother-in-law John Hall Osborne) continued to provide some financial support and friendly offices to Tubman in her later years, when most of her other early associates had died. After both Eliza and John Hall Osborne died in 1911, Josephine F. Osborne, a niece of Eliza's, continued to help Tubman manage her money in her final illness.

29. According to Kate Larson's research, Tubman and her father provided timber for a shipyard in Cambridge, Maryland. The identity of the John Stewart mentioned by Sanborn as their employer has not yet been definitely established (personal communication, July 2002).

30. The property was on South Street, a mile or so from the Seward household, at the city boundary. Later it was determined to be within the neighboring township of Fleming. According to the research of Rebecca Green (1998) in the Seward Papers, kindly conveyed to me in a personal communication by Beth Crawford (March 10, 2002), a contract with Seward dated May 25, 1859, promises Tubman a seven-acre lot "with house thereon." Seward gave Tubman a mortgage loan for the price of the property, $1,200, and charged quarterly interest. When he died in 1872 she had not yet been able to complete the purchase of the property—as a matter of fact, she had borrowed more money from Seward in the meantime. Seward's son Frederick, who inherited the property as part of the estate of his father, sold it to Tubman (in a deed recorded May 29, 1873) for the original price of $1,200. He also forgave her the rest of the debt she owed the Seward estate.

31. She began to mention this mortgage as early as May or June 1859, on her first visit to Boston.

32. "Catherine Stewart," perhaps a sister-in-law, was a member of the household in Auburn by the immediate postwar period when Bradford visited the household. See appendix A, "A Note on Harriet Tubman's Kin," for more discussion.

33. Though Douglass does not record Tubman's name in his writings about his own Underground Railroad work, he did write a warm testimonial letter to her when she and Bradford were working on the biography in 1868. A passage in the 1892 edition of his *Life and Times of Frederick Douglass, Written by Himself* suggests that he

sheltered one of her larger parties of eleven fugitives. Kate Larson believes this may have been in January 1855, after the daring Christmas rescue of 1854.

34. Loguen managed the Syracuse Fugitive Aid Society from its founding in 1850, and by 1857 he devoted his full time to this work (Quarles, 1969, 154). He had participated in the highly publicized rescue of a fugitive slave in Syracuse in 1853, and like Douglass he was the author of an ex-slave narrative. John Brown was delighted to read Loguen's letter expressing resistance to federal prosecution under the Fugitive Slave Act in *Frederick Douglass's Paper* (Quarles, 1974, 66).

35. Despite Douglass's initial involvement, he did not ultimately support the Radical Abolitionist candidate, Gerrit Smith, in the 1856 election—presumably on the pragmatic assumption that this fringe party had no chance of actually winning.

36. Franklin Sanborn was the first and most prolific nineteenth-century historian of John Brown. He never wavered in his view of John Brown as one of the great heroes of the age. Sanborn was also one of the earliest architects of Tubman's celebrity, writing the first major biographical sketch to appear in print and continuing to write briefly about her many times thereafter. He often mentioned her in the context of his later works justifying the Harpers Ferry Raid.

37. During this time Brown wrote the provisional constitution that he would present to a secret gathering of African Canadian and African American men in Chatham, Canada West, in May 1858. Loguen was evidently well informed about Brown's plans, at least in a general way. Sanborn undoubtedly refers to Loguen when he mentions "a colored clergyman who heard him [John Brown] unfold his plan in 1858, at a secret meeting of colored people in one of the western cities" (Sanborn, 1878, 76).

38. The "Secret Six" co-conspirators were Theodore Parker, Samuel G. Howe, and George L. Stearns (all of Boston), Gerrit Smith of Peterboro, New York, Franklin B. Sanborn of Concord and Boston, and Thomas W. Higginson of Worcester.

39. Wyman wrote: "Loguen found Harriet's house in this town, and informed her privately that Brown was in the place, and asked her whether she would go to the hotel and see him or whether it would do for him to come see her. Harriet declares that she was forewarned by dreams that John Brown was to come to her, and she answered Loguen that the old man might visit her home. She also sent for some of the colored people in the neighborhood to come and see him" (Wyman, 1896). For discussions of John Brown's organizing for the Virginia campaign, see Benjamin Quarles (1974), Jane H. Pease and William H. Pease (1974), and Stephen J. Oates (1984).

40. Thomas W. Higginson, in the *Liberator*, May 28, 1858; quoted in Quarles (1974), 41.

41. They met on April 12 and April 14, and possibly on other occasions as well (J. Brown, 1858a, 185–189). William Howard Day, an African Canadian printer and abolitionist, was instrumental in setting up the meeting of Harriet Tubman and John Brown (Quarles, 1974, 48). Day explained in a letter to John Brown why Tubman had missed a meeting with him: "Jackson had put her on the cars, from what I could gather, she must have gone to Toronto." In the same letter, Day provided Brown with the names of potential African Canadian recruits for the Virginia campaign (Day, 1858).

42. Loguen did send an expression of support to John Brown: "My wife & all unite in wishing you all great success in your glorious undertaking" (Loguen, 1858).

43. "Brown had been unsuccessful in getting in touch with the elusive, on-the-move Harriet Tubman," according to Benjamin Quarles (1974, 44). John Brown biographer Stephen J. Oates definitely asserts that she was not there (1984, 241–243). In the absence of new documentation to the contrary, I agree that we should not assume that she was there.

44. Hugh Forbes, whom Quarles characterizes as "an English soldier of fortune who had seen military experience in Italy under Garibaldi," had been briefly hired by Brown to help train his band of followers. When he was not paid promptly enough, he began to solicit funds from abolitionist associates of Brown's and to threaten exposure of Brown's Secret Six financial backers. In May 1858 he actually contacted three members of the U.S. Senate, including William H. Seward, with some information about Brown's Virginia campaign plans. This alarmed the Secret Six, who held a secret meeting and decided to force Brown to put off the campaign for the time being and return to Kansas. Seward apparently dismissed the warning without seeing a need to take action (J. Taylor, 1991, 111).

45. Osborne Anderson, the Canadian recruit, was lucky enough to be one of the four of Brown's band who escaped from Harpers Ferry alive—he returned to Canada immediately after the failed raid. For an excellent discussion of the many reasons why John Brown's recruitment of blacks to his cause seems to have been relatively unsuccessful, see Quarles (1974, especially 44, 72–83).

46. During the war Tubman met Higginson again when she was stationed at Beaufort, South Carolina, and he had been commissioned commanding officer of a newly organized Union army regiment made up of recently freed former slaves.

47. Quarles points out that Brown's failure to share his plans more widely and in a more timely manner may have contributed to the relative failure of his recruitment effort among blacks (1974, 81–82).

48. In Sanborn's letters from 1859 through 1862, the period when he acted as Tubman's Concord and Boston chaperone, he served as her enthusiastic publicist and also basked somewhat in her reflected glory. Sanborn brought Tubman to meet Ralph Waldo Emerson, who was at this period speaking and writing against slavery. She also met Bronson Alcott and his family, recently settled in Concord. Other prominent people to whom Sanborn introduced her included Mary Peabody Mann (Mrs. Horace Mann) and Phillip Brooks and family (Sanborn, 1868).

49. Sanborn's first wife was a close girlhood friend of Cheney's. Ednah Cheney proved to be an important friend of Tubman's during the Civil War in her role as secretary of the New England Freedmen's Aid Society. Cheney's early biographical sketch of Tubman appeared in that society's journal, the *Freedmen's Record*, in 1865.

50. Chapman acted as recording secretary of Garrison's New England Non-Resistance Society, helped edit this organization's journal as well as the *Liberator*, and with her sisters ran antislavery fairs to raise funds for the cause in the 1830s and 1840s. See Alma Lutz (1971).

51. At the end of the letter Chapman refers to "former letters" that contained Tubman's "history in brief." I have not as yet been able to locate any of these. Mrs. Arnold was Sarah Rotch Arnold, married to James Arnold, a whaling merchant who

was "a great friend of runaway slaves, whom he aided with money and in other ways," according to John M. Bullard (1947, 410). New Bedford, a prosperous cosmopolitan whaling seaport originally founded by Quakers, attracted a sizable, well-educated, independent-minded free black community during the nineteenth century, in part because of the employment opportunities offered free black men and boys on whaling ships. See Kathryn Grover (2001).

52. Rock spoke at a meeting held at Boston's Fanueil Hall on March 5, 1858, protesting the Dred Scott decision, in 1857, and was among those, including Garrison, Loguen, and Tubman, who made fiery speeches at the New England Colored Citizens Convention held in Boston in early August 1859 (Quarles, 1969, 230–234).

53. Brown's *Narrative of William W. Brown, A Fugitive Slave, Written by Himself,* was published in 1847 in Boston, revised in 1848, and reissued in 1849, the year of Tubman's escape. Brown's later brief tribute to Tubman's work offered a fascinating glimpse of the larger-than-life place she occupied in the imaginations of some of those she had rescued: "While in Canada, in 1860, we met several whom this woman had brought from the land of bondage, and they all believed she had supernatural power" (W. W. Brown, 1874).

54. Although William Wells Brown recalled that Tubman first came to Boston in 1854 and frequented the antislavery fairs and other events, I have not been able to locate any documentation of her public appearance on antislavery platforms prior to the spring and summer of 1859.

55. Many whites supported establishing colonies of U.S.-born blacks in Africa as a conservative strategy for making emancipation politically palatable. However, there were also some African American leaders who had given up on the United States as a possible homeland and were actively supporting efforts to create colonies in Haiti or Africa for Americans of African descent. Tubman supported the anticolonization side of this divisive debate within the African American political leadership in the antebellum period.

56. The pseudonym "Harriet Garrison" may have been meant to protect her from the attention of the slave catchers assumed to be on her trail.

57. Letters by L.[ewis] H.[ayden] and Franklin Sanborn suggest that she was expected to help support the Harpers Ferry enterprise but could not be located at the crucial time. See H[ayden] (1859a, b); Sanborn, 1859e, Sanborn, 1859f and Sanborn, 1859g.

58. Relying on two of Sanborn's many accounts of these events, Benjamin Quarles suggests that because Brown moved the date up a week, perhaps "Brown's raid caught Harriet Tubman unaware, coming while she was engaged in recruiting followers for him. Harriet's absence stemmed more from poor advance information than from poor health" (Quarles, 1974, 83).

59. A story in the *New York Herald* for October 20, 1859, indicated that "Brown has made a full statement, implicating Gerrit Smith . . . and Frederick Douglass" (quoted in Quarles, 1968, 180). Frederick Douglass had met with Brown in a quarry near Harpers Ferry on August 19, 1859. There he heard the full plan for the uprising for the first time. He refused to accompany Brown on what he saw as a suicidal mission. A note from Douglass to John Brown was found in the documents at the Brown hideout near Harpers Ferry, and Douglass was charged with treason by Governor

Wise of Virginia. Douglass fled to Canada and sailed for Europe from Quebec, as he had previously planned to do, on November 12, 1859 (McFeely, 1991, 175–184). Franklin Sanborn and George L. Stearns fled to Canada, where they remained six days before returning. Gerrit Smith, reported to have experienced an emotional break-down, was confined to the Utica Asylum until after John Brown's execution. Samuel Howe denied foreknowledge of the raid and then, after criticism from associates, decided to testify before the congressional investigating committee chaired by Mason. When he and Stearns ultimately testified, in February of 1860, they were evasive. The committee abetted their evasiveness in order to avoid publicizing the fact that respectable Northerners could condone a plan for a violent slave uprising. Sanborn fled again to Canada to avoid testifying to the Mason committee. Back in Concord in April, he was nearly arrested for refusing to cooperate with the committee. His Con-cord neighbors protected him from arrest, which allowed him to emerge as a "hero of the hour." Higginson refused either to flee or to destroy evidence of his complicity in Brown's plans, but he was not called to testify (Rossbach, 1982, 210–266).

60. According to one recent historian's interpretation, the Southerners on the Mason committee wound up writing a masterful "cover-up" report designed to reas-sure the public that no deep Northern sentiment for a violent solution to the slavery "problem" existed (Rossbach, 1982).

61. According to Quarles (1974), John Brown used the press very wisely during the month between his trial and his execution in order to educate the Northern public about his viewpoint on the necessity of militant action against the evil of slavery. He granted many interviews to reporters, and he wrote over one hundred letters to various correspondents, almost all of which rapidly "found their way into print" (109–111).

62. It is not yet clear why Tubman was in the Troy area at this time. A letter dated March 19, 1860, from Beriah Green (1860) to an antislavery associate introduces her as a "heroic woman" carrying papers from the Rev. Samuel J. May of Syracuse. This suggests that she was visiting among antislavery workers in the New York networks just prior to the visit to Troy—possibly fund-raising for a future trip south.

63. Several other African American women who had begun political work within the Garrisonian antislavery societies were already veterans of the campaign for women's suffrage in the 1860s. Sojourner Truth had appeared at a women's suffrage convention as early as 1850, in Worcester, Massachusetts (Painter, 1996, 114). The Forten sisters had taken an important role in the Philadelphia women's suffrage conference of 1854 (Terborg-Penn, 1998, 17). Also see Yee (1992, 86–111).

64. Louisa May Alcott's antislavery stories included "M. L.," written in 1860, and "The Brothers" (published as "My Contraband" in the *Atlantic Monthly* in 1863). After a brief stint as a Union army nurse, cut short by her own illness, she had hoped to go to Port Royal as a teacher of freed people later in the year, but she was told that unmarried women were not being sent there. She did receive "a pleasant letter from Col. Higginson praising 'The Contraband,' which he had just read in Port Royal," according to her journal for November 1863, when Tubman was still there (Baum, 1984, 250–255; Myerson & Shealy, 1987, 121; and Saxton, 1977, 267).

65. One Alcott biographer writes that "She heard Harriet Tubman, the escaped slave called Moses, speak of her many trips south to rescue other slaves. Louisa was profoundly stirred by the woman's courage and patience. Unfortunately, her rendition

of the woman in her late novel, *Work,* is dismayingly sentimental" (Saxton, 1977, 40). Another is somewhat more generous: "In *Work,* published in 1873, the character Hepsey is a noble and self-sacrificing freedwoman who needs only friendship and an education, both of which are provided by Alcott's heroine, to erase 'the tragedy of her race written in her face'" (Baum, 1987, 252).

66. Following Sarah Bradford's 1869 biography, most later biographers of Tubman have repeated the assertion that Tubman made nineteen trips south and personally rescued over three hundred fugitives. However, the documentary record produced during the 1850s and early 1860s by Tubman's friends and supporters indicates that these figures are very likely highly inflated. See appendix B, "A Note on the Numbers," for an extended discussion of the early evidence.

67. D. E. Collins reported the "sister's" death in a letter to Franklin B. Sanborn from Auburn (1861): "We were much pleased that Harriet succeeded in assisting even a few of her suffering friends to escape from bondage, but her sister was not among the number, she having been released from her labors some time since by that friend of the poor slave, the Angel of Death."

THE WAR YEARS

1. Seward had been part of the antislavery leadership in the Senate for much of the decade, though he was never "a flaming abolitionist in the mould of Charles Sumner," according to a recent biographer (J. M. Taylor, 1991, 110). Seward had been out of the country when the Harpers Ferry Raid took place in October and had returned just after the execution of John Brown in December 1859 to plunge into the thick of the now hysterical national debate. In February 1860 he gave a major address in the Senate supporting the admission of Kansas under an antislavery constitution but compromising his formerly strong antislavery views with a pro-Union position that did not threaten slavery in existing states.

2. For example, Lydia Maria Child wrote to Charles Sumner, "I thank you for the [pam]phlet you sent me last week, because any attention from you is always pleasant; but deem me not ungracious, if I ask you never again to send me anything bearing the name of William H. Seward. . . . It is an immeasurable crime for a public man to chill the moral enthusiasm of his countrymen, to lower the standard of the public conscience, to make it impossible for honest minds to trust in political leaders" (Child, 1861).

3. Sanborn was highly critical of Seward's politics during the secession crisis of 1860–1861, when he wrote his sketch of Tubman in the summer of 1863: "It was the mad winter of compromises, when State after State, and politician after politician, went down on their knees to beg the South not to secede. Mr. Seward went over to the side of compromise. He knew the history of this poor woman; he had given his enemies a hold of him, by dealing with her; it was thought he would not scruple to betray her. The suspicion was an unworthy one, for though the Secretary could betray a cause, he could not surely have put her enemies on the track of a woman who was thus in his power, after such a career as hers had been. But so little confidence was then felt in Mr. Seward, by men who had voted for him and with him, that they hurried Harriet off to Canada, sorely against her will" (Sanborn, 1863).

4. As it turned out, her confidence in Seward's personal loyalty to her was not misplaced. As Martha Coffin Wright's letter to her sister indicates, the Seward family was kept fully informed of events that threatened the safety of Tubman and her family and other fugitives in Auburn, and in her absences they were part of the support network upon which she could rely to provide material assistance to her family. Both Seward's family (especially his wife, Frances Miller Seward, and her sister Lazette Miller Worden) and Seward himself would continue to support her work in a variety of ways at the war's end, as well. Later his son William H. Seward II and daughter-in-law Janet Seward also provided various kinds of assistance to Tubman.

5. The source Conrad cited for this view was the assertion of William Wells Brown that Tubman "at once left for the South" when the war broke out (1874, 538). However, in the absence of corroborating testimony or documentation, this assertion, as well as Brown's other report that she followed Sherman's march "and witnessed the attack on Petersburg" (549), must still be considered speculative.

6. The relevant passages are these: "The war broke out, for which she had been long looking, and she hastened to her New England friends to prepare for another expedition to Maryland, to bring away the last of her family. Before she could start, however, the news came of the capture of Port Royal [December 8, 1861]. Instantly she conceived the idea of going there and working among her people on the islands and the mainland. Money was given her, a pass was secured through the agency of Governor Andrew, and she went to Beaufort" (Sanborn, 1863); "When the war broke out Harriet was very anxious to go to South Carolina to assist the contrabands" (Cheney, 1865).

7. Brickler says that her mother's father was a "brother" of Tubman's and was a former slave, living in Maryland. "One thing she knew, and that was that neither she, her brothers, or her mother had ever been slaves. . . . Her mother's marriage to Harriet's brother, an ex-slave, seems not to have hindered the family's progress for Mother said they had a pair of slick chestnut horses and a shiny carriage in which they rode to church. That was all she remembered of her home." See appendix A, "A Note on Harriet Tubman's Kin."

8. This certainly suggests that Tubman had been gathering information from Underground Railroad networks in the late summer or fall of 1861—but it does not clearly establish whether she had returned to Maryland to do so, or whether she had as yet had any contact with the Union army. In a September 1861 letter to Gerrit Smith, Sanborn reported himself to be "looking for Harriet Tubman soon; she promised to be here before this, but has not appeared" (1861a).

9. Tubman had already spoken against emigration at the New England Colored Citizens Convention held two years earlier in August 1859 (quoted earlier in this chapter).

10. I have removed from the passage the heavy dialect attributed to Tubman. Child commented to Whittier that Tubman's opinion was "wiser than the plans of politicians."

11. For more details on the politics of the colonization movement during the war, see McPherson (1965), 77–97.

12. Emma Paddock Telford quotes Tubman as saying that her antislavery friends "changed their program" when the Port Royal Experiment on the Sea Islands began—in other words, they changed Tubman's war service assignment (Telford, n.d.).

13. It was certainly becoming increasingly clear to those responsible for Union strategy that former slaves were in the best position to gather and deliver valuable information obtained from behind Confederate lines. For examples of Union army satisfaction with the use of blacks as spies, see McPherson (1965), 146–149. In May 1862 William H. Seward wrote to a London-based compatriot that "everywhere the American General receives his most useful and reliable information from the Negro, who hails his coming as the harbinger of Freedom." Seward's dispatch to Charles Francis Adams, written May 28, appeared in "Papers Relating to Foreign Affairs, Communicated to Congress, December 1, 1862," and is quoted in McPherson (1965), 150.

14. Earl Conrad, writing from a progressive anti-racist political perspective during World War II, boldly highlighted the uniqueness of Tubman's military service, calling the Combahee River Raid in which she played a key role "the only military engagement in American history wherein a woman, black or white, 'led the raid and under whose inspiration it was originated and conducted'" (Conrad, 1943a, 170).

15. This was a status created in May 1861 when Union General Butler refused to return fugitive slaves entering the Union army camp at Fort Monroe, near Washington, D.C. This status was ratified by the Confiscation Act passed by Congress on August 6, which listed slaves as among the "property" that could legitimately be seized from those in rebellion against the Union (McPherson, 1965, 28).

16. Although the Northern volunteers in the Port Royal Experiment were predominantly white, Charlotte Forten, the schoolteacher daughter of abolitionist James Forten of Philadelphia, was a notable exception. Black organizations and individuals also sent missionaries and donations to the freed people (McPherson, 1965). For a balanced evaluation of the problems and achievements of the Port Royal Experiment, see especially Willie Lee Rose (1976).

17. Sanborn was under the mistaken impression in early February that Tubman was already on her way to Port Royal to "look after" the newly freed "contrabands." He wrote to a friend, "There is a meeting of ladies at Mrs. Emerson's this P.M. to sew for the contrabands at Port Royal, who are in need of clothes. Harriet Tubman, my black heroine, has gone there to look after them" (Sanborn, 1862).

18. The *Liberator*, reporting on a speech by Tubman at a "donation festival" in Boston a few days before she left the city, regretted that the money raised for Tubman was "not large, as the ladies had but a short time to prepare" ("Donation Festival" Notice, 1862). Cheney may have helped put together this event.

19. Martha Coffin Wright reported: "Mrs. Worden was just here—she has taken a contraband 10 yrs old to live with her, a niece of Harriet Tubman" (M. C. Wright, 1862). This arrangement appears to have been made just before Tubman left for the South earlier in May. Wright may have been incorrect in calling Margaret Stewart "a contraband." Alice Brickler told Conrad that her mother said that "neither she, her brothers, or her mother had ever been slaves."

20. The speech, published in *Douglass' Monthly* (August 1862), 692–693, is excerpted in McPherson (1965, 46), along with more diplomatic criticism by John Rock of Boston.

21. For a detailed discussion of the somewhat contradictory information that has come down to us about the size of the reward offered for Tubman's capture, see appendix B, "A Note on the Numbers."

22. The African American troops in the North were recruited with the promise from the War Department of equal pay. This was a promise Secretary of War Stanton had no congressional authority to make. Under the Militia Act of July 17, 1862, "Negroes would be paid ten dollars per month, three dollars of which could be deducted for clothing. White privates received thirteen dollars per month plus a clothing allowance of $3.50. At the time this law was passed the government planned to enroll Negroes primarily as laborers rather than as combat soldiers. . . . Beginning in June 1863, all Negro soldiers were paid at this rate" (McPherson, 1965, 196–197). Black soldiers in the two South Carolina regiments from Massachusetts (54th and 55th) resisted the discrimination by refusing to accept the lower pay, despite the hardship this brought to themselves and their families. It took another year of lobbying, with the support of Governor Andrew in Massachusetts, Secretary Stanton, and Thaddeus Stevens in Congress, to get an equal pay bill through Congress on June 15, 1864 (193–203).

23. Robert Gould Shaw, the white Bostonian colonel of the 54th Massachusetts Regiment who died in the attack at Fort Wagner shortly after the regiment arrived in South Carolina, was very critical of Montgomery's slash-and-burn tactics. For more details on the policy and style differences among the three antislavery colonels, Montgomery, Shaw, and Higginson, see Rose (1976), 242–260.

24. Forten had to miss the party in the evening in order to get to the ferry that would take her back to another island, although "we wanted dreadfully to see the 'shout' and grand jubilee which the soldiers were going to have that night" (1863).

25. The passage adds: "During her absence with an important expedition in Florida this wash-house was destroyed or appropriated by a Reg't of troops fresh from the north to make shelter for themselves but without any compensation whatever to Harriet" (Wood, 1868).

26. By March 1863 she had communicated to her Northern friends about her catering enterprise. Martha Wright mentioned seeing a notice in the *Commonwealth* "that Harriet Tubman is keeping a little store and doing a good work for the freedmen in Beaufort, S. C." (M. C. Wright 1863).

27. Curiously, Gooding does not mention the role of Tubman, though as an African American man he might be expected to be proud of her unusual contribution.

28. The Wisconsin correspondent who wrote the first newspaper account of the raid to be printed in the *Commonwealth* claimed that she "led the raid," and that she had been the one "under whose inspiration it was originated and conducted." Although he made some errors about her past life (mistakenly recording Virginia as her birthplace, for example) it seems likely that as an eyewitness to the victory celebration, his testimony about the raid itself should weigh heavily in the historical record, as Conrad rightly assumed ("From Florida: Colonel Montgomery's Raid," 1863).

29. A list of the names of seven scouts and two pilots who worked with Tubman was part of the documentation Tubman gave to Charles P. Wood in 1868.

30. Sanborn later said that both Montgomery and Tubman had been a little too freewheeling for the strait-laced Higginson, and both had received "censures" from him (Sanborn, 1913a). I have not been able to determine why Tubman received Higginson's "censure." Higginson expressed privately his disapproval of Montgomery's guerilla tactics including "burning private houses" in a letter to his mother, dated June

3, 1863 (cited in Rose [1964] 244). Similar negative remarks about Montgomery occur in Higginson's 1863 Journal. See entries for June 16, June 27 and July 7. Robert Gould Shaw and the 54th Volunteers joined Montgomery on a massively destructive raid on Darien, Georgia, on June 10, 1863. Shaw afterward complained directly to Governor Andrew about Montgomery's tactics. Higginson also reported negatively on Montgomery to U.S. senator Charles Sumner (Rose, 1976, 247–255).

31. Sanborn's reprint introduced a few minor verbal changes—I am following the wording of the original here.

32. Robert Taylor reported that Tubman told him she had prepared Shaw's last breakfast (Taylor, 1901, 13).

33. Charles A. Smith, who fought in the Massachusetts 54th Colored Regiment at Fort Wagner, told an Auburn newspaper reporter at the time of Tubman's death that he "had known Aunt Harriet for over 50 years. . . . After [Col. Robert Gould] Shaw fell dead in the trenches, Harriet Tubman was assigned by Colonel Montgomery to assist in nursing the Fort Wagner victims, and Mr. Smith became acquainted with the famous Negress" ("At Church of Zion," 1913).

34. There were at least two types of "colored hospitals" that served refugees in the Port Royal area: a regular "colored hospital" consisting of five houses in Beaufort with space for twenty-five to thirty people and a "contraband smallpox hospital" at Bell Farm (Guterman, 2000, 165). Tubman told Sanborn in the letter written shortly after the Combahee River Raid that "among other duties which I have, is that of looking after the hospital here for contrabands."

35. Clara Barton spent eight months in the Sea Islands. Susie King Taylor, who worked as a laundress in the African American regiment led by Higginson, observed her and afterward wrote, "Miss Barton was always very cordial toward me, and I honored her for her devotion and care for those men" (Taylor, 1902, 67). Taylor does not mention Tubman in her memoir, but it seems likely that their paths may have crossed as well.

36. Though Telford probably picked up some of the details of this story from Bradford, this version is the only one to emphasize Tubman's ability to cure the doctor.

37. See Guterman (2000) for a discussion of Tubman's participation in the "traffic in foodstuffs" in Camp Saxton—which led her and one of her scouts to testify briefly in the court-martial trial of a superintendent convicted of the illicit sale of army rations.

38. Cheney explained in the biographical sketch published at this time: "This society consider her labors too valuable to the freedmen to be turned elsewhere, and have therefore taken her into their service, paying her the small salary of ten dollars per month that she asks for. She is not adopted by any branch as she could not fulfill the condition of correspondence with them" (Cheney, 1865).

39. If Tubman told any stories about work done in 1865 under the authority of the New England Freedmen's Aid Society as a "practical teacher," they do not appear to have survived. She may not have been able to communicate her change in plans to the society during the chaotic months at the war's end. This is suggested by a letter sent from the society's secretary, Hannah Stevenson, to Frances Seward, dated November 7, 1865—when Tubman had already returned north and Frances Seward had been

dead for several months. In this letter Stevenson hoped for news of Tubman's where-abouts and said that Tubman had received no money from the Society since April.

40. William Wells Brown (1874) later placed Tubman at the assault on Petersburg, Virginia (536–539). The siege of Petersburg, which began June 15, 1864, lasted through April 3, 1865. She was in the North for most of that time but was back in Washington, meeting Martin Delany, a few weeks before April 3, 1865. Her war service documents included a letter from Surgeon General V. K. Barnes to Seward, verifying that "the Medical Director Dept. of Virginia has been instructed to appoint Harriet Tubman Nurse or Matron at the Colored Hospital, Fort Monroe, Va.," and a pass to Fort Monroe on government transport dated July 22, 1865. Charles P. Wood stated that "it does not appear that she rec'd the appointment above indicated, and soon after this date she returned to Washington—and thence home" (Wood, 1868).

41. According to a letter dated April 6, 1865, from A. B. to the editor of the A.M.E. Church newspaper the *Christian Recorder*, Tubman had just recently visited the encampment of African American soldiers at Camp William Penn, in Philadelphia. "On last Saturday evening we had a very entertaining homespun lecture, from a colored woman, known as Harriet Tubman. . . . She seems to be very well known by the community at large, as the great Underground Rail Road woman, and has done a good part to many of her fellow creatures, in that direction. During her lecture, which she gave in her own language, she elicited considerable applause from the soldiers of the 24th regiment, U.S.C.T., now at the camp. She gave a thrilling account of her trials in the South, during the past three years, among the contrabands and colored soldiers, and how she had administered to thousands of them, and cared for their numerous necessities. . . .The lecture was interspersed with several gems of music. . . . After a liberal collection for the lecturer, the meeting adjourned" ("For the Christian Recorder. From Camp Wm. Penn." April 15, 1865). Thanks to Kate Larson for this reference.

42. We do not know the details of the "dreadful abuses" on which she might have been reporting in the segregated hospitals, but it is noteworthy that she felt confident of an open door at the War Department in Washington.

43. Delany had received a commission as major of infantry from the War Department in February 1865, having persuaded Lincoln and then Stanton of the potential value of recruiting slaves as soldiers in the South before the Confederacy put into practice its own plans for a slave army. Delany received his commission as major in the army on February 26, 1865—the first black army officer. According to Dorothy Sterling (1971) in a biography of Delany, "Harriet Tubman, who had served as an army scout earlier in the war, agreed to meet him in South Carolina" (247).

44. Was Tubman present with the Beaufort contingent at this event? The documentary record, so far, is silent.

45. Backed by influential friends, Tubman began a campaign to lobby the government for her back wages and for an adequate veteran's pension began before the war's end. Ednah Cheney had concluded the biographical sketch published in the *Freedmen's Record* in March with an account of Tubman's financial condition that was obviously intended to prick the consciences of the antislavery readers in the North: "She has had no regular support from Government; and she feels that she must have some certain income, which she wishes to apply to her parents' support" (Cheney, 1865).

46. In 1898, she made a claim for $1,800 for her services "as nurse and cook in hospitals, and as commander of several men" (Tubman [Davis], 1898).

POSTWAR YEARS IN AUBURN

1. "Copperhead" originally meant a venomous snake; by extension, it referred to a Northerner who sympathized with the Confederacy during the Civil War.

2. This quotation provides an interesting sidelight on the etiquette of racial terminology at an early postwar period, at least from Tubman's perspective. Tubman rejected the term "colored" (later adopted by civil rights organizations such as the NAACP as conveying more respect than the terms "black" or "Negro") because it suggested a lack of racial pride.

3. *Proceedings of the Eleventh Women's Rights Convention* (1866), 45–48. Tubman met Frances Watkins Harper again many years later at a suffrage reception in Boston in 1897 ("Editorial Notes," 1897).

4. Emancipation began with the wartime presidential order that took effect January 1, 1863, but it was not completed and finally put on a secure constitutional basis until the Thirteenth Amendment was ratified by the Union states in December 1865.

5. The president and Congress had clashed during Lincoln's administration over which of them had the authority to bring the former Confederate states, once they were defeated, back into the Union (Quarles, 1976, 223).

6. Frederick Douglass later remembered that when Lincoln pointed Douglass out to Johnson, at the inauguration of President Lincoln and Vice President Johnson in March 1865, Johnson's face seemed to express "bitter contempt and aversion" (Douglass, *Life and Times,* 442; cited in Quarles, 1976, 226).

7. The Fourteenth Amendment did not include a specific universal suffrage provision because congressional Republicans were divided on this issue. Because of this omission, Wendell Phillips, William Lloyd Garrison's successor as president of the American Anti-Slavery Association, initially opposed it.

8. The fact that Stanton and Anthony had unblushingly associated with the overtly racist Train helped persuade white antislavery feminist Lucy Stone to cast her lot with black male suffrage (Mayer, 1998, 604–610). For two other useful discussions of the historic split in the women's rights wing of abolitionism in 1868–1869, see DuBois (1978) and Terborg-Penn (1998).

9. For fuller discussions of this history, see especially Terborg-Penn (1998), 54–80.

10. I am indebted to Earl Conrad's research for the coverage of John Tubman's death in the Maryland newspapers.

11. The original building on the seven-acre property on the Fleming town line was listed as a "frame house" in census years 1865, 1870, and 1875; but at some point thereafter, possibly because of a fire in 1883, it was replaced with a brick dwelling.

12. One of Tubman's brothers, John Stewart, who lived in close proximity and worked as a teamster, may have been able to assist Tubman and her household to some degree. See appendix A, "A Note on Harriet Tubman's Kin," for further details.

13. Tubman told William Lloyd Garrison that "they would have suffered for food the past winter as she was disabled, if it had not been for the work of a woman in the house" (M. C. Wright, 1866a).

14. Margaret Stewart Lucas testified to her many years' association as a close neighbor and kinswoman in connection with Tubman's widow's pension claim (Lucas and Newton, 1893).

15. Helen Woodruff Tatlock told Conrad of a "white child, left on her doorstep," which she took care of for some time, as well as "an incorrigible white woman with an illegitimate child." When identifying the members of the Tubman household in the photograph (Illustration 19) to Conrad, Tatlock referred to "the children Harriet always had—usually waifs—sometimes possibly the children of employed mothers who paid Harriet a trifle for their care" (Tatlock, 1939b).

16. Mrs. Birney may have been Elizabeth Fitzhugh Birney, niece of Gerrit Smith and widow of abolitionist James G. Birney (who died in 1857). Martha Coffin Wright chatted about delivering annual payments of $50 from Mrs. Birney in correspondence and diary entries: "I have a letter from Caroline, asking what Harriet Tubman needs most, as Mrs. Tallman has her money from Mrs. Birney, ready for her, so I have to paddle down to Mr. Wise's and see if it is needed most on the Mortgage or in the household. He has been so active in selling her Life [the Bradford book], he may know" (M. C. Wright, 1869f). Also see Martha Coffin Wright Diary entry, November 9, 1869, in which she refers to $50 received from Mrs. Birney's estate for Harriet Tubman.

17. Tubman cared for children in the family of Theodore M. Pomeroy, a congressman from Auburn who had married Elizabeth Watson, sister of Janet Seward (Mrs. William H. Seward Jr.) in 1855. The couple had five children, and when Tubman attended Pomeroy's funeral in 1905, she was "cordially received by the family—the children whom she had rocked and cared for in infancy" (Telford, n.d.).

18. Eight Southern states had been readmitted to the United States by the summer of 1868. The black male Republican votes in the fall helped elect Republican presidential candidate Ulysses S. Grant. Black voters were in the majority in three Southern states: South Carolina, Mississippi, and Louisiana (Sterling, 1976, 139).

19. During the 1870s fifteen black men served as congressmen from the South. One important achievement of the Radical Reconstruction period in Congress was the passage of a Civil Rights Act outlawing public segregation in 1875. This bill, originally introduced by antislavery veteran Charles Sumner of Massachusetts in 1870, was passed after his death "largely through the efforts of the black congressmen" (Sterling, 1976, 200). For other discussions of the accomplishments and problems of Reconstruction, see W. E. B. Du Bois (1910, 781–799; 1966) and Eric Foner (1988).

20. Elsa Barkley-Brown argues that ex-slaves drew upon a tradition of "collective responsibility" when they began to build social service institutions and to act politically in support of civil rights in the postwar Southern states. Her research suggests that women participated in Republican Party and constitutional conventions as part of a process of expressing community consensus. Barkley-Brown argues that "throughout the South exclusion from legal enfranchisement did not prevent African American women from affecting the vote and the political decisions." She cites instances of women continuing to attend Republican meetings even after exclusion and of "initiating sanctions" against men who voted Democratic. "African American women, unable to cast a separate vote, viewed African American men's vote as equally theirs," she argues, using a wealth of interesting evidence (Barkley-Brown, 1997, 80).

21. This was the second such event organized that year in Auburn antislavery networks. See Martha Coffin Wright (1868b) for a description of a Freedmen's Fair at Central Church that raised over $400: "Munson and Mr. Merriman bo't several things [at auction], ham, cakes etc. & presented to Harriet Tubman."

22. William G. Wise, one of the Wrights' antislavery friends in Auburn, raised the money to pay for publishing the Bradford book by subscription (pledges made in advance of publication). In an account of an evening spent at the home of William and Anne Wise in September 1868, Martha Coffin Wright recorded some of these pledges: from "Mr. Seymour $25, Mr. Will.[iam] Seward [Jr.] $25, D. M. Osborne & two or three others the same—pretty well for a beginning." A fuller list of thirty-four subscribers and the amounts donated appeared at the back of the 1869 edition. Among the $25 contributors not mentioned in Wright's diary entry were Gerrit Smith, Wendell Phillips, and Charles P. Wood. Those making $10 donations included William Wise, T. M. Pomeroy, and David Wright.

23. For a more detailed discussion of the dynamics of the Bradford/Tubman collaboration, see part 2, "The Life Stories."

24. Martha Coffin Wright reported in a letter to her nieces (1868g) that Tubman had visited recently: "She wanted I should ask Mrs. Mott if she would not write a letter, telling what she knew of her, for Mrs. Bradley [sic] to put in a book she was writing about her—She had letters from Thos. Garret, Gerritt Smith & others, & Mr. Mott and Mrs. M. came to see her in Phila. & assisted her." Apparently Lucretia Mott did send a letter, but it arrived too late to be included. Wright wrote again to her sister (1868j): "[Tubman] was grateful for the letter & the $5— ... she wanted me to read the letter to her, & sd. it should go somewhar in the book—for Mrs. Mott stood by them when there was no one else."

25. A letter by James A. Bowley (1868) to Tubman was also apparently written for the Bradford volume, though it was never included. Thanks to Milt Sernett and Kate Larson for calling this letter in private hands to my attention.

26. More reminiscent of the social justice arguments from the antebellum antislavery literature were those made in the "Essay on Woman-Whipping" included at the end of the 1869 Bradford volume (117–129). Evidently someone in the antislavery networks who was closely following Reconstruction-era racial politics wrote this essay, which refers scornfully to the Ku Klux Klan. In my opinion Bradford was probably not the author of this essay. Referring briefly to the whipping stories included in the biography of Tubman, the author of this piece indicts the institution of slavery for fostering a culture of violence among white Southerners and especially for turning the white "mistress" into "a domestic devil with horns and claws."

27. Robert Purvis was a noted African American antislavery activist in the Philadelphia networks. He is depicted in the photograph of the Executive Committee of the Pennsylvania Anti-Slavery Society (Illustration 4).

28. Although the mortgage debt was discharged shortly after Seward's death through a payment of $1200 to his son Frederick on May 29, 1873, Tubman was forced to remortgage the seven-acre property (Green, 1998). By 1892 she owed D. Edwin French a mortgage loan of $500 (C. G. Adams, 1894).

29. Conrad believed that Tubman might have met Davis in the South during the war, but Tubman explicitly testified: "I did not [know] him till after he was discharged

from the service and came to my house to live" (Tubman, 1894b). Margaret Stewart Lucas testified that she had known him for about three years as a boarder in Tubman's home before he married Tubman (Lucas and Newton, 1893).

30. Tubman, 1890, 1894b; Lucas and Newton, 1893.

31. After a congressional investigation of Klan activities, three "Force Acts" passed by Congress in 1870 and 1871 authorized the use of federal troops to enforce the Fifteenth Amendment, and President Grant did send in extra troops. Despite the virtual disappearance of the Klan itself by 1872, violence and intimidation aimed at keeping blacks from the polls continued.

32. When the recently elected President Hayes ordered federal troops stationed outside the state houses of South Carolina and Louisiana to return to their barracks, Washington was assisting in the process of eroding black political and civil rights in the Southern states and facilitating the return of white supremacy, already well underway. For a fuller history of the end of Reconstruction, see Eric Foner (1988).

33. According to Earl Conrad, Representatives MacDougall and Hazelton introduced bills on Tubman's behalf at this time (*Congressional Record,* 43rd Congress, 1st session, p. 2618; H.R. 3786, 43rd Congress, 1st session; cited in Conrad, 1943a, 210, 237).

34. This is probably a variant spelling of Bowley, the family name of Harkless Bowley.

35. Anti-Semitism may be behind the hostile portrait of Shimer in the retrospective newspaper accounts of the gold swindle after Tubman's death. He is referred to as "the Auburn miser," and the writer seems to enjoy his losses: "Shimer, who was the 'goat,' probably for the first time in his life, almost suffered heart disease at the loss. He attempted in his characteristic manner to hold Harriet and her brother responsible for his loss, charging that they had 'borrowed' the money from him. He was never able to collect the money" ("Harriet Tubman Is Dead," 1913). In contrast, Alice Brickler's version of the story as told to Conrad, which mentions that Shimer was a Jew, nevertheless had a happy ending: Shimer "released her and scolded her for being so trusting of strangers. The story ended with the return of the money and Aunt Harriet nursing a bruised head" (Brickler, 1939b).

36. The *Auburn Citizen* reported at the time of her death, relying no doubt on their own former coverage, that she had "narrated a story that included hypnotism and ghosts to account for the loss of the money and her injuries" ("Harriet Tubman Is Dead," 1913). The *Auburn Daily Bulletin* at the time reported that while waiting for the men to return with the gold, "She became nervous, thinking of the stories about ghosts haunting buried treasures, and finally became so 'worried' that she took a walk in the woods. Here she saw something white, and thought it was a ghost" ("Gold Swindle and the Greenback Robbery," 1873). Alice Brickler, retelling the story for Conrad, said, "She did not turn back because she felt sure some one had been watching her. She said the most weird sounds were to be heard, then she would catch a glimpse of a gray something in the distance" (Brickler, 1939b).

37. Shimer would have realized a 15 percent profit by the exchange. The lack of sympathy expressed for Shimer in either the newspaper accounts or the private correspondence of Tubman's friends suggests that the community may have enjoyed seeing the nouveau riche and possibly Jewish Shimer forced to swallow his losses.

38. For a discussion of Tubman's relationships with her white friends as affected by money issues, see part 2, "The Life Stories."

39. I am not assuming in this interpretation that Tubman and her brother actually were in league with the swindlers or intended to profit by theft. I do think it probable that Tubman may have feared for her brother's physical safety. At the very least she would have realistically anticipated possible imprisonment or crushing debt, if criminal responsibility for the loss of Shimer's $2,000 were to be fixed on herself and her brother. In this dangerous situation, I believe, she adopted the stratagem of distracting the attention of the adversary with a good laugh at her expense, as in the story she told Emily Howland. See part 2, "The Life Stories," for a fuller discussion of Tubman's relationships with her white associates during the post-Reconstruction "nadir" era in U.S. racial politics.

THE LATER YEARS

1. See Paula Giddings (1984), 75–77, and Deborah Gray White (1999).

2. Some white philanthropists made notable contributions to black educational institutions, and some white women continued to work as teachers or social workers among the freed people in the South after the end of Reconstruction. For a discussion of the contributions particularly of Northern white Baptists, including organized Baptist women, to the development of collegiate education for black women in the South, see Evelyn Brooks Higginbotham (1993), 21–46.

3. The Presbyterian Church in Auburn split over the slavery issue. Among the trustees of the antislavery Central Presbyterian church when it organized separately in 1861 were David Munson Osborne and Charles P. Wood, both important community members and steadfast friends of Tubman's (O'Hara 1992).

4. Florence Carter was the widow of A.M.E. Zion pastor and Harriet Tubman Home superintendent George C. Carter. She remembered Tubman as "a devout Christian" who made "frequent visits to my house when I lived at 18 Parker Street, Auburn, N.Y." The Thompson A.M.E. Zion church building on Parker Street was not constructed until the early 1890s. An A.M.E. Zion congregation began to meet in the home of Betsey Smith at 9 Washington Street on August 24, 1846 (P. C. Johnson, 1992, 39).

5. When writing a tribute to Tubman in June 1914, Mason referred to this meeting as "over 35 years" in the past.

6. Moses Stewart may be the son of her brother John Stewart. See appendix A, "A Note on Harriet Tubman's Kin."

7. Tubman was still referring to it as the John Brown Hall as late as 1905 (Telford, n.d.), but the A.M.E. Zion Church renamed it the Harriet Tubman Home when they assumed financial responsibility in 1903.

8. Dorothy Salem cites Harriet Tubman's project as one that illustrates the problems of those funded by individuals: "Despite her widespread popularity and her constant fund-raising on the lecture circuit, maintaining the home was a continuing struggle" (Salem, 1990, 69).

9. Tubman may have been counting on the sales of the new Bradford biography, which came out in October, but as she told the story, the purchase was spontaneous.

10. The amount the farm cost is variously said in different sources to have been $1,250 (Brooks, n.d.), $1,350 ("Dedication of Harriet Tubman Home," 1908), and $1,450 (Bradford, 1901).

11. I gratefully acknowledge the plausible suggestion made by Rebecca Green that the property purchase may have been linked with the publication of the revised Bradford book (personal communication from Beth Crawford, March 2002).

12. See part 2, "The Life Stories," for more details.

13. For a photograph that may have been taken on this occasion, see page 82.

14. If she also sought support from church-based charitable and self-help societies, which have been documented by Stephanie Shaw and others as forming a social infrastructure in the black community prior to the period of the national club movement, no documentation of this has as yet surfaced (Shaw, 1995). It was over a decade after her purchase of the property, in 1899, that the Phillis Wheatley Club (later affiliated with the National Association of Colored Women) was formed in Buffalo. Later the Phillis Wheatley Club and other African American women's clubs in New York State were sources of financial support for the ailing Tubman herself (Williams, 1995).

15. By 1888 two national women's suffrage organizations had been at work for a generation, without much substantial change to show for it. Susan B. Anthony's strategy of testing the genderless concept of "citizen" in the Fourteenth Amendment by attempting to vote in 1872 had led to her dramatic imprisonment and trial, but when in 1874 the Supreme Court upheld the right of the St. Louis, Missouri, Registrar to refuse the right to vote to Virginia Minor, it became clear that further skirmishes in this campaign would be fruitless. Three African American women, at least, were among those who also pursued the strategy of attempting to register to vote in the early 1870s: Mary Ann Shadd Cary in Washington, D.C., in 1871; Mrs. Beatty of Portland, Oregon; and Sojourner Truth, who attempted to vote in Battle Creek, Michigan (Terborg-Penn, 1998, 40–41).

16. Howland was also a school classmate of the Miller sisters, Frances and Lazette, who, as Mrs. Seward and Mrs. Worden, had befriended Tubman and her protégées. In *Eighty Years and More*, Elizabeth Cady Stanton reminisced about Frances Miller Seward's interest in women's rights (Stanton, 1971, 194–199).

17. When Earl Conrad corresponded with Carrie Chapman Catt, the elderly former national leader of the reunified suffrage organization NAWSA (the National American Woman Suffrage Association), he was very disappointed at her failure to recognize Tubman as a leading feminist activist and chided her for her attitude toward blacks. (Excerpts from this correspondence appear in part 3, "Stories and Sayings.") On the other hand, Harriet Stanton Blatch, the suffragist daughter of Elizabeth Cady Stanton, remembered fondly two or three visits with Tubman from her childhood, once in the company of Elizabth Smith Miller, "out near Geneva, New York" (Blatch, 1939). African American women's suffrage activists, including the Rollin sisters of South Carolina, Sojourner Truth, Mary Ann Shadd Cary, Josephine St. Pierre Ruffin, Frances Watkins Harper, and Hattie Purvis, worked with both the AWSA and the NWSA during the 1870s and 1880s. Terborg-Penn has identified nine African American women affiliated with the AWSA and six with the NWSA during the 1870s (Terborg-Penn, 1998, 42). Tubman met Sojourner Truth at least once during the Civil War in Boston and may have had other unrecorded contacts with her.

18. A mortgage was "executed by Harriet T. Davis to D. Edwin French, dated April 21, 1892 . . . covering a parcel of land situated in town of Fleming, on the east side of South Street, containing 7 acres of land, more or less, and that the same is yet unsatisfied of record." Her new debt was $500 (C. G. Adams, 1894).

19. Jane Kellogg sent Cheney a thank-you note dated June 25, 1894, in which she conveyed Cheney's "wish."

20. The incorporation of the Tubman Home may have been facilitated by some of Tubman's white friends in Auburn. John Hall Osborne, the brother-in-law of Eliza Wright Osborne, acted as treasurer of this organization for a number of years. The A.M.E. Zion church did not formally take over the title to the property, with its three outstanding mortgages, until June 1903. Four more years passed before the church was prepared to open the home to clients.

21. It is notable that Tubman continued to work for both white (Methodist Episcopal) and black (African Methodist Episcopal) church-based children's relief efforts. Both churches recognized her work upon her death with services and speeches.

22. Cheney apparently obliged in this project. At any rate, she presided at the reception for Tubman in Boston in April 1897 that was probably timed to publicize a reprinting of the 1886 Bradford biography.

23. Margaret Murray Washington, Booker T. Washington's wife and the Lady Principal of Tuskegee Institute, had been elected president of the newly created National Federation of Afro-American Women in 1895. School founder and racial uplift activist Mary Church Terrell became the first president of the National Association of Colored Women formed the following year in Washington, when the NFAW merged with Terrell's National League of Colored Women.

24. The term "nadir" was influentially used by Rayford Logan (1954). Evelyn Brooks Higginbotham has explored the apparent paradox of "a period that has come to be known simultaneously as the 'woman's era' and the 'nadir' in American race relations" in her study of organized women in the black Baptist Church from 1880 through 1920 (Higginbotham, 1993, 1).

25. Some local clubs and regional associations admitted black members when the General Federation of Women's Clubs was founded in 1890. The participation of black women became controversial at the 1900 national meeting in Milwaukee, when Josephine St. Pierre Ruffin came as representative of both a black club (the Woman's Era Club of Boston) and the white New England Federation of Women's Clubs. Because of both prejudice among the white clubwomen and fears of the loss of Southern white clubs, the GFWC leadership maneuvered to "eliminate recognition of the black women's club" by designating Ruffin a representative from the white New England organization (Salem, 1990, 42–44). African American clubwoman Fannie Barrier Williams exposed the prejudice in the white Chicago Women's Club when she applied to join in 1894. Club members did ultimately vote to admit her "after fourteen months of controversy" (Terborg-Penn, 1998, 119).

26. Douglass-Sprague provided a wish list for women's social service work that included industrial schools: "Our wants are numerous. We want homes in which purity can be taught, not hovels that are police-court feeders; we want industrial schools where labor of all kinds is taught, enabling our boys and girls to become skilled in the trades; we want the dram shops closed; we want the pool rooms and the

gambling dens of every variety swept out of existence; we want reform schools for our girls in such cities where the conscience of the white Christian is not elastic enough to take in the Negro child. . . . This is indeed the women's era, and we are coming." Industrial education became controversial within the black political leadership in the early years of the twentieth century.

27. See Linda Gordon (1995) for a comprehensive discussion of the similarities and differences in the approaches to social welfare activism of African American and white progressive women.

28. The event was briefly covered in "Editorial Notes" of the Boston-based *Woman's Journal,* April 17, 1897. "Mr. F. J. Garrison planned the reception, Mrs. Ednah D. Cheney presided, and the survivors of the old abolitionists in this vicinity, with the children of those who have passed on, gathered to do Harriet honor. She told the story of her life in simple words, that left her hearers feeling braver and better. Mrs. Frances E. Harper also was present."

29. Harper may have lived briefly in William Still's household in 1854, when she first took up antislavery work full-time (Foster, 1990, 10). Harper traveled as an anti-slavery lecturer for the Maine Anti-Slavery Society for three years, visiting Boston, New Bedford, Rev. Jermain Loguen's house in Syracuse, and the fugitive community in Canada in the summer of 1856. Her poems on abolitionist themes, published in the 1850s, brought her high visibility. Back in Philadelphia in 1857, the year Tubman brought her parents from Maryland through Wilmington and Philadelphia to the North, Harper may have personally assisted fleeing fugitive slaves. Harper wrote a letter dated April 23, 1858, to the *Liberator* about her own experience of discrimination on the city railroads of Philadelphia.

30. The new property included "25 aces of land, with a large orchard, two houses of ten rooms each, one brick and one frame, together with two large barns and other out-houses" (Wheeler, 1903). Emma Paddock Telford said that "there is a good garden cultivated by the inmates who are able to help, a number of fruit trees which Harriet has set out, a well filled poultry yard and a stalwart peripatetic flock of geese who greet the visitor with embarrassing cordiality" (Telford, n.d.).

31. Taylor referred to her depending upon earnings from an "older" brother (Taylor, 1901). John Stewart died in 1889, so this was evidently the younger brother, William Henry Stewart, who died in 1912.

32. It is possible that she was encouraged to do this by her friend Robert Taylor, a professor and financial agent of the Tuskegee Institute in Alabama, who had established a visiting relationship with her as early as 1894. Taylor had raised money toward retiring a second mortgage on the John Brown Hall property through publication of his biographical sketch *Harriet Tubman: The Heroine in Ebony* (Taylor, 1901). She asked him to receive the property in his own name, when she was reluctant to deed it to the church organization—this suggests a high level of trust in his willingness to follow her plan for the home (Wheeler, 1904).

33. At the dedication ceremony in 1908, the local newspaper coverage mentioned that $150 would bring "lifetime privileges." Tubman was quoted as early as 1909 as scoffing at the idea of asking the indigent to pay a fee. "When I gave the Home over to Zion Church what [do] you suppose they done? Why, they make a rule that nobody should come in without they have a hundred dollars. Now I wanted to make

a rule that nobody should come in unless they didn't have no money at all" ("Moses of Her People," 1909). Another version of this story appears in "Harriet Tubman Is Dead," 1913.

34. Thanks to Kate Larson for calling this reference (NACW, 1899) to my attention.

35. One can imagine a scenario in which Tubman's white friends took it upon themselves to challenge a financial arrangement that appeared to leave Tubman in a paupered condition, an action that the A.M.E. Zion church viewed as unwarranted interference in the negotiations in which they had engaged with her for many years.

36. This position was famously articulated in "Of Mr. Booker T. Washington and Others," in Du Bois (1903b).

37. The NAACP was founded in 1910 by an interracial alliance including white anti-racist philanthropist Oswald Garrison Villard, a grandson of William Lloyd Garrison (see Meier, 1963, 171–184).

38. Paula Giddings (1984) provides a well-researched and accessible account of how the African American clubwomen, in particular, related to the Washington–Du Bois split (102–117).

39. For further discussion of the Baptist Women's Convention's support of the National Training School for Women and Girls, headed by Nannie Helen Burroughs, see Evelyn Books Higginbotham (1993, 211–221).

40. Possibly some of Tubman's white associates on the board of the Tubman Home supported the dual use of the site, which would certainly have made fund-raising among conservative wealthy whites much easier.

41. The story announced: "as a memorial to her it is proposed to expand this home into an industrial school of the type of Tuskegee and Hampton. Some of the leaders of her race will assemble here in June next to make plans for a canvass to secure funds for buildings and endowment. Bishop R. C. Harris of Salisbury N. C. who was here recently making preliminary arrangements, will head the meeting, and prominent negroes will be asked to establish auxiliaries to aid in the movement." It also recounted the dispute between Tubman and the trustees over the proposed $100 entrance fee: "Harriet had objected and was willing to go about Auburn continuing her efforts to solicit alms. At present she has become reconciled with the trustees" ("Moses of Her People," 1909).

42. She is said to have wanted to "bequeath" the property "free of debt, to her race, to be used forever as an old folks home" (R. W. Taylor, 1901). However, the deed by which she conveyed it two years later specifies that it could be used in addition for other "charitable" and "industrial" purposes. Her "white friends" may have added this change, as Rev. B. F. Wheeler suggested, but Tubman would have been fully involved in the negotiations before the agreement was signed.

43. Frank Drake (1907) also referred to the Tubman Home as "an industrial home for the deserving of her race."

44. Mrs. Jerome Jeffreys of Rochester was an African American clubwoman and suffragist and a longtime friend of Susan B. Anthony—so much so that when anti-suffrage campaigns heated up in the last years before the passage of the Susan B. Anthony amendment, her picture was reproduced on a Southern "anti" flyer, along with NAWSA leaders Carrie Chapman Catt and the Rev. Anna Howard Shaw, in an attempt to discredit the suffrage campaign in the minds of prejudiced white

Southerners (Terborg-Penn, 1998, 128–129). At the time she rode in the carriage with Tubman and her brother to the dedication of the Tubman Home, Jeffreys was president of the Colored Women's Clubs of New York State (soon to be replaced in this office by Mary Talbert).

45. The trustees listed the newspaper story were Rev. E. U. A. Brooks, Bishop A. Walter, Bishop C. R. Harris, Rev. J. E. Mason, secretary of Livingstone College in North Carolina, Rev. J. C. Walters of Rochester, Rev. M. H. Ross of Norwich, Rev. T. A. Auten of Ithaca, Rev. C. A. Smith, Thomas Freeman, James Dale, Asa Lewis, and Harriet Tubman Davis.

46. The newspaper coverage of the dedication ceremonies reveals the extent to which Jim Crow attitudes and behavior had polarized Tubman's black and white supporters during the period when the Tubman Home was under development. The celebration is described as affecting only the "colored" community, and there is no reference to any of her white antislavery network friends and supporters attending the celebrations.

COPING WITH POVERTY

1. The initial claim filed June 27, 1890, was denied because Nelson Davis had served under the name Nelson Charles. She had to submit new documents testifying to his identity, as did her niece (Tubman, 1892; Lucas and Newton, 1893).

2. Among those who supported the new pension appeal in 1898 were William H. Seward, Jr., John H. Osborne, and Thomas Matt Osborne. The debate was published in the *Congressional Record* in 1899. Conrad suggests that the congressman who introduced the bill wilted under the questioning of a committee member from South Carolina, who asked belligerently whether she was to have both a widow's pension *and* a nurse's pension. One member of the committee on invalid pensions did state that the committee on War Claims should have decided her case, but he also acknowledged that the quicker way to get the needed funds to her was to increase the amount of the widow's pension. The committee report recommended that her pension be increased to $25 (Petition for Harriet Tubman) but "five dollars was whittled off of the twenty-five dollar request, and she was granted twenty dollars a month for the rest of her life" (Conrad, 1943a, 220).

3. Florence Carter told Conrad that "just a couple of years before she died, I wrote to the Auburn Advertiser-Journal a communication entitled, 'Lest We Forget,' in which I pointed out Harriet was aged and sick and penniless and needed help. After that Mrs. Osborne and Mrs. Seward, and other old friends, helped her to get to the hospital, which she needed" (Florence Carter, 1939).

4. The description suggests trepanation, a surgical procedure to relieve pressure on the brain.

5. Bradford's increasingly overt racism seemed to co-exist with a strong feeling of personal responsibility for Tubman based on their many years of acquaintance. See further discussion in part 2, "The Life Stories."

6. Howland had a lifelong interest in promoting black education. In the prewar era she had volunteered to teach in Myrtilla Miner's school for free black girls in Washington, D.C. During the war and in the early postwar period she taught in a

school established for freed people on land purchased by her father, a Quaker aboli-
tionist. She later provided financial support for the Emily Howland School in rural
Virginia, as well as thirty other schools (Hazzard, 1971, 229–231). She was close to
Frances Miller Seward and Eliza Wright Osborne and helped support the New York
Woman Suffrage Association with money and time.

7. Undaunted, both Tubman and Howland attended the New York Woman
Suffrage Association convention in Rochester a few weeks later. Tubman missed the
evening session of the conference because her train arrived late. She stayed overnight
at the train station, then located some of her friends among the delegates (presumably
including Howland and Eliza Wright Osborne), and "addressed the convention
briefly" ("With the Suffragists," 1905).

8. The next day's paper carried the story of a young man who was arrested as a
suspect, but apparently he had a credible explanation for his absence and his extra
money. Here we get a glimpse of Tubman's rules for guests in her home: "He explained
that he did not sleep in the house Thursday night, as Aunt Harriet had told him that
he must be in by ten o'clock. It was later than that when he reached home so he slept
in the barn" ("Christmas Money Still Missing," 1907).

9. Two historians who sought her out were Albert Bushnell Hart and William H.
Siebert. Siebert told Conrad that he had arranged to interview Tubman when she was
visiting Boston in the fall of 1894. The interview took place in Cambridge, Massachusetts, at the home of Dr. Harriet Cobb. Cobb was a friend of the Sieberts' and also
knew Sarah Bradford, which suggests that Bradford facilitated the meeting (Siebert,
1940). Either Siebert misremembered the 1894 date, or he interviewed Tubman more
than once, because he refers elsewhere to conversations with her in April 1897 (Siebert,
1898, 189) and in August 1897 (Siebert, 1897).

10. Works by Lillie Buffum Chace Wyman (1896), Robert Taylor (1901), Frank
Drake (1907), James B. Clarke (1911), and Anne Fitzhugh Miller (1912) are all based
on interviews or personal acquaintance, as well as Bradford. Osborne family members
interviewed Tubman with a stenographer present in 1899, and Emma Paddock Telford
interviewed her again in about 1905, but none of this new interview material found
its way into print. See part 2, "The Life Stories," for a more detailed discussion of
some of these interview-based sources.

11. The Harriet Tubman Home of Boston, a social settlement house in Boston's
South End, may have begun operation at this time—although the article does not
specifically mention it. Twenty years later "Harriet Tubman uplift and betterment
clubs" were "maintained by our women in Boston, Philadelphia and Greater New
York" (H. Q. Brown, 1926).

12. Helen Woodruff Tatlock, who knew Tubman in Auburn from 1880 through
1898, identified those household members who appeared in a group photo (see page
87). One of these was "the old blind woman whom Harriet took care of several years"
(Tatlock, 1939b).

13. The appeal letter is included in the published correspondence of Washington;
there is no record of whether he responded with a donation.

14. The biographical article by Charles Dennis that appeared in the *Americana
Magazine* in November 1911 is one indication of the efforts made by the Tubman
Home to reach a wide audience with appeals for funds.

15. Tubman was on the list of "nationally renowned black activist figures" who "made donations or were members of the [White Rose Mission and Industrial] association in 1911 and 1912" (Weisenfeld, 1997, 46–47). The mission was founded in New York City in 1897 by Victoria Earle Matthews "to establish and maintain a Christian, non-sectarian Home for Colored Working Girls and Women where they may be trained in the principles of practical self-help and right living" (quoted in Weisenfeld, 1997, 45). The Empire State Federation of Women's Clubs was founded at the White Rose Mission in 1908 (Wesley, 1984, 201).

16. Mary Burnett Talbert (1866–1923) was an Oberlin graduate, a teacher, and a charter member of both the Buffalo Phillis Wheatley Club (1899) and the Empire State Federation of Women's Clubs (1909). She was president of the Empire State Federation of Women's Clubs (1912–1916) and then president of the National Association of Colored Women (1916–1920). Later she was national director of the NAACP's Anti-Lynching Campaign (Williams, 1993, 370–375).

17. See National Association of Colored Women's Clubs, *National Association Notes* (1911 and 1912). At the time of Tubman's death, newspapers reported that the Empire State Women's Clubs had contributed $141 toward her support in her final days at the Tubman Home ("Aunt Harriet Was Very Old," 1913).

18. The visitors that day were James B. Clarke, a young Cornell scholar from the British West Indies, and Anne Fitzhugh Miller, a granddaughter of Gerrit Smith. Tubman wished to send a letter congratulating King George V of England on the occasion of his coronation. Miller agreed to help but suggested that her friend Clarke, "as a British subject . . . might be more familiar with the proper form of address" (Clarke, 1911). Miller published her own biographical sketch of Tubman in 1912.

19. This annuity is probably the annual gift of $50 from Mrs. Birney distributed by Martha Coffin Wright in the late 1860s.

20. The presence of the national superintendent of "temperance work among colored people" for the Women's Christian Temperance Union at Tubman's bedside suggests the value of her name to this influential women's organization. Frances Watkins Harper initially hesitated to join an organization that did not seem to welcome black leadership, especially in the South, but she later did outreach for the WCTU to the black community in articles for the *African Methodist Episcopal Church Review*. In one essay, "The Women's Christian Temperance Union and the Colored Woman," she wrote: "I hold that the Women's Christian Temperance Union has in its hands one of the grandest opportunities that God ever pressed into the hands of the womanhood of any country. . . . Whether or not the members of the farther South will subordinate the spirit of caste to the spirit of Christ, time will show" (Harper, 1888, 281–285).

21. In this way her later life story contrasts strongly with the career of Sojourner Truth, the restless itinerant preacher who interpreted her call from God as a command to leave her family and go on the road. Truth searched throughout her life for the ideal community. She also involved herself in public political campaigns on a sustained basis after the war. See Mabee (1993) and Painter (1996).

22. Bishop G. L. Blackwell of the A.M.E. Zion Church gave the featured sermon, and the Auburn newspapers duly indicated his prominence in the African American community nationally: "Bishop Blackwell, in opening, said that when he had received

news of Harriet's death he was in the midst of preparations to introduce Col. Theodore Roosevelt to the largest congregation of colored people in Philadelphia, but that he felt his duty calling him to Auburn to honor the late Aunt Harriet, and he had to forego the pleasure of presenting the former president to the colored people of Philadelphia."

23. He revealed that "The boys of my time always regarded her as a sort of super-natural being; our youthful imaginations were fired by the tales we had heard of her thrilling adventures, and we came to believe that she was all-wise, and we stood in great awe of her. . . . I never knew a person whose daily life was so filled with religious thought and religious observances" ("To Aunt Harriet Hundreds Pay Tribute at Funeral Service," 1913).

24. The author of this assessment was one Dr. Marshall W. Taylor, who was quoted in Monroe A. Majors (1893) and later quoted in Collier-Thomas (1997, 41, 62). Amanda Berry Smith was a noted Holiness movement missionary who is not as well known today.

25. For a sample of thirty-four twentieth-century biographies aimed at African American readers, see Randall Burkett et al. (1991). The children's literature, including books aimed at young readers and picture books for pre-readers, is immense. African American visual artists have also contributed significantly to Tubman memorial iconography during the twentieth century, in part through books aimed at children. Notable examples are Jacob Lawrence (1968) and Faith Ringgold (1992).

26. Washington had also written an introduction for Robert Taylor's *Harriet Tubman: The Heroine in Ebony* in 1901, and he responded promptly to a request to write a memorial paragraph for the *Syracuse Post-Standard* when she died (B. T. Washington, 1913).

27. Later in the speech, Washington pointed proudly to the economic achievements of the emancipated population after the war and again used Tubman as a kind of ancestor to be honored by black virtue in the present: "We have not only survived, but from a material point of view we have supported ourselves. We have not become beggars. We have asked no appropriation from Congress to provide food, clothing or shelter for our race, and it is very seldom that in any part of America a black hand is reached out from a corner of a street asking for personal charity. We have done more, however, than to support ourselves. We have accumulated land and houses; we own and operate businesses. . . . Progress in these directions will indicate that the work of Harriet Tubman was not in vain" (B. T. Washington, 1914).

28. The headline for the newspaper summary of this speech suggests an assumption of conservative white attitudes: "Booker T. Washington Urges Colored Men to Go on Farms, Declares That Opportunity for Success Is in Country, Not in City—Advises Them to Be Optimistic and Advertise Their Progress, Not Their Troubles."

29. The article is unsigned. If not actually penned by Du Bois, it would certainly have reflected his sentiments as editor of the *Crisis*.

30. The program available at the ceremony included a description of the Tubman Home (with a photograph of its residents, including Tubman, outside the building; see the illustrations), photographs of Booker T. Washington and a Tuskegee Institute building, and a list of individual and organizational contributors to the memorial project, including Rev. and Mrs. John Quincy Adams, Mayor Charles W. Brister,

William Freeman, Isabel and Emily Howland, General William H. Seward (son of the senator), and Emma Paddock Telford ("Souvenir Harriet Tubman Memorial," 1914).

31. The *National Association Notes* for March–April 1915 announced that the Harriet Tubman Club of New York had "taken the initiative" of planning a monument: "It was decided to ask every club woman of the state to save and send 10 cents toward that monument, which will be unveiled July 4, 1915." The Empire State Federation of Colored Women sponsored a three-day convocation in Auburn over the Fourth of July when the tombstone was erected ("Town Correspondence, Auburn, NY," 1915).

32. Laird reported $1,425 received from sale of real estate and rents totaling $102; funeral expenses and related costs of $234.30, and debts paid (including an outstanding mortgage) of $996.74, leaving a balance of $295.86. He also reported on a number of claims by creditors that he disputed, amounting to another $607. 65 (Laird, 1915).

33. According to Conrad's notes on his interview with Frances Smith, one of her caretakers during her story in the Harriet Tubman Home, Tubman had wanted two boards of directors for the Home, "a white and a colored board. Did not get her way" (Smith, n.d. [1939?]).

34. Funds were raised in the late 1940s to build a replica of the former structure, which had by then decayed beyond restoration. In 1953 a dedication ceremony for the new building was held, and a Harriet Tubman history quilt made by the San Francisco National Council of Negro Women was exhibited in the Cayuga County Court House in Auburn (Walls, n.d. [1954?]). For more on the twentieth-century history of the Tubman Home, see "Tubman Home Tag Day on Thursday," 1821; "Home of Civil War Heroine in Auburn Is Decaying Fast," 1939; "Harriet Tubman Home, Historic Local Landmark,"1943; "Harriet Tubman Home 'Rescued,'" 1943; "Restoration of Tubman [Home] Definite," 1949; Walls (n.d. [1950?]); "Home of Harriet Tubman Dedicated as a National Shrine," 1953; and "Tubman Home Recognition Honors Blacks' Historic Role," 1974. Bishop William J. Walls played a major role in pushing for the restoration of the property by the church in the early 1950s.

HARRIET TUBMAN'S PRACTICES AS A LIFE-STORYTELLER

1. Oral life storytelling is a performance art with rules and conventions very distinct from those governing written narrative, as Walter J. Ong has shown (1982). Lawrence Levine (1977) and Roger D. Abrahams (1985) provide important folkloristic studies of traditional African American verbal performance arts.

2. Marion Starling (1988) points out that written slave narratives were very frequently adaptations of oral testimony on the antislavery circuit. Through many repetitions as a paid lecturer, and through structured and predictable question-and-answer sessions after the lecture, former slave narrators honed the narrative material that would then be published in text form with the aid of an abolitionist amanuensis.

3. Oral performances of slave narrative material on the antislavery lecture circuit were effective both as political propaganda and as entertainment, "in the creation of hair-raising and blood-curdling effects" (Starling, 1988, 222).

4. As noted in part 1, "The Life," Sanborn said that Anne Whiting worked with Tubman on reading and writing during an 1859 visit to Concord. Ednah Cheney

also met Tubman in Boston in 1859 and 1860 and may well have been one of those "friends" who encouraged her at that time.

5. This was also true of Sojourner Truth, who relied on two empathetic scribes/ editors, first Olive Gilbert and later Frances Titus, in creating two versions of an auto-biographical narrative. See Humez (1996, 29–52) and Douglass-Chin (2001, 58–93) for discussions of the collaboration between Truth and Gilbert.

6. John Sekora's essay (1988) is a useful review of the many types of "slave narra-tive" text generated over three centuries and a discussion of their relationship to the genres of autobiography as understood by literary historians.

7. On the authority and reliability of slave narratives, see discussions in Starling (1988), Blassingame (1975), Olney (1985), and Stepto (1985).

8. John Blassingame, a pioneer in studying slave experience through critical examination of the sources in which slave testimony is preserved, found that even in the most reliable narratives there are many literary "elements that cannot be attributed to the blacks," including long dialogues and direct appeals to the reader, as well as philosophical, religious, and historical arguments (Blassingame, 1975, 79–82). Marion Starling has estimated that "16 of 100 book-length narratives between 1836 and 1863 may be accepted as literally self-authored, because all of these narrators have had a story to tell of serious struggle to acquire their equipment for authorship" (Starling, 1988, 247).

9. Among the publications drawing on this material is a valuable anthology edited by Clifton H. Johnson presenting interview material gathered by Fisk Univer-sity researchers on the religious conversion experiences of former slaves (Johnson, 1993).

10. A recent study of the Mississippi WPA slave narrative material reveals that in both interviewing and editing practices, the social and aesthetic criteria promoted by those in charge of the project led to an emphasis on "folkloric" material rather than racial politics and concealed the power dynamics between the interviewer and the speaker. See Sharon Ann Musher (2001, 1–31).

11. Blassingame points out that the interviews as typed had often been revised and the language altered. "Indications of deliberate distortion and interpolation of the views of the WPA staffers pose a serious challenge to historians who rely on the inter-views" (1975, 87).

12. Marion Starling has pointed out the wide variety of Southern English dialects Harriet Tubman is made to speak in the texts that have come down to us. Compar-ing the way Tubman speaks in Benjamin Drew's published rendition (1856) with the dialect she uses in Lydia Maria Child's letter to Whittier (1862a), Starling writes, with generous resignation: "Which of these jobs of editorship is closer to Harriet Tubman's original utterance is a moot question. Both seem to have caught the same spirit and, in the absence of any words from her own hand, must be accepted with thanks" (1988, 246–247). Literary critic Douglass-Chin has noted the same phenomenon in the various renditions of Sojourner Truth's speech, but he links this to Truth's clever "manipulativeness as performer." As he points out, "Truth spoke alternately with a Dutch accent, in black dialect, and in standard English—an astute selection of speech presentations that she could use as she chose or as the occasion warranted" (Douglass-Chin, 2001, 74)

13. I have been able to identify only four dictated letters and one (not fully legible) postcard greeting (see part 4, "Documents"). Undoubtedly persistent (and lucky) historians and biographers will discover more examples of Tubman's correspondence in future research.

14. Kate Larson has called my attention to a touching example dated 1888, written opposite the frontispiece of a copy of the 1886 Bradford book and addressed (probably in Jane Kellogg's handwriting) to a "Miss Margie" (personal communication).

15. The emphasis on fund-raising reflects the reality of her life, of course. It may also be an accident of documentary preservation, because her letters to prominent white associates (many of whom helped her out with donations) would more likely be saved and donated to an archive than the correspondence she undoubtedly exchanged on other subjects with family members and personal friends. The postcard in the St. Catharines Museum collection is a precious example of family correspondence that somehow, against all the odds, made its way into a public document repository.

16. One example of a fascinating story of dubious authority is contained in a letter to Conrad from George S. Schuyler, to whom Conrad had sent a query about Tubman. Schuyler wrote on September 1, 1939, that although he "never saw Aunt Harriet Tubman," he had been told "of her exploits" by his mother and maternal grandmother. "One vivid recollection is a story about Harriet having to hide fugitives in a manure pile with straws in their mouths to enable them to breathe. This may have been merely a tale, yet it profoundly impressed me not only with the woman's ingenuity but with the hardships of 'following the north star.'"

17. See the bibliography for a full list of Sanborn's writings about Tubman.

18. According to an obituary for Cheney in a Boston newspaper, "During the Civil War [Cheney] was one of the first to espouse the cause of the Negro and when Negro regiments were formed to go to the front she was made secretary of the commission which was to furnish them with comforts. For ten years she was secretary of the Freedmen's Aid Society" (Perry, 1904).

19. Tubman's pass to return south was dated March 20, 1865; the article appeared in the *Freedmen's Record* for March 1865.

20. Shirley Phillips Ingebritsen, "Edna Cheney," in Edward T. James et al. (1971), 1:325–327.

21. This story, published in Bradford's *Ups and Downs; or Silver Lake Sketches* (1855), involved a slave girl who was separated from her beloved young Christian white mistress by the death of the master. When sold to a dissipated new master in Louisiana, she considered suicide but then decided it would be no sin to attempt escape. She boarded a steamer bound for New York, and there she met an "old lady" with antislavery sentiments who opposed the Fugitive Slave Law and who arranged to hide her in a village in New York. In the denouement, after the dissipated master died in a duel, Nina voluntarily arranged to return south so that her white former mistress and friend (now again her legal owner) could nurse her on her deathbed. The "old lady" back in New York paid a fine for violating the Fugitive Slave Act but was not imprisoned. Bradford's narrator in this story, as in the Tubman biography, defends slaves from the accusation that they have no affectionate feeling for their kindred (282).

22. Although Bradford included some new material about Tubman's Auburn years in her later editions and altered some of the "facts" she had given in her 1869 book,

she added only two new stories about Tubman's "heroic" years: the 1860 escape with the drugged twins and the story of "Tillie."

23. The narrators in the 1930s had been children during the very last years of slavery. Their contribution to our understanding of the child's experience of sexuality is explored in Anthony S. Parent Jr. and Susan Brown Wallace (1993).

24. Even Bradford had a hard time believing the story of the Troy mob rescue of Charles Nalle. After giving Tubman's account she added: "This is the story Harriet told to the writer. By some persons it seemed too wonderful for belief, and an attempt was made to corroborate it. Rev. Henry Fowler, who was at the time at Saratoga, kindly volunteered to go to Troy to ascertain the facts" (Bradford, 1869, 92).

25. Bradford wrote, "The writer here finds it necessary to apologize for the very desultory and hasty manner in which this little book is written. Being herself pressed for time, in the expectation of soon leaving the country, she is obliged to pen down the material to be used in the short and interrupted interviews she can obtain with Harriet, and also to use such letters and accounts as may be sent her, as they come, without being able to work them in, in the order of time" (Bradford, 1869, 47). Bradford ultimately did not use a letter by Lucretia Mott and another by James A. Bowley, as noted in part 1, "The Life." This passage suggests that letters were not used if they arrived too late for Bradford to insert them easily in chronological sequence in her manuscript.

26. Sanborn includes more "factual" information about Tubman's earlier life (such as the names of her parents, names of the slaveholding family, number of siblings) and first rescues. Sanborn and Bradford differed on her likely date of birth (not surprisingly) and on the sequence of her various employments in her younger life, and they gave different accounts of John Tubman's role in her escape and mission, among other things.

27. Johnson gave Bradford a story about Thomas Garrett, but overall Bradford found that Johnson could tell her little about Tubman: He "said he wished he could recall to me other incidents connected with her. But during those years, there were such numbers of fugitive slaves coming into the Anti-Slavery Office, that he might not tell the incidents of any one group correctly. No records were kept, as that would be so unsafe for the poor creatures, and those who aided them" (Bradford, 1886, 90). Bradford also reported, "He remembers Harriet with great pleasure, though he has not seen her for many years. He speaks, as all who knew her do, of his entire confidence in her truthfulness and in the perfect integrity of her character" (53–54).

28. James McGowan (1994) has made a systematic list of those changes in the 1886 version that led later biographers astray. McGowan also takes Earl Conrad to task for finding "reason to excuse, ignore, or overlook" Bradford's inaccuracies and deficiencies as a writer. I am inclined to view Bradford as an inexperienced collaborator with Tubman on an oral history project, rather than as a would-be professional historian. I judge her failings somewhat less severely. In my discussion here, I incorporate some of McGowan's critique, as well as some points from my own earlier essay (Humez, 1993).

29. These omissions included a revealing anecdote Tubman had told of refusing to see a dramatic version of *Uncle Tom's Cabin* playing in Philadelphia in the early 1850s (Bradford, 1869, 22), the anecdote about the conductor's assault on the New Jersey

railroad car (46–47), and the 1863 dictated letter to Sanborn in which she asked for bloomers and referred proudly to the heroism of the African American soldiers in the Combahee River Raid.

30. A particularly noteworthy example is the interruption of a dramatic story (the 1854 Christmas rescue of the brothers) with a gratuitous and defensive editorial insert about how the duplicity of slaves may be morally justified (Bradford, 1886, 68–69, 71–72).

31. I have already mentioned one example—the elimination of Tubman's joke about the way Joe's excessive emotional display cuts him off from the real world. In the 1886 version the story ends with high sentimentality. Bradford also toned down Tubman's expressed pride in her own cleverness when sparring with her white oppressors. For example, Tubman no longer makes a fool of the master the night before her escape.

32. In 1886 Bradford omitted two anecdotes that involve Tubman asking her friends for money. Presumably in the more white supremacist climate of the post-Reconstruction era Bradford wished to protect Tubman from the insult of being thought a "beggar" (Bradford, 1869, 111, 112).

33. Bradford referred in a derogatory manner to refugee communities clustered around Washington, D.C., in the immediate postwar period, calling them the "swarm of idle darkies." Bradford's racism includes a heavy dose of "classism" as well—the middle-class fear of and contempt for the poor.

34. The stories added in 1901 include one from childhood, one about her attendance at a women's suffrage meeting, one about her providing food for her family in a time of near starvation, one about her bidding on the property for the Tubman Home, and one about her skull surgery in Boston.

35. It is not clear why Bradford did not simply ask Tubman (or Eliza Wright Osborne or Franklin B. Sanborn) for the addresses of these "friends and correspondents."

36. For an overview of some of the connections between the revivalism of the Second Great Awakening and the subsequent social reform (and perfectionist communitarian) movements in New York State, see Cross (1950), T. L. Smith (1957), McLoughlin (1978), Reuther and Keller (1981), Butler (1990), and Sernett (2002).

37. In 1886, Bradford defended herself specifically for including the account of Tubman's spirituality in her book, saying that "Had I not known so well her deeply religious character, and her conscientious veracity, and had I not since the war, and when she was an inmate of my own house, seen such remarkable instances of what seemed to be her direct intercourse with heaven, I should not dare to risk my own character for veracity by making these things public in this manner. But when I add that I have the strongest testimonials to her character for integrity from William H. Seward, Gerrit Smith, Wendell Phillips, Fred. Douglass, and my brother, Prof. S. M. Hopkins, who has known her for many years, I do not fear to brave the incredulity of any reader" (Bradford, 1886, 75–76).

38. Those who mention personal conversations or interviews with Tubman include Rosa Belle Holt (1886), Lillie Buffum Chace Wyman (1896), Robert W. Taylor (1901), Frank C. Drake (1907), James B. Clarke (1911), Anne Fitzhugh Miller (1912), and several anonymous authors of Auburn newspaper articles in the years immediately before and after her death in 1913.

39. Conrad mistakenly thought that Elizabeth Smith Miller had accompanied Clarke on the visit to Tubman in 1911.

40. Holt noted that Tubman had already in effect begun to operate a home for the elderly by this time: "Her home is in Auburn—a very plain little house which is an asylum for the poor people of her own color."

41. Holt also collected some conversation with Tubman about her gradually changing view of Lincoln, in part brought on by a conversation with Sojourner Truth. Otherwise, however, Holt relied quite heavily on Bradford's book (which had just appeared that same year)—though without clear attribution.

42. Lillie Buffum Chace Wyman refers to a four-hundred-page manuscript, "the first draft of my anti-slavery female sketches nearly finished," in a letter to Frank ackson Garrison (Wyman, n.d.). Wyman mentions in the sketch that "a few friends assist [Tubman] and wonder at her. 'She would have died long ago but for her indomitable courage and will,' writes one of these" (Wyman, 1896, 118). She may have been quoting Eliza Wright Osborne.

43. According to Wyman, Tubman reported that she had "stood on her doorstep and gazed after him as long as she could see him, and then watched the omnibus which he had entered till it was out of sight" (1896, 117). Wyman's information on Tubman's meeting with John Brown in St. Catharines is much more detailed than Bradford's account, but it is not clear how reliable Wyman's research was. For example, Wyman confidently passed on the misinformation in Bradford that Thomas Garrett was a "shoe dealer." Earl Conrad and Boyd Stutler (a John Brown historian) debated strenuously in their correspondence about Wyman's information on Tubman and John Brown (see the Conrad-Stutler correspondence in the Conrad/Tubman collection).

44. Although African American novelist and journalist Pauline E. Hopkins included an extensive biographical sketch of Tubman in her "Famous Women of the Negro Race" series in *The Colored American* (1902), there is no evidence within the article that suggests she interviewed Tubman. Her article relies primarily on William Still, William Wells Brown, Franklin Sanborn, and Sarah Bradford.

45. In making his bid for donations, Taylor outlined his relationship to Tubman and her present situation: "For the past seven years I have called to see her on my annual visit to Auburn, N.Y., in the interest of Tuskegee; and each time I have found strangers under her roof—aged, maimed, blind, or orphans" (R. W. Taylor, 1901, 15–16).

46. Taylor provided detail about the goods Tubman's parents needed to bring with them during their escape to Canada and relayed that she said she prepared the last breakfast for Colonel Robert Gould Shaw of the 54th Massachusetts Regiment, who died in the assault at Fort Wagner.

47. Clarke, who was at Cornell from 1908 through 1912, had published an article in the *Cornell Era* protesting the plan to exclude "colored girls" from the women's dormitory. He apparently became interested in supporting a building fund for the Tubman Home after his visit in 1911 (106–107). My thanks to Milt Sernett for calling my attention to Clarke's history.

48. Conrad continued to work on topics related to black history and anti-racist activism, and his publications included *Scottsboro Boy* (1950), the facilitated autobiography of Haywood Patterson, one of the convicted defendants in the controversial

Scottsboro trial of the 1930s, in which two Southern white women falsely accused a group of young black men of rape.

49. Conrad evidently believed that the rejections of his book manuscript by several publishers were related to the racial politics of the era. He told one of the Tubman descendants, "I am having the greatest difficulty in trying to interest a publisher in the product [of his research]. They do not wish to handle a Negro subject, and I, though white, am experiencing Jim Crow with this as much as any Negro might in his search for a job" (Conrad, 1940f). In the dedication to his book, Conrad referred to it as "the one that the white publishers would not issue" (Conrad, 1990, vii). In the foreword to the 1990 reprint, Conrad's widow Anna Alyse Conrad said: "When Earl Conrad wrote General Harriet Tubman the white publishers didn't want to publish a book about a black person, particularly a black woman. White editors remarked that there was no interest in such a subject, but Dr. Carter Woodson had the perception and wisdom to undertake to publish this biography" (Conrad, 1990, xiii).

50. Conrad told Alice Brickler that one of the publishers reviewing his book man-uscript asked him to emphasize Tubman's religious dreams, but that he refused to "turn her into anything 'exotic'"(Conrad, 1939z).

51. Brickler and Bowley were descendants of kinfolk; Florence Carter, then living in New York City, had known Tubman very well over many years in her role as the wife of the pastor of the Thompson Memorial A.M.E. Zion Church in Auburn. Con-rad interviewed Carter and produced a five-page transcript of their talk. Bowley and Brickler were too far away to visit, but each was willing to engage in an extended exchange of letters over the course of more than a year while Conrad worked on his research. Conrad also interviewed Frances Smith, the widow of the Rev. Charles A. Smith. The Smiths knew Tubman well in her last years when they were helping to manage the Tubman Home. Frances Smith cooked meals for the inmates, and both Smiths were present when Tubman died. According to Conrad's interview notes, Frances Smith thought that the "most outstanding thing about her was the interest she took in her people. Interest in higher education" (Smith, Frances A., [n. d.]). (One wishes Conrad had fleshed out this last skimpy note a bit more.)

52. Conrad interviewed Tatlock in New York City and then typed up a narrative based on the interview for her to review, correct, and sign. According to the hand-corrected typescript in Conrad's correspondence, Tatlock "lived in Auburn, New York, the early part of my life, on Ross Place, which is off West Genesee Street, and some distance away from the residence of Harriet Tubman. I knew Harriet during this period, and until my removal from Auburn, upon my marriage. I knew Harriet from about 1880 to 1898" (Tatlock, 1939a).

53. When he disagreed with her, however, Brickler did not continue the debate.

54. The documentary record is silent, at least so far, on her perspective on this division—or on that between Douglass and his former ally, William Lloyd Garrison, over antislavery politics in the 1850s.

55. Andrews (1989) reads postwar narratives as protesting against the "objectifica-tion" of the figure of the slave in the classic antebellum narrative "by demonstrating the evolution of a liberating subjectivity in the slave's life, up to and including the act of writing autobiography itself." For example, in contrast to Frederick Douglass's

narrative's view of slavery as a "tomb," Booker T. Washington's autobiography could characterize it as a "school."

56. But see my discussion of her prayer for the master's death, pp. 181–182.

57. Again, however, the documentary record does not yet make it clear how she may have related to organizational and political divisions within the organized women's movement, in the aftermath of the Fourteenth Amendment campaign. As on the question of the complex politics within the anti-racist communities, she seemed to have friends and associates in both the Stanton-Anthony and Stone-Douglass camps.

58. Painter (1991) writes: "We surely cannot translate twentieth-century psychology directly into the mentalities of eighteenth- and nineteenth-century societies, because many aspects of life that we regard as psychological were, in earlier times, connected to religion. . . . Despite differences of mentality wrought by greater or lesser religiosity, psychology—when used carefully, perhaps gingerly—provides a valuable means of understanding people and families who cannot be brought to the analyst's couch" (128).

59. As Painter (1991) points out, "to speak of black people in psychological terms can be problematical, for this history has a history," and she reviews the fierce twentieth-century debate among historians over what kind of psychological impact the oppressive institution of slavery had on "the slave personality." Nevertheless, she argues, insights derived from today's research on physical and psychological abuse within families can deepen our understanding of the continuing impact of slavery on our culture today.

60. Helen Tatlock claimed that Tubman possessed a repertoire of traditional folktales: "Harriet told many plantation stories and sang the old songs, like 'Swing Low Sweet Chariot,' 'Inching Along,' etc. Her stories, many of them, were closely related to the Uncle Remus stories of Joel Chandler Harris. With the same animal characters—full of quaint sayings and native wit" (Tatlock, 1939a). It is possible that Tatlock was mistaken, given that no other commentator mentions anything but Tubman's autobiographical stories. It is true, however, that some of her autobiographical stories use "trickster" plots. Tatlock was certainly accurately remembering that the theme of trickery in resistance to slavery was featured in Tubman's stories, whether traditional folkloric or autobiographical.

61. Puzzlingly, Cheney appears to be saying that Tubman did not resent racial "indignities" to herself when they came from friends—though she "knows and claims her rights" in resisting public racial discrimination.

62. Bradford included a similar "defense" of the heroine from white prejudice in her 1855 antislavery story, "Poor Nina, the Fugitive": "There are those who attempt to school themselves to the belief, that the slave has no strong feeling of affection towards his kindred; that the ties of blood with him are weak, easily severed, and lightly forgotten. We know not how it may be in general, with that oppressed and despised race, but we do know, that with all this is not the case; we know that there is no free white child, beloved and idolized by a fond and doting mother, whose heart would be torn by more bitter and despairing anguish, than was poor Nina's, when dragged from her mother's arms" (Bradford, 1855, 282).

63. Higginson uses the word "comedian" in the old-fashioned sense of "actor on the stage"; he is not necessarily implying that he admired Tubman's sense of humor.

64. It is remarkable that while Higginson understood the wearing of a "mask" as part of a dramatic performance, he still could believe that "Nature" was responsible for the former slave's concealment of the authentic self.

65. Sanborn may have been indulging in a legalistic maneuver by qualifying his testimony as he did. He stated he never doubted what she said "in regard to her own career"—but perhaps he had heard her utter untruths on other subjects.

66. For useful discussions of the kinds of indirect forms of resistance to the slave owner's power that were cultivated in slavery and available for building the self-esteem of the enslaved person, see Deborah Gray White (1985) and Clifton Johnson (1993). One valuable essay on how a woman's slave narrative represents resistance, is Valerie Smith's (1990).

READING THE CORE STORIES
FOR HARRIET TUBMAN'S OWN PERSPECTIVE

1. This mirrors the contrasting emphases of antebellum and postwar accounts, pointed out by William L. Andrews (1989) and discussed in the previous chapter. The stories Emma Paddock Telford also include more detail about the material culture of Tubman's childhood (cradles, pacifiers, hand-me-down clothing, beds) than we get in the early biographies.

2. Parenthetically, this story also exemplifies how the core story structure provides resistance to editorial censorship. Although Cheney interferes with the exact language of the storyteller by summarizing in the third person, the "punch line" to which the story aims is preserved as a first-person quotation. The direct critique of the "slave-holder's religion" in the first line results from Cheney's mediation, we can be fairly sure. But the ending, which shows Tubman as a child rejecting the hypocrisy of a "family" prayer service, while retaining the power of prayer for her own purposes, is clearly determined by the internal logic of the story of a child's intelligent and purposeful action on her own behalf. The internal logic of the story is the storyteller's—not the scribe's.

3. Nell Irvin Painter argues that in Sojourner Truth's case, there is evidence in the kind of language used about her experiences in the Dumont family to suggest sexual abuse by the white mistress in addition to physical abuse by the white master (Painter, 1996, 14–18). Margaret Washington does not take a position on the question of sexual abuse in the introduction to her edition of the *Narrative of Sojourner Truth*. Although she agrees that "anyone who studies the Narrative and is familiar with the plight of female slaves can easily read between the lines—and should do so whenever reading narratives of black women unable to write for themselves," she also cautions that the narrative "must be evaluated more for what it says than for what it does not say" (M. Washington, 1993, xxxi, xxxiii).

4. For an excellent analysis of the power dynamics between nineteenth-century sexual predators and targets, based on the Harriet Jacobs narrative *Incidents in the Life of a Slave Girl* and the trial narrative of a man accused of the rape of his white indentured servant, Rachel Davis, see Sharon Block (1999).

5. Parent and Wallace (1993) develop in more detail the "soul murder" concept as applied to the rearing of African American children by white "surrogate parents" under slavery. As part of a strategy of paternalism, slave owners often "deliberately manipulated and exaggerated their role as caretaker during childhood years" and used "systematic degradation" techniques on children, such as depriving them of underwear, in order to "compromise the separate identity of another person."

6. The gendered division of labor within plantation slavery was a far cry from that of nineteenth-century middle-class white America, in which women were expected to work solely to maintain family life in the domestic sphere, while men performed agricultural, industrial, and business work outside the home. Female slaves were expected to routinely participate in agricultural labor and were punished for failing to meet planter expectations, despite childbearing and childcare responsibilities. Nevertheless, work assignments did vary according to the gender, age, and physical capabilities of individuals. See Deborah Gray White (1985) passim.

7. In her 1886 recasting of this material, Bradford tried to lay more emphasis on the cruelty of the master, but she also noted explicitly that the providential view of this strength-developing work was Tubman's, and not her own: "This cruelty *she looks upon as a blessing in disguise* . . . for by it she was prepared for after needs" (Bradford, 1886, 21–22; italics mine).

8. An impressive needlework depiction of this shower of meteors as rendered by another former slave woman, folk artist Harriet Power, who was born in Georgia in 1837, juxtaposes scenes from sacred history with pictorial renditions of spectacular weather phenomena, interpreted as divine warnings of oncoming judgment. See Marie Jeanne Adams (1996).

9. Compare the accounts of visionary experience during illness in Rebecca Jackson's writings, in Jean McMahon Humez (1981).

10. For introductions to African American women's spiritual and visionary autobiography in the nineteenth century, see Andrews (1986a), Humez (1981; 1984), Dodson (1981), Braxton (1989), and Douglass-Chin (2001).

11. For overview studies of African American religious culture, see Du Bois (1903a), Frazier (1974), Genovese (1974), Raboteau (1978), Lincoln and Mamiya (1990), Wilmore (1989), and Fulop and Raboteau (1997).

12. Sanborn and Cheney failed to do justice to the reality of Tubman's spiritual experience in their brief accounts, but perhaps because of her own more conventional Christian religiosity, Sarah Bradford took this aspect of Tubman's experience more seriously.

13. In the 1886 biography Bradford attempted to censor Tubman's open admission that she had prayed for—and believed that her prayer had actually caused—the death of the master. This suggests that there was little, if any, editorial interference from Bradford with the original self-contained mini-narrative told by Tubman in the 1868 interviews.

14. In Sanborn's version of the visions before her escape, there is a dream of flying to freedom "like a bird" and seeing "ladies dressed in white" (Sanborn, 1863). Whether it is the ladies themselves or their clothes that are "white," it seems a clear reference after the fact to the antislavery women who did render aid of various kinds as Tubman escaped and afterward. In telling this story of seeing them in vision, she may be graciously acknowledging this aid.

15. For example, the holiness evangelist Amanda Berry Smith recorded a similar wonderment in describing her sanctification experience: "Then I sprung to my feet, all around was light, I was new, I looked at my hands, they looked new . . . I went into the dining room; we had a large mirror that went from the floor to the ceiling, and I went and looked in it to see if anything had transpired in my color, because there was something wonderful had taken place inside of me, and it really seemed to me it was outside too" (A. Smith, 1893). Also see Brereton (1991), C. H. Johnson (1993), and Humez (1984).

16. Because it links Tubman's acceptance of her role as liberator to the moment she crossed the Mason-Dixon line—long before she experienced rejection by John Tubman—Bradford's version of the story projects a far saintlier image of Tubman than does Cheney's. Bradford does not actually mention Tubman's discovery of John Tubman's infidelity at all. However, she is the only one of the early biographers to report that John Tubman "did his best to betray her" prior to Tubman's escape, and this may suggest that she had heard Tubman tell about his infidelity but chose not to mention it in the book out of delicacy.

17. I have developed this interpretation in more detail in Humez (1993).

18. Bradford's version of the story of Tubman's Christmas rescue of her brothers also underlines Ritta Ross's emotionality, treating it as a weakness. Interestingly, Sanborn and the Wright family also seem to have seen Ritta Ross as demanding and selfish—as violating, in other words, the version of motherhood they themselves saw as sacred. For a discussion of a similar clash of motherhood values between Sojourner Truth and her biographer Olive Gilbert, see Humez (1996).

19. Unfortunately, we have only a very few stories from Tubman's repertoire that relate to her mother or her father that have not passed through Sarah Bradford's pen. My reading of Tubman's feelings for her mother is based on details gathered by Sanborn and Telford about Ritta Ross's efforts to protect her daughter from the weaver's family as well as the story of the adolescent Tubman's efforts to reunite with her mother the night the stars fell, both previously discussed.

20. Thomas Garrett retold several stories Tubman had told him about her experience with divine guidance. For example, he reported in an awestruck tone to Bradford about an occasion when Tubman followed divine instructions to change course in the middle of a rescue: "She mostly had her regular stopping places on her route, but in one instance, when she had two stout men with her, some 30 miles below here, she said that God told her to stop, which she did; and then asked him what she must do. He told her to leave the road, and turn to the left; she obeyed, and soon came to a small stream of tide water; there was no boat, no bridge; she again inquired of her Guide what she was to do. She was told to go through. It was cold, in the month of March; but having confidence in her Guide, she went in; the water came up to her arm-pits; soon after which she came to a cabin of colored people, who took them all in, put them to bed, and dried their clothes, ready to proceed next night on their journey. Harriet had run out of money, and gave them some of her underclothing to pay for their kindness" (Garrett, 1868).

21. Cheney's summary of some of these precautions is familiar Tubman folklore: "She always came in the winter when the nights are long and dark, and people who

have homes stay in them. She was never seen on the plantation herself, but appointed a rendezvous for her company eight or ten miles distant, so that if they were discovered at the first start she was not compromised. She started on Saturday night; the slaves at that time being allowed to go away from home to visit their friends—so that they would not be missed until Monday morning" (Cheney, 1865).

22. The story was not included in sketches by white writers Holt (1886) and Wyman (1896). Frank Drake (1907) did include it.

23. Bradford included what is almost an ethnographic report by Tubman on the funeral customs of the Gullah-speaking Sea Island people (Bradford, 1869, 42–46).

24. Telford's retelling is generally taken from Bradford, but it inserts a few extra lines she may have derived from a more recent interview with Tubman. I have italicized these insertions by Telford in the text.

25. Valerie Smith (1987) has argued that the antebellum slave narrative "enshrines cultural definitions of masculinity . . . by mythologizing rugged individuality, physical strength, and geographic mobility." McDowell (1991) believes that much contemporary scholarship on slavery has been concerned with "making the slave a man, according to cultural definitions of masculinity (214). She points out that the most anthologized part of Frederick Douglass's 1845 *Narrative* is the fight with the master, Covey. The male slave's defeat of the white master in battle "serves to incarnate a critical/political view that equates resistance to power with physical strength" (52).

26. Mamie Garvin Fields remembered Terrell describing Tubman with two guns! She was wearing "a bandana on her head and boots on her feet, a pistol on her hip and a rifle in her hand" (Fields, 1983, 190).

27. For interesting commentary on the value of public life history storytelling for the elderly, see Myerhoff (1994).

STORIES AND SAYINGS

1. In most cases when newspaper or magazine writers of the late nineteenth and early twentieth centuries included stories that had already appeared in print, they did not use currently accepted techniques for avoiding plagiarism, such as quotation marks and citation of their sources. The result is that it is often very difficult to decide whether a given rendition of a story is really a later-told version collected by that interviewer or simply a lightly rewritten paraphrase from an earlier printed source such as Bradford.

2. Bradford gave this figure as $12,000 in 1869. See appendix B, "A Note on the Numbers."

3. This is an interesting indication of Tubman's ability to play with the idea of violating racial taboos in order to entertain and divert potential enemies.

4. Aunt Lidy is Eliza Wright Osborne, who was evidently trying to capture in writing some of Tubman's life stories at this time. If it still exists, this manuscript generated by Osborne's stenographer has not as yet come to light.

5. Adams is coyly suggesting that Tubman implied that she stole the horse and buggy.

6. Bradford was in error here, apparently. Mary Pattison lived to marry twice, and she bore one son, Edward Brodess. See the introduction.

7. I have not preserved the nonstandard spelling and punctuation of Harkless Bowley's manuscript letters to Conrad.

8. This is the only version of the escape story in which John Tubman actually collaborates in the effort to prevent her escape. While not impossible, it seems unlikely that she would have returned for him later, had she believed in this betrayal.

9. Sanborn renders this as "ladies all dressed in white."

10. This expression of fear that Ritta Ross "would raise an uproar and prevent her going, or insist upon going with her," may suggest an ambivalent mother-daughter relationship at this period. However, as I note in the introduction, it may be Bradford who is editorializing in a negative way here. Ritta Ross appears in the 1863 testimony of Tubman's brother as a fiercely protective parent who was prepared to defend her children in open confrontation with the slave owner, if need be (H. Stewart , 1863).

11. Tubman's quilting ("patchwork") in the context of the rescue missions is also mentioned by Cheney.

12. This is a memorable restatement of a classic moment in Protestant evangelical religious rebirth experience. Tubman apparently feels that her sense of spiritual transformation through self-emancipation should also be reflected in the physical transformation of her body. The "glory" is both the sunshine's glow and the emotional and spiritual exaltation of new personhood.

13. This is an excellent example of Tubman's use of extended metaphors reminiscent of New Testament teaching parables.

14. Harkless Bowley is the only source I have found to suggest that she was directly recruited as an Underground Railroad operative.

15. This was Tubman's niece, Keziah Bowley. See appendix A, "A Note on Harriet Tubman's Kin," for further discussion.

16. This poignant story suggests that Tubman was still very passionately attached to John Tubman at this point, two years after her escape to the North. It seems unlikely that she believed at this time that he had collaborated with those trying to prevent her escape.

17. Compare the report from December 29, 1854, in William Still (1872).

18. In her 1886 revision, Bradford added here: "John assured her that wherever he went she should come. He might not come for her, but he would send Moses, and then he hurried away" (Bradford, 1886, 64–72). This suggests Bradford's understanding that John's wife and her children were among those Tubman rescued later.

19. In the first edition of the Bradford book, "swine's flesh" was mistakenly printed as "sinner's flesh." Ellen Wright Garrison joked about the error in a letter to her mother Martha Coffin Wright, as an instance of Bradford's hasty and sloppy work. See part 4, "Documents," for excerpts from the letter.

20. In the first version of the book, Bradford thought that all three brothers escaped with Harriet at the same time. However, in 1886 she detached the story of the escape of "William Henry" and "Catherine" from that of the Christmas rescue (61–64, 72–73). See appendix A, "A Note on Harriet Tubman's Kin," for further discussion of the somewhat contradictory evidence about the number (and names) of the brothers who participated in the Christmas rescue.

21. This is the rescue described in Thomas Garrett's letter of October 24, 1856 (in part 4, "Documents").

22. The prayer is quite different in Ednah Cheney's earlier version of this story: "The clerk of the boat declined to give her tickets, and told her to wait. She thought he suspected her, and was at a loss how to save herself and her charge, if he did; so she went alone into the bow of the boat, and she says, "I drew in my breath, and I sent it out to the Lord, and I said, O Lord! You know who I am, and where I am, and what I want; and that was all I could say; and again I drew in my breath and I sent it out to the Lord, but that was all I could say; and then again the third time, and just then I felt a touch on my shoulder, and looked round, and the clerk said, 'Here's your tickets'" (Cheney, 1865, 36). A later version, retold just after Tubman's death by the pastor of the M.E. Church, includes a vision: "On one occasion when she was standing on a steamer sailing North, she did not have the passports for her runaway girls. On the shore she saw men that were looking for her, she had asked the captain for passports and he had refused them. She went to the stern of the vessel and leaned over and said, "Lord, I am serving thee and I want them passports," and suddenly she saw in the water the face of the thorn-crowned Jesus and heard him say, "My child, your passports are all right." She went to the captain and asked again, and he handed them out and she walked off in triumph" ("Two Timely Topics Discussed by Doctor Rosengrant," 1913).

23. A letter by Thomas Garrett (1856d) gives an abbreviated account of the arrival of the four men and one woman in New York, where Oliver Johnson of the New York Office of the American Anti-slavery Society saw to their safety. William Still identified three of the male fugitives as Josiah Bailey, William Bailey, and Peter Pennington (Still, 1872, 272).

24. This may have been her seventh or eighth rescue mission *since her own escape*—given what she told antislavery friends in Boston in 1859. See appendix B, "A Note on the Numbers."

25. In William Still's account, Josiah Bailey decided to escape because of a dispute with another slave (Still, 1872, 272). Bradford's version is obviously more heroic.

26. In 1886, Bradford changed the $12,000 figure to $40,000, probably influenced by the figure given in Sallie Holley's printed 1867 letter. See appendix B, "A Note on the Numbers."

27. This abolitionist song was evidently sung to the popular tune, "Oh, Susanna."

28. In the 1886 revision of this story Bradford omitted Joe's expression of determination to resist physical punishment and pride in his own strength.

29. This is Oliver Johnson, of the New York Anti-Slavery Society. When preparing the second version of the biography, Bradford interviewed Johnson and reported, "He remembers Harriet with great pleasure, though he has not seen her for many years. He speaks, as all who knew her do, of his entire confidence in her truthfulness and in the perfect integrity of her character" (Bradford, 1886, 90).

30. Garrett may not have been aware of the fact that Benjamin Ross had purchased Ritta Ross from Eliza Ann Brodas in 1855.

31. Jehu was a King of Israel in the Old Testament (2 Kings 9). His swift chariot driving had become proverbial.

32. Others remembered Harriet Tubman's stories about her parents' reluctance to leave possessions behind: "She told me that, when she found her mother unwilling to leave behind her feather-bed tick, and her father his broad-axe and other tools,

she bundled up bed-tick, broad-axe, mother, father, all, and landed them in Canada" (R. W. Taylor, 1901). "Meantime, she had stolen her aging parents from Maryland, an extra-hazardous venture, since her mother had insisted upon taking along her feather bed and a hencoop full of chickens. Harriet had found it necessary to steal a horse and wagon to carry them" (Adams 1989, 271).

33. This story was new in Bradford's 1886 edition; it also appears, very closely paraphrased from Bradford, in Wyman (1896).

34. In Tatlock's version of the escape story, she gives a quilt to the white woman who helped her escape.

35. It is notable that Tubman paid the poor people who acted as her impromptu hosts. No doubt she was keenly aware that they could not afford to feed extra company uncompensated—and that there was a strong temptation to go to the authorities for a reward.

36. Bradford gives the lyrics as she heard them in this version of the songs (putting the "correct" or original word in parentheses). Here "anger" makes a particularly apt substitution for the "anguish" of the original. Early collectors of African American folk songs of slavery had already pointed to the creative adaptations of lyrics from Methodist and other Protestant hymns (Allen et al., 1995). In the 1886 revision, both songs are changed a bit. After giving the lyrics for the first one, Bradford comments, "The air sung to these words was so wild, so full of plaintive minor strains, and unexpected quavers, that I would defy any white person to learn it, and often as I heard it, it was to me a constant surprise." The second song becomes a version of "Go Down Moses," which she gives as: "Oh go down, Moses / Way down into Egypt's land / Tell old Pharaoh / Let my people go / Oh Pharaoh said he would go cross / Let my people go / And don't get lost in the wilderness / Let my people go / . . . / You may hinder me here, but you can't up there / Let my people go / He sits in the Heaven and answers prayer / Let my people go!" (Bradford 1886, 37–38).

37. I have normalized the spelling in this hymn, removing the efforts at dialect made by Bradford.

38. William Lloyd Garrison II (1897b) recalled being impressed as a child with this missing front tooth when he met Harriet Tubman in the company of Wendell Phillips.

39. See the discussion of the various versions of the revolver story in part 2, "The Life Stories."

40. The $40,000 reward figure is probably an exaggeration, originating with Tubman's abolitionist friends. See appendix B, "A Note on the Numbers."

41. Here Bradford's point is that the slave system condoned the enslavement of "near-white" people, usually the offspring of white slave owners and "mulatto" slave women. White readers were expected to find this particularly shocking.

42. This account by Lillie B. Chace Wyman (1896) was based in part on published accounts of John Brown's life. Wyman had also asked Eliza Wright Osborne to interview Tubman on her behalf for a book of "anti-slavery female sketches" (Wyman, n.d.) Wyman's article on Tubman indicates that they met at least once in person, but does not specify when.

43. One wonders how Tubman understood the mystical three handshakes and comments by Brown, another religious visionary.

44. For a discussion of John Brown's plans for inciting an armed slave insurrection, see part 1, "The Life." Wyman's paraphrase of Tubman's understanding of John Brown's "rules" for the protection of life and property is close to that recorded by Martha Coffin Wright's letter (1869a) to her son-in-law William Lloyd Garrison II.

45. The phrase "It is stated, moreover" suggests that Wyman relied on her reading about John Brown for this assertion, rather than direct testimony from Tubman.

46. This phrase suggests that Wyman did get some of her material from Tubman in person.

47. As one of the six John Brown co-conspirators himself, Sanborn knew that Tubman figured in John Brown's recruiting plans, but he may not have wished to reveal this fact in this sketch, written only four years after the raid, and before the Union victory was assured.

48. Sanborn, a Harvard graduate and associate of Concord's transcendentalist luminaries, seemingly had a condescending attitude toward Tubman's spiritualism.

49. If Sanborn's account is correct, this places Tubman in the state of New York, in the house of a friend, on the day of the raid, October 16, 1859. The story implies that communication between her and Brown had not been established in September.

50. Tubman was evidently staying in Boston with Ednah Cheney on December 16, 1859. In all likelihood, she had met Cheney through Sanborn in the spring of 1859, just a few months before the Harpers Ferry Raid. Cheney may have heard Sanborn mention Tubman's knowledge of John Brown's plans, or she may have been relying on Sanborn's 1863 sketch here.

51. Cheney interrupts the flow of the biographical sketch here to speak emotionally about Emancipation to the Northern abolitionist reader: "Oh how sanguine and visionary it seemed then! but now four little years, and Maryland is free by her own act, and the bells are ringing out the declaration, that slavery is abolished throughout the land; and our Moses may walk, no longer wrapped in darkness, but erect and proud in her native State; and the name of him who was hung on the gallows is a rallying cry for victorious armies; and the stone which the builders rejected has become the head of the corner. What shall we fear whose eyes have seen this salvation?" (Cheney, 1865, 37).

52. Telford evidently followed Bradford's 1869 account very closely, in some places almost word for word. She also included some important details that are not in Bradford. For the reader's convenience, I have italicized these details.

53. For a discussion of Tubman's campaign after the war to receive just compensation for her services, see the part 1, "The Life."

54. Telford may have picked up some of the details of this story from Bradford. However, this version is the only one to emphasize Tubman's ability to cure the doctor—a touch that may reflect Tubman's own sense of humor.

55. This is the only reference to Tubman's visiting Mary Todd Lincoln of which I am aware.

56. The pay disparity was a galling denial of equal respect for African American soldiers in the Union army.

57. Carlton Mabee with Susan Mabee (1993) includes an extensive discussion of the evidence for Sojourner Truth's meeting with Lincoln in October 1864, shortly after this meeting with Tubman in Washington.

58. This quoted phrase refers to retreating into a private place for prayer.

59. "Catherine" may have been a sister-in-law. See appendix A, "A Note on Tubman's Kin."

60. Tubman attended and addressed the New York Woman's Suffrage Association meetings in Rochester in 1896.

61. This young girl was Katy Stewart, later Northrup, whom Harkless Bowley referred to as "the lady Aunt Harriet reared" (H. Bowley, 1939d).

62. In the original, the word was "gin."

63. Here Tubman refers to her poverty in later years, which she attributed in part to the failure of the U.S. government to acknowledge the justice of her claim for a veteran's pension. At this time she did receive a small pension as Nelson Davis's widow. See part 1, "The Life."

64. I can shed no light on this term.

65. In Bradford's original dialect rendition, the phrase is "Good Friday, and five Fridays hand gwine from Good Friday" (Bradford, 1869, 108). While the exact sense is not clear, Tubman evidently refers to a period of fasting on Fridays leading up to the Good Friday of Easter week, as a rite of purification similar to the Roman Catholic fasting during Lent.

66. Frances Adeline Seward, daughter of William and Frances Miller Seward, died in 1866, aged twenty-two.

67. Oddly enough, the writer, Rosa Belle Holt, included two slightly different versions of this story within one magazine article—perhaps simply because of inattentive editing. The other version precedes this one, and reads: "Harriet was known among her people as 'Moses,' and in conversation she says, 'I felt like Moses. The Lord told me to do this. I said, "O Lord, I can't—don't ask me—take somebody else." Then I could hear the Lord answer, "It's you I want, Harriet Tubman"—just as clear I heard him speak—and then I'd go again down South and bring up my brothers and sisters'" (Holt, 1886, 461).

68. Holt evidently remembered Tubman as saying that the Lord addressed her as "Harriet," or "Harriet Tubman," on the occasion of her call. In contrast, Samuel Hopkins Adams, the grandson of Samuel Hopkins, remembered her as having said that God addressed her by her original name, Araminta. "Her relations with the Deity were personal, even intimate, though respectful on her part. He always addressed her as Araminta, which was her christened name. Harriet was her slave name, which she accepted for convenience" (Adams, 1989, 278).

69. This is a reference to the vision of the new Jerusalem or heavenly city in the New Testament Book of Revelation (21:10–27). The Book of Revelation was believed to contain the mystical writing of the evangelist John.

70. Cheney's footnote indicates that "God's time" was commonly understood among abolitionists as a code term for Emancipation (82).

71. In her *Reminiscences* (1902) Cheney expanded on her own earlier article (Cheney, 1865).

72. Tatlock's comment supports a wary interpretation of the "ghost stories" Tubman told during the gold swindle publicity of 1873. See part 1, "The Life."

73. Cheney elaborated on this in 1902: "She had a natural love for beauty and art, especially in sculpture. I never left her alone a little while in my room but I found her

standing in admiration before a cast or a picture, and she was overwhelmed with delight at the present of a little statue" (Cheney, 1902, 81–82).

74. Tubman's story of striking out her own tooth was also recorded by Wyman (1896).

75. Bradford may have been mistaken in her belief that the mortgage to Seward was fully paid by the book sales. See part 1, "The Life."

76. David Munson Osborne, Eliza Wright Osborne's husband, served as mayor of Auburn for two consecutive terms in 1879 and 1880. He died in 1886, the year Bradford's new version of the Tubman biography appeared, but his brother John Hall Osborne seems to have taken over his role in supporting the John Brown Hall project. See part 1, "The Life," for more details.

77. Tubman may have brought Margaret Stewart north just as the Civil War was beginning, in the fall of 1861. See part 1, "The Life." Evidently the "trip by water" was from Baltimore.

78. In a portion of the letter I have omitted, Brickler speaks of a split between Tubman's Northern and Southern relatives and says "several brothers were sold into the deep south during slavery." Since she is the only person who speaks of "brothers" sold south, whereas all the other documentary and testimonial evidence suggests that it was two sisters sold south, I believe she may be misremembering family history in this instance.

DOCUMENTS

1. Because this testimony reads like a series of answers to questions put to her by an interviewer, I have inserted paragraph markers to bring out this quality.

2. This account suggests that the first escape attempt the brothers made on their own probably took place in early 1853, at least eighteen months before the successful Christmas rescue of 1854.

3. The account gives no reason why the brothers, though eager to escape and having already made one try, "wouldn't go" when Harriet Tubman first came for them. It seems to indicate that Tubman stayed in the vicinity of the Brodess plantation for several months, perhaps beginning in fall 1854. Very likely this was the time when she met "the master," Dr. Thompson, and diverted his attention by making chickens flutter, a favorite story she told afterward.

4. This seems to indicate that "a party of ten" participated in the Christmas rescue. Still's account mentions only six arriving in Philadelphia, but it is possible that the party split up before arriving in Philadelphia and arrived in two groups.

5. The Harpers Ferry Raid publicity had suggested that she was involved, though probably ill at the time of the raid itself. Presumably she sent her family a dictated letter to relieve their anxieties about her at this time. She had been absent from Auburn at least since June.

6. "Brother John" may refer to John Bowley, who was married to their niece Keziah.

7. This phrase was inserted over the line in the manuscript.

8. Sarah Bradford helped Tubman's parents send dictated letters to Tubman during the war. See part 1, "The Life."

9. The original manuscript of this letter, listed among Sanborn's papers in *Libbie's Sale Catalogue* in 1917, seems to have been bought for a private collection. I have been unable to locate it. This text is based on the portion of the letter printed by Sanborn in "Harriet Tubman" in the *Boston Commonwealth* (1863). Sanborn added, after the printed excerpt: "it appears that she needs some contributions for her work. We trust she will receive them, for none has better deserved it. She asks nothing for herself, except that her wardrobe may be replenished, and even this she will probably share with the first needy person she meets." Tubman's extra personal request to Sanborn for financial aid was not printed, but it was quoted in Kenneth Walter Cameron (1982), 24.

10. Cheney did send a check for $20 to Kellogg, a friend of Eliza Wright Osborne, asking that the money be given to Tubman, with the wish "that she should use the money for her own comfort," and Kellogg wrote again to acknowledge the gift on June 25 (Kellogg, 1894b).

11. Jane B. Kellogg wrote the April 9 letter at the Osborne house on South Street in Auburn; her later thank you note to Cheney was sent from 17 High Street, Orange, New Jersey.

12. This letter was dictated in Syracuse, New York.

13. Under the title of this section, William Still included the names "John Chase, Alias Daniel Floyd; Benjamin Ross, Alias James Stewart; Henry Ross, Alias Levin Stewart; Peter Jackson, Alias Staunch Tilghman; Jane Kane, Alias Catherine Kane; and Robert Ross."

14. For a discussion of the evolution of the wording of her threat here, see part 2, "The Life Stories."

15. *Ex parte*, a legal term meaning "from one side only," refers to bias in testimony. Still uses the term ironically here.

16. This "sister," Mary Ann Williamson, may be the daughter of an older sister sold south. See appendix A, "A Note on Harriet Tubman's Kin."

17. Robert Ross, Tubman's elder brother, was working for Dr. Anthony Tompson in 1853. Robert Ross later took the name John Stewart.

18. This would appear to be an otherwise undocumented rescue of one person. See appendix B, "A Note on the Numbers."

19. "Table rappings" refers to the way spirits of the dead communicated with the living in the type of séance spiritualism made popular in the later 1840s and 1850s by the Fox sisters of Rochester, New York. Many Garrisonian abolitionists were drawn to spiritualism at this time.

20. This is a fascinating example of the use of Tubman stories as cultural currency among her abolitionist friends many years before published accounts were available. It also indicates that James and Lucretia Mott were acquainted with Tubman at least by 1856, and probably several years earlier.

21. This is the only case I am aware of in which Tubman's mother's first name is recorded as anything other than Harriet (or its nicknames, Ritta, Rit, Ritty, and Rittia). Perhaps she used "Catherine" as an alias for the escape.

22. The identity of this man referred to as the "master" is not yet clear. Given that Benjamin Ross described Anthony C. Thompson in completely negative terms to William Still, it seems unlikely to have been Thompson who warned him to flee.

Garrett's assertion (which he repeated in his letter to Bradford in 1868) that Harriet Ross "belonged to another plantation" at this time is erroneous. She had been purchased by her husband from Eliza Ann Brodess in 1855.

23. I have not as yet located these letters.

24. Sanborn is writing in the coded language used by the co-conspirators in case the letters should fall into the wrong hands. The "missionary" work may refer to her fund-raising for further Maryland trips to rescue slaves, but it could also refer to recruiting for John Brown's planned Harpers Ferry expedition. I have not located any sources that show direct contact between Tubman and John Brown during the summer months of 1859, however—and several sources suggest that they were not in communication. See part 1, "The Life."

25. The original gave Tubman's speech in very heavy dialect. I have normalized spelling and punctuation in the passages that represent themselves as quotations.

26. Child used another version of Tubman's comment in a letter, written two weeks later, to Joseph Carpenter: "Harriet Tubman, the fugitive slave whom we call Moses, because she brings so many out of bondage, says, 'God's ahead of Master Lincoln. God never let Master Lincoln beat the south, till he do the right thing.' I confess about all the hope and trust I have, is that 'God's ahead of Master Lincoln'" (Child, 1862b).

27. Sanborn reprinted portions of this report in the *Commonwealth* issue for July 10, 1863, commenting that "the above, . . . will remind many of our readers of their interviews with the heroine here mentioned—Harriet Tubman. She has a more remarkable history than any fugitive we have ever met, some portions of which we shall give in our next issue" ("Harriet Tubman," 1963).

28. This would seem to be the first estimate of the number of rescued slaves that exceeds 100—though the number of trips is still listed as nine. The journalist here, evidently meeting Tubman for the first time, was probably mistaken (after all, if there were only nine trips, she would have had to average 20 people per trip.). The number may be a simple misprint for 80.

29. Charlotte Forten also recorded Tubman's wish to go north, as early as January 1863. Her anxiety over the support of her parents and other dependents living in Auburn during the war was evidently very strong.

30. I have retained the dialect Martha Coffin Wright used to represent Tubman's speech in this letter because it sheds light on the unconscious condescension of even her very strongest white antislavery supporters.

31. Along with Wood's manuscript of the oral history narrative, copies of letters from General Hunter, Secretary Seward, Colonel Montgomery, General Saxton, and several others were originally sent to Congress by Seward through Auburn's Congressman Clinton MacDowell, sometime between 1868 and Seward's death in 1872. The documents were ultimately used in the final successful effort to obtain a Civil War widow's pension in 1897–1898 (Conrad, 1950, 90).

32. If Phillips is correct, Tubman may have made more than one trip to Maryland sponsored by her New England antislavery friends (after 1859). At least one of these has been amply documented—a trip from which she returned in December 1860 (and for which she prepared by asking Wendell Phillips for funds). She may also have made an otherwise undocumented trip to Baltimore in the fall of 1861, from which

she returned with Margaret Stewart. This is suggested by her bringing Sanborn news about escapes from Maryland when she visited him that fall.

33. Bradford's original text had "1845," but this is evidently a misprint for 1854— after all, Tubman didn't leave Maryland until 1849, and she only began to appear in Garrett's letters in 1854.

34. Sanborn later qualified his vague overstatement in this testimonial letter with a more precise estimate of how many days Tubman had spent in Concord altogether from 1859 (Sanborn, 1913a). Apparently in later years he felt that his testimonial letter to Bradford had led some biographers to exaggerate greatly the degree of her intimacy with the Concord transcendentalist literary luminaries.

35. In the obituary sketch (1913a), Sanborn portrayed the relationship between Higginson, Montgomery, and Tubman as more complicated than in this testimonial letter.

36. Douglass addressed his testimonial letter directly to Tubman, but he was answering the question Bradford asked of all the testimonial writers—whether Tubman was trustworthy as a witness to her own adventures.

37. If James A. Bowley was Ritta Ross's great grandson, this would confirm the hypothesis that the visitor's mother, Keziah Bowley, was Tubman's niece, the daughter of an elder sister. James Bowley had himself written a testimonial letter for the Bradford book that was not ultimately included—nor was the letter Lucretia Mott wrote in response to Martha Coffin Wright's request.

38. Martha Coffin Wright frequently used humor to make her letters to family members more entertaining. In this postwar period when the financial and other needs of recently freed slaves were great, Wright's tone of comic exasperation suggests some of the ambivalence generated in the white antislavery community of the North, as it extended itself to help raise funds for freedmen's aid.

39. Earlier in the same year, Martha Coffin Wright reported on another fair for freedmen's aid that raised over $400, held at the Central Church (M. C. Wright, 1868d).

40. Martha Coffin Wright was more generous about the Bradford book than was her daughter Ellen Wright Garrison, who made fun of Sarah Bradford's work with Tubman's interview material.

41. This may be Elizabeth Fitzhugh Birney, niece of Gerrit Smith and widow of abolitionist James G. Birney, who died in 1857.

42. Tubman and her husband Nelson Davis operated a brickyard on the back section of their seven-acre property at this time (Kate Larson, personal communication, December 2002).

43. James A. Bowley's testimonial letter (June 1868) describes the same self-sacrifice on Tubman's part as is summarized by Wright here. Perhaps this is the letter Tubman brought to show her friends. Thanks to Kate Larson for calling my attention to the existence of this letter.

44. By "How funny it must seem to him," Wright presumably means that the vast transformation in his station in life, from slave to legislator, must seem "peculiar" to the nephew.

45. Again, Wright imitates Tubman's Southern rural pronunciation of words here, perhaps fondly, in the privacy of her correspondence with her daughter. Wright

obviously admires Tubman's self-sacrificial labor on behalf of her grandnephew's education, as well as the care lavished on the grandnephew's mother, yet her attitude does seem condescending. Note that if Wright is correct, the grandnephew's escape from Baltimore happened as much as two years before Tubman had saved enough money to "get his Ma away." See appendix B, "A Note on the Numbers."

46. One of the ways David and Martha Wright helped Tubman support herself and her dependents during this period was to offer some occasional employment in housework.

47. Harriet Tubman was taken to the Howland home to recuperate.

48. David Munson Osborne, the husband of Eliza Wright Osborne, owned an increasingly successful agricultural implements business at this time. John Stewart had obtained employment there in part because of his sister's close connection with the Wright and Osborne families.

49. "Ringing in" is contemporary slang for getting the victim to trust the confidence man (the trickster or hustler).

50. Tubman's celebrity status clearly had its disadvantages.

51. An earlier news account of the robbery had probably appeared on October 2, the day after the evening robbery.

52. Evidently the confidence men were referring to James A. Bowley, the Reconstruction South Carolina legislator who was Tubman's grandnephew. See appendix A, "A Note on Harriet Tubman's Kin," for further discussion.

53. The first paragraph of this newspaper account was also included in Isabel Howland (1896).

54. This quotation has not been recorded elsewhere, so far as I am aware.

55. Rev. B. F. Wheeler reported to the church conference in 1904 that "The deed conveying the property to the church stipulates that when the trustees see their way clear to do so, they shall establish on the ground besides the home, a school of domestic science where girls may be taught the various branches of industrial education. This feature of the work is particularly popular with the white people in this western part of the state of New York" (Walls, 1974, 442).

56. According to Wheeler's 1904 report, again, Tubman deeded the property to the church "reluctantly," only after unsuccessfully attempting to deed it to a trusted individual instead. She first asked Robert Taylor, the Tuskegee financial agent, to receive it, and then made the same request of B. F. Wheeler. "As some of Aunt Harriet's white friends were bitterly opposed to her deeding the property to us, we had to make generous provisions for her in drawing the deed," he said—including giving her "life interest in all money accruing from rents." The church also had to pay off three outstanding mortgages on the property as a condition of the deed—one held by Tubman's brother William H. Stewart for $371 (Walls, 1974, 441, 442).

57. Tubman's opposition to charging residents a fee was one of reasons she did not want to give over management to the church. See discussion in part 1, "The Life."

58. I have placed in brackets a few additional details found in the competing newspaper's similar account of the funeral ("To Aunt Harriet," 1913).

59. A more complete text of the eulogy sermon by Bishop Blackwell was printed the next day in the *Auburn Citizen*, under the title "A Race of Harriets Would Secure the Future of the Negro, Says Bishop Blackwell" (1913).

60. The phrase in brackets appears in the typescript version of this sketch, "The late Araminta Davis" (Sanborn, 1913a), but not in the published version (Sanborn, 1913b).

61. The surviving documentary evidence suggests that Tubman actually first met Sanborn in Boston in May 1859.

62. This is the only assertion I have been able to locate that Tubman was "censured" in some way during her war service.

63. This song is usually associated with her singing to the freed people to keep them from swamping the boats during the Combahee River Raid.

64. Alice Lucas Brickler mentioned her memory of this event to Earl Conrad (A. Brickler, 1939a).

APPENDIX A

1. I gratefully acknowledge the generosity of fellow researchers James McGowan and Kate Larson, both of whom provided me with important documents and personal communications as I was completing work on this book. Larson's forthcoming book, *Bound for the Promised Land: Harriet Tubman, Portrait of an American Heroine*, will be an invaluable guide to the complex histories of Tubman kinfolk.

2. Larson believes that Thompson's 1853 list of Ritta Ross's children cannot be regarded as absolutely reliable. She has found evidence suggesting that there may have been another daughter mentioned by Thompson.

3. Thompson also testified in 1853 as to their monetary value: "Witness had in his possession at one time three of them, two boys and a girl, for which he paid $120.00 a year, he has now Robert in his possession for which he pays $55.00 per year.... Witness thinks Robert, Harry & Ben would sell for $800.00 each in the County. If Mose was in the County now he would sell for $500.00. Minty being always sickly I don't think she would bring over $200—or $250."

4. Kate Larson believes this is the case with the "Mary" who worked in the kitchen at the time of Tubman's escape (personal communication, June 2002).

5. Tubman said in 1855, "I had two sisters carried away in a chain-gang—one of them left two children." Her brother said in 1863, "I had a sister, who had a young child, about two or three months old, & the master came after her to sell her to Georgia.... And he comes & gets her & sells her down to Georgia, and leaves that young child; and on his death-bed, sometime after the mother was sold, his greatest cry was 'Take this young child away from me!'"

6. Kate Larson has identified John Bowley's wife's first name as Keziah (personal communication, June 2002).

7. Bradford's 1869 account of the Christmas rescue included all three brothers. When she rewrote it in 1886, just two brothers escaped at Christmas, and Bradford was vague about when the third brother escaped, bringing his sweetheart "Catherine," dressed as a boy. She implied that it was at a different time. A Canadian newspaper story after Tubman's death quoted the Rev. R. A. Ball of the British Methodist Episcopal Church as remembering that on Tubman's "first escape from slavery" she brought two of her brothers; and then on a subsequent rescue she brought "William and his wife and child" ("This is British Soil," 1913). Some biographers, including Conrad, following Sanborn, believe that one brother was rescued along with two other men

prior to 1851, probably from Baltimore. Conrad inferred, probably mistakenly, that the brother who later was called "John Stewart" had escaped several years earlier than the other two who came to Canada. Kate Larson's research suggests the possibility that the youngest brother, Moses, may have reached Canada by 1850 or 1851 (personal communication, June 2002).

8. John Stewart (or Steward) was listed in the Auburn City street directories as a "teamster" with a house on South Street (near Hamilton), in 1867–1868; as a "teamster" with a house on South (near Swift) in 1873–1874; and as a "teamster" with a house at 101 South Street in 1876–1877. "John Stewart" also appears in the Cayuga County Census for 1880 as a sixty-five-year-old black male residing in Fleming with a sixty-one-year-old black female (Millie) and a twenty-seven-year-old black male (Moses). This Moses Stewart, whose age means that he was born around the year of the 1854 Christmas escape, may have been one of the two sons of John Stewart that were brought north by John Bowley later on.

9. William Henry Stewart's name appears linked with Tubman's as early as 1861, in a reference in the *Liberator* to a fugitive slave relief fund in St. Catharines (December 1861).

10. William Henry Stewart Jr. settled in 1880 in a house on Garrow Street that is currently occupied by some of his descendants, according to a personal communication from Kate Larson (June 2002).

11. I am grateful to Kate Larson for supplying the death dates of the brothers in Auburn

12. In 1886 Bradford detached this story from her account of the 1854 Christmas rescue story and said that it occurred on "one of" Tubman's rescues. She also added that Catherine was a "pretty mulatto." Kate Larson's research indicates that Catherine (who was the Jane Kane listed by William Still in the 1854 Christmas rescue party) was actually the wife of James Stewart (formerly Benjamin Ross). She came to Auburn in 1865 with two or three children to live temporarily in Tubman's household, later remarrying and relocating in Auburn with her second husband (personal communication, June 2002).

13. John and Keziah Bowley's family returned south after the war, staying with Tubman for a year in Auburn on the way. The older grandnephew, James Bowley, was mentioned in a letter from Martha Coffin Wright to her nieces, dated September 11, 1868. "He lived in Canada till the War, & now teaches the freedmen in S. Carolina—He was one of the first that Harriet rescued from slavery" (1868g). In the following year, writing to her daughter in Boston, Wright noted that Tubman had visited with a letter "from her nephew whom William met here, once—he is a member of the S. Carolina legislature!—His letter was well written—How funny it must seem to him—Harriet, after getting him from de Souf—worked out two years at a dollar a week & paid 50 cts a week for his board, & sent him to school—then she saved up enough to get his Ma away & nursed her thro' a fit of sickness after she came Norf" (M. C. Wright, (1869h).

14. At Lucas's death the newspapers said that she was born in Baltimore, but "brought to this city when a young girl by Harriet Tubman, for whom the Harriet Tubman Home was named, and who was her foster-mother" ("Foster Child of Harriet Tubman Dies," 1930).

15. Kate Larson develops an interesting theory as to the identity of the family from which Margaret Stewart came (Larson, forthcoming).

16. Conrad discovered that there were divisions within the branches of the family of Tubman sibling descendants when he corresponded with Brickler and Bowley. Harkless Bowley knew Katy Stewart Northrup well, but Alice Brickler did not recognize her married name, although they had known each other in childhood in Auburn.

17. Bradford includes in her 1901 report of Tubman's visit to a suffrage convention the following note: "She was led into the church by an adopted daughter, whom she had rescued from death when a baby, and had brought up as her own."

APPENDIX B

1. James McGowan first pointed out Bradford's unreliability with numbers several years ago and challenged historians to correct the record (McGowan, 1994, 5).

2. One bit of evidence to support my guess is that Sanborn underestimated the number of rescues of her middle career. He says, "Between 1852 and 1857, she made but two of these journeys" (1863). If we assume that he is referring to the years 1853–1856, he is missing at least four trips documented in Garrett's letters and Still: one in 1854, one in 1855, and at least two and possibly three in 1856, depending upon whether the Tillie rescue from Baltimore is counted separately.

3. This grandnephew in the Bowley family was one of Tubman's earliest rescues, according to Martha Coffin Wright—perhaps preceding the rescue of John Bowley's wife and other children by as much as two years (M. C. Wright, 1868g). Perhaps he was one of the party including "a brother and two men" given by Sanborn as an 1851 rescue from Baltimore. Alternatively, the rescue of this grandnephew may have been a separate event not noted by Sanborn, perhaps as early as 1850.

4. Tubman tended to bring out parties numbering between one and nine—the largest number recorded in contemporary documents is eleven. In one case, she is said to have collected a large group of thirty-nine and sent them on "in the care of others, as from some cause she was prevented from accompanying them" (Bradford, 1869, 25). Perhaps Bradford counted this larger group in the total numbers, but I have not done so.

5. William Still confirmed these figures of the rewards offered for "Joe" (Josiah Bailey) and two others in the party, William Bailey ($300) and Peter Pennington ($800) and included the advertisement in his book (Still, 1872, 272). (Garrett uses the old-fashioned term "shilling" for "dollar.")

6. In 1886, Bradford changed the figures given for the escalating reward for the members of the Joe party to $1,000, then $1,500, and finally $2,000 (43); she also changed the reward for Tubman from her original figure of $12,000 to $40,000. She apparently decided to take Sallie Holley's printed article as a more reliable source than Tubman's memory.

BIBLIOGRAPHY

ARCHIVES AND MANUSCRIPT COLLECTIONS

AL   Alma Lutz Collection, Schlesinger Library, Harvard University, Cambridge, Massachusetts

BPL   Boston Public Library Rare Book Room, Manuscript Division

BS   Boyd B. Stutler Collection, West Virginia Division of Culture and History, Charleston, West Virginia

BU   Brock University Special Collections, St. Catharines, Ontario

CCC   Cayuga County Clerk's Office, Auburn, New York

CM   Cayuga Museum and Case Research Lab Museum, Auburn, New York

DCC   Dorchester County Courthouse, Dorchester, Maryland

EC-CCC Earl Conrad Collection, Cayuga Community College, Auburn, New York

EC-NY   Earl Conrad / Harriet Tubman Collection, Schomburg Center for Research in Black Culture, New York Public Library (Collection available on microfilm)

EDC   Ednah D. Cheney Papers, Rare Book Room, Manuscript Division, Boston Public Library

EH-CU   Emily Howland Papers, Division of Rare and Manuscript Collections, Cornell University Library, Ithaca, New York

EHF   Emily Howland Family Papers, Friends' Historical Library, Swarthmore College, Swarthmore, Pennsylvania

FBS-AAS Franklin B. Sanborn Papers, American Antiquarian Society, Worcester, Massachusetts

FBS-BU   Franklin B. Sanborn Collection, Special Collections, Boston University Library

FBS-CFPL Franklin B. Sanborn Papers, Concord Free Public Library, Concord, Massachusetts

FBS-HSP Franklin B. Sanborn Papers, Historical Society of Pennsylvania, Philadelphia

FBS-HU   Franklin B. Sanborn Letters, Houghton Library, Harvard University

FBS-LC   Franklin B. Sanborn Papers, Manuscript Division, Library of Congress, Washington, D.C.
FD-LC   Frederick Douglass Papers, Manuscript Division, Library of Congress
FD-MS   Frederick Douglass Papers, Moorland-Spingarn Research Center, Howard University, Washington, D.C.
FD-NYHS   Frederick Douglass Letters, New York Historical Society
FHL   Friends' Historical Library, Swarthmore College
FWH-CU   Florence Woolsey Hazzard Papers, Cornell University Library
FWH-HU   Florence Woolsey Hazzard Papers, Schlesinger Library, Harvard University
GF   Garrison Family Papers, Sophia Smith Collection, Smith College, Northampton, Massachusetts
GHS   Geneva Historical Society, Geneva, New York
GS-LC   Gerrit Smith Letters, Manuscript Division, Library of Congress
GS-SU   Gerrit Smith Papers, George Arrents Research Library, Syracuse University, Syracuse, New York
HR   Records of the House of Representatives, National Archives and Records Administration, Washington, D.C.
HTH   Harriet Tubman Home Museum, Auburn, New York
JAG   Records of the Office of the Judge Advocate General (Army), National Archives and Records Administration
JB   John Brown Papers, Kansas State Historical Society, Topeka
JMC   Jean Mahoney Collection, Harriet Tubman Materials, Seymour Public Library, Auburn, New York
LC   Library of Congress, Washington D.C.
LMC-CU   Lydia Maria Child Papers, Cornell University Library
LMC-LC   Lydia Maria Child Papers, Manuscript Division, Library of Congress
MHS   Massachusetts Historical Society, Boston
NACWC   National Association of Colored Women's Clubs Records, 1895–1992, microfilm, 26 reels
NEFA   New England Freedmen's Aid Society Collection, Massachusetts Historical Society, Boston
OF   Osborne Family Papers, George Arrents Research Library, Syracuse University
PEM   Peabody Essex Museum, Salem, Massachusetts
QC   Quaker Collection, Haverford College, Haverford, Pennsylvania
RLA   Rochester Ladies' Anti-Slavery Society Papers, William L. Clements Library, University of Michigan, Ann Arbor
SC   Siebert Collection of Underground Railroad Manuscripts, Houghton Library, Harvard University
SCC   Surrogate's Court, Cayuga County, Auburn, New York
SCM   St. Catharines Museum, St. Catharines, Ontario
SSC   Sophia Smith Collection, Smith College
SFP   Smith Family Papers, New York Public Library
SH   Seward House Museum, Auburn, New York
SMA   Samuel May Anti-Slavery Collection, Cornell University Library

SPL   Seymour Public Library, Auburn, New York
TFP   Talbert Family Papers, Buffalo and Erie County Historical Society,
             Buffalo, New York
TPC   Thomas P. Cope Family Papers, Quaker Collection, Haverford College
             Library
TWH-AAS   Thomas Wentworth Higginson Papers, American Antiquarian Society
TWH-H   Thomas Wentworth Higginson Papers, Houghton Library, Harvard
             University
UR   University of Rochester, Rochester, New York
VP   Villard Papers, Columbia University, New York
WHS   William H. Seward Papers, Rare Books Department, Rush Rees
             Library, University of Rochester
WP   Papers of Wendell Phillips, Houghton Library, Harvard University
WS   William Still Papers, Historical Society of Pennsylvania

PRINTED SOURCES

Note: Individual primary sources containing references to Harriet Tubman are designated with an asterisk (*). Especially valuable sources based on eyewitness accounts
and/or interviews are designated with a double asterisk (**).

Abbott, Martin. (1967). *The Freedmen's Bureau in South Carolina, 1865–1872.* Chapel
    Hill: University of North Carolina Press.
*Abbott, W. E. (1856, November 29). Letter to Maria G. Porter. RLA.
Abrahams, Roger D. (1985). *Afro-American Folktales: Stories from Black Traditions in
    the New World.* New York: Pantheon.
Acquittal of a Murderer. (1867, December 23). *Baltimore American.*
Acquittal of a Murderer. (1867, December 23). *Cambridge (Maryland) Intelligencer.*
*Adams, Charles G. (1894, September 4). Certificate of Harriet Tubman's mortgage
    debt to D. Edwin French. Filed with Harriet Tubman Vital Records, CCC.
Adams, Marie Jeanne. (1996). The Harriet Powers Pictorial Quilts. In Weisenfeld and
    Newman (1996), 21–31.
**Adams, Samuel Hopkins. (1989). A Slave in the Family. In *Grandfather Stories,* 268–
    279. (Rev. ed.) Syracuse: Syracuse University Press. (Original work published 1947)
Adams, Virginia M. (Ed.). (1991). *On the Altar of Freedom: A Black Soldier's Civil War
    Letters from the Front.* Amherst: University of Massachusetts Press.
Affray in Boston. (1860, December 15). *Harper's Weekly,* 788.
Alcott, Louisa May. (1960). *Hospital Sketches.* Cambridge: Harvard University Press.
    (Original work published 1863)
*All This Since '81. (1914, June 8). *Auburn (N.Y.) Citizen,* 5.
Allen, William Francis, Charles Pickard Ware, and Lucy McKim Garrison (Eds.).
    (1995). *Slave Songs of the United States.* Bedford, Mass.: Applewood Books. (Origi-
    nal work published 1867)
*A. M. E. Zion Church Plans Pilgrimage (1982, May 26). *Auburn (N.Y.) Citizen.*
Anderson, James D. (1988). *The Education of Blacks in the South, 1860–1935.* Chapel
    Hill: University of North Carolina Press.

Andrews, William L. (1982). The First Fifty Years of the Slave Narrative, 1760–1810. In Sekora and Turner (1982), 6–24.

———. (Ed). (1986a). *Sisters of the Spirit.* Bloomington: Indiana University Press.

———. (1986b). *To Tell a Free Story: The First Century of Afro-American Autobiography, 1760–1865.* Urbana: University of Illinois Press.

———. (1988). Dialogue in Antebellum Afro-American Autobiography. In James Olney (Ed.), *Studies in Autobiography.* New York: Oxford University Press, 89–98.

———. (Ed.). (1989). The Representation of Slavery and the Rise of Afro-American Literary Realism, 1865–1920. In McDowell and Rampersad (1989), 62–80.

———. (Ed.). (1991). *Critical Essays on Frederick Douglass.* Boston: Twayne.

———. (Ed.). (1993). *African American Autobiography: A Collection of Critical Essays.* Englewood Cliffs, N.J.: Prentice-Hall.

———. (Ed.). (1996). *The Oxford Frederick Douglass Reader.* New York: Oxford University Press.

*Anthony, Susan B. (1903, January 1). Inscription on flyleaf of Bradford biography. Susan B. Anthony Collection, Library of Congress.

*At Church of Zion Body of Harriet Tubman Will Lie in State. (1913, March 12). *Auburn (N.Y.) Citizen.*

*Auburn, N.Y., city deeds.

*Auburn, N.Y., city directories, 1857–1913.

*Aunt Harriet Was Very Old. (1913, March 12). *Auburn (N.Y.) Daily Advertiser.*

*Aunt Harriet's Funeral. (1913, March 13). *Auburn (N.Y.) Daily Advertiser,* 6.

Bacon, Margaret Hope. (1980). *Valiant Friend: Life of Lucretia Mott.* New York: Walker.

*Bailie, Helen Tufts. (1897, April 6). Journal entry. SSC.

**Baird, Mrs. Gen. A. (1864, November 24). Testimonial letter. In Bradford (1869), 66.

Baker, Houston A., Jr. (1991). *Workings of the Spirit: The Poetics of Afro-American Women's Writings.* Chicago: University of Chicago Press.

Barkley-Brown, Elsa. (1997). To Catch the Vision of Freedom: Reconstructing Southern Black Women's Political History, 1865–1880. In A. Gordon (1997), 66–99.

**Barnes, V. K. (N.d. [1865]). Letter to Hon. William H. Seward. In Wood (1868), 5.

Bartlett, Irving. (1961). *Wendell Phillips: Brahmin Radical.* Boston: Beacon Press.

Baum, Freda. (1984). The Scarlet Strand: Reform Motifs in the Writings of Louisa May Alcott. In Stern (1984), 250–255.

Benstock, Shari. (1988). *The Private Self: Theory and Practice of Women's Autobiographical Writings.* Chapel Hill: University of North Carolina Press.

Berkeley, Kathleen C., 1985. "Colored Ladies Also Contributed": Black Women's Activities from Benevolence to Social Welfare. In Walter J. Fraser Jr. et al. (Eds.), *The Web of Southern Social Relations: Women, Family and Education,* 181–185. Athens: University of Georgia Press.

Berlin, Ira. (1998). *Many Thousands Gone: The First Two Centuries of Slavery in North America.* Cambridge: Harvard University Press.

Berlin, Ira, et al. (Eds.) (1982, 1985). *The Destruction of Slavery:* Vol. 1, *Freedom: A Documentary History of Emancipation.* Vol. 2, *The Black Military Experience.* New York: Cambridge University Press.

Berlin, Ira, et al. (Eds.). (1998). *Remembering Slavery: African Americans Talk about Their Personal Experiences of Slavery and Emancipation.* New York: New Press.

Blackett, R. J. M. (1983). *Building an Antislavery Wall: Black Americans in the Atlantic Abolitionist Movement, 1830–1860*. Baton Rouge: Louisiana State University Press.

*Blackwell, Alice Stone. (1939a, July 24). Letter to Earl Conrad. EC-NY.

*Blackwell, Alice Stone. (1939b, July 25). Letter to Earl Conrad. EC-NY.

Blassingame, John W. (1975, November). Using the Testimony of Ex-Slaves: Approaches and Problems. *Journal of Southern History 41*, 473–492.

———— (Ed.). (1977). *Slave Testimony.* Baton Rouge: Louisiana State University Press.

———— (Ed.). (1979–1991, 1999). *The Frederick Douglass Papers.* Series One, Speeches, Debates and Interviews, 4 vols. Series Two, Autobiographical Writings, 1 vol. New Haven: Yale University Press.

Blassingame, John W., et al. (1984). *Antislavery Newspapers and Periodicals.* 5 vols. New York: G. K. Hall, 1984.

*Blatch, Harriet Stanton. (1939, May 31). Letter to Earl Conrad. EC-NY.

Block, Sharon. (1999). Lines of Color, Lines of Service: Comparative Sexual Coercion in Early America. In Martha Hodes, (Ed.), *Sex, Love, Race: Crossing Boundaries in North American History,* 141–163. New York: New York University Press.

Blockson, Charles L. (1987). *The Underground Railroad.* New York: Berkley.

*Booker T. Washington Urges Colored Men to Go on Farms. (1914, June 15). *Auburn (N.Y.) Advertiser-Journal.*

Botume, Elizabeth Hyde. (1893). *First Days among the Contrabands.* Boston: Lee and Shepard.

**Bowley, Harkless. (1939a, August 8). Letter to Earl Conrad. EC-NY.

**————. (1939b, August 15). Letter to Earl Conrad. EC-NY.

**————. (1939c, August 24). Letter to Earl Conrad. EC-NY.

**————. (1939d, November 26). Letter to Earl Conrad. EC-NY.

**————. (1940a, January 4). Letter to Earl Conrad. EC-NY.

**————. (1940b, May 1). Letter to Earl Conrad. EC-NY.

**Bowley, James A. (1868, June). Testimonial Letter to Harriet Tubman. HTH.

Bracey, John H., et al. (Eds.). (1971). *Blacks in the Abolitionist Movement.* Belmont, Calif.: Wadsworth.

Bradford, Sarah Hopkins. (1855). *Ups and Downs; or Silverlake Sketches.* Auburn, N.Y.: Alden, Beardsley.

**————. (1869). *Scenes in the Life of Harriet Tubman.* Auburn, N.Y.: W. J. Moses.

**————. (1886). *Harriet, the Moses of Her People.* New York: George R. Lockwood and Son. (Reprinted 1897)

**————. (1901). *Harriet, the Moses of Her People.* (Rev. ed.) New York: J. J. Little.

**————. (N.d. [1900? 1901?], May 11). Letter to Franklin B. Sanborn. FBS-BU.

*Bragg, George Freeman. (1914). *Men of Maryland.* Baltimore: Church Advocate Press.

Braude, Ann. (1989). *Radical Spirits: Spiritualism and Women's Rights in Nineteenth-Century America.* Boston: Beacon.

*Brawley, Benjamin Griffith. (1919). *Women of Achievement.* Chicago: Women's American Baptist Home Mission Society.

————. (1937). Harriet Tubman and Her "Underground Railroad." In *Negro Builders and Heroes,* 67–72. Chapel Hill: University of North Carolina Press.

Braxton, Joanne. (1989). *Black Women Writing Autobiography: A Tradition within a Tradition.* Philadelphia: Temple University Press.

Breault, Judith Colucci (1974). *The World of Emily Howland, Odyssey of a Humanitarian.* Millbrae, Calif. Les Femmes.

Brereton, Virginia. (1991). *From Sin to Salvation: American Women's Conversion Narratives, 1800–1980.* Bloomington: Indiana University Press.

**Brickler, Alice H. (Mrs. Alexander D. Brickler). (1939a, July 19). Letter to Earl Conrad. EC-NY.

**———. (1939b, July 28). Letter to Earl Conrad. EC-NY.

**———. (1939c, August 14). Letter to Earl Conrad. EC-NY.

**———. (1939d, September 6). Letter to Earl Conrad. EC-NY.

**———. (1939e, November 7). Letter to Earl Conrad. EC-NY.

**———. (1940a, January 13). Letter to Earl Conrad. EC-NY.

**———. (1940b, January 27). Letter to Earl Conrad. EC-NY.

**———. (1940c, April 16). Letter to Earl Conrad. EC-NY.

**———. (1940d, April 23). Letter to Earl Conrad. EC-NY.

**———. (1940e, September 4). Letter to Earl Conrad. EC-NY.

**———. (1940f, November 26). Letter to Earl Conrad. NYNYPL.

*Brodess, Eliza. (1855, June 11). Bill of sale issued to Benjamin Ross for the purchase of Ritta Ross. County Court House, Dorchester County, Md.

**Brooks, E. U. A. (1911, June 7). Letter to Booker T. Washington. In Harlan and Smock (1980), 195.

**———. (N.d. [1950?]). In Memory of Harriet Tubman, By One Who Knew Her. In Walls (n.d.), *Harriet Tubman Home,* [1–5].

Brown, Elsa Barkley. (1997). To Catch the Vision of Freedom: Reconstructing Southern Black Women's Political History, 1865–1880. In A. D. Gordon (1997), 66–99.

*Brown, Hallie Q. (1926). Harriet the Moses. In *Homespun Heroines and Other Women of Distinction.* Xenia, Ohio: Hallie Q. Brown.

**Brown, John. (1858a). Diary, 1855–1859. BPL.

**———. (1858b, April 8). Letter to John Brown Jr. In Sanborn (1969) 452.

Brown, Sterling A. (1985). On Dialect Usage. In Davis and Gates (1985), 37–39.

Brown, William Wells (1848). *Narrative of William W. Brown, A Fugitive Slave, Written by Himself. Boston: American Anti-Slavery Society.* Reprinted in William L. Andrews (Ed.) (1993). *From Fugitive Slave to Free Man: The Autobiographies of William Wells Brown.* New York: Mentor.

**Brown, William Wells. (1874). Moses. In *The Rising Son: or The Antecedents and Advancement of the Colored Race,* 536–539. Boston: A. G. Brown.

*Bryant, Gladys. (1965, January 14). Letter to Lorne Barnes. SCM.

Buckmaster, Henrietta. (1941). *Let My People Go.* New York: Harper.

Bullard, John M. (1947). *The Rotches.* New Bedford, Mass.

Bullock, Penelope L. (1981). *The Afro-American Periodical Press, 1838–1909.* Baton Rouge: Louisiana State University Press.

Burkett, Randall K., Nancy Hall Burkett, and Henry Louis Gates Jr. (Eds.). (1991). *Black Biographical Dictionaries, 1790–1950.* Alexandria, Va.: Chadwyck-Healey.

Butler, Jon. (1990). *Awash in a Sea of Faith: Christianizing the American People.* Cambridge: Harvard University Press.

Byerman, Keith. (1982). We Wear the Mask: Deceit as Theme and Style in Slave Narratives. In Sekora and Turner (1982), 70–82.

Cain, William E. (1995). *William Lloyd Garrison and the Fight against Slavery: Selections from* The Liberator. New York: St. Martin's Press.

Cameron, Kenneth Walter (Ed.). (1978). *Young Reporter of Concord.* Hartford, Conn.: Transcendental Books.

——— (Ed.). (1981). *Transcendental Youth and Age: Chapters in Biography and Autobiography by Franklin Benjamin Sanborn.* Hartford, Conn.: Transcendental Books.

——— (Ed.). (1982). *Correspondence of Franklin Benjamin Sanborn the Transcendentalist.* Hartford, Conn.: Transcendental Books.

*Campbell, Jan. (1975, June 7). S. S. *Tubman*, Like Its Namesake, Fought for Freedom. *Syracuse Post-Standard.*

Carby, Hazel V. (1987). *Reconstructing Womanhood: The Emergence of the Afro-American Woman Novelist.* New York: Oxford University Press.

*Carey, Shawn. (N.d. [1991?]). Ancestor Provides Inspiration. *Syracuse Herald.*

**Carter, Florence L. (1939). Interview statement to Earl Conrad. EC-NY

**Carter, Rev. G[eorge] C. (1908, August 1). Harriet, the Moses of Her People. *(Boston) Woman's Journal.*

*———. (1913, November 9). To the Colored Race, Mrs. Seward Was Always a True Friend Declares This Negro. *Auburn (N.Y.) Citizen.*

*Catt, Carrie Chapman. (1939a, June 1). Letter to Earl Conrad. EC-NY.

*———. (1939b, June 8). Letter to Earl Conrad. EC-NY.

*———. (1939c, June 27). Letter to Earl Conrad. EC-NY.

*———. (1939d, August 11). Letter to Earl Conrad. EC-NY.

*———. (1939e, August 19). Letter to Earl Conrad. EC-NY.

*———. (1940a, January 17). Letter to Earl Conrad. EC-NY.

*———. (1940b, January 25). Letter to Earl Conrad. EC-NY.

*——— (1940c, February 17. Letter to Earl Conrad. EC-NY.

*Cayuga County, N.Y.. Census.

Chace, Elizabeth Buffum. (1891). *Anti-slavery Reminiscences.* Central Falls, R.I.: E. L. Freedman and Son.

Chadwick, John White. (1899). *A Life for Liberty: Anti-slavery and Other Letters of Sallie Holley.* New York: G. P. Putnam's.

*Chapman, Maria Weston. (1859, June 4). Letter to Mrs. [Sarah Rotch] Arnold. AL.

**[Cheney, Ednah] (1865, March). Moses. *Freedmen's Record,1,* 34–38.

**Cheney, Ednah Dow. (1902). *Reminiscences.* Boston: Lee and Shepard.

Child, Lydia Maria. (1861, January 28). Letter to Charles Sumner. In Meltzer and Holland (1982), 372–373.

**———. (1862a, January 21). Letter to John Greenleaf Whittier. LMC-LC.

**———. (1862b, February 8). Letter to Joseph Carpenter. MHS.

*Christmas Money Still Missing. (1907, December 28). *Auburn (N.Y.) Daily Advertiser.*

*City Asked to Aid Tubman Home. (1972, January 5). *Auburn (N.Y.) Citizen-Advertiser.*

*Clarence Stewart Dies; Nephew of Harriet Tubman. (1972, March 30). *Auburn (N.Y.). Citizen-Advertiser.*

**Clarke, James B. (1911). An Hour with Harriet Tubman. In William Edgar Easton (Ed.), *Christophe: A Tragedy in Prose of Imperial Haiti.* Los Angeles: Grafton.

Clarkson, Kenneth Wheeler, Jr. (1973). *An Annotated Checklist of the Letters of Franklin Benjamin Sanborn (1831–1917)*. Ph.D. dissertation, Columbia University.

Cleghorn, Sarah N. (1933). *The True Ballad of Glorious Harriet Tubman*. Manchester, Vt.: Sarah N. Cleghorn.

Clinton, Catherine. (1994). "With a Whip in His Hand": Rape, Memory and African-American Women. In Genevieve Fabre and Robert O'Meally (Eds.), *History and Memory in African-American Culture*, 205–218. New York: Oxford University Press.

Coleman, Willi. (1997). Architects of a Vision: Black Women and Their Antebellum Quest for Political and Social Equality. In A. D. Gorden (1997), 24–40.

Coles, Howard W. (1941). Harriet Tubman, the Joan of Arc of America and the Moses of Her People. In *The Cradle of Freedom: A History of the Negro in Rochester, Western New York and Canada*, 91–99. Rochester, N.Y.: Oxford Press.

Collier-Thomas, Bettye. (1997). Frances Ellen Watkins Harper: Abolitionist and Feminist Reformer, 1825–1911. In A. D. Gordon (1997), 41–65.

*Collins, D. E. (1861, January 25). Letter to Franklin B. Sanborn. FBS-AAS.

*Committee Plans Tubman Program. (1914, June 9). *Auburn (N.Y.) Advertiser-Journal*, 4.

**Concerning Women. (1897, April 17). *(Boston) Woman's Journal*, vol. 28, no. 16, p. 1.

*Conrad, Earl. (1939a, June 7). Letter to Harriet Stanton Blatch. EC-NY.

*———. (1939b, June 7). Letter to Louise Bradford Varnum. EC-NY.

*———. (1939c, June 16). Letter to Carrie Chapman Catt. EC-NY.

*———. (1939d, June 16). Letter to Louise Bradford Varnum. EC-NY.

*———. (1939e, June 29). Letter to Florence L. Carter. EC-NY.

*———. (1939f, July 7). Letter to Carrie Chapman Catt. EC-NY.

*———. (1939g, July 19). Letter to Isabel Howland. EC-NY.

*———. (1939h, July 20). Letter to Alice Brickler. EC-NY.

*———. (1939i, July 23). Letter to Alice Stone Blackwell. EC-NY.

*———. (1939j, August 3). Letter to Harkless Bowley. EC-NY.

*———. (1939k, August 3). Letter to Alice Brickler. EC-NY.

*———. (1939l, August 8). Letter to Carrie Chapman Catt. EC-NY.

*———. (1939m, August 12). Letter to Harkless Bowley. EC-NY.

*———. (1939n, August 14). Letter to Alice Stone Blackwell. EC-NY.

*———. (1939o, August 14). Letter to Carrie Chapman Catt. EC-NY.

*———. (1939p, August 20). Letter to Mrs. James [Helen Osborne] Storrow. EC-NY.

*———. (1939q, August 20). Letter to Mrs. William [Helen Woodruff] Tatlock. EC-NY.

*———. (1939r, August 22). Letter to Harkless Bowley. EC-NY.

*———. (1939s, August 22). Letter to Alice Brickler. EC-NY.

*———. (1939t, August 23). Letter to Emily Hopkins Drake. EC-NY.

*———. (1939u, August 31). Letter to Harkless Bowley. EC-NY.

*———. (1939v, September 17). Letter to Emily Hopkins Drake. EC-NY.

*———. (1939w, September 17). Letter to Mrs. William [Helen Woodruff] Tatlock. EC-NY.

*———. (1939x, September 22). Letter to Emily Hopkins Drake. EC-NY.

*———. (1939y, November 10). Letter to Harkless Bowley. EC-NY.

*———. (1939z, n.d. November ?). Letter to Alice Brickler. EC-NY

*———. (1939aa, November 13). Letter to Mrs. E. S. [Katie Stewart] Northrup. EC-NY.

*———. (1939bb, November 14). Letter to Carrie Chapman Catt. EC-NY.

*———. (1939cc, December 20). Letter to Carrie Chapman Catt. EC-NY.

*———. (1940a, February 3). Letter to Carrie Chapman Catt. EC-NY.

*———. (1940b, February 26). Letter to Carrie Chapman Catt. EC-NY.

*———. (1940c, March 11). Letter to Harkless Bowley. EC-NY.

*———. (1940d, March 11). Letter to Alice Brickler. EC-NY.

*———. (1940e, April 2). Letter to Carrie Chapman Catt. EC-NY.

*———. (1940f, n.d., after April 1). Letter to Mrs. E.S. [Katie Stewart] Northrup. EC-NY

*———. (1940g, April 17). Letter to Alice Brickler. EC-NY.

———. (1940h, August). A Great Leader—Harriet Tubman. *Negro World Digest.* 46–50.

———. (1940i, November). Most of a Man. *Negro World Digest* 1–88

———. (1940j, December). General Tubman on the Combahee. *Negro World Digest,* 13–16.

———. (1941, March). General Tubman at Troy. *The Crisis,* 78, 91.

———. (1942a). *Harriet Tubman, Negro Soldier and Abolitionist.* New York: International.

———. (1942b, May). General Tubman, Composer of Spirituals. *Etude V.* (60) 305, 344, 352.

———. (1943a). *General Harriet Tubman.* Washington, D.C.: Associated Publishers. Reprinted 1990.

———. (1943b, April 13). The Fighting Slave. *Americana Magazine.*

*———. (1950, January). Charles P. Wood Manuscripts of Harriet Tubman. *Negro History Bulletin, 13* (4), 90–95.

———. (1970, January–February). I Bring You General Tubman. *Black Scholar,* 2–7.

*———. (N.d. [May 1939?]). Letter to Harriet Stanton Blatch. EC-NY.

A Considerable Amount of Excitement (1884, October 13). *Auburn (N.Y.) Daily Advertiser.*

Cornish, Dudley Taylor. (1966). *The Sable Arm: Negro Troops in the Union Army, 1861–1865.* New York: W. W. Norton.

*Courthouse Ceremonies End Tubman Home Dedication. (1953, May 1). *Auburn (N.Y.) Citizen Advertiser.*

Crawford, Beth (2002). Tubman Chronology Primarily Relating to Auburn sites. Prepared by Crawford and Stearns. In progress. Syracuse, N.Y.: Crawford and Stearns, Architects and Preservation Planners.

Cromwell, Otelia. (1958). *Lucretia Mott.* Cambridge: Harvard University Press.

Cross, Whitney. (1950). *The Burned-Over District: The Social and Intellectual History of Enthusiastic Religion in Western New York, 1800–1850.* Ithaca: Cornell University Press.

Davis. (1888, October 18). Obituary of Nelson Davis. *Cayuga County (N.Y.) Independent.*

Davis, Charles T. (1985). The Slave Narrative: First Major Art Form in an Emerging Black Tradition. In Davis and Gates (1985), 83–119.

Davis, Charles T., and Henry Louis Gates Jr. (Eds.). (1985). *The Slave's Narrative*. New York: Oxford University Press.

Davis, Sue. (1970. Spring). Harriet Tubman: The Moses of Her People. *Women: A Journal of Liberation*, 12–15.

**Day, William Howard. (1858, April 17). Letter to John Brown. VP. Reprinted in Sterling (1973), 274.

*Death of Aunt Harriet, "Moses of Her People." (1913, March 11). *Auburn (N.Y.) Daily Advertiser*, 4, 6.

*Death of "Queen of the Underground." (1913, March 15). *Baltimore Afro-American Ledger*.

*Dedication of Harriet Tubman Home. (1908, June 24). *Auburn (N,Y,) Daily Advertiser*, 5.

*Dennis, Charles. (1911, November 6). The Work of Harriet Tubman. *Americana Magazine 6*, 1067–1071.

Dodson, Jualynne. (1981). Nineteenth-Century A. M. E. Preaching Women. In Hilah F. Thomas and Rosemary Skinner Keller (Eds.), *Women in New Worlds: Historical Perspectives on the Wesleyan Tradition*. Vol. 1, 276–292. Nashville: Abingdon Press.

*Donation Festival Notice. (1862, February 21). *Liberator*.

Dorwart, Jeffery M. (1992). *Cape May County, New Jersey: The Making of an American Resort Community*. New Brunswick, NJ: Rutgers University Press, 1993.

*Douglass, Frederick. (1858, January 8). Letter to Ladies Irish Anti-Slavery Association. Reprinted in P. Foner, (1950–1955), 46–47.

**———. (1868, August 29). Testimonial letter to Harriet Tubman. In Bradford (1869), 6–8.

———. (1987). *My Bondage and My Freedom* (William L. Andrews, Ed.). Urbana: University of Illinois Press. (Original work published 1855)

Douglass-Chin, Richard J. (2001). *Preacher Woman Sings the Blues: The Autobiographies of Nineteenth-Century African American Evangelists*. Columbia: University of Missouri Press.

**Drake, Emily Hopkins. (1939, August 21). Letter to Earl Conrad. EC-NY.

**———. (1939, August 24). Letter to Earl Conrad. EC-NY.

**———. (1939, September 21). Letter to Earl Conrad. EC-NY.

**Drake, Frank C. (1907, September 22). The Moses of Her People. *New York Herald*.

**Drew, Benjamin. (1856). Harriet Tubman. In *The Refugee: or the Narratives of Fugitive Slaves in Canada*, 30. Boston: J. P. Jewett.

DuBois, Ellen Carol. (1978). *Feminism and Suffrage: The Emergence of an Independent Women's Movement in America, 1848–1869*. Ithaca: Cornell University Press.

Du Bois, W. E. B. (1903a). *The Negro Church*. Atlanta: Atlanta University Press.

———. (1903b). *The Souls of Black Folk: Essays and Sketches*. Chicago: A. C. McClurg.

———. (1909). *John Brown*. Philadelphia: George W. Jacobs.

———. (1910, July). Black Reconstruction and Its Benefits. *American Historical Review*, 15, 781–799.

*[———]. (1913, March). David Livingston and Harriet Tubman. *The Crisis*.

————. (1966). *Black Reconstruction in America*. New York: Russell and Russell. (Original work published 1935)

*Durrant, Henry R. (1862, August 28). Note to Captain Warfield. In Bradford (1869), 69.

*————. (1864, May 3). Testimonial letter. In Bradford (1869), 67–68.

*Earle [Mathews], Victoria. (1896, June). Harriet Tubman. *(Boston) Woman's Era*, 8.

Edelstein, Tilden G. (1968). *Strange Enthusiasm: A Life of Thomas Wentworth Higginson*. New Haven: Yale University Press.

*Editorial Notes (April 17, 1897). *(Boston) Woman's Journal*. vol. 28, no. 16, p. 1.

Emilio, Luis F. (1968). *History of the Fifty-fourth Regiment of Massachusetts Volunteer Infantry, 1863–1865*. New York: Johnson Reprint Corporation. (Original work published 1894)

Escott, Paul D. (1979). *Slavery Remembered: A Record of Twentieth Century Slave Narratives*. Chapel Hill: University of North Carolina Press.

————. (1985). The Art and Science of Reading WPA Slave Narratives. In Davis and Gates (1985), 40–48.

*Exercises Honoring Harriet Tubman to Be Held Here. (1953, April 29). *Auburn (N.Y.) Citizen-Advertiser*, 13.

Fatal Shooting Affray. (1867, October 4). *Baltimore Sun*.

*Featherstonhaugh, Thomas. (1900, December 31). Letter to Franklin B. Sanborn. FBS-BU.

*————. (1901, March 20). Letter to Franklin B. Sanborn. FBS-BU.

*Fields, Mamie Garvin, with Karen Fields (1983). *Lemon Swamp and Other Places: A Carolina Memoir*. New York: Free Press.

*The Fight for the Ballot. (1896, November 19). *Rochester (N.Y.) Democrat and Chronicle*, 12.

Finkelman, Paul (Ed.). (1995). *His Soul Goes Marching On: Responses to John Brown and the Harpers Ferry Raid*. Charlottesville: University Press of Virginia.

*Fisk, R. (1868, January 22). Harriet Tubman. *Auburn (N.Y.) Daily Advertiser*.

Fleischner, Jennifer. (1996). *Mastering Slavery: Memory, Family, and Identity in Women's Slave Narratives*. New York: New York University Press.

Foner, Eric. (1988). *Reconstruction: America's Unfinished Revolution, 1863–1877*. New York: Harper and Row.

————. (1993). *Freedom's Lawmakers*. New York: Oxford University Press.

Foner, Philip S. (Ed.). (1950–1955). *The Life and Writings of Frederick Douglass*. 5 vols. New York: International.

———— (Ed.). (1972). *The Voice of Black America: Major Speeches by Negroes in the United States, 1797–1971*. New York: Simon and Schuster.

———— (Ed.). (1974). *Organized Labor and the Black Worker, 1619–1973*. New York: Praeger.

Foner, Philip S., (Ed.), with Yuval Taylor. (1999). *Frederick Douglass: Selected Speeches and Writings*. Chicago: Lawrence Hill Books.

**Forten, Charlotte. (1863, January 31). Diary entry. In Stevenson (1988), Journal 3, 442–443.

————. (1864, May and June). Life on the Sea Islands. *Atlantic Monthly*, 587–596, 666–676.

**For the *Christian Recorder*. (1865, April 15). From Camp Wm. Penn. *Christian Recorder.*

*For the Harriet Tubman Home. (1907, October 12). *Auburn (N.Y.) Daily Advertiser*, 5.

*For the Tubman Home. (1908, June 18). *Auburn (N.Y.) Citizen*, 5.

*For Tubman Memorial. (1914, June 9). *Auburn (N.Y.) Citizen*, 5.

*Foster Child of Harriet Tubman Dies. (1930, May 19). *Auburn (N.Y.) Advertiser-Journal.* (Article also appeared in *Auburn (N.Y.) Citizen*)

Foster, Frances Smith. (1994). *Witnessing Slavery: The Development of Ante-Bellum Slave Narratives.* Second edition. Madison: University of Wisconsin Press.

———— (Ed.). (1990). *A Brighter Coming Day: A Frances Ellen Watkins Harper Reader.* New York: Feminist Press at the City University of New York.

**Fowler, Rev. Henry. (1868, June 23). Testimonial letter to Sarah Bradford. In Bradford (1869), 71.

Fox-Genovese, Elizabeth. (1988). *Within the Plantation Household: Black and White Women of the Old South.* Chapel Hill: University of North Carolina Press.

————. (1990). My Statue, My Self: Autobiographical Writings of Afro-American Women. In Gates (1990), 176–203.

*Frank, Katy. (1982, May 30.). Relatives Join in Pilgrimage. *Auburn (N.Y.) Citizen*, 4.

Franklin, John Hope. (1971). Harriet Tubman. In E. James et al. (1971), 3:481–483.

Frazier, E. Franklin. (1974). *The Negro Church.* New York: Schocken Books. (Original work published 1964)

Fredrickson, George M. (1975). A Man but Not a Brother: Abraham Lincoln and Racial Equality. *Journal of Southern History, 41*, 39–58.

————. (1988). *The Arrogance of Race: Historical Perspectives on Slavery, Racism and Social Inequality.* Middletown, Conn.: Wesleyan University Press.

**From Florida: Colonel Montgomery's Raid. (1863, June 20). *(Madison) Wisconsin State Journal*, vol. 11, no. 237, p. 2. Reprinted with minor alterations in *Boston Commonwealth*, July 10, 1863, as Harriet Tubman.

**Fugitive Slave Rescue in Troy. (1860, April 28). *Troy (N.Y.) Whig.*

Fulop, Timothy E., and Albert J. Raboteau (Eds.). (1997). *African-American Religion: Interpretive Essays in History and Culture.* New York: Routledge.

*Funeral of Mrs. Lucas. (1930, May 21). *Auburn (N.Y.) Citizen.*

*Future of Harriet Tubman Home Discussed by Clergy. (1972, April 10). *Auburn (N.Y.) Citizen-Advertiser*, 10.

Galen, Mercy. (1973, August). Harriet Tubman, the Moses of Her People. *Ms. Magazine, 2* (2), 16–18.

Gara, Larry. (1961). *The Liberty Line: Legend of the Underground Railroad.* Lexington: University of Kentucky Press.

Garfield, Deborah, and Rafia Zafar (Eds.). (1993). *Harriet Jacobs and Incidents in the Life of a Slave Girl: New Critical Essays.* Cambridge: Cambridge University Press.

**Garrett, Thomas. (1854, December 29). Letter to J. Miller McKim. In Still (1872), 296.

**————. (1855, December 16). Letter to Eliza Wigham. QC. In McGowan (1977), 123–138.

**————. (1856a, May 11). Letter to J. Miller McKim and William Still. In Still (1872), 387.

**————. (1856b, September 12). Letter to Eliza Wigham. QC. In McGowan (1977), 126–129.

———. (1856c, October 24). Letter to Eliza Wigham. QC. In McGowan (1977), 129–131.

**———. (1856d, November 29). Letter to Joseph A. Dugdale. FHL. In McGowan (1977), 148–149.

**———. (1856e, December 16). Letter to Eliza Wigham. QC. In McGowan (1977), 123–138.

**———. (1856f, December 27). Letter to Eliza Wigham. QC. In McGowan (1977), 132–134.

**———. (1857a, March 27). Letter to William Still. In McGowan (1977), 95, and Still (1872), 638–39.

**———. (1857b, March 29 or 30?). Letter to William Still. In McGowan (1977), 96, and Still (1872), 639.

**———. (1857c, March 29). Letter to Mary Edmundson. QC. In McGowan (1977), 138–143.

**———. (1857d, August 11). Letter to Mary Edmundson. QC. In McGowan (1977), 143–145.

**———. (1860, December 1). Letter to William Still. In McGowan (1977), 107–8, and Still (1872), 530.

**———. (1868, June). Testimonial letter to Sarah Hopkins Bradford. In Bradford (1869), 48–53.

**Garrison, Agnes. (1899a, November 25). Letter to Ellen Wright Garrison. GF. (Original missing)

**———. (1899b, November 26). Letter to Ellen Wright Garrison. GF. (Original missing)

**Garrison, Eleanor. 1948, November 10). Letter to M. S. Grierson. GF.

**Garrison, Ellen Wright. (1861, November 16). Letter to Lucy McKim. GF.

**———. (1866, April 23). Letter to Martha Coffin Wright. GF.

**———. (1868, December 26). Letter to Martha Coffin Wright. GF.

**———. (1869, December 19). Letter to Martha Coffin Wright. GF.

**———. (1872, November 4). Letter to Martha Coffin Wright. GF.

**———. (1873, October 14). Letter to Martha Coffin Wright. GF.

**———. (1894, June 12). Letter to William Lloyd Garrison II. GF.

**———. (1895, May 30). Letter to David Wright. GF.

**———. (1906, October 22). Letter to William Lloyd Garrison II. GF.

**Garrison, George. (1864, February 10). Letter to William Lloyd Garrison II. GF.

**Garrison, Wendell. (1864, June 20). Letter to William Lloyd Garrison II. GF.

**Garrison, William Lloyd II. (1897a). Diary entries for March 14 and April 14, 1897. GF.

**———. (1897b, April 13). The Story of Harriet Tubman. *Boston Evening Transcript*, 6.

Gasper, David Barry, and Darlene Clark Hine. (1996). *More Than Chattel: Black Women and Slavery in the Americas*. Bloomington: Indiana University Press.

Gates, Henry Louis, Jr. (Ed.). (1990). *Reading Black, Reading Feminist: A Critical Anthology*. New York: Penguin.

Genovese, Eugene. (1974). *Roll, Jordan, Roll: The World the Slaves Made*. New York: Pantheon.

*Giddings, Paula. (1984). *When and Where I Enter: The Impact of Black Women on Race and Sex in America.* New York: William Morrow.

[Gilbert, Olive.] (1993). *Narrative of Sojourner Truth, A Northern Slave, Emancipated from Bodily Servitude by the state of New York in 1828....* Reprinted in Margaret Washington (Ed.), *Narrative of Sojourner Truth.* New York: Random House. (Original work published 1850)

Ginzberg, Lori D. (1986, December). "Moral Suasion Is Balderdash": Women, Politics and Social Activism in the 1850s. *Journal of American History, 73,* 601–622.

Glassman-Hersh, Blanche. (1978). *The Slavery of Sex: Feminist-Abolitionists in Nineteenth-Century America.* Urbana: University of Illinois Press.

**The Gold Swindle and the Greenback Robbery. (1873, October 6). *Auburn (N.Y.) Daily Bulletin.*

Gooding, Corporal James Henry. (1863, June 8). Letter to *New Bedford Mercury,* published June 19. In V. M. Adams (1991).

Goodson, Martia Graham. (1979, Summer). The Slave Narrative Collection: A Tool for Reconstructing Afro-American Women's History. *Western Journal of Black Studies, 3,* 116–122.

Gordon, Ann D. (Ed.), with Bettye Collier-Thomas et al. (1997). *African-American Women and the Vote, 1837–1965.* Amherst: University of Massachusetts Press.

Gordon, Linda. (1995). Black and White Visions of Welfare: Women's Welfare Activism, 1890–1945. In Hine et al. (1995), 449–485.

Gougeon, Len. (1990). *Virtue's Hero: Emerson, Antislavery and Reform.* Athens: University of Georgia Press.

Gougeon, Len, and Joel Myerson (Eds.). (1995). *Emerson's Antislavery Writings.* New Haven: Yale University Press.

*Great Day in Auburn. (1908, June 20). *Auburn (N.Y.) Daily Advertiser.*

*Green, Beriah. (1860, March 19). Letter to Samuel Campbell. RLA.

Green, Rebecca (1998). History of Harriet Tubman and Her Brick House. Ithaca: Cornell University. Unpublished paper.

*Greenberg, Wendy. (1991, February 17). Sharing the Life of Tubman. *Philadelphia Inquirer.*

*Griffin, Fred G. (1924, January 19). Toronto Minister the Son of a Slave. *Toronto Star Weekly.*

Grover, Kathryn (2001). *The Fugitive's Gibraltar: Escaping Slaves and Abolitionism in New Bedford, Massachusetts.* Amherst: University of Massachusetts Press.

**Guterman, Benjamin. (2000, Fall). "Good Brave Work": Harriet Tubman's Testimony at Beaufort, South Carolina. *Prologue: Quarterly of the National Archives and Records Administration, 32,* 155–165.

Gwin, Minrose C. (1985). *Black and White Women in the Old South: The Peculiar Sisterhood in American Literature.* Knoxville: University of Tennessee Press.

———. (1986). Green-Eyed Monsters of the Slavocracy: Jealous Mistresses in Two Slave Narratives. In Marjorie Pryse and Hortense Spillers (Eds.), *Conjuring: Black Women, Fiction and Literary Tradition.* Bloomington: Indiana University Press.

Hall, Jacqueline Dowd. (1979). *Revolt against Chivalry: Jessie Daniel Ames and the Women's Campaign against Lynching.* New York: Columbia University Press.

Hallowell, Anna Davis (Ed.). (1884). *James and Lucretia Mott, Life and Letters*. Boston: Houghton Mifflin.

Hansen, Debra Gold. (1993). *Strained Sisterhood: Gender and Class in the Boston Female Anti-Slavery Society*. Amherst: University of Massachusetts Press.

Hardy, Gayle J. (1993). *American Women Civil Rights Activists: Biobibliographies of 68 Leaders, 1825–1992*. Jefferson, N.C.: McFarland.

Harlan, Louis R. (1983). *Booker T. Washington: The Wizard of Tuskegee, 1901–1915*. New York: Oxford University Press.

Harlan, Louis R., and Raymond W. Smock (Eds.). (1980). *The Booker T. Washington Papers*. 14 vols. Urbana: University of Illinois Press.

Harley, Sharon. (1990, Winter). For the Good of Family and Race: Gender, Work and Domestic Roles in the Black Community, 1880–1930. *Signs, 15*, 338.

Harley, Sharon, and Rosalyn Terborg-Penn (Eds.). (1978). *The Afro-American Woman: Struggles and Images*. Port Washington, N.Y.: Kenikat.

*Harper, Frances Ellen Watkins. (1866, May). Speech. In *Proceedings of Eleventh Women's Rights Convention* (1866), 45–48.

———. (1888). The Woman's Christian Temperance Union and the Colored Woman. In Foster (1990), 281–285.

**Harriet Tubman. (1863, July 10). *Boston Commonwealth*.

*Harriet Tubman. (1864a, August 4). *Boston Commonwealth*.

*Harriet Tubman. (1864b, August 12). *Boston Commonwealth*.

*Harriet Tubman. (1869, January 9). *Boston Commonwealth*.

*Harriet Tubman: A Colored Woman with a Remarkable History Revisits Boston. (1886, October 31). *Boston Sunday Herald*, 10.

*Harriet Tubman at the Hospital. (1907, May 10). *Auburn (N.Y.) Daily Advertiser*, 6.

*Harriet Tubman at the Hub. (1905, May 30). *Auburn (N.Y.) Daily Advertiser*. (Originally published as Oldest Ex-Slave Given Reception in *Boston Journal*, May 26, 1905, 8.

*Harriet Tubman Davis. (1913, March 13). *Springfield (Mass.) Republican*, 10.

*Harriet Tubman Davis. (1913, March 14). *New York Times*.

*Harriet Tubman Davis, Ex-Slave. (1913, March 13). *Boston Evening Transcript*.

*Harriet Tubman Dies Monday at Auburn, N.Y. (1913, March 13). *New York Age*, 1–2.

*Harriet Tubman Dying. (1913, March 11). *New York Times*, 17.

*Harriet Tubman Home and Christening of John Brown Hall. (1903, June 20). *Auburn (N.Y.) Daily Advertiser*, 8.

*Harriet Tubman Home Free from Debt. (1918, November 2). *New York Age*.

*Harriet Tubman Home Granted National Landmark Status. (1974, July 5). *Auburn (N.Y.) Citizen-Advertiser*.

*Harriet Tubman Home Historic Local Landmark, on Block for Unpaid Taxes. (1943, June 16). *Auburn (N.Y.) Citizen-Advertiser*, 5.

*Harriet Tubman Home Meeting. (1907, June 14).*Auburn (N.Y.) Daily Advertiser*, 7.

*Harriet Tubman Home "Rescued": Church to Keep It. (1943, June 17). *Auburn (N.Y.) Citizen-Advertiser*, 13.

*Harriet Tubman Ill and Penniless. (1911, June 8). *New York Age*.

**Harriet Tubman Is Dead. (1913, March 11). *Auburn (N.Y.) Citizen*, 5.

* *Harriet Tubman*, New Liberty Ship, Launched in Maine. (1944, June). (Clipping from unknown newspaper source, in SPL)

*Harriet Tubman, Noted Negress, Dead. (1913, March 11). *Albany (N.Y.) Evening Standard.*

*Harriet Tubman's Hogs (1884, July 11). *Evening Auburnian*, 1.

*Harriet Tubman's Money Gone. (1907, December 27). *Auburn (N.Y.) Daily Advertiser*, 6.

*Harriet Tubman Penniless. (1911, June 2). *New York Times*, 18.

*Harriet Tubman's Tribute. (1905, April 3). *Auburn (N.Y.) Daily Advertiser.*

**Hart, Albert Bushnell. (1906). *Slavery and Abolition, 1831–1841.* New York: Harper and Brothers.

Haviland, Laura S. (1881). *A Woman's Life-Work: Labors and Experiences.* Cincinnati: Walden and Stowe.

*H[ayden], L[ewis]. (1859a, September 16). Letter sent to John Brown via Kagi at Chambersburg, Pa. Printed in *New York Herald*, October 25, 1859.

*Hayden, Lewis (1859b, September 16). Letter to Gerrit Smith. Printed in *Boston Evening Transcript*, October 26, 1859.

*Haynes, Elizabeth Ross. (1921). Harriet Tubman, the Moses of Her People, 1820–1913. In *Unsung Heroes*, 87–102. New York: Du Bois and Dill. Also reprinted in Elizabeth Davis, *Lifting As They Climb*, 254–262. Washington, D.C.: National Association of Colored Women, 1933.

Hazzard, Florence Woolsey. (1971). Emily Howland. In James et al. (1971), 229–31.

Hernstadt, Richard L. (Ed.). (1969). *The Letters of A. Bronson Alcott.* Ames: Iowa State University Press.

Hewitt, Nancy A. (1984). *Women's Activism and Social Change: Rochester, New York, 1822–1872.* Ithaca: Cornell University Press.

Higginbotham, Evelyn Brooks. (1989, Spring). Beyond the Sound of Silence: Afro-American Women in History. *Gender and History, 1,* 50–67.

———. (1993). *Righteous Discontent: The Women's Movement in the Black Baptist Church.* Cambridge: Harvard University Press.

———. (1994). Rethinking the Subject of African American Women's History. In Susan Ware (Ed.), *New Viewpoints in Women's History: Working Papers from the Schlesinger Library 50th Anniversary Conference, March 4–5, 1994.* 64–70. (A bound copy of the conference papers was made available to interested scholars by the Schlesinger Library.)

Higginson, Mary Thacher (Ed.). (1969). *Letters and Journals of Thomas Wentworth Higginson, 1846–1906.* New York: Negro Universities Press. (Original publication in 1906)

**Higginson, Thomas W. (1859, June 17). Letter to Louisa Storrow Higginson. In Mary Thacher Higginson (Ed.) (1906). 81.

**———. (1862a, November 27). Diary entry. In Howard Mumford Jones (Ed.) (1960), 9–10.

**———. (1862b, December 10). Letter to Mary Channing Higginson. TWH-H.

———. (1863) Journal. TWH-H.

**———. (1898). *Cheerful Yesterdays.* Boston: Houghton Mifflin.

*———. (1960). *Army Life in a Black Regiment.* East Lansing: Michigan State University Press. (original publication in 1870)

*High Tribute Paid to Harriet Tubman as Memorial Tablet Is Unveiled in Her Honor. (1914, June 13). *Auburn (N.Y.) Advertiser-Journal,* 5, 10.

Hills, Patricia. (1993). Jacob Lawrence as Pictorial Griot: The Harriet Tubman Series. *American Art,* 7(1), 40–59.

Hinding, Andrea, et al. (1979). *Women's History Sources: A Guide to Archives and Manuscript Collections in the United States.* New York: Bowker.

Hine, Darlene Clark. (1986). *The State of Afro-American History.* Baton Rouge: Louisiana State University Press.

———. (1989, Summer). Rape and the Inner Lives of Black Women in the Middle West: Preliminary Thoughts on the Culture of Dissemblance. *Signs, 14,* 912–920.

——— (Ed.). (1990). *Black Women in American History: From Colonial Times through the Present.* 4 vols. Brooklyn, N.Y.: Carlson.

———. (1994). *Hine Sight: Black Women and the Reconstruction of American History.* Brooklyn, N.Y.: Carlson.

Hine, Darlene Clark, et al. (Eds.). (1993). *Black Women in America: An Historical Encyclopedia.* 2 vols. Brooklyn, N.Y.: Carlson.

Hine, Darlene Clark, et al. (Eds.). (1995). *We Specialize in the Wholly Impossible: A Reader in Black Women's History.* Brooklyn, N.Y.: Carlson.

Hine, Darlene Clark, and Kathleen Thompson. (1999). *A Shining Thread of Hope: The History of Black Women in America.* New York: Broadway Books.

*Holberg, Eve. (1983a, August 19). Tribute Targets Women. *Auburn (N.Y.) Citizen.*

*———. (1983b, August 21). Tubman's Life Inspires Women. *Auburn (N.Y.) Citizen.*

Holland, Rupert Sargent (Ed.). (1969). *Letters and Diary of Laura M. Towne, Written from the Sea Islands of South Carolina, 1862–1884.* New York: Negro Universities Press. (Original publication in 1912)

*Holley, Sallie. (1867a, November 4). Letter to unknown recipient. Excerpt in Chadwick (1899), 205.

*———. (1867b, November 30). Letter to Mr. Powell. In *National Anti-Slavery Standard.*

*———. (1868, March 4) Letter to "Mrs. ———. Excerpt in Chadwick (1899), 207–208.

*Holman, Julia A. (1896, August 1). National Federation of Colored Women. *Richmond (Va.) Planet.*

**Holt, Rosa Belle. (1886, July). A Heroine in Ebony. *Chautauquan, 23,* 459–462.

*Home of Civil War Heroine in Auburn Is Decaying Fast. (1939, March 16). *Syracuse Post-Standard.*

*Home of Harriet Tubman Dedicated as a National Shrine. (1953, May 6). *Ithaca Journal,* 8.

*Hopkins, Pauline E. (1902, January–February). Famous Women of the Negro Race. III. Harriet Tubman (Moses). *Colored American Magazine,* 210–216.

**Hopkins, Samuel Miles (1886, March 16). Testimonial letter published in Bradford (1886), 9–11.

**Howland, Emily. (1873, October 4). Typescript diary entry, FHW-CU.

**———. (1901–1902). Diary entries for December 21, 1901, to November 18, 1902. Diary 1901–2 and Diary 1902–3. EHF.

———. (1904–1905). Diary entries for October 31, 1904, and October 14, 16, 17, and 27, 1905. Diaries for 1904–5 and 1905–6. EHF.

*Howland, Isabel. (1896, December 5). New York State Annual Convention. *(Boston) Woman's Journal.*

*———. (1939, July 11). Letter to Earl Conrad. EC-NY.

Huggins, Nathan (1980). *Slave and Citizen: Life of Frederick Douglass.* Boston: Little Brown.

*Hughes, Langston. (1958). Harriet Tubman, Liberator. In *Famous Negro Heroes of America.* New York: Dodd Mead, 103–116.

Humez, Jean McMahon. (1981). *Gifts of Power: The Life and Writings of Rebecca Cox Jackson, Black Preacher, Shaker Eldress.* Amherst: University of Massachusetts Press.

———. (1984). "My Spirit Eye": Some Functions of Spiritual and Visionary Experience in the Lives of Five Black Women Preachers, 1810–1880. In Barbara J. Harris and Joann K. McNamara (Eds.), *Women and the Structure of Society: Selected Research from the Fifth Berkshire Conference on the History of Women.* Durham, N.C.: Duke University Press, 129–143.

———. (1993, Summer). In Search of Harriet Tubman's Spiritual Autobiography. *NWSA* (National Women's Studies Association) *Journal, 3,* 162–182.

———. (1995). Harriet Tubman. In Richard Wrightman Fox and James T. Kloppenberg (Eds.), *A Companion to American Thought,* 690–691. Cambridge, Mass.: Blackwell.

———. (1996, Spring). Reading the Narrative of Sojourner Truth as a Collaborative Text. *Frontiers: A Journal of Women's Studies, 16,* 29–52.

Hunter, Carol. (1993). *To Set the Captives Free: Reverend Jermain Wesley Loguen and the Struggle for Freedom in Central New York, 1835–1872.* New York: Garland.

*[Hunter, Gen. David.] (1863, February 19). Military Pass, Ensuring Free Government Transport. In Wood (1868). Reprinted in Bradford (1869), 68–69.

Hutton, Frankie. (1993). *The Early Black Press in America, 1827 to 1860.* Westport, Conn.: Greenwood Press.

Ingebritsen, Shirley Phillips (1971). Ednah Dow Littlehale Cheney. In James et. al. (1971) 1:325–327.

*In Honor of Harriet Tubman. (1914, June 15). *Auburn (N.Y.) Citizen,* 94.

Jacobs, Donald M. (Ed.). (1993). *Courage and Conscience: Black and White Abolitionists in Boston.* Bloomington: Indiana University Press.

James, Edward T., et al. (Eds.). (1971). *Notable American Women, 1607–1950: A Biographical Dictionary.* 3 vols. Cambridge: Harvard University Press.

James, William (1958). *The Varieties of Religious Experience.* New York: New American Library. (Original publication in 1902)

Jelinek, Estelle C. (1986). *The Tradition of Women's Autobiography: From Antiquity to the Present.* Boston: Twayne.

**Johnson, Alida Stewart. (1940, April 1). Interview summary. In Dorothy E. Snow, *Early Cayuga Days: Folk Lore and Local History of a New York County,* 61–65. Master's thesis, New York State College for Teachers, Albany, N.Y. (Reprinted 1993 by Genoa Historical Association, Aurora, N.Y.)

*——— (Mrs. Carroll Johnson). (1940, October 14). Letter to Earl Conrad. EC-NY.

Johnson, Clifton H. (Ed.). (1993). *God Struck Me Dead: Voices of Ex-Slaves*. Cleveland: Pilgrim Press. (Original publication in 1969)

Johnson, Guion Griffis. (1930). *A Social History of the Sea Islands, with Special Reference to St. Helena Island, South Carolina*. Chapel Hill: University of North Carolina Press. Reprint, New York: Negro Universities Press, 1969.

Johnson, Oliver. (1881). *William Lloyd Garrison and His Times*. Boston: Houghton Mifflin.

*Johnson, Pauline Copes. (1992). Harriet Tubman and Thompson Memorial African Methodist Episcopal Zion Church. In O'Hara (1992), 39, 93.

Johnston, Malcolm Sanders. (1944, October 2, 3, 4). Sarah Hopkins Bradford: Author, Historian, Teacher. *Geneva (N.Y.) Daily Times*.

Jones, Jacqueline. (1985). *Labor of Love, Labor of Sorrow: Black Women, Work, and the Family from Slavery to the Present*. New York: Basic Books.

Jones, Peter Lloyd, and Stephanie E. Przybylek. (1995). *Images of America: Around Auburn*. Dover, N.H.: Arcadia.

Kashatus, William C. (2002). *Just over the Line: Chester County and the Underground Railroad*. West Chester, Pa.: Chester County Historical Society.

**Kellogg, Jane B. [for Harriet Tubman]. (1894a, April 9). Letter to Ednah Cheney. EDC.

**Kellogg, Jane B. (1894b, June 25). Letter to Ednah Cheney. EDC.

King, Wilma. (1995). *Stolen Childhood: Slave Youth in Nineteenth Century America*. Bloomington: University of Indiana Press.

*Kolberg, Rebecca. (1984, June 11). Tubman Gets Little Official Attention in Home Town. *Cambridge (Md.?) Herald Journal*. Clipping in JMC.

Ladner, Joyce A. (1975, August). The Woman. *Ebony*, 76–77.

*Laird, Louis K. (1915, July 28). In the Matter of the Settlement of the Estate of Harriet Tubman Davis. Revised Executor's Account. Filed with Harriet Tubman [Davis's] last will and testament (1912).

Launching of SS Harriet Tubman. (1944, June 3). Souvenir program. Portland, Maine.

Larson, Kate Clifford (forthcoming). *Bound for the Promised Land: Harriet Tubman, Portrait of an American Heroine*. New York: Ballantine Books.

*Lawrence, Jacob. (1968). *Harriet and the Promised Land*. New York: Simon and Schuster.

Lerner, Gerda. (1972). *Black Women in White America: A Documentary History*. New York: Random House.

———. (1979). The Community Work of Black Clubwomen. In *The Majority Finds Its Past*. New York: Oxford University Press.

Lewis, David Levering. (1993). *W. E. B. Du Bois: Biography of a Race, 1868–1919*. New York: Henry Holt.

Levine, Lawrence. (1971). Slave Songs and Slave Consciousness: An Exploration in Neglected Sources. In Fulop and Raboteau (1977), 59–87.

Levine, Lawrence. (1977). *Black Culture and Black Consciousness: Afro-American Folk Thought from Slavery to Freedom*. Oxford: Oxford University Press.

Levine, Robert S. (1997). *Martin Delany, Frederick Douglass, and the Politics of Representative Identity*. Chapel Hill: University of North Carolina Press.

*Liberty Ship Harriet Tubman Launched with Many Celebrities Participating. (1944, June 17). *New York Amsterdam News.*

Lincoln, C. Eric, and Lawrence H. Mamiya. (1990). *The Black Church in the African American Experience.* Durham, N.C.: Duke University Press.

Litwack, Leon F. (1979). *Been in the Storm So Long: The Aftermath of Slavery.* New York: Vintage.

Logan, Rayford. (1954). *The Negro in American Life and Thought: The Nadir, 1877–1901.* New York: Dial Press.

*Loguen, Rev. Jeremiah W. (N.d. [1856?]). Letter to Frederick Douglass. In *Frederick Douglass' Paper* (Rochester, N.Y.), April 4, 1856.

**———. (1858, May 6). Letter to John Brown. JB.

*Lopez, Michael. (1985 [May?]). Annual Pilgrimage Honors the "Moses of Her People." *Auburn (N.Y.) Citizen.* Clipping in JMC.

**Lucas, Maggie [Margaret Stewart], and Thornton Newton. (1893, June 15). Neighbors' affidavit. Filed with Harriet Tubman Vital Records, CCC.

Lutz, Alma. (1971). Maria Weston Chapman. In James et al. (1971), 324–325.

Mabee, Carleton, with Susan Mabee Newhouse. (1993). *Sojourner Truth, Slave, Prophet, Legend.* New York: New York University Press.

Majors, Monroe A. (1893). *Noted Negro Women, Their Triumphs and Activities.* Chicago: Donahue and Henneberry.

Maryland Affairs: Outrage in Talbot County (1867, October 7). *Baltimore American,* 4. (Reprinted from the *Eastern Gazette*)

**Mason, Rev. James E. (1920, October 14). *Then and Now: The Soldier Spirit of Harriet Tubman.* Address at Harriet Tubman Homecoming. A.M.E. Zion Church, Auburn, N.Y.

**———. (N.d. [after 1915]). *Tribute to Harriet Tubman, The Modern Amazon.* Auburn, N.Y.: Harriet Tubman Home.

*May, Samuel J. (1869). *Some Recollections of Our Antislavery Conflict.* Boston: Fields, Osgood.

Mayer, Henry. (1998). *All On Fire: William Lloyd Garrison and the Abolition of Slavery.* New York: St. Martin's Press.

McCarthy, Nick. (1995, Summer). Authority, Orality and Specificity: Resisting Inscription in Sojourner Truth's Ar'n't I a Woman? *Sage, 9,* 30–35.

McDougall, Marion Gleason. (1891). *Fugitive Slaves.* Boston: Ginn.

McDowell, Deborah. (1991). In the First Place: Making Frederick Douglass and the Afro-American Narrative Tradition. In Andrews, (1991), 192–214.

McDowell, Deborah, and Arnold Rampersad (Eds.). (1989). *Slavery and the Literary Imagination.* Baltimore: Johns Hopkins University Press.

McFeely, William S. (1991). *Frederick Douglass.* New York: Norton.

McGovern, Ann. (1965). *Runaway Slave: The Story of Harriet Tubman.* New York: Four Winds Press.

McGowan, James A. (1977). *Station Master on the Underground Railroad: The Life and Letters of Thomas Garrett.* Moylan, Pa.: Whimsie Press.

———. (1994, January). Harriet Tubman: According to Sarah Bradford. *Harriet Tubman Journal, 2,* 1–10.

McHenry, Beth (1943, September 13). Newspaperman Is Inspired by Heroine of His Book on Harriet Tubman. *New York Daily Worker*.

McKay, Nellie Y., and Frances Smith Foster (Eds.). (1991). *Incidents in the Life of a Slave Girl: Contexts, Criticism*. New York: W. W. Norton.

*McLaughlin, Mrs. W. H. (1886, October 31). Letter to Franklin B. Sanborn. FBS-BU.

McLoughlin, William C. (1978). *Revivals, Awakenings and Reform*. Chicago: University of Chicago Press.

McPherson, James M. (1965). *The Negro's Civil War: How American Negroes Felt and Acted during the War for the Union*. New York: Pantheon Books.

———. (1975). *Abolitionist Legacy: From Reconstruction to the NAACP*. Princeton, N.J.: Princeton University Press.

Measday, Walter (1975, June). Cape May and the Underground Railroad, *Cape May County Magazine of History and Genealogy*, 139–145.

Meier, August (Ed.). (1963). *Negro Thought in America, 1880–1915*. Ann Arbor: University of Michigan Press.

Meltzer, Milton, and Patricia G. Holland (Eds.). (1980). *The Collected Correspondence of Lydia Maria Child, 1817–1880*. Microfiche.

———. (Eds.). (1982). *Lydia Maria Child: Selected Letters, 1817–1880*. Amherst: University of Massachusetts Press.

*Memorial to Harriet Tubman. (1914, June 18). *New York Age*, 1, 5.

*Memorial to Harriet Tubman to Be Unveiled. (1914, June 12). *Auburn (N.Y.), Advertiser-Journal*.

*Metcalf, George R. (1971, November 17). Tubman. *Syracuse Post-Standard*.

*———. (1983, October 3). City Should Preserve Its Priceless Treasures. *Auburn (N.Y.) Citizen*.

*Military Pass. (1865a, March 20). To Hilton Head and Charleston, S.C. By order of Secretary of War, Washington D.C. Reprinted in Bradford (1869), 69.

*Military Pass (1865b, July 22). To Fort Monroe, Washington D.C. In Wood (1868), 5. Reprinted in Bradford (1869), 70.

**Miller, Anne Fitzhugh. (1912, August). Harriet Tubman. *American Magazine, 74*, 420, 422.

Mitchell, Rev. W. M. (1970.) *The Underground Railroad*. Westport, Conn.: Negro Universities Press. (Original publication in 1860)

*Mitchell, William Donald. (1914, May 25). Describes Tablet to Be Unveiled in Memory of Harriet Tubman. *Auburn (N.Y.) Advertiser-Journal*.

**Montgomery, Colonel James. (1863, July 6), Letter to Brigadier General Gilmore. In Bradford (1869), 65–66.

*Monument over Harriet Tubman Grave Unveiled. (1937, July 8). *Auburn (N.Y.) Citizen-Advertiser*, 14.

Moody, Jocelyn K. (1990). Ripping Away the Veil of Slavery: Literacy, Communal Love, and Self-Esteem in Three Slave Women's Narratives. *Black America Literature Forum, 24*, 633–648.

———. (2001). *Sentimental Confessions: Spiritual Narratives of Nineteenth Century African American Women*. Athens, Georgia: University of Georgia Press.

*Mortgage on the Tubman Home Is But Memory Now. (1918, October 5). *Auburn (N.Y.) Citizen*, 6.

*Morton, [Edwin]. (1859, June 1). Letter to Franklin B. Sanborn. Excepted in Sanborn (1969), 468 and Sanborn (1909), 165.

Morton, Patricia. (1991). *Disfigured Images: The Historical Assault on Afro-American Women*. New York: Praeger.

*The Moses of Her People: Proposed Memorial to Harriet Tubman, a Negress. (1909, May 2). *New York Sun*, 2.

*Moses of Her Race Ending Her Life in Home She Founded. (1911, June 25). *New York World*.

*The Moses of the Negroes. (1913, April 19). *Literary Digest, 46*, 913–915.

**Mott, Lucretia Coffin. (1867, January 1). Letter to Martha Coffin Wright. GF.

**———. (N.d. [1873, October?]). Letter to Pattie Lord. GF.

Musher, Sharon Ann. (2001, March). Contesting "The Way the Almighty Wants It": Crafting Memories of Ex-Slaves in the Slave Narrative Collection. *American Quarterly, 53*, 1–31.

Myerhoff, Barbara G. (1994). *Number Our Days: Culture and Community among Elderly Jews in an American Ghetto*. New York: Meridian. (Original work published 1978)

Myerson, Joel, and Daniel Shealy (Eds.). (1987). *The Journals of Louisa May Alcott*. Boston: Little, Brown.

*Name Liberty Ship for Noted Auburn Woman. (1944, May 13). *Auburn (N.Y.) Citizen-Advertiser*, 5.

*National Association of Colored Women's Clubs. (1899). *Minutes of the Second Convention of the NACW Held at Quinn Chapel . . . Chicago, Ill., August 14th, 15th and 16th, 1899*. NACWC.

**———. (1902). *Official Minutes of National Federation of Afro-American Women Held in Washington D.C., July 20, 21, 22, 1896)*. NACWC.

*———. (1911, November –January 1912). Personals. *National Association Notes, 4*, 13. NACWC.

*———. (1915, March–April). Report of the Empire State Federation of Women's Clubs Made at Wilberforce, Ohio. *National Association Notes, 12*. NACWC.

*National Grapevine by Charley Cherokee: It's the Truth, Brother. (1944, June 17). *Chicago Defender*, 11. Clipping in JMC.

*Nelson, Dorothy O. (1991, August 25). Harriet Tubman, Alive in Historic Auburn. [*Auburn (N.Y.) Citizen?*]. Clipping in JMC.

Neverdon-Morton, Cynthia. (1989). *Afro-American Women of the South and the Advancement of the Race, 1895–1925*. Knoxville: University of Tennessee Press.

*New England Colored Citizens' Convention. (1859, August 26). *Liberator*, 136.

New England Woman's Club (1905). Memorial Meeting. Ednah Dow Cheney, 1824–1904. Boston: George H. Ellis Co.

*News of Greater New York. (1911, September 21). *New York Age*, 7.

*Northrup, Mrs. E. S. [Katie Stewart]. (1939, November 9). Letter to Earl Conrad. EC-NY.

*———. (1940, April 1). Letter to Earl Conrad. EC-NY.

Oates, Stephen B. (1984). *To Purge This Land with Blood: A Biography of John Brown*. Amherst: University of Massachusetts Press.

*O'Brien, Nancy. (1993, February 8). Family "Very Proud," Plaque Honors Memory of Harriet Tubman. *St. Catharines (Ont.) Standard.*

O'Hara, Ward (Ed.). (1992). *Auburn, NY: Two Hundred Years of History, 1793–1993.* Auburn, N.Y.: Auburn Bicentennial Committee.

*Oldest Ex-Slave Given Reception. (1905, May 26). *Boston Journal,* 8. (Reprinted as Harriet Tubman at the Hub in *Auburn [N.Y.] Daily Advertiser,* May 30, 1905)

Olney, James. (1985). "I Was Born": Slave Narratives, Their Status as Autobiography and as Literature. In Davis and Gates (1985), 148–175.

———— (Ed.). (1988). *Studies in Autobiography.* New York: Oxford University Press.

*Once a Union Spy. (1903, June 6). *Auburn (N.Y.) Daily Advertiser.*

Ong, Walter J. (1982). *Orality and Literacy: The Technologizing of the Word.* London: Methuen.

*Osborne, Eliza Wright. (1890, January 28) Letter to Ellen Wright Garrison. GF.

**Osborne, J. F. [Josephine F.] (1913, February 19). Letter to Emily Howland. EH-CU.

**Osgood, Lucy. (1859, June 2). Letter to Lydia Maria Child. LMC-CU.

Painter, Nell Irvin. (1991). Soul Murder: Toward a Fully Loaded Cost Accounting. In Linda K. Kerber et al. (Eds.), *U. S. History as Women's History: New Feminist Essays.* Chapel Hill: University of North Carolina Press.

————. (1996). *Sojourner Truth: A Life, a Symbol.* New York: W. W. Norton.

Parent, Anthony S., Jr., and Susan Brown Wallace. (1993). Childhood and Sexual Identity under Slavery. In Fout, John C. and Tantillo, Maura Shaw (eds). *American Sexual Politics: Sex, Gender, and Race Since the Civil War.* Chicago: University of Chicago Press, 19–57.

Parrish, Anne. (1948). *A Clouded Star.* New York: Harper.

Pasternak, Martin B. (1995). *Rise Now and Fly to Arms: The Life of Henry Highland Garnet.* New York: Garland.

*Pattison, Athow. (1791, January 18). Last will and testament. DCC.

*Pays Tribute to Harriet Tubman. (1914, June 6). *Auburn (N.Y.) Advertiser-Journal,* 4.

Pearson, Elizabeth Ware (Ed.). (1906). *Letters from Port Royal, Written at the Time of the Civil War.* Boston: W. B. Clarke.

Pease, Jane H., and William H. Pease. (1974). *They Who Would Be Free: Blacks' Search for Freedom, 1830–1861.* Urbana: University of Illinois Press.

*Pendleton, Mrs. Leila Amos. (1912). *A Narrative of the Negro.* Washington, D.C.: Press of R. L. Pendleton.

Perry, Olin A. (1904, November 19). Mrs. Ednah Dow Cheney Dead. (Boston newspaper clipping in author's possession)

**Petition for Harriet Tubman (1897–1899). File of documents related to pension claim. Record Group 233, HR 55A-D1. HR.

*Petry, Ann. (1955). *Harriet Tubman, Conductor of the Underground Railroad.* New York: Thomas Y. Crowell.

*————. (1960). *The Girl Called Moses: The Story of Harriet Tubman.* London: Methuen.

**Phillips, Wendell. (1868, June 16). Testimonial letter to Sarah Hopkins Bradford. In Bradford (1869), 5–6.

**————. (N.d. [1868, June?]). Letter to Franklin B. Sanborn. FBS-CFPL.

Pierce, Edward L. (1863, September). The Freedmen at Port Royal. *Atlantic Monthly*, 291–315.

*Pilgrimage Honors Harriet Tubman's Life. (1984, May 27). *Auburn (N.Y.) Citizen*.

*Plans for Tubman Home. (1907, February 9). *Auburn (N.Y.) Daily Advertiser*, 5.

Porter, Dorothy. (1964). Harriet Tubman. *Dictionary of American Biography*, 10:27. American Council of Learned Societies. New York: Scribner's Sons. (Original publication in 1936)

Proceedings of the Eleventh National Woman's Rights Convention . . . New York, May 10, 1866. (1866). New York: Robert J. Johnston.

*Putnam, Caroline. (1903, December 31). Letter to Mrs. Miller. EH-CU.

Quarles, Benjamin (Ed.). (1968). *Frederick Douglass*. Englewood Cliffs, N.J.: Prentice-Hall.

———. (1969). *Black Abolitionists*. New York: Oxford University Press.

———. (1974). *Allies for Freedom: Blacks and John Brown*. New York: Oxford University Press.

———. (1976). *Frederick Douglass*. New York: Atheneum. (Original publication in 1948)

———. (1990). Harriet Tubman's Unlikely Leadership. In Hine (1990), 4:43–57.

Raboteau, Albert J. (1978). *Slave Religion: The "Invisible Institution" in the Antebellum South*. New York: Oxford University Press.

*A Race of Harriets Would Secure the Future of the Negro, Says Bishop Blackwell. (1913, March 14). *Auburn (N.Y.) Citizen*, 5, 12.

*Rademacher, Jean. (1983a, May 29). Visitors Stop in City Saturday for Annual Tubman Pilgrimage. *Auburn (N.Y.) Citizen*.

*———. (1983b, June 1). Group Plans Building near Tubman Home. *Auburn (N.Y.) Citizen*.

Rawick, George P. (Ed.). (1972, 1979). *The American Slave: A Composite Autobiography*. Series one, 12 vols. Series two, 10 vols. Westport, Conn.: Greenwood.

*Reception to Booker T. and Mrs. Mary B. Talbert. (1914, June 11). *Auburn (N.Y.) Citizen*.

Redpath, James. (1860). *The Public Life of Capt. John Brown*. Boston: Thayer and Eldredge.

*Relief of Fugitives in Canada. (1861a, October 25). *Liberator*, 170.

*Relief of Fugitives in Canada. (1861b, December 20). *Liberator*, 203.

**Report of the Committee of Teachers. (1865, April). *Freedmen's Record*, 1, 54–55.

*Restoration of Harriet Tubman [Home] Definite. (1949, June 27). *Auburn (N.Y.) Citizen-Advertiser*.

Reuther, Rosemary Radford, and Rosemary Skinner Keller (Eds.). (1981). *Women and Religion in America*. 2 vols. New York: Harper and Row.

*Ringgold, Faith. (1992). *Aunt Harriet's Underground Railroad in the Sky*. New York: Crown.

Ripley, Peter, and George Carter (Eds.). (1986). *Black Abolitionist Papers*. Chapel Hill: University of North Carolina Press.

*Rochester Ladies' Antislavery [Sewing] Society. (1851–1868). Annual Reports and Account books. RLA.

Roediger, David R. (1991). *The Wages of Whiteness: Race and the Making of the American Working Class*. London: Verso.

Roediger, David R., and Philip S. Foner (Eds.). (1989). *Our Own Time: A History of American Labor and the Working Day.* New York: Greenwood Press.

Rollins, Frank [Frances] A. (1868). *Life and Public Services of Martin R. Delany.* Boston: Lee and Shepard.

Rose, Willie Lee. (1976). *Rehearsal for Reconstruction: The Port Royal Experiment.* New York: Oxford University Press. (Original publication in 1964)

Rosell, Lydia J. (2001). *Images of America: Auburn's Fort Hill Cemetery.* Charleston, S.C.: Arcadia Publishing Company.

Rossbach, Jeffery. (1982). *Ambivalent Conspirators: John Brown, The Secret Six, and a Theory of Slave Violence.* Philadelphia: University of Pennsylvania Press.

*S. S. Tubman Building Plates Presented during Ceremonies. (1973, August 16). *Auburn (N.Y.) Citizen-Advertiser.*

Sadlier, Rosemary. (1997). *Tubman: Harriet Tubman and the Underground Railroad.* Toronto: Umbrella Press.

Salem, Dorothy. (1990). *To Better Our World: Black Women in Organized Reform, 1890–1920.* Brooklyn, N.Y.: Carlson.

**Sanborn, Franklin B. (1859a, May 30). Letter to Thomas W. Higginson. BPL.

**———. (1859b, June 4). Letter to Thomas W. Higginson. BPL. Excerpted in Sanborn (1909), 167.

**———. (1859c, June 8). Letter to Benjamin Smith Lyman. FBS-HSP. Excerpted as Letter 68 in Cameron (1978), 17.

**———. (1859d, June 18). Letter to Benjamin Smith Lyman. FBS-HSP. Excerpted as Letter 1682 in Cameron (1982), 15.

**———. (1859e, August 27). Letter to John Brown (Taken from Kennedy Farm). In *Report of the Select Committee of the Senate Appointed to Inquire Into the Late Invasion and Seizure of the Public Property at Harpers Ferry.* Washington D.C.: Mason Committee, 1860, 67–68.

**———. (1859f, September 14). Letter to Thomas W. Higginson. BPL

**———. (1859g, September 23). Letter to John Brown Jr. In *Report of the Select Committee* (1860).

**———. (1859h, December 20). Letter to Thomas W. Higginson. BPL. Excerpted as Letter 1719 in Cameron (1982), 17.

**———. (1860, June 10–11). Letter to Benjamin Smith Lyman. FBS-HSP. Excerpted as Letter 101 in Cameron (1978), 25.

**———. (1861a, September 8). Letter to Gerrit Smith. GS-SU.

**———. (1861b, November 3). Letter to Benjamin Smith Lyman. FBS-HSP. Excerpted as Letter 129 in Cameron (1978), 33.

**———. (1862, February 2–6). Letter to Benjamin Smith Lyman. FBS-HSP. Excerpted as Letter 133 in Cameron (1978), 35.

**———. (1868, June?) Testimonial letter excerpted in Bradford (1869), 53–55.

**———. (1863, July 17). Harriet Tubman. *Boston Commonwealth.*

**———. (1868, July 7). Letter to C. W. Slack. BPL. Letter 1961 in Cameron (1982), 28.

**———. (1869, January 25). A Negro Heroine—Scenes in the Life of Harriet Tubman. *Springfield Republican,* 2. In Cameron (1981), 16–17.

*———. (1875, January–May, December). The Virginia Campaign of John Brown. *Atlantic Monthly,* 16–24, 224–233, 323–331, 453–465, 591–600, 704–721.

**———. (1878). *Memoirs of John Brown, Written for Rev. Samuel Orcutt's History of Torrington, Ct* . . . Concord, Mass.: J. Munsell.

**———. (1886, November 1). Letter to unknown recipient. BS. Typescript in EC-NY.

———. (1905, October). A Concord Note-Book: Gerrit Smith and John Brown. *Critic*, 349–356.

**———. (1909). *Recollections of Seventy* Years. 2 vols. Boston: R. G. Badger.

**———. (1913a, March 13). The Late Araminta Davis . . . . Typescript obituary sketch. FBS-AAS. (Also see Sanborn [1913b])

**———. (1913b, March 19). Concerning Harriet Tubman and Fugitive Slaves. *Springfield (Mass.) Republican*, 17. In Cameron (1981), 150–151.

**———. (1969). *Life and Letters of John Brown, Liberator of Kansas and Martyr of Virginia.* New York: Negro Universities Press. (Original publication in 1885)

**———. (N.d. [June 1868]). Testimonial letter to Sarah Bradford. In Bradford (1869), 53–55.

Saville, Julie. (1994). *The Work of Reconstruction: From Slave to Wage Laborer in South Carolina, 1860–1870.* New York: Cambridge University Press.

Saxton, Martha. (1977). *Louisa May: A Modern Biography of Louisa May Alcott.* Boston: Houghton Mifflin.

*Saxton, Rufus (1868, March 21). Letter to a lady of Auburn on Tubman's war service. In Bradford (1869), 64.

*Saxton, R[ufus]. (N.d.) List of names of Harriet Tubman's scouts and pilots. In Bradford (1869), 70–71.

*Schuyler, George S. (1939, September 1). Letter to Earl Conrad. EC-NY.

Schwartz, Marie Jenkins. (2000). *Born in Bondage: Growing Up Enslaved in the Antebellum South.* Cambridge: Cambridge University Press.

*Scott, Lee (1981, October). Black History Is a Family Affair for Ithacan Eleanor Washington. *Ithaca Journal.*

*Scout Project Grows. (1983, May 25). *Auburn (N.Y.) Citizen.*

*Scruggs, Lawson A. (1893). Harriet, the Modern Moses. In *Women of Distinction: Remarkable in works and invincible in character*, 65–68. Raleigh: L. A. Scruggs, 1893.

Sekora, John. (1988). Is the Slave Narrative a Species of Autobiography? In Olney (1988), 99–111.

Sekora, John, and Darwin T. Turner (Eds.). (1982). *The Art of the Slave Narrative.* Macomb: Northern Illinois University Press.

Sernett, Milton. (2002). *North Star Country: Upstate New York and the African American Freedom Struggle.* Syracuse: Syracuse University Press.

**Seward, William H. (1865, July 25). Letter to Major-General David Hunter [Misdated 1868]. In Bradford (1869), 65.

*———. Family Papers. WHS. Microfilm available.

Sewell, Richard H. (1976). *Ballots for Freedom: Antislavery Politics in the United States, 1837–1860.* New York: Oxford University Press.

———. (1988). *A House Divided: Sectionalism and Civil War, 1848–1865.* Baltimore: Johns Hopkins University Press.

Shaw, Stephanie J. (1994). Mothering under Slavery in the Antebellum South. In

Evelyn Nakano Glenn et al. (Eds.), *Mothering: Ideology, Experience, Agency.* New York: Routledge.

————. (1995). Black Club Women and the Creation of the National Association of Colored Women. In Hine et al. (1995), 432–447.

————. (1996). *What a Woman Ought to Be and to Do: Black Professional Women Workers during the Jim Crow Era.* Chicago: University of Chicago Press.

Shepard, Odell (Ed.). (1966). *The Journals of Bronson Alcott.* 2 vols. New York: Kennikat Press.

**Siebert, Wilbur (1897). Notes on Interview with Tubman, August 1897. SUC, vol. 40.

**Siebert, Wilbur H. (1898). Harriet Tubman, the Moses of Her People. In *The Underground Railroad from Slavery to Freedom,* 185–189. New York: Macmillan.

**————. (1940, September 4). Letter to Earl Conrad. EC-NY.

 *Smedley, R. C. (1883). *History of the Underground Railroad in Chester and the Neighboring Counties of Pennsylvania.* Lancaster, Pa.: Office of the *Journal.*

Smith, Amanda. (1893). *An Autobiography: The Story of the Lord's Dealings with Mrs. Amanda Smith, the Colored Evangelist* . . . Chicago: Meyer.

**Smith, Frances A. (n.d., 1939?). Typed notes from interview with Earl Conrad. EC-NY.

**Smith, Frances A. (1939, October 23). Letter to Alice Brickler. EC-NY.

**Smith, Gerrit. (1861a, January [29?]). Letter to Franklin B. Sanborn. FBS-LC.

**————. (1861b, February [20?]). Letter to Franklin B. Sanborn. FBS-LC.

**————. (1864, November 22). Testimonial letter. In Bradford (1869), 67.

**————. (1867, November 4). Testimonial letter. In Bradford (1869), 66–67.

**————. (1868, June 13). Testimonial letter to Sarah Hopkins Bradford. In Bradford (1869).

Smith, Timothy L. (1957). *Revivalism and Social Reform.* Nashville: Abindgon Press.

Smith, Valerie. (1987). *Self-Discovery and Authority in Afro-American Narrative.* Cambridge: Harvard University Press.

————. (1990). Loopholes of Retreat: Architecture and Ideology in Harriet Jacobs's Incidents in the Life of a Slave Girl. In Gates (1990), 212–226.

Soderlund, Jean. (1985). *Quakers and Slavery: A Divided Spirit.* Princeton: Princeton University Press.

 *Souvenir Harriet Tubman Memorial. (1914, June). Souvenir program. Harriet Tubman Home for Aged and Indigent Colored Persons.

 Sponsors of SS Tubman. (1944, May 28). New York PM Sunday.* Clipping in JMC.

 *St. Catharines, Canada West. (1858). Assessment Roll. BU.

Stampp, Kenneth M. (1971). Triumph of the Conservatives. In Robert C. Twombley (Ed.), *Blacks in America since 1865.* New York: David McKay.

Stanton, Elizabeth Cady (1971). Eighty Years and More: Reminiscences 1815–1897. New York: Shocken Books. (Original publication in 1898).

 *Stanton, Elizabeth Cady, et al. (1881–1922). *History of Woman Suffrage.* 6 vols. Rochester: Susan B. Anthony; New York: National American Woman Suffrage Association.

Starling, Marion Wilson (1988). *The Slave Narrative: Its Place in Literary History.* 2nd ed. Washington, D.C.: Howard University Press. (Original publication in 1981)

**Stearns, George L. (1861, April 26). Letter to Franklin B. Sanborn. FBS-CFPL.

Stepto, Robert Burns. (1979). *From behind the Veil: A Study of Afro-American Narrative.* Urbana: University of Illinois Press.

———. (1985). I Rose and Found My Voice: Narration, Authentication, and Authorial Control in Four Slave Narratives. In Davis and Gates (1985), 225–241.

*Sterling, Dorothy. (1954). *Freedom Train: The Story of Harriet Tubman.* Garden City, N.Y.: Doubleday.

———. (1971). *The Making of an Afro-American, Martin Robison Delany, 1812–1885.* Garden City, N.Y.: Doubleday.

——— (Ed.). (1973). *Speak Out in Thunder Tones: Letters and Other Writings by Black Northerners, 1787–1865.* Garden City, N.Y.: Doubleday.

——— (Ed.). (1976). *The Trouble They Seen: Black People Tell the Story of Reconstruction.* Garden City, N.Y.: Doubleday.

———. (1984). *We Are Your Sisters: Black Women in the Nineteenth Century.* New York: W. W. Norton.

———. (1991). *Ahead of Her Time: Abby Kelley and the Politics of Anti-Slavery.* New York: W. W. Norton.

Stern, Madeleine B. (Ed.). (1984). *Critical Essays on Louisa May Alcott.* Boston: G. K. Hall.

Stevenson, Brenda (Ed.). (1988). *The Journals of Charlotte Forten Grimke.* New York: Oxford University Press.

———. (1996). *Life in Black and White: Family and Community in the South.* New York: Oxford University Press.

**Stevenson, Hannah E. (1865, November 7). Letter to Frances Seward. HTH.

**Stewart, Henry. (1863). Testimony to American Freedmen's Inquiry Commission. In Blassingame (1977), 414–416.

Stewart, James Brown. (1986). *Wendell Phillips, Liberty's Hero.* Baton Rouge: University of Louisiana Press.

Stewart, Jeffrey C. (Ed.). (1991). *Narrative of Sojourner Truth.* New York: Oxford University Press.

**Stewart, John. (1859, November 1). Letter to Harriet Tubman. RLA.

**Stewart, William H. (1892, July 21). Affidavit. [Location unknown: Mentioned in Harriet Tubman *Affidavit*, November 10, 1894, q.v.]

**Still, William (1854–1856). Underground Railroad Journal "C," entries for August 28, 1854 and May 13, 1856, 99, 263, WS.

**Still, William. (1872). Samuel Green, Alias Wesley Kinnard, August 28, 1854. "Moses" Arrives with Six Passengers. Benjamin Ross, and His Wife Harriet. In *The Underground Rail Road,* 246–250, 296–299, 395–396. Philadelphia: Porter and Coates.

*Storrow, Helen Osborne. (1939, August 29). Letter to Earl Conrad. EC-NY.

Straub, Deborah A. (1981). Earl Conrad. In *Contemporary Authors,* New Revision Series. vol. 10, 114–16.

*The Suffragists: Proceedings at Their Meeting Held Yesterday. (1888, March 15). *Auburn (N.Y.) Morning Dispatch,* 8.

*Swift, Hildegarde Hoyt. (1932). *The Railroad to Freedom: A Story of the Civil War.* New York: Harcourt Brace and World.

*———. (1939, September 8). Letter to Earl Conrad. EC-NY.

*———. (1940, January 12). Letter to Earl Conrad. EC-NY.

* *Syracuse Post Standard.* (1913, March 11). Telegram to Booker T. Washington. EC-NY.

* *Tallman, Irene C. (1980, March 21). "Unforgettable Person" Reflects Black History. *Auburn (N.Y.) Citizen.*

*———. (1981, July 7). Tubman Kin Visits Area. *Auburn (N.Y.) Citizen.*

** Tatlock, Mrs. William [Helen Woodruff]. (1939a, August 15). Interview statement to Earl Conrad. EC-NY.

** ———. (1939b, September 9). Letter to Earl Conrad. EC-NY.

Taylor, Clare. (1995). *Women of the Anti-Slavery Movement: The Weston Sisters.* New York: St. Martin's Press.

Taylor, John M. (1991). *William Henry Seward, Lincoln's Right Hand.* New York: HarperCollins.

* Taylor, Robert W. (1901). *Harriet Tubman: The Heroine in Ebony.* Boston: George H. Ellis.

Taylor, Susie King (1902). *Reminiscences of My Life in Camp with the 33rd U.S. Colored Troops.* Boston: S. K. Taylor. Reprinted as *A Black Woman's Civil War Memoirs: Reminiscences of My Life in Camp with the 33rd U S. Colored Troops.* Patricia Romero and Willie Lee Rose (Eds.). New York: Markus Weiner, 1988.

** Telford, Emma Paddock. (N.d. [circa 1905]). Harriet: The Modern Moses of Heroism and Visions. Typescript. CM.

Terborg-Penn, Rosalyn. (1995). *Discontented Black Feminists: Prelude and Postscript to the Passage of the Nineteenth Amendment.* In Hine et al. (1995), 487–503.

———. (1998). *African-American Women in the Struggle for the Vote, 1850–1920.* Bloomington: Indiana University Press.

* [There is no more tyrannical master than custom.] (1869, March 19). *Auburn (N.Y.) Morning News.*

* This Is British Soil. (1913, April 2). *Toronto Globe.*

* Thomas, Adah B. (1929). *Pathfinders.* New York: Kay Printing House.

Thomas, Owen A. (1999). *Niagara's Freedom Trail: A Guide to African-Canadian History on the Niagara Peninsula.* Available from Niagara Economic and Tourism Corporation, Thorold, Ontario.

** Thompson, Anthony C. (1853). Testimony. In *Gourney Pattison vs. Brodess and Others, Oct. 1, 1853 and Oct. 8, 1853.* DCC.

Thompson, Priscilla (1986, Spring/Summer). Harriet Tubman, Thomas Garrett, and the Underground Railroad. *Delaware History, 22.*

[Titus, Frances, ed. and Olive Gilbert] (1991). *Narrative of Sojourner Truth, A Bondswoman of Olden Time, With a History of Her Labors and Correspondence Drawn from Her "Book of Life."* Reprinted in Jeffrey C. Stewart (Ed.), *Narrative of Sojourner Truth.* New York: Oxford University Press. (Original work published 1878)

* To a Most Heroic Negress. (1914, June 13). *Auburn (N.Y.) Citizen,* 6, 14.

* To Aunt Harriet Hundreds Pay Tribute at Funeral Service. (1913, March 13). *Auburn (N.Y.) Citizen,* 6.

* To Harriet Tubman, Former Auburn Woman Pays Deserved Tribute. (1914, June 11). *Auburn (N.Y.) Citizen,* 5.

* Town Correspondence: Auburn, N.Y. (1915, July 8). *New York Age.*

**Townsend, Martin I. (1868). Statements made by Martin I. Townsend Esq. of Troy. In Bradford (1869), 100–103.

*A Tribute by the White Race to the Black Race. (1914, June 13). *Auburn (N.Y.) Citizen*, 4.

*Tribute Paid to Harriet Tubman. (1914, June 11). *Auburn (N.Y.) Advertiser-Journal.*

**Tubman, Harriet. (1856). Testimony given in Canada in 1855. In Benjamin Drew, *The Refugee: or, A North-Side View of Slavery*, 30–31. Boston: J. P. Jewett, 1856. Reprinted as *The Refugee; or, The Narratives of Fugitive Slaves in Canada Related by Themselves.* New York: Negro Universities Press, 1968.

**————. (1860, August 4). Dictated letter to Wendell Phillips. WP.

**————. (1863a, June 5). Testimony in Beaufort, S.C. U.S. Army, Department of South. In Civil War Court-Martial File LL566, *U.S. v. Private John E. Webster*, Co. G., 47th Regiment Penn. Records of the Office of the Judge Advocate General (Army), Record Group 153, NA, Washington, D.C. Text published in Guterman (Fall 2000).

**————. (1863b, June 30). Dictated letter to Franklin B. Sanborn. Excerpts in Sanborn (1863, July 17); also in Bradford (1869), 85–87; also see Cameron (1982), 24.

**Tubman [Davis], Harriet. (1890, July 14). Declaration for Widows Pension. In Harriet Tubman Vital Records, CCC.

**————. (1892, May 28). Affidavit. Filed with Harriet Tubman Vital Records, CCC.

**————. (1894a, April 9). Dictated letter to Ednah Cheney. EDC. See Kellogg (1894a).

**————. (1894b, November 10). Affidavit. In Harriet Tubman Vital Records, CCC.

**————. (1896, May 29). Dictated letter to Mary Wright. EDC.

**————. (1898, January 1). Affidavit. In Petition for Harriet Tubman, HR.

**————. (1903, June 11). Deed to African Methodist Episcopal Church of America, City Deed #33, CCC.

**————. (1908, November 15). Dictated postcard to Mrs. Carrie Barnes. SCM.

**————. (1912, November 18) Last will and testament. In Harriet Tubman Davis Proof of Will Papers. SCC. Filed with Harriet Tubman Vital Records, CCC.

*Tubman Artifacts Received. (1973, August 16). *Syracuse Post-Standard*, 6.

*Tubman Boosters Urge Action by Supervisors. (1971, November 9). *Syracuse Post-Standard.*

*Tubman, Conductor on Greatest Railroad. (1911, June 15). *New York Age.*

*The Tubman Home. (1908, June 23). *Auburn Citizen*, 5.

*Tubman Home Dedicated. (1908, June 23). *Auburn (N.Y.) Daily Advertiser.*

*Tubman Home Open. (1908, June 24). *Auburn (N.Y.) Citizen*, 7.

*Tubman Home Opening. (1908, June 17). *Auburn (N.Y.) Daily Advertiser.*

*Tubman Home Recognition Honors Blacks' Historic Role, (1974, July 14). *Syracuse Herald-American.*

*Tubman Home Tag Day on Thursday. (1921, October 8). *Auburn (N.Y.) Citizen*, 6.

*Tubman Memorial Tablet Is Here. (1914, June 5). *Auburn (N.Y.) Advertiser-Journal.*

*Tucker, Sheila. (1975, May 4). The "Gold Man," Tubman, Shimer. *Auburn (N.Y.) Citizen.*

*————. (1977, February 21). Tubman Held Messianic Beliefs about Brown. *Auburn (N.Y.) Citizen.*

*Two Timely Topics Discussed by Doctor Rosengrant at First M. E. (1913, March 17). *Auburn (N.Y.) Citizen*, 5.

*Unveil "Tubman" Memorial. (1915, July 17). *Cleveland Advocate*, 2, 1.

**Varnum, Louise Bradford. (1939, June 10). Letter to Earl Conrad. EC-NY.

Venet, Wendy Howard. (1991). *Neither Ballots nor Bullets: Women Abolitionists and the Civil War*. Charlottesville: University Press of Virginia.

Villard, Oswald Garrison. (1966). *John Brown, 1800–1859: A Biography Fifty Years After*. Gloucester: Peter Smith. (Original publication in 1910)

Voss, Frederick S. (1995). *Majestic in His Wrath: A Pictorial Life of Frederick Douglass*. Washington, D.C.: Smithsonian Institution.

*Walls, William J. (1974). *The African-Methodist Episcopal Zion Church*. Charlotte, N.C.: A. M. E. Zion Church.

*———. (N.d. [1946?]). *Harriet Tubman*. Charlotte, N.C.: A. M. E. Zion Church.

*——— (Ed.). (N.d. [1954?]) *Harriet Tubman Home: Its Present and Its Future*. Charlotte, N.C.: A. M. E. Zion Church.

*Wanted to Buy Tubman Property. (1914, June 9). *Auburn (N.Y.) Advertiser-Journal*, 10.

*Washington, Booker T. (1907, November 1). Letter to A. O. Stafford. In Harlan and Smock (1980), 9:389.

*———. (1909). *The Story of the Negro*. 2 vols. New York: Doubleday, Page.

*———. (1913, March 12). Telegram about Harriet Tubman to *Syracuse Post-Standard*.

*———. (1914, June 12). Extracts from an Address at the Unveiling of the Harriet Tubman Memorial. In Harlan and Smock (1980), 13:58–62.

Washington, Margaret (Ed.). (1993). *Narrative of Sojourner Truth*. New York: Random House.

Washington, Mary Helen. (1987). *Invented Lives: Narratives of Black Women, 1860–1960*. Garden City, N.Y.: Doubleday.

Weisenfeld, Judith. (1997). *African American Women and Christian Activism: New York's Black YWCA, 1905–1945*. Cambridge: Harvard University Press.

Weisenfeld, Judith, and Richard Newman (Eds.). (1996). *This Far by Faith: Readings in African-American Women's Religious Autobiography*. New York: Routledge.

Wesley, Charles Harris. (1984). *History of the National Association of Colored Women's Clubs: A Legacy of Service*. Washington, D.C.: Association of Colored Women's Clubs.

**Wheeler, B. F. (1903, June 20). Harriet Tubman Home and Christening of John Brown Hall. *Auburn (N.Y.) Daily Advertiser*, 8.

**———. (1904). Minutes, Twenty-Second Quadrenniel Session, A. M. E. Zion General Conference, 1904. In Walls (1974), 439–444.

Whelchel, Love Henry. (1985). *My Chains Fell Off: William Wells Brown, Fugitive, Abolitionist*. Lanham, Md.: University Press of America.

———. (2002). *Hell without Fire: Conversion in Slave Religion*. Nashville: Abingdon Press.

When Slaves Were Spirited to Canada. (1911, June 10). *New York Evening Sun*.

White, Deborah Gray. (1985). *Ar'n't I a Woman? Female Slaves in the Plantation South*. New York: W. W. Norton.

———. (1999). *Too Heavy a Load: Black Women in Defense of Themselves, 1894–1994*. New York: W.W. Norton.

*Whiting, Helen Adele. (1956, April). Slave Adventures: Harriet and Her Caravans. *Negro History Bulletin,* 164.

Williams, Lillian S. (1993). Mary Burnett Talbert. In Hardy (1993), 370–375.

———. (1995). And Still I Rise: Black Women and Reform, Buffalo, New York, 1900–1940. In Hine et al. (1995),, 521–541.

Williamson, Joel. (1965). *After Slavery: The Negro in South Carolina during Reconstruction, 1861–1877.* Chapel Hill: University of North Carolina Press.

———. (1986). *A Rage for Order: Black/White Relations in the American South since Emancipation.* New York: Oxford University Press.

Wilmore, Gayraud. (1989). *Black Religion and Black Radicalism.* Maryknoll, N.Y.: Orbis Books.

Wilson, Harriet E. (1983). *Our Nig: or Sketches in the Life of a Free Black, in a Two-Story White House, North.* Henry Louis Gates Jr. (Ed.). New York: Vintage. (Original publication in 1859)

*Wilson, Rev. Hiram. (1857, May 9). Canada Mission Semi Annual Report. PEM.

Winch, Julie. (1988). *Philadelphia's Black Elite: Activism, Accommodation and the Struggle for Autonomy, 1787–1848.* Philadelphia: Temple University Press.

Winks, Robin W. (1997). *Blacks in Canada: A History.* Montreal: McGill-Queens University Press.

Winks, Robin W. (1985). The Making of a Fugitive Slave Narrative: Josiah Henson and Uncle Tom—A Case Study. In Davis and Gates (1985), 112–146.

*With the Suffragists. (1905, October 28). *Auburn (N.Y.) Daily Advertiser.*

Wixom, Elbert Cook. (1903). The Underground Railroad of the Lake Country of Western New York. B.A. thesis, Cornell University.

Woloch, Nancy. (1996). *Women and the American Experience: A Concise History.* New York: McGraw-Hill.

*Women's Clubs Will Dedicate Harriet Tubman Memorial. (1937, July 7). *Auburn (N.Y.) Citizen-Advertiser,* 5.

*Woman's Rights Meetings. (1860, July 6). *Liberator.*

**Wood, Charles P. (1868). Manuscript Narrative and Copy of Harriet Tubman War Service Testimonial Materials. Filed with Petition for Harriet Tubman, HR. Also reprinted in Conrad (1950).

Woodson, Carter Goodwin. (1972). *The History of the Negro Church.* Washington, D.C.: Associated Publishers.

**Wright, David. (1861, February 9). Letter to Martha C. Wright. GF.

**———. (1866, April 3). Letter to Martha C. Wright. GF.

**Wright, Martha Coffin. (1860, December 30). Letter to Ellen Wright Garrison. GF.

**———. (1862, May 28). Letter to Frank Wright. GF.

**———. (1863, March 31). Letter to David Wright. GF.

**———. (1865, November 7). Letter to Marianne Pelham Mott. GF.

**———. (1866–1870). Diary entries for April 7, 18–19, 1866; May 24, September 3, 1867; January 4, 30–31, February 14–15, September 19, 28, 29, October 14, November 1868; November 9, 10, 1869; May 2, 3, 4, 1870. GF.

**———. (1866a, April 2). Letter to David Wright. GF.

**———. (1866b, April 9). Letter to Ellen Wright Garrison. GF.

**———. (1866c, April 12). Letter to Frank Wright. GF.

**———. (1866d, June 2). Letter to David Wright. GF.

———. (1866e, November 1). Letter to Ellen Wright Garrison. GF.

**———. (1867a, May 19). Letter to Ellen Wright Garrison. GF.

**———. (1867b, September 6). Letter to Ellen Wright Garrison. GF.

**———. (1868a, January 19). Letter to William Pelham Wright. GF.

**———. (1868b, February 5). Letter to William Pelham Wright. GF.

**———. (1868c, February 9). Letter to Ellen Wright Garrison. GF.

**———. (1868d, February 24). Letter to William Pelham Wright. GF.

**———. (1868e, March 22). Letter to Ellen Wright Garrison. GF.

**———. (1868f, August 31). Letter to her sisters. GF.

**———. (1868g, September 11). Letter to Anna and Patty Lord. GF.

**———. (1868h, September 24). Letter to Ellen Wright Garrison. GF.

**———. (1868i, October 8). Letter to Ellen Wright Garrison. GF.

**———. (1868j, October 8). Letter to her sisters. GF.

**———. (1868k, December 16). Letter to Ellen Wright Garrison. GF.

**———. (1869a, January 10). Letter to William Lloyd Garrison II. GF.

**———. (1869b, January 27). Letter to David Wright. GF.

**———. (1869c, March 7). Letter to David Wright. GF.

**———. (1869d, March 22). Letter to David Wright. GF.

**———. (1869e, October 7). Letter to Ellen Wright Garrison. GF.

**———. (1869f, October 19). Letter to Anna Brown. OF.

**———. (1869g, October 20). Letter to Ellen Wright Garrison. GF.

**———. (1869h, December 22). Letter to Ellen Wright Garrison. GF.

**———. (1870, May 5). Letter to Ellen Wright Garrison. GF.

**———. (1871, November 29). Letter to Frank Wright. GF.

**———. (1872, October 2). Letter to Ellen Wright Garrison. GF.

**———. (1873a, October 2). Letter to Ellen Wright Garrison. GF.

**———. (1873b, October 9). Letter to Ellen Wright Garrison. GF.

**———. (N.d. [fragment, February 1861?].) Letter to Lucretia Mott. GF.

**———. (N.d. [fragment, probably February or March 1861?]). Letter to Lucretia Mott. GF.

**———. (N.d. [fragment, probably November 1869?]). Letter probably to Lucretia Mott. GF.

**Wyman, Lillie B[uffum] Chace. (1896, March). Harriet Tubman. *New England Magazine, 6*, 110–118.

**———. (N.d. [1889?], November 24). Letter to Frank Jackson Garrison. GF.

Yee, Shirley J. (1992). *Black Women Abolitionists: A Study in Activism, 1828–1860.* Knoxville: University of Tennessee Press.

Yellin, Jean Fagan. (1985). Texts and Contexts of Harriet Jacobs' *Incidents in the Life of a Slave Girl: Written by Herself.* In Davis and Gates (1985), 262–282.

——— (Ed.). (1990). *Women and Sisters: Antislavery Feminists in American Culture.* New Haven: Yale University Press.

**Yerrington, James M. W. (1859, July 8). The Fourth at Framingham. *Liberator.*

*Zionists Are Active. (1911, June 5). *Auburn (N.Y.) Daily Advertiser,* 6.

INDEX

abolitionists: in Civil War, 50; and
  emancipation, 51–52; Garrisonian, 20,
  150, 156, 179, 193, 362n. 50, 364n. 63,
  402n. 19; and stories of Tubman,
  402n. 20; and suffrage, 364n. 63; and
  Tubman's political and social agenda,
  156. *See also* antislavery movement;
  specific person or organization
Adams, C. G., 286, 339, 377n. 18
Adams, Charles Francis, 367n. 13
Adams, Fannie Frances, 121
Adams, John Quincy, 121, 383n. 30
Adams, Samuel Hopkins, 137, 144, 151,
  162, 176, 203–204, 248, 256–257,
  267, 355n. 6, 395n. 5, 398n. 32, 400n.
  68
Addams, Jane, 100
African American women: as club
  women, 98–101, *127*, 379n. 38; and
  funding/support for Tubman, 115;
  and tributes to Tubman, 120–121; and
  Washington–Du Bois split, 379n. 38.
  See also specific person or organization
African American Women's Clubs, *127*
African Methodist Episcopal (A.M.E.)
  Church: in Canada, 359n. 24; relief
  efforts of, 98, 286, 377n. 21; and
  visionary experiences, 180; women in,
  180. *See also specific church or minister*
African Methodist Episcopal (A.M.E.)

Zion Church: beginnings of, 375n. 4;
  Davis as trustee of, 92; and funding/
  support for Tubman, 94; and Mason-
  Tubman meeting, 334; relief work for,
  98, 286; and Tubman Home, 102–
  103, 106, 126, 128, 324, 325, 326, 375n.
  7, 377n. 20, 378n. 33, 379n. 35, 405nn.
  55, 56, 57; and Tubman's death and
  funeral, 117, 121, 328, 329, 331; and
  Tubman's later years, 92; and
  Tubman's property, 94, 251–252, 347;
  Washington's speech at, 123, 338–339
Agnew, Allen, 288
Aiken, E. Clarence, 123, 125, 335, 336
Albany, New York: Underground
  Railroad activities in, 359n. 26
Alcott, Bronson, 37, 42, 145, 146, 306,
  362n. 48
Alcott, Louisa May, 41–42, 364n. 64,
  364–365n. 65
Alcott family, 332
American Anti-Slavery Society, 20, 27,
  76, 85, 86, 371n. 7, 397n. 23
American Equal Rights Association, 75,
  76
American Missionary Society, 25
American Woman Suffrage Association
  (AWSA), 76, 101
Amnesty Act (1872), 87
Anderson, Osborne, 39, 362n. 45

443

Stevens, Thaddeus, 368n. 22
Stevenson (aka Johnson), 310, 311–313, 314
Stevenson, Hannah, 369–370n. 38
Stewart, Bell, 311
Stewart, Catherine (sister-in-law), 28, 78, 222, 282, 347, 359n. 20, 360n. 32, 396n. 20, 402n. 13, 406n. 7, 407n. 12
Stewart, Charles H., 331
Stewart, Dora, *87*
Stewart, Elijah, 271
Stewart, Henry (brother), 23, 24, 185–186, 280–282, 344, 345, 346, 356n. 14, 396n. 10
Stewart, James (brother), 271, 344, 345, 346, 358n. 11, 359n. 20, 402n. 13, 406n. 3, 407n. 12
Stewart, John (brother): in Auburn, 28, 271, 282–283, 346, 371n. 12, 407n. 8; and care for parents, 28, 282, 346; children of, 272, 346, 375n. 6, 407n. 8; death of, 378n. 31; as dependent on Tubman, 113; and Drew's interviews, 359n. 20; escape of, 220, 221, 406–407n. 7; and family tree, 246, 271, 272, 344, 345; and gold swindle scheme, 88, 89–90, 310–311, 314, 346, 375n. 39; letters of, 143, 279, 282–283; name change of, 358n. 11, 402nn. 13, 17; Thompson places monetary value on, 406n. 3; and Tubman's financial affairs, 28, 282; Tubman's relationship with, 282; and Underground Railroad activities of Tubman, 143, 282; and Wright and Osborne families, 405n. 48
Stewart, John (builder), 14–15, 27, 179, 211, 346, 359n. 18, 360n. 29
Stewart, Judge, 41
Stewart, Katie. *See* Northrup, Katie Stewart
Stewart, Levin (brother), 344, 345, 358n. 11, 402n. 13, 406n. 3
Stewart, Margaret (niece): appearance of, 271; and Davis-Tubman marriage, 374n. 29; death of, 407n. 14; and family tree, 271, 272; and gold swindle scheme, 155; marriage of, 78, 366n. 7;

picture of, *119;* with Seward/Worden family, 51, 270, 367n. 19; and stories of Tubman, 203; and Tubman family, 408n. 15; in Tubman's household, 78, 271; Tubman's "kidnapping" of, 24, 47–48, 160, 269–270, 272, 348, 401n. 77, 404n. 32; and veteran's pension for Tubman, *119*, 372n. 14
Stewart, Moses (brother), 93, 344, 346, 358n. 11, 375n. 6, 406n. 3, 407nn. 7, 8
Stewart, William Henry (brother): antislavery activism of, 25–26, 407n. 9; in Auburn, 272, 346–347; in Canada, 25–26, 222, 271, 282, 346, 407n. 9; children of, 347; death of, 222, 272, 346, 347, 378n. 31; and dedication of Tubman Home, 106, 324, 347; escape of, 222, 333, 396n. 20, 406–407n. 7; and family tree, 268, 271, 346–347; and financial affairs of Tubman, 347, 405n. 56; and funding/support for Tubman, 101; letters to, 282; and name change of, 358n. 11
Stewart, William Henry, Jr., 407n. 10
Stiles, Deputy Sheriff, 93
Still, William: antislavery activities of, 20–21, *21*, 292; documentary evidence about Tubman left by, 288–290, 353n. 2; and escape of Rosses (Benjamin and Ritta), 293–294, 402n. 22; and escape of Tubman, 357n. 25; and funding/support for Tubman, 292; and Harper, 378n. 29; notes on testimony of, 293–294; picture of, *21;* as source for other biographers, 389n. 44; and Tubman's family tree, 344, 345, 402n. 13; Underground Railroad activities of, 359n. 26; and Underground Railroad activities of Tubman, 20–21, 143, 279, 288–290, 293–294, 349, 351, 358n. 5, 397n. 23, 397n. 25, 401n. 4, 407n. 12, 408nn. 2, 5
Stone, Lucy, 76, 101, 371n. 8, 391n. 57
stories: as autobiography, 6; and Bible, 135, 161; body language when telling,

Wisconsin Studies in Autobiography

WILLIAM L. ANDREWS
General Editor

ROBERT F. SAYRE
The Examined Self: Benjamin Franklin, Henry Adams, Henry James

DANIEL B. SHEA
Spiritual Autobiography in Early America

LOIS MARK STALVEY
The Education of a WASP

MARGARET SAMS
Forbidden Family: A Wartime Memoir of the Philippines, 1941–1945
Edited, with an introduction, by Lynn Z. Bloom

CHARLOTTE PERKINS GILMAN
The Living of Charlotte Perkins Gilman: An Autobiography
Introduction by Ann J. Lane

MARK TWAIN
Mark Twain's Own Autobiography: The Chapters from the North American Review
Edited, with an introduction, by Michael Kiskik

Journeys in New Worlds: Early American Women's Narratives
Edited by William L. Andrews

American Autobiography: Retrospect and Prospect
Edited by Paul John Eakin

CAROLINE SEABURY
The Diary of Caroline Seabury, 1854–1863
Edited, with an introduction, by Suzanne L. Bunkers

MARIAN ANDERSON
My Lord, What a Morning
Introduction by Nellie Y. McKay

American Women's Autobiography: Fea(s)ts of Memory
Edited, with an introduction, by Margo Culley

FRANK MARSHALL DAVIS
Livin' the Blues: Memoirs of a Black Journalist and Poet
Edited, with an introduction, by John Edgar Tidwell

JOANNE JACOBSON
Authority and Alliance in the Letters of Henry Adams

CORNELIA PEAKE MCDONALD
A Woman's Civil War: A Diary with Reminiscences of the War, from March 1862
Edited, with an introduction, by Minrose C. Gwin

KAMAU BRATHWAITE
The Zea Mexican Diary: 7 Sept. 1926–7 Sept. 1986
Foreword by Sandra Pouchet Paquet

GENARO M. PADILLA
My History, Not Yours: The Formation of Mexican American Autobiography

FRANCES SMITH FOSTER
Witnessing Slavery: The Development of Ante-bellum Slave Narratives

Native American Autobiography: An Anthology
Edited, with an introduction, by Arnold Krupat

American Lives: An Anthology of Autobiographical Writing
Edited, with an introduction, by Robert F. Sayre

CAROL HOLLY
*Intensely Family: The Inheritance of Family Shame and the
Autobiographies of Henry James*

People of the Book: Thirty Scholars Reflect on Their Jewish Identity
Edited by Jeffrey Rubin-Dorsky and Shelley Fisher Fishkin

G. THOMAS COUSER
Recovering Bodies: Illness, Disability, and Life Writing